MO☾N

HANDBOOKS

# ATLANTIC CANADA

ANDREW HEMPSTEAD

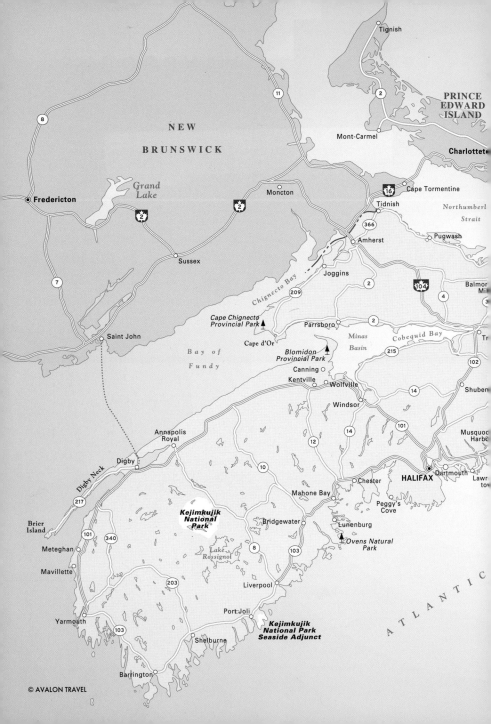

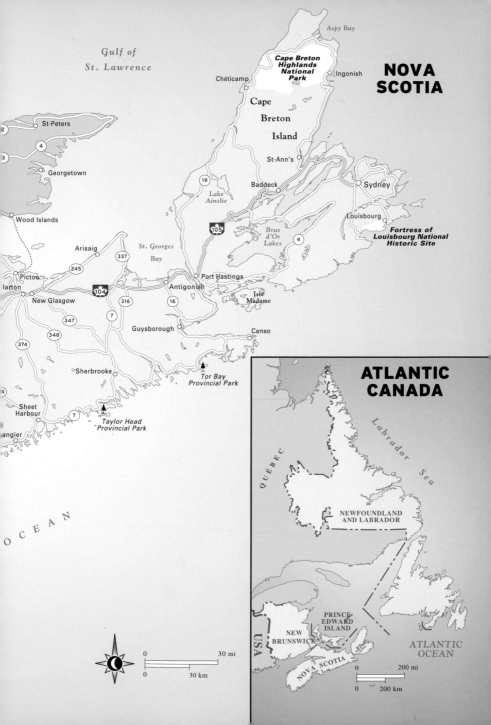

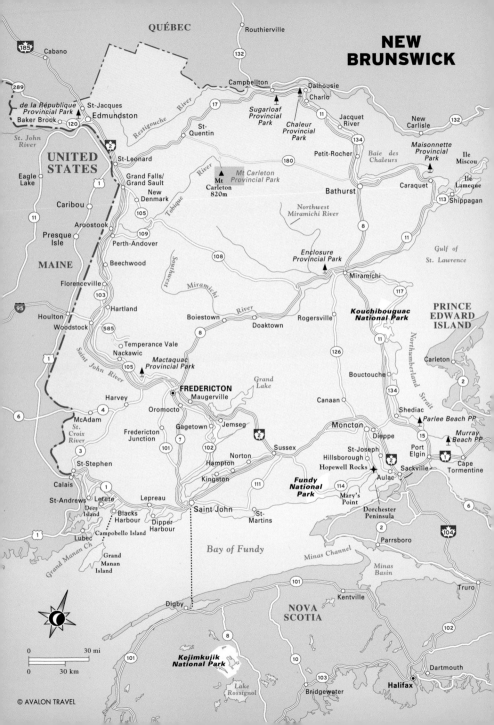

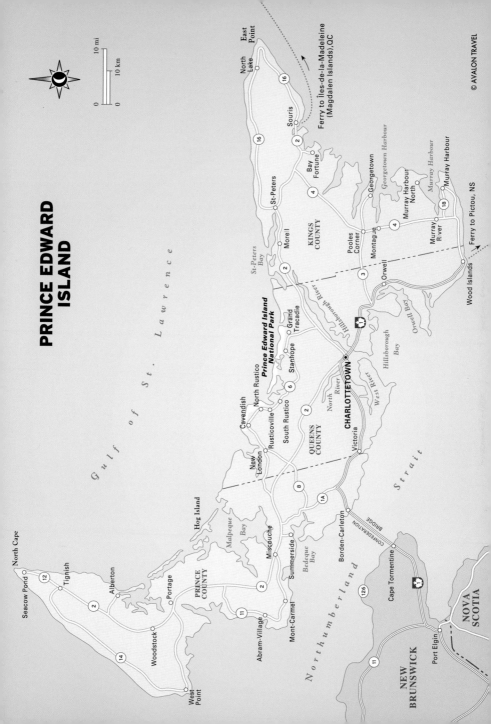

# Contents

# Discover Atlantic Canada

Atlantic Canada, the sea-bound northeastern corner of North America, comprises four provinces that have their own personalities but that are inextricably entwined in history, people, and place. Each province holds the promise of fabulous scenery and rich history. The scene at Peggy's Cove on a still morning is alone worth the trip, and similarly memorable views of rugged coastline, forest-encircled lakes, and ancient landscapes present themselves at almost every turn. You can hike through flower-filled alpine meadows, stride the fairways of some of the world's best golf courses, and bike along red clay lanes – or just take it easy, stepping back in time at historic attractions and soaking up culture in cosmopolitan cities.

The ocean is a defining feature of Atlantic Canada. It permeates all aspects of life on the edge of the continent, as it has done for centuries. Kayaking to an uninhabited island for a picnic lunch and searching out the world's rarest whales are just two of the watery adventures that await you. Long stretches of remote sand are perfect for beach walking, and the warm waters of Northumberland Strait encourage summer swimming. The surrounding waters also offer a veritable smorgasbord of seafood.

The joys of visiting Atlantic Canada are many, but some of your most treasured memories will be of the people. For centuries, the folk of

Atlantic Canada have gone down to the sea in ships to ply their trade on the great waters. The hard seafaring life has given them what so much of the modern world has thoughtlessly let slip through its fingers: nearness to nature's honest rhythms, replete with the old values of kindness, thrift, and rugged self-reliance. In a world crowded with too many people and too much development, Atlantic Canada remains a refuge of sorts, and its friendly people will make you feel welcome and comfortable.

Sure, you'll remember the sight and sound of bagpipers marching across Halifax's Citadel Hill, you'll snap the requisite photo of the lighthouse at Peggy's Cove, and you won't want to miss walking along the beaches of Prince Edward Island National Park. But there are many unexpected pleasures in Atlantic Canada. It's not about specific places, but rather personal experiences that come about through intangible ingredients beyond the scope of any guidebook and revolve around adventures of your own making.

# Planning Your Trip

## ▶ WHERE TO GO

Atlantic Canada is made up of four provinces, which makes dividing the region into manageable areas easy. But even among Canadians, there is sometimes confusion about the definition of Atlantic Canada versus the Maritimes. The latter comprises New Brunswick, Nova Scotia, and Prince Edward Island, while Atlantic Canada comprises the Maritime provinces together with Newfoundland and Labrador.

### Nova Scotia

Nova Scotia typifies Atlantic Canada, with a dramatic, 7,459-kilometer-long coastline notched with innumerable coves and bays holding scores of picturesque fishing villages. It would be easy to spend an entire vacation exploring Nova Scotia yet still leave feeling you hadn't seen everything. The cosmopolitan streets of Halifax, the colorful port of Lunenburg, the historic ambience of Annapolis Royal, and the wilds of Cape Breton Island are just a taste of what you can expect in this diverse province.

historic Annapolis Royal

11-meter-long, cast-iron lobster sculpture, Shediac, New Brunswick

- **A WEEKEND:** Spend your time in Halifax.
- **ONE WEEK:** Visit Halifax, the South Shore, and the Fundy Coast.
- **TWO WEEKS:** Add Prince Edward Island.
- **THREE WEEKS:** Add Newfoundland.

## New Brunswick

New Brunswick is the largest of the Maritime provinces, but is the least known to outsiders. Although mostly forested, it is the province's coastline and fertile Saint John River valley that attract the most attention. Here you find the elegant resort town of St. Andrews, the phenomenal Fundy tides, and pristine beaches such as Parlee. These attractions, along with the three main cities—Fredericton, Saint John, and Moncton—and a distinct Acadian flavor to the north coast, create a destination with something for everyone.

## Prince Edward Island

Little PEI ranks as Canada's smallest province, as well as its most densely populated, most cultivated, most ribboned with roads, and most bereft of original wilderness. PEI also has the country's smallest provincial capital—Charlottetown, with a population of just 32,000. The tourist's island revolves around Cavendish, but the island's low-key charm is found elsewhere, along rural roads that end at the ocean and through neat villages that have changed little over the last century.

## Newfoundland and Labrador

Three times the size of the Maritimes put together, this province redefines the region as Atlantic Canada. It comprises the island of Newfoundland as well as Labrador on the mainland. The Maritimes share a kindred climate, history, and lineage, but Newfoundland is different. About half of the mountainous island is boreal forest, while much of the rest is rocky, barren, or boggy. The people in some ways seem more akin to their Irish or English forebears than culturally blended or archetypically Canadian.

Trinity, Bonavista Peninsula, Newfoundland

# ► WHEN TO GO

Summer revolves around outdoor activities such as hiking, biking, swimming, canoeing, and fishing. July and August are especially busy. This is the time of year when school is out and the parks come alive with campers, the lakes and streams with anglers, the beaches with swimmers and sunbathers, the woods with wildlife, and the roadsides with stalls selling fresh produce.

Unless you're governed by a schedule, spring and fall are excellent times to visit Atlantic Canada. While May-June is considered a shoulder season, in many ways the province is at its blooming best in spring. After the first weekend in September, there is a noticeable decrease in travelers across the province. But early fall (Sept.-Oct.) provides pleasant daytime temperatures, reduced room rates, and uncrowded attractions. By late September, fall colors are at their peak, creating a minisurge in visitors.

Officially, winter extends from late December to March, but in reality, most attractions and visitor information centers, as

Public Gardens, Halifax, Nova Scotia

well as accommodations in resort towns, start closing in mid-October.

# ► BEFORE YOU GO

## Passports and Visas

To enter Canada, a passport is required by citizens and permanent residents of the United States. At press time, the U.S. government was developing alternatives to the traditional passport. For further information, see the website http://travel.state.gov/travel. For current entry requirements to Canada, check the Citizenship and Immigration Canada website (www.cic.gc.ca).

All other foreign visitors must have a valid passport and may need a visa or visitors permit depending on their country of residence and the vagaries of international politics. At present, visas are not required for citizens of the United States, British Commonwealth, or Western Europe. The standard entry permit is for six months, and you may be asked to show onward tickets or proof of sufficient funds to last you through your intended stay.

## Transportation

Visitors to Atlantic Canada have the option of arriving by road, rail, ferry, or air. The main gateway city for flights from North America and Europe is Halifax. Ferries cross to Yarmouth from Maine while the main rail line enters the region from Quebec and terminates at Halifax. Driving, whether it be your own vehicle or a rental car, is by far the best way to get around Atlantic Canada, although some towns are served by bus.

# Explore Atlantic Canada

## ▶ THE BEST OF ATLANTIC CANADA

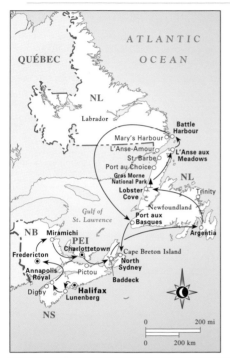

Two weeks is an excellent length of time for visiting each of the four provinces and not feeling too rushed along the way. You could of course just spend the entire two weeks in the three Maritimes provinces, or only explore the far reaches of Newfoundland and Labrador, but this itinerary has it all.

### Day 1

After arriving in Halifax, settle in at a historic downtown bed-and-breakfast such as The Halliburton. Spend the afternoon taking in sights such as Halifax Citadel National Historic Site and the Maritime Museum of the Atlantic, and make dinner reservations at a waterfront restaurant.

### Day 2

Drive south through Peggy's Cove (take the obligatory lighthouse photo) and Mahone Bay (browse the arts and crafts shops, eat lunch at the Saltspray Café) to Lunenburg. There's plenty to see en

Lunenburg, Nova Scotia

route, but arrive in time for an afternoon walk through the UNESCO-protected core of downtown, which is filled with colorful buildings. For the views alone, the Spinnaker Inn is my favorite Lunenburg lodging.

## Day 3

Drive across to Annapolis Royal and plan visits to Fort Anne and Port-Royal National Historic Sites. Stop in Digby for a meal of plump Digby scallops and board the afternoon ferry for New Brunswick and

# FRESH FROM THE SEA

While the down-home cooking found across Atlantic Canada is irresistible, it is seafood that is the star. You'll find white-glove service at some seafood restaurants, but your most memorable meals will be less formal, including the following favorites.

## NOVA SCOTIA

Almost completely surrounded by the sea, Nova Scotia offers up a wide variety of ocean delicacies.

- **Muddy Rudder:** This roadside stand near Ingonish features the freshest seafood you could imagine.
- **O'Neil's Royal Fundy Market:** This combined café-market is the perfect place to try Digby's famed scallops.

## NEW BRUNSWICK

Look for lobsters in the north and scallops along the Bay of Fundy.

- **Lobster Tales:** Step aboard a working fishing boat, haul up your own lobster, and have it cooked onboard during this tasty cruise that departs from Shediac.
- **Butlands:** In the village of Alma, try Butlands, where you choose a lobster, boiled to perfection, and enjoy an outdoor feast overlooking the Bay of Fundy.

## PRINCE EDWARD ISLAND

- **New Glasgow Lobster Supper:** Lobster suppers are an island tradition. You'll see them advertised locally, or head to the popular New Glasgow Lobster Supper for a full lobster with all the trimmings.
- **Flex Mussels:** Flex Mussels in Charlottetown has tasty mussels steamed

to order in more than 50 flavors.

- **Seaweed Pie Café:** At Seaweed Pie Café a slab of seaweed pie will set you back just $4, so don't feel too guilty if you decide this local Mimingash delicacy is not for you.

## NEWFOUNDLAND AND LABRADOR

Seal-flipper pie, moose burgers, and roasted wild game – partridge, rabbit, and caribou – are Newfoundland and Labrador highlights.

- **Lighthouse Picnics:** Head to the restaurant Lighthouse Picnics in Ferryland and order a picnic of crab cakes and other gourmet goodies.
- **Norseman Restaurant:** In L'Anse aux Meadows, this restaurant offers fresh, creative seafood dishes.

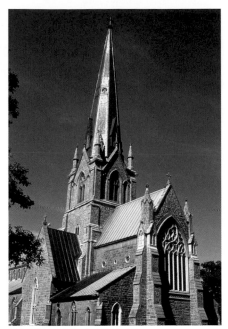

Christ Church Cathedral, Fredericton

an overnight at one of two lodgings in Fundy National Park.

## Day 4

Mornings are a delight in Fundy National Park, so plan on a hike and then drive through to Fredericton. Here, the Historic Garrison District packs in the past (and art lovers will want to schedule a stop at Beaverbrook Art Gallery), but the highlight of this day will be watching Loyalist history come to life at Kings Landing Historical Settlement. There's no advantage to staying right downtown, so reserve a room at On the Pond.

## Day 5

Drive down the Miramichi River to Miramichi. You'll learn about Acadians and their struggles at Village Historique Acadien. Soak up some of the arts at Le Pays de la Sagouine dinner theater.

## Day 6

Drive to Prince Edward Island via the Confederation Bridge. Check in early to Charlottetown's Shipwright Inn and spend the afternoon on a rural jaunt through Cavendish, passing through Prince Edward Island National Park and stopping at Green Gables House.

## Day 7

Rise early to catch the ferry from Wood Islands to Caribou. Learn about the arrival of the early Scottish settlers at Hector Heritage Quay in Pictou, and drive through to Baddeck, on Cape Breton Island. Squeeze in a visit to Alexander Graham Bell National Historic Site. Most rooms at Baddeck's Water's Edge Inn have balconies with views of the sun setting over the lake.

## Day 8

Spend the day driving the famously scenic Cabot Trail, choosing between hiking coastal trails, relaxing on the beach, and a whale-watching trip. Catch the evening ferry to Argentia (reserve a cabin for extra comfort).

## Day 9

You'll wake to your first views of Newfoundland as the ferry pulls into Argentia.

Signal Hill National Historic Site, St. John's, Newfoundland

There's plenty to see on the way to the capital, including the archaeological dig at the Colony of Avalon. Once in St. John's, head to the The Rooms to learn about local history and Signal Hill National Historic Site for the views. Still feeling energetic? The lively downtown bars of George Street come alive after dark.

## Day 10

Head west, stopping at Trinity, a tiny fishing village where little has changed in over a century, en route to Gros Morne National Park, where you will have time for a walk through the Tablelands and still be at Lobster Cove Head in time to watch the sunset. Mountain Range Cottages is a centrally located base in Rocky Harbour.

## Day 11

Join a morning boat tour of Western Brook Pond and drive north along the Northern Peninsula. Make sure to stop at Port au Choix National Historic Site and the thrombolites of Flowers Cove en route to Southwest Pond Cabins in L'Anse aux Meadows. Dinner at the Norseman Restaurant is a must.

## Day 12

Visit L'Anse aux Meadows National Historic Site, then drive to St. Barbe, and put your feet up for a couple of hours on the ferry crossing to Labrador. Head north along the Labrador Straits to Mary's Harbour. Park your vehicle and pack an overnight bag for the short boat trip to Battle Harbour, an "outport" (remote fishing village) that was abandoned in the 1960s, but where restoration efforts include a restaurant and an inn.

## Day 13

Return to the mainland and spend the day exploring this remote stretch of coast. Red Bay

## A FAMILY AFFAIR

The most important thing to remember when traveling with children is not to try to fit too much in. Instead, sacrifice covering great distances for enjoying specific sights and towns for extended periods of time, and try to fit as many of these family-friendly attractions and activities into your itinerary as possible:

- **Harbour Hopper Tours,** Halifax, Nova Scotia
- **Museum of Natural History,** Halifax, Nova Scotia
- **Shubenacadie Wildlife Park,** near Truro, Nova Scotia
- **Hector Heritage Quay,** Pictou, Nova Scotia
- **Hopewell Rocks,** Fundy Coast, New Brunswick
- **Historic Garrison District,** Fredericton, New Brunswick
- **Magnetic Hill,** Moncton, New Brunswick
- **Parless Beach,** Shediac, New Brunswick
- **Anne of Green Gables attractions,** Cavendish, Prince Edward Island
- **Prince Edward Island National Park,** Prince Edward Island
- **Attend a lobster supper,** Prince Edward Island
- **The Rooms,** St. John's, Newfoundland and Labrador
- **Norstead,** near St. Anthonys, Newfoundland and Labrador

Green Gables House, Cavendish, Prince Edward Island

thrombolites of Flowers Cove, Newfoundland

National Historic Site should definitely be on your itinerary, as should the lighthouse at L'Anse Amour. Catch the ferry back to St. Barbe and continue south to Port aux Basques in time for the evening ferry back to Nova Scotia.

## Day 14

Arriving in North Sydney around dawn, you have plenty of time to make an afternoon flight home from Halifax. If you're not flying out until the following morning, take Marine Drive along the Eastern Shore and spend your 14th night along this remote stretch of coast, where Sherbrooke Village is a historical highlight and where the beaches of Taylor Head Provincial Park are perfect for a walk.

# ▶ THE WHIRLWIND TOUR

It may be possible to touch down in all four provinces in one week, but such a rushed schedule is neither practical nor enjoyable. Therefore, in this itinerary, we'll stick to the three Maritime provinces (Nova Scotia, New Brunswick, and Prince Edward Island). This itinerary and those that follow assume you have your own vehicle or a rental.

## Day 1

Arrive in Halifax and spend the afternoon exploring the downtown precinct; include a visit to the Maritime Museum of the Atlantic and a tour of Alexander Keith's Brewery. Enjoy your first evening in the city by tucking into seafood at an outdoor waterfront restaurant such as Salty's. For lodging, choose The Halliburton for historic charm or the Prince George Hotel for modern conveniences.

## Day 2

Rise early to beat the crowd to Peggy's Cove, then follow the scenic coastal route through Chester to Mahone Bay. After lunch, spend time admiring the local arts and crafts scene and walk along the waterfront

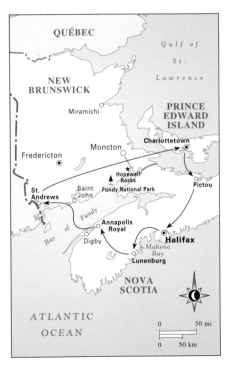

to view the trio of waterfront churches. At nearby Lunenburg, you'll find enough time

Mahone Bay, Nova Scotia

for a sunset harbor cruise before turning in for the night at the Spinnaker Inn.

## Day 3

Drive across southwestern Nova Scotia to Annapolis Royal and spend the afternoon exploring North America's oldest downtown street as well as attractions like Port-Royal National Historic Site. Guest rooms at the Queen Anne Inn reflect the town's gracious past.

## Day 4

Catch the ferry from Digby to Saint John and drive down the coast to St. Andrews, where you do what visitors have done for over a century—browse through the boutiques, enjoy Kingsbrae Garden, and dine on seafood. Have a room reserved at Seaside Beach Resort, unless it's a special occasion, in which case you'll want to spend the night at the Inn on the Hiram Walker Estate.

## Day 5

Drive along the Fundy Coast to Fundy National Park. Plan on at least one hike (Dickson Falls is an easy walk) and time your early afternoon departure for low tide at Hopewell Rocks, where you can "walk on the ocean floor." Continue north across the Confederation Bridge to Charlottetown's Shipwright Inn.

## Day 6

Spend some time in the island capital, where Province House and Founders' Hall are highlights, but also head north to Cavendish to soak up the legend of *Anne of Green Gables* at Green Gables House and to explore the beachfront national park. Either way, the last ferry of the day departs Wood Islands at 7:30 P.M., and you'll need to be on it to reach Pictou and your room at the waterfront Consulate Inn.

## Day 7

Drive to Halifax. If time allows, fit in a few more city sights. The Halifax Citadel National Historic Site and the Public Gardens should be at the top of your list.

Founders' Hall, Charlottetown, Prince Edward Island

Halifax Citadel National Historic Site, Nova Scotia

# TOP 10 PLACES TO STAY

While most visitors who choose Atlantic Canada for their vacation do so for the outdoors, there are a number of unique and upscale lodgings that are well worth a splurge.

## NOVA SCOTIA

- **Lunenburg Inn,** Lunenburg
- **Whispering Waves Cottages,** Shelburne
- **Queen Anne Inn,** Annapolis Royal
- **Keltic Lodge,** Ingonish

## NEW BRUNSWICK

- **Kingsbrae Arms,** St. Andrews
- **Hotel Paulin,** Caraquet

## PRINCE EDWARD ISLAND

- **Shipwright Inn,** Charlottetown
- **Kindred Spirits Country Inn,** Cavendish

## NEWFOUNDLAND AND LABRADOR

- **Artisan Inn,** Trinity
- **Elizabeth J Cottages,** Bonavista

Keltic Lodge

# ► RUGGED ATLANTIC CANADA

This 12-day itinerary is suited for outdoor enthusiasts with a love of nature. It is impossible to discuss adventures in the region without including Newfoundland, and so three days are spent on that island. If you have less time, plan on dedicating your next trip to Atlantic Canada to exploring the region's largest province. In keeping with the theme, I've added accommodation recommendations that keep you close to nature, but if cabins and cottages aren't your thing, you will find plenty of alternatives along the way.

## Day 1

Pick up your rental car in Halifax and head for the Eastern Shore. Try surfing at Lawrencetown Beach or sea kayaking at Tangier. Regardless, pick up smoked salmon at J. Willy Krauch and Sons for a beachside picnic at Taylor Head Provincial Park. Stay at Paddlers Retreat Bed and Breakfast and rent a kayak for an evening jaunt around the bay.

## Day 2

Drive across Cape Breton Island, stopping for an outdoor lunch of boiled lobster at the Muddy Rudder, and then spend the afternoon swimming and sunbathing at Ingonish Beach. Even if you don't pay for a room with water views at Glenghorm Beach Resort, the water is just a short walk from your front door.

## Day 3

Day three is spent in Cape Breton Highlands National Park. In the process of reaching the best hikes, you'll drive the spectacular Cabot Trail. Leave the pavement behind on the Skyline Trail, a moderate hike

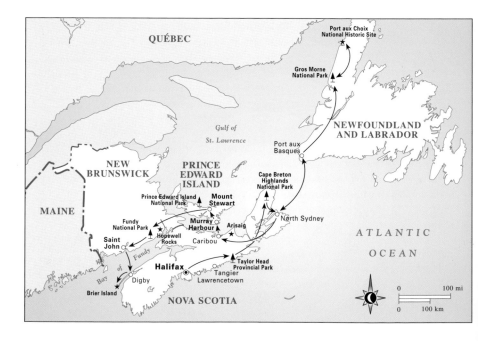

sunset at Gros Morne National Park, Newfoundland

that leads to a stunning headland with sweeping water views. For a less energetic option, plan on walking to Benjie's Lake, and spend the extra time exploring Black Brook Cove. Either way, allow three hours to reach North Sydney for the overnight ferry to Port-aux-Basques.

## Day 4

The ferry arrives in Newfoundland as the sun rises, which makes the early morning drive north to Gros Morne National Park even more enjoyable. In the afternoon, choose between exploring the Tablelands on foot and driving out to Trout River for rugged coastal scenery. Fresh seafood cooked on your barbecue at Mountain Range Cottages ends out this long day.

## Day 5

The boat tour on Western Brook Pond is an absolute must, but allow time to reach the dock, which is only accessible on foot through a typical northern forest. Stop in at the Discovery Centre to learn about the park's geology and then hike to Green Gardens. Spend another night at Mountain Range Cottages.

## Day 6

Even the adventurous need a day off, and this is it. Personally, I'd spend the time driving up the Northern Peninsula (Port au Choix National Historic Site makes a solid day trip while still allowing plenty of time for scenic stops), but you could also stay within the park and tackle the summit of Gros Morne Mountain. Drive back south to Port-aux-Basques and catch the evening ferry back to Nova Scotia.

## Day 7

Hopefully you've not spent all night on the ferry being entertained by the Celtic musicians in the lounge, because the ferry docks just before dawn and the morning is spent driving to Caribou, where you board the ferry to Prince Edward Island. The fossil cliffs of

Arisaig make a worthwhile detour en route. Once on the island, stop at Rossignol Estate Winery for a bottle of wine and continue to Murray Harbour's Fox River Cottages, where you can relax with a glass of chardonnay on your screened porch.

## Day 8

Yes, you've seen the tourist brochures espousing the touristy wonders of the island, but on this visit you're chasing a more nature-oriented experience. In this regard, spend the morning on a seal-watching trip, stroll along the singing sands of the beach below Basin Head, and walk through the disappearing coastal forests of Prince Edward Island National Park. The Trailside Inn, at Mount Stewart, is your overnight stop.

## Day 9

The Trailside Inn rents bikes, so go for an early morning pedal along the Confederation Trail. Strike out for the Confederation Bridge to New Brunswick and head to Sackville Waterfowl Park for its bird-watching opportunities. Walking through the flowerpots at Hopewell Rocks is tide dependent, but you can always kayak as a high-tide alternative. Spend the night in Fundy National Park.

## Day 10

Continue down the coast to Saint John, where Irving Nature Park is a good example of what the entire coastline would have looked like before European settlement. You're staying in a city, so you may as well take advantage of the delightful harborfront Hilton Saint

Hopewell Rocks, Fundy Coast, New Brunswick

John (which isn't as much of a splurge as you might imagine).

## Day 11

Catch the ferry across the Bay of Fundy and drive out to Brier Island. An afternoon whale-watching trip can be combined with an evening of bird-watching. Stay at Brier Island Lodge, and dine in-house.

## Day 12

The outdoor-oriented vacation is nearly over, but there's one more activity to try, and Atlantic Canada is the only place in the world you can do so—riding the tidal bore down the Shubenacadie River.

# NOVA SCOTIA

# HALIFAX

Halifax (pop. 370,000), the 250-year-old provincial capital, presents Nova Scotia's strikingly modern face wrapped around a historic heart. It's one of the most vibrant cities in Canada, with an exuberant cultural life and cosmopolitan population. The tourist's Halifax is tidily compact, concentrated on the manageable, boot-shaped peninsula the city inhabits. Its prettiest parts are clustered between the bustling waterfront and the short, steep hillside that the early British developed two centuries ago. In these areas you'll find handsomely historic old districts meshed with stylishly chic new glass-sheathed buildings.

Halifax is more than a city, more than a seaport, and more than a provincial capital. Halifax is a harbor with a city attached, as the Haligonians say. Events in the harbor have shaped Nova Scotia's history. The savvy British military immediately grasped its potential when they first sailed in centuries ago. In fact, Halifax's founding as a settlement in 1749 was incidental to the harbor's development. From the first, the British used the 26-kilometer-long harbor as a watery warehouse of almost unlimited ship-holding capacity. The ships that defeated the French at Louisbourg in 1758—and ultimately conquered this part of Atlantic Canada—were launched from Halifax Harbour. A few years later, the Royal Navy sped from the harbor to harass the rebellious colonies on the Eastern Seaboard during the American Revolution. Ships from Halifax ran the blockades on the South's side during the American Civil War. And during World Wars I and II, the harbor bulged with troop convoys destined for Europe.

© ANDREW HEMPSTEAD

# HIGHLIGHTS

**( Historic Properties:** The oldest waterfront warehouses in Canada have been brought to life with an impressive restoration project and are now filled with bustling boutiques and restaurants (page 35).

**( Maritime Museum of the Atlantic:** If you visit just one museum in Nova Scotia, make it this one, which tells the many stories of the region's links to the ocean, from the *Titanic* tragedy to fishing the Grand Banks (page 35).

**( Alexander Keith's Brewery:** Tours of North America's oldest working brewery go beyond describing the beer-making process, delving deep into Halifax's history and its most colorful characters (page 37).

**( Point Pleasant Park:** On the southern tip of the Halifax Peninsula, this urban park is a favorite for walking and biking (page 37).

**( Halifax Citadel National Historic Site:** Canada's most visited historic site lies atop downtown Halifax's highest point. It provides a glimpse into the city's past as well as sweeping harbor views (page 38).

**( Public Gardens:** Strolling through these formal Victorian gardens is a morning rite of passage for many locals (page 39).

**( Fairview Cemetery:** Varying from three-digit numbers to moving family messages, the inscriptions on the headstones of more than 100 *Titanic* victims make this suburban cemetery a poignant place to visit (page 41).

**( McNabs Island:** Not a place to make a casual stop, spending the day exploring McNabs Island is a good way to get back to nature within city limits (page 42).

**( Bedford Institute of Oceanography:** Looking rather institutional from the outside, this government facility has provided an array of scientific and exploratory services that will awe anyone with an interest in the ocean (page 43).

**( Fisherman's Cove:** If you're not planning to travel beyond Halifax, a visit to this historic fishing village will give you a taste of what you'll be missing farther afield (page 44).

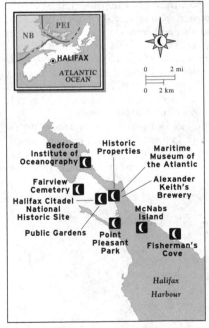

LOOK FOR **(** TO FIND RECOMMENDED SIGHTS, ACTIVITIES, DINING, AND LODGING.

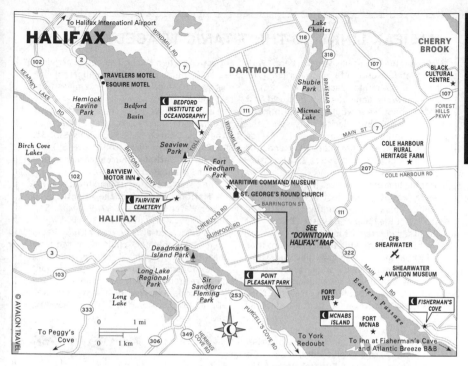

## PLANNING YOUR TIME

Everyone will have his or her own idea as to how best to spend time in Halifax. History buffs will want to spend an entire week exploring the city's oldest corners, while outdoorsy types will want to hit the highlights before moving through to the rest of the province. Halifax has three attractions no one will want to miss, even if you have just one day. The first of these is the **Historic Properties,** a group of waterfront warehouses converted to restaurants and boutiques, while the nearby **Maritime Museum of the Atlantic** is the place to learn about the city's seafaring traditions. The third is **Halifax Citadel National Historic Site.** Any self-respecting beer drinker will want to join a tour of **Alexander Keith's Brewery,** but the brewery is also interesting for its history. These four attractions, along with time exploring the waterfront, would fill one day.

As it's both a gateway for air travelers and as the hub of three highways, chances are you'll be passing through Halifax more than once on your travels through Nova Scotia. This allows you to break up your sightseeing and to plan your schedule around the weather. If, for example, the sun is shining when you first arrive, plan to visit **Point Pleasant Park,** the **Public Gardens,** and **Fairview Cemetery.** These spots and historic downtown attractions should fill two full days. If you have a third day and the forecast is for fine weather, plan to spend time on **McNabs Island,** a delightful destination for hiking just a short ferry ride from the city.

Across the harbor from downtown is the city of Dartmouth, where the **Bedford Institute of Oceanography** overlooks the water. A guided tour of this government facility followed by lunch at the nearby fishing village of **Fisherman's Cove** makes a perfect half-day combination.

# HALIFAX LINKS TO THE *TITANIC* TRAGEDY

"My God, the *Titanic* has struck a berg." With these fateful words, uttered on April 14, 1912, by wireless operator Jack Goodwin of Cape Race, Newfoundland, the outside world first heard about what would develop into the world's best-known maritime disaster – the sinking of the unsinkable ship on its maiden voyage between Southampton, England, and New York City. On board were 2,227 passengers and crew.

At the time of the wireless transmission, the vessel was 500 miles east of Halifax. Three Halifax ships were promptly chartered to search for the foundering vessel. By the time the first had arrived, the *Titanic* was lying on the bottom of the Atlantic Ocean. More than 1,500 passengers and crew perished while 702 lucky souls, mostly women and children, were rescued. Bodies were bought ashore at Karlsen's Wharf (2089 Upper Wharf St.) and **Coaling Wharf No. 4** (north of the MacDonald Bridge), both of which are not open to the public. They were then transported in coffins to a variety of locations, including a curling rink (now an army surplus store, at 2660 Agricola St.) and **Snow's Funeral Home** (1750 Argyle St.), which is now a seafood restaurant. Some bodies were claimed by families, but most were buried in three local cemeteries. The largest concentration is in a plot donated by the White Star Line within **Fairview Cemetery** (corner of Connaught and Chisholm Aves.). Most of the black headstones simply note the date of the tragedy and a number that relates to the order in which bodies were pulled from the ocean. Others have moving tributes to the bravery of loved ones. John Clarke, a band member famous for continuing to play as the ship was sinking, is buried at **Mount Olivet Cemetery** (Mumford Rd. off Joesph Howe Dr.).

The *Titanic*'s owners, the White Star Line, maintained an office in Halifax at 1682 Hollis Street that still stands. It became a hive of activity when the bodies began arriving, as staff members were an important link between the victims and their families from around the world.

Funerals and services were held at a number of downtown churches, including **St. George's Anglican Church** (222 Brunswick St.), **St. Paul's Anglican Church** (1749 Argyle St.), and **St. Mary's Catholic Church** (corner Spring Garden Rd. and Barrington St.).

The best place to learn about the tragedy is the **Maritime Museum of the Atlantic** (1675 Lower Water St., 902/424-7490; Mon.-Sat. 9:30 A.M.-5:30 P.M., Sun. 1-5:30 P.M.), which has a dedicated display area with artifacts such as the only deck chair recovered from the vessel. For archival records, including travel documents, photos, and correspondence related to *Titanic* passengers, visit the **Nova Scotia Archives** (6016 University Ave., 902/424-6060; Mon.-Fri. 8:30 A.M.-4:30 P.M., Sat. 9 A.M.-5 P.M.).

© ANDREW HEMPSTEAD

# HISTORY

The French learned about the area in the early 1700s, when local Mi'Kmaq Indians escorted the French governor on a tour of what they called Chebuctook, the "Great Long Harbor," and adjacent waterways. But it was the British who saw the site's potential; in 1749 Colonel Edward Cornwallis arrived with about 2,500 settlers on 13 ships and founded Halifax along what is now Barrington Street. The settlement was named for Lord Halifax, then president of Britain's Board of Trade and Plantations.

Early Halifax was a stockaded settlement backed by the Grand Parade, the town green where the militia drilled. The first of four citadels was built on the hilltop. St. Paul's Church, the garrison church at Grand Parade's edge, opened in 1750, making it Canada's first Anglican sanctuary. It was a gift from King George III. More English settlers arrived in 1750 and founded Dartmouth across the harbor. By 1752 the two towns were linked by a ferry system, the oldest saltwater ferry system in North America. Nova Scotia was granted representative government in 1758.

## The Royal Military

The completion of Her Majesty's Royal Dockyard in 1760 was the prelude to Louisbourg's absolute destruction the same year. The harbor's defensibility was ensured by a ring of batteries at McNabs Island, Northwest Arm, Point Pleasant with its Martello Tower, and the forts at George's Island and York Redoubt. In 1783 the settlement got another massive Anglo infusion with the arrival of thousands of Loyalists from the United States. Among them was John Wentworth, New Hampshire's former governor. He received a baronet title for his opposition to the revolution in the American colonies and was appointed Nova Scotia's lieutenant governor. Sir John and Lady Wentworth led the Halifax social scene, hobnobbing with Prince Edward (the Maritimes' military commander in chief, who would later sire Queen Victoria) and his French paramour Julie St. Laurent (to the chagrin of propriety-minded local society).

## Prosperous Times

The seaport thrived in the 1800s. By 1807 the city's population topped 60,000. A proper government setting—the sandstone Colonial Building (now Province House)—opened in 1819, followed by a number of noteworthy academic institutions. The harbor front—which during the War of 1812 served as a black-market trade center for Halifax privateers—acquired commercial legitimacy when native Haligonian Samuel Cunard, rich from lumbering, whaling, and banking, turned his interests to shipping. By 1838 the Cunard Steamship Company handled the British and North American Royal Mail, and by 1840 Cunard's four ships provided the first regular transport between the two continents.

The seaport's incorporation in 1841 ushered in a prosperous mercantile era. Granville Street, with its stylish shops, became in its day Atlantic Canada's Fifth Avenue. Less stylish brothels and taverns lined Brunswick, Market, and Barrack Streets, and the military police swept through the area often, breaking up drunken fistfights and reestablishing order.

## The Modern Era

By the 1960s, Halifax looked like a hoary victim of the centuries, somewhat the worse for wear. Massive federal, provincial, and private investment, however, restored the harbor to its early luster, with its warehouses groomed as the handsome Historic Properties.

The city continued to polish its image, as sandblasting renewed the exterior of architectural treasures such as Province House. The Art Gallery of Nova Scotia moved from cramped quarters near the Public Archives and settled within the stunningly renovated former Dominion Building. Municipal guidelines sought to control the city's growth. The unobstructed view on George Street between the harbor and the Citadel was secured with a municipal mandate, and the height of the hillside's high-rise buildings was also restricted to preserve the cityscape. During this time, the waterfront evolved into a bustling tourist precinct, but one that is also enjoyed by locals.

# A LONG WEEKEND IN HALIFAX

Halifax is a major destination for conventioneers (modern facilities, well-priced accommodations, centrally located for delegates from both North America and Europe), and in this regard, you may find yourself wanting to hang around for a few days when the last meeting wraps up on Friday. Or, for leisure travelers, many flights to other parts of Atlantic Canada are routed through Halifax, so it will cost little or no extra to have a stopover, and then continue to Newfoundland, Prince Edward Island, or elsewhere. This itinerary covers both scenarios, and you don't have to worry about driving.

## DAY 1

You've been staying at an upscale downtown Halifax hotel such as Four Points by Sheraton Halifax, and suddenly it's not business anymore. No worries; rates drop dramatically come the weekend, so you won't break the bank by staying another two nights. Join the after-work crowd at the **Seahorse Tavern**, and then plan on dining next door at the **Economy Shoe Shop.**

## DAY 2

Visit **Halifax Citadel National Historic Site** to get a feel for the city's colorful history and then walk over to the **Public Gardens.** After lunch at the **Harbourside Market,** learn about the *Titanic* tragedy at the **Maritime Museum**

**of the Atlantic** before visiting the graves of some of the victims at **Fairview Cemetery.** A two-minute walk from the Sheraton is **Bish,** one of the city's best restaurants, or if it's casual seafood you're after, continue along the waterfront to **Salty's.**

## DAY 3

The local tour company Ambassatours operates an excellent full-day trip along the South Shore. It hits the highlights – scenic **Peggy's Cove** and the beautiful waterfront **churches of Mahone Bay** – while also allowing time to wander through the historic streets of downtown **Lunenburg,** where there's time for shopping and lunch. You'll be back in Halifax in time for dinner at **Chives Canadian Bistro,** which features lots of fresh seasonal produce.

## DAY 4

Check the sailing schedule of the *Bluenose II* and make reservations for a morning cruise if this grand old lady is in port. Otherwise, you could start out with breakfast and checking your email at the **Paper Chase News Café,** followed by shopping at downtown stores as varied as **Nova Scotian Crystal** and **Rum Runners Rum Cake Factory.** Golfers may want to squeeze in a tee time at **Glen Arbour Golf Course,** which is on the way out to the airport.

# Sights

Halifax is packed with attractions, all reasonably priced or absolutely free. The biggest concentration is within walking distance of the waterfront precinct and many accommodations. Beyond the downtown core are a number of interesting sights that are easy to miss but easy to reach by public transportation. Whatever your interests—searching out *Titanic*-related sights or exploring coastal parks—you will find plenty to do and see in the capital.

## GETTING ORIENTED

The layout of Halifax is easy to grasp. **Downtown** lines the western side of **Halifax Harbour.** Lower and Upper Water Streets and Barrington Street run through downtown parallel to the water. This is the core of the city, chock-full of historic attractions, the city's finest accommodations, and a wonderful choice of restaurants. The waterfront itself bustles day and night. From Historic Properties' wharves at the waterfront,

# DOWNTOWN HALIFAX

*Halifax Harbour*

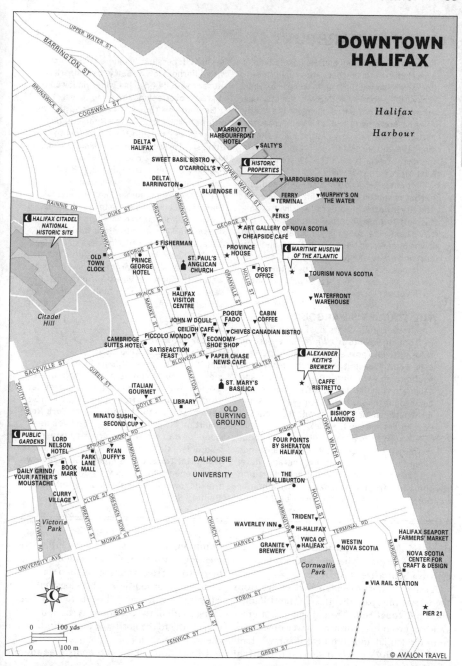

MARRIOTT HARBOURFRONT HOTEL
SALTY'S
DELTA HALIFAX
SWEET BASIL BISTRO
O'CARROLL'S
HISTORIC PROPERTIES
DELTA BARRINGTON
HARBOURSIDE MARKET
BLUENOSE II
FERRY TERMINAL
MURPHY'S ON THE WATER
PERKS
ART GALLERY OF NOVA SCOTIA
CHEAPSIDE CAFÉ
HALIFAX CITADEL NATIONAL HISTORIC SITE
5 FISHERMAN
PROVINCE HOUSE
MARITIME MUSEUM OF THE ATLANTIC
OLD TOWN CLOCK
PRINCE GEORGE HOTEL
ST. PAUL'S ANGLICAN CHURCH
POST OFFICE
TOURISM NOVA SCOTIA
Citadel Hill
HALIFAX VISITOR CENTRE
WATERFRONT WAREHOUSE
POGUE FADO
CABIN COFFEE
JOHN W DOULL
CEILIDH CAFÉ
CHIVES CANADIAN BISTRO
PICCOLO MONDO
ECONOMY SHOE SHOP
CAMBRIDGE SUITES HOTEL
SATISFACTION FEAST
PAPER CHASE NEWS CAFÉ
ALEXANDER KEITH'S BREWERY
ITALIAN GOURMET
ST. MARY'S BASILICA
CAFFE RISTRETTO
LIBRARY
OLD BURYING GROUND
BISHOP'S LANDING
MINATO SUSHI
SECOND CUP
PUBLIC GARDENS
LORD NELSON HOTEL
FOUR POINTS BY SHERATON HALIFAX
RYAN DUFFY'S
PARK LANE MALL
DAILY GRIND/ YOUR FATHER'S MOUSTACHE
BOOK MARK
DALHOUSIE UNIVERSITY
THE HALLIBURTON
CURRY VILLAGE
Victoria Park
TRIDENT
WAVERLEY INN
HI-HALIFAX
HALIFAX SEAPORT FARMERS' MARKET
GRANITE BREWERY
YWCA OF HALIFAX
WESTIN NOVA SCOTIA
NOVA SCOTIA CENTER FOR CRAFT & DESIGN
Cornwallis Park
VIA RAIL STATION
PIER 21

0    100 yds
0    100 m

© AVALON TRAVEL

UPPER WATER ST
BARRINGTON ST
BRUNSWICK ST
COGSWELL ST
RAINNIE DR
LOWER WATER ST
DUKE ST
ARGYLE ST
BARRINGTON ST
GEORGE ST
BRUNSWICK ST
GEORGE ST
PRINCE ST
GRANVILLE ST
HOLLIS ST
MARKET ST
PRINCE ST
BLOWERS ST
GRAFTON ST
SALTER ST
SACKVILLE ST
QUEEN ST
DOYLE ST
SOUTH PARK ST
BISHOP ST
LOWER WATER ST
SPRING GARDEN RD
BIRMINGHAM ST
BRENTON ST
DRESDEN ROW
CHURCH ST
BARRINGTON ST
HOLLIS ST
TERMINAL RD
TOWER RD
MORRIS ST
HARVEY ST
MARGINAL RD
UNIVERSITY AVE
CLYDE ST
SOUTH ST
QUEEN ST
TOBIN ST
FENWICK ST
KENT ST
GREEN ST

# HALIFAX HARBOUR

From a maritime standpoint, Halifax Harbour is a jewel, the world's second-largest natural harbor (after Sydney Harbour in Australia). High rocky bluffs notched with coves rim the wide entrance where the harbor meets the frothy Atlantic. **McNabs Island** is spread across the harbor's mouth and is so large that it almost clogs the entrance. Many an unwary ship has foundered on the island's shallow, treacherous Eastern Passage coastline.

On the western side of McNabs Island, the harbor is split in two by Halifax's peninsula. The Northwest Arm, a fjord-like sliver of sea, cuts off to one side and wraps around the city's back side. Along its banks are the long lawns of parks, estates, yacht clubs, and several university campuses. The main channel continues inland, shouldered by uptown Halifax on one side and its sister city of Dartmouth on the other.

## THE TOURIST'S HARBOUR

The harbor puts on its best show directly in front of downtown. White-hulled cruise ships nose into port and dock alongside Halifax's **Point Pleasant Park** at the peninsula's southern tip. Freighters, tugs, tour boats, and sailboats skim the choppy waters, and ferries cut through the sea traffic, scurrying back and forth between the two cities with their loads of commuters and sightseers.

The scene has a transfixing quality about it. Tourist season unofficially starts and ends when the harborfront Halifax Sheraton hotel sets tables and chairs for alfresco dining on the waterfront promenade. Stiff summer breezes usually accompany lunch, but the view is worth it. Less hardy diners jostle for tables with a harbor view at **Salty's,** the nearby restaurant with its enviable wide-windowed dining room overlooking the same scene.

Beyond the tourist's realm and the two cities' harbor-fronts, the spacious harbor compresses itself into **The Narrows.** Two high-flung steel expressways – the **MacDonald** and **MacKay Bridges** (toll $0.75) – cross the Narrows at either end. The MacDonald Bridge permits pedestrians and provides an aerial view of the **Maritime Command** and **Her Majesty's Canadian Dockyard** along the Halifax side.

The slender Narrows then opens into 40-square-kilometer **Bedford Basin,** 16 kilometers long and as capacious as a small inland sea. Sailboats cruise its waters now, but the expanse has seen a parade of ships cross its waters through the years – from the white-sailed British warships of centuries ago to the steel-hulled vessels of the Allies during both World Wars.

## HALIFAX HARBOUR FROM VARIED ANGLES

Halifax Harbour reveals itself in different views. Its pulse can be probed from one of the ferries or from the harborfront in either city. The approach from the Atlantic can be seen best from the historic fort at **York Redoubt** on Purcells Cove Road. And you get a good view of Northwest Arm's ritzy estate and university scene from Fleming Park's **Memorial Tower** on the same road. **Seaview Park** beneath the MacKay Bridge overlooks the Narrows where that slender strait meets Bedford Basin.

---

sightseeing boats explore the harbor. The splendid Maritime Museum and Art Gallery of Nova Scotia are close by.

A series of short streets rise like ramps from the waterfront, past the grassy Grand Parade and up **Citadel Hill.** Around the hill, a great swath of green space provides a welcome break from residential and commercial sprawl. Laid out by the city's original surveyor, **Central Common,** on the west side of the hill, marks a meeting of roads. Major thoroughfares merge here (Robie Street running north to south, Bell Road running southeast, and Cogswell Street running east to west). Locals refer to everything south of the commons as the South End, everything to the north the North End, and to the west the West End.

In the South End is the city's **academic**

area, site of Dalhousie University, University of King's College, St. Mary's University, and the Atlantic School of Theology. At the southern tip of the downtown peninsula is **Point Pleasant Park,** an oasis of green surrounded by the grays of sprawling loading docks to the north and the sparkling blue waters of Halifax Harbour on all other sides.

The **Northwest Arm** of Halifax Harbour nearly cuts the downtown area off from the rest of the city. At the head of this waterway is the **Armdale Rotary,** from where Herring Cove Road spurs south to **Purcells Cove Road,** which passes yacht-filled marinas, Sir Sandford Fleming Park, and York Redoubt National Historic Site.

Across Halifax Harbour from downtown is the city of **Dartmouth.** Linked to downtown by ferry and bridge, this commercial and residential area has a smattering of sights and is also worth visiting for the views back across to Halifax. Beyond the two bridges spanning Halifax Harbour is Bedford Basin, a large body of water surrounded by development. At the head of the basin is the residential area of Bedford and suburbs, including Lower Sackville and Waverly. Traveling down Highway 102 from Truro and **Halifax International Airport** (38 kilometers north of downtown), you'll pass exits to these and other towns.

## DOWNTOWN

The following sights are within walking distance of each other from the waterfront. You could easily spend a full day exploring this part of the city, taking time out to lunch at an outdoor harborfront restaurant.

### ⟨ Historic Properties

Canada's oldest surviving group of waterfront warehouses is also one of the city's main tourist attractions, with excellent shopping and dining spread along a three-block expanse on Upper and Lower Water Streets. The wooden and stone warehouses, chandleries, and buildings once used by shipping interests and privateers have been restored to their early 1800s

glory. They now house restaurants, shops, and other sites impressively styled with Victorian and Italianate facades. The history of the precinct is cataloged halfway along the Privateer Wharf building (on the inside) with interpretive panels.

### ⟨ Maritime Museum of the Atlantic

The seaport's store of nautical memorabilia lies within this sleek, burnished-red waterfront museum (1675 Lower Water St., 902/424-7490; summer daily 9:30 A.M.–5:30 P.M., the rest of the year Tues.–Sat. 9:30 A.M.–5 P.M., Sun. 1–5 P.M.; adult $9, senior $8, child $5). The museum is one of the crowning achievements of the city's Waterfront Development Project. Most visitors find the *Titanic* display room most interesting. It contains the world's largest collection of artifacts from the floating palace deemed unsinkable by its owners; you will see the only deckchair recovered at the time of the sinking, a cribbage board, lounge paneling, and more. Also on display is a model of the *Titanic,* the wireless log taken as the vessel floundered, and a variety of information boards that tell the story of ship's construction. **Titanic 3D,** a National Geographic documentary created from footage taken from the wreck, shows continuously.

Outside, two historic vessels are tied up at the wharf. One of these, the **CSS Acadia,** spent its life as Canada's first hydrographic vessel, its crew surveying the east coast using sextants and graphing shoreline features. The other, **HMCS Sackville,** is the last remaining Canadian World War II convoy escort corvette. Admission is $1 to each, or free with proof of admission to the maritime museum.

### Art Gallery of Nova Scotia

Atlantic Canada's largest and finest art collection is housed in two buildings separated by a cobbled courtyard just up from the harbor (1723 Hollis St., 902/424-7542; daily 10 A.M.–5 P.M.; adult $10, senior $8, child $4). The main entrance is within Gallery South (also home to an excellent little café).

Art Gallery of Nova Scotia

The vast majority of the collection is displayed in Gallery North, the sandstone Dominion Building. Some 2,000 works in oils, watercolors, stone, wood, and other media are exhibited throughout its four floors of spacious galleries. The permanent collections give priority to current and former Nova Scotia residents and include works by Mary Pratt, Arthur Lismer, Carol Fraser, and Alex Colville. The mezzanine-level regional folk-art collection is a particular delight. The ground-floor Gallery Shop trades in the cream of provincial arts and crafts and sells books, cards, and gifts.

## Province House

The seat of the provincial government, Province House (1726 Hollis St., 902/424-4661; July–Aug. Mon.–Fri. 9 A.M.–5 P.M., Sat.–Sun. 10 A.M.–4 P.M., the rest of the year Mon.–Fri. 9 A.M.–4 P.M.; free) was completed in 1819. It's the smallest and oldest provincial legislature building in the country and features a fine Georgian exterior and splendid interior, resembling a rural English mansion more than an official residence. On his visit to modest but dignified Province House in 1842, author Charles Dickens remarked, "It was like looking at Westminster through the wrong end of a telescope…a gem of Georgian architecture."

## St. Paul's Anglican Church

This stately white wooden church (1749 Argyle St., 902/429-2240) was styled on the Palladian style of St. Peter's Church on Vere Street in London, England. Dating to 1749, it is the oldest surviving building in Halifax and was the first Anglican church in Canada. The interior is full of memorials to Halifax's early residents. Notice the bit of metal embedded above the door at the back of the north wall—it's a piece of shrapnel hurled from the *Mont Blanc,* two kilometers away, during the Halifax Explosion. The church is between Barrington and Argyle Streets at the edge of the Grand Parade; look for the square belfry topped by an octagonal cupola.

## Old Burying Ground

Designated a national historic site in 1991, this cemetery (June–Sept. daily 9 A.M.–5 P.M.) sits opposite Government House at Barrington Street and Spring Garden Road. Its history goes back to the city's founding. The first customer, so to speak, was interred just one day after the arrival of the original convoy of English settlers in 1749. Also among the thicket of age-darkened, hand-carved, old-fashioned headstones is the 1754 grave of John Connor, the settlement's first ferry captain. The most recent burial took place more than 160 years ago, in 1844.

## St. Mary's Basilica

Two popes and hundreds of thousands of parishioners have filed through the doors of this Gothic Revival church (1508 Barrington St., 902/423-4116), whose spires cast an afternoon shadow over the Old Burying Ground. It was built in 1860; the title "Basilica" was bestowed during a visit by Pope Pius XII in 1950. The stained-glass windows, replaced after the originals were destroyed by the 1917 Halifax Explosion, are particularly impressive.

## ◖ Alexander Keith's Brewery

Keith's, at the south end of downtown and one block back from the water (1496 Lower Water St., 902/455-1474) is North America's oldest operating brewery. Keith arrived in Halifax in 1795, bringing with him brewing techniques from his English homeland and finding a ready market among the soldiers and sailors living in the city. Although main brewing operations have been moved to the Oland Brewery, north of downtown, the original brewery, an impressive stone and granite edifice extending along an entire block, produces seasonal brews using traditional techniques. Tours led by costumed guides depart June–October Monday–Saturday 11 A.M.–8 P.M., Sunday noon–5 P.M., November–April Friday 5–8 P.M., Saturday noon–8 P.M., Sunday noon–5 P.M. Adults pay $16, seniors $14, and children $8, with the tour ending with a traditional toast to the "Father of Great Beer."

## Pier 21

As you continue south along Lower Water Street from the brewery (take the Harbourwalk for the full effect), beyond the statue of Samuel Cunard, the waterfront is dominated by Halifax's massive cruise-ship terminal. This 3,900-square-meter structure has a long and colorful history of welcoming foreigners in its original capacity as an "immigration shed," where more than a million immigrants, refugees, and war brides first set foot on Canadian soil between 1928 and 1971. It was also the main departure point for 500,000 Canadians who fought in World War II. Upstairs within the building is the **Exhibition Hall** (1055 Marginal Rd., 902/425-7770; May–Nov. daily 9:30 A.M.–5:30 P.M., Dec.–Apr. Tues.–Sat. 10 A.M.–5 P.M.; adult $8.50, senior $7.50, child $5). This immigration museum does a wonderful job of bringing to life the stories of those who traveled across the ocean to make a new home in Canada. The firsthand accounts begin with the decision to leave home and go through the voyage and arrival to describe onward journeys by rail across Canada. Allow time to view *Oceans of Hope,* a 30-minute film narrated by a fictional immigration officer.

Beside the street-level reception area is the **Research Centre,** which can be used by individuals whose families arrived in Canada through Pier 21. It contains a wide variety of documents, passenger logs, and historic images of passenger vessels.

## Nova Scotia Centre for Craft and Design

Provincial crafts development and innovation are nurtured at this workshop ensconced in the cruise-ship terminal (1061 Marginal Rd., 902/492-2522; Mon.–Sat. 9 A.M.–4 P.M.; free), geared to weaving, woodworking, metal, and multimedia production.

## ◖ Point Pleasant Park

Before dawn on September 29, 2003, Hurricane Juan hit Halifax like no other storm in living memory. Seventy-five–hectare Point Pleasant Park, at the southern tip of the Halifax peninsula, took the full brunt of the storm. By daybreak the next morning the full extent of the damage was first seen—more than 75,000 of the park's 100,000 trees had been destroyed, and the park's ecology had been changed forever. After the cleanup, a massive rejuvenation project that continues to this day began.

Although much of the forest may be gone, the park is still well worth visiting. To get to the main entrance, take South Park Street south from Sackville Street. South Park becomes Young Avenue, a tree-lined boulevard graced by magnificent mansions; turn left on Point Pleasant Drive. Marginal Road from downtown also terminates at the same waterside entrance. Views from the parking lot itself sweep across the harbor, with container terminals on one side and green space on the other. Forty kilometers of trails, many paved, allow for hiking, jogging, and cross-country skiing in winter. Bikes are allowed only Monday–Friday. Most of the main trails have reopened since the storm, allowing access to all corners of the spread, with terns, gulls, and ospreys

# HALIFAX EXPLOSION

On the morning of Thursday, December 6, 1917, Halifax experienced a catastrophic explosion – at the time the largest man-made explosion in history, unrivaled until the detonation of the first atomic bomb. On that fateful morning, Halifax Harbour was busy with warships transporting troops, munitions, and other supplies bound for the war in Europe. A French ship, the *Mont Blanc*, filled to the gunwales with explosives – including 400,000 pounds of TNT – was heading through the narrows toward the harbor mouth when it was struck by a larger vessel, the *Imo*, which was steaming in the opposite direction, and caught fire. The terrified crew of the *Mont Blanc* took immediately to the lifeboats, as the burning ship drifted close to the Halifax shore.

A short time later, at 9:05 A.M., the *Mont Blanc* cargo blew up, instantly killing an estimated 2,000 people, wounding another 10,000, and obliterating about 130 hectares of the North End of downtown Halifax. So colossal was the explosion that windows were shattered 80 kilometers away, and the shock wave rocked Sydney on Cape Breton, 430 kilometers northeast. The barrel of one of the *Mont Blanc*'s cannons was hurled 5.5 kilometers, while its half-ton anchor shank landed more than three kilometers away in the opposite direction.

Serving as a memorial to the tragedy is **Fort Needham Memorial Park,** along Gottingen Street north from downtown. Here, a 14-bell carillon is on a high point of land from where the site of the original explosion can be seen. While the harborfront **Maritime Museum of the Atlantic** has an exhibit dedicated to the explosion, one of the most interesting reminders is up the hill at **St. Paul's Anglican Church** (1749 Argyle St.), where a chunk of metal from the doomed *Mont Blanc* is embedded in the north-facing wall.

---

winging overhead. A bit of real-estate trivia: The park is still rented from the British government, on a 999-year lease, for one shilling per year.

Point Pleasant's military significance is evidenced by the 1796 Prince of Wales Martello Tower (July–early Sept. daily 10 A.M.–6 P.M.) and Fort Ogilvie, built in 1862, both part of Halifax's defensive system. The former, a thick-walled round tower, based on those the British were building at the time to repel Napoleon's forces, was the first of its kind to be built in North America.

## CITADEL HILL AND VICINITY

Walk up George Street from the harbor front to reach Citadel Hill. You'll know you're on the right street by the **Old Town Clock,** framed by the buildings of George Street at the base of Citadel Hill. Originally constructed as the official timekeeper for Halifax, the four-faced clock tower was completed in 1803 by order of the compulsively punctual Prince Edward. It is not open to the public but instead stands as a city landmark.

## ( Halifax Citadel National Historic Site

Halifax's premier landmark (Sackville St., 902/426-5080; May–Oct. daily 9 A.M.–5 P.M., until 6 P.M. in summer; adult $12, senior $10.50, child $6) is also the most visited National Historic Site in Canada. The Citadel crowns the hill at the top of George Street, commanding the strategic high ground above the city and harbor, with magnificent views of the entire area. This star-shaped, dressed-granite fortress, the fourth military works built on this site, was completed in 1856. In its heyday, the Citadel represented the pinnacle of defensive military technology, though its design was never tested by an attack.

In summer, students in period uniforms portray soldiers of the 78th Highlanders and the Royal Artillery, demonstrating military drills, powder magazine operation, changing of the sentries, and piping. At the stroke of noon each day, they load and fire a cannon with due military precision and ceremony, a shot heard round the city. Most of the fortress is open for exploration; exhibits include a museum, barrack rooms, a powder magazine, and a 50-minute audiovisual presentation on the fort's history. Guided tours are included in the admission price, while within the grounds are a gift shop and café.

The grounds are open year-round, but no services are offered November–April.

## Museum of Natural History

This museum (1747 Summer St., 902/424-7353; June–mid-Oct. Mon.–Sat. 9 A.M.–5 P.M., Sun. noon–5 P.M., mid-Oct.–May Tues.–Sat. 9 A.M.–5 P.M., Sun. noon–5 P.M.; adult $5, senior $4.50, child $3) is a five-minute walk from Citadel Hill, but it also has plenty of its own parking. The rather plain exterior belies a treasure trove of exhibits that bring the province's natural world to life. Opposite the ticket desk is a kid-friendly nature center, with small critters in enclosures and tanks, and staff on hand to answer any questions. Beyond this point are exhibits that tell the story of Nova Scotia's first human inhabitants, Palaeo Indians, who moved into the region 11,000 years ago. The dinosaur displays are a major draw for young and old. You'll also learn about modern-day creatures in a room full of stuffed animals and a large hall dominated by a pilot whale skeleton. Other highlights include a gem and mineral display and artifacts from Acadian culture.

## ( Public Gardens

South across Sackville Street from the Citadel grounds, the Public Gardens (May–mid-Oct. daily 8 A.M.–dusk) are an irresistibly attractive oasis spread over seven hectares in the heart of the city. Bordered by Spring Garden Road, South Park Street, Summer Street, and Sackville Street, what started in 1753 as a private garden is now considered one of the loveliest formal

Halifax Citadel National Historic Site

© ANDREW HEMPSTEAD

gardens in North America and is reminiscent of the handsome parks of Europe.

Inside the wrought-iron fence (main entrance at the corner of South Park Street and Spring Garden Road), the setting revels in tulips that flower late May through early June, followed by rhododendrons and roses, and the roses and perennials through summer. Other highlights are the exotic and native trees, fountains, and lily ponds where ducks and geese make their home. The ornate bandstand dates from Queen Victoria's Golden Jubilee and is the site of free Sunday afternoon concerts in July and August. Also during the summer, vendors of arts and crafts hawk their wares outside the gardens along Spring Garden Road.

## NORTH OF DOWNTOWN

The following sights are north of Cogswell Street. It's a two-kilometer walk from downtown to Fort Needham Memorial Park. Fairview Cemetery is not within walking distance.

© ANDREW HEMPSTEAD

St. George's Round Church

### St. George's Round Church

Architect William Hughes designed this unusual and charming timber-frame church, which at once accommodated the overflow of parishioners from the nearby Dutch Church on Brunswick Street and satisfied Prince Edward's penchant for round buildings. The cornerstone was laid in 1800, and the chancel and front porch were added later. A fire in 1994 destroyed the dome, but it has since been replaced. St. George's is a few blocks north of downtown at Brunswick and Cornwallis Streets.

### Maritime Command Museum

On the grounds of Canadian Forces Base Halifax, this museum (Gottingen St. between North St. and Russell St., 902/721-8250; Mon.–Fri. 10 A.M.–3:30 P.M.; free) is ensconced in the 30-room Admiralty House, built in the 1840s as a residence for the base's admiral. Exhibits include presentation swords, memorabilia from the World War II Battle of the Atlantic, a military gun collection, uniforms, ship models, and other artifacts relating to the

history of the Canadian Maritime Military Forces.

### Fort Needham Memorial Park

Continue north along Gottingen Street from the maritime museum and veer right onto Dartmouth Street to reach this park, a high point of land with views across the head of Halifax Harbour. The park's most distinctive feature is a 14-bell carillon, a monument to the Halifax Explosion of 1917, at the time the largest man-made explosion the world had ever known. Stand in the break between the memorial's two halves and you get views through a clearing to the harbor and the actual site of the explosion.

### Seaview Park

Halifax's peninsula is bookended by a pair of expansive green spaces. Seaview Park is at the north end, overlooking Bedford Basin from the foot of the A. Murray McKay Bridge. This was once the site of Africville, a community of black Haligonians established in the 1840s but since demolished. George Dixon, holder of three world boxing titles, was born here in 1870. As you head north from downtown along Barrington Street, access is along Service Road. A boat launch provides the only water access.

### ◖ Fairview Cemetery

Take Windsor Street north from Quinpool Road to reach Fairview Cemetery, final resting place of 121 *Titanic* victims. When the bodies were pulled from the Atlantic Ocean, they were given a number. These numbers, along with the date of the disaster, April 15, 1912 (it is assumed no one could have survived any longer than a day in the frigid ocean), adorn a majority of the simple black headstones paid for by the White Star Line, owners of the *Titanic*. Where identification was possible, a name accompanies the number, such as victim 227, J. Dawson, the origin of the character Jack Dawson played by Leonardo DiCaprio in the movie *Titanic*. Some headstones are engraved with moving tributes, such as that to Everett Edward Elliott, aged 24, which reads, "Each man stood at his port while all the weaker ones went by, and showed once more to all the world how Englishmen should die."

The turn into the cemetery is easy to miss; get in the left lane by Connaught Avenue and be prepared to turn against oncoming traffic to reach the cemetery's main entrance. The other option is to take Connaught Avenue off Windsor Street and park at the end of Chisholm Avenue. Once you're at the cemetery, the plot is well signposted, with an interpretive board describing events leading up to identifying victims long after they were buried. The cemetery is open from dawn to dusk.

### Hemlock Ravine Park

This rugged tract of forest lies beside the western side of Bedford Basin between the busy Bedford and Bicentennial highways—but you'd never know urban civilization is so close as you walk along the five interconnecting walking trails. The park's namesake ravine, with its towering hemlocks, takes about 20 minutes to reach from the main parking lot, at the end of Kent Avenue, which branches off the Bedford Highway (Highway 2) one kilometer north of the Kearney Lake Road intersection. Beside the parking lot is a heart-shaped pond designed by Prince Edward, who spent his summers here with his companion Julie St. Laurent.

### Uniacke Estate Museum Park

This splendid 930-hectare estate (758 Main Rd., Mount Uniacke, 902/866-0032; June–mid-Oct. Mon.–Sat. 9:30 A.M.–5:30 P.M., Sun. 11 A.M.–5:30 P.M.; adult $3, child $2) is along Highway 1 beyond city limits 20 kilometers northwest from the intersection of Highway 102 (the easiest way to get there is to take Exit 3 from Highway 101). The home's interior features original furnishings, including four-poster beds and family portraits. The grounds offer seven hiking trails.

## WEST SIDE OF NORTHWEST ARM

Carefully make your way onto the Armdale Rotary at the west end of Quinpool Road and take the Herring Cove Road exit. A short distance south along this road, Purcells Cove Road veers off to the left. This winding road hugs the Northwest Arm for nine kilometers to the fishing village of Herring Cove. Along the way are two yacht clubs filled with glistening white sailboats, and these two sights.

### Sir Sandford Fleming Park

A 38-hectare grassy spread, this delightful piece of parkland is mostly forested, sloping to a seawall promenade fringing a quiet waterway. The land was donated by the Scottish-born Fleming, best known for establishing time zones. It is said a missed train led the enterprising Fleming to begin formulating a plan that would see the entire world operate on a 24-hour clock with time zones that related to longitude. Fleming, who also designed Canada's first postage stamp, lived in Halifax from the 1880s until his death in 1915.

On a slight rise above the bay is the 10-story **Dingle Tower** (June–Aug. daily 9 A.M.–5 P.M.). A stairway winds up the

© ANDREW HEMPSTEAD

The high point of Sir Sandford Fleming Park is the Dingle Tower.

interior of this stone edifice, presenting great views from the top.

The park is open daily 8 A.M.–dusk. The main entrance is off Purcells Cove Road; Dingle Road leads down through the wooded park to the waterfront.

### York Redoubt National Historic Site

Set on a bluff high above the harbor entrance, York Redoubt National Historic Site (Purcells Cove Rd., 902/426-5080; grounds mid-May–Oct. daily 9 A.M.–6 P.M., buildings mid-June–Aug. daily 10 A.M.–6 P.M.; free) is six kilometers south of downtown. The setting draws visitors with walking paths that lead down the steep incline to picnic tables and protected coves. Up top are strategic fortifications dating to 1793, when Britain went to war with the French. Most of the fort is from later times, including massive muzzle-loading guns that were designed to fire nine-inch shells capable of piercing armored vessels.

## MCNABS ISLAND

Whatever your interests, this five-kilometer-long island at the entrance to Halifax Harbour is a wonderful place to spend a day. The island is mostly wooded, its forests filled with bird-life and its shoreline dotted with beaches and tidal pools. Archaeological evidence points to habitation by the Mi'Kmaq at least 1,600 years ago, but the most obvious signs of human development are more recent, including two forts and the remains of a number of residences (including the summer home of Frederick Perrin, of Lea & Perrins Worcestershire sauce fame). Although many of the early residences have disappeared, signs of their formal gardens remain; look for ash, oak, and apple trees.

### Recreation

Most visitors come to the island to go hiking. Ferries land at Garrison Pier, from where trails radiate in all directions. The top of Jenkin's Hill, easily reached in 10 minutes, is a good place to get oriented while also enjoying sweeping harbor views. At the 1864 **Fort Ives,** an easy 30-minute walk from the pier, cannons are still in place. **Fort McNab,** a similar distance south of the pier, was built in 1889 and is protected as a National Historic Site. Sandy **Mauger's Beach,** just south of Garrison Pier, is the best and most accessible of many island beaches.

### Getting There

Year-round access to the island is provided by **McNabs Island Ferry** (902/465-4563), which departs from Fisherman's Cove, on the Dartmouth side of the harbor. Round-trip fare is adult $14, senior and child $11.50. Ask at the Halifax Visitor Centre for ferries departing from downtown Halifax. No services are available on the island, so bring your own food and drink and be prepared for changeable weather by bringing a rain jacket.

## DARTMOUTH

Dartmouth is a large residential, commercial, and industrial area across the harbor from Halifax. The two cities are joined by a bridge and Metro Transit's Halifax–Dartmouth ferry from the foot of downtown's George Street to the Alderney Gate Complex in Dartmouth. Ferries operate year-round Monday–Saturday 6:30 A.M.–midnight, and daily in summer. The fare is adult $2, senior and child $1.40 each way. The ferry arrives within walking distance of Dartmouth Heritage Museum properties and various shops and restaurants.

## Dartmouth Heritage Museum

The Dartmouth Heritage Museum comprises two historic homes within walking distance of Alderney Gate. The 1867 **Evergreen House** (26 Newcastle St., 902/464-2300; summer Tues.–Sun. 10 A.M.–5 P.M., the rest of the year Tues.–Sat. 10 A.M.–5 P.M.; adult $2), filled with period antiques, is the grander of the two. Built by a cooper (barrel maker) in 1785, **Quaker House** (57 Ochterloney St., 902/464-5823; summer Tues.–Sun. 10 A.M.–5 P.M.) is one of Dartmouth's oldest residences. In addition to period furnishings, exhibits tell the story of the Quakers, who were drawn to Nova Scotia for the abundance of whales.

## ◖ Bedford Institute of Oceanography

This government-run facility (Baffin Blvd., 902/426-4306; Mon.–Fri. 9 A.M.–4 P.M.; free) has a mandate that includes everything from helping maintain Canada's sovereignty to federal fisheries, but is best known for its work on the sunken *Titanic*. On a guided tour (summer, by appointment only), you'll get to learn about all this work, as well as step aboard a simulated ship's bridge and get up close and personal at the Touch Tank. To get there from downtown Halifax, cross the Narrows and take the Shannon Park exit of the MacKay Bridge (immediately after the toll gates); turn right and then left onto Baffin Boulevard, which crosses under the bridge to the institute.

## Shubie Park

In 1858, construction began on an ambitious canal system that linked Halifax Harbour with the Bay of Fundy via a string of lakes and the Shubenacadie River. The canal was abandoned just 12 years later. The canal between Lake Micmac and Lake Charles has been restored, complete with one of nine original locks. The park is laced with hiking and biking trails, but many visitors take to the water in canoes and kayaks, paddling from the main day-use area to Lake Charles. Access is signposted from Braemar Drive, which branches north from Exit 6 of Highway 111.

## Cole Harbour Rural Heritage Farm

Surrounded by a residential subdivision, this outdoor attraction (471 Poplar Dr., 902/434-0222; mid-May–mid-Oct. Mon.–Sat. 10 A.M.–4 P.M., Sun. noon–4 P.M.; donation) is a great place for children. Buildings include a 200-year-old farmhouse, a blacksmith shop, various barns, and a tearoom, while garden plots represent early crops, with the produce used in the tearoom. Livestock is fenced, but rabbits, geese, and ducks roam free.

# EASTERN PASSAGE

The Eastern Passage is a narrow waterway running between the Dartmouth side of Halifax Harbour and McNabs Island. From downtown Dartmouth take Pleasant Street south to Highway 322. This route passes oil refineries and Canadian Forces Base Shearwater before reaching the delightful Fisherman's Cove. Beyond this point, Highway 322 continues through an oceanfront residential area to Southeast Passage Provincial Park.

## Shearwater Aviation Museum

At the entrance to Canadian Forces Base Shearwater, this museum (12 Wing, Pleasant St., 902/460-1083; June–Aug. Tues.–Fri. 10 A.M.–5 P.M., Sat.–Sun. noon–4 P.M., Apr.–May and Sept.–Nov. Tues.–Thurs. 10 A.M.–5 P.M., Sat. noon–4 P.M.; free) is home to 10 restored aircraft and an impressive collection of air force memorabilia. The museum is off Pleasant Street (Highway 322); turn left at the first set of lights beyond the Imperial oil refinery.

## ◖ Fisherman's Cove

Fisherman's Cove is no different from the hundreds of picturesque fishing villages that dot the Nova Scotia coastline, with one exception—it's within the city limits of the capital. Lying along the Eastern Passage two kilometers southeast of Dartmouth along Highway 322, the cove mixes the needs of working fishing vessels with a constant flow of curious visitors. You can drive along Government Wharf Road, which spurs right at the traffic lights in Eastern Passage, onto the main dock area, but it's much more enjoyable to explore the area on foot from the parking lot just beyond the cove's main entrance.

Opened in 2004, **Fisherman's Cove Marine Interpretative Centre** (Government Wharf Rd., 902/465-6093; Tues.–Sun. 11 A.M.–7 P.M.; $2) is the first building you come to after entering Fisherman's Cove. This museum tells the story of the village and its colorful history, and aquariums are filled with local underwater species. The interpretive center is the only official sight. Plan also to spend time browsing craft shops and soaking up the sights, sounds, and smells of this authentic fishing village.

**Fisherman's Cove Visitor Information Centre** (30 Government Wharf Rd., 902/465-8009; mid-May–mid-Oct. daily 9 A.M.–6 P.M.) is along the main street of touristy shops. Ask for the historic walking tour brochure.

# NORTH OF DOWNTOWN
## Atlantic Canada Aviation Museum

Across the highway from the airport (take Exit 6 from Hwy. 102), this museum (20 Sky Blvd., 902/873-3773; May–Oct. daily 9 A.M.–5 P.M.; adult $5) is a good place to visit on the way north to Truro or before your flight home. On display are around 30 aircraft—everything from fighter planes to a homemade helicopter—and a couple of simulators.

# Recreation

## WALKING AND HIKING

Even if you're not feeling overly energetic, plan to take a stroll along the downtown waterfront. A **seawall promenade** winds past docks filled with all manner of boats—tall ships, tugboats, and visiting yachts—harborfront restaurants, the Maritime Museum of the Atlantic, Historic Properties, and south to Pier 21. While it's possible to do all your downtown sightseeing on foot, an easier option is to catch a cab to Citadel Hill, from where it's downhill all the way back to the harbor. At Citadel Hill, take the time not only to visit the fort, but to walk around the perimeter, and then cross Sackville Street to the **Public Gardens,** a delightful place for a flower-filled stroll.

For information on **McNabs Island,** a popular destination for day-tripping hikers, see the *McNabs Island* section in this chapter.

## Parks

**Point Pleasant Park,** 2.5 kilometers south of downtown off Young Avenue, is laced with hiking and biking trails. The obvious choice is to stick to the water, along a two-kilometer (each way) trail that hugs the shoreline, passing Point Pleasant itself before winding around to the Northwest Arm. Other trails lead inland to historic fortifications and through the remains of forests devastated by Hurricane Juan in 2003.

Across the Northwest Arm from downtown, **Sir Sandford Fleming Park** flanks the water in an upscale neighborhood. Again, it's the seawall walk that is most popular, but another pleasant trail leads up through the forest to Frog Lake.

Take the Bedford Highway north from downtown and then one kilometer north of the Kearney Lake Road junction and watch

© ANDREW HEMPSTEAD

Walking trails in Sir Sandford Fleming Park hug the water's edge.

for Kent Avenue (to the left), which leads into a dense old-growth forest protected as **Hemlock Ravine Park.** From the pond and picnic area, a world away from surrounding development, five trails branch off into the forest. Some are short and perfect for younger and older walkers, while others, including the trail to the hemlock-filled ravine, are steeper and can be slippery after rain.

## BICYCLING

The local municipality, with its many lakes and harbor-side coves, has put considerable effort into making the city as bike-friendly as possible. The Halifax Regional Municipality website (www.halifax.ca) has a PDF file bike map, or pick one up at the information center. A centrally located source for rentals and advice is **Harbour Bike and Sea Rentals** (1781 Lower Water St., 902/423-1185). Standard bikes cost $10 per hour or $42 for a full day.

**Freewheeling Adventures** (902/857-3600 or 800/672-0775, www.freewheeling.ca) is a local tour company that runs recommended guided bike trips along the South Shore, starting from Hubbards, just south of the city. Guests ride for up to six hours per day, stay in cottages or bed-and-breakfasts, and have all meals included in rates starting at $1,600 per person.

## WATER SPORTS
### Swimming and Sunbathing

Municipal swimming pools include **Northcliffe Pool** (111 Clayton Park Dr., 902/490-4690) and **Needham Pool** (3372 Devonshire Ave., 902/490-4633).

**Crystal Crescent Beach Provincial Park** lies a half hour south of Halifax off Highway 349 and is the locals' favorite Atlantic beach. Its sand is fine, and the sea is usually cold, but summer crowds heat up the action. Nature lovers will enjoy the 10-kilometer trail to remote Pennant Point while naturists will want to gravitate to the farthest of the park's three beaches—one of Canada's few official nude beaches.

If you're visiting Fisherman's Cove, head east for eight kilometers along Cow Bay Road to reach **Rainbow Haven Provincial Park.** The park protects wetlands at the mouth of Cole Harbour and an ocean-facing beach. The beach is often windy (it's not uncommon to see people sunbathing back in the dunes), but on calm days it's a delightful place to soak up some rays and maybe, if you're brave, take a dip in the water. At the end of the park access road are change rooms and a concession selling beachy food such as ice cream and hot dogs.

### Canoeing and Kayaking

Based on the Northwest Arm, **Saint Mary's Boat Club** (1641 Fairfield Rd., 902/490-4688) rents canoes for $8 per hour on a limited basis through summer. Rentals are available June–Sept. Sat.–Sun. 11 A.M.–7 P.M.

## GOLFING

Halifax and surrounding area is home to more than a dozen courses varying from nine-hole public courses to exclusive 18-holers. The **Nova Scotia Golf Association** website (www.nsga.ns.ca) has links to all provincial courses.

## The Courses

Host of a 2005 LPGA event, **Glen Arbour Golf Course** (Glen Arbour Way, off Hammonds Plains Rd., 1 km west of Bedford, 902/835-4653) is one of Canada's finest links. Choose from five sets of tees to a maximum of 6,800 yards. The course has abundant water hazards, 90 bunkers, and fairways lined by hardwood forests. Greens fees top out at $155 in midsummer, dropping as low as $75 for twilight golf in October.

**Lost Creek Golf Club** (902/865-4653) enjoys the same forested environment as Glen Arbour, but without the valet parking and high greens fees, which are just $42 at Lost Creek. To get there, take Exit 2 from Highway 101 and follow Beaverbank Road north for 10 kilometers; turn right on Kinsac Road and then left on William Nelson Drive.

One of the region's most enjoyable layouts is **Granite Springs** (25 km west of downtown off Hwy. 333 at 4441 Prospect Rd., Bayside, 902/852-4653). This challenging course winds through 120 hectares of mature forest, with distant ocean views. Greens fees are $55 ($38 twilight).

## WINTER SPORTS

In winter, walking paths become **cross-country ski trails** at Point Pleasant Park, Sir Sandford Fleming Park, and Hemlock Ravine. Dartmouth maintains groomed surfaces at Lake Charles, and several lakes in Halifax are great for skating.

### Skiing and Snowboarding

The closest downhill skiing and boarding is at **Ski Martock** (902/798-9501), an hour's drive northwest of Halifax off Highway 101 (signposted from Exit 5). It's a popular family hill, with mostly beginner runs accessible by two lifts rising 180 vertical meters. Snowmaking covers the entire resort while lights keep runs open nightly until 10 P.M. Day tickets are adult

© ANDREW HEMPSTEAD

Life in Halifax revolves around the water, and nowhere is this more apparent than the downtown harbor, where sailing ships like the famous *Bluenose II* are often tied up.

$35, child $25. Ski or snowboard rental packages are $22.

### Hockey

Through the long winter, when outside activities are curtailed by the weather, there is much interest in ice hockey (known in Canada simply as "hockey"). When they're not watching the National Hockey League on television (the closest teams are in Boston, Montreal, and Toronto), local fans flock to the Halifax Metro Centre to cheer on their own **Halifax Mooseheads** (5284 Duke St., 902/429-3267, www.halifaxmooseheads.ca), who play mid-September to mid-March in the Quebec Major Junior Hockey League. Tickets start at $15.

## HARBOR CRUISES AND LAND TOURS

If you don't have a lot of time to explore Halifax or just want an introduction to the city, consider one of the many tours available—they'll maximize your time and get you to the highlights with minimum stress.

## Bluenose II

The harborfront's premier attraction, the magnificent schooner *Bluenose II,* divides her summertime between Halifax, her home port Lunenburg, and goodwill tours to other Canadian ports. The vessel is an exact replica of the famous *Bluenose.* It is operated by the Lunenburg Marine Museum Society on behalf of the Province of Nova Scotia. When in Halifax, two-hour harbor tours are available twice daily from the Maritime Museum's wharf. Check www.museum.gov.ns.ca/bluenose for a schedule. Departures are at 9:30 A.M. and 1 P.M. and the cost is adult $35, child $20. Each sailing has 75 spots—40 spots can be reserved by calling 902/634-4794 or 800/763-1963, with the remaining 35 going on sale 90 minutes before departure. Without a reservation, expect to line up for a spot.

## Harbour Hopper Tours

This company (902/490-8687) picks up passengers from the north side of the maritime museum for a quick trip around the historic streets of Halifax, and then the fun really starts, as the company's distinctive green and yellow amphibious vehicles plunge into the water for a cruise around the harbor. The trip lasts around one hour, with up to 20 departures daily May–October between 9 A.M. and 9:30 P.M. The ticket kiosk is on Cable Wharf. Tickets are adult $25, senior $24, child $15.

## Other Harbor Cruises

Many other sightseeing craft also offer harbor tours. **Murphy's on the Water** (Cable Wharf, 1751 Lower Water St., 902/420-1015) operates several vessels through a sailing season that runs mid-May–late October. The 23-meter wooden sailing ketch *Mar* departs up to six times daily on cruises that cost adult $23, senior $22, child $17. The *Harbour Queen I* is a 200-passenger paddle wheeler offering a narrated harbor cruise (adult $22, senior $21, child $17) and a variety of lunch and dinner cruises ($44 for dinner).

## Bus Tours

**Ambassatours** (902/423-6242 or 800/565-7173) has the local Grayline franchise. The

© ANDREW HEMPSTEAD

Harbour Hopper Tours combine street touring with a harbor cruise.

three-hour Deluxe Historic Halifax City Tour includes stops at the Public Gardens, Halifax Citadel National Historic Site, and Fairview Cemetery. The tour also passes all major downtown attractions, working precincts of the harbor, and various university campuses. This tour departs June–mid-October daily at 9 A.M. and 1 P.M. and costs adult $36, child $18. Another option with Ambassatours is a downtown loop tour aboard an old English double-decker bus (mid-June–mid-Oct.; adult $44, child $31). You can get on and off as you

please at any of the 11 stops on the one-hour loop and tickets are valid for two days (a good plan is to ride the entire loop once, and then plan your stops for the second go-round. This same company also has a three-hour trip to Peggy's Cove (departs June–mid-Oct. Tues., Thurs., and Sun. at 1 P.M.; adult $48, senior $44, child $34) and a full-day trip that combines a stop in Mahone Bay with time in Lunenburg (departs June–Oct. Mon., Wed., Fri., and Sat. at 9 A.M.; adult $98, senior $89, child $69).

# Entertainment and Events

Halifax has a reputation as a party town, partly because of a large population of students. The city has dozens of pubs, many with local brews on tap and Celtic-inspired bands such as the Kilkenny Krew and the Navigators performing to small but raucous crowds. Most pubs close around midnight. The city also has a notable performing arts community. Although most seasons run through the cooler months, many companies put on events especially for summer crowds.

For complete listings of all that's happening around Halifax, pick up the free *Coast* (www .thecoast.ca). Friday and weekend editions of the *Halifax Herald* offer comprehensive entertainment listings. The website www.halifaxlocals.com is a user-driven vehicle for discussions on the local music scene.

## NIGHTLIFE
### Pubs
If you're going to have just one beer in Halifax, make it at the **Stag's Head Tavern,** part of the Keith's Brewery complex (Lower Water St., 902/455-1474). Best known as North America's oldest working brewery, Keith's still uses traditional British brewing techniques. Its famous India Pale Ale is widely available as draft and in bottles across the country, but it's best enjoyed in the Stag's Head, surrounded by the

convivial atmosphere and with traditional Maritime music in the background.

In the vicinity of Keith's, the **Granite Brewery** (1662 Barrington St., 902/422-4954; daily from 11 A.M.) is ensconced in a historic stone building a couple of blocks back from Alexander Keith's Brewery. Its own excellent English-style ales are brewed on-site, using natural ingredients such as black malt imported from England. The pub itself attracts a slightly older crowd of well-dressed locals.

Live music at the **Lower Deck** (Upper Water St., 902/425-1501; daily from 11:30 A.M.) keeps the crowds humming nightly at this waterfront pub within the historic Privateers Warehouse.

**Tug's Pub,** in the Waterfront Warehouse complex (1549 Lower Water St., 902/425-7610; daily 11:30 A.M.–midnight), is a refined English-style pub with a tartan color scheme, lots of polished mahogany furnishings, and walls lined with historic photos.

As you move away from the harborfront, **Pogue Fado** (1581 Barrington St., 902/429-6222; daily from 11 A.M.) is one of the busiest Irish pubs in Halifax. The atmosphere is friendly and welcoming, there's live music on weekends, and the food is good—so it's easy to see why.

**The Maxwell's Plum** (1600 Grafton St., 902/423-5090) has an excellent selection of imported draft beers (notably Beamish Irish Stout, John Courage, and Newcastle Brown Ale) and single-malt scotches. That alone may be reason enough to visit there, but it's also a good venue for straight-ahead jazz, including Sunday afternoon jam sessions.

**Your Father's Moustache** (5686 Spring Garden Rd., 902/423-6766) puts on excellent live, usually local, music most evenings. On Saturday afternoon it hosts its popular Blues Matinee.

## Bars

Along the lively stretch of Argyle Street between Blowers and Sackville Streets is the **Seahorse Tavern** (1665 Argyle St., 902/423-7200), which has been around since 1948. Horsepower Beer, produced by the local Propeller Brewery, is available on tap only at the Seahorse, but most patrons are here for the music. Monday through Thursday are theme nights such as Mullet Mondays (retro rock and roll) and Indie Wednesdays while weekends are devoted to live music. Part of the same complex is the **Economy Shoe Shop** (1663 Argyle St., 902/423-8845; daily 11 A.M.–2 A.M.), a drinking and dining venue incorporating three restaurants and the Belgian Bar, with a gaudy but appealing tropical vibe.

**Stayner's Bar and Grill** (5075 George St., 902/492-1800) is in the heart of the tourist district, but as it's away from the water, the casual visitor often misses this bar that remains quiet until local Celtic bands hit the stage.

## Nightclubs

Around midnight, when the pubs start closing their doors, the crowds move on to nightclubs spread through downtown.

The **Dome** (1741 Grafton St., 902/422-6907; Wed.–Sun. 10 P.M.–3:30 A.M.) is a mass of young heaving bodies who dance the night away in sync to one of Canada's most dynamic sound and light systems. It's also a bit of a pickup place (locals often refer to it as the Do-Me). Under the same roof is **Cheers** (902/421-1655), which attracts an older crowd. Another multivenue nightclub

is **Pacifico** (corner Barrington and Salter Streets, 902/422-3633), where **Crave** attracts serious dancers and the **Capitol** holds a stylish martini bar.

Starting out as a gay bar, **Reflections** (5184 Sackville St., 902/422-2957) now attracts an eclectic mix of locals of all sexual persuasions. Each night has a theme—Tuesday is house and techno, bands play Wednesday, Thursday is an anything-goes talent show—but the biggest crowds are on weekends, when the resident DJ spins his favorite tunes until 4 A.M.

**The Palace** (1721 Brunswick St., 902/420-0015) has a huge dance floor with a dynamic light and sound system. It's a bit rough around edges and busiest in the wee hours of morning when everywhere else is closing.

## Jazz and Blues

The **Seahorse Tavern** (1665 Argyle St., 902/423-7200) hosts a blues jam every Thursday night. Next door, the Belgian Bar, within the **Economy Shoe Shop** (1663 Argyle St., 902/423-8845; daily 11 A.M.–2 A.M.) features no-charge Monday evening jazz.

The best blues bar in town is **Bearly's House of Blues and Ribs** (1269 Barrington St., 902/423-2526). As the name suggests, ribs ($16 for a full rack) are the dining specialty, but it is the music that draws the enthusiastic crowd. Weekends feature local talent while weekdays except Monday and Wednesday the stage is turned over to traveling talent. On Saturday afternoons through winter, bluegrass musicians strum their stuff.

# PERFORMING ARTS

Haligonians have a sweet and sometimes bittersweet Canadian sense of humor (somewhat like the British), and local theater revels in their brand of fun. A $37 admission will get you into dinner-theater musical productions at **Grafton Street Dinner Theatre** (1741 Grafton St., 902/425-1961), which operates daily except Monday in summer and three times a week through the rest of the year. **Halifax Feast Dinner Theatre** (Maritime Centre, corner Barrington and Salter Sts., 902/420-1840) costs a few dollars more, but the production often has a historic Halifax angle. A lot of food is served very quickly at both venues, but the quality remains excellent.

At the **Neptune Theatre** (1593 Argyle St., 902/429-7070), private companies such as Legends of Broadway take to the boards during summer with musicals and Gilbert and Sullivan shows.

# FESTIVALS AND EVENTS

Halifax hosts a number of well-known events that visitors plan their trips around, as well as many you probably haven't heard of but that are well worth attending if the dates correspond with your own travels. The most popular festivals are held outdoors and in summer, but the cooler months are the season of performing arts. For details and exact dates of the events listed, use the contacts given or check out the Tourism Nova Scotia website (www.novascotia.com).

## Spring

The **Scotia Festival of Music** centers on the Music Room (6181 Lady Hammond Rd., 902/429-9467, www.scotiafestival.ns.ca) for two weeks in late May and early June. Chamber musicians present piano, cello, and violin recitals in a dignified yet casual atmosphere.

The **Nova Scotia Multicultural Festival** (Alderney Gate Complex, Dartmouth, 902/423-6534, www.multifest.ca) fills the Dartmouth waterfront precinct with the sounds, sights, and smells of various cultures the middle weekend of June. You can feast on barbecued Korean short ribs while watching Polish folk dancing or tap your feet to Celtic highland dancers while juggling a plate of German sausages. Ferries dock right at Alderney Gate, making this the best way to travel to the festival from downtown.

## Summer

Nothing reflects Halifax's long military heritage better than the **Nova Scotia International Tattoo** (902/420-1114, www.nstattoo.ca), held annually for 10 days at the beginning of July

at the Halifax Metro Centre (5284 Duke St.). A "tattoo" is an outdoor military exercise presented as entertainment. Here it involves competitions, military bands, dancers, gymnasts, and choirs. The event has grown to be regarded as one of the world's greatest indoor events, bringing together thousands of performers from around the world. You can buy tickets (around $32–50) through the Halifax Metro Centre Box Office (902/451-1221).

In mid-July, jazz fans descend on Halifax for the **Atlantic Jazz Festival** (902/492-2225, www.jazzeast.com), the largest music festival east of Montréal. More than 400 musicians from around the world gather at venues as intimate as the Economy Shoe Shop and as character-filled as the old schoolhouse at Peggy's Cove to perform traditional and contemporary jazz.

Halifax and Dartmouth come together to celebrate their birthdays with a civic holiday known as **Natal Day** (902/490-6773, www.natalday.org) on the first Monday of every August. Events take place through the entire weekend, including a Saturday parade, talent shows, sporting events, and a grand finale fireworks presentation on the harbor Monday night.

Street performers fill five stages spread along the downtown waterfront for 11 days in early August during the **Halifax International Buskers Festival** (902/471-0550, www.buskers.ca).

Summer finishes with the **Atlantic Fringe Festival** (902/435-4837, www.atlanticfringe.ca), featuring 200 shows at various downtown venues through the first week of September.

## Fall

The mid-September **Atlantic Film Festival** (902/422-3456, www.atlanticfilm.com) has been wowing moviegoers for more than a quarter of a century. It features the very best films from around the world, but the emphasis is on local and Canadian productions. Venues are mostly downtown theaters.

Celebrate **Alexander Keith's birthday** (902/455-1474, www.keiths.ca) on October 5 with hundreds of enthusiastic locals. Or pull up a bar stool at any local pub and raise a toast of India Pale Ale to "The Great Man of Beer," who began brewing beer in Halifax in 1820. The event (check the website for locations) is the epicenter of celebrations, with plenty of foot-stomping, beer-drinking East Coast music.

For 10 days from the first Friday in October, the country comes to the city for the **Maritime Fall Fair** (Exhibition Park, 200 Prospect Rd., 902/876-8221, www.maritimefallfair.com). It has everything a fall fair should—a craft marketplace, agricultural competitions, vegetable judging, a rodeo, and a midway. Exhibition Park is off Highway 333, the main road to Peggy's Cove.

## Winter
The first full weekend of November, the **Christmas Craft Village** (902/463-2561, www.atlanticchristmasfair.com) fills Exhibition Park with hundreds of crafty booths selling everything from homemade preserves to self-published books to East Coast antiques.

# Shopping

Shopaholics will love Halifax. Most shops and all major department stores are generally open Monday–Saturday 9:30 A.M.–5:30 P.M. Stores along the touristy harborfront usually have longer hours and also are open Sunday.

## Arts and Crafts
The city's art galleries are superb. The newest fine arts trends are on exhibit at Nova Scotia College of Art and Design's **Anna Leonowens Gallery** (5163 Duke St., 902/494-8223; Tues.–Fri. 11 A.M.–5 P.M., Sat. noon–5 P.M.). The gallery displays and sells the work of Nova Scotia College of Art and Design students. This downtown university, one of North America's oldest cultural institutions, was founded by the gallery's namesake, Anna Leonowens, in 1887. Leonowens, a one-time English teacher who was governess to the King of Siam in the 1860s (the movie *Anna and the King,* starring Jodie Foster, tells her life story), spent 20 years in Halifax, during which time she established NSCAD.

Hundreds of clan fabrics and tartans in kilts, skirts, vests, ties, and other apparel are stocked at **Plaid Place** (1903 Barrington St., 902/429-6872). The capital's definitive crafts source is **Jennifer's of Nova Scotia** (5635 Spring Garden Rd., 902/425-3119), an outlet for 120 provincial producers of handicrafts such as patchwork quilts, pottery, and soaps. **Studio 21** (1223 Lower Water St., 902/420-1852) is a good source of contemporary paintings by local artists. For the unique combination of hand-built furniture and porcelain dog dishes, head to **Henhouse** (5533 Young St., 902/423-4499).

## Crystal
Canada's only traditional glassworks is **Nova Scotian Crystal** (5080 George St., 902/492-0416), which is ensconced in a waterfront building that contains a showroom and workshop. You can watch master craftspeople at work every day, but Tuesday, Thursday, and Saturday are the days you won't want to miss—this is when the actual glassblowing takes place. Rather than taking a tour, interested folks crowd around open factory doors to watch the goings-on inside. The shop sells pieces such as Christmas ornaments, stemware, toasting flutes, candleholders, and bowls, many with Nova Scotian–inspired designs.

## Markets
**Halifax Seaport Farmers' Market** happens every Saturday 7 A.M.–1 P.M. at Pier 20 (Marginal Rd., 902/492-4043). North America's oldest such market, its stands are filled with

local crafts and produce that make the perfect memento of your time in Nova Scotia.

In the same vicinity, **Pavilion 22** (May–Oct.) is designed as a market-style shopping experience for cruise-ship visitors, but it is also worth stopping by if you are at this end of town.

### Local Delicacies

You'll no doubt eat a lot of seafood while in Nova Scotia, but it can also make a great souvenir to take home for friends and family. Or plan a get-together upon your return and impress everyone with a Nova Scotian feast.

**Clearwater** (757 Bedford Hwy., 902/443-0550) is a high-profile supplier with a huge shop front along the Bedford Highway waterfront. The outlet is anchored by a massive lobster tank divided into sections that make choosing the right-size lobster easy (from $8 per pound). You can also pick up cooked crab legs to go, attend cooking demonstrations, and buy all manner of seafood cookbooks. Better still for those departing Halifax International Airport, Clearwater has an airport location (902/873-4509) with a lobster tank. For an additional fee, live lobsters can be packaged

for air travel. Clearwater also sells crabs, scallops, clams, and shrimp.

The days of Prohibition, when smuggling rum into the United States was a way to make a living for seafaring Nova Scotians, may be a distant memory, but at the **Rum Runners Rum Cake Factory** (facing the harbor at 1479 Lower Water St., 902/421-6079) you can buy rum cakes whose recipe was passed down from a rum-running family. The cakes are deliciously rich and sweet, and travel well.

### Outdoor and Camping Gear

Halifax's largest outdoor equipment store is **Mountain Equipment Co-op** (1550 Granville St., 902/421-2667; Mon.–Wed. 10 A.M.–7 P.M., Thurs.–Fri. 10 A.M.–9 P.M., Sat. 10 A.M.–6 P.M.). Like the American REI stores, it is a cooperative owned by its members; to make a purchase, you must be a member (a once-only charge of $5). The store holds a massive selection of clothing, climbing and mountaineering equipment, tents, backpacks, sleeping bags, books, and other accessories. To order a copy of the mail-order catalog, call 800/663-2667 or go online to www.mec.ca.

# Accommodations and Camping

Accommodations in Halifax vary from a hostel and budget-priced roadside motels to luxurious bed-and-breakfasts. Downtown is home to a number of full-service hotels catering to top-end travelers and business conventions. In general, these properties offer drastically reduced rates on weekends—Friday and Saturday nights might be half the regular room rate. No matter when you plan to visit, arriving in Halifax without a reservation is unwise, but especially in the summer, when gaggles of tourists compete for a relative paucity of rooms. If you do arrive without a confirmed reservation, staff at the **Halifax Visitor Centre** (1598 Argyle St., 902/490-5946; daily 9 A.M.–6 P.M.) will try their best to find you somewhere to stay.

All rates quoted below are for a double room in summer.

## DOWNTOWN
### Under $50

Also known as the Halifax Heritage House Hostel, **HI-Halifax** (1253 Barrington St., 902/422-3863, www.hihostels.ca) has 75 beds two blocks from the harbor and a 15-minute walk to attractions such as the maritime museum and Citadel Hill. Facilities include a communal kitchen, laundry room, television in the common room, and a storeroom for bikes. Beds in four- to eight-bed dorms are $25 per night ($30 for nonmembers) while those in private rooms are $57 s or d.

## $100-150

Oscar Wilde and P. T. Barnum both slept (not together) at the **Waverley Inn** (1266 Barrington St., 902/423-9346 or 800/565-9346, www.waverleyinn.com), which, at its completion in 1866, was one of the city's grandest residences. Rates for the 34 rooms ($125–229 s, $165–229 d) include breakfast; tea, coffee, and snacks are offered all day and evening in the hospitality suite. Rooms are furnished with Victorian-era antiques, and deluxe rooms contain whirlpool tubs and feather beds. The least expensive single rooms are very small while the deluxe twins are spacious and extravagantly luxurious.

## $150-200

**C** **Cambridge Suites Hotel** (1583 Brunswick St., 902/425-4076 or 800/565-1263, www.cambridgesuiteshalifax.com; $155–205 s or d) is a modern, centrally located, all-suite hotel with 200 rooms. Even the smallest have separate bedrooms, and continental breakfast is included in the rates. Rooms are packed with amenities, including high-speed Internet, beautiful bathrooms, lounge and work areas, and basic cooking facilities. The rooftop patio, a fitness center, and a bistro-style restaurant are pluses. Ask about rates that include free parking, full breakfast, and extras for traveling families.

**C** **The Halliburton** (5184 Morris St., 902/420-0658 or 888/512-3344, www.thehalliburton.com; from $185 s or d) is a beautiful heritage property transformed into a boutique hotel. The 29 rooms come with super-comfortable beds topped with goose-down duvets and luxurious en suite bathrooms. Rates include continental breakfast, and wireless Internet is available throughout the building. The acclaimed in-house dining room, Stories, is open nightly for dinner.

Halifax is home to two Delta properties. In both cases, click on the "Packages and Specials" link at www.deltahotels.com for the best rates. **Delta Barrington** (1875 Barrington St., 902/429-7410 or 888/890-3222, www.deltahotels.com; from $190 s or d) shares space with Barrington Place Mall in the historic area and has 200 comfortable rooms. Amenities include a fitness room, indoor pool, business center, a street-side café (with a summer seafood menu), and a lounge bar. Rack rates are around $190 s or d midweek and $160 on weekends. Nearby, the **Delta Halifax** (1990 Barrington St., 902/425-6700 or 877/814-7706, www.deltahotels.com; $190 s or d) was one of the city's first grande dame hotels, and the old girl's still a handsome dowager. A highlight is the lavish indoor pool complex, complete with whirlpools and a sauna, as well as an adjacent fitness room.

## $200-250

In any other Canadian capital, you'd pay a lot more for a room of similar standard as those at the full-service **Prince George Hotel** (1725 Market St., 902/425-1986 or 800/565-1567, www.princegeorgehotel.com; from $205 s or d), one block below the Halifax Citadel and seven blocks uphill from the harbor. The rooms feature contemporary furnishings, and amenities include a midsize indoor pool, a business center with Internet access, a restaurant, a lounge, and quiet public areas off the main lobby. Although rack rates start at just over $200, check the website for weekend specials or upgrade to the Crown Floor for an extra $30.

Part of the Casino Nova Scotia complex, **Marriott Harbourfront Hotel** (1919 Upper Water St., 902/421-1700 or 800/943-6760, www.marriott.com; $220 s or d) is a modern edifice designed to resemble the garrison that once occupied the waterfront. Although many guests are from Atlantic Canada and are staying especially to play the tables, it is also a convenient choice for leisure travelers. In addition to the casino, there are multiple restaurants, a stylish English-style pub, and live entertainment. Almost no one pays rack rates. Instead, check the website for a world of options starting at $149 s or d. For information on the casino, go to www.casinonovascotia.com.

## Over $250

If you're after modern accommodations,

consider **Four Points by Sheraton Halifax** (1496 Hollis St., 902/423-4444, www.star-woodhotels.com; from $255 s or d), one block back from the harbor. Guest rooms are filled with modern conveniences (free high-speed Internet, 27-inch TVs, multiple phones, and well-designed work areas) while other facilities include an indoor pool and fitness room. Disregard the rack rates, book online, and you'll pay as little as $150 s or d, even in midsummer.

Opened in 1930 to coincide with the arrival of the first passenger trains to Halifax, the station's adjacent **Westin Nova Scotian** (1181 Hollis St., 902/421-1000 or 877/993-7846, www.westin.ns.ca; from $275 s or d) was extensively renovated in 2008. Linked to the railway station—many guests are still rail passengers—it oozes Old World charm throughout public areas (poke your head into the Atlantic Ballroom) and the 300 guest rooms. Amenities include a fine-dining restaurant featuring contemporary cooking, a hip lounge, café, fitness room, indoor pool, spa services, and a shuttle to the central business district (one kilometer away).

## CITADEL HILL AND VICINITY

The following accommodations are in the vicinity of Citadel Hill, from where it's downhill all the way to the harbor. Even the fittest visitors may not feel like tramping back up to the Citadel Hill area after a full day sightseeing or a big meal at a downtown restaurant—no worries; a cab will cost around $6.

### $50-100

A rambling old house directly opposite North Common has been renovated as **Fountain View Guest House** (2138 Robie St. between Williams St. and Compton Ave., 902/422-4169 or 800/565-4877; $25 s, $50 d). The seven rooms share bathrooms, there is no kitchen or laundry, and parking is limited to what you can find on the street.

### $100-150

Across North Common from Citadel Hill is the **Commons Inn** (5780 West St., 902/484-3466 or 877/797-7999, www.commonsinn.ca; $110–150 s or d), an older three-story building with basic 40 guest rooms. The rooms are on the small side, but are well-decorated with comfortable beds, en suite bathrooms, free local calls, and cable TV. The spacious suite, complete with a separate sitting area and jetted tub, is excellent value. Other pluses are free parking, a rooftop patio, and a continental breakfast.

### $150-200

The grandiose ◖ **Lord Nelson Hotel** (1515 S. Park St., 902/423-6331 or 800/565-2020, www.lordnelsonhotel.com; from $199 s or d) presides over a busy Spring Garden Road intersection and overlooks the famous Public Gardens. Originally opened in 1928, the Lord Nelson underwent a transformation in the late 1990s, reopening as one of the city's finest hotels. It is probably a little too far for some to walk from downtown, but location aside, it is one of Halifax's best and best-value accommodations. Beyond the extravagant marble-floored lobby are 260 elegantly furnished rooms, each with large bathrooms, high-speed Internet access, coffeemakers, and irons. Other amenities include a fitness room, restaurant, English-style pub, and room service. Parking is $14 per night. Check the website for specials under $140 year-round.

## BEDFORD HIGHWAY

Running along the western edge of the Bedford Basin, the Bedford Highway (Highway 2) is the original route north from downtown to the airport and beyond. A few motels from prebypass days exist, providing inexpensive accommodations a 10-minute or quicker drive from the city center. If you make this part of the city your base, you'll need a vehicle, or be prepared to ride transit buses. To get there from the north, take Exit 3 from Highway 102 and follow the signs toward downtown.

### $50-100

Nestled in treed grounds on the harbor side

of the Bedford Highway is the **Travelers Motel** (773 Bedford Hwy., 902/835-3394 or 800/565-3394, www.travelersmotel.ca). It is a classic 1950s park-at-the-door roadside motel where rates start at $82 for smallish rooms with dated decor, cable TVs, and phones. Summer-only cabins with TV but no phones are $58–90 s or d. This place is surprisingly busy, so you'll need reservations in summer.

Over the rise toward the city from the Travelers and opposite a busy diner of the same name is the **Esquire Motel** (771 Bedford Hwy., 902/835-3367 or 800/565-3367, www.esquiremotel.ca; $85–145 s or d). Amenities are similar to its neighbor's, with the only real difference a small outdoor pool and free local calls. Outside of summer, rates start at $65.

## NEAR THE AIRPORT

No accommodations are right at the airport, but it's only 40 minutes to downtown on the Airporter, which operates daily 5 A.M.–1 A.M. Here are a few options just in case you *must* stay in the vicinity.

### $100-150

Across the highway from the airport and linked by free shuttle is the **Airport Hotel Halifax** (60 Sky Blvd., 902/873-3000 or 800/667-3333, ww.airporthotelhalifax.com; $130 s or d), which has regularly revamped rooms, an indoor and outdoor pool, a fitness room, a restaurant, and a desk for Discount car rentals.

### $150-200

Four kilometers south of the airport, **Hilton Garden Inn** (200 Pratt & Whitney Dr., Enfield, 902/873-1400, www.hilton.com; from $179 s or d) offers 24-hour shuttle service for guests. It's a newer property with a high standard of guest rooms, as well as a restaurant and fitness room.

Around halfway between the airport and downtown is **Inn on the Lake** (3009 Hwy. 2, Fall River, 902/861-3480 or 800/463-6465, www.innonthelake.com; from $169 s or d), which has expanded from a 1970s roadside motel into a full-blown resort, complete with multiple dining rooms, recreational opportunities spread over two hectares of landscaped lakefront, and even a white sandy beach.

## FISHERMAN'S COVE

If you don't need to be right downtown, consider the following oceanfront accommodation—which is both excellent value and a world away from the bustle of the city.

### Under $100

Overlooking the historic fishing village, **⟨ Inn at Fisherman's Cove** (1531 Shore Rd., Eastern Passage, 902/465-3455 or 866/725-3455, www.theinnatfishermanscove.com; $75–125 s or d) is a modern three-story building with its own private dock on the "crick" that has been chock-full of fishing boats for more than 200 years. Each room has an en suite bathroom and TV while downstairs is a breakfast room that opens to the dock. Four of the eight guest rooms face the water and have private balconies. Rates include a light breakfast.

Inn at Fisherman's Cove

# CAMPGROUNDS

You won't find any campgrounds in the city center area, but a few commercial campgrounds lie within a 30-minute drive of downtown. Farther out are two provincial parks that offer camping without hookups.

## Dartmouth

The closest camping to downtown is at **◖ Shubie Park Campground** (Jaybee Dr., Dartmouth, 902/435-8328, www.shubiecampground.com; mid-May–mid-Oct.). Facilities such as the washrooms have been recently renovated, while public Internet access and landscaping have been added. The adjacent beach on Lake Charles comes with supervised swimming, and the campground is linked to walking trails along the Shubenacadie Canal. On the downside, sites offer little privacy. Unserviced sites are $27, hookups $32–40. To get there, take Exit 6 from Highway 111 and follow Braemer Drive north for 2.5 kilometers to Jaybee Drive. Coming from the north, take Exit 5 from Highway 102 and follow Highway 118 to Highway 111; from this point, it's a short way east to the Braemer Drive exit.

## West

**Woodhaven RV Park** (1757 Hammonds Plains Rd., 902/835-2271, www.woodhavenrvpark.com; May–mid-Oct.; $28–36) is 18 kilometers from downtown and handy for an early-morning start out to the South Shore. To get there, take Exit 3 from Highway 102 and follow Hammonds Plains Road west for eight kilometers. From the South Shore,

you bypass the city by taking Exit 5 from Highway 103. Facilities include coin-operated showers, two launderettes, a swimming pool, a playground, a games room, and wireless Internet access.

**Halifax West KOA** (3070 Hwy. 1, Upper Sackville, 902/865-4342, www.koa.com; mid-May–mid-Oct.; $31–49, cabins with shared bathrooms $60) is northwest of the city, farther out than Woodhaven and a 45-minute drive from downtown. To get there, take Exit 4B from Highway 102 and follow Highway 1 (Sackville Road) for 15 kilometers. If you're traveling toward Halifax from Windsor along Highway 101, take Exit 3 and follow the signs.

## North

Take Exit 5 from Highway 102 and head north beyond Fall River for 10 kilometers to reach **Laurie Provincial Park** (coming from the north, take Exit 7 south to Highway 2), which lies on the southern shore of Grand Lake. Here, 71 sites are spread around a treed loop. Each site has a picnic table and fire pit, while park amenities include toilets, a short walking trail, and a day-use area, but no showers or hookups. The campground is open mid-June to early September and sites are $18 per night.

**Dollar Lake Provincial Park** (mid-May–early Sept.; $24) is farther from the city than Laurie Provincial Park, but it has showers and a concession, as well as a nicer beach, with swimming, boating, walking trails, and a playground. Sites are spread around three loops, with Loop A closest to the water.

# Food

Halifax may not have a reputation as a gastronomical wonderland, but the dining scene has improved greatly during the last decade. Not only is the standard of food high in many of the better restaurants, but prices are generally reasonable, with mains in even the very best restaurants rarely more than $30. The many pubs are a good place to start looking for an inexpensive meal, but you can also find old-style diners, cheap ethnic meals, and the usual choice of city-style coffeehouses.

Naturally, **seafood** dominates many menus—especially lobster, crab, mussels, scallops, shrimp, halibut, and salmon, all of which are harvested in Nova Scotia. Some of the best seafood is, surprisingly, found along the touristy waterfront precinct. You can also buy it fresh from trawlers at Fisherman's Cove and even pick up live lobsters packed for flying out at the airport.

## DOWNTOWN
### Cafés

You can get a caffeine hit at outlets of Second Cup and Tim Hortons spread throughout the city (for fancily named Starbucks brews, your choices are limited to two mall locations, both well outside downtown), but the absence of coffeehouse chains in downtown Halifax is refreshing.

**Perks** (1781 Lower Water St., 902/429-9386; daily 6:30 A.M.–11:30 P.M.) is always busy. Sure, the coffee is good, food such as chicken Caesar salad is well priced ($6), there's wireless Internet, and the service efficient, but it's the location—at a busy waterfront intersection where ferries from Dartmouth unload—that ensures a constant lineup.

Serious coffee-lovers gravitate to **Just Us!** (1678 Barrington St., 902/422-5651; Mon.–Fri. 7:30 A.M.–5:30 P.M., Sat. 9 A.M.–5:30 P.M.,

dining along the downtown waterfront

© ANDREW HEMPSTEAD

# BOOTHS AND BURGERS

Beyond the white linens and perfectly presented seafood of Halifax's finer restaurants are a smattering of old-style diners. The following are my favorites – one downtown, another overlooking the city's most notorious intersection, and another handy for those traveling into downtown from the north.

In the heart of the central business district, the venerable **Bluenose II** (1824 Hollis St., 902/425-5092; daily from 7 A.M.) is named for the famous schooner that calls Halifax home on a part-time basis. The booths fill with an eclectic crowd of locals for breakfast, but the space is bright and welcoming, meaning many regulars are families. Eggs Benedict is $7.50, steak and eggs $8.50, while the rest of the day choices vary from a lobster sandwich ($10) to Greek specialties ($9-14).

Overlooking the confusing-even-for-the-locals Armdale Rotary is **Armview Restaurant** (7156 Chebucto Rd., 902/455-4395; Mon.-Sat. from 7 A.M., Sun. from 9 A.M.), an old-style breakfast and lunch spot where everything is less than $10. Cooked breakfasts are from $6.50 and burgers from $2.80.

On Monday, Tuesday, and Wednesday, coupon-clipping retirees fill **Esquire Restaurant** (772 Bedford Hwy., 902/835-9033; daily 7 A.M.-9 P.M.) for specials such as home-style pork dinners for $6. It's across from the Bedford Basin, and there's plenty of parking, or, if you're staying across the road at the Esquire Motel, you need only to negotiate traffic zooming along the busy Bedford Highway.

and comfortable couches inside, but it's the coffee that shines—as good as it gets in Halifax.

At **( Paper Chase News Café** (5228 Blowers St., 902/423-0750; Mon.–Thurs. 8 A.M.–8 P.M., Fri.–Sat. 8 A.M.–9 P.M., Sun. 9 A.M.–8 P.M.), a narrow stairway leads upstairs to a funky space where windows roll up garage door–style and seating spreads from one side of the building to the other, with a split level and slightly arty decor in between. The food is remarkably inexpensive; scrambled eggs and toast is $5, a Swiss melt is $4.75, and vegetarian lasagna is $4.50. The café also has Internet access.

Off to one side of the reception area for the Art Gallery of Nova Scotia, **( Cheapside Café** (1723 Hollis St., 902/425-4494; Tues.–Sat. 10 A.M.–5 P.M.) is not named for the prices, but rather for a historic designation for the cobbled area out front where vendors once peddled their wares. Fittingly, the room itself is a work of art, decorated with colorful paintings that hang on bright orange walls. Lunches such as warm Thai chicken salad and seared salmon on coconut-drizzled spinach range $10–14, or stop by for just a coffee and a generous slab of raspberry mousse torte ($7).

On the south side of downtown, **Trident** (1256 Hollis St., 902/423-7100; Mon.–Fri. 8 A.M.–5 P.M., Sat. 8:30 A.M.–5 P.M., Sun. 11 A.M.–5 P.M.) is a secondhand bookstore on one side and an old-fashioned café with leather-backed chairs on the other—the perfect place to relax with a newly bought literary treasure.

## Harbourside Market

Multiple dining choices and food-court seating that spreads outside onto the adjacent wharf make Harbourside Market, at the waterfront end of the Privateers Warehouse along Lower Water Street, the perfect place for lunch on the run or a casual dinner. At the **( Captain John's** (902/420-9255, daily lunch and dinner) outlet, order fish-and-chips (from $10), a huge plate of steamed mussels to share ($10), or the grilled fish special of the day (around $13).

**Brisket Boardwalk Deli** (902/423-7625) and **Loaf, Leaf N Ladle** (902/422-1137) both

Sun. 10 A.M.–5 P.M.), which does an admirable job of sourcing fair-trade coffee from Mexico.

If you take a walk south along the harborfront, **( Caffe Ristretto** (1475 Lower Water St., 902/425-3087; daily 7 A.M.–10 P.M.), tucked into the back of Bishop's Landing, is a good turnaround point. It has a few outdoor tables, make sandwiches and wraps to order, with the latter open daily at 8 A.M. for breakfast.

Tucked into a corner of the market is **John Shippey Brewing Company** (902/423-7386), a microbrewery (look up in the rafters to see the brew tanks) pouring traditional English ales.

## Seafood Along the Waterfront

While **Captain John's** in the Harbourside Market is a good choice for inexpensive seafood in a food-court setting, the following places are excellent choices for a sit-down meal with water views. Whereas other downtown restaurants have spotty weekend openings, you'll find each of the following open every day for lunch and dinner.

In the Historic Properties, **Salty's** (1869 Lower Water St., 902/423-6818) mixes seafood with succulent meat dishes in a sublime setting. But first, kick back with a margarita and watch the boats sail in and out of the harbor. Then sit indoors or out to enjoy some of the city's best food in a casual atmosphere. And don't miss the scrumptious desserts.

Just north of Salty's, diners at **Murphy's on the Water** (1751 Lower Water St., 902/420-1015) also enjoy panoramic harbor views. This restaurant fills a converted warehouse, with outside tables at the end of the pier. Naturally, the emphasis is on seafood, with lunches starting at around $12 and rising to $17 for a lobster sandwich. Dinner mains range $18–32, or share the impressive Taste of Nova Scotia platter for $70.

Continue south along the harborfront to **Waterfront Warehouse** (1549 Lower Water St., 902/425-7610; May–Oct. daily for lunch and dinner), which is exactly that—a converted waterfront warehouse where tugboats were once repaired. The setting is more upscale than you might imagine from the outside, with white linens, nautical-themed furnishings, and an oversized fireplace. The seafood chowder ($12) is a hearty starter while seafood-oriented mains ($22–32) include bouillabaisse served in an iron pot and the signature dish—maple-glazed salmon grilled on a cedar plank.

## Other Seafood Restaurants

◖ **5 Fishermen** (1740 Argyle St., 902/422-4421, daily lunch and dinner) occupies one of Halifax's oldest buildings—it was built in 1816 and once used by famed governess Anna Leonowens (of *Anna and the King* fame) for her Victorian School of Art and Design. The restaurant is popular with seafood-loving Haligonians for its 68-dish menu, which includes swordfish, Louisiana shrimp, Malpeque oysters, and Digby scallops, as well as chicken and Alberta steaks. All entrées ($35–50) come with all-you-can-eat mussels, steamed clams, and salad bar at no extra charge.

## Pub Dining

**Pogue Fado** (1581 Barrington St., 902/429-6222; daily from 11 A.M.) is Irish in more than name only. The long and narrow room with a couple of sidewalk tables out front offers a menu that includes traditional treats such as Tipperary chicken caudle (chicken stew served

5 Fishermen is one of Halifax's better seafood restaurants.

on a bed of mashed potato), Guinness steak pie, and cottage pie. Almost everything except the steak is under $10.

**Tug's Pub** (Waterfront Warehouse, 1549 Lower Water St., 902/425-7610; daily 11:30 A.M.–midnight) is a comfortable place for a pint of ale before heading to the adjacent restaurant, but the food in the pub itself is excellent, including warm crab dip ($9) and maple-glazed salmon cooked on a cedar plank ($19).

It's a little away from the tourist precinct, but the **( Granite Brewery** (1662 Barrington St., 902/422-4954; daily from 11 A.M.) offers some excellent food. Melt-in-your-mouth baby back ribs ($21 with Caesar salad) are a house specialty, or choose healthy options such as a salmon baked in crushed cashews ($20). On Sunday 11 A.M.–3 P.M. you can indulge in an all-you-can-eat brunch for $12 or tasty treats such as a smoked salmon and goat cheese omelet for $10.

## Bistros
Affiliated with the excellent Cheapside Café, **Sweet Basil Bistro** (1866 Upper Water St., 902/425-2133; daily 11:30 A.M.–9 P.M.) serves fresh and flavorful cooking in a casual and cheerful room—basically everything that a bistro should be. You could start with seared Digby scallops on an avocado salad, move on to walnut-crusted chicken breast stuffed with gorgonzola and pear and basil cream, and then finish with blueberry cheesecake. Dinner starters are mostly under $12, mains range $16–28, and all desserts are $8. Unusually, the lunch menu is not simply a recycled version of dinner, with dishes such as shrimp pad thai for $9–16.50.

**( Chives Canadian Bistro** (1537 Barrington St., 902/420-9626; daily 5–9:30 P.M.) is well worth searching out, and even though it's away from the touristy waterfront, you'll need a reservation. The menu revolves around seasonal ingredients and produce sourced from throughout Nova Scotia. Add immaculate presentation to fresh and healthy cooking styles, and you have a meal

to remember. Mains such as lamb shepherd's pie range $19–26 and desserts such as buttered rhubarb cake are under $10.

## A Halifax Original
The stretch of Argyle Street between Sackville and Blowers Streets has emerged as a dining hotspot, with the utterly original **( Economy Shoe Shop** (1663 Argyle St., 902/423-8845; daily 11 A.M.–2 A.M.) anchoring the strip. The unusual name originated when one of the owners was starting out in the restaurant business; with little cash to spare, he found an old neon sign bearing the name and hung it out front. The original space has grown to encompass three very different restaurants and a bar—one a bohemian-themed space, another a glass-roofed room enclosing a jungle of rainforest that adds a tropical vibe even in the dead of winter. On offer is everything from run-of-the-mill hamburgers ($6) to baked halibut and scallop mornay ($18). Throw entertaining servers into the mix and you get a unique dining experience without spending a fortune.

## Steakhouse
For carnivorous cravings, prepare to splurge at **Ryan Duffy's** (1650 Bedford Row, 902/421-1116; Mon.–Sat. lunch, daily dinner). Some cuts, such as the signature strip loin, are wheeled to your table by a waitperson wielding a carving knife who asks how much of the loin you'd like before carving the cut and telling you the price (around $30 for an average-size serving). Back in the kitchen it is cooked exactly the way you ordered it over charcoal coals. American visitors will be pleased to know that the better cuts come from corn-fed steers raised south of the Canadian border, with prices topping out at $75 for the tomahawk steak. As in many upscale steakhouses, you'll be charged extra for accompanying vegetables.

## Italian
Pasta is a ubiquitous and usually bland choice

on menus throughout North America, but to taste the real thing, you need to find a truly traditional Italian restaurant. Downtown Halifax has two such choices.

( **Da Maurizio** (1496 Lower Water St., 902/423-0859; Mon.–Sat. 5–10 P.M.) is the most upscale of the two. In the historic brewery building, the character-filled room is decorated in mellow hues, its walls lined with Italian art, the wine rack filled with thoughtfully selected bottles from around the world, and the linen-draped tables highlighted by vases of fresh flowers. The menu represents the best of northern Italian cooking, with mains such as veal delicately sautéed with lobster in a tomato and sherry base topping out at $33.

Among a strip of restaurants with outdoor tables, **Piccolo Mondo** (1580 Argyle St., 902/429-0080; daily for lunch and dinner) is casual Italian dining at its best. Pasta is made in-house every morning and, when combined with local seafood such as calamari or shrimp, is divine. Expect to pay up to $15 for a lunchtime main and $24–31 in the evening.

## Asian
Halifax doesn't have a concentration of Asian restaurants, but throughout downtown you'll find a smattering of good choices. One of the best is **Cheelin** (1496 Lower Water St., 902/422-2252; Mon.–Sat. 11:30 A.M.–2:30 P.M. and Tues.–Sun. 5:30–10 P.M.), within the Alexander Keith's Brewery complex. The atmosphere is informal, with chefs in an open kitchen churning out flavorful Chinese favorites in the $12–18 range. The seafood-stuffed eggplant is a unique treat.

**Hamachi Steakhouse** (Bishop's Landing, 1477 Lower Water St., 902/422-1600; daily lunch and dinner) is a contemporary Japanese restaurant specializing in *teppan* cooking. In the center of communal tables are grills where chefs slice, dice, and then grill your choice of beef, chicken, or seafood main ($24–38) as you sample starters such as *niku balu*

(tenderloin meatballs with pineapple chili dipping sauce). For dessert, the Mount Fuji (a combination of brownie, ice cream, cream, and chocolate sauce) is an easy choice.

# SPRING GARDEN ROAD
This restaurant-lined thoroughfare begins at Barrington Street and heads uphill past the main library and the Sexton Campus of Dalhousie University to the Public Gardens. Downstairs in **Spring Garden Place** is one of the city's better food courts.

## Cafés
The Canadian coffeehouse chain **Second Cup** has a popular location here (5425 Spring Garden Rd., 902/429-0883; daily 6:30 A.M.–11 P.M.) with comfortable couches and wireless Internet access.

At the other end of the food-filled strip, opposite the Lord Nelson Hotel, is **Daily Grind** (5686 Spring Garden Rd., 902/429-6397; Mon.–Fri. 7 A.M.–10 P.M., Sat.–Sun. 8 A.M.–10 P.M.), tucked away in the back corner of a newsagent. Cooked breakfasts are small, but sandwiches, hot dishes such as lasagna, and muffins are all delicious and inexpensive.

## Delis
One block off Spring Garden Road at its downtown end, ( **Italian Gourmet** (5431 Doyle St., 902/423-7880; Mon.–Sat. 9 A.M.–7 P.M., Sun. 10 A.M.–5 P.M.) is an absolute delight. Along one side is a deli counter with premade dishes while another side is home to the desserts and drinks. In between, the shelves are lined with goodies imported from around the world. But back to the counters, where you choose from cabbage rolls, quiche, meatloaf meatballs, sun-dried tomato–crusted chicken breasts, smoked salmon pâté, and more. Prices are reasonable (less than $10 for lunch) and there are tables inside and out.

## Restaurants
**Your Father's Moustache** (5686 Spring Garden Rd., 902/423-6766) is a casual favorite

with a reasonably priced menu of seafood, steaks, and pasta. It's open year-round daily for lunch and dinner, and a popular brunch is served Sunday 11 A.M.–3 P.M.

My favorite Indian restaurant in Halifax is **Curry Village** (5677 Brenton Pl., 902/429-5010; Mon.–Sat. lunch, daily dinner), which prepares chicken tandoori, *biryanis,* lamb *vindaloo,* and other Indian dishes to order for around $15. It's just off Spring Garden Road at the Public Gardens end.

For no-frills Japanese and Korean cooking at reasonable prices, consider a meal at **Minato Sushi** (1520 Queen St., 902/420-0331; Mon.–Sat. 11:30 A.M.–9:30 P.M.). Dishes such as sautéed scallops and mushrooms in a butter sauce are all under $15 and *bulkokee* (a sweet beef teriyaki), the unofficial national dish of Korea, is $16.

# DARTMOUTH AND VICINITY

From **MacAskill's** (88 Alderney Dr., 902/466-3100; Mon.–Fri. 11:30 A.M.–2 P.M., Mon.–Sat. 5–10 P.M.), views extend back across Halifax Harbour to downtown, a real treat when the night lights of downtown are sparkling across the water. The menu is dominated by simple yet stylish seafood dishes, all reasonably priced (some under $20) and well presented. The seafood Cajun sampler is a good starter to share while the pan-fried haddock ($17) is a tasty yet inexpensive main. MacAskill's is on the upper floor of the Alderney Gate complex, where ferries from Halifax terminate. With ferries running until midnight, there's plenty of time to enjoy a meal before returning to your downtown accommodation.

## Fisherman's Cove

At this historic fishing village, two kilometers southeast of Dartmouth alongside the Eastern Passage, it's no surprise that seafood dominates local menus. The most obvious place to eat is **Boondocks** (200 Government Wharf Rd., 902/465-3474; daily lunch and dinner), a big red-roofed building with a pleasant oceanfront patio. The menu offers the usual collection of seafood, including pan-seared halibut and chips for $18 and a rich lobster stew for $16. For a more authentic atmosphere, continue to smaller places such as **Fish Basket** (100 Government Wharf Rd., 902/465-5902), which is primarily in business selling fresh seafood, but which also sells lobster sandwiches for $8.50. **Wayne's World Lobster** (Government Wharf Rd., 902/465-6686) is a larger seafood shop, with fresh lobster, crab, scallops, clams, mussels, halibut, and salmon—perfect if you have cooking facilities at your accommodation. **Sea Gulps** (18 Government Wharf Rd., 902/461-8007; May daily 10 A.M.–5 P.M., June–Sept. daily 10 A.M.–8 P.M.) is a friendly little coffee shop set among the fishing shacks.

# Information and Services

As always when traveling, do as much research as you can before leaving home. **Tourism Nova Scotia** (902/425-5781 or 800/565-0000, www.novascotia.com) is a wealth of information, and it sends out free information packs and maps on request. For information specific to Halifax, contact **Destination Halifax** (902/422-9334 or 877/422-9334, www.destinationhalifax.com). The **Halifax Regional Municipality** website (www.halifaxinfo.com) has general information about the city, such as festivals and events, transportation, and park programs.

## INFORMATION CENTERS
### Downtown
Make your first stop the **Halifax Visitor Centre** (1598 Argyle St., 902/490-5946; daily 9 A.M.–6 P.M., the rest of the year daily, but shorter hours), a few blocks up from the waterfront but still central to many attractions.

Tourism Nova Scotia operates an information center along the downtown waterfront at Sackville Landing (1655 Lower Water St., 902/424-4248; daily 8:30 A.M.–6 P.M.). Its shelves are filled with provincewide information, so this is the place to get help planning your travels beyond the capital.

### Fisherman's Cove
Along the Eastern Passage, two kilometers southeast of downtown Dartmouth, **Fisherman's Cove Visitor Information Centre** (30 Government Wharf Rd., 902/465-8009, www.fishermanscove.ns.ca; mid-May–mid-Oct. daily 9 A.M.–6 P.M.) has information on the historic fishing village, as well as general Halifax information.

### Airport
After retrieving your bags from the luggage carousels, you'll pass right by the **Airport**

**Visitor Information Centre** (902/873-1223; daily 9 A.M.–9 P.M.), which is a provincially operated facility. Most questions thrown its way relate to Halifax, but the center represents the entire province.

## BOOKS AND BOOKSTORES
### Libraries
**Halifax Public Libraries** (www.halifaxpubliclibraries.ca) has 14 branches across the city. The largest and most central is **Spring Garden Road Memorial Public Library** (5381 Spring Garden Rd., 902/490-5700; Tues.–Thurs. 10 A.M.–9 P.M., Fri.–Sat. 10 A.M.–5 P.M., and outside of summer Sun. 2–5 P.M.), which has a pleasant tree-shaded park out front. Inside, you'll find more than 280,000 volumes, historical documents, newspapers from around the world, magazines from around North America, and free Internet access.

### General Bookstores and Maps
In the Historic Properties, **Maps and Ducks** (1869 Upper Water St., 902/422-7106; daily 10 A.M.–9 P.M.) has a wide range of antique maps, globes, nautical charts, road atlases, guidebooks, and specialty travel guides. As the name suggests, it also has ducks, as in duck decoys.

Upstairs in the Park Lane Mall, **Frog Hollow Books** (5640 Spring Garden Rd., 902/429-3318) is a comfortable store that occasionally hosts visiting literati. A few doors farther from downtown is **Bookmark** (5686 Spring Garden Rd., 902/423-0419), a small independent with a solid collection of Nova Scotian reading.

The **Trail Shop** (6210 Quinpool Rd., 902/423-8736, Mon.–Wed. 9 A.M.–6 P.M., Thurs.–Fri. to 9 P.M.) is an outdoor sports shop with a wide selection of maps. **Binnacle** (15 Purcell's Cove Rd., 902/423-6464) specializes in nautical charts.

## Secondhand Bookstores

**John W. Doull** (1684 Barrington St., 902/429-1652, www.doullbooks.com; Mon.–Tues. 9:30 A.M.–6 P.M., Wed.–Fri. 9:30 A.M.–9 P.M., Sat. 10 A.M.–5 P.M.) is the most centrally located of Halifax's secondhand bookstores. Its shelves are literally stocked to the ceiling, making finding specific titles difficult.

**Schooner Books** (5378 Inglis St., 902/423-8419, www.schoonerbooks.com; Mon.–Thurs. 9:30 A.M.–6 P.M., Fri. 9:30 A.M.–9 P.M., Sat. 9:30 A.M.–5 P.M.) fills two stories of a converted Victorian-era home off Barrington Street. Specialties include Atlantic Canada history and literature, early Canadiana, and Canadian art.

At the south end of downtown, **Trident** (1256 Hollis St., 902/423-7100; Mon.–Fri. 8 A.M.–5 P.M., Sat. 8:30 A.M.–5 P.M., Sun. 11 A.M.–5 P.M.) is stacked from floor to ceiling with everything from 1970s best-selling romances to titles that will have political historians salivating.

## Media

The daily *Halifax Herald* circulates throughout the province and *Coast* is a free arts and entertainment weekly.

## EMERGENCY SERVICES

The city's hospital services are coordinated under the auspices of the **Queen Elizabeth II Hospital** (1796 Summer St., 902/473-3383).

Municipal **police** are assigned to Halifax and Dartmouth; in emergencies, dial 911, and for nonemergency business call 902/490-5026. The **RCMP** can be reached by calling 911 or 902/426-1323.

## ACCESS FOR TRAVELERS WITH DISABILITIES

The good news about Halifax specifically is that the major attractions as well as a small percentage of rooms in most major hotels are wheelchair-accessible. Theaters and performing arts venues are also usually wheelchair-

accessible. Halifax's public transit system, Metro Transit, has low-floor buses along all major routes as well as the **Access-A-Bus** program, providing wheelchair-accessible transportation on a door-to-door basis. Register at 902/490-6681.

## MONEY AND COMMUNICATIONS

### Banks

As Nova Scotia's capital, Halifax has banks by the dozens. **Scotiabank** has nine city branches and does not charge to convert foreign currency to Canadian dollars. The fee for cashing traveler's checks is $2, so it pays to convert several checks at one time. Branches are open Monday–Wednesday and Saturday 10 A.M.–3 P.M., Thursday–Friday until 5 P.M.

Hotel desks also exchange currency, but rates are more favorable at the banks.

### Postal Services

The city has three post offices open Monday–Friday 8 A.M.–5 P.M., including the General Post Office (1680 Bedford Row, 902/494-4734); branches are at 6175 Almon Street and 1969 Upper Water Street.

### Public Internet Access

Internet access is free at the **Spring Garden Road Memorial Public Library** (5381 Spring Garden Rd., 902/490-5700; Tues.–Thurs. 10 A.M.–9 P.M., Fri.–Sat. 10 A.M.–5 P.M., and outside of summer Sun. 2–5 P.M.), as well as at other city libraries, but you may have to wait for a terminal. Right downtown, **Ceilidh Connection** (1672 Barrington St., 902/422-9800; Mon.–Fri. 10 A.M.–10 P.M., Sat.–Sun. noon–8 P.M.) charges around $10 per hour for access. **Paper Chase** (5228 Blowers St., 902/423-0750; Mon.–Thurs. 8 A.M.–8 P.M., Fri.–Sat. 8 A.M.–9 P.M., Sun. 9 A.M.–8 P.M.) combines public Internet access with good-value healthy food.

The **Community Access Program (CAP)**

provides free Internet access to members of the public across Nova Scotia. To find out addresses and hours of the 30-odd locations within Halifax call 866/569-8428 or go to www.hrca.ns.ca.

## PHOTOGRAPHY

General photography shops are plentiful throughout downtown and are all up on digital technology, allowing you to print from memory cards or transfer your images to compact disc. Reliable equipment and hard-to-find films are stocked at **Carsand-Mosher Photographic** (1559 Barrington St., 902/421-

1980). **Camera Repair Centre** (2342 Hunter St., 902/423-6450; Mon.–Fri. 9 A.M.–5 P.M.) handles repairs.

## LAUNDRIES

You'll find coin-operated laundries around the fringes of downtown. These include **Murphy's Laundromat** (corner North and Robie Sts., 902/454-6294) and **Spin and Tumble** (1022 Barrington St., 902/422-8099).

**Bluenose Laundromat** (2198 Windsor St., 902/422-7098; Mon.–Sat. 7:30 A.M.–7:30 P.M.) will wash, dry, and fold your clothes with same-day service.

# Getting There

## AIR

**Halifax International Airport (YHZ)** is beside Highway 102, 38 kilometers north of Halifax. It is Atlantic Canada's busiest airport, handling more than 3.4 million passengers annually.

The airport is easy to navigate on foot. Beside the baggage carousels is the **Nova Scotia Visitor Information Centre** (902/873-1223; daily 9 A.M.–9 P.M.), which helps out with all the usual tourist information and maps. Beyond this point are the car-rental desks and an information counter specifically for helping out with airport transportation. The arrivals area is linked to the rest of the terminal by a short concourse. In between is the main concentration of food and retail shops, including a currency exchange (daily 7 A.M.–9 P.M.); **Clearwater Seafood,** which plucks live lobsters from a tank and packs them for air travel; a bookstore; and a variety of souvenir shops. There are also a play area and wireless Internet hotspots.

The Halifax International Airport Authority operates two websites: www.hiaa.ca has lots of information about the airport itself, while www.flyhalifax.com has general travel-planning information, as well as a nifty virtual

flight map that tracks flights in real time as they arrive and depart from Halifax.

### Airport Transportation

The **Airporter** (902/873-2091) runs between the airport and major downtown hotels ($18 one-way) 1–2 times every hour between 5 A.M. and 1 A.M. You need reservations only when returning to the airport from your hotel.

Taxi and limousine services are available curbside in the Domestic Arrivals area for all arriving flights. A one-way trip to Halifax city center is $53 by taxi or limousine.

### Airport Car Rental

Once you've picked up your bags from the baggage carousels, you'll find a row of check-in desks for major car-rental companies immediately behind you. Airport phone numbers are: **Avis** (902/429-0963), **Budget** (902/492-7551), **Enterprise** (902/873-4700), **Hertz** (902/873-2273), **National/Alamo** (902/873-3505), and **Thrifty** (902/873-3527). **Discount** (902/468-7171) operates out of a nearby motel; call for a pickup upon arrival.

Along the airport access road is **Petro Canada,** perfect for ensuring that you are not hit with outrageous charges for not returning the vehicle with a full tank of gas.

## Parking

Short-term airport parking within walking distance of the terminal costs $3 per hour to a maximum of $12 per day and $70 per week. For long-term parking, nearby **Park'N Fly** (668 Barnes Dr., 902/873-4574, www .parknfly.ca) charges $9 per day and $43 per week, inclusive of a free ride to and from the airport. (Check the Park'N Fly website for a discount coupon.)

## RAIL

Halifax is served by **VIA Rail** (416/366-8411 or 888/842-7245, www.viarail.ca) passenger trains from Montréal.

The **VIA Rail Station** is one kilometer south of downtown at the corner of Barrington and Cornwallis Streets. It's a classic old terminal, with a colonnaded facade, high ceiling, and tiled floors, but it is only ever busy when a train rolls in. **Hertz** has a desk at the terminal, and a concourse links the terminal to the grand Westin hotel.

## BUS

Long-distance bus services arrive and depart from the **VIA Rail Station** (corner of Barrington and Cornwallis Sts.), one kilometer south of downtown and within walking distance of HI–Halifax. The main carrier is **Acadian Lines** (902/454-9321 or 800/567-5151, www.smtbus.com), which has departures from Halifax to points throughout the province and beyond. Acadian Lines services run as far as Montréal, Toronto, and Bangor, Maine, from where connections can be made to Greyhound buses.

# Getting Around

## PUBLIC TRANSPORTATION

**Metro Transit** (902/490-4000, www.halifax .ca/metrotransit) buses saturate city streets, charge adult $2, senior and child $1.40 (exact change only) with free transfers, and operate daily 6 A.M.–midnight. Main bus stops are on Water, Barrington, Cornwallis, Cogswell, and Duke Streets, Spring Garden Road, and Gottingen Street, with service to Quinpool Road and Bayers Street. If you're at a stop waiting for a bus, dial 465 followed by the four-digit route number (marked in red at every stop) for real-time information on when the next bus will be arriving.

**FRED** (an acronym for "Free Rides Everywhere Downtown") is a free July–late October bus service that makes 18 stops on a circuit that begins northbound along Lower Water Street and then heads along Barrington Street and Spring Garden Road before returning to Water Street on South Street.

### Ferries

Metro Transit runs the **Halifax-Dartmouth ferry** from the foot of George Street (beside Historic Properties) to Alderney Drive in Dartmouth. It is the oldest saltwater passenger service in North America, having transported its first passengers by rowboat more than 200 years ago. Today, three modern vessels ply the route in just 12 minutes. The service runs year-round, Monday–Saturday 6:30 A.M.–midnight, and June–September on Sunday, same hours. The one-way fare is the same as by bus—adult $2, senior and child $1.40.

### Taxi

Cabs are easiest to flag outside major hotels

and Dartmouth, the A. Murray MacKay and the Angus L. MacDonald; the toll is $0.75 one-way for vehicles, free for bicyclists and pedestrians.

## Downtown Parking

Metered parking costs $1 per 30 minutes but is difficult to find during business hours. Most major hotels have underground public parking, and a few multistory parking lots are scattered throughout the city core. The most convenient parking lots are along Lower Water Street, at the foot of Prince and Salter Streets, but these are also the most costly ($5 per hour). If you're staying at a downtown hotel, expect to pay up to $24 per day for parking (ask about free parking for weekend reservations).

© ANDREW HEMPSTEAD

The ferry trip between downtown and Dartmouth makes for an inexpensive harbor cruise.

or transportation hubs, such as the VIA Rail Station. All rides start at $2.75, with an additional $2.25 charged for each mile plus $0.50 for each additional person. Taxi fares within downtown usually run under $8 while the trip between the airport and downtown is set at $53. Major companies include: **Airport Taxi** (902/455-2232), **Co-op Taxi** (902/444-0001), **Halifax Taxi** (902/877-0404), and **Yellow Cab** (902/420-0000).

## DRIVING

Getting into the city is made easy by a number of major arteries that spill right into downtown. Once in the commercial core, Haligonians are painstakingly careful and slow drivers—a wise way to go as hillside streets are steep, and many roads are posted for one-way traffic. Pedestrians have the right-of-way on crosswalks. Two **bridges** link Halifax

## DRIVING IN HALIFAX

The compactness of downtown Halifax means driving is not essential. If you're planning to spend a few days in the capital before heading out to explore the rest of the province, delay renting a vehicle and plan to explore the city on foot.

If you do plan to drive, the good news is that locals are remarkably accommodating to other drivers – allowing others to merge, stopping for pedestrians even where no crosswalk exists, and generally keeping to the speed limits. The most confusing meeting of roads is the **Armdale Rotary,** a large traffic circle west of downtown along Quinpool Road. Officially now a roundabout (meaning that vehicles on the circle have right of way over those joining the flow), locals continue to alternate and ignore the traffic lights, creating an intimidating intersection that is remarkably simple to use – although it may not seem so at first glance.

## Car Rental

Each of the major car-rental companies is represented at the airport and downtown. As always, book as far in advance as possible, and use the Internet to find the best deals. Vehicles rented from downtown are generally the same price as out at the airport, but the final bill comes with fewer taxes.

# SOUTH SHORE

Nova Scotians must have had this region in mind when they coined the province's motto, "So Much to Sea." The crashing Atlantic lays itself out in foaming breakers along the deeply scored Atlantic coastline that extends from Lunenburg to Yarmouth. It's a three-hour drive between these two towns, but you'll want at least two days and preferably more to explore the hidden corners of this quintessential corner of Nova Scotia. The seaports and towns follow one another, like a series of glossy, life-size picture postcards. There are those that outsiders will know by name—Peggy's Cove, Mahone Bay, and Lunenburg—but one of the joys of touring the South Shore is discovering your own Peggy's Cove (and I give you some ideas throughout this chapter).

The South Shore ends at Yarmouth, where the Atlantic meets the Bay of Fundy. Locals say the Vikings came ashore a thousand years ago and inscribed the boulder that now sits at the Yarmouth County Museum's front door. Yarmouth's ragged coastline impressed early explorer Samuel de Champlain, who named the seaport's outermost peninsula Cap Forchu ("Forked Cape"). Like the Vikings, Champlain arrived and departed, as do thousands of visitors who arrive on the ferries and quickly disperse on routes to distant provincial destinations. Their loss is the gain of the tourist who stays. Cyclists like to bike the Yarmouth area's backcountry coastal roads. At Chebogue Point south of the seaport, pink, purple, and white lupines bloom in June, and

© ANDREW HEMPSTEAD

# HIGHLIGHTS

◖ **Peggy's Cove:** Nova Scotia's most famous village is a photogenic gem that you
won't want to miss (page 72).

◖ **The Churches of Mahone Bay:**
Lining up along the waterfront, three historic
churches reflect across the waters of charming Mahone Bay (page 78).

◖ **Classic Boat Festival:** In early August,
Mahone Bay fills with wooden boats and the interesting characters who build and sail them
(page 79).

◖ **Historic Downtown Lunenburg:**
Designated a World Heritage Site by UNESCO,
Lunenburg is as interesting as it is charming
(page 82).

◖ **Blue Rocks:** A world away from the
crowds of Peggy's Cove, this picture-perfect
fishing village clings to the shore of a rocky
harbor (page 84).

◖ *Bluenose II:* Lunenburg is a wooden-
ships kind of town, and what better way to tour
the harbor than aboard one (page 84)?

◖ **LaHave Islands:** Just a short detour
from the busy South Shore highway, these
small islands are dotted with a colorful collection of cottages and cabins (page 90).

◖ **Shelburne Historic District:** A wonderful collection of 200-year-old wooden
buildings brings the shipbuilding era to life
(page 93).

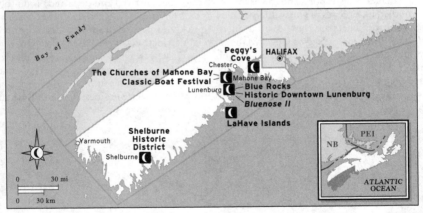

LOOK FOR ◖ TO FIND RECOMMENDED SIGHTS, ACTIVITIES, DINING, AND LODGING.

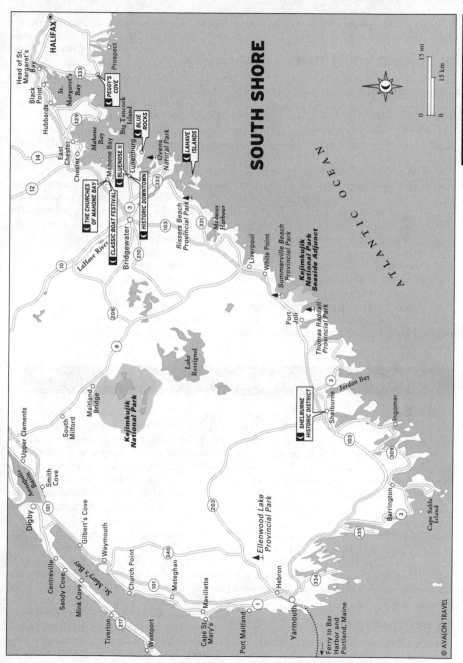

SOUTH SHORE

© AVALON TRAVEL

in summertime white-winged willets roam the marshes.

## PLANNING YOUR TIME

It is possible to visit the best-known towns along this stretch of coast in a day and return to Halifax. But don't. More realistically, plan a day in each place that interests you. As elsewhere in Nova Scotia, dining at its best is superb, and the region's specialty is its abundance of top-notch country inns with public dining rooms. Many lodgings are in historic houses and mansions converted to country inns and in categories best described as better, best, and beautiful. But it is the towns themselves that are this region's highlight. Even with just one week to explore the entire province, plan to spend at least one night in **Mahone Bay** or **Lunenburg,** the former recognized for its three waterfront churches and the latter as a UNESCO World Heritage Site. While the detour to **Peggy's Cove** is almost de rigueur, you should work into your itinerary less publicized villages such as **Blue**

**Rocks,** near Lunenburg. Taking part in two highlights of the South Shore involves some planning—Mahone Bay's **Classic Boat Festival** requires a visit in early August, while a sailing trip on the *Bluenose II* calls for reservations.

Travelers on a tight schedule make Lunenburg a turnaround point, but the rest of the South Shore is well worth exploring and sets you up for exploring the Fundy Coast. This stretch of coast is dotted with coastal provincial parks and hideaways such as the **LaHave Islands,** which a few hundred souls call home. The major historic attraction between Lunenburg and Yarmouth is **Shelburne Historic District.** If you are planning to circumnavigate southwestern Nova Scotia, or if you're arriving by ferry at Yarmouth from Maine, Shelburne is an ideal location for an overnight stay. Coupled with a night in Lunenburg or Mahone Bay, give yourself three days for the South Shore—not enough time to see everything, but a chance to spend quality time visiting each of the highlights.

# Halifax to Mahone Bay

From downtown Halifax, it's 105 kilometers along Highway 103 to Lunenburg, but for the most scenic views and interesting insights, forget the expressway and drive the secondary coastal routes. The best-known village in all of Nova Scotia is Peggy's Cove, a 40-minute drive south from downtown Halifax along Highway 333. Meanwhile, Highway 103 takes a direct route across to St. Margaret's Bay, from where secondary Highway 3 passes the charming towns set around Mahone Bay and its islands. One of these, Oak Island, looms large in the world of treasure-hunting legends—pirates are believed to have buried incalculable booty on it in the 1500s.

## ◖ PEGGY'S COVE

Atlantic Canada's most photographed site is a 40-minute drive along Highway 333 southwest

from Halifax, and the place is everything its fans say it is. With the houses of the tiny fishing village clinging like mussels to weathered granite boulders at the edge of St. Margaret's Bay, the Atlantic lathering against the boulder-bound coast, the fishing boats moored in the small cove, and the white octagonal lighthouse overlooking it all, the scene is the quintessence of the Nova Scotia coast.

Sightseers clog the village during the daytime (to miss the worst of the crowds, get there before 9 A.M. or after 5 P.M.), wandering along the wharves and around the weathered granite boulders surrounding the photogenic lighthouse. Peggy's Cove has a population of just 60 souls, so don't come expecting the services of a tourist town. The village has just one bed-and-breakfast, a restaurant, and the **deGarthe Gallery** (902/823-2256; mid-May–mid-Oct.

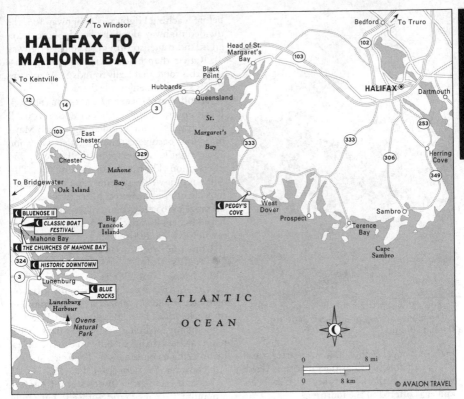

# HALIFAX TO MAHONE BAY

To Windsor

To Kentville

To Bridgewater

Bedford    To Truro

Head of St. Margaret's Bay

Black Point

Hubbards

Queensland

**HALIFAX**    Dartmouth

Herring Cove

East Chester

Chester

Mahone Bay

Oak Island

St. Margaret's Bay

West Dover

Prospect

PEGGY'S COVE

Sambro

Terence Bay

Cape Sambro

BLUENOSE II

CLASSIC BOAT FESTIVAL

Mahone Bay

THE CHURCHES OF MAHONE BAY

Big Tancook Island

HISTORIC DOWNTOWN

Lunenburg

BLUE ROCKS

Lunenburg Harbour

Ovens Natural Park

A T L A N T I C

O C E A N

0    8 mi

0    8 km

© AVALON TRAVEL

daily 9 A.M.–5 P.M.). The latter, along the main road through town, displays the work of well-known artist William deGarthe, whose stunning nautically themed oil paintings grace galleries the world over. Behind the gallery, deGarthe sculpted a 30-meter-long frieze on a granite outcropping. It depicts 32 of the seaside village's fishermen and families.

On a sad note, the town received worldwide attention in September 1998, when a Swissair MD-11 jetliner bound from New York City to Geneva crashed in shallow waters off the coast here, killing all 229 people aboard. A small memorial overlooks the ocean along Highway 333, two kilometers west of the village.

## Accommodations

The only accommodation has just five guest rooms, so book well ahead if you'd like to stay overnight in this delightful village. At the head of the actual cove, ◖ **Peggy's Cove Bed and Breakfast** (17 Church Rd., 902/823-2265 or 877/725-8732, www.peggyscovebb .com; $125–145 s or d including breakfast) has five well-furnished guest rooms with Wi-Fi Internet, a living area, a dining room, and a deck with magnificent views across the cove. It's open year-round; rates are discounted to $95–115 in winter.

## Food

The road through the village ends at the **Sou'wester Restaurant** (178 Peggy's Point Rd., 902/823-2561; June–Sept. daily 8 A.M.–9 P.M., Oct.–May daily 9 A.M.–8 P.M.), a cavernous room with a menu designed to appeal to the tourist crowd. And as the only place in town to eat, attract them it does—try to

© ANDREW HEMPSTEAD

Peggy's Cove, just a short drive from Halifax, is the most famous of all Nova Scotian fishing villages.

plan your meal before 10 A.M. or after 5 P.M. The menu does have a distinct maritime flavor, with dishes such as fish cakes, pickled beets, and eggs offered in the morning.

## Tours

If you are in Halifax without transportation, there are two options for visiting Peggy's Cove. **Peggy's Cove Express** (902/422-4200; June–Sept.) is a boat service that departs Halifax's Cable Wharf daily at 10 A.M. for the 2.5-hour run down the coast to Peggy's Cove and returns at 4:15 P.M. The fare is adult $70, senior $63, child $50, which includes a walking tour of the village. **Ambassatours** (902/423-6242 or 800/565-7173) offers a three-hour trip to Peggy's Cove (departs Halifax June–mid-Oct. daily at 12:30 P.M.) for adult $48, child $34.

## PEGGY'S COVE TO CHESTER

Highway 333 beyond Peggy's Cove winds north past a string of small fishing villages

before reaching Highway 3 (Highway 103, the divided highway along the South Shore, takes an inland route, so turn at the older Highway 3). Rather than places that you simply must stop, this route that lazily rounds St. Margaret's Bay is simply an enjoyable drive.

**Grand View Motel and Cottages** (Hwy. 3, Black Point, 902/857-9776 or 888/591-5122, www.grandviewmotelandcottages.com; May–mid-Nov.) occupies a prime waterfront location about eight kilometers from the Highway 333 intersection. The row of 10 motel rooms ($80–100 s or d) is well maintained and has windows looking out on the water. Three two-bedroom cottages ($165 s or d) are more spacious and have kitchens and decks. Outdoor furniture is set along the waterfront.

Continue west to **Hubbards,** where the ◖ **Trellis Café** (22 Main St., 902/857-1188; Mon.–Thurs. 9 A.M.–4 P.M., Fri.–Sun. 10 A.M.–9 P.M.) is a casual restaurant with colorful decor and occasional live entertainment on weekends. The namesake trellised deck is a good spot for lunch on warmer days. Most mains are less than $20, but you can spend less by ordering a combination of starters, such as fish chowder ($9) with fish cakes ($8).

Beyond Hubbards, **Queensland Beach** is a popular stretch of sand with safe but chilly swimming and a freshwater lagoon that attracts lots of birdlife.

## CHESTER AND VICINITY

The bayside town of Chester, first settled by New Englanders in 1759, lies at the northern head of Mahone Bay, just off Highway 103 (take Exit 8). Its first hotel was built in 1827, and the town, with its ideal sailing conditions and many vacation homes, has been a popular summer retreat ever since. Getting oriented beyond the downtown core can be confusing, so start your visit at the **Tourist Information Centre** (Hwy. 3, 902/275-4616; May–early Oct. daily 10 A.M.–5 P.M.), which is on the Mahone Bay side of town (coming into town from Halifax, continue up the hill to the right of the downtown turnoff).

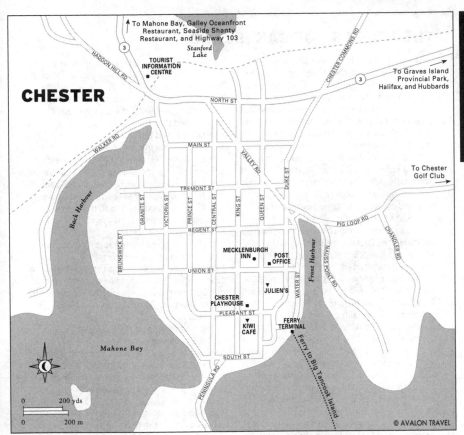

To Mahone Bay, Galley Oceanfront
Restaurant, Seaside Shanty
Restaurant, and Highway 103

Stanford
Lake

HADDON HILL RD

TOURIST
INFORMATION
CENTRE

CHESTER COMMONS RD

To Graves Island
Provincial Park,
Halifax, and Hubbards

**CHESTER**

NORTH ST

WALKER RD

MAIN ST

VALLEY RD

DUKE ST

To Chester
Golf Club

TREMONT ST

Back Harbour

GRANITE ST

VICTORIA ST

PRINCE ST

CENTRAL ST

KING ST

QUEEN ST

PIG LOOP RD

CHANDLER RD

REGENT ST

BRUNSWICK ST

MECKLENBURGH
INN

POST
OFFICE

Front Harbour

NAUSS POINT RD

UNION ST

JULIEN'S

WATER ST

CHESTER
PLAYHOUSE

PLEASANT ST

KIWI
CAFÉ

FERRY
TERMINAL

Mahone Bay

SOUTH ST

PENINSULA RD

Ferry to Big Tancook Island

0        200 yds
0        200 m

© AVALON TRAVEL

## Sights and Recreation

Most visitors to Chester are content to browse through downtown shops and wander lazily along the Front Harbour waterfront.

An easy excursion is to **Big Tancook Island** (adult $5, vehicle $21 round-trip) via ferries departing regularly from Front Harbour. The islands are mostly residential, but it's a pleasant trip across and walking parks lace the island.

Dating to 1914, **Chester Golf Club** (Golf Course Rd., Prescott Point, 902/275-4543) is an old-style golf course that opens up along the oceanfront to give sweeping views on holes lapped by the water. Greens fees are a good value at $50.

**Chester Playhouse** (22 Pleasant St., 902/275-

3933 or 800/363-7529, www.chesterplayhouse. ca) hosts some form of live entertainment weekly between March and December. Its Summer Theatre Festival draws professional talents in July and August. Past seasons have included musicals, Broadway-style revues, comedy improv, puppet shows, and children's programs.

## Accommodations and Camping

The most noteworthy of Chester's inns is ◖ **Mecklenburgh Inn** (78 Queen St., 902/275-4638, www.mecklenburghinn.ca; May–Dec.; $95–155 s or d), a 100-year-old sea captain's home that has been given a bohemian-chic look. Guests tend to gather on the wide veranda to watch the world of Chester go

# THE MYSTERY OF OAK ISLAND

In 1795, on Oak Island, a small island in Mahone Bay, a young man came upon an area where the forest had been cut away. Besides the stumps, he found a large forked limb with an old tackle block and a "treenail," and the ground nearby was sunken in a pit. His first thought would have been buried treasure, as the bay was a known haunt for pirates such as "Captain" William Kidd, Sir Henry Morgan, and Edward "Blackbeard" Teach 100 years previously. After hours of digging, McGinnis and two farmer friends reached a depth of 10 feet and hit wood. It turned out, however, to be not the rotted lid of a treasure chest but rather a platform of logs. So the men pressed on, convinced that the treasure lay just below. At the depth of 25 feet, digging became difficult, and they halted.

The first organized dig occurred in 1804, when a boat loaded with equipment arrived. Along with McGinnis and his friends, another log platform was uncovered at the 30-foot level, others at 40 and then 50 feet from the surface. At 60 feet the men uncovered a layer of coconut fiber, which hinted at cargo from warmer climes. At the 90-foot level, a large slab of granite that was later verified as being from Europe was uncovered. The next morning, the men returned to the pit to find it had filled with water. Having no success pumping the water out, the search was abandoned until the following spring. In 1805 a second shaft was dug, and at the 100-foot mark a horizontal tunnel was dug in the hope of reaching the treasure, but the search was abandoned. It would be another 40 years before the next serious attempt was made to retrieve whatever lay deep below Oak Island. While the secondary shafts filled with water only when linked to the original pit, it had been noted that the level of water in all three shafts rose and fell with that of the tide. This deepened the mystery even further, but what the men found next amazed everyone present. Along the adjacent bay, just below the low-tide mark, were five drains that, it was later found, converged on a single tunnel. While it was understood that this simple manmade flooding system had been put in place after the treasure pit had been dug, this didn't help solve the mystery. Nor did it help the next round of investors, who spent the summer of 1863 in a futile attempt to reach below the 100-foot level, or the numerous other treasure seekers who attempted to get to the bottom of the pit during the next 140 years.

The saga has cost six lives, sent many investors broke, and created numerous feuds between island property owners. Two treasure hunters, Dan Blankenship and Fred Nolan, spent a combined 100 years trying to outsmart those who designed the "Money Pit" many centuries ago. In 2005, Blankenship, who had sole road access to the island via a causeway, sold his share of the island to the government of Nova Scotia in the hopes that it would be opened to tourism. Incredibly, one of the world's great mysteries and longest treasure hunts continues to this day.

by, and then after dinner at a local restaurant gravitate to the comfortable couches set around two fireplaces in the living room. Three of the four rooms have en suite bathrooms with clawfoot tubs while a fourth has a private bathroom down the hall. A big breakfast of pancakes or smoked salmon eggs Benedict will set you up for a day of sightseeing.

Signposted from Highway 3 three kilometers northeast of Chester, **Graves Island Provincial Park** (mid-May–mid-Sept.; $24)

covers a small island connected to the mainland by a causeway. An open area at a high point of the island allows for pull-through RVs while tent sites are scattered around the surrounding forest. If you're just visiting for the day, plan on a picnic at the waterfront day-use area just across the causeway.

## Food

In downtown Chester, the **Kiwi Café** (19 Pleasant St., 902/275-1492) opens daily at

© ANDREW HEMPSTEAD

charming Chester

8:30 A.M. for simple healthy breakfasts and lunches along with a wide range of hot drinks, including chai tea and creamy hot chocolate. It's painted a cheery blue and kiwifruit green, with outside tables down one side. Around the corner and up the hill, **Julien's** (43 Queen St., 902/275-2324; Tues.–Sun. daily 8 A.M.–5 P.M.) serves delectable fresh breads, pastries, desserts, as well as more substantial healthy cooking.

# Mahone Bay

The town of Mahone Bay (pop. 1,200), on the island-speckled bay of the same name, is one of the most charming in all of Nova Scotia. The town's prosperous past is mirrored in its architecture, with Gothic Revival, Classic Revival, and Italianate styles in evidence. Many of these buildings have been converted to restaurants specializing in seafood and shops selling the work of local artisans. The distinctive bayside trio of 19th-century churches reflected in the still water has become one of the most photographed scenes in Nova Scotia.

## SIGHTS AND EVENTS

Most visitors to Mahone Bay are quite happy to spend their time admiring the architecture, browsing through the shops, and enjoying lunch at one of the many cafés. If you are interested in the town's architectural highlights, ask for the three walking-tour brochures at the museum.

## Mahone Bay Settler's Museum

Inside a 150-year-old wooden house, this museum (578 Main St., 902/624-6263; June–early Sept. Tues.–Sat. 10 A.M.–5 P.M., Sun. 1–5 P.M.; donation) describes the town's 250-year history. One room is dedicated to settlement of the area in the mid-1700s by German, French, and Swiss Protestants and the story of how they were enticed by the British government's offer of free land, farm equipment, and a year's "victuals." You also learn about the importance of shipbuilding, which thrived in a dozen shipyards from the 1850s to the early part of last century, and you can admire historic arts and crafts.

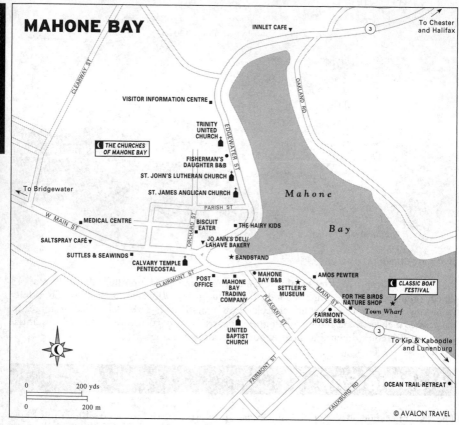

MAHONE BAY

INNLET CAFE ▼

To Chester
and Halifax

VISITOR INFORMATION CENTRE ■

TRINITY
UNITED
CHURCH ♦

❨ THE CHURCHES
OF MAHONE BAY

FISHERMAN'S
DAUGHTER B&B ■

ST. JOHN'S LUTHERAN CHURCH ♦

ST. JAMES ANGLICAN CHURCH ♦

PARISH ST.

W. MAIN ST.

MEDICAL CENTRE ■

BISCUIT
EATER ■

■ THE HAIRY KIDS

SALTSPRAY CAFÉ ▼

JO ANN'S DELI/
LAHAVE BAKERY

SUTTLES & SEAWINDS ■

★ BANDSTAND

CALVARY TEMPLE
PENTECOSTAL ♦

POST
OFFICE ■

■ MAHONE
BAY B&B

■ AMOS PEWTER

❨ CLASSIC BOAT
FESTIVAL

MAHONE
BAY
TRADING
COMPANY

SETTLER'S ★
MUSEUM

FOR THE BIRDS
NATURE SHOP ★

UNITED
BAPTIST
CHURCH ♦

FAIRMONT ★
HOUSE B&B

Town Wharf

To Kip & Kaboodle
and Lunenburg

To Bridgewater

Mahone

Bay

CLEARWAY ST.

EDGEWATER ST.

OAKLAND RD.

ORCHARD ST.

CLAIRMONT ST.

PLEASANT ST.

MAIN ST.

FAIRMONT ST.

FAUXBURG RD.

3

OCEAN TRAIL RETREAT ●

0        200 yds
0        200 m

© AVALON TRAVEL

## ❨ The Churches of Mahone Bay

From the flower-bedecked bandstand on Main Street, three churches can be seen shoulder to shoulder across the water. The oldest (and farthest from this viewpoint) is the **Trinity United Church** (Edgewater St., 902/624-9287), which dates to 1861 and was dragged by oxen to its current site in 1885. **St. John's Lutheran** (Edgewater St., 902/624-9660) is a symmetrical wooden structure standing in the middle of the three. Right on the corner is the Gothic Revival **St. James Anglican Church** (Edgewater St., 902/624-8614). This is the only one of the three open for tours (July–Aug. Thurs.–Sat. 11 A.M.–3 P.M.).

**Music at the Three Churches** is a series of classical music concerts hosted by the churches on select Friday nights through summer. The cost is adult $15, child free. Visit www.threechurches.com or check with the information center for a schedule and pay at the door.

If you walk along the waterfront beyond the information center, you'll see a different angle on the churches, as well as two others. Completed in 1875, the white spire you see rising above the trees is the **United Baptist Church** (56 Maple St., 902/624-9124), open for services Sunday at 11 A.M. The **Calvary Temple Pentecostal** (at the traffic circle where Main and Edgewater Sts. meet, 902/624-8420) opens its doors Sunday at 7 P.M. for hymn singing.

Mahone Bay is famous for its photogenic churches.

### Classic Boat Festival

Mahone Bay's annual Classic Boat Festival (902/624-0348, www.mahonebayclassicboatfestival.org) centers on the Town Wharf the weekend closest to August 1. This annual event draws thousands of spectators, who gather to take part in workshops, marvel over boatbuilding demonstrations, listen to tales from the sea, and cheer on competitors in boat-race series that vary from classic old yachts to floating contraptions constructed in less than four hours. A parade of sail, live entertainment, and the re-creation of a boat-launching using oxen are other highlights. Best of all, everything is free.

## SHOPPING

Many artists are attracted to Mahone Bay for its scenic setting, and the main street has developed into a hub for shoppers. Most shops are open from late spring to Christmas.

At **Amos Pewter** (589 Main St., 902/624-9547), you can watch artists at work as they cast, spin, and finish pewter pieces. **Mahone Bay Trading Company** (544 Main St.,

Plan on spending time browsing through the many shops along Mahone Bay's Main Street.

902/624-8425) is a large old-fashioned general store, but in keeping with the town's nautical feel, the sales clerks work from behind a boat-shaped counter. Tea connoisseurs will be in their element at the **Tea Brewery** (525 Main St., 902/624-0566) while birders are attracted to the **For the Birds Nature Shop** (647 Main St., 902/624-0784; closed Tues.), which sells binoculars, field guides, and related arts and crafts. Up the hill from the Tea Brewery, **Suttles and Seawinds** (466 Main St., 902/624-8375) sells stylish but colorful clothing. Even our four-legged friends aren't forgotten; **The Hairy Kids** (21 Edgewater St., 902/624-9097) is stocked with doggy fashions and treats.

## ACCOMMODATIONS

Through summer, and especially on weekends, demand is high for a limited number of rooms, so plan accordingly and book as far in advance as possible.

### Under $50

Mahone Bay is home to one of Nova Scotia's only privately operated backpacker lodges, ( **Kip and Kaboodle** (9466 Hwy. 3, Mader's Cove, 902/531-5494 or 866/549-4522, www.kiwikaboodle.com; $25 per person), which is three kilometers from the center of town toward Lunenburg. It's small, with facilities to match, but everything is well maintained, including a communal kitchen, living area, and outdoor pool. Other amenities include a barbecue and Wi-Fi Internet access. Rates include linen and a light breakfast.

### $50-100

Opposite the Town Wharf, you can sit on the veranda of **Fairmont House B&B** (654 Main St., 902/624-8089, www.fairmonthouse.com; $85–150 s or d) and watch the world of Mahone Bay go by. A local shipbuilder built this Gothic Revival home in 1857, and it was converted to a bed-and-breakfast in 1991. In the ensuing years its exterior has been given a coat of stately blue paint, and three guest rooms have been outfitted in stylish colored

themes. All rooms have en suite bathrooms, air-conditioning, and niceties such as hair dryers and irons. Downstairs is a library with board games and a TV. Rates include a continental breakfast.

Set right in the shopping heart of town, **Mahone Bay B&B** (558 Main St., 902/624-6388; $75–120 s or d) is a bright-yellow two-story home with a wraparound veranda bedecked in gingerbread trim—in other words, impossible to miss. The building, dating to 1860, is filled with antiques. The four guest rooms have a distinct grandmotherly look, and a full breakfast is served in the grand dining room.

### $100-150

Nestled amid the famous three churches is ( **Fisherman's Daughter B&B** (97 Edgewater St., 902/624-0483, www.fishermansdaughter.com; $100–125 s or d). Built in 1840 by a local shipbuilder, the home is understated but shows a restrained Gothic Revival style. A couple of the four guest rooms have funky layouts (such as beds nestled under the eaves), but this adds to the charm. Throw in a host of modern amenities and a full breakfast to make this place an excellent choice.

Two kilometers southeast of town toward Lunenburg, **Ocean Trail Retreat** (Hwy. 3, Mader's Cove, 902/624-8824 or 888/624-8824, www.oceantrailretreat.com; Apr.–Nov.) is set on a large grassed chunk of land that slopes down to the highway and Mahone Harbour. Two modern wings contain 17 motel-style rooms ($110–130 s or d) with big windows that take full advantage of the water views. Closer to the road are three two-bedroom chalets with full kitchens, living areas with propane fireplaces, and decks along the ocean-facing sides ($1,200 per week, but ask for nightly rates outside of summer). The outdoor heated pool is always a hit for families.

## FOOD

Mahone Bay's main street is lined with cafés, but most close in the late afternoon.

## Cafés

With a bag of carrots serving as a counter-weight on the front door, ◖ **Jo Ann's Deli** (9 Edgewater St., 902/624-6305; late May–Oct. daily 9 A.M.–7 P.M.) is a welcoming food shop filled with goodies. Locals come for organic produce, but everyone comes out with something—gourmet sandwiches, filled bagels, oatmeal cakes, brownies, homemade jams and preserves, and more. If you're planning a picnic, this is the place to get everything together.

Of the many places to eat in the village, the ◖ **Saltspray Café** (436 Main St., 902/624-9902; daily 7:30 A.M.–6 P.M.), uphill from the waterfront, stands out for value and quality. The café offers cooked breakfasts for less than $7, *including* bottomless cups of coffee. Chowder is a lunchtime mainstay, but also check the blackboard for daily specials. As you'd imagine, the Saltspray is perpetually busy.

## Restaurant

More of a restaurant than a café, ◖ **Innlet Cafe** (249 Edgewater St., 902/624-6363; daily 11:30 A.M.–9 P.M.) sits at the head of the bay, a 10-minute waterfront walk from downtown and with a classic view of all five Mahone Bay churches and tables on a stone patio perfect for warmer weather. Most mains are under $20, including Irish-inspired seafood stews and a wide range of fettuccini. Leave room for a slice of the delicious mud cake.

## INFORMATION AND SERVICES

The **Visitor Information Centre** (Edgewater St., 902/624-6151; summer Mon.–Sat. 9 A.M.–5 P.M., Sun. 11 A.M.–5 P.M.) is in a small building just before you reach the first church.

The **post office** is at the corner of Main and Clairmont Streets. Also along Main Street is a grocery store, pharmacy, and bank, while up West Main Street is a small medical center and launderette. Opposite the gazebo is the town's lone gas station.

Check your email over a coffee, and then browse the collection of used books at **Biscuit Eater** (16 Orchard St., 902/624-2665; 8:30 A.M.–5:30 P.M., Sun. 11 A.M.–5 P.M.).

# Lunenburg

Lunenburg (pop. 2,400) lies about equidistant between Halifax and Shelburne off Highway 103. Sited on a hilly peninsula between two harbors, this is one of the most attractive towns in Nova Scotia, with a wealth of beautiful homes painted in a crayon box of bold primary colors. In 1991 Lunenburg's Old Town was designated a national historic district, and in December 1995 the town received the ultimate honor when UNESCO designated it a World Heritage Site—one of only two cities in North America to enjoy that status (the other is Quebec City). More recently, in 2005, the provincial government stepped in and bought a chunk of waterfront buildings and wharves, saving them from development that would take away from the town's well-preserved history.

## History

To understand what the fuss is all about, you have to go back in time a couple of centuries. Protestant German, Swiss, and French immigrants, recruited by the British to help stabilize their new dominion, settled the town in 1753; their influence is still apparent in the town's architectural details. With its excellent harbor—a protected inner arm of the Atlantic embraced by two long, curving peninsulas—Lunenburg became one of Nova Scotia's premier fishing ports and shipbuilding centers in the 19th century. In 1921 the famous schooner *Bluenose* was built here. The 49-meter fishing vessel won the International Fisherman's Trophy race that same year, and for the next 18 years it remained the undefeated champion

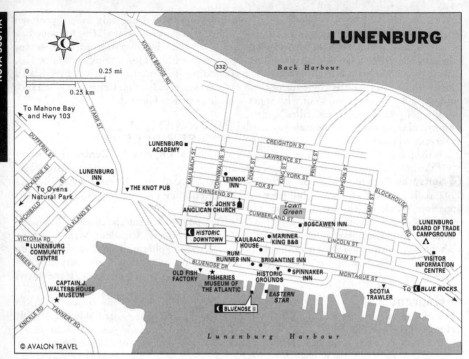

LUNENBURG

*Back Harbour*

*Lunenburg Harbour*

© AVALON TRAVEL

of the Atlantic fleets. The ship has become the proud symbol of the province, and its image is embossed on the back of the Canadian dime.

Today, the fishing industry that fostered the town's growth and boatbuilding reputation is comatose, and the Atlantic fisheries are mere shadows of their former selves. But here in Lunenburg, the townspeople carry on the shipbuilding and shipfitting skills of their ancestors. The port is still known as a tall ship mecca, and big multimasted sailing ships, old and new alike from around the world, continue to put in here for repairs, shipfitting, or provisions—whatever excuse the owners can come up with. Underneath the tourist glitz, the community pride in this tradition runs strong and deep, and the town's international reputation among mariners remains formidable. Strike up a conversation with a local about sailing ships and see what happens.

## ◖ HISTORIC DOWNTOWN

The port's oldest part is set on the hillside overlooking the harbor. The nine blocks of Old Town, designated a World Heritage Site by UNESCO, rise steeply from the water, and the village green spreads across the center. Bluenose Drive, the narrow lane along the harbor, and Montague Street, a block uphill, define the main sightseeing area. A mesh of one-way streets connects Old Town with the newer area built with shipbuilding profits. One of the pleasures of Lunenburg is strolling the residential and commercial streets, admiring the town's many meticulously preserved architectural gems. At the northern end of the harbor is the **Scotia Trawler Shipyard,** where the *Bluenose* was built. This shipyard and 16 other properties and most of the wharves are off-limits, but in 2005 the provincial government bought

© ANDREW HEMPSTEAD

Life in Lunenburg revolves around the colorful harborfront.

this entire precinct from a private company, and as the years go by they will be opened to the public.

### Fisheries Museum of the Atlantic

This spacious bright-red museum (68 Bluenose Dr., 902/634-4794; early May–mid-Oct. daily 9:30 A.M.–5:30 P.M., adult $10, senior $7, child $3; mid-Oct.–early May Mon.–Fri. 9:30 A.M.–4 P.M.; free) boasts a trove of artifacts and exhibits on shipbuilding, seafaring, rum-running, and marine biology. This thoroughly fascinating museum engages the visitor with demonstrations on fish filleting, lobster-trap construction, dory building, net mending, and other maritime arts. Inside are aquariums, tanks with touchable marine life, a gallery of ship models, full-size fishing vessels from around Atlantic Canada, a theater, a restaurant, and a gift shop. Tied up at the wharf outside are the fishing schooner *Theresa E. Connor,* built in Lunenburg in 1938; the steel-hulled trawler *Cape Sable,* an example of the sort of vessel

that made the former obsolete; the *Royal Wave,* a Digby scallop dragger; and, when it's in its home port, the *Bluenose II.* All the vessels may be boarded and explored.

### St. John's Anglican Church

This church (Cumberland and Cornwallis Sts., 902/634-4994; May–Oct. Mon.–Sat. 10 A.M.–5 P.M., Sun. noon–7 P.M.) stood for almost 250 years. In 2001, at the time the second-oldest church in Canada, it was destroyed by fire. It has now been rebuilt and can be visited on volunteer-led tours.

### Lunenburg Academy

High above the port and surrounded by parkland, the imposing Lunenburg Academy (97 Kaulbach St.) is easily spotted from afar. Dating to 1885, this black and white wooden building, with its mansard roof and worn wooden stairways, was originally a prestigious high school. Today, it is the local elementary school, but it remains as one of the oldest academy schools in Canada.

## Captain J. Walters House Museum

Captain Walters was the captain of the *Bluenose* during its racing days and was alive to sail aboard the *Bluenose II.* On the edge of the historic precinct, his modest home (37 Tannery Rd., 902/634-4410; July–Aug. Mon.–Sat. 10 A.M.–4 P.M.; $2.50) was donated to the town by his son and is now a museum. Displays center on the captain and his famous ship, but others describe the importance of shipbuilding to the local economy and the early fishing industry in general.

## OTHER SIGHTS
### ( Blue Rocks

Follow any of Lunenburg's downtown streets eastbound to link with a road that leads eight kilometers to Blue Rocks, toward the end of the peninsula. This tiny fishing village is set along a jagged coastline wrapped with blue-gray slate and sandstone, and the combination of color and texture will inspire photographers. Blue Rocks has no official attractions or services. Instead, drive to the end of the road, from where you need to explore on foot to get the full effect of a part of Nova Scotia far removed from touristy Lunenburg and Peggy's Cove. The shoreline is littered with boats and fishing gear such as nets and traps in various states of repair while simple but colorful homes cling to the rocky foreshore.

## Ovens Natural Park

A 15-minute drive south of Lunenburg on Highway 332, spectacular sea caves have been scooped out of the coastal cliffs. Early prospectors discovered veins of gold embedded in the slate and white quartz cliffs, sparking a small gold rush in 1861. During the following several decades, the cliffs surrendered 15,500 grams of the precious metal, while the Cunard family, of shipping fame, had the beach sand transported to England to retrieve the gold. Today, the site is privately owned, combining camping, cabins, hiking trails, and a restaurant on a 75-hectare site. Below the main parking lot, visitors can try their hand at panning for gold along Cunard's Beach. A trail leads along the sea cliffs and into one of the "ovens," and you can jump aboard an inflatable boat to get a sea-level view of the caves. The day-use fee is adult $8, senior and child $4. Call 902/766-4621 for information.

## RECREATION
### ( *Bluenose II*

Without a doubt, to immerse yourself fully in the Lunenburg experience you should set sail aboard the *Bluenose II,* an exact replica of the famous sailing ship.

When not in Halifax or visiting other Canadian ports, the *Bluenose II* (902/634-4794 or 866/579-4909, www.museum.gov.ns.ca/bluenose) can be found here at her home berth, outside the Fisheries Museum. Rather than separating you from the maritime experience with cushy reclining seats, acrylic plastic windows, and a cocktail lounge, the *Bluenose II* takes you to sea as a sailor. Cruising out of the harbor under a fresh breeze—the sails snapping taut and the hull slicing through the chilly waters—you'll begin to understand, to actually feel the history and lifeblood of Lunenburg.

When in Lunenburg she departs twice daily (9:30 A.M. and 1 P.M.; adult $35, child $20) for a two-hour harbor cruise. A total of 75 spots are offered on each sailing. Of these, 40 can be reserved through the phone numbers or website. The remaining 35 are offered on a first-come, first-served basis from the booth at the entrance to the Fisheries Museum 90 minutes before departure. (Tickets are always in high demand, so making a reservation well in advance is essential). Check the website for a sailing schedule.

## Other Boat Tours

The *Bluenose II* isn't always in port, and when she is, tickets sell fast. An excellent alternative is the ***Eastern Star,*** a character-imbued 48-foot wooden ketch lovingly tended by an amiable and knowledgeable crew passionately intent on perpetuating the seafaring tradition that put Lunenburg on the map. The *Eastern Star* makes four 90-minute cruises a

## THE FAMOUS *BLUENOSE*

Featured on Nova Scotian license plates and the back of the Canadian dime, the original *Bluenose* was launched from Lunenburg in 1921. Built as a fishing schooner, she was designed specifically for competing in the International Fishermen's Trophy, a racing series that pitted working ships from Canada and the United States against each other. Much to the joy of Canadians, the *Bluenose* won every racing competition she entered, while also serving as a working fishing boat. In 1942 the era of the sail-powered fishing industry was giving way to that of modern steel-hulled trawlers. The great *Bluenose* was sold to carry freight in the West Indies. Four years later, she foundered and was lost on a Haitian reef.

The ship herself was black. The name is thought to have originated from local fishermen, who, when conditions were cold and wet, would wipe their noses with their blue mittens, and the dye would consequently run.

In July 1963, the *Bluenose II* was re-created from the plans of the original and launched at Lunenburg. Some of the same craftspeople who had built the first *Bluenose* even participated in her construction.

day June–October, with a two-hour sunset cruise added in July and August. These tours cost adult $24–27, child $11–14, and the boat is operated by **Star Charters** (902/634-3535), which has a ticket booth down at the east end of the Fisheries Museum.

For a chance to see a lobster boat at work, sign up with **Lobstermen Tours** (902/634-3434 or 866/708-3434) for a two-hour trip that allows the chance to see local fishermen at work as they set traps and then bring them to the surface (preferably filled with lobsters). Departures are through summer daily at 11 A.M. and 1:30 P.M., and the cost is reasonable (adult $34, child $14). Even though it's a working boat, conditions are comfortable, with indoor seating and a washroom.

**Lunenburg Whale Watching Tours** (902/527-7175) depart Government Wharf May–October four times daily. While whales are definitely the highlight, regular sightings are also made of sunfish, turtles, dolphins, seals, and puffins. The cost is adult $45, child $30.

## ENTERTAINMENT AND EVENTS
### Nightlife

The seaport is usually quiet evenings and Sundays. Locals frequent **The Knot Pub** (4 Dufferin St.; daily noon–11 P.M.), a comfortable and lively place where you can get "knotwurst" and kraut with your draft beer. Up from the harbor, the **Lunenburg Arms** (94 Pelham St., 902/640-4040) has a lounge bar with tables that spill out onto a quiet patio.

### Performing Arts

Drama, dance, puppet shows, children's theater, and music performances regularly take place at **Pearl Theatre** (37 Hall St., 902/634-8716). **Lunenburg Opera House** (290 Lincoln St., 902/640-6500) hosts gigs by musicians from throughout Atlantic Canada. Cover charges are up to $20.

### Lunenburg Folk Harbour Festival

For four days from the first Thursday in August, a roster of traditional, roots, and contemporary folk musicians come together for the Lunenburg Folk Harbour Festival (902/634-3180, www.folkharbour.com). They perform under a tent atop Blockhouse Hill, at the Opera House, in the downtown bandstand, and out on the wharf. Many performances are free, with big-name acts under the big tent costing $20.

## SHOPPING

The **farmers' market** at Lunenburg Community Centre (corner Victoria Rd. and Green St.; July–Oct. Thurs. 8 A.M.–noon) lures crowds for fresh produce, smoked meats, and crafts at the former railroad depot grounds; wares are high quality and priced accordingly.

**Houston North Gallery** (110 Montague St., 902/634-8869) specializes in folk art, Inuit crafts and sculptures, and imported sculpture. Nautical gifts are available at the **Yacht Shop** (280 Montague St., 902/634-4331), which is also a full-service marine-supply center, and at the nonprofit **Bluenose II Company Store** (121 Bluenose Dr., 902/634-1963), which sells all manner of *Bluenose* clothing, gifts, and art to support preservation of the vessel.

## ACCOMMODATIONS AND CAMPING

Whatever Mahone Bay may lack in accommodation is more than made up for in Lunenburg, where more than 60 bed-and-breakfasts—more than Halifax, which has more than 100 times the population—clog the historic streets. Still, you should try to make reservations ahead of time in summer, but be prepared for an answering machine in winter, when many lodgings are closed.

### $50-100

Many of the bed-and-breakfasts in the $100–150 range have rooms under $100 outside of summer, but in July and August, your choices are limited. One of the best is the ( **Lennox Inn** (69 Fox St., 902/521-0214 or 888/379-7605, www.lennoxinn.com; May–Oct.; $95–120 s or d), which dates to 1791, making it Canada's oldest inn. The present owners breathed life into the building through a meticulous restoration using the original plans. Two guest rooms share a single bathroom, and the other two have en suites. Breakfast in what was originally the tavern is included in the rates.

Right downtown, above Grand Banker Restaurant, the tidy **Brigantine Inn and Suites** (82 Montague St., 902/634-3300 or 800/360-1181, www.brigantineinn.com; $75–160 s or d) provides excellent value. It offers seven nautically themed rooms, each with a private bathroom and named for a famous sailing ship. The smallest of the rooms is the brightly decorated Cutty Sark room, while

the much larger Brigantine Romance room features a jetted tub on a glass-enclosed balcony overlooking the harbor. Part of the inn is a complex of seven suites one block from the main inn. These have separate bedrooms, as well as sitting areas, coffeemakers, microwaves, and fridges.

Incorporating two (circa 1888 and 1905) buildings, the **Boscawen Inn and McLachlan House** (150 Cumberland St., 902/634-3325 or 800/354-5009, www.boscawen.ca; $95–205 s or d) also has a couple of rooms under $100, but most are more. This European-style hotel occupies a scenic perch above the harbor and is surrounded by gardens. The five guest rooms in McLachlan House are less expensive than those across the road at what was originally known as the Boscawen Manor, but all guests enjoy a light breakfast included in the rates. Other amenities include a formal dining room and sun-soaked terrace, both open to the public for meals.

### $100-150

**Kaulbach House** (75 Pelham St., 902/634-8818 or 800/568-8818, www.kaulbachhouse.com; mid-Mar.–Oct.; $112–169 s or d) is one of Lunenburg's many historic treasures (circa 1880) converted to an inn, complete with the unique "Lunenburg bump" architectural feature. Two blocks up from the harbor but with partial water views, the six antiques-filled rooms have en suite or private bathrooms and wireless Internet. A full breakfast is included in the rates.

The ornately detailed **Mariner King B&B** (15 King St., 902/634-8509 or 800/565-8509, www.marinerking.com; $110–220 s or d) is also right downtown. Its cheaper rooms are a little more threadbare than those at Kaulbach House, but the character-filled Attic Suite is a gem. It even has its own rooftop patio. Public areas include two sitting rooms and a small stone patio.

**Rum Runner Inn** (66 Montague St., 902/634-9200 or 888/778-6786, www.rumrunnerinn.com; $109–169 s or d) is right along the busy restaurant strip opposite the waterfront. It's a historic building, but the 13

© ANDREW HEMPSTEAD

Lunenburg Inn

rooms are thoroughly modernized and look no different from a regular motel. Each has a coffeemaker, fridge, air-conditioning, and Internet connections. The most expensive rooms have a king bed and glassed-in veranda. A light breakfast is included.

If you're looking to stay in a historic building with a modern feel, consider the centrally situated **( Spinnaker Inn** (126 Montague St., 902/634-4543 or 888/777-8606, www.spinnakerinn.com; $125–175 s or d). Overlooking the harbor, all four guest rooms have polished hardwood floors and antique-style beds. Two are split-level with jetted tubs in the en suite bathrooms and harbor views.

The **Lunenburg Inn** (26 Dufferin St., 902/634-3963 or 800/565-3963, www.lunenburginn.com; Apr.–Oct.; $155–195 s or d) is an elaborate Victorian home that has been taking in guests since 1924. It underwent serious renovations in the mid-1990s and now provides some of the nicest rooms in town. If I had a choice, I'd stay in the Hillside Suite, which has a sitting area with a TV, a jetted tub in the en suite bathroom, and a private entrance

from the veranda. Guests enjoy a sitting room with a fireplace, a private bar, and high-speed Internet access.

## Campgrounds

The **Lunenburg Board of Trade Campground** (Blockhouse Hill Rd., 902/634-8100; May–Oct.; $22–28) sits on Blockhouse Hill, high above downtown and beside the information center. It's on the small side (55 sites) but facilities are adequate (showers, views, Internet access).

A lot more than a campground, **( Ovens Natural Park** (off Hwy. 332, 902/766-4621, www.ovenspark.com; mid-May–mid-Oct.) has campsites (tents $25, hookups $38–55) and cabins varying from those with shared bathrooms ($60 s or d) to self-contained two-bedroom chalets ($180). Amenities include lawn games, a playground, evening bonfires, a restaurant, and a gift shop. Relations of Harry Chapin (of *Cat's in the Cradle* fame) own and operate the property, making the evening sing-alongs a real treat. On the middle weekend of August, the entire Chapin family comes together as a tribute to the singer, with everyone welcome to join in the fun.

## FOOD

Lunenburg has a great number of restaurants, nearly all serving seafood in a casual setting. Local specialties appearing on some menus include Solomon Gundy (pickled herring, usually served with sour cream), Lunenburg pudding (pork sausage), and fish cakes topped with rhubarb relish. Beyond the tourist precinct, **Scotia Trawler** (266 Montague St., 902/634-4914) is where fishermen come for their supplies. Beyond the rows of dry goods and canned food are salted cod, Solomon Gundy and Lunenburg pudding, as well as many other "treats" you won't find in your local grocery store.

### Café and Pub Dining

**◖ Historic Grounds** (100 Montague St., 902/634-9995; June–mid-Sept. Mon.–Fri. 7:30 A.M.–10 P.M., Sat.–Sun. 8 A.M.–10 P.M., the rest of the year daily 7:30 A.M.–5:30 P.M.) is Lunenburg's best place for a coffee concoction (especially if you nab one of two tables on the balcony overlooking the harbor). But this café is a lot more than a coffeehouse. It also serves sandwiches made to order, chowder, and salads.

Away from the waterfront, **Knot Pub** (4 Dufferin St., 902/634-3334; daily noon–9:30 P.M.) is a small space with decent pub grub, including battered fish-and-chips for $10.

### Restaurants

In the big red building down on the water, the **Old Fish Factory** (68 Bluenose Dr., 902/634-3333; May–Oct. 11 A.M.–10 P.M.) is a large restaurant in a converted fish storehouse. Specialties include creamy seafood chowder, beer-battered haddock, and fish baked on a cedar plank. After Solomon Gundy (pickled herring), a sour-tasting local specialty, you'll be ready for Blueberry Grunt, sweet dumplings floating in a blueberry compote and topped with whipped cream. Nonseafood dishes with a Canadian twist are also offered, such as maple-

glazed chicken for $18.50. All other dinner entrées are similarly priced, while lunches run $8–15.

One block back from the harbor, several restaurants line Montague Street. All have decks or floor-to-ceiling windows facing the water. **Big Red's Family Restaurant** (80 Montague St., 902/634-3554; daily 9 A.M.–10 P.M., until 11 P.M. on weekends) is exactly that—a cavernous family-friendly restaurant with a standard seafood menu. Portions are generous and prices reasonable.

The **◖ Grand Banker Seafood Bar & Grill** (82 Montague St., 902/634-3300; daily 8:30 A.M.–9 P.M.) offers similarly great views from an enclosed dining room and serves a wide-ranging menu of seafood, salads, pastas, and sandwiches. The food is well prepared and the atmosphere pleasant—it feels a little more relaxed and a little less tourist-driven than some of its neighbors. Mains ranging $10–20 include crab cakes, Acadian seafood stew, and maple-pecan glazed salmon. A half dozen good beers and a couple of Nova Scotia wines are available. The Grand Banker puts on a fine brunch (weekends 11 A.M.–2:30 P.M.) that includes lobster eggs Benedict ($12).

## INFORMATION AND SERVICES

**Lunenburg Visitor Information Centre** (Blockhouse Hill Rd., 902/634-8100; May–Oct. daily 9 A.M.–8 P.M.) stocks locally written, informative literature about the port's historic architecture. *Understanding Lunenburg's Architecture* describes the design elements, and *An Inventory of Historic Buildings* provides details on almost every seaport building, organized street by street. Staff will help those without reservations find accommodation. For the uninitiated, the office can be a little hard to find; as you enter town, stay on Lincoln Street as it passes the signs for the waterfront and you'll soon find yourself on Blockhouse Hill.

**Fishermen's Memorial Hospital** (14 High St., 902/634-8801) is between Dufferin and Green Streets. For the **RCMP**, call 902/634-8674.

Banks dot King Street, while the **post office** is on the corner of King and Lincoln Streets. **Soap Bubble Cleanette** (39 Lincoln St., 902/634-4601; Mon.–Sat. 8 A.M.–8 P.M., Sun. 10 A.M.–8 P.M.) is the local launderette.

## GETTING THERE AND AROUND

Along divided Highway 103, it takes a little more than one hour to reach Lunenburg from Halifax, taking Exit 10 via Mahone Bay for the final stretch. Most visitors arrive this way, as part of a tour, or in their own or a rental car. If you're in Halifax without a vehicle, consider a six-hour tour with **Ambassatours** (902/423-6242 or 800/565-7173). These depart June–October Wednesday, Friday, and Saturday at 8:30 A.M. for adult $98, senior $88.20, child $69.

Bridgewater-based **Try Town Transit** (902/521-0855) operates an on-demand shuttle between Halifax and Lunenburg for about $120 for up to eight passengers.

# Lunenburg to Shelburne

Beyond Lunenburg, the divided highway continues south to Bridgewater, but the crowds thin out quickly. This is one of the best reasons to continue south—the coastline is dotted with Peggy's Cove–like villages steeped in history but unaffected by tourism and a rugged coastline where parks with designated hiking trails and sandy beaches beckon.

The 140-kilometer drive between Lunenburg and Shelburne takes less than two hours nonstop. As accommodations are limited along this stretch of coast, a sensible schedule is to plan to leave Lunenburg after breakfast, spend the day exploring the following parks and towns, and have a room booked in Shelburne for that night.

## BRIDGEWATER

Situated on the LaHave River, west of Lunenburg, Bridgewater (pop. 7,000) is the main service town of the South Shore. Industry revolves around a Michelin tire plant, and if you're traveling south, this is the last place to fill up on fast food (if you must) and do your mall shopping.

### Sights

The 1860 **Wile Carding Mill** (242 Victoria Rd., 902/543-8233; June–Sept. Mon.–Sat. 9:30 A.M.–5:30 P.M., Sun. 1–5:30 P.M.; adult $4, child $2) was once a wool-processing mill. The wool was carded for spinning and weaving or made into batts for quilts. The original machinery is still in operation, powered by a waterwheel, and now demonstrates old carding methods. It's on the south side of the river (take Exit 13 from Highway 103).

Surrounded by parkland on the east side of downtown, **DesBrisay Museum** (130 Jubilee Rd., 902/543-4033; July–Sept. Mon.–Sat. 9 A.M.–5 P.M., Sun. 1–5:30 P.M., the rest of the year Wed.–Sun. 1–5 P.M.; adult $3:50, senior $2.25, child $2) tells the story of Bridgewater's first European settlers and the importance of local industries. Highlights include Mi'Kmaq quilting and a wooden plough dating to 1800.

### Accommodations and Food

Nova Scotia's oldest accommodation is Bridgewater's **Fairview Inn** (25 Queen St., 902/543-2233 or 800/725-8732, www .thefairviewinn.ca; $95–145 s or d), a gracious three-story wooden building that dates to 1863. It has been beautifully restored, now with 24 stylish guest rooms that vary from simple but comfortable to a nautically themed suite. In-room niceties include plush linens, bathrobes, and room service, while other amenities include an outdoor pool and hot tub, a restaurant, a lounge, and even room service. To get there from Highway 103, take Exit 13 and follow Victoria Road to Queen Street. About six kilometers east of town along

Highway 331 is the **Lighthouse Motel** (1101 Hwy. 331, Pleasantville, 902/543-8151, www .lighthousemotel.ca; May–Oct.; $75–100 s or d). It occupies a prime riverside location, and guests have access to a private beach, a picnic area, and a playground.

**Cranberry's** (Fairview Inn, 25 Queen St., 902/543-2233; daily 7 A.M.–9 P.M.) is an inviting space with a creative menu to match. It's very popular in the morning ($6 for a full cooked breakfast with coffee or $9 for eggs Benedict with smoked salmon), but it is lunch and dinner that set this restaurant apart. You could start with Solomon Gundy (a local delicacy of pickled herring), and then choose a main as simple as curried shrimp or as rich as baked haddock stuffed with asparagus and smoked salmon. Just make sure to save room for the divinely rich chocolate mousse.

# HIGHWAY 331 TO LIVERPOOL

Highway 331, which begins in downtown Bridgewater as King Street, follows the LaHave River to its mouth and then winds along the coast to Exit 17 of Highway 103. It adds just 30 minutes to the trip between Bridgewater and Liverpool, but you'll want to allow longer—it's a beautiful introduction to the untouristy South Shore beyond Lunenburg.

## ◖ LaHave Islands

A causeway from **Crescent Beach** crosses to Bush Island, from where quirky old iron bridges provide access to Bell Island and LaHave Island. Just three of dozens of islands in the group, they are dotted with old fishing cottages inhabited by those who have escaped the rat race. On Bell Island, a museum filled with local history is in the church, while Bush Island Provincial Park is little more than a boat launch, but for the rugged scenery and funky fishing cottages the drive to the end of the road makes a delightful detour from the main South Shore tourist route.

Just one of many parks along this stretch of coast, **Rissers Beach Provincial Park** boasts a beach of finely ground quartz sand and an area of pristine salt marsh laced with boardwalks. The park campground (902/688-2034; mid-May–mid-Oct.; $24) fills every weekend through summer, but midweek even sites close to the sandy beach remain empty. The park is right by the causeway leading across to the islands.

# LIVERPOOL

This historic town, at the mouth of the Mersey River 50 kilometers south of Bridgewater, doesn't get as much attention as it deserves. Throughout the compact downtown core are a number of interesting attractions, while Privateer Days (early July) provide a lively glimpse of the town's colorful past.

## Sights and Events
### THE PORT OF PRIVATEERS

Privateers were government-sanctioned pirates who had permission to capture enemy vessels. American privateers found their way to Nova Scotia during the American Revolution, but the British responded by attacking American boats. Privateers were required by law to take captured vessels to Halifax's Privateers Wharf, where the boats and cargo were auctioned off, a portion of which was handed back to the privateer and his crew. Liverpool local Simeon Perkins had a share in a privateering boat, along with dozens of others who used Liverpool as their home port. The most prolific of the privateer vessels was the *Liverpool Packet* captained by Joseph Barss, which captured an estimated 200 vessels during its lifetime. With plundered goods from a single vessel selling for up to $1 million at auction, Liverpool became a wealthy town, and many of the grand homes still standing were financed from privateering.

### SHERMAN HINES MUSEUM OF PHOTOGRAPHY

Renowned landscape and portrait photographer Sherman Hines developed this photography museum (219 Main St., 902/354-2667; mid-May–mid-Oct. Mon.–Sat. 10 A.M.–5:30 P.M. and July–Aug. also Sun. noon–5:30 P.M.; adult $4, child $3) to display the work of prominent Nova Scotian photographers, including the museum's namesake. The wooden building, a 1901 National Historic Site in itself, also holds the re-creation of a Victorian-era photography studio, a gallery of changing exhibits, a research library, and a gift shop. In the foyer is an impressive mounted tuna—at 400 kilograms, the largest of its species ever caught on rod and reel.

## OTHER SIGHTS

In addition to his photography museum, Sherman Hines has injected his own resources into developing the **Rossignol Cultural Centre** (205 Church St., 902/354-3067; mid-May–mid-Oct. Mon.–Sat. 10 A.M.–5:30 P.M. and July–Aug. also Sun. noon–5:30 P.M.; adult $4, child $3) in a school building once slated for demolition. One block south of Main Street along Old Bridge Street, it encompasses multiple small museums, including one devoted to outhouses (Hines is well known for his outhouse photography), and others to folk art, the Mi'Kmaq, and wildlife.

Built by an infamous privateer, **Perkins House** (105 Main St., 902/354-4058; mid-May–mid-Oct. Mon.–Sat. 9:30 A.M.–5:30 P.M., Sun. 1–5:30 P.M.; free) is a classic example of a New England planter's adaptation to Nova Scotia. Built in 1766, it is furnished with antiques and displays that tell the story of Perkins's colorful life on the high seas.

Country music legend Hank Snow, who sold 70 million records, was born in nearby Brooklyn. Across the river from downtown, a railway station has been converted to the **Hank Snow Country Music Centre** (148 Bristol St., 902/354-4675; mid-May–mid-Oct. Mon.–Sat. 9 A.M.–5 P.M., and July–Aug. also Sun. noon–5:30 P.M.; $3) in his memory. Displays catalog his life, from the earliest performances in Halifax through details of his seven number 1 hits from 120 albums, to his Grand Ole Opry performances, his role in introducing Elvis Presley to the entertainment world, and, finally, the huge collection of awards accumulated through six decades of performing. To get there from Highway 103, take Exit 19; from downtown, cross the Mersey River via Bristol Street.

## PRIVATEER DAYS

There's no better place to immerse yourself in the colorful history of Nova Scotia's privateers than **Privateer Days** (902/354-4500, www .privateerdays.com), a Liverpool tradition held the first weekend in July. Walking tours led by locals in period dress and a re-creation of when two American privateer boats invaded the town are highlights, but events go on all week, culminating with a bang during final night's fireworks.

## Accommodations and Food

Once home to a privateer, **Lane's Privateer Inn** (27 Bristol Ave., 902/354-3456 or 800/794-3332, www.lanesprivateerinn.com; $90–120 s, $105–135 d) has everything you need for an overnight stay under one roof. The 27 rooms all have en suite bathrooms and air-conditioning while some have king beds and balconies overlooking the Mersey River. Downstairs is an excellent restaurant. Breakfast includes all the usual options, with Nova Scotian specialties such as smoked salmon sausage as a substitute for bacon. The lunch and dinner includes haddock topped with fruit salsa for $16 and lamb chops doused in blueberry-brandy sauce for $20.

## Information and Services

The **Visitor Information Centre** (28 Henry Hensey Dr., 902/354-5421, www.queens.ca; mid-May–Sept. daily 9:30 A.M.–5:30 P.M.) is on the riverfront right downtown. **Snug Harbour Books** (Lane's Privateer Inn, 27 Bristol Ave., 902/354-3456) is a welcoming spot at street level of the town's best accommodation. This is the place to pick up books on privateering, but you will find the many Nova Scotian cookbooks also make great souvenirs. The bookstore is part café, sharing the same menu as the affiliated restaurant.

# LIVERPOOL TO PORT JOLI

If you've left Highway 103 to explore Liverpool, continue south through town along the older Highway 3 to reach White Point before rejoining the main route south at Summerville.

## White Point

Activities at **White Point Beach Resort** (White Point Beach, 902/354-2711 or 800/565-5068, www.whitepoint.com) make this lodging a destination in itself. Stretching along a wide stretch of white sand, it has indoor and outdoor pools, swimming in a freshwater lake, surfboard and kayak rentals, tennis courts, a nine-hole golf course, a games room, two restaurants, and nightly entertainment in the lounge. Most guests are families, many returning annually for summer vacation. Comfortable motel-like rooms are $140–165 s or d depending on the view, and cottages are $265–310.

Continue along Highway 3 from White Point to Hunts Point is **Hunts Point Beach Cottages** (Hwy. 3, 902/683-2077, www.huntspointbeach.com; mid-May–mid-Oct.), a much quieter spot, where guests laze their time away on the grassed grounds, which extend to the beach. The cottages have one or two bedrooms ($135 and $145 s or d respectively), kitchens, covered decks, and living rooms with TVs.

## Summerville Beach Provincial Park

Just before Highway 3 rejoins Highway 103, a turnoff leads to this small provincial park, which protects a spit of sand jutting across Port Mouton. It's a day-use park with picnic tables and plenty of room to spread your towel on the beach.

## Kejimkujik National Park Seaside Adjunct

About 25 kilometers southwest of Liverpool is one of the largest remaining undisturbed areas of Nova Scotian coastline. Affiliated with the inland Kejimkujik National Park (along Highway 8 between Liverpool and Annapolis Royal), this section of the park encompasses unspoiled beaches and offshore isles. The park is accessible only on foot. The main access is along an easy three-kilometer trail beginning at the parking lot on St. Catherine's Road (turn off in Port Joli) and ending at the southwest end of St. Catherine's River Beach.

Some sections of this beach close late April–late July to protect piping plover nesting sites. The Seaside Adjunct has no visitor facilities, and camping is not permitted.

## PORT JOLI

It's another picturesque coastal village with another seaside park that gets busy only on the hottest of summer weekends.

## Thomas Raddall Provincial Park

This gem of a park protects rock formations suggesting it was the point where the Gondwana and North American continents collided many millions of years ago. But for most, the beaches are the main draw. Left behind by the retreating ice cap at the end of the last ice age, banks of sand have washed ashore, forming beautiful stretches of beach now protected by the park.

The park has an 11-kilometer trail system, half of which is paved and set aside for both cyclists and walkers. The most popular destination is Sandy Bay, a short beach bookended by rocky headlands. If you can pull yourself away from the beach, follow the **Sandy Bay Trail** over the northern headland to the **Herring Rock Trail,** where the remains of a 1700s fishing station can be seen. Take both these trails and you'll be back on your beach towel within an hour. In the north of the park, beaches are lapped by the protected waters of Port Joli Harbour. Starting from the top end of the campground, the **Port Joli Trail** (one kilometer each way) winds south past interpretive panels to Scotch Point Beach. To the north, a string of beaches spread out well beyond the park boundary.

The park campground (902/683-2664; mid-May–mid-Oct.; $24) has 82 large sites, including a few designated for tents. Each site has a picnic table and fire pit, while other amenities include washrooms with showers, a playground, and firewood sales.

To get to the park continue along Highway 103 south from Port Joli and turn south on East Port L'Herbert Road; it's three kilometers from the highway.

# Shelburne and Vicinity

Like Lunenburg, 140 kilometers to the northeast, Shelburne (pop. 2,300) sits at the innermost end of a long harbor formed between two peninsulas. The seaport was established in 1783 when Loyalists fleeing the newly independent American colonies settled here by the thousands, establishing shipbuilding and fish processing businesses—but eventually the seaport began to show its age. Then Hollywood came to town. In 1992, the motley collection of historic buildings along the waterfront was used as a setting for Fairfield, Connecticut, circa 1780 in the American Revolution movie *Mary Silliman's War*. In 1995 Shelburne again hit the big screen as the setting for 1600s Boston in *The Scarlet Letter*, an adaptation of Nathaniel Hawthorne's novel. Demi Moore and Robert Duvall may be long gone, but the two movies created an impetus for preservation. While some "historic" buildings were added to the mix, many original buildings were spruced up, power lines were buried, and generally the town came together to promote its past.

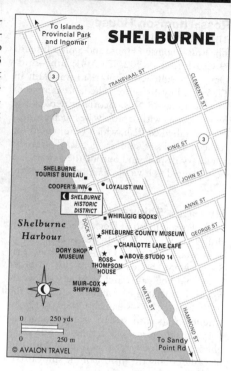

## ◖ SHELBURNE HISTORIC DISTRICT

Dock Street is dotted with some of Canada's oldest wooden buildings. The **Shelburne Historical Society** (902/875-3219) has done a wonderful job of breathing life into the precinct, while businesses such as a cooperage and a boatbuilder help bring the history to life. In between are grassed areas, a waterfront pathway, and kayak rentals. Admission to each of the buildings run by the Shelburne Historical Society is $3, or buy a ticket for $8 to visit all four.

## Shelburne County Museum

The Shelburne County Museum (8 Maiden La., 902/875-3219; June–mid-Oct. daily 9:30 A.M.–5:30 P.M., mid-Oct.–May Mon.–Fri. 10 A.M.–5 P.M.) is the best place to make your first stop. It contains exhibits covering Shelburne's Loyalist heritage and shipbuilding history. One highlight is the 250-year-old fire engine, believed to be the oldest in Canada.

## Dory Shop Museum

First used in the mid-1800s, dories were small, skifflike wooden boats that were essential to the success of fishing the Grand Banks. Rather than fishing from the mother vessel, a dozen or more would be transported to the fishing grounds, allowing hundreds of hooks to be laid out at once. Adding to their usability, they were inexpensive to make and stackable. On the waterfront across from the county museum, the Dory Shop (11 Dock St., June–Sept. daily 9:30 A.M.–5:30 P.M.) is the last of seven once-thriving boat factories in town. The seven shops turned out thousands of handcrafted wooden fishing dories between 1880 and 1970.

The shop now houses interpretive displays and gives demonstrations on the dying art.

## Ross-Thomson House and Store Museum

The Ross-Thomson House and Store Museum (9 Charlotte La., 902/875-3141; June–mid-Oct. daily 9:30 A.M.–5:30 P.M.) was built in 1785 as a Loyalist store. The last example of its kind today in Nova Scotia, it depicts the period setting with sample wares such as lumber and salted codfish, which were traded for tobacco, molasses, and dry goods. Upstairs is a military display, and outside the garden has been planted as it would have been in the late 1700s.

## Muir-Cox Shipyard

At the far south end of Dock Street, this small shipyard (902/875-5310; June–Sept. daily 9:30 A.M.–5:30 P.M., Oct.–May Mon.–Fri. 8 A.M.–4 P.M.) builds boats on a custom-order basis, and you can watch men at work year-round. It operated continuously between the 1820s and the 1980s launching square-rigged barques in its earliest days and wooden racing yachts in more modern times. Inside is the Shipbuilding Interpretation Centre, with displays describing the history of the shipyard.

## ACCOMMODATIONS AND CAMPING
## $50-100

The centrally located **Loyalist Inn** (160 Water St., 902/875-3333; $84–89 s or d) is a late-1800s wooden hotel with 11 rooms on the top two floors and a downstairs bar and restaurant.

Better value is **Shelburne Harbour-side Cottages** (10 George St., 902/875-4555, www .shelburneharboursidecottages.com; $95 s or d). Each of two modern cottages enjoys harbor views and has cooking facilities, a separate bedroom, TV, and a deck. Extras include bike rentals ($18 per day) and kayak rentals ($25 per day).

Off historic Water Street is **Above Studio 14** (14 George St., 902/875-1333, www.studio14

.ns.ca; $95 s or d), a folksy two-bedroom suite with its own kitchen, living room, and balcony. Downstairs, owner Mary Lou Keith spends her time painting sailcloth, a Maritimes tradition dating from the days when old canvas sails were painted in nautical themes and used as floor coverings.

## $100-150

**Cooper's Inn** (36 Dock St., 902/875-4656 or 800/688-2011, www.thecoopersinn.com; Apr.–Oct.; $100–185 s or d) is a two-story colonial beauty overlooking the harbor and next to the tourist bureau and museum. Built in 1784 by a merchant and restored and opened in 1988, the lodging has six rooms all with private baths ($100–150), and a large top-floor suite with water views ($185). Rates include a full breakfast in a cheery dining room.

◖ **Whispering Waves Cottages** (Black Point Rd., Ingomar, 902/637-3535 or 866/470-9283, www.whisperingwavescottages.com; $149 s or d) may be out of town, but an overnight stay at this welcoming waterfront property is as enjoyable as one could imagine. The modern cottages are stylishly furnished in wilderness, nautical, or romance themes, and each has a separate bedroom, kitchen, lounge room with a fireplace, and a deck with ocean views. Hosts Jo-Anne and Paul Goulden organize activities such as sea kayaking, fishing, and spa days. A lobster dinner, delivered to your cottage door, is a delicious extra.

## Campground

Rustic and pretty **The Islands Provincial Park** (off Hwy. 3, 5 km west of Shelburne, 902/875-4304; mid-May–early Sept.; $24) faces the town across the upper harbor. It offers 64 unserviced sites with table shelters and grills, pit toilets, running water, and a spacious modern shower room.

## FOOD

With an established reputation for fine dining is the ◖ **Charlotte Lane Café** (13 Charlotte La., 902/875-3314; May–early Dec. Tues.–Sat. 11:30 A.M.–2:30 P.M. and 5–8 P.M.), between

Water and Dock Streets. Its Swiss owner-chef, Roland Glauser, specializes in local seafood prepared using cooking techniques from around the world. The seafood chowder is one of the best I've tasted.

The dining room at the **Loyalist Inn** on Water Street (reservations are wise, call 902/875-2343) is usually jammed with bus-tour diners. A table is easiest to get before noon, during midafternoon, or after 8 P.M. The specialty is seafood ($9–15) prepared any way you like it.

## INFORMATION AND SERVICES

While Dock Street is the historic heart of Shelburne, Water Street, running parallel one block to the west, is lined with all the services of a small town, including banks and the post office.

**Shelburne Visitor Information Centre** (34 King St., 902/875-4547; June–Oct. daily 10 A.M.–6 P.M., July–Aug. daily 9 A.M.–7 P.M.) stocks literature and self-guided tour maps. The website www.historicshelburne.com is loaded with up-to-date information about the town. **Whirligig Books** (135 Water St., 902/875-1117) stocks a good selection of local and Nova Scotian literature.

## SHELBURNE TO YARMOUTH
### Barrington and Vicinity

Highway 103 takes a mainly inland route between Shelburne and Yarmouth. One place where it does come in contact with the ocean is near Barrington, just off the main highway along Highway 3, where coastal views are exquisite. In Barrington itself, the **Old Meeting House Museum** (2408 Hwy. 3, 902/637-2185; June–Sept. Mon.–Sat. 9:30 A.M.–5:30 P.M., Sun. 1–5:30 P.M.; free) is a variation on planter life. Built by 50 Cape Cod families in 1765, the New England–style church is Canada's oldest nonconformist house of worship.

Beyond Barrington, at Villagedale, is **Sand Hills Beach Provincial Park,** so named for a complex dune system where wide tidal flats extend into the ocean. Time your arrival for high tide, and the water is warm enough for swimming—in summer only, of course.

### Cape Sable Island

At Barrington West, Cape Sable Island is well worth the detour. Connected to the mainland by a causeway, the island forms the southernmost point in Nova Scotia. Feared by early sailors because of its jagged shores, the island was settled by brick-making Acadians during the 17th century. The island also served as a summer base for fishermen from New England, and fishing prevails today as the community's main industry, with tourism a close second.

The island's four main beaches offer surfing, clam digging, swimming, fishing, and bird-watching. At **Hawk Beach,** on the eastern side (turn at Lower Clark's Harbour at Hawk Road and go left), you can see the **Cape Lighthouse** on a small nearby sandbar. The original tower, built in 1861, was Canada's first eight-sided structure; the present lighthouse, a protected heritage building, was constructed in 1923. At low tide on Hawk Beach you can also see the remains of a 1,500-year-old forest.

**Causeway Beach** (turn right at the Corbett Heights subdivision) is a prime sunbathing and fishing (for mackerel) spot. **Stoney Island Beach,** as the name implies, is not as popular with sunbathers as it is with seals, which like to sun themselves on the rocks. **South Side Beach** (turn on Daniel's Head Road in South Side) is also popular as a seal-watching and beachcombing locale.

Services and accommodations are limited. **Cape Sable Cottages** (37 Long Point Rd., Newellton, 902/745-0168, www.capesablecottages.com) are my favorite. These five spacious and modern cottages sit on a private peninsula jutting into Barrington Passage. Each cottage has water views, a separate bedroom, a living area, a kitchen, a wide deck furnished with a barbecue and outdoor furniture, and its own fire pit. Rates range $165–250 in summer (when there is also a two-night minimum). The property is open year-round, with cottages dropping to $125 in winter. Check the website for specials.

# Yarmouth

Yarmouth (pop. 7,500) was the center of a ship-building empire during Canada's Great Age of Sail, when it ranked as the world's fourth-largest port of registry. Still the region's largest seaport, the town is a prosperous and orderly place supported by shipping—primarily lumber products, Irish moss, and Christmas trees—and fishing. Yarmouth's herring fleet is a major contributor to the local economy. The fleet sails at night and anchors with all its lights blazing farther up the Fundy coast, creating a sight known as "herring city." Tourism also helps the port thrive; two ferry lines bring visitors to town in numbers sufficient to establish Yarmouth as the busiest ferry landing in the province.

## SIGHTS

If historic architecture interests you, take a leisurely walk along Main Street, where the commercial buildings are styled in late-19th-century Classic Revival, Queen Anne Revival, Georgian, and Italianate. At the tourist information center on Forest Street, pick up the *Walking Tour of Yarmouth* brochure, which details about two dozen points of architectural and historical interest on a self-guided four-kilometer walk.

### Firefighters' Museum

The Firefighters' Museum of Nova Scotia (451 Main St., 902/742-5525; June–Sept. Mon.–Sat. 9 A.M.–5 P.M., July–Aug. Mon.–Sat. 9 A.M.–9 P.M. and Sun. 10 A.M.–5 P.M.; adult $4, child $2) is Atlantic Canada's only museum dedicated solely to firefighting equipment. Among the extensive vintage collection is an 1819 Hopwood and Tilley hand pump and other sparkling equipment.

### Yarmouth County Museum

An enjoyable walk from downtown through a tree-lined residential area east of Main Street is Yarmouth County Museum (22 Collins St., 902/742-5539; June–mid-Oct. Mon.–Sat.

9 A.M.–5 P.M., Sun. 1–5 P.M., the rest of the year Tues.–Sat. 2–5 P.M.; adult $5, child $2). It showcases Canada's largest ship-portrait collection and exhibits a trove of seafaring lore, musical instruments, ship models, furniture, and more. The research library and archives store extensive records and genealogical materials.

## Scenic Drive to Cape Forchu

The region's most scenic drive is to Cape Forchu, where the red and white **Cape Forchu Light Station** guides ships into the harbor. Follow Main Street north and turn left at Vancouver Street. Just past the hospital complex, turn left on Grove Road. The Faith Memorial Baptist Church marks the site where the famous Yarmouth Runic Stone, believed to have been inscribed by Leif Eriksson's men, was found. Next you come to the lighthouse (July–Aug. daily 9 A.M.–9 P.M.) perched on a stone promontory. The actual lighthouse is

**Yarmouth County Museum**

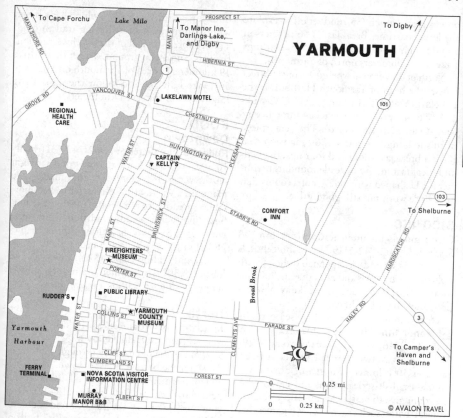

To Cape Forchu
Lake Milo
PROSPECT ST
To Digby
MAIN SHORE RD
MAIN ST
To Manor Inn,
Darlings Lake,
and Digby
**YARMOUTH**
HIBERNIA ST
1
VANCOUVER ST
GROVE RD
101
LAKELAWN MOTEL
REGIONAL
HEALTH
CARE
CHESTNUT ST
WATER ST
PLEASANT ST
HUNTINGTON ST
103
CAPTAIN
KELLY'S
To Shelburne
BRUNSWICK ST
COMFORT
INN
STARR'S RD
HARDSCATCH RD
MAIN ST
FIREFIGHTERS'
MUSEUM
PORTER ST
Broad Brook
PUBLIC LIBRARY
RUDDER'S
HALEY RD
Yarmouth
Harbour
WATER ST
COLLINS ST
YARMOUTH
COUNTY
MUSEUM
CLEMENTS AVE
PARADE ST
3
CLIFF ST
To Camper's
Haven and
Shelburne
CUMBERLAND ST
FERRY
TERMINAL
NOVA SCOTIA VISITOR
INFORMATION CENTRE
FOREST ST
0          0.25 mi
MURRAY
MANOR B&B
ALBERT ST
0        0.25 km
© AVALON TRAVEL

open to climb, and you get good views from the top. Beyond the parking lot, a trail leads down to **Leif Ericson Picnic Park,** overlooking the rocky coast.

## ACCOMMODATIONS AND CAMPING
### $50-100

If you are looking to spend less than $100 for accommodations, the **Murray Manor B&B** (225 Main St., 902/742-9625 or 877/742-9629, www.murraymanor.com; $95–139 s or d), just one block from the ferry terminal, is a good choice. In this Regency-style heritage property dating to 1820 and kept in the same family for 140 years, you find three guest rooms with a shared bath and one with an en suite, a dining room, as well as a beautiful garden and greenhouse secluded behind a low stone wall. A unique feature is the "prayer windows," so named because you must kneel to see through them.

**Churchill Mansion Country Inn** (Hwy. 1, Darlings Lake, 902/649-2818 or 888/453-5565, www.churchillmansion.com; May–mid-Nov.; $80–140 s or d) was the hilltop summer home of Aaron Flint Churchill, who made his fortune in the shipping trade after establishing the Churchill Line out of Savannah, Georgia. Overlooking a lake and with distant ocean views, it was converted to an inn in the 1980s. The most expensive room is Churchill's master bedroom, with a balcony overlooking a lake. Guests can rent a bike ($10 per day), order a picnic lunch ($5), and set off to explore the local coastline. Breakfast is $6 per person and the nightly seafood buffet is $15. Darlings Lake is 15 kilometers north of Yarmouth.

North of downtown, where Vancouver Street crosses the head of Yarmouth Harbour, is the **Lakelawn Motel** (641 Main St., 902/742-3588 or 877/664-0664, www.lakelawnmotel.com; May–Oct.; $70–100 s or d). The centerpiece of this lodging is a grand 1864 mansion that holds a breakfast room and four upstairs bed-and-breakfast rooms. Spread around its perimeter is a U-shaped wing of 27 motel rooms that are a little worn but still good value.

### $100-150

Chain motels include the **Comfort Inn** (96 Starrs Rd., 902/742-1119, www.choicehotels .ca; $115–145 s or d), a dependable choice with well-equipped rooms and rates that include free local calls, Internet access, weekday newspapers, and a light breakfast.

Once the home of a wealthy sea captain, ( **Manor Inn** (Hwy. 101, 902/742-2487 or 888/626-6746, www.manorinn.com; $129–199 s or d) sprawls across five magnificent hectares 10 kilometers north of downtown. Formal English-style gardens and a grand dining room give the estate an upscale ambience, while activities such as tennis, lawn games, biking, and canoeing from the private dock keep guests busy. Guest rooms are spread through multiple buildings, including the Coach House and the original mansion. Rates include a light breakfast; check the website for American-plan meal packages.

### Campgrounds

The closest campground to Yarmouth is **Campers' Haven** (5 km east of Yarmouth off Hwy. 3 in Arcadia, 902/742-4848, www .campershavencampground.com; mid-May–mid-Oct.; $15–35). The lakeside campground offers more than 200 sites ($16–27), as well as canoe rentals, a pool, a camp store, a launderette, and a recreation hall with a fireplace.

For a wilderness experience, travel a little farther out to **Ellenwood Lake Provincial Park**

(mid-June–mid-Oct.; $24), which has a beach with swimming, a short hiking trail through a mixed forest typical of the southwest region, showers, and a playground. To get there, drive 19 kilometers north of Yarmouth on Highway 101, take Exit 34, and follow the signs along Highway 340 for seven kilometers.

## FOOD
### Downtown

**Rudder's** (96 Water St., 902/742-7311; daily 10 A.M.–10 P.M.) is a large brewpub set right on the water. It's a big room that manages to maintain a warm atmosphere, with even more tables spread across a veranda facing the harbor. The menu blends traditional pub food with Nova Scotian specialties. Think maple-glazed salmon baked on a cedar plank ($21), lobster and scallop crepes ($22), and steak and lobster ($30). In summer the nightly lobster supper (4–9 P.M.; $30) is a major draw.

### North of Downtown

In a two-story mansion at the north end of Main Street, **Captain Kelley's** (577 Main St., 902/742-9191) opens daily through summer at 7 A.M. for the best breakfast in town. The lunch and dinner menu features seafood dishes accompanied by local produce (mains $12–22). After your meal, ask to see the 200-year-old "captain's table" in the private dining room; it's built of solid oak and measures six meters in length.

The ( **Commodore Dining Room** (Manor Inn, Hwy. 101, Hebron, 902/742-2487; daily for lunch and dinner) is named for the sea captain who once lived here. The room is filled with richly elegant furnishings, and service is very professional, which makes the prices a pleasant surprise. For example, you could start with scallop wraps and then order salmon topped with a maple-mustard glaze and baked on a cedar plank for just $25 combined. Wines ($24–30) are also sensibly priced.

Beyond the Manor Inn, **Churchill Mansion Country Inn** (Hwy. 1, Darlings Lake, 902/649-2818 or 888/453-5565, www.churchillman sion.com; May–Oct.; daily 6:30–9 P.M.) offer a buffet for $15. It includes salads, seafood casserole, mussels, grilled fish, vegetables, and dessert. Nonguests should make reservations.

## INFORMATION AND SERVICES

Greeting visitors as they arrive by ferry is the cavernous **Nova Scotia Visitor Information Centre** (228 Main at Forest St., 902/742-5033; June–mid-Oct. daily 9 A.M.–5 P.M., July–Aug. Thurs.–Tues. 9 A.M.–9 P.M., Wed. 9 A.M.–5 P.M.), where you'll find literature and information on just about everything imaginable in the city and the province. In advance of your visit, visit www.goyarmouth.com.

The **public library** (405 Main St., 902/742-5040; Mon.–Fri. 9 A.M.–9 P.M., Sat. 9 A.M.–5 P.M.) is a good place to check your email.

The **Regional Health Centre** is at 50 Vancouver Street (902/742-1540). For the **RCMP,** call 902/742-8777. The town has seven banks downtown and at the malls, and there's also a currency-exchange counter (exchange rates are better at the banks) at the visitors center. The **post office** is at 15 Willow Street.

## GETTING THERE AND AROUND

*The Cat* (902/742-6800 or 888/249-7245, www.catferry.com), a super-fast vehicular ferry, crosses to Yarmouth from Portland (Maine) in 5.5 hours and from Bar Harbor (Maine) in three hours. It runs three or four times weekly from each port June–mid-October. From Portland, peak-season (July–Aug.) one-way fares are adult US$99, senior US$79, child US$55, vehicle under 6.6 feet US$164. From Bar Harbor, fares are adult US$69, senior US$58, child US$48, vehicle under 6.6 feet US$115. After clearing immigration and customs at the downtown Yarmouth terminal, the information center is straight up the hill, and the main drag is off to the left. From Yarmouth it's 123 kilometers (90 minutes) to Shelburne, 340 kilometers (four hours) to Halifax, and 105 kilometers (70 minutes) to Digby.

**Avis** (902/742-3323) and **Budget** (902/742-9500) have desks at the ferry terminal, but reserve a vehicle before arriving.

# FUNDY COAST

The natural beauty of Nova Scotia's Fundy coast is sublime. Sea breezes bathe the shore in crisp salt air, and the sun illuminates the seascape colors with a clarity that defies a painter's palette. Wildflowers bloom with abandon, nourished by the moist coastal air. And fog, thick as cotton, sometimes envelops the region during the summer. This is the Fundy Coast, which stretches from Yarmouth in the west to the farthest reaches of the Bay of Fundy in the east. Quietly and relentlessly, twice a day, a tidal surge that has its beginnings far away pours into the bay, creating the highest tides on the planet. Fishing boats are lifted from the muddy sea floor, and whales in pursuit of silvery herring hurry along the summertime currents, their mammoth hulks buoyed by the 100 billion tons of seawater that gush into the long

bay between Nova Scotia and New Brunswick. The cycle from low to high tide takes a mere six hours. The tide peaks, in places high enough to swamp a four-story building, and then begins to retreat. As the sea level drops, coastal peninsulas and rocky islets emerge from the froth, veiled in seaweed. The sea floor reappears, shiny as shellac and littered with sea urchins, periwinkles, and shells. Where no one walked just hours ago, local children run and skip on the beaches, pausing to retrieve tidal treasures. Locals take the Fundy tides for granted. For visitors, it's an astounding show.

To a great extent, the history of the province's Fundy Coast is the story of all of Nova Scotia, and this is reflected in the region's wealth of historic and cultural wonders. France's colonial ambitions began at Port-Royal and clashed

© ANDREW HEMPSTEAD

# HIGHLIGHTS

**◖ Église de Sainte-Marie:** A pocket of Acadian villages along the Fundy Coast allows visitors to immerse themselves in this uniquely French culture by trying Acadian cooking at Rapure Acadienne, visiting the local museums, and straining their necks below Église de Sainte-Marie, the tallest wooden church in North America (page 104).

**◖ Whale-Watching on the Bay of Fundy:** Use Digby Neck and the adjacent islands as a base for whale-watching trips into the Bay of Fundy (page 110).

**◖ Fort Anne National Historic Site:** After centuries of changing hands between the British and the French, the site of numerous fortifications and onetime capital of Nova Scotia is in the hands of the government as a tourist attraction (page 112).

**◖ Historic Gardens:** The name doesn't do them justice. Garden styles from the Middle Ages through to modern times have been carefully planted at this downtown Annapolis Royal attraction (page 112).

**◖ Port-Royal National Historic Site:** The oldest European settlement north of St. Augustine, Florida, has been re-created at this important national historic site (page 113).

**◖ Grand Pré National Historic Site:** This outdoor museum brings the Henry Wadsworth Longfellow story of Evangeline, a young girl caught up in the Acadian deportation, to life (page 122).

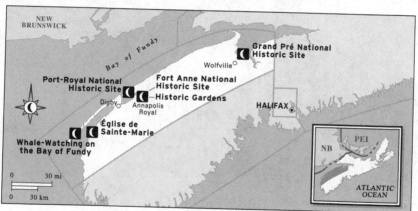

LOOK FOR ◖ TO FIND RECOMMENDED SIGHTS, ACTIVITIES, DINING, AND LODGING.

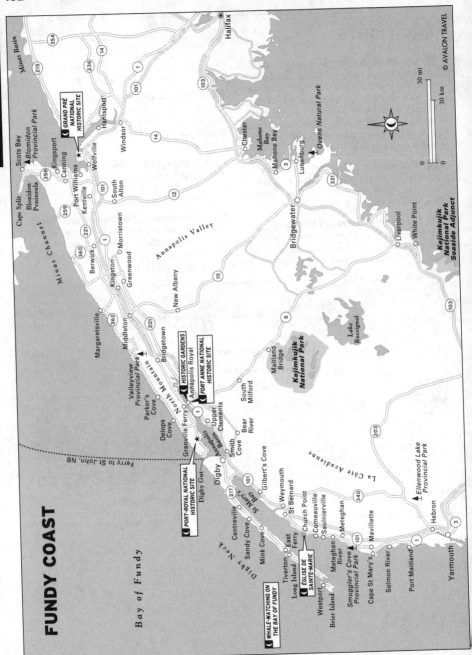

# FUNDY COAST

© AVALON TRAVEL

head-on with England's quest for New World dominance, and multiple national historic sites along the coast lie in testament to these troubled times. The trim Acadian villages of La Côte Acadienne, the historic streetscape of Annapolis Royal, and the gracious towns of Wolfville and Windsor add to the appeal.

## PLANNING YOUR TIME

You can drive between Yarmouth and Halifax in a single day, but you should allow a minimum of two days, which would mean you could reserve a room at one of Annapolis Royal's many historic inns. This small town is definitely the historic heart of the Fundy Coast, with sights such as **Fort Anne National Historic Site,** the **Historic Gardens,** and **Port-Royal National Historic Site** easily filling out a full day of sightseeing. For this reason, two days and two nights should be allotted for exploring the Fundy Coast. At the western end, the detour through La Côte Acadienne and stops at Acadian icons such as **Église de Sainte-Marie** add only slightly to the length of the drive. The most impressive Acadian attraction, **Grand Pré National Historic Site,** is farther east, and it deserves at least three hours of your time. At some time during your travels through the region you'll want to focus on the Bay of Fundy (digging into a plate of plump Digby scallops doesn't count). Taking the above into consideration, if you have two nights planned for the Fundy Coast, and you are traveling east from Yarmouth, spend the first morning meandering along La Côte Acadienne, order scallops for lunch in Digby, and continue to Annapolis Royal. Spend the rest of the afternoon and the first part of the next morning exploring this town before moving on to Wolfville. Spend the night, rise early for a short hike through Blomidon Provincial Park, and then move on to Grand Pré National Historic Site. You'll be back in the capital by late afternoon. With an extra day and night, plan on driving along Digby Neck and going **whale-watching.**

# La Côte Acadienne

Those who zoom along Highway 101 between Yarmouth and Digby will be missing the charming La Côte Acadienne (Acadian Coast), also known as the **Municipality of Clare,** a 50-kilometer coastal stretch populated by descendants of the French who resettled here after the Acadian expulsion of 1755.

To get there, follow Highway 1 north through Yarmouth or take Highway 101 to Exit 32 to save a little time. Between Rivière-aux-Saumon (Salmon River) in the south and Weymouth in the north, the place-names, the soaring Catholic churches, and the proud Acadian flags (a French tricolor with a single yellow star) announce that you're in the largest francophone enclave in Nova Scotia.

## MAVILLETTE AND VICINITY

For a look at the dynamic Fundy, check out **Mavillette Beach Provincial Park,** on the south side of Cap Sainte-Marie (Cape St. Mary's). The sign for Cape View Restaurant signals the turn from Highway 1; the road peels down to the sea and runs alongside high dunes. Boardwalks cross the dunes to the mile-long beach, where sandbars trap water into warm pools at low tide. On sunny days, beachcombers walk the expanse and hunt for unusual seashells. Though this is one of the finest beaches in all Nova Scotia, crowds are nonexistent.

### Accommodations and Food

Along the beach access road you'll find **Cape View Motel and Cottages** (902/645-2258, www.capeviewmotel.ca; June–Sept.). The motel's 10 basic rooms ($80 s or d) and five cottages ($90–120) overlook sand dunes and the provincial park.

Across the road from the Cape View Motel and with wonderful views of the beach and its stunning sunsets is **Cape View Restaurant** (157

John Doucette Rd., 902/645-2519; mid-May–Oct. daily for breakfast and dinner), which dishes up breakfasts such as scrambled eggs with lobster ($13) and seafood with an Acadian twist the rest of the day (mains $12–22).

## Smuggler's Cove Provincial Park

From Mavillette Beach, it's 16 kilometers north to Smuggler's Cove Provincial Park. Walkways here lead to great bluff-top views of the coast and down steep tree-lined steps to the rocky shoreline. The coastal cliffs in this area are notched with caves, which were used by Prohibition-era rumrunners. Some of the caves can be explored at low tide. The park also holds numerous picnic tables, making it an ideal lunch stop, but no campsites.

## METEGHAN AND VICINITY

Settled in 1785, the seaport of Meteghan, 15 kilometers north of Mavillette, is the district's commercial hub, although the population still numbers fewer than 1,000. The main wharf is a hive of activity throughout the day, but the official attraction is **La Vieille Maison** (Old House Museum) on Highway 1 (902/645-2389; July–Aug. daily 9 A.M.–7 P.M., June and Sept. daily 10 A.M.–6 P.M.; donation). In the Robicheau family's former homestead, this museum features 18th-century furnishings and exhibits explaining the area's history, with help from bilingual guides in traditional Acadian costume. Part of the museum is operated as the **Meteghan Visitor Centre.**

### Accommodations and Food

For a place to overnight, the tidy **Bluefin Motel** (7765 Hwy. 1, 902/645-2251 or 888/446-3466, www.bluefinmotel.ns.ca; $79–139 s or d) is a good choice. Situated on the south side of town, the rooms don't take full advantage of its cliff-top setting, but a few outdoor chairs can be found on a deck behind the restaurant. The view, the lobster traps strung across the adjacent lot, and scallop trawlers making their way slowly across the bay all add to the appeal. The motel restaurant is open daily from 8 A.M. for breakfast, lunch, and dinner.

A seafood cornucopia is brought in daily by the seaport's scallop draggers, herring seiners, and lobster boats. **Blue Rock Restaurant** (Hwy. 1 near the museum, 902/645-3453) is a good place for seafood dining.

## North from Meteghan

The village of **Meteghan River,** north of Meteghan, is Nova Scotia's largest wooden ship-building center. One of the nicest lodgings along La Côte Acadienne is **L'Auberge au Havre du Capitaine** (9118 Hwy. 1, 902/769-2001, www.havreducapitaine.ca), a country-style inn with hardwood floors and a sitting area set around a large stone fireplace. Choose from rooms with private baths and TVs ($85–100 s or d) or larger suites with whirlpool tubs ($110 d). The inn's licensed dining room is open daily for breakfast, lunch, and dinner.

Also in Meteghan River, lobster lovers should stop in at **Wright's Lobster** (Hwy. 1, 902/645-3919; Mon.–Fri. 9 A.M.–5 P.M.), where you can buy live lobsters kept in flow-through crates at the large warehouse—perfect if you're camping or if your accommodation has cooking facilities.

### Comeauville

The village of Comeauville, a bit farther north, is notable for **La Galerie Comeau** (761 Hwy. 1, 902/769-2896; June–Aug. Mon.–Sat. 10 A.M.–5 P.M., Sun. noon–5 P.M.), where artist Denise Comeau displays and sells her watercolors that reflect the region and its Acadian roots.

## POINT DE L'ÉGLISE (CHURCH POINT)

This aptly named community is the last major Acadian community for northbound travelers, but it's also the most interesting.

### ◖ Église de Sainte-Marie

Built between 1903 and 1905, the enormous Église de Sainte-Marie (St. Mary's Church), the largest and tallest wooden church in North America, dominates this village of 490 inhabitants. The building is laid out in the shape of

The soaring Église de Sainte-Marie is the architectural highlight of La Côte Acadienne.

a cross, and its soaring 56-meter steeple has been ballasted with 40 tons of rock to withstand the winter wind. Inside, **Le Musée Sainte-Marie** (902/769-2808; June–mid-Oct. daily 9 A.M.–5 P.M.; adult $2, child free) exhibits religious artifacts and historical documents and photos. Mass takes place Sunday at 10:30 A.M.

## Accommodations and Camping

Accommodations are available at **Le Manoir Samson** (1768 Hwy. 1, 902/769-2526 or 888/769-8605, www.manoirsamson.com; May–Aug.; $75–125 s or d), a red brick roadside motel where most rooms have a microwave and fridge. A light breakfast is included.

Campers can head to the full-service **Belle Baie Park** (Hwy. 1, 902/769-3160, www.belle-baiepark.ca; mid-May–Sept.), an oceanfront campground with its own beach, an outdoor pool, a playground, and a launderette. Tent sites are $20, hookups range $25–35, and the more expensive ones sit right on the edge of the ocean. Friday night events include potluck dinners and live music.

## Food

Through town to the south is 🌙 **Rapure Acadienne** (1443 Hwy. 1, 902/769-2172; Mon.–Sat. 8 A.M.–5:30 P.M.), the most authentic place in all of Nova Scotia to try rappie pie, a traditional Acadian chicken dish with a rather unusually textured potato filling. The pies are massive (and also come with beef and clam fillings) and cost just $6, including a side of butter or molasses. Order at the inside window (where you can peek through at the big ovens) and eat at the one indoor table or the picnic tables outside.

## CONTINUING TO DIGBY

The last of the Acadian communities is **Grosses Coques,** a small village immediately north of Pointe de l'Église that takes its name from the huge bar clams harvested here on the tidal flats, an important food source for early settlers.

### Gilbert's Cove

A short unpaved road leads from Highway 101 to **Gilbert's Cove Lighthouse.** Built in 1904 to help vessels navigate the upper reaches of St. Mary's Bay, it has been restored and is open to the public in July and August.

Gilbert's Cove Lighthouse

# Digby and Vicinity

The port of Digby (pop. 2,300), 105 kilometers northeast of Yarmouth and 235 kilometers west of Halifax, is the terminus for the ferry from Saint John (New Brunswick) and home for the world's largest scallop fleet. The Mi'Kmaq name for the area is Te'Wapskik, meaning "flowing between high rocks," a reference to Digby Gut, a narrow opening in the Annapolis Basin to the north of town. Digby derived its English name from Admiral Robert Digby, who sailed up the Fundy in 1793 and settled the place with 1,500 Loyalists from New England. The scallop fleet ties up off Fishermen's Wharf off Water Street; be there at sunset when the pastel-painted draggers lie at anchor in a semicircle, backlit by the intense setting sun.

Lying outside the area's main roads, Digby is easily bypassed. High-speed Highway 101 lies south of Digby and routes sightseers up the St. Mary's Bay coastline into the Annapolis Valley. More scenic Highway 1, the pastoral route through the valley, starts beyond Digby to the west. Even the site of Digby's ferry terminal diverts traffic around town, and if you enter the province from New Brunswick, street signs will direct you from Shore Road to Highway 101 via Victoria Street and Highway 303.

## SIGHTS AND RECREATION

A couple of worthwhile attractions are scattered along the waterfront, but the highlights are farther afield—Digby Neck and Kejimkujik National Park, both covered in this section.

### Lady Vanessa

On the boardwalk in front of the Fundy Restaurant (Water St.) is the dry-docked 98-foot *Lady Vanessa*. This locally built scallop boat is open to the public (June–Sept. daily 9 A.M.–7 P.M.; $2), allowing visitors the opportunity to step aboard and experience the workplace of local fishermen. You can explore the entire boat—above and below

deck, the shucking room, the wheelhouse, and the living quarters. Interpretive panels describe the scallop fishing process, while the claws of a 45-pound lobster are one of the more eye-catching displays. A 30-minute documentary screened on board is surprisingly interesting. It is mostly underwater footage, including of a lobster entering a trap and scallops being scooped up by the dragnets.

### Admiral Digby Museum

Digby's place in history is on display at the harborfront Admiral Digby Museum (95 Montague Row, 902/245-6322; mid-June–Aug. Mon.–Sat. 9 A.M.–5 P.M., Sun. 1–5 P.M.; donation), housed in a trim two-story Georgian-era residence with exhibits of old photographs, interesting maps, and maritime artifacts.

### Bear River

Calling itself the "Switzerland of Nova Scotia" may be a stretch, but this small village straddling the Bear River eight kilometers south of Digby is nestled in a delightful little valley, where the trees turn glorious colors in late September. Along the main street are a motley collection of wooden buildings in various states of repair, many built on stilts above the river far below. Those that have been restored now hold craft shops.

## ENTERTAINMENT AND EVENTS

Montague Row to Water Street is the place for people-watching, especially at sunset. **Club 98 Lounge** (28 Water St., 902/245-4950) in the Fundy Restaurant has a band (cover charge) or disc jockey Friday–Saturday. The lounge at the **Pines Resort** (103 Shore Rd., 902/245-2511; closed Sun.) is known for tamer pursuits, low lighting, a comfortable ambience, and finely tuned mixed drinks.

The port's famed scallops attract appropriate

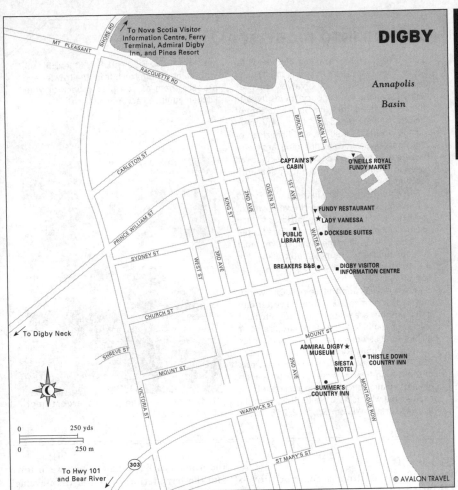

**DIGBY**

*Annapolis*

*Basin*

To Nova Scotia Visitor Information Centre, Ferry Terminal, Admiral Digby Inn, and Pines Resort

MT PLEASANT
SHORE RD
RACQUETTE RD
CARLETON ST
PRINCE WILLIAM ST
SYDNEY ST
CHURCH ST
SHREVE ST
MOUNT ST
VICTORIA ST
WARWICK ST
ST MARY'S ST
KING ST
2ND AVE
WEST ST
3RD AVE
MOUNT ST
2ND AVE
MONTAGUE ROW
BIRCH ST
MAIDEN LN
QUEEN ST
1ST AVE
WATER ST

CAPTAIN'S CABIN
O'NEILLS ROYAL FUNDY MARKET
FUNDY RESTAURANT
LADY VANESSA
PUBLIC LIBRARY
DOCKSIDE SUITES
BREAKERS B&B
DIGBY VISITOR INFORMATION CENTRE
ADMIRAL DIGBY MUSEUM
SIESTA MOTEL
THISTLE DOWN COUNTRY INN
SUMMER'S COUNTRY INN

To Digby Neck

0    250 yds
0    250 m

303

To Hwy 101 and Bear River

© AVALON TRAVEL

## ACCOMMODATIONS AND CAMPING

fanfare during **Digby Scallops Days** (www.digbyscallopdays.com) with a parade, scallop-shucking competitions, street vendors, the crowning of the Scallop Queen and Princesses, music, fireworks, and a parade of the scallop fleet in the second week of August.

Digby has a few motel rooms under $100, including the **Siesta Motel** (81 Montague Row, 902/245-2568; $70–95 s or d), but there are no real bargains in town.

### $50-100

Two blocks from the waterfront, **Summer's Country Inn** (16 Warwick St., 902/245-2250, www.summerscountryinn.com; May–Oct.; $65–95 s or d) has 11 guest rooms in an 1830s home. Each room has a private bath and comfortable bed, although the decorations in some are a little flowery for my tastes.

# DIGGING INTO DIGBY SCALLOPS

Digby is known for its scallops, so there is no better place to try them than this small Fundy Coast port. Unlike other bivalves (such as clams), scallops do not bury themselves in the sand. Instead, they live on the bottom of the Bay of Fundy and "swim" by quickly opening and closing their shells. The fishermen of Digby harvest scallops by dragging large wire baskets over the sea floor. They are shucked (opened) immediately and put on ice until reaching the shore.

The water temperature in the Bay of Fundy varies only slightly through the year, which, combined with the tides' creating lots of nutrient movement, creates ideal conditions for the scallops. The result is the plumpest yet most delicate and succulent meat you could imagine. As a bonus, scallops are low in fat and full of protein.

Across Nova Scotia and beyond, Digby scallops appear on menus by name. In better dining rooms they are sautéed in butter with light spices, or combined in seafood casseroles or dishes such as bouillabaisse. Local eateries such as the **Fundy Restaurant** (34 Water St., 902/245-4950; 8 A.M.-10 P.M.), which has views of the fishing fleet, get creative with scallop omelets, scallop chowder, and scallop fettuccine. At the wharfside **O'Neil's Royal Fundy Market** (Prince William St., 902/245-6528;

Mon.-Fri. 9 A.M.-5:30 P.M., Sat. 10 A.M.-5 P.M.), you can buy them fresh from the trawler and prepare them as you please back at your kitchen-equipped accommodation.

© ANDREW HEMPSTEAD

Digby is home to the world's largest fleet of scallop trawlers.

## $100-150

Digby's only waterfront accommodation is **◖ Thistle Down Country Inn** (98 Montague Row, 902/245-4490 or 800/565-8081, www.thistledown.ns.ca; May–Oct.; $105–130 s or d), where a landscaped garden extends right to water's edge. It comprises six rooms in an Edwardian-era home and six regular motel rooms in a new addition that occupies the back half of the property. A full breakfast is included in the rates, and dinner is available with a reservation.

The **Admiral Digby Inn** (441 Shore Rd., 902/245-2531 or 800/465-6262, www.digbyns.com; mid-May–Oct.) is across the road from

the Annapolis Basin halfway between town and the ferry terminal. Better-than-average motel rooms start at $110 s or d, and for $135 you get a balcony with water views. Cottages with one and two bedrooms are $150 and $200 respectively. All rates include a light breakfast. Amenities include a restaurant, a lounge, an indoor pool, and a laundry.

**Breakers Bed and Breakfast** (5 Water St., 902/245-4643 or 866/333-5773, www.thebreakersbb.com; May–Oct.; $125–145 s or d, including full breakfast) is a 150-year-old two-story home across from the waterfront. The three guest rooms are extra large and furnished in keeping with a heritage theme. A covered front porch with water views and the book-filled sitting room add to the charm.

**Dockside Suites** (26 Water St., 902/245-4950, www.fundyrestaurant.com; $129–159 s or d) is part of the Fundy Restaurant complex. Each of the six units is air-conditioned and has a balcony with harbor views and a separate bedroom. Other in-room amenities include a TV/DVD combo and high-speed Internet access.

## $150-200

Appealing to visitors looking for an old-fashioned resort experience, the baronial **Pines Resort** (103 Shore Rd., 902/245-2511 or 800/667-4637, www.digbypines.ca; mid-May–mid-Oct.; from $198 s or d) peers down over the port from the brow of a hill on the town's outskirts. The French Norman manor of stucco and stone was built in 1903 and served as a Canadian Pacific Railway hotel until the province bought it in 1965. The accommodations include more than 80 rooms in the manor and 30 cottages shaded by spruce, fir, and pine. The hotel offers a dining room of provincial renown, an 18-hole golf course (greens fees $65), an outdoor pool, a fitness center, tennis courts, hiking trails, and afternoon tea. Most guests stay as part of a package, paying, for example, $120 per person for accommodation, golf, and breakfast.

### Campgrounds

Close to town is **Digby Campground** (Smith's Cove, 230 Victoria St., 902/245-1985; mid-May–mid-Oct.; $20–26). To get there, take Exit 26 from Highway 101 and follow the signs toward the ferry for three kilometers. Within walking distance of downtown, it has an outdoor pool, Laundromat, and hookups.

## FOOD

Right downtown, **Fundy Restaurant** (34 Water St., 902/245-4950; 8 A.M.–10 P.M.) is a large casual restaurant overlooking the scallop fleet. Seating is inside in a main dining room, in a solarium, or out on the balcony. Digby scallops are the specialty, prepared any way you'd like them or in combination with other seafood—the Fundy (scallop) omelet ($11) is an interesting breakfast choice, while the rest of the day dishes such as scallop chowder ($9) and a platter of scallops cooked in various ways ($18) are good ways to sample this tasty treat.

One block back from the water, **Captain's Cabin** (Water St., 902/245-4868; 11:30 A.M.–10:30 P.M.) is a little more of a locals' hangout, but it still specializes in seafood. Dishes are a little less creative but a couple of dollars less expensive. A half lobster with a side of scallops is $25.

Check out ◖ **O'Neil's Royal Fundy Market** (Prince William St., 902/245-6528; Mon.–Fri. 9 A.M.–5:30 P.M., Sat. 10 A.M.–5 P.M.) for fresh seafood for those staying somewhere with cooking facilities. Otherwise, order pan- or deep-fried scallops, seafood chowder, fresh mussels and salmon, cooked lobster, and smoked cod, haddock, mackerel, and Digby chicks (smoked herring) to eat in or take out.

## INFORMATION

Downtown, the **Digby Visitor Information Centre** (110 Montague Row, 902/245-5714) is open June–early October daily 9 A.M.–5 P.M. Along the road between the ferry terminal and town is the **Nova Scotia Visitor Information Centre** (237 Shore Rd., 902/245-2201; early May–Oct. daily 9 A.M.–5 P.M., until 9 P.M. daily in July and Aug.), which represents tourism regions throughout the province.

**Digby Public Library** (corner of 1st and Sydney Sts.; Tues.–Fri. 3–5 P.M., Sat. 10 A.M.–1 P.M.) has public Internet access.

## GETTING THERE AND AROUND

The terminus of the *Princess of Acadia* is through town near the mouth of the Annapolis Basin. Operated by **Bay Ferries** (902/245-2116 or 888/249-7245, www.nfl-bay.com), the large vessel plies the Bay of Fundy between Saint John (New Brunswick) and Digby (Nova Scotia) one or two times daily throughout the year. High-season one-way fares are adult $40, senior and child $30, vehicle $100. The crossing takes 3.5 hours, and reservations are essential if you're traveling with a vehicle.

The **Acadian Lines** bus pulls into the convenience store at 77 Montague Row (902/245-2048) on its route between Digby and Halifax.

## DIGBY NECK

The Digby Neck is a long spindly peninsula reaching like an antenna for almost 80 kilometers back down the Bay of Fundy from Digby. Beyond the end of the peninsula are two small islands. Off the main tourist path, the peninsula will appeal to those interested in nature and spending time in tiny coastal villages where the pace of live is much slower than elsewhere along the Fundy Coast.

### Driving Digby Neck and Beyond

From Digby, Highway 217 runs down the center of Digby Neck, through the villages of **Centreville, Sandy Cove,** and **Mink Cove.** At picturesque Sandy Cove, houses cling to the shoreline while a nearby trail leads to Nova Scotia's highest waterfall. At East Ferry, a ferry departs every 30 minutes on the half hour for **Long Island.** The trip across takes just five minutes and costs $5 per vehicle inclusive of passengers. Beyond Tiverton, the main town on Long Island, a two-kilometer (30-minute) each-way trail leads along sea cliffs to **Balancing Rock.** This volcanic outcrop rises precariously from a narrow ledge, looking as if it will topple at any time.

### Brier Island

A second ferry (also $5) connects Long Island to Brier Island, Nova Scotia's westernmost extremity. The island has a bustling little fishing port at **Westport** and a tourism business that revolves around spring wildflowers, summer whale-watching, and year-round bird-watching. The island's most famous inhabitant was Joshua Slocum (the two vehicle ferries are named for him and his famous sailing boat, *Spray*), who spent his childhood on the island before taking to the high seas and becoming the first person to sail around the world solo. A small monument on a headland south of Westport commemorates the feat.

### ◖ Whale-Watching on the Bay of Fundy

Digby Neck is the base for a thriving whale-watching community. Companies generally offer half-day excursions between mid-June and early October, with regular sightings of finback, right, humpback, and minke whales, as well as Atlantic white-sided dolphins and porpoises. **Ocean Explorations,** based on Long Island at Tiverton (902/839-2417 or 877/654-2341), is notable for guide Tom Goodwin, a well-known biologist who takes interested visitors out into the bay aboard high-speed but stable inflatable Zodiac boats. In addition to the most common species, Goodwin searches out North Atlantic right whales when they gather in the middle of the bay (usually August). Estimated to number fewer than 300, these are the world's rarest whales, so named because they were the "right" whales to hunt. Rates are adult $59, child $40. Other operators include **Brier Island Whale and Seabird Cruises** (Westport, Brier Island, 902/839-2995 or 800/656-3660) and **Mariner Cruises** (Westport, Brier Island, 902/839-2346 or 800/239-2189).

### Accommodations and Food

◖ **Brier Island Hostel** (Water St., Westport, Brier Island, 902/839-2273, www.brierisland-hostel.com; adult $18, child $9) is in a prime position across from the harbor and adjacent to a grocery store stocked with local delicacies and deli items. The lodge has just 12 beds spread through three rooms. The communal kitchen, sitting area, and wide deck are all excellent.

Between the ferry and Westport (one kilometer from each), **Brier Island Lodge** (Northern Point Rd., 902/839-2300 or 800/662-8355, www.brierisland.com; May–Oct.; $60–150 s or d) sits on a bluff overlooking the sea. The 40 motel-style rooms are spacious and bright; most have water views, and some have king beds. The lodge's pine-paneled restaurant is my favorite island dining room. You can order old-fashioned roast turkey dinner or local specialties such as smoked pollack chowder and steamed periwinkles.

## Information
The website www.brierisland.org has information about the island, but before driving out along Digby Neck, stop by the **Provincial Visitor Centre** (902/742-6639; May–mid-Oct. daily 9 A.M.–5 P.M., July–Aug. daily 9 A.M.–9 P.M.) along Highway 303 between the ferry terminal and downtown Digby.

# Annapolis Royal

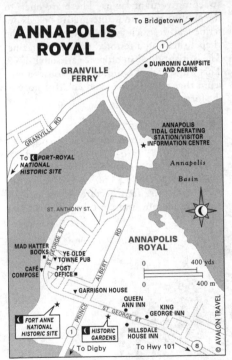

The history of Annapolis Royal (pop. 500) spans four centuries, with much of the past preserved along a main street that is lined with the finest collection of pre-1800 buildings in Canada. The town and surrounding area has 150 registered historic buildings, three national historic sites, and Canada's oldest wooden building. Add to the mix one of the world's only tidal power generating plants, Nova Scotia's largest fun park and its smallest pub, and a selection of gracious accommodations and you find a town like no other place in the province.

## History
In 1605, Samuel de Champlain and the survivors of the bitter winter in New Brunswick moved across the Bay of Fundy and established the fortified Port-Royal across Annapolis Basin from modern-day Annapolis Royal. It was the first permanent European settlement north of St. Augustine, Florida. After eight years the settlement came to an abrupt end when it was attacked and destroyed by New Englanders. In the 1630s, the French governor Charles de Menou d'Aulnay built a new Port Royal on the south shore of the Annapolis Basin, attracting French settlers who came to be known as Acadians. The site would remain capital of Acadie for the next eight decades. The British captured the fort in 1710, renaming it Fort Anne and rechristening the town as Annapolis Royal in honor of their queen. It would serve as Nova Scotia's first capital until 1749, when it was succeeded by the new town of Halifax.

## SIGHTS
It's easy to spend a half day wandering through Fort Anne National Historic Site and the adjacent St. George Street, which curves downhill to the waterfront. For Annapolis Royal's other attractions, you'll need a vehicle.

## Annapolis Tidal Generating Station

It may not be the town's oldest attraction, but it contains the local tourist information center, so it makes a sensible starting place for your visit. Near the head of Annapolis Basin, signposted to the right as you come into town off Highways 1 or 101, the **Tidal Power Plant** (Hwy. 1, 902/532-5769; May–mid-Oct. daily 9 A.M.–5 P.M., July–Aug. 9 A.M.–8 P.M.; free) is the only facility in North America that generates electricity from the tides. Originally built as an experiment, the plant still operates and is capable of generating 20 kilowatts of electricity (enough to power 4,000 homes). The facility harnesses the energy of the massive Fundy tides, which fill a head pond twice daily and then pass through a turbine as they flow back out toward the ocean. The plant's top floor is dedicated to describing the process, with windows allowing views down the bay and of the head pond.

## ◖ Fort Anne National Historic Site

This 18th-century fort and grounds, Canada's first national historic site (St. George St., 902/532-2397; mid-May–mid-Oct. daily 9 A.M.–5:30 P.M.; adult $4, senior $3.50, child $2), overlook Annapolis Basin from the heart of Annapolis Royal. Considered the key stronghold for possession of Nova Scotia, as the British knew the region—it was Acadie to the French—the site had particular importance to both parties. It has been fortified on at least eight occasions since Scots built Fort Charles in 1629. The earliest French fort, dating to 1630, was designed with a star-shaped layout. Earthwork from the French fort of 1702 remains today, impressively banked with sweeping verdant lawns. These are open to the public year-round. Interpretive boards describe features such as the parade ground, the chapel site, and a restored powder magazine. The British added an officers' garrison in 1797. This whitewashed building now houses a museum that tells the long and colorful story of the fort.

## ◖ Historic Gardens

The Historic Gardens (441 St. George St., 902/532-7018; mid-May–mid-Oct. daily 9 A.M.–5 P.M., extended July–Aug. daily 8 A.M.–dusk; adult $8.50, senior and child $7.50) comprise four hectares of theme gardens, a restaurant, and a gift shop. The gardens

cannon at Fort Anne National Historic Site

©ANDREW HEMPSTEAD

are undeniably beautiful, but they are also interesting. The Acadian Garden, complete with an Acadian house and outdoor oven, replicates that of the earliest European settlers. Vegetables such as beets, carrots, parsnips, onions, and cabbages are surrounded by a hedge to keep out wild animals, and off to one side is a hedge-encircled orchard of apple and pear trees. Other highlights include the Knot Garden, styled after a hedge garden of the Middle Ages; the Governor's Garden, laid out as a formal garden in the 1750s, when Annapolis Royal was the capital; and a striking Rose Garden with more than 200 varieties, including early English and modern hybrids. The gardens are at their most spectacular in summer, with roses peaking mid-July–September.

## ❰ Port-Royal National Historic Site

The first lasting settlement north of Florida, the 1605 fort at Port-Royal has been reconstructed at what is believed to be the original site (902/532-2898; mid-May–mid-Oct. daily 9 A.M.–5:30 P.M.; adult $4, senior $3.50, child $2). The French settlement of 1605 has been reconstructed from Samuel de Champlain's plan using 17th-century construction techniques; the rustic buildings—governor's house, priest's dwelling, bakery, guardroom, and others, furnished with period reproductions—form a rectangle around a courtyard within the palisaded compound. The original outpost boasted many historic firsts: Canada's first play, *Le Théâtre de Neptune,* was written and produced here by the young Parisian lawyer Marc Lescarbot; the continent's first social club, l'Ordre de Bon Temps (the Order of Good Cheer) was founded here in 1606; and the New World's first grain mill was built here to grind meal from the first cereal crops. The story of these is brought to life by knowledgeable staff dressed in period costume. To get to Port-Royal, cross Annapolis Basin by the generating station and turn left at Granville Ferry. It's 10 kilometers along the road (two kilometers beyond Melanson Settlement National Historic Site).

## RECREATION
### Hiking

Delaps Cove, 24 kilometers west of Annapolis Royal (cross Annapolis Basin, head south toward Port Royal for eight kilometers, and turn right on the unpaved road that ends at the Bay of Fundy), is a small fishing village that is the start of the **Delap's Cove Wilderness Trail,** one of the few longer hiking trails along this stretch of coast. From the wharf at the end of the road, the trail meanders southwest along the coast for 15 kilometers. It takes about eight hours round-trip, but you can hike for just an hour or so before turning around if time is an issue.

### Fun Park

**Upper Clements Parks** (Hwy. 1, Upper Clements, 902/532-7557; mid-June–early Sept. daily 11 A.M.–7 P.M.) is Nova Scotia's largest theme park. Its style is thoroughly Nova Scotian, featuring a train ride on a historic replica, a minigolf course designed as a map of the province, and the re-creation of a fishing village. The park also has a roller coaster, flume ride, carousel, pedal boats, live entertainment, dinner theater Friday–Saturday evenings, a crafts area with demonstrations and a shop, and dining rooms. Everyone pays $8 to get through the gate, plus $3 per ride or $22.50 for everything. Tickets also include entry to the adjacent **Upper Clements Wildlife Park,** featuring indigenous wildlife of the province such as black bears, white-tailed deer, moose, and cougars, as well as farm animals and Sable Island horses.

## ACCOMMODATIONS AND CAMPING
### $50-100

Aside from the cabins at **Dunromin Waterfront Campground and Cabins,** few places offer rooms for less than $100 in July and August. One option is **Grange Cottage** (102 Richie St., 902/532-7993; $65 s, $75 d), where the three guest rooms share one bathroom. The rear deck has river views and the front porch is a relaxing place to cool off on hot afternoons. Rates include a full breakfast.

Swimming, hiking, wagon rides, canoeing, and lawn games fill the day at **Mountain Top Cottages** (888 Parker Mountain Rd., 902/532-2564 or 877/885-1185, www.mountaintopcottages.com; May–Oct.; $97–127 s or d), in a forested setting atop North Mountain. Seventeen simple cottages with one or two bedrooms overlook a private lake. Each has a microwave and fridge. To get there, cross Annapolis Basin at the tidal plant, follow Highway 1 through Granville Ferry, and take Parker Mountain Road off to the north (left).

## $100-150

**Hillsdale House Inn** (519 Upper St. George St., 902/532-2345 or 877/839-2821, www.hillsdalehouseinn.ca; May–Dec.; $109–149 s or d) is on a six-hectare estate that has been graced by kings and prime ministers. The main house has 11 guest rooms and the adjacent coach house another three. Antiques fill public areas, including a cozy lounge. A cooked breakfast is included in the rates.

**King George Inn** (548 Upper St. George St., 902/532-5286, www.kinggeorgeinn.20m.com; mid-May–mid-Nov.; $90–160 s or d) is a ship captain's home, built circa 1868 and furnished with Victorian-era antiques. It offers eight luxurious guest rooms, including a two-room family suite. Amenities include a library, pianos, free use of bicycles, and evening tea and coffee.

Set on two hectares of landscaped grounds, **❰ Queen Anne Inn** (494 Upper St. George St., 902/532-7850 or 877/536-0403, www.queenanneinn.ns.ca; May–Oct.; $119–210 s or d) is a restored 1865 Victorian mansion with a grand mahogany staircase that sweeps upstairs to 10 guest rooms outfitted with period furnishings. Room 10 is significantly smaller than the remaining nine, which are extra large ($159–189 s or d). Behind the main house, the carriage house contains two two-bedroom units, perfect for two couples traveling together or a family. Rates include a full three-course breakfast and afternoon tea.

© ANDREW HEMPSTEAD

The Queen Anne Inn is one of many gracious accommodations in Annapolis Royal.

## Campgrounds

Running right down to a private beach on the Annapolis Basin, **Dunromin Waterfront Campground and Cabins** (902/532-2808, www.dunromincampsite.com; May–mid-Oct.) is the perfect place for families. With a fort-themed playground, an outdoor pool, minigolf, lawn games, canoe rentals, and a café, the biggest problem will be dragging the children off for a day of sightseeing. The campground has 165 sites, most of them serviced ($26–38.50). Canvas tepees with shared bathrooms are $45 s or d, and cabins range from $65 for shared bathroom to $110 for a two-bedroom waterfront cottage.

Enjoying an absolutely stunning location right on the Bay of Fundy, **❰ Cove Oceanfront Campground** (Parker's Cove, 902/532-5166, www.oceanfront-camping.com; mid-May–late Oct.; $29–95) has modern facilities including a pool, a playground, a games room, and a small café. But it's the views that make this an excellent choice, with grassed terraces ensuring everyone can see the water. To get to Parker's Cove, cross the Annapolis Basin at the generating station, turn right at Granville Ferry, and then take the first left, up and over the low wooded peninsula to Parker's Cove.

## FOOD

St. George Street has many dining choices, including diner-style cafés and fine-dining restaurants. If you're staying at a campground or have chosen an accommodation with cooking facilities, head over North Mountain to Parker's Cove and pick up fresh seafood such as scallops, lobster, and crab from **R. R. Shellfish** (902/532-7301), across the road from the water.

Facing Annapolis Basin from behind the main row of shops, **Café Compose** (235 St. George St., 902/532-1251; Mon.–Sat. 11 A.M.–7 P.M., Sun. 1–7 P.M.) is easy to miss. This European-style café pours good coffee and has a menu of light and sweet lunches, including delicious strudels.

Locals gather for afternoon beer and pub grub on the outdoor patio or for nightcaps in the cozy interior of English-style **Ye Olde Towne Pub** (11 Church St., 902/532-2244; Mon.–Sat. 11 A.M.–11 P.M., Sun. noon–8 P.M.), beside the outdoor Farmers Market at the bottom end of St. George Street. Built in 1884 as a bank and reputed to be the smallest bar in Nova Scotia, its meals are typical pub fare, but the portions are generous. Look to the blackboard for seafood specials.

**Garrison House** (350 St. George St., 902/532-5501; daily from 6 P.M.) is a refined restaurant spread through three connected rooms of an 1854 inn. The chef is renowned for sourcing seasonal produce, while year-round specialties include fish cakes ($14) and Acadian jambalaya ($17). With its impressive wine list and professional service, this is the best place in town for fine dining.

## INFORMATION AND SERVICES

**Annapolis Royal Visitor Information Centre** (Hwy. 1, 902/532-5769; May–mid-Oct. daily 9 A.M.–5 P.M., July–Aug. daily 9 A.M.–8 P.M.; free) is at the Tidal Power Plant, on the north side of downtown. Coming into town from Exit 22 along Highway 101, turn right before the historic main street.

**Mad Hatter Books** (213 St. George St., 902/532-2070) is an inviting bookstore that stocks a large collection of literature on local history and culture, coffee-table books, and travel guides.

The **post office** is at 50 Victoria Street. At the back of Sinclair Mews is a self-serve **laundry** (daily 9 A.M.–9 P.M.).

# Kejimkujik National Park

Deep in the interior of southwestern Nova Scotia, Kejimkujik (kedji-muh-KOO-jick, or "Keji" or "Kedge" for short) National Park lies off Highway 8, about midway between Liverpool and Annapolis Royal. Encompassing 381 square kilometers of drumlins (rounded glacial hills), island-dotted lakes—legacies of the last ice age—and hardwood and conifer forests, the park and the adjacent Tobeatic Game Sanctuary are an important refuge for native wildlife and town-weary Nova Scotians.

Wildlife enthusiasts visit the park for bird-watching (including barred owls, pileated woodpeckers, scarlet tanagers, great crested flycatchers, and loons and other waterfowl) and may also spot black bears, white-tailed deer, bobcats, porcupines, and beavers. The many lakes and connecting rivers attract canoeists and swimmers in warm weather, as well as anglers (particularly for perch and brook trout). Hikers can choose from a network of trails, some leading to backcountry campgrounds; some of the campgrounds are also accessible by canoe. In winter, cross-country skiers take over the hiking trails.

© ANDREW HEMPSTEAD

The Mersey River is one of many waterways within Kejimkujik National Park.

## RECREATION

The two most popular park activities are hiking and canoeing. The **Beech Grove Trail** on a two-kilometer loop starts at the visitors center and wends along the Mersey River, where it climbs a drumlin hilltop swathed in an almost-pure beech grove. The **Farmlands Trail** is another drumlin variation, and the 45-minute hike makes its way up a drumlin to an abandoned farm on the hilltop. A little further south along the park access road is the trailhead for the one-kilometer **Rogers Brook** loop, which passes through a forest of red maple and hemlock trees.

You can rent canoes, rowboats, and bicycles ($5 per hour, $24 per day) at Jakes Landing on the northeast side of large Kejimkujik Lake; the adjacent stretch of the Mersey River is placid and suitable for beginning paddlers.

## ACCOMMODATIONS AND CAMPING

Within the park, **Jeremy's Bay Campground,** on the north side of Kejimkujik Lake, has 360 unserviced sites for tents and trailers ($25.50), with washrooms and showers, fire pits, and

firewood ($7), a playground, picnic areas, and an interpretive program. Another 46 wilderness sites ($18) are scattered in the woodlands with toilets, tables, grills, and firewood. A percentage of sites can be booked through the **Parks Canada Campground Reservation Service** (905/426-4648 or 877/737-3783, www.pccamping.ca) for $11 per reservation.

Hostelling International's **Raven Haven Hostel** (902/532-7320, www.hihostels.ca; mid-June–Aug.) is in South Milford, about 20 kilometers north of the park toward Annapolis Royal. Members pay $15, nonmembers $17. Family rooms are available, and you can go swimming or canoeing at adjacent Sandy Bottom Lake. Check-in is any time after 1 P.M.

## INFORMATION

The **Visitor Reception Centre** (902/682-2772; mid-June–Aug. daily 8:30 A.M.–8 P.M., Aug.–mid-June daily 8:30 A.M.–4:30 P.M.) is just beyond the park entrance. This is the place to buy day passes (adult $6, senior $5, child $3) and fishing licenses ($10 per day, $35 annual) and pick up literature on the park, including hiking trail descriptions. For more information on the park, click through the links at www.pc.gc.ca.

# Annapolis Valley

The Annapolis Valley, which spreads along the Annapolis River east from Annapolis Royal, is a haze of white when its apple orchards bloom in late May to early June. The valley, extending northeast from Annapolis Royal, supports more than magnificent apple orchards, however; if you look closely, you'll also see hectares of strawberries, plums, peaches, pears, and cherries, as well as crops of hay, grain, and tobacco.

The Annapolis Valley has a legion of fans, among them the Mi'Kmaq, who first settled this region. According to Mi'Kmaq legend, Glooscap, a deity taking the form of a giant man, roamed the areas of the upper Fundy. He made his home atop the basalt cliffs of the peninsula—the lofty hook-shaped cape that finishes in sea stacks at Cape Split—and buried jewels on the Fundy beaches. (Today's tides still claw at the coastline to reveal agate, amethyst, and zeolite from Hall's Harbour to Cape Split's tip.)

## ANNAPOLIS ROYAL TO CANNING

From Annapolis Royal, Highway 101 heads northeast, crossing the Annapolis River near Bridgetown and continuing east for 100 kilometers to Wolfville. You don't see a great deal from the highway, so plan to travel Highway 1 (cross the Annapolis Basin at Annapolis Royal to get going). Along this route, you pass through the villages and apple orchards now bypassed by Highway 101.

### Bridgetown

About 28 kilometers from Annapolis Royal, this town has wide streets lined with grand old homes and stately trees. **James House Museum** (12 Queen St., 902/665-4530; mid-May–Sept. daily 9 A.M.–4 P.M.; free) is an 1835 residence sandwiched between modern shops along the main street. As well as predictable displays on early settlers, there's an old-fashioned tearoom.

Take Church Street north out of town and you reach **Valleyview Provincial Park** after five kilometers. This small park sits atop North Mountain, an ancient ridge of lava that forms a cap over softer shale and sandstone that has been gouged away to the south, forming the Annapolis Valley. From the park, views extend across the valley to the province's remote interior. The park campground (mid-June–mid-Oct.; $24) has just 30 sites, but it only ever fills on summer weekends. It has toilets and drinking water but no showers.

### Kentville

The commercial hub of the Annapolis Valley is Kentville (pop. 6,000), 120 kilometers east of Annapolis Royal. The town is on the north side of Highway 101 (take Exits 14 or 13 from the west and Exit 12 from the east) and at the junction of Highway 12, which cuts south through the Nova Scotia interior to Mahone Bay and Lunenburg. In the historic heart of town is **King's County Museum** (37 Cornwallis Ave., Mon.–Fri. 9 A.M.–4 P.M.; free), which contains an art gallery and small theater within a two-story red brick courthouse.

On the outskirts of town, you'll find a couple of inexpensive motels, including **Allen's Motel** (384 Park St., 902/678-2683, www .allensmotel.ns.ca; mid-Mar.–mid-Dec.; $70–105 s or d), two kilometers west of downtown. Here, 10 rooms are separated from the highway by well-tended gardens and a picnic area with a gas barbecue.

**South Mountain Park** (Hwy. 12, South Alton, 902/678-0152 or 866/860-6092, www .southmountainparkcampground.com; $33–38, cabins $70) fills with holidaying families through its mid-May to mid-October season. A few kilometers south of Kentville, it's not really set up for quick overnight stays. But if you have children and are looking for a break from touring, it's a great place to kick back for a few days. The activities offered could easily fill a week of fun—everything from fishing to tennis and wagon rides to walking paths. Amenities include a par 3 golf course, games room, TV room, library, Internet access, Olympic-size outdoor pool, and more, lots more. On the downside, campsites offer little privacy.

## Starr's Point

**Prescott House Museum** (1633 Starr's Point Rd., 902/542-3984; June–mid-Oct. Mon.–Sat. 9:30 A.M.–5:30 P.M., Sun. 1–5:30 P.M.; adult $4, senior $3, child $2) harks back to the valley's orchard beginnings, when horticulturist Charles Ramage Prescott imported species to add to the provincial store of fruit trees. His profits built this Georgian-style homestead. The restored mansion, constructed circa 1812, displays period furnishings and sits amid beautiful gardens. Its special events celebrate the fall harvest. It's along Highway 358, which leads north from Greenwich (Exit 11 from Highway 101).

## Canning

The east end of the Annapolis Valley has a smattering of emerging boutique wineries, including **Blomidon Estate Winery** (10318 Hwy. 221, 902/582-7565; June–Oct. daily 10 A.M.–5 P.M.). This winery was the first in Nova Scotia to produce classic varietals such as chardonnay, pinot noir, and shiraz. The winery and a small cellar door are two kilometers east of Canning along Highway 221.

# BLOMIDON PENINSULA

The Blomidon Peninsula is the sphincter-shaped northern end of North Mountain. Extending into the Minas Channel and with Minas Basin to its back, it features more fantastic Fundy scenery and a couple of good campgrounds. From Exit 11 of Highway 101, it's 40 kilometers to the end of the road.

## The Look-Off

On the north side of Canning, **Look-Off Family Camping** (Hwy. 358, 902/582-3022, www.lookoffcamping.com; May–Sept.) lives up to its name with a long list of activities—think hayrides, bingo, and fitness classes—and workshops such as kite-making and cookie painting. Other facilities include a café open daily at 9 A.M., a playground, a pool, and a launderette. Unserviced sites around the shaded edge of the campground are $25, hookups are $30, and camping cabins (no linen supplied) are $60 s or d. The namesake Look-Off (a Nova Scotian term for a lookout) is across the road and has wonderful views across the bucolic Annapolis Valley.

## Blomidon Provincial Park

This dramatically positioned 759-hectare park is along the eastern side of the Blomidon Peninsula, facing Minas Basin. To get there, turn off Highway 358 three kilometers north of the Look-Off and follow the secondary road north for 14 kilometers. The red shale and sandstone that make the park so striking was laid down millions of years ago and then eroded by glacial and water action to form 180-meter-high bluffs that are topped by coastal forest. Fundy tides sweep up to the cliff face twice daily, but as the water recedes, you can walk along the red-sand beach, searching for semiprecious stones such as amethyst and agate. The uplands area is covered in forests of sugar maple, beech, and birch, yet also present are alpine plants such as maidenhair.

The best place for a walk is along the beach, but check at the park office (902/582-7319) or information boards for tide times. Four official trails wind their way through the park. The best views are from the Look-Off Trail, an easy one-kilometer walk to a lookout high atop the cliffs. The 5.6-kilometer **Jodrey Trail** fringes the cliffs while the **Interpretive Trail** passes information boards describing the forest and its inhabitants. The main day-use area is where the access road enters the park. It's one of the few places along the Fundy Coast where the water gets warm enough for swimming.

Beyond the day-use area, the access road climbs to the campground (early June–early Oct.; $24), where sites are spread through the forest on two short loops. Facilities include showers, a playground, and drinking water.

## To Cape Split

At the tip of the Blomidon Peninsula is Cape Split. To get there, continue north on Highway 358 from the Look-Off to Scots Bay, where there's a small provincial park with a pebbly beach fronting Minas Channel. The road ends just beyond Scots Bay, from where it's 13 kilometers on foot to Cape Split. It's a long way to walk (and make the return trek) in one day, but there is no elevation gain and the rewards are total wilderness and sweeping views from the cliff top at the end of the trail.

# Wolfville and Vicinity

At the eastern end of the Annapolis Valley, the genteel town of Wolfville (pop. 3,700) began with the name Mud Creek, an ignoble tribute from the founding New England planters who wrestled with the Fundy coastal area once farmed by early Acadians. Now the town sits in the lushest part of the Annapolis Valley, and you won't want to miss it. Highway 1 runs through town as Main Street, where large houses with bay windows and ample porches sit comfortably beneath stately trees. Acadia University's ivy-covered buildings and manicured lawns lie along Main and University.

The town, just six blocks deep, has an uncomplicated layout alongside Highway 1 and Highway 101.

## SIGHTS
### Along the Main Street

Wolfville's refined nature is apparent to anyone walking along the main street, which is dotted with grand stone buildings and, at the eastern end, stately trees.

**Randall House Museum** (259 Main St., 902/542-9775; mid-June–mid-Sept. Mon.–Sat. 10 A.M.–5 P.M., Sun. 1:30–5 P.M.; donation) is a historic home (built in 1815) with period furnishings and local artifacts from the 1760s to the 20th century.

**Acadia University Art Gallery** (Beveridge Arts Centre, at Highland Ave. and Main St., 902/585-1373; summer Tues.–Sat. 1–4 P.M., the rest of the year daily 1–4 P.M.; free) has a fine-arts collection of local and regional works, highlighted by Alex Colville's oils and serigraphs.

### Wolfville Waterfront

Most visitors miss Wolfville's waterfront, but the town does have one, one block north of the main street across Front Street. Trails and a small park have been developed at the mouth of the Cornwallis River, which was once lined with busy shipyards. Views extend across the Minas Basin to the red cliffs of Blomidon Provincial Park.

Along Front Street to the west is **Robie Tufts Nature Centre,** which is a series of covered interpretive boards describing the flora and fauna native to the area. The main purpose of the structure is to provide a home for chimney swifts, which make their home in the red brick chimney rising through the roof.

## SHOPPING

The **Harvest Gallery** (462 Main St., 902/542-7093) displays the work of local artists. Especially eye-catching are the colorful oil paintings of Jeanne Aisthorpe-Smith.

Although apples get all the glory, lots of other farming happens in the Annapolis Valley. **Gaspereau Valley Fibres** (830 Gaspereau River Rd., 902/542-2656) highlights the local wool industries, with knitting, weaving, and spinning, as well as the raw materials sold as is. The shop is on a farm on the south side of Highway 101; to get there from town, take Gaspereau Road south.

## ACCOMMODATIONS

Most Wolfville accommodations are grand heritage homes, so there are no bargains.

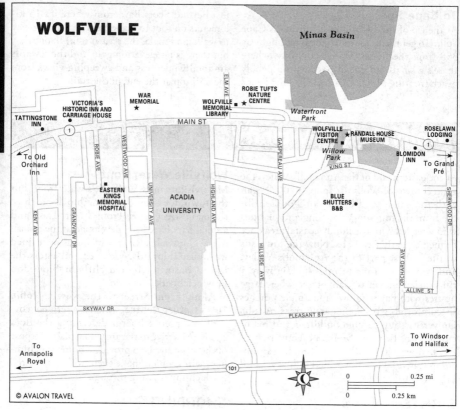

## $50-100

On the hill behind the information center, **Blue Shutters Bed and Breakfast** (7 Blomidon Terr., 902/542-3363; $80–110 s, $100–125 d) has three well-equipped guest rooms. Each has an en suite bathroom, TV/DVD combo, wireless Internet, and an electric fireplace. Rates include a full breakfast.

**Roselawn Lodging** (32 Main St., 902/542-3420, www.roselawnlodging.ca) is a modest motel on the east side of downtown. Facilities include an outdoor pool, launderette, barbecues and picnic tables, a tennis court, and a playground. The 28 motel rooms ($80–120 s or d) are clean and comfortable, and 12 adjacent cottages come with kitchens ($100–150 s or d).

## $100-150

If you're a garden lover, you won't want leave the expansive grounds of **🄲 Blomidon Inn** (127 Main St., 902/542-2291 or 800/565-2291, www.blomidon.ns.ca; $100–270 s or d), which is surrounded by more than one hectare of cacti, roses, rhododendrons, azaleas, ponds, a croquet lawn, and a terraced vegetable garden that doubles as an outdoor eating area. The home itself, built in 1882 by a shipbuilder, reflects the wealth of its original owner. Mahogany and teak dominate, and local antiques are found throughout public areas and the 29 guest rooms. The least expensive rooms are on the small side, but all have en suite bathrooms. Rates include a continental breakfast and afternoon tea. Tennis courts, a restaurant, and a lounge round out this elegant accommodation.

A registered historic property (1893), **Victoria's Historic Inn and Carriage House** (600 Main St., 902/542-5744 or 800/556-5744, www.victoriashistoricinn.com; $108–245 s or d) combines a grand Victorian house with an adjacent carriage house. Rooms vary in character greatly; my favorite is the Hunt Room ($138 s or d), on the upper floor of the carriage house, which has a smart green and burgundy color theme and a vaulted cathedral ceiling. Like the other rooms, it has an en suite four-piece bathroom, TV, telephone, bathrobes, and a CD player. Rates include a cooked breakfast and afternoon tea.

Dating to 1874 and within walking distance of downtown, **Tattingstone Inn** (630 Main St., 902/542-7696 or 800/565-7696, www.tattingstone.ns.ca; $118–178 s or d) is casually formal with 10 guest rooms spread through the main house and adjacent carriage house. All are decorated with antiques and some have whirlpool tubs. The inn also offers a music room, dining room, steam room, heated outdoor pool, and tennis court. Rates include a cooked breakfast.

The **Old Orchard Inn** (153 Greenwich Rd., 902/542-5751 or 800/561-8090, www.oldorchardinn.com) is a sprawling resort near Exit 11 of Highway 101. It comprises more than 100 motel-style guest rooms ($150–195 s or d) and 29 cabins (May–Oct.; $150–225 s or d) spread through the forest. Tennis courts, an indoor pool, saunas, spa services, hiking trails, and a stone patio with sweeping valley views add to the appeal. The resort also has a dining room and lounge.

# FOOD

For a small town, Wolfville has a surprising number of eateries. If you're in town on a Saturday, it's worth browsing the **Wolfville Farmers Market.** In summer it's outdoors (Robie Tufts Nature Centre, Front St.; mid-May–Sept. 8:30 A.M.–1 P.M.) while the rest of the year, everything is moved indoors (Acadia Student Union Building, Highland Ave.; Oct.–mid-May 8:30 A.M.–1 P.M.).

## Cafés

**Just Us** (450 Main St., 902/542-7731; Mon.–Fri. 7 A.M.–9 P.M., Sat. 8 A.M.–6 P.M., Sun. 10 A.M.–5 P.M.) pours organic coffees and a wide range of teas from the front of a historic theater building, with seating spread through the lobby. Meals are very inexpensive ($4 for soup and sandwich), and the muffins are baked fresh daily. A little farther along, the **Coffee Merchant** (472 Main St., 902/542-4315; daily 8 A.M.–10 P.M.) has some of the best coffee concoctions in town.

## Restaurants

In a restored 1860 home one block from Main Street, the kitchen at **❨ Tempest** (117 Front St., 902/542-0588; daily for lunch and dinner and Fri.–Sat. until 10:30 P.M.) prepares the most creative and well-presented cooking in the Annapolis Valley, although it's also a little more expensive than other local restaurants. The menu features cuisine from around the world that makes use of local seafood and produce. The origin of dishes is truly global—Indian butter chicken, lobster risotto, potato-crusted haddock, and the highlight for me, lobster and corn chowder. Starters range $7–15 while mains are $18–31. Lunch is an excellent deal, with most dishes under $10. The tree-shaded patio fills on warmer evenings and jazz musicians play on Friday night.

The dining rooms at the local inns are good bets for meals. One of the best of the dining rooms associated with local accommodations is the **Acadian Room** (Old Orchard Inn, 153 Greenwich Rd., 902/542-5751; daily 7 A.M.–9 P.M.), which draws diners to its large restaurant with stunning views and good food. Before 11 A.M., the French toast with whipped cream and blueberry sauce is a delight. Local fare such as cedar-plank salmon basted with dark rum and maple syrup is an evening standout. Most dinner mains are less than $20. The wine list allows the opportunity to taste Nova

Scotian wine by the glass. Sunday brunch (Oct.–May 11 A.M.–2 P.M.; $18) is a grand affair, with a huge array of hot and cold foods laid out on a buffet table.

## INFORMATION AND SERVICES

At the east end of town is **Wolfville Visitor Centre** (Willow Park, Main St., 902/542-7000; May–mid-Oct. daily 9 A.M.–5 P.M.). **Wolfville Memorial Library** (21 Elm St., 902/542-5760; Tues.–Sat. 11 A.M.–5 P.M., Sun. 1–5 P.M.) is a red brick building that was once the local railway station. As with most public libraries through Nova Scotia, public Internet access is free.

Box of Delights Bookshop (328 Main St., 902/542-9511; Mon.–Sat. 9 A.M.–5:30 P.M., Sun. noon–5 P.M.) has a good collection of Canadiana and Acadian history and field guides. In business since the 1970s, the **Odd Book** (112 Front St., 902/542-9491; Mon.–Thurs. 9:30 A.M.–5:30 P.M., Fri. 9:30 A.M.–9 P.M., Sat. 9:30 A.M.–5 P.M., Sun. 1–5 P.M.) is where locals go to search out hard-to-find used and antiquarian books.

Eastern Kings Memorial Hospital is at 23 Earnscliffe Ave. (902/542-2266). Call the **police** at 902/542-3817 or the **RCMP** at 902/679-5555.

Banks and the **post office** are along Main Street. **Wile's** (210 Main St.; daily 8 A.M.–10 P.M.) has coin-operated laundry machines.

## GETTING THERE AND AROUND

**Acadian Lines** stops up at the university twice daily on the route between Digby and Halifax. Buy tickets at the information desk (15 Horton Ave., 902/585-2110).

## GRAND PRÉ

Continue east through Wolfville on Highway 1 for six kilometers (or take Exit 10 from Highway 101) to reach this small village that was the epicenter of one of the most tragic events in Canadian history, the expulsion of the Acadians from their homeland. First settled

Grand Pré National Historic Site

in 1680 by an Acadian family who moved from the confines of nearby Port Royal, Grand Pré grew to become the largest Acadian settlement in Nova Scotia. The main attraction is Grand Pré National Historic Site, but also worth visiting is **Grand Pré Wines** (Hwy. 1, 902/542-1753; Mon.–Sat. 10 A.M.–6 P.M., Sun. 11 A.M.–6 P.M.), where grapes are grown on 60 hectares of former Acadian farmland. In the main building you'll find a restaurant, wine shop, and crafts corner. Winery tours ($6) are offered through summer daily at 11 A.M., 3 P.M., and 5 P.M.

## ◖ Grand Pré National Historic Site

Commemorating the Acadian deportation, this living museum (2242 Grand Pré Rd., 902/542-3631; mid-May–mid-Oct. daily 9 A.M.–6 P.M.; adult $7.80, senior $6.60, child $4) brings Acadian history and the deportation to life. It wasn't until Henry Wadsworth Longfellow wrote the poem *Evangeline* in 1847 that the English-speaking world became aware of the expulsion, but by then nothing remained of Grand-Pré (Great Meadow), the setting for the story of the Acadian heroine separated from her lover by the deportation.

In 1922 an interested benefactor with Acadian roots built a small stone church on the presumed site of Grand Pré, and this was the genesis for the historic site of today. Visitors enter through a large museum complex, where there's a bookstore and gift shop, along with information panels describing Acadian life, the deportation, and the return of the Acadians to Nova Scotia. Outside are sprawling grounds crisscrossed by pathways that lead to vegetable gardens, a blacksmith shop, an orchard, a lookout over the diked farmland, and a statue of Henry Wadsworth Longfellow. In the middle of the site is a statue of Evangeline, who was born at Grand Pré and whose life has become an icon of the struggle of her people. Directly behind the statue is the 1922 church. It houses an exhibit of paintings that showcase the history of the people, a copy of the original expulsion order that was read to a congregation within the original church, as well as stained-glass windows with a story to tell. Guided tours of the grounds (included with admission) are highly recommended. A guide is also stationed within Église Saint-Charles to lead you through the story of each painting.

### Accommodations and Food

The best choice of accommodations are in nearby Wolfville, but the centrally located **Evangeline Inn and Motel** (11668 Hwy. 1, 902/542-2703 or 888/542-2703, www .evangeline.ns.ca; May–Oct.) provides comfortable accommodations right at the turnoff to the historic site. Choose from motel rooms ($75–95 s or d) or rooms in the adjacent boyhood home of Sir Robert Borden, prime minister of Canada for nine years early last century ($95–115 s or d). All guests have use of a landscaped pool. Also on the grounds is a café open daily for breakfast and lunch, where cooked breakfasts are less than $5 and dishes such as haddock chowder with a warmed scone on the side are $4–7.

Across the road from the entrance to Grand Pré National Historic Site is **Le Panier D'Evangéline** (2208 Grand Pré Rd., 902/542-1543; Tues.–Fri. 8 A.M.–8 P.M., Sat.–Sun. 10 A.M.–8 P.M.), a large country-style café serving healthy foods, local and organically grown whenever possible. The freshly squeezed juices are especially good.

## WINDSOR

If you've toured along the South Shore and then traveled along the Fundy Coast, the temptation may be to stay on the highway and give Windsor, just 60 kilometers northwest of Halifax, a miss. But this gracious town on the banks of the Avon River is well worth the short detour from busy Highway 101. To get there

---

### HOLY PUMPKINS!

Windsor may be famous as the birthplace of hockey, but no attraction is bigger than the pumpkins grown on the south side of town at **Howard Dill Enterprises** (400 College Rd., 902/798-2728). Dill is renowned in the giant pumpkin-growing business for developing seeds that go on to produce some of the world's largest pumpkins, some of which grow to over 700 kilograms (1,540 pounds).

You won't find the pumpkins grown from Dill's seeds on grocery-store shelves. They are used for fall fairs and pumpkin-growing competitions, and as jack-o-lanterns by folks with strong porches. Most of the company's business is done online; through the website www.howarddill.com you can order the precious seeds and books such as *How to Grow World Class Giant Pumpkins* and *How To Grow World Class Giant Pumpkins Volume II*, as well as download growing tips. At Dill's farm, visitors are encouraged to drop by and see his own pumpkin patch, where even the smallest pumpkins are in the 180- to 230-kilogram (400- to 500-pound) range leading up to the late September–early October harvest.

from the main highway, take Exit 6, which leads into downtown. Before town is a small **information center** (902/798-2690; mid-May–mid-Oct. daily 9 A.M.–5 P.M.).

## Fort Edward National Historic Site

Dating to 1750, Fort Edward National Historic Site (King St., 902/542-3631; mid-June–late Sept. daily 10 A.M.–6 P.M.; free) preserves the last 18th-century blockhouse in Nova Scotia. Fort Edward was one of the main assembly points for the deportation of the Acadians from the province in 1755. Although the building is open only during summer, touring the grounds will give a good feel for the location of the fort and the chance to see earthen mounds where the rest of the fort once stood.

## Historic Homes

**Haliburton House** (414 Clifton Ave., 902/798-5619; June–mid-Oct. Mon.–Sat. 9:30 A.M.–5:30 P.M., Sun. 1–5:30 P.M.; adult $3, child $1.50) was owned by 19th-century author, humorist, and historian Judge Thomas Chandler Haliburton, who was born in Windsor in 1796. Among the sayings that originated in Haliburton's writings are "It's raining cats and dogs," "barking up the wrong tree," "Facts are stranger than fiction," and "quick as a wink." The Victorian mansion on 10 hectares is open to the public, as are the surrounding gardens. For hockey fans, his written memories of childhood have special meaning. In them, he reminisced about children "playing ball on ice" behind Haliburton House, which is the earliest mention of the game of ice hockey.

On Ferry Hill, **Shand House** (389 Avon St., 902/798-8213; June–mid-Oct. daily 9:30 A.M.–5:30 P.M., Sun. 1–5:30 P.M.; adult $3, child $1) is another vintage beauty and marks the wealthy Shand family's prominence in Windsor. When it was built in the early 1890s, the Queen Anne–style mansion was one of the first residences in the area fitted with electric lights and indoor plumbing.

© ANDREW HEMPSTEAD

Nova Scotia's oldest remaining blockhouse, protected within Fort Edward National Historic Site

# CENTRAL NOVA SCOTIA

This chapter encompasses a wide swath of Nova Scotia extending north from Halifax to Truro (the geographical center of the province) and then west to the New Brunswick border and east to the causeway leading to Cape Breton Island. This region, at once the most traveled and least known part of the province, is perfect for those looking for low-key attractions as varied as ancient fossils, beautiful beaches, and remote parks.

The region can roughly be divided into manageable sections—each very different in look and feel. The TransCanada Highway slices through the region's northwest corner and extends to Cape Breton Island in the east. But this route promises little besides uninterrupted speed. Detour south to explore an area that was once the realm of Glooscap, the Mi'Kmaq god

who roamed this part of Nova Scotia as a man as large as Gulliver among the Lilliputians. A legend relates that Glooscap slept stretched out over the region's northern portion and used Prince Edward Island as his pillow. While the Northumberland Strait has long been the domain of vacationing locals—attracted by warm water and long stretches of beautiful beach— other visitors on a fast track often see the region as a flash of landscape from the TransCanada Highway. The other option for reaching Cape Breton Island from Halifax is to drive along the Eastern Shore, which is as rugged as the Northumberland Strait shore is tame. This super-scenic road unfurls itself at a leisurely pace, and it's worth slowing down and taking two or three days to travel its length. Passing tiny fishing ports reminiscent of seafaring life

© ANDREW HEMPSTEAD

# HIGHLIGHTS

**◖ Watching the Tidal Bore:** The tidal bore phenomenon occurs in only a few places in the world. Locals call it the Total Bore, and I'll admit it's not exactly exciting, but it's unusual enough to be worth timing your visit to Truro to coincide with the twice-daily tidal bore (page 130).

**◖ Balmoral Grist Mill:** Surrounded by rich green foliage, the reflection of this bright red building in an adjacent pond creates a scene of tranquility (page 138).

**◖ Hector Heritage Quay Museum:** Step aboard a full-size replica of the *Hector,* upon which Pictou's first settlers arrived, to get a taste of the hardships that were endured crossing the Atlantic Ocean (page 139).

**◖ Arisaig:** The unassuming cliffs at Arisaig

are filled with fossils that have helped scientists understand the evolution of life on earth 400 million years ago (page 143).

**◖ Taylor Head Provincial Park:** Marine Drive passes dozens of protected areas, but Taylor Head stands out for its ease of access and interesting geology (page 148).

**◖ Sherbrooke Village:** History comes alive at this living museum. For the full effect, join the Hands on History program by dressing up in period costume (page 150).

**◖ Canso Islands National Historic Site:** The focus of this attraction is Grassy Island, home to a thriving fishing community in the early 1700s. But the best part for budget-conscious travelers will be the price – just $5 including a boat trip (page 152).

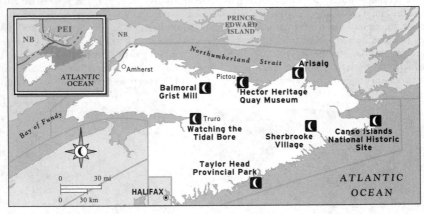

LOOK FOR ◖ TO FIND RECOMMENDED SIGHTS, ACTIVITIES, DINING, AND LODGING.

NOVA SCOTIA

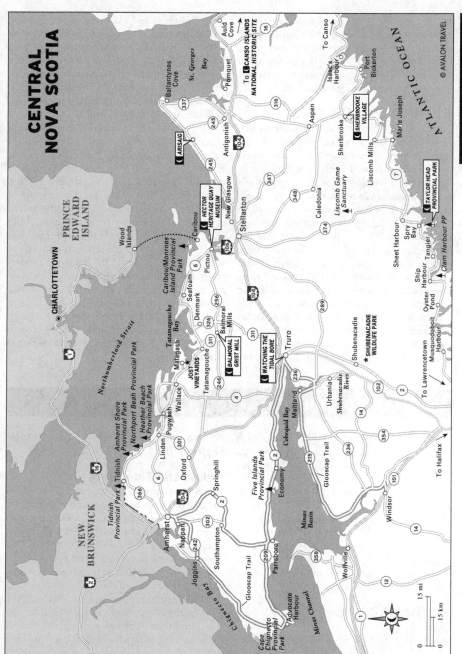

CENTRAL NOVA SCOTIA

© AVALON TRAVEL

decades ago and rock-bound coves where the forest grows right down to the sea, the road's services are few and far between (Canso, with a population of 1,000, is the largest town), so plan ahead by making accommodation reservations and keeping your gas tank full.

## PLANNING YOUR TIME

Central Nova Scotia is not a destination like Cape Breton Island, where you would plan your visit around an itinerary that lasted a certain length of time. Instead, you will surely find yourself passing through central Nova Scotia on more than one occasion—for example driving from New Brunswick through to Halifax and then again on the way to Cape Breton Island. If you've been touring through New Brunswick, you'll already be well aware of the massive Fundy tides. In central Nova Scotia, you can **watch the tidal bore** at Truro. Along Northumberland Strait, beaches lapped by warm water will tempt you to linger while historic attractions such as **Balmoral Grist Mill** and Pictou's **Hector Heritage Quay Museum** keep the past alive. From Halifax, you could plan on spending two days reaching

Cape Breton Island via the above-mentioned attractions, which would also allow time for a detour to **Arisaig,** a fossil hot spot protected by a small provincial park. If you have an extra day or two, consider taking Marine Drive to or from Cape Breton Island. The distance (320 kilometers) is deceiving when planning how long the drive will take. Add a ferry trip to a winding, often narrow road that passes through dozens of small townships, and you should expect the journey to take at least six hours. From Canso it will take another 90 minutes to reach Port Hastings, the gateway to Cape Breton Island. But of course, this estimate of 7.5 hours to complete the Marine Drive is sans stops, and if you're only interested in reaching Cape Breton Island from Halifax, the Highway 102/104 route via Truro takes around half as long. Leaving Halifax in the morning, an ideal scenario would be to spend one night en route and plan on reaching Cape Breton Island later the following day. This would allow time to explore **Taylor Head Provincial Park,** to step back in time at **Sherbrooke Village,** and to take the boat trip to **Canso Islands National Historic Site.**

# Halifax to Truro

As you head north from Halifax, suburbia is quickly left behind as divided Highway 102 speeds north to Truro, which is easily reached in an hour from downtown. The original route between these two cities (Highway 2) may look appealing on the map, but the scenery is no different from what you'll see from Highway 102—it simply takes longer. If you've traveled the Fundy Coast from west to east, take Highway 22 from Windsor as a shortcut, or Highway 215, also from Windsor, to follow the Bay of Fundy to its head.

## SHUBENACADIE

If you're willing to try something new or you have an animal-loving family, there

are two good reasons to take Exit 10 from Highway 102.

### Riding the Tidal Bore

The **Shubenacadie River,** which drains into the Bay of Fundy at Cobequid Bay, is not just a good place to view the tidal bore but also to *ride* it. **Tidal Bore Rafting Park** (Urbania, Hwy. 215, 902/758-4032 or 800/565-7238, www.tidalboreraftingpark.com) operates two- and four-hour Zodiac raft excursions May–September. You board the rafts at low tide and head downstream, just in time to catch the tidal bore back upriver. The driver rides the wave, and then doubles back to blast through its face, finding rapids along the way to keep the adrenaline pumping. Rates range $60–75. Departures are dependent on the tides; check the website for times.

## Shubenacadie Wildlife Park

Upstream of Highway 102 (signposted from Exit 11), families will enjoy Shubenacadie Wildlife Park (902/758-2040; mid-May–mid-Oct. daily 9 A.M.–7 P.M., mid-Oct.–mid-May Sat.–Sun. 9 A.M.–3 P.M.; adult $4.25, child $1.50), a zoological facility operated by the provincial government. Throughout the spacious grounds are Canadian animals you are unlikely to see in the wild (fishers, mink, and more), ones that you don't want to meet face to face (bears, cougars, bobcats, and lynx), and those you'll see only at Christmas (reindeer). The Sable Island horses may look like regular horses, but they are one of the world's few wild horse populations.

## Accommodations and Camping

⊂ **Rafters Ridge Cottages** (Urbania, Hwy. 215, 902/758-4032 or 800/565-7238, www .raftersridgecottages.com; $145–190 s or d) is part of the Tidal Bore Rafting Park complex, so it's no surprise that many guests come for the rafting (booked as part of an accommodation package). Enjoying a riverside location, you can also rent canoes or hang out around the outdoor pool. Lodging is in one- and two-bedroom cottages. The cottages have decks, barbecues, and pleasant views across a lightly treed hillside.

In the vicinity of the rafting park and also right on the Shubenacadie River is **Wide Open Wilderness Campground** (Urbania, 902/261-2228 or 866/811-2267, www.wowcamping .com; mid-May–mid-Oct.). You can watch the tidal bore, walk marked hiking trails, relax around the pool, or try your hand at the horseshoe pits. Campsites are $20–26, and cabins are $60 s or d.

## MAITLAND

If you've been moseying eastbound along the Bay of Fundy and don't particularly want to detour back through Halifax, turn at Windsor

(take Exit 5 from Highway 101) and follow Highway 215 along the edge of Minas Basin to Maitland, crossing the Shubenacadie River to meet busy Highway 102 at Truro.

Maitland, at the mouth of the Shubenacadie River, was where Canada's largest wooden ship, the three-masted *William D. Lawrence,* was built. Documentaries, ship portraits, and memorabilia are kept at the shipbuilder's former homestead, the **Lawrence House Museum,** which overlooks Cobequid Bay (8660 Hwy. 215, 902/261-2628; June–mid-Oct. Mon.–Sat. 9:30 A.M.–5:30 P.M., Sun. 1–5:30 P.M.; adult $3.25, senior and child $2.25). The actual 1874 launching is commemorated on the middle Saturday of each September with a parade of period-dressed locals, a symbolic launch, and seafood suppers hosted throughout the village.

## TRURO

Situated at the convergence of the province's major expressways and served by VIA Rail, Truro (pop. 12,000) is called the hub of Nova Scotia. It is the province's third-largest town, with an economy based on shipping, dairy products, and the manufacture of clothing, carpets, plastic products, and wines. Truro's academic side includes a teachers' college in town and an agricultural college on the outskirts.

## Town Sights

The access road leading into 400-hectare **Victoria Park** (corner Brunswick St. and Park Rd.) ends at a wide-open day-use area where beds of tulips flower through June, a colorful highlight of the town. At other times of year the park is still worth visiting—forests of spruce, hemlock, and white pine are spliced with hiking trails that lead along a deep canyon and past two waterfalls.

In a quiet residential area, **Colchester Society Museum** (29 Young St., 902/895-6284; June–Sept. Mon.–Fri. 10 A.M.–5 P.M., Saturday 2–5 P.M.; adult $4, child $2) does a fine job entwining exhibits on Fundy eccentricities and the area's natural history.

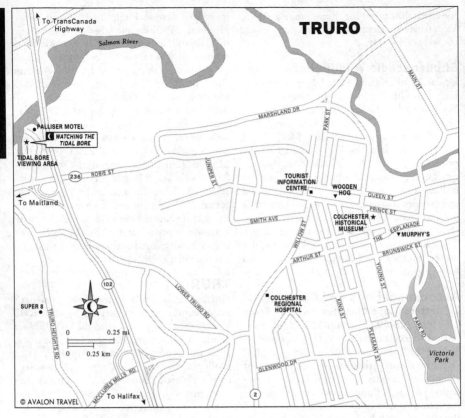

## ⟨ Watching the Tidal Bore

Tidal bores only occur in a few places in the world, and one of the most accessible is the **Salmon River,** which flows through Truro. Best described as a small wave, the bore is particularly high along the Salmon River as it is at the head of Cobequid Bay, where the incoming tide pushing up the Bay of Fundy is forced into a narrow funnel. At Truro, the lead wave travels up the river as it pushes toward town beneath the Highway 102 overpass. If you want a close-up look at the tidal bore, take Robie Street west out of town toward Highway 102 and turn off on one of the roads leading to the river. Tidal-bore arrival times are listed in the *Truro Daily News* and at the town's visitor information center (902/893-2922).

## Accommodations

Lodgings in Truro are plentiful and reasonably priced. Motels line all the main routes into town, and you shouldn't have a problem finding a room at short notice.

Occupying a prime site for watching the tidal bore, the **Palliser Motel** (902/893-8951; May–Oct.; $79–99 s or d) is west of downtown off Robie Street (Highway 2), or take Exit 14 from Highway 102. It's on the banks of the Salmon River, and the bore-watching area is lit at night. The rooms are basic and old-fashioned, but rates include a breakfast buffet at the motel restaurant.

As usual, the **Super 8** (85 Treaty Trail, 902/895-8884 or 877/508-7666, www .super8truro.com; $140 s or d) is close to a main artery and is filled with clean, comfortable air-conditioned rooms packed with amenities. Here you also get an indoor pool with a waterslide and hot tub. A light breakfast is included, and you can walk next door to the Capricorn Restaurant for dinner. Call for last-minute specials.

## Food

In a nondescript strip mall near the heart of downtown, **◖ Murphy's** (the Esplanade, 902/895-1275; daily 11 A.M.–8 P.M.) serves some of the best-priced seafood anywhere in this part of the province. I had the deep-fried haddock and chips—cooked to perfection—for just $8. A variety of fish is offered—pan-fried, poached, or "Texas style"—amid bright nautical-themed decor.

Another favorite is the **Wooden Hog** (627 Prince St., 902/895-0779; Mon.–Fri. 9 A.M.–10 P.M., Sat. 11 A.M.–10 P.M.). While locals often stop by just for coffee and one of the many delicious pastries, the lunch and dinner menu provides good value, with all dinner mains less than $20 (including poached salmon smothered in hollandaise sauce for $14).

Many motels have in-house dining rooms, including the **Palliser Motel Restaurant** (off Robie St., 902/893-8951), where you can combine inexpensive dining with tidal bore–watching.

© ANDREW HEMPSTEAD

At the Truro Tourist Information Centre ask for a brochure detailing the tree-trunk sculptures scattered around the town.

## Information

At the **Truro Tourist Information Centre** (Victoria Sq., Court St., 902/893-2922; Apr.–mid-Oct. daily 9 A.M.–5 P.M.), ask for a map of the tree-trunk sculptures scattered through town and check your email at the public computer terminal. Driving out from Victoria Square and ending up heading out of town in the right direction can be confusing, so get the staff to point the way.

# Glooscap Trail

Named for the mighty Glooscap, a mythical Mi'Kmaq legend who controlled the tides, this region is far enough from the main highway that it is missed by most visitors, which is a shame, because it is dotted with interesting seaside villages, has beaches that occasionally give up precious gemstones, and has been the site of some amazing dinosaur discoveries. According to the tourist brochures, the Glooscap Trail extends along the Bay of Fundy from as far west

as Windsor, but in the name of organization, this section divulges the best of Highway 2, which follows the coast west from Truro to Cape Chignecto and then north to Amherst.

## TRURO TO PARRSBORO

Take Exit 14A from Highway 102 and you'll quickly find yourself on Highway 2, heading west along Cobequid Bay. En route to Parrsboro are a string of small fishing villages,

NOVA SCOTIA

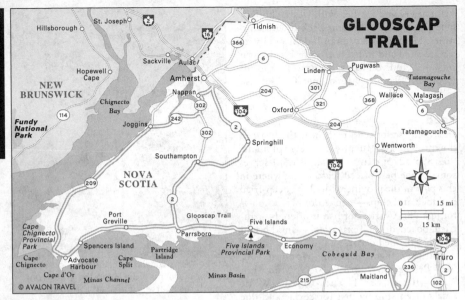

lookout points, and a couple of spots where beach access is possible at low tide.

### Five Islands Provincial Park

As the name suggests, Five Islands Provincial Park does protect five islands, but it also encompasses more than 600 hectares of the mainland between Economy and Parrsboro. Along the park's coastal extremes are high cliffs and beaches, the latter giving up gems such as agate, amethyst, and jasper as the huge Fundy tides sweep across the bay. The five-kilometer (round-trip; allow 90 minutes) **Red Head Trail** reaches almost a dozen lookouts, including the Old Wife, a point of land that enjoys views across to the five islands.

## PARRSBORO

The sea's erosive force has opened a window on the ancient world along the coastlines of Chignecto Bay and Minas Basin. Archaeological digs have yielded 100,000 fossilized bone fragments of ancient dinosaurs, crocodiles, lizards, sharks, and primitive fish.

Learn about local geology at Parrsboro Rock and Mineral Shop and Museum.

© ANDREW HEMPSTEAD

## Sights
### FUNDY GEOLOGICAL MUSEUM

Cross the bridge from downtown via Two Island Road to reach Fundy Geological Museum (162 Two Islands Rd., 902/254-3814; June–mid-Oct. daily 9:30 A.M.–5:30 P.M.; adult $5, senior and child $3.50). It highlights the Bay of Fundy, with displays describing how the tides have eroded the bedrock to expose numerous geological wonders, such as precious gemstones, and the fossilized remains of dinosaurs.

### PARRSBORO ROCK AND MINERAL SHOP AND MUSEUM

Parrsboro Rock and Mineral Shop and Museum (39 Whitehall Rd., 902/254-2981, May–Dec. Mon.–Sat. 9 A.M.–9 P.M., Sun. 9 A.M.–5 P.M.) is famed local geologist Eldon George's pride. The museum displays dinosaur, reptile, and amphibian footprint fossils. The shop stocks fossil and gem specimens, rock-hound supplies, books, and maps.

### OTTAWA HOUSE

Through town, beyond the mineral shop, is Ottawa House (902/254-2376; June–Sept. daily 10 A.M.–5 P.M.; donation), a 21-bedroom waterfront home dating to 1775. All that remains on the beach in front of the home are broken-down pylons, so it's hard to believe that this was once an important shipbuilding port. Now cared for by the local historical society, Ottawa House has two floors of historic displays and a tearoom.

Linked to the mainland by a narrow strip of rocky beach that begins below Ottawa House, archaeological evidence points to Mi'Kmaq occupation of Partridge Island 10,000 years ago. A rough road ends just before the island, from where a hiking trail winds to the summit and views across the Minas Basin to Cape Split (allow 30 minutes round-trip).

## Accommodations

**Riverview Cottages** (3575 Eastern Ave., 902/254-2388 or 877/254-2388, www.riverviewcottages.ca; mid-Apr.–mid-Nov.; $60–90 s or d) lie along Farrells River on the

Ottawa House

east side of town. They are older and only a few have cooking facilities, but canoes are available for guest use, and the price is right.

Within walking distance of downtown, the **Maple Inn** (2358 Western Ave., 902/254-3735, www.mapleinn.ca) subtly combines two historic homes into an accommodation with 11 regular rooms and a spacious two-bedroom suite. The building was originally a hospital, and so the inn has special meaning to those visitors returning to the town where they were born (Room 1 was the delivery room). The inn is surrounded by well-tended gardens, while inside is a lounge with a TV and a library of books. Rates are $90–170 including a full breakfast served in a cheery dining room.

Dating to a similar era is **Gillespie House Inn** (358 Main St., 902/254-3196 or 877/901-3196, www.gillespiehouseinn.com; May–Oct.; $99 s, $119 d). The rooms ooze Old World charm and each has an en suite bathroom. The Elderkin Room has a wooden sleigh bed and looks over the front garden, which catches the morning sun.

## Food

As you cruise the main street, **Glooscap Restaurant** (758 Upper Main St., 902/254-3488, daily breakfast, lunch, and dinner) is obvious, but a better choice is the **( Harbour View Restaurant** (476 Pier Rd., 902/254-3507, summer daily 11 A.M.–9 P.M.), which has uninterrupted water views from off Two Island Road. It's a friendly place, with all the usual seafood choices, including daily specials that are sourced from seasonal seafood. The lobster dinner ($25) is a favorite.

## WEST TO CAPE CHIGNECTO

At Parrsboro, most travelers head north to Springhill on Highway 2, but Highway 209 along Minas Channel makes for a pleasant drive. It's 50 kilometers to the last village of any consequence, Advocate Harbour. At the halfway mark is Port Greville, once home to four shipbuilding companies. Today, take Wagstaff Street to the cliff edge and you can peer down at the river mouth that 100 years ago would have been filled with ships in various stages of construction. Across the water, Cape Split is plainly visible.

### Advocate Harbour

At Spencers Island, Highway 209 turns inland to Advocate Harbour, a quiet corner of the province first visited by Europeans in 1604 when Samuel de Champlain came ashore. Just before town, take the signposted road to Cape d'Or, where a light-keeper's residence has been converted into **( The Lighthouse at Cape d'Or** (902/670-0534, www.capedor.ca; May–mid-Oct.; $80–110 s or d). Perched on high cliffs overlooking the Bay of Fundy, this four-room lodge is a wonderful place to kick back and do absolutely nothing at all. One room has an en suite bathroom while the other three share two bathrooms, and the common room is stocked with books and board games. The attached restaurant (cash only) serves light lunches and creative dinners in the $16–30 range.

### Cape Chignecto Provincial Park

As the crow flies, this park isn't far from the TransCanada Highway or the city of Saint John (New Brunswick), but it is a world away from civilization, protecting an arrow-shaped headland jutting into the Bay of Fundy. Cliffs up to 185 meters high are lapped by the world's highest tides, which pour into Chignecto Bay on one side and Minas Basin on the other. No roads penetrate the park. Instead, from the end of the road at Red Rocks, just beyond the village of West Advocate and 46 kilometers from Parrsboro, a hiking trail leads around the cape and loops back through the forested interior. Most backpackers complete the circuit in three days, packing their own food and water and pitching their tents at backcountry campgrounds. Cabins along the way at Arch Gulch and Eatonville provide an alternative to camping (call 902/392-2085 for reservations). All hikers should be experienced in backcountry travel and totally self-sufficient.

## JOGGINS

This town on the Chignecto Bay coast is 40 kilometers southwest from Amherst. From Parrsboro, take Highway 2 north to Southampton and then follow Highways 302 and 242 north and then west for 38 kilometers.

### Joggins Fossil Cliffs

Declared a UNESCO World Heritage Site in 2008, the sea cliffs here have yielded thousands of fossils from the Carboniferous period (350 million to 280 million years ago). Plants are most common, but a forest of upright petrified tree stumps is what the site is best known for. First discovered in the 1850s, the hollow stumps contained the fossilized remains of *Hylonomous,* the earliest reptile ever discovered. It is supposed that these 30-centimeter-long critters fell inside and were unable to escape. The site has also revealed a two-meter arthropod with 30 sets of legs, as well as dinosaur footprints.

In conjunction with the UNESCO designation, the opening of the **Joggins Fossil Centre** (100 Main St., off Hwy. 302, 902/251-2727; mid-May–mid-Nov. daily 9:30 A.M.–5:30 P.M.;

adult $8, senior and child $6) in 2008 cemented the town as an important stop in central Nova Scotia. In addition to displays of ferns, fish scales, reptile footprints, and gastropods, visitors can watch lab technicians at work. Daily two-hour guided tours to Coal Mine Point ($10 per person) are dependent on the tides.

## SPRINGHILL

The sultry voice of crooner Anne Murray is known the world over, but the folks in the small town of Springhill, on a slight rise just off Highway 104, take special pride in this local girl who has gone on to sell 50 million albums and win more awards than any other female vocalist.

### Anne Murray Centre

You probably already guessed that Springhill would provide a home for the Anne Murray Centre (36 Main St., 902/597-8614; mid-

May–mid-Oct. daily 9 A.M.–4:30 P.M.; adult $7.50, senior and child $5.50). The museum pays tribute to the beloved local warbler who hit the Top 40 in the 1970s with "Snow Bird" and is still going strong. Exhibits include photos, clothing, and other memorabilia, and an audio-visual display catalogs her career.

## AMHERST AND VICINITY

Amherst (pop. 9,000) is built on high ground above Amherst Marsh—part of the larger 200-square-kilometer Tantramar Marshes—on the isthmus joining Nova Scotia to the mainland of Canada. The fertile marshes were first diked and farmed by the Acadians in the 1600s and are still productive today, mainly as hayfields.

### Sights

Amherst is at its architectural best along Victoria Street, where the profits of industry and trade were translated into gracious

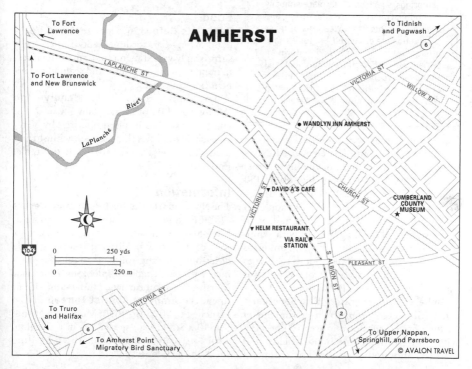

## THINKER'S LODGE

Recognized mostly for its delightful name, Pugwash (from the Mi'Kmaq word *pagweak*, meaning "shallow water"), 50 kilometers east of Amherst, is best known as the origin of the **Pugwash Conferences on Science and World Affairs** (www .pugwash.org). The first of these took place in 1955 in Pugwash after Albert Einstein called for a meeting to discuss the dangers of a nuclear war. Cyrus Eaton, who had made his fortune in the United States as an industrialist, offered to sponsor the event on the condition it was held in his hometown of Pugwash, Nova Scotia. And so in 1957 it came to be that 13 Cold War nuclear scientists, including three from the USSR, met at what became known as the Thinker's Lodge, a large but otherwise unremarkable residence on the Pugwash foreshore. It was the first of many such gatherings, which now take place annually in London, Washington, Rome, Tokyo, and even still in Pugwash. Weapons of mass destruction are discussed, but topics have broadened to include breaking down international borders, the environment, and economic prosperity. To get to Thinker's Lodge, follow Durham Street to its eastern end and turn right down Water Street.

houses and commercial buildings garnished in Tudor, Gothic, and Queen Anne Revival styles. A few blocks south of the historic district, **Cumberland County Museum** (150 Church St., 902/667-2561; Feb.–Dec. Tues.–Fri. 9 A.M.–5 P.M., Sat. noon–5 P.M.; adult $3) is in an 1838 residence. The museum does an impressive job of tracking the past with exhibits on early Acadian settlements, Amherst's Anglo background, and spicy tidbits relating to Russian revolutionary Leon Trotsky, who was interned in an Amherst POW camp in 1917.

**Amherst Point Migratory Bird Sanctuary,** a few kilometers from town at the end of Victoria Street, spreads out over 190 hectares with trails through woodlands, fields, and marshes, and around ponds. The sediment-rich Cumberland Basin lures 200 bird species, including Eurasian kestrels, bald eagles, hawks, and snowy owls.

## Accommodations

If you've just arrived in Nova Scotia by highway from New Brunswick, the **Fort Lawrence Inn** (La Planche St., 902/667-3881) is a basic but convenient choice on the western outskirts of Amherst. It charges $55–85 for older motel rooms and has a restaurant, a lounge, and laundry facilities. To get there, take the Nova Scotia Visitor Information Centre exit and continue east along La Planche Street for a few hundred meters.

**Wandlyn Inn Amherst** (Victoria St. off Hwy. 104 at Exit 3, 902/667-3331 or 800/561-0000, www.wandlyninns.com; from $90 s or d), the town's largest lodging, has 88 air-conditioned rooms, a restaurant, a café, a lounge, and an indoor pool.

## Food

**David A's Café** (125 Victoria St., 902/661-0760; Mon.–Sat. for lunch and dinner) has a surprisingly varied menu for a small-town restaurant, with local produce and seafood prominent in most dishes.

The dining room at the **Wandlyn Inn** (Victoria St., 902/667-3331; daily 7 A.M.–2 P.M. and 5–9 P.M.) has inspired offerings by a creative chef who likes flamed steak with shrimp sauce and Caesar salad tossed at the table. Entrées range $15–29.

## Information

The **Nova Scotia Visitor Information Centre** (902/667-8429; daily 8:30 A.M.–4:30 P.M., May–Sept. 8 A.M.–8 P.M.) is a large complex west of downtown. Adjacent is a promenade describing driving routes through the province, with picnic tables overlooking Tantramar Marshes. In a rail carriage on the same side of town, the **Amherst Tourist Bureau** (51 La Planche St., 902/667-0696; May–Aug. Mon.–Sat. 10 A.M.–6 P.M.) specializes in the region, with lots of information for those heading south to the Glooscap Trail.

# Sunrise Coast to Pictou

The quickest way to reach Pictou from Amherst is to take Highway 104 via Truro, but Highway 6 is more scenic. Throughout the region, the land dips and sweeps in manicured farmlands extending to the red beaches and cliffs of Northumberland Strait. The villages are small, and the backcountry roads are scenic. This is rural Nova Scotia at its best. Allow three hours plus stops.

## TIDNISH AND VICINITY

Highway 366 branches off Highway 6 a few kilometers northeast of Amherst and reaches the Northumberland Strait at Tidnish, which lies right on the provincial border between Nova Scotia and New Brunswick.

### Tidnish Dock Provincial Park

Across the Tidnish River from town is Tidnish Dock Provincial Park. This small day-use park protects the northern terminus of an ambitious railway construction project that was designed to transport vessels across the isthmus between the Bay of Fundy and Northumberland Strait. The initial proposal had been for a canal link, but the government decided constructing a rail line would be easier. The plan called for the construction of hydraulic presses at either end to lift the boats into cradles that were to be pulled across the 28-kilometer rail line by locomotives. In 1891, after nearing completion, the entire project was abandoned. The park protects remains of the dock and a short length of the rail bed.

### Continuing East Along Highway 366

Head east from Tidnish to **Amherst Shore Provincial Park.** From the day-use area, a short trail follows Annebelles Brook to a short beach, while on the other side of the highway is a campground (mid-May–mid-Sept.; $24) with flush toilets, showers, and fire pits. Continue east for seven kilometers to **Northport Beach Provincial Park,** renowned for its excellent

beach and water warmed by shallow sandbars. Next up, and equally popular for swimming, is **Heather Beach Provincial Park.**

## PUGWASH

Recognized mostly for its delightful name, Pugwash (from the Mi'Kmaq word *pagweak,* meaning "shallow water") lies at the mouth of Pugwash Basin 50 kilometers east of Amherst. Durham Street (Highway 6) is the main drag. Here you find a summer-only information center and the usual array of small-town businesses. Across the water to the south of downtown is a salt mine. Current production is 90,000 tons annually (10 percent of Nova Scotia's total mineral value). The best opportunity to get an idea of the operation's scope is to watch the freighters being loaded at the downtown dock.

### Accommodations and Food

Downtown, the Irish-themed **Shillelagh Sheila's Country Inn** (10340 Durham St., 902/243-2885, www.shillelaghsheilasinn .com; June–mid-Oct.; $65–75 s or d) has a distinctive green and red exterior and four guest rooms with older furnishings. Breakfast is included, and dinner is offered with notice.

**Hidden Jewel Café** (10163 Durham St., 902/243-4059; Mon.–Sat. 9:30 A.M.–5 P.M.) has tables along a covered veranda and a menu of healthy choices.

## PUGWASH TO PICTOU

It's 110 kilometers between Pugwash and Pictou along Highway 6, but there are many worthwhile detours; the first, Gulf Shore Road, starts from downtown Pugwash.

### Along Gulf Shore Road

From downtown's Durham Street, Gulf Shore Road spurs north and then follows the edge of Northumberland Strait in an easterly direction before rejoining Highway 6 at Wallace. About four kilometers from Pugwash is **Gulf Shore**

© ANDREW HEMPSTEAD

Toney River is one of many fishing villages between Pugwash and Pictou.

**Picnic Park,** a day-use area with fireplaces and picnic tables spread across a grassed area that slopes to a red-sand beach.

Near where Gulf Shore Road loops south to Wallace is **Fox Harb'r Golf Resort and Spa** (1337 Fox Harbour Rd., 902/257-1801 or 866/257-1801, www.foxharbr.com). While the resort and its facilities wouldn't look out of place in Arizona or the Atlantic Coast, it's certainly unique in rural Nova Scotia. At $225 for a round of golf, the greens fee is too high for a humble travel writer such as myself (no, we don't get everything for free), but I'm told it's a beautiful course. Other facilities include an Olympic-size indoor pool, spa services, guided kayaking, and formal dining (jacket required) in the Great Room. Guests soak up pure luxury in suites (from $325 s or d) contained within 12 chalets that line the fairways and look out over Northumberland Strait.

## Jost Vineyards

About 34 kilometers west of Pugwash, Jost Vineyards (902/257-2636; mid-June–mid-Sept. daily 9 A.M.–6 P.M., the rest of the year daily 9 A.M.–5 P.M.) is signposted off Highway 6. The creation of the Jost (pronounced "yost") family from Europe's Rhineland, this 18-hectare vineyard produces fine white wines that are sold throughout the province, including at many better restaurants. The best-known blends are the Jost ice wines. To produce this style, grapes are left on the vines until after the first frost, and then gently pressed to produce just a few drops of concentrated juice from each grape. The result is an intensely sweet wine that is perfect as an after-dinner treat. Free guided tours are given daily in summer at noon and 3 P.M., and a deli is stocked with picnic treats—the perfect compliment to Jost wines.

## 🍷 Balmoral Grist Mill

Best known for its gristmill, Balmoral Mills lies along Highway 311 south of Tatamagouche 10 kilometers and 38 kilometers north of Truro. Nestled at the base of a wooded vale, bright red Balmoral Grist Mill (660 Matheson Brook Rd., 902/657-3016; June–mid-Oct. Mon.–Sat. 9:30 A.M.–5:30 P.M., Sun. 1–5:30 P.M.; adult $3.25, senior and child $2.25) is a photographer's ideal setting. Wheat, oats, and barley are still ground using 19th-century methods at this historic gristmill-cum-museum built in 1874. Milling demonstrations are at 10 A.M. and 2 P.M. The mill is busiest the first Sunday in October—an Open Day drawing a crowd of hundreds with activities such as milling demonstrations and popular taste testing of oatmeal cakes.

## Seafoam

At this coastal village 24 kilometers east of Tatamagouche, you find the 🍷 **Seafoam Campground** (Harris Ave., 902/351-3122; mid-May–Sept.; $18), a large facility with direct access to the beach and warm swimming water. Amenities include lawn games, a playground, showers, and a laundry. On the west side of the campground, a side road leads to an abandoned dock, where a concrete wall has created a natural barrier for shifting sand. The result is a wide stretch of beach, perfect for lazing away a few hours on a warm summer day.

# Pictou

Pictou (PIC-toe), 160 kilometers west of Amherst and 14 kilometers north of Exit 22 from Highway 104, is a historic port town on Northumberland Strait. It is also the ferry gateway to Prince Edward Island, meaning plenty of traffic passes through.

Nearly everything in Pictou happens at the waterfront, which is home to the main museum, restaurants, and historic accommodations. Some of the older buildings have a distinct Scottish vernacular style, designed to reflect local lineage. The residential streets also have numerous fancier styles; you'll see examples of stone Gothic and Second Empire designs along Water, Front, and Church Streets.

## History

In 1773, 33 families and 25 unmarried men arrived from the Scottish Highlands aboard the *Hector,* and Pictou (pop. 3,800) quickly became known as the "birthplace of New Scotland." The flamboyant Presbyterian minister and doctor Thomas McCulloch, en route to ministerial duties on Prince Edward Island, arrived here with his family by accident in 1803 when a storm blew his ship into Pictou Harbour. Local immigrants asked him to stay, and McCulloch agreed. In addition to providing medical care to the immigrants, McCulloch tried to reform the province's backward educational system.

## SIGHTS
### ◖ Hector Heritage Quay Museum
At the heart of the downtown waterfront, Hector Heritage Quay Museum (33 Caladh Ave., 902/485-6057; mid-May–late Oct. Mon.–Sat. 9 A.M.–6 P.M., Sun. noon–6 P.M.; adult $5, senior $4, child $2) is home to a three-floor interpretation center detailing the Scottish immigrants' arrival and early years. An elevated outdoor walkway overlooks the harbor. Admission includes access to the *Hector,* a replica of the sailing ship that transported Scottish settlers from across the Atlantic.

Take time to look over the *Hector.* The three-masted black-and-off-white replica is a splendid vessel, wide-hulled and round-ended.

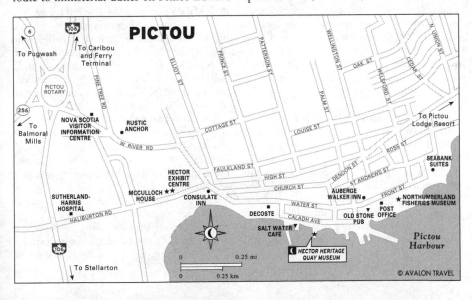

© AVALON TRAVEL

NOVA SCOTIA

© ANDREW HEMPSTEAD

Climbing aboard this replica of the *Hector* is a highlight of visiting Pictou.

From the shape of the ship, though, you'll easily see that the voyage from Scotland was not so splendid. The ship's hull is unusually wide, and indeed the *Hector,* owned by the Dutch and chartered by the Scots for the voyage, was built as a freighter and modified only slightly to carry human cargo. Remarkably, the 200-plus immigrants from the Highlands survived, and Nova Scotia owes its Scottish heritage to those seaworthy voyagers.

## Northumberland Fisheries Museum

This fascinating museum (71 Front St., 902/485-4972; mid-June–mid-Oct. Mon.–Fri. 10 A.M.–5 P.M., Sun. noon–5 P.M.; adult $5, senior $4, child $2) is within a red brick railway station, away from the redeveloped waterfront precinct and easy to miss. Displays tell the story of the local fishing industry through a vintage lobster boat, an aquarium holding local marine species, a mock fisherman's bunkhouse, period photos, and other memorabilia.

## Hector Exhibit Centre

The next two attractions are east of downtown along Old Haliburton Road. The Hector Exhibit Centre (86 Old Haliburton Rd., 902/485-4563; mid-May–mid-Oct. Tues.–Sat. 8:30 A.M.–4:30 P.M.) showcases fine arts as part of the national arts exhibit circuit. The site is also one of the province's best genealogical libraries. Admission to the exhibits is $1; admission to the genealogical library is $5 first visit, $2 subsequent visits.

## McCulloch House

A path leads uphill from the Hector Exhibit and Research Centre to McCulloch House (100 Old Haliburton Rd., 902/485-1150; June–mid-Oct. Wed.–Sat. 9:30 A.M.–4:30 P.M.; $1), the early 1800s home of Thomas McCulloch. With distant water views, it holds period antiques and a small library. The print of a Labrador falcon downstairs was a gift to McCulloch from artist-naturalist John James Audubon.

## ENTERTAINMENT AND EVENTS

The local performing arts scene is based at **deCoste** (Water St., 902/485-8848), a modern waterfront entertainment complex that puts on upward of 100 shows each year. In July and August, the center hosts the Summer Sounds of Nova Scotia series. These concerts highlight top Celtic dancers, singers, and fiddlers, who hit the stage Tuesday–Thursday at 8 P.M. Tickets are generally under $20.

The **Hector Festival** (902/485-8848, www.decostecentre.ca) celebrates the 1773 arrival of Pictou's Scottish ancestors through five mid-August days. Most of the action takes place along the waterfront, including concerts, pipe bands, Highland dancing, and workshops. The second Sunday in August is the final day and also the highlight. A reenactment of the historic landing takes place at 4 P.M., drawing thousands to the waterfront. This is followed by a *ceilidh* (Celtic music concert).

Hector Heritage Quay Museum

## ACCOMMODATIONS AND CAMPING

Pictou has cheap motels such as the **Rustic Anchor Motel** (132 W. River Rd., 902/485-4423, www.rustyanchormotel.com; $60 s, $65 d), but I encourage you to take advantage of the wonderful choice of historic lodgings, many within walking distance of the waterfront and all well priced.

### $50-100

Right on the water and within walking distance of downtown, the **Consulate Inn** (157 Water St., 902/485-4554 or 800/424-8283, www.consulateinn.com) dates to 1810. It's a historic building styled in Scottish and Georgian vernacular that was once the U.S. consulate. The restored inn has five guest rooms ranging from the low-ceilinged Lower Garden Suite ($80 s or d) to the spacious Harbour View Suite, which has a kitchen and private balcony ($140). In a modern annex are five additional guest rooms, with the largest,

the Bermudiana Suite ($160), providing excellent value. All rooms have en suite bathrooms, and a self-serve–style breakfast is included in the rates.

The three units at **Seabank Suites** (68 Front St., 902/485-4274 or 866/877-2988, www.seabanksuites.com; May–Dec.; $95–140 s or d) have private entrances and full kitchens. The 1854 home, built for a local shipping merchant, has been thoroughly modernized, with rooms also featuring TV/DVD combos.

The restored 1876 **Auberge Walker Inn** (34 Coleraine St., 902/485-1433 or 800/370-5553) has 11 guest rooms ($79–159 with a light breakfast), some with harbor views, and a fully licensed dining room.

### $100-150

Dating to the 1920s, **Pictou Lodge Resort** (Braeshore Rd., 5 km east of town, 902/485-4322 or 800/495-6343, www.pictoulodge.com; mid-May–mid-Oct.; $139–423 s or d) sits on a 67-hectare oceanfront estate overlooking Northumberland Strait. The roomy lodge has

© ANDREW HEMPSTEAD

Reserve a room at the Consulate Inn and you'll be close to everything in Pictou.

been restored with rustic comforts and features a long outside porch, dining in the high-ceilinged rotunda, and a nearby pond with canoes. The 59 guest units include six three-bedroom chalets, 21 suites of various sizes and configurations, and 20 standard motel rooms. All units have private baths, and many have fireplaces, kitchens, and separate living rooms. Resort amenities include canoe rentals, a driving range, an outdoor pool, and a playground.

## Campground
**Caribou/Munroes Island Provincial Park** (mid-June–mid-Oct.; $24) has 87 campsites (Loop B is closest to the beach), cooking shelters, flush toilets, and fire pits. It fronts a long red-sand beach, which at low tide links Munroes Island to the mainland. The park is six kilometers west of town, signposted from Highway 6.

## FOOD
For waterfront ambience, head to the **Salt Water Cafe,** next to Hector Heritage Quay

Museum (67 Caladh Ave., 902/485-2558; daily 11 A.M.–8:30 P.M.). Sit inside or out on the screened deck while enjoying the house specialty—seafood, moderately priced. The **Old Stone Pub** (38 Dept St., 902/485-4546; daily from 11 A.M.) has an inviting Scottish ambience, but the menu takes from many countries—lobster bruschetta, lasagna, and spaghetti and meatballs are all under $20.

Several local lodgings offer excellent public dining rooms. **The Vines** (Consulate Inn, 157 Water St., 902/485-4554; daily for dinner) has intimate dining June–September. The specialty is seafood, with some beef and chicken dishes. Five kilometers out of town, the dining room at the **( Pictou Lodge Resort** (Braeshore Rd., 902/485-4322; mid-May–mid-Oct. daily for lunch and dinner) is a woodsy, old-fashioned space. You'll enjoy strait views from an intimate setting, with tables centered around a massive stone fireplace. The menu features entrées such as ginger-fried chicken, sauced poached salmon, and smoked trout, with prices ranging $18–29.

## INFORMATION AND SERVICES
At the Pictou Rotary (where Highway 106 meets Highway 6), the **Nova Scotia Visitor Information Centre** (902/485-6213 or 800/565-0000; mid-May–mid-Oct. daily 8 A.M.–9 P.M.) is primarily in place for those arriving in Nova Scotia via the ferry from Prince Edward Island, but it is also a good source of local information. The website www.townofpictou.com will help plan your trip.

**Sutherland-Harris Hospital** is at 1059 Haliburton Road (902/485-4324). Locals do their banking in style at architecturally resplendent places; the **Bank of Nova Scotia** is in a Second Empire–style building at the corner of Front and Colerain Streets (902/485-4378). The **post office** is at 49 Front Street.

## GETTING THERE
If you're combining your travels through Nova Scotia with a visit to Prince Edward Island, you have the choice of driving across the

Confederation Bridge or catching the ferry. From Caribou, a short drive north of Pictou, **Northumberland Ferries** (902/566-3838 or 800/565-0201, www.nfl-bay.com) operates 5–9 sailings May to mid-December daily to the eastern side of Prince Edward Island. Taking just longer than one hour, the fare is $61 round-trip per vehicle, regardless of the number of passengers (you pay when leaving the island).

# Pictou to Cape Breton Island

The TransCanada Highway promises little besides uninterrupted speed on its route across the northeastern mainland. The best vistas, beaches, camping, and other attractions lie off the expressway, along the strait's coastal roads between Tatamagouche and Cape Breton. Shallow pools of seawater among sandbars turn warm in the sun, making for comfortable wading and swimming at Rushton's **Beach Provincial Park, Tatamagouche Bay,** and **Melmerby Beach Provincial Park,** east of Pictou.

## CAPE GEORGE SCENIC DRIVE

The route to fossil hunting at Arisaig and Cape George's ruggedly beautiful eastern coastline lies along Highways 245 and 337 between New Glasgow and Antigonish. From Exit 27 east of New Glasgow, allow half a day to reach Antigonish, which is enough time to spend time at the sights detailed here.

### 🄲 Arisaig

Like many other places in Nova Scotia, Arisaig, 57 kilometers northeast of New Glasgow, is an unassuming place that is much more interesting than the casual visitor may imagine. The cliffs on the west side of the village tell the story of a 4-million-year period of life on earth 400 million years ago—one of the only places in the world where such a long period of time is exposed in a single layered cliff line. Four hundred million years ago, this area was a shallow sea, and as the layers of sediment built up on its floor, brachiopods (shells), nautiloids (related to squid), trilobites (ancient crabs), crinoids (a filter-feeder that attached itself to the sea bed), and bryozoans (coral) were buried. As

ocean levels dropped, cliffs were formed along the shoreline, and as erosion broke the sediment down further, fossils from the Silurian Period were exposed, perfectly preserved in bands of rock that represent specific time periods all those millions of years ago. Added to the mix is the upper cliff face, which is topped with up to four meters of sand and gravel left behind when glaciers retreated across the area at the end of the last ice age. Geologists have studied the site since the mid-1800s, and as the erosion process continues and more fossils are uncovered, interest continues. You can walk to the cliffs from the wharves of Arisaig, but

© ANDREW HEMPSTEAD

Cape George Lighthouse is the high point of the Cape George Scenic Drive.

the official access is from **Arisaig Provincial Park,** on the east side of the town. From the park, steps descend steeply to the beach far below, ending near Arisaig Brook, where the largest concentration of fossils is found. It is illegal to dig at the cliff face, but scavenging through fallen rock is permitted.

## Cape George

At Malignant Cove, Highway 337 branches north from Highway 245 and climbs steadily before peaking at an elevation of 190 meters at Cape George. The setting is a bicyclist's favorite scene and a just reward after the steep coastal climb. The panorama from the lighthouse at the cape's tip takes in the manicured farmlands of the Pictou–Antigonish highlands to the south as well as the misty vision of Prince Edward Island across the strait.

Along Cape George's eastern side, Highway 337 peels down from the peak alongside St. Georges Bay. Nestled below the cape is **Ballantynes Cove.** From the town wharf, a rough walking trail climbs back to the lighthouse. The 1.8-kilometer route takes less than one hour each way and makes reaching the cape more satisfying than simply driving to its summit.

# ANTIGONISH

First impressions of Antigonish (An-tee-guh-NISH), from a Mi'Kmaq name meaning "place where the branches are torn off by bears gathering beechnuts," are not promising. Main Street is a thicket of fast-food restaurants and service stations—but the town is not without its charms. Dig deeper and you'll find a bustling university town with nearby beaches and hiking trails, a good choice of places to stay and eat, and two popular festivals.

## Sights

In a downtown railway building dating to 1908, **Antigonish Heritage Museum** (20 E. Main St., 902/863-6160; Mon.–Fri. 10 A.M.–5 P.M.; free) tells the town's story through donated items and historical photographs. Farther along the main street is the **County Courthouse** (168 Main St.), still in use even though it has been designated a

National Historic Site. Although no tours are offered, the landscaped grounds of gracious **St. Francis Xavier University** (take Exit 32 north from Highway 104) are pleasant for a stroll, especially in summer when the campus is deserted.

## Festivals and Events

The second week of July, the town hosts the **Antigonish Highland Games** (902/863-4275, www.antigonishhighlandgames.com)—the longest-running in North America, celebrated since 1863. Highlights include Celtic music, pipe bands, dancing, heavy sports such as caber tossing, and a kilted golf tournament. Throughout July and August, the **Festival Antigonish** (800/563-7529), Nova Scotia's largest and most successful professional summer theater program, features a variety of drama, musicals, comedies, cutting-edge improv, and children's entertainment at the university campus.

## Accommodations

**Maritime Inn Antigonish** (158 Main St., 902/863-4001 or 877/768-3969, www.maritimeinns.com; $125–175) is open year-round. It has 32 units and a dining room, lounge, and café. **Antigonish Victorian Inn** (149 Main St., 902/863-1103 or 800/706-5558, www.antigonishvictorianinn.ca; $125–170 s or d) is a splendid bed-and-breakfast occupying a William Critchlow Harris–designed Queen Anne–style mansion. Each of the 12 guest rooms has a private bath and TV. Rates include full homemade breakfast.

## Food

Antigonish offers a surprising number of good dining options. **Sunshine on Main** (332 Main St., 902/863-5851; Sun.–Thurs. 7 A.M.–9 P.M., Fri.–Sat. 7 A.M.–10 P.M.) has a homey atmosphere and a good menu of inexpensive healthy fare, including a number of choices for vegetarians and tasty thin-crust pizza.

Being close to the university, **Piper's Pub** (33 College St., 902/863-2590; daily from 11 A.M.) is a popular student hangout. The typical pub grub is well priced (mains $10–16), and bands play Saturday night.

# Marine Drive

From Halifax, it's 320 kilometers along the Eastern Shore to Canso, at the eastern tip of mainland Nova Scotia. From this point, it's another 80 kilometers to the Canso Causeway, gateway to Cape Breton Island. It is a scenic alternative to the TransCanada Highway via Truro—longer and beyond the main tourist path, but with interesting stops around every bend.

## LAWRENCETOWN

If you have enough time to take the Marine Drive, you have enough time to kick off the drive by following Cole Harbour Road from Exit 7 of Highway 111 in Dartmouth to **Lawrencetown Beach,** one of Canada's best-known surf spots. Easily reached in 30 minutes from Dartmouth, this long stretch of sand backed by high dunes is an enjoyable stop even if you don't plan to take to the water.

### Surfing at Lawrencetown Beach

The waves of "L-town," as it's known to locals, break along the length of the beach and off a rocky headland that breaks the main beach in two. They are best November–May, when winter swells provide large and consistent waves. These waves also coincide with the coldest ocean temperatures—and I mean *cold*. Even with water temperatures of 0°C (32°F) and air temperatures that drop to –20°C (–4°F), it's not unusual to see footprints leading down a snow-covered beach to the breakers beyond. Summer is not devoid of waves. They are just likely to be smaller and less consistent. Hardy locals swim in the ocean in the warmer months, when water temperatures rise to 15°C (59°F), but for surfing, be prepared with a wetsuit. The beach's southern headland provides an ideal vantage point for watching the action.

From an unlikely spot in the heart of downtown Halifax, **DaCane Surf Shop** (5239 Blowers St., 902/431-7873, www.hurricane-surf.com) rents surfboards ($25 for 24 hours), wetsuits ($20), gloves and booties ($10), and bodyboards ($15). The company also has a rental outlet behind the dunes at Lawrencetown Beach Provincial Park (June–Sept.); three-hour rates are surfboards, $20; wetsuits, $20; booties and gloves, $15; bodyboards, $15. Surf lessons are $90 per hour.

## Accommodations

Room rates at **Seaboard Bed and Breakfast** (2629 Cromwell Rd., East Lawrencetown, 902/827-3747 or 866/599-8094, www .seaboardbb.com; $100–115 s or d) have been creeping up, but this converted farmhouse one kilometer from the beach is still a relaxing place to spend one or more nights. Bikes are available for guest use, as is a canoe tied up at Porters Lake, which lies directly across the road. Other amenities include games such as bocce ball and horseshoes, a library with a fireplace, and a TV room. Rates include a

Lawrencetown Beach is Nova Scotia's premier surf spot.

© ANDREW HEMPSTEAD

NOVA SCOTIA

# FABLED SABLE ISLAND

COURTESY OF SABLE ISLAND GREEN HORSE SOCIETY

Just less than 200 kilometers off Nova Scotia's eastern coastline is a 40-kilometer-long sliver of sand that was known for generations of seafarers as the Graveyard of the Atlantic and is today inhabited by a herd of horses that have taken on almost mythical proportions.

The island is made up entirely of sand. The sand is part of a terminal moraine left behind by the receding ice cap at the end of the last ice age 11,000 years ago. Hardy marram grass stabilizes the central part of the island, while seals and birds are also native. The island's most famous residents are horses; they were introduced in the late 1700s, some say to feed shipwreck victims, while others claim they were aboard ships that came to grief. Today, Sable Island is home to about 300 horses. They are of special interest since they are one of the world's few truly wild horse populations, without feral intruders (such as domestic horses gone wild), and are free to roam, feed, and reproduce without human interference.

Since Sable Island was first mapped in the late 1500s, more than 350 vessels have been wrecked along its fog-shrouded shore (the last was a small yacht, the *Merrimac*, in 1999). In 1801 a station manned with a lifesaving crew

was established on the island. This government-operated service soon expanded to five stations and continued until 1958. Today, the island has a year-round population of fewer than 20 people – mostly scientists who study the weather and monitor the island's environment.

The island is under the control of the Canadian Coast Guard, with Sable Island Station jointly funded by provincial and federal agencies. Aside from those in the scientific and government communities, about 50 or so intrepid travelers visit Sable Island each year. If you'd like to visit, the first step is to obtain permission from the Canadian Coast Guard. Once permission is granted, make accommodation arrangements in the staff quarters of **Sable Island Station** (not always available) and arrange fixed-wing air charters from Halifax through **Maritime Air** (902/873-3330, www.maritimeair.com). The charter company is charged a $500 landing fee (which of course will be passed on to you). The best source of island information is the website of the **Sable Island Preservation Trust** (www.sabletrust.ns.ca), which includes a visitor guide.

breakfast made up of homemade bread, jam, waffles, and more.

Ocean views from **Moonlight Beach Inn** (Hwy. 207, north end of Lawrencetown Beach, 902/827-2712, www.moonlightbeachinn.com; $139–350 s or d) are nothing short of stunning. The three guest rooms are decorated in a nautical theme, and each has a private deck, jetted tub, and TV/VCR combo, while thoughtful extras include binoculars and beach towels. The largest of the three rooms is massive and has a huge private deck with sweeping water views. Rates include a full breakfast.

# MUSQUODOBOIT HARBOUR TO TANGIER

With just 900 people, Musquodoboit Harbour is nevertheless the largest community between Dartmouth and Canso. The only real attraction in town is **Musquodoboit Harbour Railway Museum** (Hwy. 7, 902/889-2689; summer only; free), housed in a 1918 railway station and three vintage rail cars. The **tourist information center** is in the same building. Five kilometers south of Musquodoboit Harbour on Petpeswick Road, **Martinique Beach Provincial Park** protects the southern end of Nova Scotia's longest beach. The beach is often windy, but it's still a relaxing place for a long, easy walk.

## Salmon River Bridge

Cross the bridge for which this village, 13 kilometers east of Musquodoboit Harbour, is named and you reach a neat little lodge nestled between a forested hill and the river. Dating to 1850 and operating as a guesthouse since 1920, **Salmon River House Country Inn** (9931 Hwy. 7, 902/889-3353 or 800/565-3353, www.salmonriverhouse.com) has seven guest rooms ($108–144 s or d), all with en suite bathrooms and some with water views, and a riverfront cottage ($144) with a fireplace. Part of the inn is the **Lobster Shack** (Apr.–Nov. daily 8 A.M.–9 P.M.), a seafood restaurant with seats that spill outside to a large riverfront

© ANDREW HEMPSTEAD

Salmon River House Country Inn is one of the best-located lodgings along the Marine Drive.

deck. Lobsters kept in the tank are often larger than five pounds, but there's a wide choice of other seafood, including supercreamy lobster chowder.

Drive three kilometers beyond Salmon River Bridge and then four kilometers north to reach ◖ **Webber Lakeside Park** (Upper Lakeville, 902/845-2340 or 800/589-2282, www.webber-slakesideresort.com), which is filled with fun things to do such as lake swimming, a floating dock, canoe and boat rentals, a playground, and a games room with table tennis. The two-bedroom cottages ($145 s or d) have kitchens and wide decks, and the campground (mid-May–mid-Oct.; $25–34) has full hookups and hot showers. Being just an hour's drive from Halifax, this place fills up every summer weekend, so you'll need reservations.

### Oyster Pond

Turn south off Highway 7 just beyond Salmon River Bridge to visit the small but interesting **Fisherman's Life Museum** (58 Navy Pool Loop, 902/889-2053; June–mid-Oct. Mon.–Sat. 9:30 A.M.–5:30 P.M., Sun. 1–5:30 P.M.; adult $3.25, senior and child $2.25). Rather than a collection of artifacts, this museum within a small homestead re-creates the life of a fisherman, his wife, and their 13 children who lived a simple self-sufficient lifestyle.

### Clam Harbour Provincial Park and Vicinity

This park along the south-facing side of Clam Bay protects a long stretch of hard white sand. The beach has supervised swimming in summer, as well as change rooms and picnic areas, but no camping (from the end of the access road, turn right to reach the nicest picnic area, where tables are nestled in windswept coastal forest).

Members of the Murphy family have lived in Murphy Cove for seven generations, involved through time in everything from rum-running to fishing. Now they operate ◖ **Murphy's Camping on the Ocean** (291 Murphy's Rd., 902/772-2700; mid-May–mid-Oct.), which sprawls across a grassy headland. The campground has all the usual facilities—showers,

boat and kayak rentals, a laundry, a playground, and more—but it's Brian's evening storytelling, boat tours (two hours for $17.50), clam-digging trips, and free mussel bakes that make this place stand apart. Tent camping is $20, hookups $25, or rent trailers for $75 s or d.

## TANGIER

Tangier is best known for the smokehouse of ◖ **J. Willy Krauch and Sons** (signposted off Hwy. 7, Tangier, 902/772-2188; Mon.–Fri. 8 A.M.–6 P.M., Sat.–Sun. 10 A.M.–6 P.M.), whose smoked salmon you'll find in better restaurants throughout the province. Willy Krauch was a Danish immigrant who settled in Tangier in the 1950s. Following a Scandinavian recipe that Krauch's sons still use, the fish is cold-smoked (salted and then smoked at low temperatures for one week), creating a divine-tasting treat of the most delicate texture. The smokehouse's retail shop stocks smoked salmon, mackerel, and eel, ready to eat or packed to travel. If you've planned well by bringing crackers and cheese from the city, stop by for a selection of salmon and continue to Taylor Head Provincial Park for a seafood snack by the seaside.

**Coastal Adventures** (84 Mason's Point Rd., 902/772-2774, www.coastaladventures .com) pushes off into the cove on full-day kayak excursions that include a visit to uninhabited islands; $110 per person includes lunch. Kayak rentals are $50 per day for a single and $75 for a double. The same people operate ◖ **Paddler's Retreat Bed and Breakfast** ($50–80 s, $55–75 d), which is an excellent spot to plan to spend one and more nights. Most guests staying in this restored 1860s fisherman's home do so as part of a kayaking instruction package or before or after participating in a day trip. Three of the four rooms share bathrooms while the fourth has an en suite bathroom and private entrance. Rates include a full breakfast.

## TANGIER TO SHERBROOKE
◖ **Taylor Head Provincial Park**

Turn off at Spry Bay, 15 kilometers beyond Tangier, to reach this interesting ocean park protecting a narrow peninsula extending six

Psyche Cove, Taylor Head Provincial Park

kilometers to Taylor Head. The west-facing side of the spit is rugged and windswept, with stunted white spruce trees clinging precariously to the rocky ground, while the east side is characterized by sandy coves lapped by calm waters. A five-kilometer unpaved road from Highway 7 hugs the west side of the peninsula before crossing to protected Psyche Cove. At the end of the road is a series of small parking lots with beach access. You can walk along the beach back toward the mainland to Bob Bluff or head in the opposite direction to a headland with sweeping views up and down the peninsula and of island-dotted Mushaboom Harbour. Taylor Head itself is four kilometers from the end of the road. If you return via rocky Spry Bay, you'll have walked 10 kilometers (allow four hours).

## Spry Bay to Liscomb Mills

Marine Drive between Spry Bay and Liscomb Mills passes a string of fishing villages with delightful names such as Ecum Secum (a Mi'Kmaq word of unknown origin) and Spanish Ship Bay (named for a nearby headland that resembles a Spanish galleon). Linked to Highway 7 by a short bridge, Sober Island's name has a more cynical origin (the first residents bemoaned the lack of alcohol).

In Liscomb Mills, **Liscombe Lodge** (Hwy. 7, 902/779-2307 or 877/375-6343, www.signatureresorts.com; mid-May–late Oct.; from $170 s or d) boasts an idyllic setting along the Liscomb River. Amenities include an indoor pool, sauna, hot tubs, a fitness center, hiking trails, tennis courts, a marina with boat, canoe, and fishing-equipment rentals, and a comfortable dining room overlooking the river.

## SHERBROOKE

Highway 7 leaves the coast at Liscomb, turning north to Sherbrooke, from where Highway 7 continues north to Antigonish and the Marine Drive spurs east, continuing along the Eastern Shore as Highway 316. Sherbrooke (pop. 400) was founded at the farthest navigable point of the St. Mary's River in the early 1800s. By 1869 gold had been discovered in the area, and the town was booming. In addition to mining, mills were established to process lumber

historic Sherbrooke Village

for export, and local farms depended on the town for services. But by 1890 the gold rush was over, and the population began slipping.

## Sherbrooke Village

By the late 1960s Sherbrooke was a shadow of its former self. Gold rush–era buildings remained in varying states of disrepair, but the only visitors were anglers chasing salmon along the river. At this point, a local trust stepped in, and under the guidance of the Nova Scotia Museum an ambitious restoration project took place. Today, Sherbrooke Village (902/522-2400; June–mid-Oct. daily 9:30 A.M.–5 P.M.; adult $10, senior $8, child $4.25) is a unique historical setting, comprising more than 80 restored buildings that are integrated with the town itself. About 20 buildings are open to the public, including an ambrotype photography studio, the colonnaded courthouse, a jail, a water-powered sawmill, the Sherbrooke Hotel, a drug store, a blacksmith shop, a church, and a farmyard. The site is brought alive by costumed interpreters who wander the village streets, tend to their crops, and go about operating each business as folks would have done in the late 1800s. To fully immerse yourself in the experience, consider participating in the Hands on History program (July–Aug. only). For $30 per person, the costume department will dress you in period clothing, and you can spend the day helping in the kitchens, trying your hand at pottery, or learning skills from the blacksmith. The Courthouse Concert Series (888/743-7845 or check the schedule at www .sherbrookenow.ca) takes place 2–3 nights a week through the summer season; entertainment varies from traditional Celtic *ceilidhs* to musical comedies. Starting time is usually around 7:30 P.M. The main parking lot and entrance are off Court Street (turn left at the end of the modern-day main street).

### Accommodations and Food

For overnight stays, Sherbrooke offers several choices. **St. Mary's River Lodge** (21 Main St., 902/522-2177, www.riverlodge.ca; Apr.–Dec.; $75–106 s or d) is across the road from the river and steps from Sherbrooke Village. It has seven guest rooms, each with an en suite bathroom. A cooked breakfast is included in the rates. On the east side of town, a 10-minute walk from the village, is **Sherbrooke Village Inn** (7975 Hwy. 7, 902/522-2235 or 866/522-3818, www .sherbrookevillageinn.ca; May–Oct.). The medium-size motel rooms are plain but comfortable ($80 s, $95–100 d) and self-contained units are $110 s or d.

In the Sherbrooke Hotel, within the historical village, the **What Cheer Tea Room** (June–mid-Oct. daily 11 A.M.–9 P.M.) is a countrified restaurant with friendly staff and basic but tasty dishes that will set you up for more historical sightseeing. You can try traditional rural dishes such as Acadian chicken pot pie ($14), or big city favorites such as a veggie burger on focaccia ($9). **Sherbrooke Village Inn Restaurant** (7975 Hwy. 7, 902/522-2235, www.sherbrookevillageinn.ca; May–Oct. daily 7:30 A.M.–9 P.M.) is a small wood-paneled restaurant on the east (Halifax) side of town. The emphasis is on simple presentations of local seafood. You could start with fish chowder ($5.50) and then choose between dishes such as deep-fried scallops and strip loin ($20) or a lobster from the tank (usually around $25). The homemade pie with ice cream (it was blueberry the night I visited) is $6.

## SHERBROOKE TO CANSO

It's only a little more than 100 kilometers between Sherbrooke and Canso, but the drive will take at least two hours, plus any time you wait for the ferry at Country Harbour.

### Nova Scotia Lighthouse Interpretive Centre

There could be no better location for a lighthouse display than in a restored light-keeper's home at the end of a windswept, often fog-enshrouded peninsula—which is exactly where this museum (Lighthouse Rd., Port Bickerton, 902/364-2000; mid-June–Sept. daily 10 A.M.–8 P.M.; adult $2) is situated. Built in 1901 and deactivated in 1962, the two-building complex, originally **Point Bickerton Lighthouse,** now holds a display describing the lonely life of Nova Scotian light-keepers and their families, the original foghorn, and a directory of Nova Scotia's lighthouses. Stairs lead to an observation tower. Outside, a trail leads past clumps of tasty blueberries and cranberries to a sandy beach. From the turn-off in Port Bickerton, 25 kilometers beyond Sherbrooke and seven kilometers before the ferry across Country Harbour, it's three kilometers to the interpretive center, the last two along an unpaved road.

## Country Harbour

The Country Harbour ferry, along Highway 316 seven kilometers north of Port Bickerton, departs the east side (Halifax side) of the bay on the half hour and the west side on the hour. During the laughably named "rush hour" (9–10 A.M. and 5–6 P.M.), ferries operate more frequently. The ferry has room for just 12 passenger vehicles or a limited number of trucks and RVs. The fare is $5 (cash only), which is paid to the attendant upon loading. From the west side of the bay, it's 86 kilometers to Canso. Aside from the short detour to Tor Bay, it's worth slowing down to admire the village of Issacs Harbour, which on a calm day is reflected across the bay of the same name from Goldboro.

## Tor Bay

Named for granite knolls that dot the region, Tor Bay is lined by three small communities established by Acadians after their deportation by the English in 1755. For visitors, the highlight is **Tor Bay Provincial Park,** on an isthmus along a peninsula that forms the southern boundary of the bay. This small day-use park encompasses one of the few sandy beaches this far east along the Marine Drive. A boardwalk leads to the beach, from where a short trail leads to a rocky headland where covered interpretive boards describe the geology that led to the creation of the beach.

## CANSO

The remote town of Canso, 320 kilometers along Marine Drive from Halifax, is the jumping-off point to an interesting historic site that

After a century of guiding shipping, Port Bickerton Lighthouse is now a museum.

protects Canada's oldest fishing village. In more recent times, Canso was an important link in trans-Atlantic communications. The most striking reminder of this era is the 1884 **Hazel Hill Cable Station,** just before town. It was from here that the distress signal from the sinking *Titanic* and news of the 1929 stock market crash were transmitted to the rest of the world.

## ( Canso Islands National Historic Site

Archaeological digs point to European settlement as early as the 1500s on this small island one kilometer offshore from Canso. Their time on the island was only temporary, and no obvious signs of this era remain today. Two hundred years later, the French and British were fighting for control of North America, with ownership of the Canso Islands in dispute even after the signing of the Treaty of Utrecht in 1713. In 1718 the French were displaced, and the same year, fearing a reprisal attack by the French, the British built a small fort on Grassy Island to protect access to cod stocks that were being harvested at the amazing rate of 10 million pounds per year. Grassy Island grew into a prosperous community, complete with wealthy merchants who built solid stone homes. The village was destroyed by a French invasion from Louisbourg in 1744 and was never rebuilt.

The site comprises a visitors center (Union St., 902/366-3136; June–mid-Sept. daily 10 A.M.–6 P.M.; $5 donation) on the Canso waterfront and the island itself. Mainland exhibits include a scale model of the settlement, fragments of French pottery dated to the early 1700s, and a short documentary. Boats run on demand between the visitors center and the island. Once safety regulations are described, the small craft is off, and you'll be on the island within 15 minutes. A mowed trail passes eight information boards describing the settlement and what remains—cellar pits, mounds of rubble from residences, and terraced vegetable plots—before looping back down to the dock. Allow around 30 minutes to walk the trail. If visitation is slow, the boat will be waiting at

© ANDREW HEMPSTEAD

**Not much remains of early settlements at Canso Islands National Historic Site, but what does is a poignant reminder of the past.**

the wharf for your return; otherwise, expect a wait of up to 30 minutes while it transports more visitors across. The only services on the island are pit toilets and a shelter, so bring warm clothes and water. The suggested donation to the visitors center includes the boat ride to the island.

## Stan Rogers Folk Festival

On the first weekend of July, the population of Canso increases 10 times as music fans descend on the town for "Stanfest" (888/554-7826, www.stanfest.com), a folk-music festival of 50 acts from around the world performing on six stages. In addition to the music, there are a food fair, craft show, and beer garden. Most visitors camp at the Acoustic Campground, set up by the organizers within walking distance of the main stage. Other temporary campgrounds take the overflow, with shuttle buses running to the grounds and to showers at the local high school. A camping pass is $60 and entry to the concert is $100 for the entire weekend.

## Accommodations and Camping

Canso is most definitely not a tourist town. The **Last Port Motel** (Hwy. 16, 902/366-2400) is just before town. It offers basic rooms in the $60–70 range as well as a restaurant open daily at 7 A.M. A much better option is ❰ **DesBarres Manor Inn** (90 Church St., 902/533-2099, www.desbarres-manor.com; $199–259 s or d), 56 kilometers east in Guysborough. Dating to 1837, the three-story inn has been beautifully restored, and the grounds remain in immaculate shape. The 10 guest rooms are stylish and come with niceties like 600-thread-count sheets on super-comfortable mattresses, plus luxurious bathrooms. Rates include a gourmet continental breakfast, with dinner available with advance reservations.

Ten kilometers before Canso along Highway 16 is **Seabreeze Campground and Cottages** (230 Fox Island Rd., Fox Island, 902/366-2352; mid-May–mid-Oct.), where modern facilities, full hookups, and views across Chedabucto Bay keep the 51 campsites full through July and August. One- and two-bedroom cottages ($90 and $110 respectively) have basic cooking facilities, a lounge area with TV, and separate bedrooms. Other resort amenities include coin-operated showers, a laundry, firewood sales, a playground, canoe rentals, and even a lobster pound (where you can buy live lobster).

## Food

You can get a meal in the restaurant at the **Last Port Motel** (Hwy. 16, 902/366-2400; daily 7 A.M.–10 P.M.), but a better choice is **Canso Rose Family Restaurant** (20 Telegraph St., 902/366-2189; daily from 8 A.M.), a sparsely decorated but cheerful room attached to the local pharmacy. A cooked breakfast is just $6, *including* coffee, while the rest of the day fish cakes with baked beans is $6, fish-and-chips is $9, and a chicken stir fry is $11.

## Information

**Whitman House** (1297 Union St., 902/366-2170; June–Sept. daily 9 A.M.–5 P.M.; donation), a handsome three-story 1885 house with displays illustrating local history, doubles as an information center.

# CAPE BRETON ISLAND

"I have traveled around the globe," wrote Alexander Graham Bell, perhaps Cape Breton Island's most renowned transplant. "I have seen the Canadian and American Rockies, the Andes and the Alps, and the Highlands of Scotland; but for simple beauty, Cape Breton outrivals them all."

Linked to the mainland by a two-lane causeway, nearly every coastal and inland backcountry road on the western half of the island leads eventually to the Cabot Trail, the scenic highway rimming the unforgettable landscape of northwestern Cape Breton. The 294-kilometer route of steep ascents, descents, and hold-your-breath switchbacks has no official beginning or end, nor, unlike every other highway in the province, is it numbered. From the south, enter the route from Highway 395 near Whycocomagh or from Exit 7 of the TransCanada Highway, eight kilometers west of Baddeck. The latter option is most scenic, passing through the Margaree River Valley.

In the far northern part of the island, magnificent Cape Breton Highlands National Park stretches from coast to coast, as wild and remote as the Highlands of Scotland. Green, steeply pitched highlands begin at the sea in the south and sweep north, cut by salmon-filled rivers. As the elevation increases, the Acadian and boreal forests give way to a taiga tableland of windswept stunted trees.

The Northumberland Strait opens into the Gulf of St. Lawrence on the western coast, while the Atlantic washes the opposite shore. The 1,098-square-kilometer Bras d'Or Lakes forms the island's heart. The saltwater "Arm of

# HIGHLIGHTS

**Glenora Distillery:** Tucked into a quiet glen along the remote west coast is North America's only single-malt whiskey distillery, complete with a restaurant and guest rooms for those looking to linger longer (page 160).

**Alexander Graham Bell National Historic Site:** Dedicated to one of the world's most prolific inventors, this museum will interest all ages (page 161).

**Boat Tours on Bras d'Or Lakes:** Sail back in time aboard Alexander Graham Bell's beautiful yacht *Elsie* (page 163).

**Driving the Cabot Trail:** This spectacular 300-kilometer circuit traverses varying landscapes, but the highlight is the section through Cape Breton Highlands National Park – the main reason for visiting the island (page 168).

**Golfing Highland Links:** Where else can you walk the fairways of one of the world's finest golf courses knowing that what you've paid to play is less than at many regular city courses (page 172)?

**Gaelic College of Celtic Arts and Crafts:** No, you don't need to sign up for a course. Instead, take in music recitals and demonstrations such as weaving (page 174).

**Celtic Colours International Festival:** Hosted at venues across Cape Breton Island, this October festival draws crowds for the opportunity to enjoy traditional music while soaking up the colors of fall (page 175).

**Fortress of Louisbourg National Historic Site:** It may be a little off the tourist path, but sprawling across 10 hectares of a remote headland is a reconstruction of a French town destroyed by the British 250 years ago (page 178).

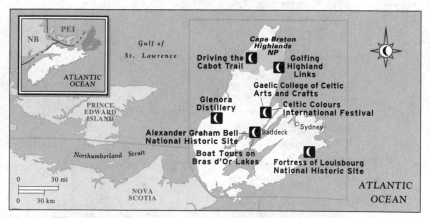

LOOK FOR **(** TO FIND RECOMMENDED SIGHTS, ACTIVITIES, DINING, AND LODGING.

NOVA SCOTIA

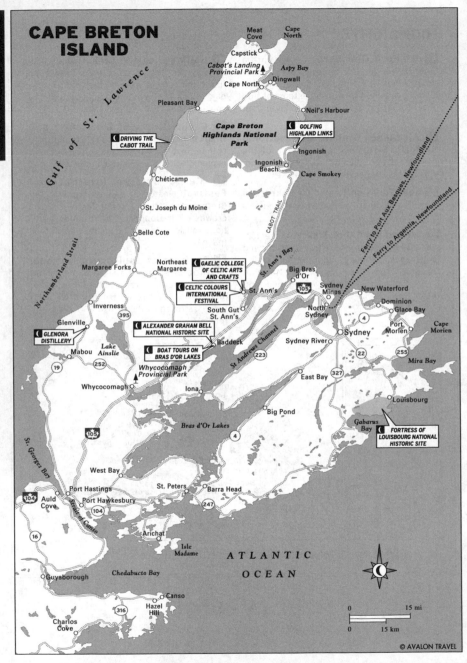

# CAPE BRETON ISLAND

Gulf of St. Lawrence

Meat Cove
Cape North
Capstick
*Cabot's Landing Provincial Park*
Aspy Bay
Cape North
Dingwall
Pleasant Bay
Neil's Harbour

☾ **DRIVING THE CABOT TRAIL**

*Cape Breton Highlands National Park*

☾ **GOLFING HIGHLAND LINKS**

Ingonish
Ingonish Beach
Cape Smokey

Chéticamp

St. Joseph du Moine

CABOT TRAIL

Belle Cote

Northumberland Strait

Margaree Forks

Northeast Margaree

☾ **GAELIC COLLEGE OF CELTIC ARTS AND CRAFTS**

☾ **CELTIC COLOURS INTERNATIONAL FESTIVAL**

St. Ann's
St. Ann's Bay

Big Bras d'Or

105

Sydney Mines

New Waterford

Ferry to Port Aux Basques, Newfoundland
Ferry to Argentia, Newfoundland

Inverness
395

South Gut St. Ann's

North Sydney

Dominion
Glace Bay
Port Morien
Cape Morien

Glenville

☾ **ALEXANDER GRAHAM BELL NATIONAL HISTORIC SITE**

Baddeck

St. Andrews Channel

Sydney River
Sydney

4

☾ **GLENORA DISTILLERY**

Mabou

*Lake Ainslie*

☾ **BOAT TOURS ON BRAS D'OR LAKES**

223

22

255

Mira Bay

19
252

*Whycocomagh Provincial Park*

327

East Bay

Whycocomagh

Iona

Big Pond

Louisbourg

St. Georges Bay

105

*Bras d'Or Lakes*

4

Gabarus Bay

☾ **FORTRESS OF LOUISBOURG NATIONAL HISTORIC SITE**

West Bay

Port Hastings

St. Peters

Barra Head

104

Auld Cove

Strait of Canso

Port Hawkesbury

104

247

16

Arichat

Isle Madame

**ATLANTIC OCEAN**

Guysborough

*Chedabucto Bay*

0        15 mi

0        15 km

316

Canso

Hazel Hill

Charlos Cove

© AVALON TRAVEL

Gold," though barely influenced by tidal cycles, is an inland arm of the Atlantic consisting of a sapphire-blue main lake with numerous peripheral channels, straits, and bays.

## PLANNING YOUR TIME

Although you can fly into the airport at Sydney, most visitors drive to Cape Breton from Halifax, reaching the causeway linking the island to the mainland in less than four hours. From the causeway, a choice of routes present themselves, including the little-traveled route up the west coast, which passes the **Glenora Distillery.** The geographic and tourist hub is Baddeck. Plan to spend at least one full day at this resort town, which is enough time to visit the **Alexander Graham Bell National Historic Site** and take a **boat tour on Bras d'Or Lakes.** Baddeck is also a good starting point for beginning the **Cabot**

**Trail,** a 300-kilometer highway that loops through the wilderness of **Cape Breton Highlands National Park.** The park scenery is the highlight of the drive, but along the way, plan on browsing the **arts and crafts of Chéticamp** and **golfing at Highland Links.** If your travels correspond with the October **Celtic Colours International Festival,** plan on taking in as many concerts as you can. At other times of the year, St. Ann's **Gaelic College of Celtic Arts and Crafts** is the place to immerse yourself in Celtic culture. To hit all the highlights—those detailed above—you should allow yourself at the very least three days from Halifax, but preferably four or five. The main reason for veering from the Cabot Trail is to visit the **Fortress of Louisbourg,** a lesser-known but impressive attraction that re-creates a French town from the mid-1700s.

# Port Hastings to Baddeck

Canso Causeway, easily reached in four hours from Halifax, links Cape Breton to the mainland. From this point, Highways 104 and 105 (the TransCanada) and Highway 19 fan out across the island from here. Highway 19 follows the west coast up to Mabou and Inverness, and then links up with the Cabot Trail in the Margaree Valley. The TransCanada Highway lies straight ahead, leading through the center of the island to Baddeck and on to Sydney. The endless stream of buses packed with tourists makes a beeline along this route, connecting with the Cabot Trail at Baddeck. Highway 4 branches off to the east (or take the more direct Highway 104 for the first 28 kilometers), passing the turnoff to Isle Madame, and then following Bras d'Or Lakes, en route to Sydney.

## PORT HASTINGS

The main reason to stop in Port Hastings, the gateway town to Cape Breton Island, is to load up with brochures at the well-stocked **Nova**

**Scotia Visitor Information Centre,** on the right as the TransCanada Highway crosses to the island (902/625-4201; May–Dec. daily 9 A.M.–5 P.M.). Behind the center, views extend back across to the mainland, and information boards describe the processes involved in constructing the causeway.

### Accommodations

Through town toward Port Hawkesbury, **EconoLodge MacPuffin Motel** (Hwy. 4, 902/625-0621 or 800/867-2212, www.macpuffin.com; Apr.–late Dec.; $89–149 s or d) has 46 air-conditioned rooms, each with comfortable beds, coffeemakers, and high-speed Internet access. Bonuses include an indoor pool, playground, fitness room, and free breakfast.

## ISLE MADAME

Take Highway 104 for 30 kilometers east from Port Hastings, and then Highway 320 south over Lennox Passage Bridge to reach this

© ANDREW HEMPSTEAD

Arichat Church, Isle Madame

43-square-kilometer island. Settled by French fishermen in the early 1700s, this was one of the first parts of the province to be settled, and it's one of the oldest fishing ports in North America. Isle Madame has four main communities—**Arichat, West Arichat, Petit Grat,** and **D'Escousse.**

The wooded island is a popular weekend getaway, with two provincial parks (**Lennox Passage** to the north and **Pondville Beach** on the east side) and plenty of picnicking, swimming, and vista spots. In Arichat, on the waterfront, **LeNoir Forge Museum** (902/226-9364; May–Sept. daily 10 A.M.–6 P.M.; donation) is a restored working 18th-century forge open to visitors.

**L'Auberge Acadienne Inn** (High Rd., Arichat, 902/226-2200, www.acadienne .com) is designed as a 19th-century Acadian-style inn, with eight inviting rooms, one with a jetted tub, in the main building ($105 s, $115 d) and nine adjacent motel units ($85 s, $95 d). The dining room serves Acadian dishes in a casual country-style atmosphere.

## BRAS D'OR LAKES SCENIC DRIVE

It's an easy two-hour drive (148 kilometers) from the Canso Causeway to Sydney via Highway 4 along the southeastern shore of Bras d'Or Lakes. The highway steers away from the lake until passing St. Peters, with nearby **Dundee Resort** (902/345-2649 or 800/565-1774, www.capebretonresorts.com; mid-May–Oct.), a destination in itself. The resort, 12 kilometers from Highway 4, is set on 223 hectares overlooking Bras d'Or Lakes. It features an 18-hole golf course (greens fees $55), an outdoor pool, a marina with all manner of watercraft for rent, an Arcade Activities Centre, summer programs for the kids, and a restaurant. Motel rooms, most with balconies, range $139–199, while cottages with limited cooking facilities and up to three bedrooms are $129–219.

### St. Peters and Vicinity

This small town lies 12 kilometers beyond the

turnoff to Isle Madame and 55 kilometers from Port Hastings.

Photography buffs should check out the **MacAskill House Museum** (7 MacAskill Dr., 902/535-2531; mid-June–Sept. daily 10 A.M.–6 P.M.; donation), in the restored childhood home of Wallace MacAskill, one of the world's preeminent marine photographers. The museum exhibits a collection of his best photographs as well as historic cameras.

Overlooking Bras d'Or Lakes, 1.5 kilometers east of St. Peters, **Joyce's Motel and Cottages** (tel. 902/535-2404, www.joyces-motel.com; mid-May–mid-Oct.; $65–110 s or d) offers the choice of regular motel rooms or larger one-bedroom cottages. Attractions include a laundry, boating, fishing, and an outdoor swimming pool. **Battery Provincial Park** (off Hwy. 4 1 km east of town, 902/535-3094; mid-June–early Sept.) has hiking trails and ocean views. Rates are $24 for the 52 open, wooded, unserviced campsites.

## Big Pond

From St. Peters, the run to Sydney takes a little more than an hour, with Highway 4 paralleling Bras d'Or Lakes for much of the way. A good halfway-point lunch stop is **Rita's,** in a converted schoolhouse at Big Pond (902/828-2667; summer daily 9 A.M.–7 P.M.). Owned by singer Rita MacNeil, who grew up in Big Pond and who continues to promote Cape Breton Island around the world, the café serves her own blend of tea, sandwiches, and salads in a country setting. An adjacent room is devoted to her distinguished career.

## HIGHWAY 19: THE CEILIDH TRAIL

This is the least traveled of the three routes north from the Canso Causeway. Highway 19 hugs the coastline and passes many small villages that haven't changed much in decades. This stretch of coastline is a bastion of Celtic music, hence the nickname Ceilidh Trail. Natalie MacMaster and the Rankins, as well as a new generation of stars headed by

### FIDDLING THE NIGHT AWAY

A *ceilidh* (KAY-lee) was originally an informal gathering, usually on a Friday or Saturday night, that would bring together young people who would dance the night away to lively Celtic music in a local hall. These social gatherings originated in Gaelic-speaking regions of Scotland and Ireland, with the tradition introduced to the New World by immigrants in the 1700s. Although nightclubs and pubs may have replaced the *ceilidh* in popularity in the city, along the west coast of Cape Breton Island and in other rural areas they remain an important part of the social scene. Most important, the music has retained its original roots, with progressive dancing in which the woman moves along a ring from man to man or everyone dancing in formation (similar to line dancing). The most skilled dancers break away from the formations to step dance.

Highway 19 is known as the Ceilidh Trail, and for good reason, as *ceilidhs* take place in towns and villages along the route year-round. Everyone is welcome, with many of the summer events especially tailored for visitors. At Mabou, the Mabou Community Hall fills with the sound of fiddle music every Tuesday through summer while the following night, the foot-stomping fun happens down the road at the local museum. Passing through on Thursday? Then plan for a lively evening of entertainment at the Inverness Fire Hall *ceilidh*.

Christine Crowley, were all born and raised in the area.

### Mabou

A 60-kilometer drive north up Highway 19 from the Canso Causeway, the town of Mabou (pop. 400) is the center of Gaelic education in Nova Scotia (the language is taught in the local school) and the location of Our Lady of Seven Sorrows Pioneers Shrine. The Mabou

Gaelic and Historical Society Museum, or **An Drochaid** (902/945-2311; July–Aug. daily 9 A.M.–5 P.M.) focuses on crafts, local music and poetry, genealogical research, and Gaelic culture.

The Mabou Mines area, near the coast, has some excellent hiking trails into a roadless section of the **Mabou Highlands.**

## ( Glenora Distillery

The Glenora Inn and Distillery (Glenville, 9 km north of Mabou, 902/258-2662 or 800/839-0491, www.glenoradistillery.com; mid-June–Oct.), is North America's only single-malt whiskey distillery (it can't be called Scotch whiskey as it's not from Scotland). The final product is marketed as Glen Breton Rare, with 250,000 liters distilled annually. Built in 1990 using impressive post-and-beam construction and traditional copper pots for the distilling process, the complex is open for tours through summer on the hour 9 A.M.–5 P.M. The cost is $7 per person. Better still, it's also a country inn with nine comfortable rooms ($155–170) and six spacious log chalets ($205–295). Also at the distillery is **Glenora Dining Room and Pub** (daily 7–9 A.M., 11 A.M.–3 P.M., and 5–10 P.M.), which serves light breakfasts and hearty lunches and dinners, the latter two accompanied by live Celtic music.

## Inverness

This Scottish settlement (pop. 2,000), the largest town along Highway 19, has decent beaches and the **Inverness Miners' Museum** (62 Lower Railway St., 902/258-2097; June–Sept. Mon.–Sat. 9 A.M.–7 P.M.; adult $2, child $1), which focuses on the region's mining history.

Ten kilometers north of Inverness on Highway 19 is **( MacLeod's Beach Campsite** (Dunvegan, 902/258-2433, www.macleods.com; June 15–Oct. 15), which slopes down to a delightful beach that rarely gets crowded. Amenities include washrooms, showers, fire pits, a store, a launderette, a games room, volleyball, basketball, horseshoes, and more. Tent sites are $25, hookups $28.

# HIGHWAY 105 TO BADDECK

From the Canso Causeway, it's 90 kilometers to Baddeck along Highway 105 (TransCanada Highway). This is the main route north to Sydney and the Cabot Trail.

## Iona

Nine kilometers northeast of Whycocomagh, Highway 223 crosses Little Narrows to Iona, and then follows the shoreline of St. Andrews Channel all the way to Sydney. It's the least traveled of the many up-island highways, but no less interesting than the other options. The route is posted as Bras d'Or Lakes Drive.

Set on 16 hectares overlooking the narrow body of water between Bras d'Or Lakes and St. Andrews Channel, Iona's **Highland Village** (Hwy. 223, 902/725-2272; June–mid-Oct. daily 9:30 A.M.–5:30 P.M.; adult $9, senior $7, child $4) features 10 historic buildings as well as many examples of working farm equipment.

# Baddeck and Vicinity

Baddeck (from *abadak*, or "place near an island," as the Mi'Kmaq called it, referring to Kidston Island just offshore) lies on the misty wooded shore of St. Patrick's Channel, a long inlet of Bras d'Or Lakes. Halfway between the Canso Causeway and Sydney, Baddeck also marks the traditional beginning and ending point for the Cabot Trail.

## SIGHTS AND RECREATION

Many visitors plan a stop in Baddeck for its heritage accommodations and fine dining, but there are also a few things to see and do, including a National Historic Site that everyone should visit.

## Alexander Graham Bell National Historic Site

At the east end of Baddeck (within walking distance of downtown) is Alexander Graham Bell National Historic Site (902/295-2069; June daily 9 A.M.–6 P.M., July–mid-Oct. daily 8:30 A.M.–6 P.M.; adult $7.80, senior $6.55, child $3.90), a tremendously satisfying museum with displays on Bell's life, family, and seemingly inexhaustible curiosity about science. The multimedia exhibits include working models of Bell's first telephones and a full-size reproduction of his speed-record–setting HD-4 hydrofoil, but some of the most interesting displays are information panels describing how Bell's interest in teaching the deaf to speak led

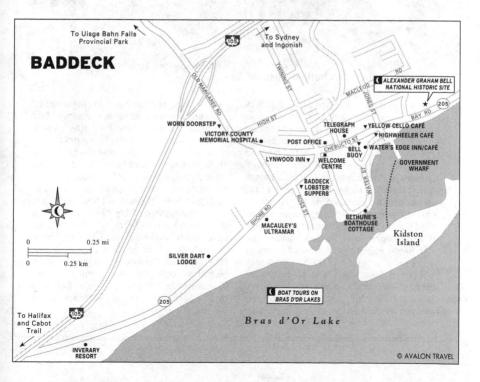

BADDECK

To Uisge Bahn Falls Provincial Park

To Sydney and Ingonish

ALEXANDER GRAHAM BELL NATIONAL HISTORIC SITE

WORN DOORSTEP
VICTORY COUNTY MEMORIAL HOSPITAL
TELEGRAPH HOUSE
YELLOW CELLO CAFÉ
HIGHWHEELER CAFÉ
POST OFFICE
WATER'S EDGE INN/CAFÉ
BELL BUOY
LYNWOOD INN
WELCOME CENTRE
GOVERNMENT WHARF
BADDECK LOBSTER SUPPERS
BETHUNE'S BOATHOUSE COTTAGE
MACAULEY'S ULTRAMAR
Kidston Island
SILVER DART LODGE
BOAT TOURS ON BRAS D'OR LAKES
Bras d'Or Lake
To Halifax and Cabot Trail
INVERARY RESORT

0    0.25 mi
0    0.25 km

© AVALON TRAVEL

NOVA SCOTIA

# ALEXANDER GRAHAM BELL

© ANDREW HEMPSTEAD

**Alexander Graham Bell National Historic Site**

Once a major shipbuilding center, Baddeck claims as its most famous resident not a sailor but an inventor – Alexander Graham Bell. The landscape, language, and people all reminded the Scotsman of his native land. He built a grand summer home, Beinn Bhreagh (Ben Vreeah), across the inlet from Baddeck (it is still owned by his descendents and is not open to the public). While the telephone is his most famous invention, Bell possessed an intellectual curiosity that is almost impossible to comprehend in today's world.

At Beinn Bhreagh, he studied heredity by breeding sheep and seeking to increase twin births. Even when separated from the rest of the world at Baddeck, he maintained friendships in high places – after the attempted assassination of President Gar-field in 1881, Bell was hastily commissioned to invent an electromagnetic device to find the bullet. When his son died after experiencing breathing problems, he developed a breathing device that was the prototype of the iron lungs used to help polio victims. More than anything else, Bell was captivated by flight. He tested propeller-driven kits as early as the 1890s, and in 1909, four years after the Wright Brothers' famous flight, the great inventor took to the air over Bras d'Or Lakes in the **Silver Dart.** But he wasn't done yet: In 1919, at the age of 72, Bell and his estate manager, Casey Baldwin, invented the hydrofoil, which set a water-speed record of more than 70 miles per hour. Bell died three years later and was buried at Beinn Bhreagh.

to the invention of the telephone. The inventor always had a soft spot for children, and the love of the younger generation is reflected in Children's Corner, a large space where kids of all ages can make and decorate kites, do experiments, and generally have fun in an educational environment. Allow at least two hours, more if you have children.

### Kidston Island

A free ferry runs from Government Wharf out to Kidston Island, just 200 meters from the mainland, which has a beach with supervised swimming. The wooded island also has numerous short walking trails, including one that leads to a lighthouse that has been guiding vessels on Bras d'Or Lakes for more than a century. The ferry operates every 20 minutes July–August Monday–Friday 10 A.M.–6 P.M., Saturday–Sunday noon–6 P.M.

### C Boat Tours on Bras d'Or Lakes

Built by Alexander Graham Bell, *Elsie* is a sleek 55-foot yacht that has spent its entire life sailing the calm waters of Bras d'Or Lakes. Now operated by Cape Breton Resorts (902/295-3500 or 800/565-5660), *Elsie* sails mid-June to mid-October daily at 10:30 A.M. and 2:30 P.M. from the Inverary Resort marina on the south side of town. The trips last three hours and cost $65 per person.

A less expensive option (adult $25, child $10) are 90-minute trips aboard *Amoeba* (902/295-2481), a 67-foot concrete-hulled yacht built by the current owner's father during a 10-year period. Departures are from Government Wharf three or four times daily mid-May through mid-October. In addition to enjoying the lake, you'll pass Alexander Graham Bell's estate and often spot bald eagles perched atop shoreline trees.

## ACCOMMODATIONS AND CAMPING
### $50-100

Owned by the same family for five generations, **Telegraph House** (479 Chebucto St., 902/295-1100 or 888/263-9840; $80–119 s or d) combines basic rooms in the grandly historic

original 1861 home with a row of modern motel units. The lodge has two historic links of note—it was once home to a telegraph office that sent some of the first trans-Atlantic messages, and Alexander Graham Bell was a frequent guest. The room that Bell called his own looks exactly like it would have in the 1880s ($109 s or d); others have been given a modern look while retaining the historic feel through antique furnishings. Amenities include a library, a sitting room, and a dining room open daily for breakfast, lunch, and dinner. Telegraph House is also one of the few downtown accommodations open year-round.

Don't expect room service at the delightful **Bethune's Boathouse Cottage** (49 Water St., 902/295-2687; mid-May–mid-Oct.; $90–110), a converted boathouse that enjoys a waterfront location with gardens that extend to the water's edge. The cottage has a separate bedroom, bathroom, TV, outdoor barbecue, and a dock where a rowboat is tied up for guest use.

### $100-150

A 10-minute walk from town, the C **Worn Doorstep** (43 Old Margaree Rd., 902/295-1997; $115 s or d) has four delightful en suite rooms, each with a private entrance, air-conditioning, basic cooking facilities, and a TV. Rates include breakfast delivered to your room.

**Water's Edge Inn** (22 Water St., 902/295-3600 or 866/439-2528, www.thewatersedgeinn.com; May–mid-Oct.; $140–170 s or d) is across the road from the lake and also within easy walking distance of downtown restaurants. Four of the six rooms have lake views and private balconies. All six are heritage-themed yet stylishly outfitted with modern touches such as air-conditioning and TV/DVD combos. The in-house café is also highly recommended.

Named for Alexander Graham Bell's famous airplane, **Silver Dart Lodge** (257 Shore Rd., 902/295-2340 or 800/565-8439, www.silverdartlodge.com; mid-May–mid-Oct.; $135–200 s or d) sits on a 40-hectare hillside overlooking the lake. Amenities include a heated outdoor pool and putting green, as well as lake cruises, boat rentals, a beach, and hiking trails.

Oatcakes and hot drinks (no extra charge) are served for early risers, followed by a buffet breakfast ($12 per person). Picnic lunches are available with notice, and the restaurant is also open for dinner.

Direct water access is a major draw at **( Inverary Resort** (Exit 8 from Hwy. 105, 902/295-3500 or 800/565-5660, www .capebretonresorts.com; May–Nov.; $110–350), a large complex that offers accommodations varying from homely bed-and-breakfast–style rooms to modern two-bedroom suites. Down on the waterfront, rent canoes and kayaks from the activity center, or go for a sailing trip aboard Alexander Graham Bell's yacht *Elsie*. Elsewhere on the grounds are an indoor pool, game rooms, a playground, spa services, two dining rooms, and a pub.

## Campgrounds

**Bras d'Or Lakes Campground** (5 km west of Baddeck on Hwy. 105, 902/295-2329, www .brasdorlakescampground.com; mid-June–Sept.) has 95 unserviced and two-way-hookup sites ($25–39, cabins $59–89 s or d). On Bras d'Or Lakes, it has showers, washrooms, a launderette, Wi-Fi Internet throughout, a pool, and a recreation area.

In the vicinity, **Adventures East Campground** (between Exits 7 and 8 of Hwy. 105, 902/295-2417 or 800/507-2228, www .adventureseast.ca; early June–mid-Oct.; campsites $26–30, cabins $115–140 s or d) has all the necessary amenities—showers, laundry, a pool, fishing, a restaurant, and tours.

## FOOD

Cafés and restaurants line Baddeck's main street, but be aware that most open only through the warmer months, and by mid-October, choices become very limited.

## Casual Dining

For breakfast, sandwiches, pizzas, and light meals, the **( Yellow Cello Cafe** (525 Chebucto St., 902/295-2303; May–Oct. daily 8 A.M.–10:30 P.M.) is centrally located and well priced, with an indoor dining room and

veranda in front. The calzones are delicious, the beer selection is good, and the people-watching can't be beat. Expect a wait in peak summer season, when live musicians grace the small indoor stage.

For the best coffee in town, head to the **Highwheeler Café** (486 Chebucto St., 902/295-3006; May–mid-Oct. daily 6 A.M.–9 P.M.). This café has an in-house bakery, so you know everything is fresh, including inexpensive yet healthy sandwiches made to order.

After a boat tour or a trip to Kidston Island, **Water's Edge Cafe** (22 Water St., 902/295-3600; June–Oct. daily 11 A.M.–5 P.M.) is the perfect place to eat a healthy bite to eat. The *tikka* (chicken curry) is as spicy as it should be and the seafood chowder is as creamy as you'd expect. Almost everything is under $12.

**Lakeside Café** (Exit 8 from Hwy. 105, 902/295-3500; Apr.–Nov. daily from 11 A.M.) is set on the waterfront within the Inverary Resort complex. The food is simple and unsurprising, but the prices are reasonable and the setting a delight when the sun is shining and you find yourself seated at an outdoor table.

**Herring Choker Deli** (Hwy. 105, 902/295-2275; daily 8 A.M.–8 P.M.) overlooks the water from 10 kilometers west of town. Instead of greasy cooked breakfasts, tuck into a scrambled egg, ham, and cheese wrap ($5). The lunchtime highlight is the thick gourmet sandwiches packed with goodies on bread baked each morning.

## Lobster Supper

Lobster suppers originated as local gatherings held in church basements and community halls. Today, they have become a little more commercialized, but they are still a fun and inexpensive way to enjoy this succulent seafood treat. One of the few regularly scheduled in Nova Scotia (Prince Edward Island is a hotbed of lobster suppers) is **Baddeck Lobster Suppers** (Ross St., 902/295-3307; mid-June–mid-Oct. daily 4–9 P.M.). A one- to 1.5-pound lobster with all-you-can-eat chowder, mussels, trimmings, dessert, and nonalcoholic drinks costs $30 per person. Substitute salmon for lobster and pay $21–25.

## Other Restaurants

Watching the sun set over Bras d'Or Lakes from a window table at the **( Bell Buoy Restaurant** (536 Chebucto St., 902/295-2581; mid-May–June daily dinner only, July–mid-Oct. daily lunch and dinner) is worth the price of dinner alone. A menu highlight is the sea-food chowder ($10), which comes chock-full of haddock, salmon, mussels, and even lobster, as well as a slab of homemade oatmeal bread as a side. Mains vary from pastas (from $14) to whole lobsters ($34).

Of many local lodges with dining rooms that welcome nonguests, none is better than the **Lynwood Inn** (24 Shore Rd., 902/295-1995; mid-May–mid-Oct. noon–8:30 P.M.), a grand 1868 home that has been converted into an inn and restaurant. The smallish dining room is tastefully decorated in Victorian-era style. The menu is less expensive than you may imagine, with most seafood mains less than $20.

## INFORMATION AND SERVICES
### Information

At the east end of the main street, the **Baddeck Welcome Centre** (corner Chebucto St. and Shore Rd., 902/295-1911, www.visitbaddeck.com; June–Sept. daily 9 A.M.–5 P.M.) is indeed welcoming. Friendly staff will help out with finding accommodations and, as always, love handing out maps and brochures.

Public Internet access is offered at **Cape Breton Regional Library** (526 Chebucto St., 902/295-2055; Mon.–Fri. 1–5 P.M., Thurs.–Fri. also 6–8 P.M., Sat. 10 A.M.–noon and 1–5 P.M.).

### Services

You'll find a couple of banks with ATMs along Chebucto Street, as well as the local **post office.** For emergencies, dial 911 or **Victoria County Memorial Hospital** (902/295-2112).

## MARGAREE RIVER VALLEY

Eight kilometers west of Baddeck (back toward the Canso Causeway), the Cabot Trail branches off the TransCanada Highway northwest through the hills and into the valley of the Margaree River, a renowned salmon-fishing stream and the namesake of seven small communities.

The peak time for fishing is mid-June to mid-July and September to mid-October; many guides are available locally. Near North East Margaree, **Margaree Salmon Museum** (60 E. Big Intervale Rd., 902/248-2848; mid-June–mid-Oct. daily 9 A.M.–5 P.M.; adult $2, child $1) tells the story of the river and its fishy inhabitants.

### Accommodations

Even though it's away from the ocean, the Margaree River Valley is a popular spot to get away from it all. Near the village of Margaree Valley, **Normaway Inn** (691 Eygpt Rd., 902/248-2987 or 800/565-9463, www.normaway.com; $99–269 s or d) is typical of the many accommodation options. This elegantly rustic 1920s resort is nestled on 100 hectares in the hills. The main lodge has nine guest rooms, and the grounds hold 19 one- and two-bedroom cabins. Activities include nightly films or traditional entertainment, tennis, walking trails, bicycling, weekly barn dances, and fiddling contests. The dining room (open for breakfast and dinner) serves dishes of Atlantic salmon, lamb, scallops, and fresh fruits and vegetables. The Normaway is about 30 kilometers along the Cabot Trail from Highway 105, and then three kilometers along Egypt Road.

On Lake O'Law, **The Lakes Resort** (902/248-2360 or 888/722-2112; May–Oct.; $98–110 s or d) comprises eight two-bedroom cottages overlooking the lake. Each cottage has a bathroom, microwave, living area, and outdoor barbecue. Recreational opportunities include boating, fishing, canoeing, minigolf, and go-karting while the resort restaurant specializes in lobster dinners. To get there, turn off the Cabot Trail at North East Margaree.

# Chéticamp

Along the Cabot Trail 90 kilometers north and then east of Baddeck, Chéticamp is an Acadian fishing village (pop. 1,000) set along a protected waterway that opens to the Gulf of St. Lawrence. Deep-sea fishing and whale-watching charter boats leave from the central Government Wharf, and the entrance to Cape Breton Highlands National Park is five kilometers north of town.

The village was first settled by Acadians expelled from the Nova Scotia mainland in the 18th century. Today, the weeklong **Festival de l'Escaouette,** in early August, celebrates aspects of Acadian culture with a parade, arts and crafts, and music.

## SIGHTS

The first stones for **St. Pierre Catholic Church** were laid in 1893, but it took almost 20 years to finish. Its tower pierces the sky at a height of more than 50 meters and can be seen from far up and down the coast. On the south side of town, the **Acadian Museum** (744 Main St., 902/224-2170; mid-May–mid-June daily 9 A.M.–6 P.M., mid-June–Sept. daily 9 A.M.–9 P.M., Oct. daily 9 A.M.–6 P.M.; donation) displays artifacts from early settler days, with an emphasis on the sheepherding past, including weaving, spinning, and rug-hooking demonstrations.

## RECREATION

At Government Wharf, **Whale Cruisers** (902/224-3376) operates two vessels, the *Whale Cruiser* and the *Bonnie Maureen III,* which take guests out on three-hour whale-watching trips three times daily July to mid-September and less frequently in May, June, and late September. Fare is adult $35, child $15.

One of the major cottage industries of this area is the production of hooked rugs, a craft developed by Acadians centuries ago. In the late 1930s, a group of Chéticamp women formed a rug-hooking cooperative that still

© ANDREW HEMPSTEAD

Each morning, the docks of Chéticamp come alive as crab fishermen begin unloading their catch.

thrives. The Co-op Artisanale de Chéticamp gives demonstrations and displays its wares at the Acadian Museum. You can also see beautiful hooked rugs and tapestries at **Les Trois Pignons** (15584 Main St., 902/224-2612; mid-May–mid-Oct. daily 9 A.M.–5 P.M., the rest of the year weekdays only; adult $5, senior and child $4), a striking red-roofed building at the northern end of Chéticamp (the building also houses the visitors information center).

A number of galleries and shops hereabouts also sell locally produced folk arts—brightly colored, whimsical carvings and paintings of fish, seabirds, fishermen, boats, or whatever strikes the artists' fancy. One kilometer north of the visitors center, the **Sunset Art Gallery** (902/224-2119) features the colorfully painted woodcarvings of William Roach.

## ACCOMMODATIONS

If you're traveling on a budget, a choice of older, inexpensive motels along the main street makes Chéticamp a good base for day trips into Cape Breton Highlands National Park. Best of the bunch is **Fraser's Motel and Cottage** (902/224-2411; mid-May–mid-Oct.; $50–80 s or d), near the main wharf.

Overlooking the ocean a few kilometers south of town, **[** **Chéticamp Outfitters Inn B&B** (13938 Cabot Tr., Point Cross, 902/224-2776; Apr.–mid-Dec.; $60–110 s or d) is a large, modern home with six guest rooms and common areas that include a deck with sweeping ocean views. The less expensive rooms share two bathrooms, while all rates include a full breakfast. The hosts operate a charter fishing business, so this is a good base for anglers.

Behind the main street and linked to the local golf course by a short trail, **Cabot Trail Sea and Golf Chalets** (902/224-1777 or 877/244-1777, ww.seagolfchalets.com; mid-May–mid-Oct.) is a complex of spacious and modern freestanding units, each with a bathroom, kitchen, deck, and barbecue. Rates range $149–299 for up to four people.

## FOOD

At the north end of town, **Hometown Kitchen** (15559 Main St., 902/224-3888; daily from 8 A.M.) is right on the water but doesn't really take advantage of the location. The food is good, though, with generous portions and inexpensive prices. Expect lots of seafood.

Dine at the **[** **Restaurant Acadien** (774 Main St., 902/224-3207; May–Oct. daily 7 A.M.–10 P.M.) for authentic Acadian food: *fricot* (souplike stew), meat pies, fresh fish, blood pudding, and butterscotch pie. Entrées range $12–22. **Evangeline** (15150 Main St., 902/224-2044; daily 6:30 A.M.–midnight) is a family restaurant specializing in homemade soups and meat pies.

## INFORMATION

On the north side of town, **Chéticamp Visitor Information Centre** (15584 Main St., 902/224-2642; mid-May–mid-Oct. daily 9 A.M.–5 P.M.) has information on tours, accommodations, and campgrounds. For national park information, continue north through town to the large visitors center complex.

# Cape Breton Highlands National Park

Protecting a swath of wilderness at the northern tip of Cape Breton Island, this national park is one of the finest in Canada. While outdoor enthusiasts are attracted for opportunities to hike and bike, anyone can enjoy the most spectacular scenery simply by driving the Cabot Trail, which spans the length of the park from Chéticamp in the west to Ingonish in the east.

## The Land

Heath bogs, a dry rocky plateau, and a high taiga 400 meters above sea level mark the interior of the 950-square-kilometer park. Rugged cliffs characterize the seacoast on the west side, where the mountains kneel into the Gulf of St.

Lawrence, and gentler but still wildly beautiful shores define the eastern side. Nova Scotia's highest point, 532-meter White Hill, is simply a windswept hump, far from the nearest road and with no formal access trail reaching it.

Typical Acadian forest, a combination of hardwoods and conifers, carpets much of the region. Wild orchids bloom under the shade of thick spruce, balsam fir, and paper birch. The **Grand Anse River** gorge near MacKenzie Mountain is the Acadian forest's showpiece. Its terrain—with sugar maples, yellow birches, and rare alpine-arctic plants—has been designated an international biological preserve. The park is also a wildlife sanctuary for white-tailed deer, black bears, beavers, lynx, mink,

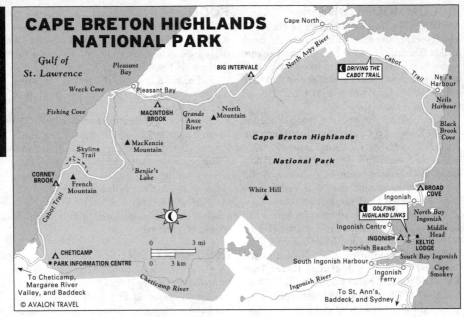

red foxes, snowshoe hare, and more than 200 bird species, including eagles and red-tailed hawks.

## Park Entry

Cape Breton Highlands National Park is open year-round, though campgrounds and the two information centers operate only mid-May–October. A **National Parks Day Pass** is adult $7.80, senior $6.80, child $3.90 to a maximum of $19.60 per vehicle. It is valid until 4 P.M. the day after its purchase. Passes can be bought at both park information centers, Chéticamp and Ingonish campgrounds, or at the two park gates.

## ☾ DRIVING THE CABOT TRAIL

The Cabot Trail extends well beyond park boundaries along its 300-kilometer length, but the most spectacular stretch is undoubtedly the 110 kilometers through the park between Chéticamp and Ingonish. By allowing a full day for the drive, you will have time to

walk a trail or two, stop at the best lookouts, and even head out on a whale-watching trip. This section describes the drive itself, with recreational opportunities discussed below. You can of course follow the Cabot Trail in either direction, but I've laid out the drive from Chéticamp to Ingonish (clockwise), meaning you pass the main park information center at the beginning of the drive and that you're driving on the safer inland side of the road the entire way.

Thousands of outdoor enthusiasts tackle the Cabot Trail under pedal power each summer. The trip is not particularly long, but it is very strenuous in sections, and lack of a wide shoulder can make for some hair-raising moments.

### Chéticamp to Pleasant Bay

Make your first stop out of Chéticamp the **Park Information Centre** (902/224-2306; mid-May–mid-Oct. 9 A.M.–5 P.M., extended July–Aug. 8 A.M.–8 P.M.). Pick up a map, ask about hiking opportunities, browse the natural history displays, and hit the highway. You can pay for park entry here or at the tollgate a little farther up the road.

This is the most impressive stretch of one of the world's most spectacular drives, with the highway clinging to the shoreline and then climbing steeply along oceanfront cliffs to a viewpoint 18 kilometers north of the information center.

## Continuing Around the Cape

From Pleasant Bay, the park's northwestern corner, the highway turns inland and wraps upward to 455-meter-high **French Mountain.** From this point, a level stretch barrels across a narrow ridge overlooking deeply scooped valleys. The road climbs again, this time to **MacKenzie Mountain,** at 372 meters, and then switchbacks down a 10–12 percent grade. Another ascent, to **North Mountain,** formed more than a billion years ago, peaks at 445 meters on a three-kilometer summit. The lookout opens up views of a deep gorge and the North Aspy River.

## Cape North and Vicinity

The northernmost point on the Cabot Trail is Cape North, the name of a small service town (as well as a geographical feature to the north). Here a spur road leads 22 kilometers north to Meat Cove. Although outside the park, this road traverses complete wilderness before reaching the open ocean at St. Lawrence Bay. En route, **Cabot's Landing Provincial Park,** the supposed landing site of English explorer John Cabot, offers a sandy beach on Aspy Bay (good for clam digging) and a picnic area and marks the starting point for hikes up 442-meter-high Sugar Loaf Mountain.

## The East Coast to Ingonish

From Cape North, it's 45 kilometers east and then south to the resort town of Ingonish. Aside from tucking into a seafood feast at Neil's Harbour, you should make time for a stop at **Black Brook Cove.** Backed by a short stretch of beach, the cove is an extremely popular spot for picnicking and swimming. To escape the

© ANDREW HEMPSTEAD

**Black Brook Cove is a protected bay with safe swimming.**

summertime crowd, walk to the north end of the beach and follow the Jack Pine Loop through open coastal forest.

## RECREATION
### Hiking

The park offers 26 established hiking trails, varying from simple strolls shorter than half a kilometer to challenging treks leading to campgrounds more than 20 kilometers away. Many of the trails are level; a few climb to awesome viewpoints. Some hug the rocky shoreline; others explore river valleys. No matter what your abilities may be, you'll be able to enjoy the park at your own speed. For details on hiking in the park, look for the book *Walking in the Highlands,* for sale at Les Amis du Plein Air, the bookstore within the Park Information Centre.

The following hikes have been arranged in a clockwise direction.

On the light side, the self-guiding **Le Buttereau Trail** leads 1.9 kilometers to wildflowers and good bird-watching opportunities.

The trailhead is just north of the park gate north of Chéticamp.

For the more hardy, the seven-kilometer (two hours one-way) **Skyline Loop** climbs a headland, from which the lucky can spot pilot whales; along the way, look for bald eagles, deer, and bears. The trail begins where the Cabot Trail heads inland at French Mountain.

On overcast or wet days, **Benjie's Lake Trail** provides an ideal break from driving. From a trailhead six kilometers beyond the start of the Skyline Loop Trail, this easy walk takes about 30 minutes each way.

Serious backpackers gravitate to the **Fishing Cove Trail** (16 km round-trip), a rugged journey to a campground and beach. You can reach the end of the trail in two hours, but allow at least three for the strenuous return trip back up to the highway.

### Whale-Watching

One of two whale-watching spots in Nova Scotia (the other is the Bay of Fundy), a number of operators depart daily through summer from Pleasant Bay. The region boasts a high success rate when it comes to spotting pilot, humpback, and minke whales, simply because of the high numbers close to the coastline. Tours last about 90 minutes and cost a reasonable $30 per person. Operators based at Pleasant Bay include **Captain Mark's** (902/224-1316 or 888/754-5112) and **Fiddlin' Whale Tours** (866/688-2424). Both have booths along the harbor, but you should book by phone in advance for July and August sailings.

## ACCOMMODATIONS AND CAMPING

As it's a national park, there are no hotel accommodations within the park boundary. Instead, visitors stay at Chéticamp for its Acadian heritage, at Ingonish for its beaches and golfing, or at one of the following choices in between the two.

### Under $50

The only backpacker lodge on Cape Breton Island is **Cabot Trail Hostel** (23349 Cabot Tr.,

902/224-1015; $26 per person), within walking distance of Pleasant Bay, 38 kilometers north of Chéticamp on the park's western side. The facility is small but friendly and comfortable, with 18 dorm beds in two rooms and an adjacent bunkhouse. Guests have use of communal washrooms, two kitchens, a deck with barbecue, and Internet access.

### $100-150

Just more than 40 kilometers north of Chéticamp, the Cabot Trail exits the park for a short distance at Pleasant Bay. Here, the distinctively pink **Midtrail Motel & Inn** (23475 Cabot Tr., 902/224-2529 or 800/215-0411, www.midtrail.com; mid-May–Oct.; from $109 s or d) offers 20 bright but basic motel rooms, some with ocean views, and a family-friendly seafood restaurant.

Set on 25 hectares of oceanfront property, **The Markland** (Dingwell, 902/383-2246 or 800/872-6084, www.marklandresort.com; May–mid-Oct.) is 52 kilometers north of Ingonish (signposted off the Cabot Trail between Cape North and South Harbour). Although it is a resort, the emphasis is on the outdoors, with most guests spending their time on the adjacent beach or lazing around the outdoor pool. Regular rooms go for $149 s or d, and the much larger and private chalets are $249–299. The resort restaurant features the freshest of fresh seafood combined with seasonal produce such as fiddleheads and wild mint.

### Campgrounds

Cape Breton Highlands National Park is the most popular camping destination in Nova Scotia. Parks Canada operates seven campgrounds within the park.

**Chéticamp Campground** (5 km north of Chéticamp) is behind the main park information center. Amenities include showers, flush toilets, kitchen shelters, playgrounds, and an outdoor theater hosting a summer interpretive program. Only some sites have fire pits. Tent sites are $25.50 per night, serviced sites $38.20. Chéticamp Campground is the park's only

© ANDREW HEMPSTEAD

Corney Brook Campground sits right on the ocean.

campground that accepts reservations. Sites can be reserved through the **Parks Canada Campground Reservation Service** (905/426-4648 or 877/737-3783, www.pccamping.ca) for $11 per reservation. If you're traveling in the height of summer and require hookups, this booking system is highly recommended.

Continue north from the park gate for 10 kilometers to ( **Corney Brook Campground** (mid-May–early Oct.; $23.50), which is not much more than a parking lot with 20 designated sites, but it has incredible ocean views that more than make up for a lack of facilities. Beyond Pleasant Bay, the 10 sites at **MacIntosh Brook Campground** (mid-May–early Oct.; $21.50) fill quickly. Ten kilometers farther east is **Big Intervale Campground** (mid-May–early Oct.; $18), also with 10 sites. Neither of these two campgrounds have drinking water. With 256 sites, **Broad Cove Campground** (mid-May–early Oct.; $27.40), on the ocean just north of Ingonish, is the park's largest campground. Campers have use of showers, flush toilets, kitchen shelters, playgrounds, and an outdoor theater. **Ingonish**

**Campground** (late June–early Sept.; $27.40) is within a finger of the park that extends to the ocean along the Ingonish coastline. Although it's close to the resort town of Ingonish, the wooded setting is quiet and private and within walking distance of a sandy beach with safe swimming. It has showers, flush toilets, and kitchen shelters.

## INFORMATION

Turn right as soon as you cross into the park for the excellent **Park Information Centre** (902/224-2306; mid-May–mid-Oct. 9 A.M.–5 P.M., extended July–Aug. 8 A.M.–8 P.M.). It features natural-history exhibits, weather reports, an activities schedule, and helpful staff. Part of the complex is **Les Amis du Plein Air** (902/224-3814), a surprisingly large bookstore with more than 1,000 titles in stock.

Parks Canada also operates a smaller information center in Ingonish for those entering the park from the east. It's open mid-May–mid-October 9 A.M.–5 P.M., extended to 8 A.M.–8 P.M. in July and August.

NOVA SCOTIA

# Ingonish and Vicinity

Ingonish (pop. 500), 110 kilometers east of Chéticamp and 100 kilometers north of Baddeck, is a busy resort center at the eastern entrance to Cape Breton Highlands National Park. The town is a lot more than somewhere simply to rest your head: It is fringed by beautiful beaches, has one of Canada's premier golf courses, and offers a delightful choice of seafood restaurants. Simply put, if you are allowing yourself some rest time on your Nova Scotia travels, this is the place to book two or more nights in the same accommodation.

## SIGHTS AND RECREATION

Ingonish has no official attractions as such. Instead, beach lovers gather on **Ingonish Beach,** where a lifeguard watches over swimmers splashing around in the shallow water that reaches enjoyable temperatures July–August.

Drag yourself away from one of Canada's finest beaches and you'll find the **Freshwater Lake Loop,** a two-kilometer circuit that encircles a shallow lake where beavers can often be seen hard at work in the evening. The trailhead is the parking lot at Ingonish Beach.

Even if you're not a guest at the Keltic Lodge, the grounds are a pleasant place for a stroll. Beyond the end of the lodge access road, a walking trail leads two kilometers to the end of Middle Head Peninsula.

### ◖ Golfing Highland Links

Highland Links (3 km north of Ingonish Beach, 902/285-2600 or 800/441-1118) is generally regarded as one of the world's top 100 golf courses, and relative to other courses of similar reputation the greens fees are a steal—$91 in high season, with twilight rates from just $55. Power carts are an additional $31. The course, which opened in 1939, was designed by Stanley Thompson, the same architect commissioned to design famous courses in Banff and Jasper National Parks.

## ACCOMMODATIONS

Accommodations are spread along the Ingonish coastline, but demand is high in July and August, so book well ahead. Also note the given open dates, as very few places are open year-round.

### $50-100

**Sea Breeze Cottages and Motel** (8 km north of the east park gate, 902/285-2879 or 888/743-4443; mid-Apr.–mid-Dec.) overlooks the ocean and boasts a playground that children will love. Accommodation options include basic motel rooms ($84 s or d) or cottages ($98–140 s or d).

### $100-150

Open year-round, **Ingonish Chalets** (36784 Cabot Tr., Ingonish Beach, 902/285-2008 or

**Highland Links is one of Canada's finest golf courses.**

888/505-0552, www.ingonishchalets.com) has access to the beach and hiking trails. Nine two-bedroom log chalets go for $150 s or d, while five motel-style rooms cost $110. The rooms are furnished in a very woodsy way, with pine paneling extending from the handcrafted furniture to the wall linings. These units also come with basic cooking facilities—microwave, kettle, and so on.

It would be difficult to claim boredom at **◖ Glenghorm Beach Resort** (Ingonish, 902/285-2049 or 800/565-5660, www.glenghormbeachresort.com; May–Oct.; $115–400 s or d), a sprawling complex that extends from the Cabot Trail to a long narrow arc of sand. Things to do include walking along the beach, relaxing around the outdoor pool, renting kayaks and paddling through quiet offshore waters, or working out in the fitness room. There are also lawn games, tennis, volleyball, and bike rentals. At the end of the day, you can relax with a glass of wine in one of the shoreline Adirondack chairs or try a Nova Scotian brew at the resort pub. Accommodation options are motel rooms, older-style cottages (some right by the ocean), and my favorite rooms in all of Cape Breton Island—casual but stylish kitchen-equipped suites with private balconies.

## $150-200

The Cabot Trail has its devoted fans, and so does the **Keltic Lodge** (902/285-2880 or 800/565-0444, www.kelticlodge.ca; mid-May–mid-Oct.; from $180 s or d), on Middle Head Peninsula. The access lane from the Cabot Trail meanders through thick stands of white birches and finishes at the lodge. The long low wood-sided lodge—painted bright white and topped with a bright red roof—is as picturesque as a lord's manor in the Highlands of Scotland. The main lodge has 32 rustic rooms off a comfortable lobby, furnished with overstuffed chairs and sofas arranged before a massive stone fireplace. Another 40 rooms are in the adjacent newer White Birch Inn. In addition, nine cottages with suite-style layouts (nice

Keltic Lodge

© ANDREW HEMPSTEAD

for families) are scattered across the grounds. Well-marked hiking trails meander through the adjacent national park woodlands and ribbon the coastal peninsula. An outdoor pool (a bit chilly), tennis courts, and a spa facility are also available.

Affiliated with one of the region's finest restaurants, **◖ Seascape Coastal Retreat** (36083 Cabot Tr., Ingonish, 902/285-3003 or 866/385-3003, www.seascapecoastalretreat.com; May–mid-Oct.; $229–249 s or d) is suited to couples looking for a quiet getaway in romantic surroundings. Within the walls of this very private resort are 10 wooden cottages, each air-conditioned and with a private deck overlooking the ocean and a separate bedroom. Bathrobes, jetted tubs, and TV/VCR combos add to the appeal. Outside, paths lead through landscaped gardens to an herb garden and courtyard where guests gather in the evening. Rates include a full breakfast and seafood snacks delivered to your door upon arrival.

## FOOD

When the sun is shining, there is no better place in all of Nova Scotia to enjoy fresh seafood than the (  **Muddy Rudder** (38438 Cabot Tr., 902/285-2280; June–Sept. daily 11 A.M.–8 P.M.), a quirky outdoor eatery south of Ingonish Beach. Place your order at the window—crab, clams, lobster, mussels, and more—and the owner simply plunks your order in a big pot of boiling water that balances on a propane burner out front. Most tables are spread out on a grassed area beside the river, while a couple are under a shelter. Expect to pay about $15 for a full crab with a side of coleslaw and a buttered roll.

Occupying a weathered wooden building on the high headland at Neil's Harbour is the (  **Chowder House** (902/336-2463; May–Sept. daily 11 A.M.–8 P.M.). Order at the inside window and wait for your number to be called. Then tuck into creamy clam chowder ($4), fish-and-chips ($8), a lobster burger ($10), or a full crab ($17). Dollar for dollar, you're doing well if you find better value than the food at the always-busy Chowder House.

(  **Seascapes Restaurant** (36083 Cabot Tr., Ingonish, 902/285-3003; May–mid-Oct. daily 6–9 P.M.) is a smart stylish dining room overlooking the ocean. Instead of a menu, a blackboard describes nightly choices, which are dependent on the seafood available. Mains range $18–25.

### Keltic Lodge

The Keltic Lodge (Middle Head Peninsula, 902/285-2880) is home to two very different restaurants. Along the access road is the **Atlantic Restaurant** (mid-May–mid-Oct. daily 11 A.M.–9 P.M.), a big family-style restaurant with seafood for all tastes and budgets. Beer-battered fish-and-chips is $11, grilled salmon is $20, and most mains except the lobster are less than $25. An excellent add-on is the salad bar ($9). The row of tables along the east side have stunning ocean views. The smart-casual **Purple Thistle Dining Room** (late May–mid-Oct. daily 7–10 A.M. and 6–9 P.M.) has one of Nova Scotia's finest reputations,

especially in seafood. Meals are five courses (about $45) rather than à la carte, with an emphasis on lobster in varied creations and other seafood. If you're tooling along Cabot Trail and hope to stop here for dinner, reservations are very wise.

## SOUTH FROM INGONISH

South of Ingonish Beach, the Cabot Trail descends hairpin turns. Stop at 366-meter-high **Cape Smokey** for a picnic or hiking along the cliff top, which has wonderful views. The steep and twisting road finishes in a coastal glide with views of the offshore Bird Islands. Lying off the northwest side of the cape at the mouth of St. Ann's Bay, these two islands are the nesting site of a multitude of seabird species.

## ST. ANN'S

During the 1850s, about 900 of St. Ann's residents, dissatisfied with Cape Breton, sailed away to Australia and eventually settled in New Zealand, where their descendants today make up a good part of the Scottish population. Despite this loss of nearly half its population, St. Ann's, 80 kilometers south of Ingonish and 30 kilometers north of Baddeck, is today the center of Cape Breton's Gaelic culture.

### (  Gaelic College of Celtic Arts and Crafts

The only institution of its kind in North America, the Gaelic College (51779 Cabot Tr., 902/295-3411) was established in 1938. Programs include highland dancing, fiddling, piping, Gaelic language, weaving, and other subjects. The summer session attracts Gaelophiles from around the world. The **Great Hall of the Clans** (July–Aug. daily 9 A.M.–5 P.M.), on the campus, examines the course of Scottish culture and history, including the migrations that brought Highlanders to Cape Breton. Activities include weaving and instrument-making demonstrations, as well as music and dance performances (July–Aug. Mon.–Fri.). The campus gift shop sells a predictable collection of kilts and tartans.

### ◖ Celtic Colours International Festival

This popular festival (902/562-6700 or 877/285-2321, www.celtic-colours.com) takes place the second full week of October. It celebrates Cape Breton's Gaelic heritage through concerts held at venues around the island, but the Gaelic College of Celtic Arts and Crafts is a focal point, especially for its nightly Festival Club, where musicians get together for an unofficial jam after performing elsewhere. The festival proper features six or seven concerts nightly, usually in small town halls, with visitors enjoying the brilliant colors of fall as they travel from venue to venue.

## The Northeast

### SYDNEY

Cape Breton Island's only city is Sydney (pop. 24,000), set around a large harbor on the island's northeast corner. In the early 1800s, it was it was the capital of the colony of Cape Breton, and then at the turn of the 20th century the Sydney area boomed, ranking as one of Canada's major steel production centers.

### Sights

Historic buildings constructed of stone quarried at nearby Louisbourg dot the streets north of downtown. One of these, the 1830 **St. Patrick's Church Museum** (87 Esplanade; June–Aug. daily 9:30 A.M.–5:30 P.M.; donation), is Cape Breton's oldest Roman Catholic sanctuary. **Cossit House** (75 Charlotte St., 902/539-7973; June to mid-Oct. Mon.–Sat. 9:30 A.M.–5:30 P.M., Sun. 1–5:30 P.M.; adult $2, senior and child $1) is almost as old as Sydney itself. The 1787 manse has been restored to its original condition.

© ANDREW HEMPSTEAD

St. Patrick's Church dates to 1830.

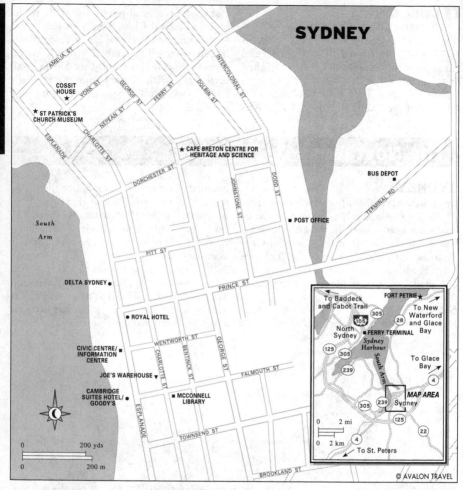

The **Cape Breton Centre for Heritage and Science** (225 George St., 902/539-1572; June–Sept. Mon.–Fri. 9 A.M.–5 P.M., the rest of the year Tues.–Fri. 10 A.M.–4 P.M.; free) offers displays on the social and natural history of eastern Cape Breton, art exhibits, and films.

## Accommodations

Motel rooms in Sydney are generally more expensive than they should be. Therefore, use the websites to search out package rates or wait until the last minute and start calling around for deals.

**Comfort Inn Sydney** (368 Kings Rd., 902/562-0200, www.choicehotels.ca; $120–140 s or d) overlooks the waterfront two kilometers south of downtown. The midsize rooms have contemporary style and modern necessities such as high-speed Internet access.

My pick in Sydney is the modern **Cambridge Suites Hotel** (380 Esplanade, 902/562-6500 or 800/565-9466, www.cambridgesuitessydney

.com), which comprises 150 spacious self-contained units, each with a kitchen and high-speed Internet access. On the roof level are a pool, sauna, exercise room, and sundeck. Summer rates are from $160 s or d, discounted to about $130 the rest of the year.

Right downtown, **Delta Sydney** (300 Esplanade, 902/562-7500 or 800/565-1001, www.deltahotels.com; $200 s or d) is a well-designed comfortable high-rise with more than 150 rooms, a restaurant with water views, an indoor pool and waterslide, a whirlpool, a sauna, an exercise room, and a gift shop. The rack rates of $200 are too high, but the $140 I was quoted for a water-view room in early June seemed about right.

## Food

**ℂ** **Goody's** (Cambridge Suites Hotel, 380 Esplanade, 902/562-6500; daily for breakfast, lunch, and dinner) stands out as the best place in town for a healthy, well-priced meal in pleasant surroundings. The continental breakfast is $8 (free for hotel guests) while later in the day lunches such as Thai chicken salad are less than $12. In the evening, tasty temptations include salmon stuffed with shrimp and scallops ($25).

Away from the hotel dining scene, **Joe's Warehouse** (424 Charlotte St., 902/539-6686; lunch and dinner daily) is a converted Canadian Tire warehouse. It's spacious enough to accommodate locals on a casual splurge, who come for the specialty prime rib, New York strip steak, and surprisingly good cheesecake.

## Information and Services

**Sydney Visitor Information Centre** is in the waterfront Civic Centre (320 Esplanade, 902/539-9876; late May–mid-Oct. Mon.–Fri. 8:30 A.M.–5 P.M.). Another source of information is the website of Destination Cape Breton (www.cbisland.com).

To get onto the Internet, head for **McConnell Library** (50 Falmouth St., 902/562-3161; Tues.–Fri. 10 A.M.–9 P.M., Sat. 10 A.M.–5:30 P.M.) and tell the staff you're visiting from

out of town. If there's an available terminal, it's yours.

**Cape Breton Regional Hospital** is at 1482 George Street (902/567-8000). For the **RCMP** call 564-7171, or 911 in emergencies.

Major banks are represented along Charlotte Street. The main **post office** is at 75 Dodd Street.

## Getting There and Around

It's just more than 400 kilometers between Halifax and Sydney—easily driven in under five hours. The main reason to fly in would be the ease of getting to Cape Breton Highlands National Park, a 90-minute drive northeast of town. Sydney Airport is 14 kilometers northeast of the city center. A taxi to town costs $18, or rent a car through Avis, Budget, Hertz, and National, all of which have rentals desks at the airport. Sydney is served by **Air Canada** (902/539-7501 or 888/247-2262) with direct flights from Halifax.

The **Acadian Lines** depot (99 Terminal Rd., 902/564-5533) is open daily 6:30 A.M.–1 A.M. and has luggage-storage lockers. Scheduled passenger buses run daily from Sydney to Halifax via North Sydney and Baddeck.

## HIGHWAY 28 TO GLACE BAY

From Sydney, the New Waterford Highway (Highway 28) spurs north off Prince Street and follows the eastern side of Sydney Harbour for 26 kilometers to the industrial town of New Waterford. Along the way is **Fort Petrie** (3479 Hwy. 28, 902/862-8367; May–Nov. 10 A.M.–6 P.M.; free), one of seven such forts constructed to protect local coal and steel production facilities from attack during World War II. Not much remains, but an interpretive display tells the story of the fort, and views of the harbor make the stop worthwhile.

### Glace Bay

At Glace Bay, 21 kilometers northeast of Sydney, **Cape Breton Miners' Museum** (42 Birkley St., 902/849-4522; June–Aug. daily 10 A.M.–6 P.M., the rest of the year weekdays

9 A.M.–4 P.M.; adult $10, child $5) is the main attraction for visitors. Retired miners guide you on an underground tour of a real mine, the Ocean Deeps Colliery, to show the rough working conditions under which workers manually extracted coal. Above the mine is an exhibit gallery where the highlight is a simulated, multimedia trip into the workings of a modern mine, using laser-disc projection and other special effects. On selected Tuesday evenings through summer (usually at 8 P.M.), the Men of the Deeps, a local singing group composed of miners dressed in their coveralls, give concerts at the museum. Also in the main building is Miners' Village Restaurant (mid-Apr.–Oct. daily noon–8 P.M.), where the food is both tasty and well priced.

## LOUISBOURG

This small fishing town (pop. 1,200), 32 kilometers southeast of Sydney along Highway 22 (take Exit 8 from Highway 125), is famous for its historic links to France and for the reconstruction of an entire walled town. Louisbourg may be well off the main Baddeck–Cape Breton Highlands National Park itinerary of many visitors, but it gets a steady flow of visitors through summer and has limited accommodations, so plan accordingly.

### ◖ Fortress of Louisbourg National Historic Site

Fortress of Louisbourg National Historic Site (902/733-2280; July–Aug. daily 9 A.M.–5:30 P.M., May–June and Sept.–mid-Oct. daily 9:30 A.M.–5 P.M.; adult $17.60, senior $15, child $8.80) is a fantastic re-creation of the original French fort. Parks Canada has reconstructed 50 of the original 80 buildings, right down to the last window, nail, and shingle, based on historical records.

Louisbourg reveals itself slowly. The seaport covers 10 hectares, and you can spend the better part of a day exploring. From the Visitor Reception Centre, it's a brief bus ride across fields and marsh to the back of the fortress. The reconstructed fortress and town

open a window on New France; they are designed to reflect Louisbourg on a spring day in 1744, the year preceding England's first attack, when the seaport hummed with activity. The houses, fortifications, ramparts, and other structures—as authentically 18th-century French as anything you will find in France—were conceived as a statement of grandeur and power in the New World. The fancy houses lining cobbled lanes belonged to the elite, who ate sumptuous meals on fine china and drank the finest French wines. The simpler houses are the rustic cottages of the working class. Guides and animators—portraying soldiers, merchants, workers, and craftspeople—are on hand to answer questions and demonstrate military exercises, blacksmithing, lace making, and other skills. The historical feel flows through to three dining rooms. Hungry visitors can feast on a slice of heavy bread and a chunk of cheese at the **King's Bakery;** at **Hotel de la Marine** servers dish up simple fare in big wooden bowls; while over in **Grandchamps Inn** the "wealthy" can dine on exquisite European cuisine served up on the finest china.

The site is open and fully staffed June to mid-October. In May and through the last two weeks of October, access is by guided tour only (departs daily 10 A.M. and 2 P.M.). There are no services during these periods, and so admission is reduced to adult $6.25, senior $5.25, child $3.25. The grounds are closed the rest of the year.

Be prepared for walking, and bring a sweater or jacket in case of breezy or wet weather. Louisbourg's reconstructed buildings stretch from the bus stop to the harbor. Remaining ruins lying beyond the re-creation are marked by trails. You can wander on your own or join a tour—usually 10 A.M. and 2 P.M. for English tours and 1 P.M. for the French-language tour.

### Accommodations and Camping

Accommodations in Louisbourg are limited, so it's wise to make reservations.

© PAUL CLARKE/123RF

Fortress of Louisbourg National Historic Site

Overlooking the fort and harbor is **Stacey House** (7438 Main St., 902/733-2317 or 888/924-2242; June–mid-Oct.; $65–95 s or d). It offers four rooms, two with private baths, and an antique-filled parlor within walking distance of town. Rates include a cooked breakfast.

With a similar outlook as Stacey House, but in the commercial core of Louisbourg, **Fortress View Suites** (7513 Main St., 902/733-3131 or 877/733-3131, www.fortress-view.ca; May–Oct.; $80–90 s or d) comprises five guest rooms, each with an en suite bathroom and television but no phone.

Perfectly situated on a high headland with sweeping views of the fortress, **C** **Point of View Suites** (15 Commercial St., 902/733-2080 or 888/374-8439, www.louisbourgpointofview.com; mid-May–Oct.) is Louisbourg's finest accommodation. The sun-filled suites ($125 s or d) and much larger apartments ($199 s or d) look as if they are straight out of a glossy architectural magazine with their crisp color schemes, hardwood floors, and sliding doors that open to balconies with ocean views. At the edge of the property is a private beach, and each evening guests are invited to a lobster supper in the "beach house."

## CAMPGROUNDS

**Louisbourg RV Park** (24 Harbourfront Cres., 902/733-3631 or 866/733-3631; June–mid-Oct.; $18–26) enjoys a downtown waterfront setting. Amenities include showers, 30-amp hookups, and modem connections.

Affiliated with Louisbourg's most upscale accommodation, **Point of View RV Park** (15 Commercial St., 902/733-2080 or 888/374-8439, www.louisbourgpointofview.com; mid-May–Oct.; $24) is an RV-only facility right on the ocean. Guests have use of showers and a laundry while breakfast is served in an on-site café, and nightly lobster dinners mean you don't need to worry about cooking.

The wilderness camping nearest to Louisbourg is at **Mira River Provincial Park** (mid-June–early Sept.), 17 kilometers before town off Highway 22. The park has showers, fire pits and firewood sales, and canoe rentals.

Sites scattered through the forest or along the river are all $24 per night.

## Food

Wander Louisbourg's main street and you'll find numerous dining choices. My favorite is **( Grubstake Restaurant** (7499 Main St., 902/733-2308; daily noon–8:30 P.M.), which has been open since the 1970s but offers an up-to-date menu of seafood such as linguine topped with shrimp, scallops, haddock, and lobster in a cream sauce ($22). If you want to take a break from seafood, this is the place to do so—the pork slow-baked in barbecue sauce ($19) just melts in your mouth.

The food at **Fortress View Restaurant** (7513 Main St., 902/733-3131 or 877/733-3131, www.fortressview.ca; mid-May–mid-Oct. 7 A.M.–9 P.M.) is a little less adventurous than the Grubstake but is still excellent. Breakfasts such as French toast with a side of bacon and bottomless coffee are just $6, poached or grilled fish dishes are $16, lobster dinner is about $25, and all children's meals are less than $5. Affiliated with the Fortress View is the adjacent **CJ's Café and Bakery** (7511 Main St., 902/733-2253), which bakes European-style breads and a tempting array of muffins and pastries.

# NEW BRUNSWICK

# SAINT JOHN AND THE FUNDY COAST

Imagine the scene: An unearthly stillness pervades. Seabirds wheel and dart across the horizon. Suddenly, the birds cry out in a chorus as the incoming tide approaches. The tidal surge, which began halfway around the world in the southern Indian Ocean, quietly and relentlessly pours into the Fundy's mouth, creating the highest tides on the planet. Fishing boats are lifted from the muddy sea floor, and whales in pursuit of silvery herring hurry along the summertime currents, their mammoth hulks buoyed by the 100 billion tons of seawater that gush into the long bay between New Brunswick and Nova Scotia.

The cycle from low to high tide takes a mere six hours. The tide peaks, in places high enough to swamp a four-story building, and then begins to retreat. As the sea level drops, coastal peninsulas and rocky islets emerge from the froth, veiled in seaweed. The sea floor reappears, shiny as shellac and littered with sea urchins, periwinkles, and shells. Where no one walked just hours ago, local children run and skip on the beaches, pausing to retrieve tidal treasures. New Brunswickers take the Fundy tides for granted. For visitors, it's an astounding show.

The Fundy Coast is a paradox: It's at once the most- and least-developed part of the province. Saint John—the province's largest city and major port—sits at the midpoint. To either side, the coastline is remotely settled and wonderfully wild. The region is best considered as two distinct areas, with Saint John interposed between them. The Lower Fundy, situated at the bay's southwestern end, includes

# HIGHLIGHTS

**◖ Prince William and Germain Streets:** Downtown Saint John oozes history at every corner, but nowhere is it as concentrated as along these two streets (page 189).

**◖ Irving Nature Park:** Nature is left to its own devices within this oceanfront park, but what makes it remarkable is its vicinity to a major shipping port (page 192).

**◖ Kingsbrae Garden:** Blending formal gardens with trails through Acadian coastal forest, Kingsbrae will soothe your senses (page 200).

**◖ Minister's Island Historic Site:** Yes, wandering through the 50-room summer home of a railway magnate is interesting, but getting there along a road exposed only at low tide is half the fun (page 202).

**◖ Grand Manan Island:** Bird-watchers will want to catch the ferry over to this Bay of Fundy island to watch the abundance of seabirds that gather each spring and fall (page 207).

**◖ Fundy National Park:** Protecting a huge swath of Fundy coastline, this park offers plenty of chances to get back to nature or, if you prefer, the opportunity to go golfing and feast on fresh seafood (page 209).

**◖ Hopewell Rocks:** This attraction, where you can "walk on the ocean floor," is a wonderful natural phenomenon helped along by the massive Fundy tides – just don't expect to find solitude (page 212).

**NEW BRUNSWICK**

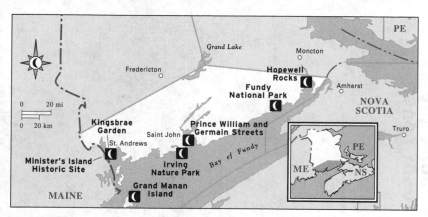

LOOK FOR ◖ TO FIND RECOMMENDED SIGHTS, ACTIVITIES, DINING, AND LODGING.

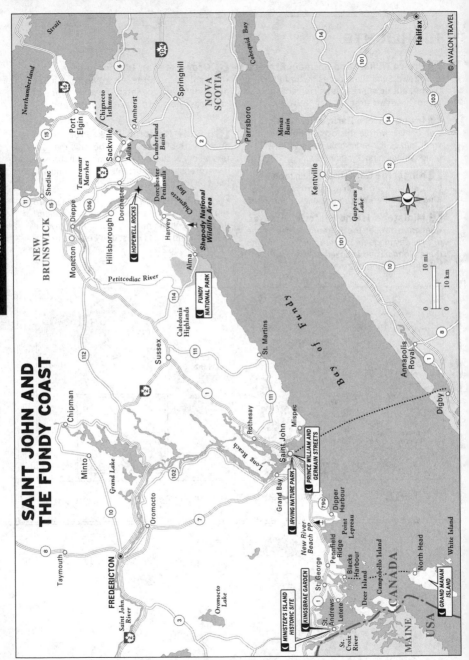

St. Andrews—the province's definitive resort town on sheltered Passamaquoddy Bay—and the Fundy Isles, the archipelago (made up of Grand Manan, Deer, and Campobello Islands) that dangles into the sea alongside Maine's northernmost coast. The Upper Fundy area, situated at the coast's northeastern end, takes in Fundy National Park and several coastal bird sanctuaries.

## PLANNING YOUR TIME

New Brunswick's 250-kilometer-long Fundy coastline is central to all of mainland Atlantic Canada, with the port city of Saint John roughly halfway between the U.S. border and the head of the bay. This is the place to explore historic **Prince William and Germain Streets,** get a taste of nature at **Irving Nature Park,** and to take advantage of fine lodgings and restaurants. Everywhere else is within day-tripping distance of Saint John, but then you'd miss out on soaking up the old-fashioned resort atmosphere of **St. Andrews.** So plan on spending at least one night here, which will also allow time to visit **Kingsbrae Garden** and **Minister's Island Historic Site.** If you're driving up through Maine to Atlantic Canada, St. Andrews makes an ideal first stop. If you've rented a vehicle in Halifax, this will mark your turnaround point on a loop that would incorporate a ferry trip from Digby to Saint John. Either way, on the north side of Saint John, plan on stops at **Fundy National Park** and **Hopewell Rocks** as you follow the Fundy Coast north to Moncton. By virtue of their location, the Fundy Isles require some extra time to reach, especially **Grand Manan Island,** but nature lovers will be rewarded by a magnificent display of birds, whales, and seals.

# Saint John and Vicinity

Saint John (pop. 71,000), 110 kilometers south of Fredericton and 155 kilometers southwest of Moncton, ranks as New Brunswick's largest city, its major port, and its principal industrial center. It is also Canada's largest city in terms of area, sprawling across 321 square kilometers. The city perches on steep hills, laid out southwest to northeast across two peninsulas that almost mesh, like two hands about to meet in a handshake. The setting is among Atlantic Canada's most unusual—Saint John looks east across the spacious Saint John Harbour to the Bay of Fundy and is backed on the west by the confluence of the Saint John River and Kennebecasis Bay.

Saint John began as a collection of small Loyalist settlements. Today these settlements maintain their identities in the form of neighborhoods within greater Saint John. This accounts for numerous street-name duplications, a confusing fact of life you will have to deal with as you sightsee across the oddly laid-out city. For example, one Charlotte Street runs through the city's historic part, while another Charlotte Street may be found in western Saint John. It helps to keep a map handy, or just ask: the locals are sympathetic to the visitor's confusion.

Locals and visitors alike take full advantage of a revitalized waterfront precinct that includes the provincial museum, dining and shopping in Market Square, live outdoor entertainment, and the 2.3-kilometer Harbour Passage, a walking and biking trail that rims the waterfront.

## HISTORY

On June 24, 1604, the feast day of St. John the Baptist, French explorer Samuel de Champlain sailed into the harbor area and named the river in the saint's honor. He dismissed the site, however, as unsuitable for settlement, and continued on to an island in the St. Croix River near St. Andrews.

Saint John as an Anglo settlement began with 14,000 Loyalists, who arrived by ship in

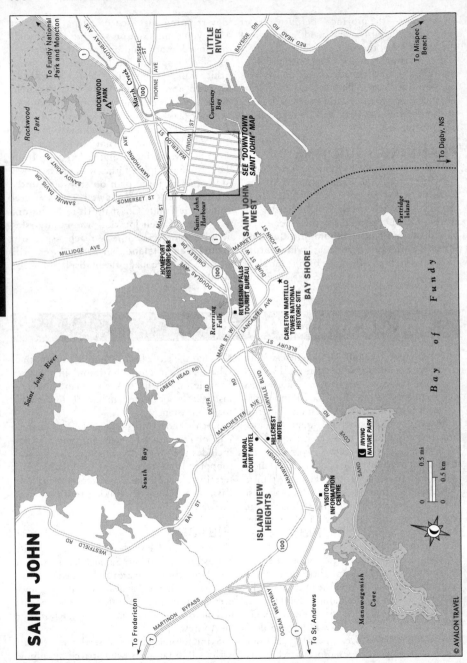

SAINT JOHN

© AVALON TRAVEL

The corner of King and Prince William Streets is a good place to begin your exploration of historic downtown Saint John.

1783. The refugees quickly settled the fledgling town and spread out to create Carleton west of the harbor and Parrtown to the east. The city was incorporated in 1785, making it Canada's oldest. The port was an immediate economic success, and the Carleton Martello Tower was built to guard the harbor's shipping approaches during the War of 1812.

The city's next great wave of immigrants brought the Irish, who were fleeing poverty and persecution at home. Saint John's reputation as Canada's most Irish city began with a trickle of Irish in 1815; before the wave subsided in 1850, the city's 150,000 Irish outnumbered the Loyalists, and Saint John's religious complexion changed from Protestant to Roman Catholic.

## Liverpool of America

Despite its early social woes, Saint John strode ahead economically and became known as the Liverpool of America. The *Marco Polo,* the world's fastest ship in its heyday, was launched in 1852 during an era when the port ranked third worldwide as a wooden ship builder. After steel-hulled steam vessels began to replace the great sailing ships in the 1860s, the city plunged into a decline, which was deepened by the Great Fire of 1877. The fire, at the Market Square area, raged for nine hours and left 18 people dead and another 13,000 homeless.

The blaze cost the city $28 million, but undaunted, Saint John replaced the damage with more elaborate, sturdier brick and stone buildings designed in the ornate Victorian style. The economic surge continued after New Brunswick joined the Confederation of Canada in 1867 and the nation's new railroads transported goods to Saint John for shipping.

## World War II and Beyond

Saint John thrived during World War I as a shipping center for munitions, food, and troops bound for the Allied offensive in Europe. The port took an economic plunge during the Depression, further worsened by another devastating fire that destroyed port facilities. Prosperity returned during World War II; the fortifications at Fort Dufferin, Partridge Island, Fort Mispec, and Carleton Martello Tower guarded the nation's shipping lifeline as German submarines roamed the Bay of Fundy.

Saint John modernized after the war. New Brunswick's native-son billionaire, K. C. Irving, diversified his petroleum empire with the acquisition and expansion of the Saint John Shipbuilding facilities. The University of New Brunswick opened a campus at the city's north end; enrollment today is 1,150 full-time and 1,500 part-time students. Canada's Confederation centennial launched Saint John's rejuvenation in 1967, which continues to this day, most recently with the ambitious Harbour Passage waterfront promenade project.

## GETTING ORIENTED

On a map, Saint John looks large and somewhat unmanageable, almost intimidating. Forget about Saint John's unusual shape and the soaring bridges that connect the city's parts.

Rather, concentrate on the main highways: The closely aligned Highway 1 and Highway 100, which parallel each other in most parts, are often the best routes for getting from one section of the city to another.

Tackle Saint John by areas. Most sightseeing is on the eastern peninsula in **uptown Saint John.** Access here is easiest from Highway 1's Exits 121 or 125; the access roads peel down into the heart of downtown, centered on Market Square. The surrounding area is **Trinity Royal,** a national heritage preservation area protecting the original 20 blocks laid out by the Loyalists. You'll also know you've arrived by the street names: The early Loyalists called the area Parrtown, and the avenues were royally named as King, Princess, Queen, Prince William, and Charlotte Streets. This precinct is easily identified by distinctive blue and gold street signs.

**Northern Saint John** (the North End) lies on the highways' other side. **Rockwood Park,** one of Canada's largest municipal parks, dominates the area with 870 wooded hectares speckled with lakes and an 18-hole golf course; numerous roads off Highway 1 feed into the park. This part of the city is also known for Saint John Harbour's best views; for a sublime overview, drive up to the **Fort Howe Lookout,** where timber blockhouses perch atop a rocky outcrop on Highway 1's northern side. Worthy hotels are nearby.

**Western Saint John** lies across the highway bridges on the western peninsula. Here you'll find some of the newer motels and a shopping mall along Highway 100, the area's commercial row, while Highway 1 heads west to St. Andrews. The residential area, with several interesting bed-and-breakfasts, spreads out closer to the water, while the Bay Ferries ferry terminal (with service to Digby, Nova Scotia) is at the harbor's edge.

# SIGHTS
## Downtown

Hills aside, the following attractions are all within walking distance of each other. If the steep streets look daunting, flag a cab in front

© ANDREW HEMPSTEAD

Barbour's General Store

of the Hilton Saint John and ask the driver to be dropped up at King's Square ($5 with tip).

Downtown sightseeing starts at **Loyalist Plaza,** an outdoor strip filled with plants and seating that ends at the waterfront. It's a good place to get oriented by visiting the information center (in Market Square) and taking the **Harbour Passage** waterfront promenade around the head of the harbor. This paved walking/biking trail leads 2.3 kilometers to a pavilion from where views extend back across to downtown.

### NEW BRUNSWICK MUSEUM

The province's prime resource for fine arts and natural-history lore is this museum inside Market Square (St. Patrick St., 506/643-2300; Mon.–Fri. 9 A.M.–5 P.M., Sat. 10 A.M.–5 P.M., Sun. noon–5 P.M.; adult $6, senior $4.75, child $3.25). One of Canada's oldest museums, its displays are spread through three floors packed with elegant ship models, shipbuilding tools, war memorabilia, stuffed birds and beasts, agricultural and domestic implements, you name

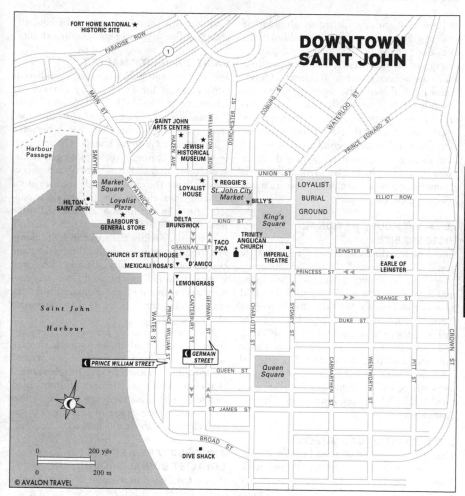

it. There's a hands-on Discovery Centre for kids and a bookstore that stocks books about the province.

## BARBOUR'S GENERAL STORE
Across Loyalist Plaza from Market Square, the essence of old-time New Brunswick is re-created at this restored country store-cum-museum (506/658-2939; June–Sept. daily 9 A.M.–6 P.M.), which was moved from upriver at Sheffield. Inside are 2,000 artifacts typical

of the period from 1840 to 1940, as well as a restored turn-of-the-century barbershop in the back room. Next door, peek into the bright red schoolhouse, which was also moved to the site from rural New Brunswick.

## 🌙 PRINCE WILLIAM AND GERMAIN STREETS
A block up from Market Square, these two parallel streets delineate the commercial heart of old Saint John. Following the devastating fire

of June 1877, the city hurried to rebuild itself in even grander style. The stone and brick edifices along Prince William Street are a splendid farrago of architectural styles, incorporating Italianate facades, Corinthian columns, Queen Anne Revival elements, scowling gargoyles, and other decorative details. One of the country's finest surviving examples of 19th-century streetscape, this was the first "national historic street" in Canada. Some good art galleries and craft shops are ensconced here among the other businesses. Two blocks east, Germain Street is the more residential counterpoint, with a number of opulent townhouses.

## LOYALIST HOUSE NATIONAL HISTORIC SITE

This simple, white clapboard Georgian-style house (120 Union St., 506/652-3590; mid-May–June Mon.–Fri. 10 A.M.–5 P.M., July–mid-Sept. daily 10 A.M.–5 P.M.; adult $3, child $1) was built between 1810 and 1817 by pioneer David Merrit, and it remained in his family for five generations. Having survived the 1877 fire and now meticulously restored, it's the oldest unaltered building in the city. The original front door with brass knocker opens into an authentic evocation of the early Loyalist years, furnished with Sheraton, Empire, and Duncan Phyfe antiques.

## JEWISH HISTORICAL MUSEUM

Half a block up the hill from Loyalist House, this modest museum (29 Wellington Row, 506/633-1833; late May–Oct. Mon.–Fri. 10 A.M.–4 P.M., Sun. 1–4 P.M.; free) has a functioning Hebrew school, chapel, and *mikvah*, sacred and secular artifacts, and exhibits about the city's small Jewish community, which dates its arrival to 1858.

## SAINT JOHN ARTS CENTRE

One block west of the Jewish museum, the grandiose former Carnegie Library (20 Hazen Ave., 506/633-4870; June–early Sept. daily 10 A.M.–5 P.M., early Sept.–May Tues.–Sun. 11:30 A.M.–4:30 P.M.; free) is now a cultural complex. Inside, six galleries (including the City of Saint John Gallery) hold frequently changing fine arts and photography exhibits.

## SAINT JOHN CITY MARKET

For a visual and culinary treat, spend some time at Saint John's Old City Market (47 Charlotte St., 506/658-2820; Mon.–Thurs. 7:30 A.M.–6 P.M., Fri. to 7 P.M., Sat. to 5 P.M.; free), spanning a whole city block between Charlotte and Germain Streets. The setting is impressive. The original ornate iron gates stand at each entrance, and there's usually a busker or two working the crowd. Inside the airy stone building, local shipbuilders framed the expansive ceiling in the form of an inverted ship's hull. "Market Street," the market's central, widest aisle, divides the space in half; alongside the adjacent aisles, the bustling stalls stand cheek-to-jowl, their tables groaning with wares. Notice the building's pitched floor, a convenient arrangement on the slanted hillside that makes hosing the floor easier after the market closes each day.

It's a great venue for people-watching and for sampling freshly baked goods, cheeses, seafood, meat, and produce. If you haven't yet tried dulse, a leather-tough purple seaweed that's harvested from the Bay of Fundy, dried, and sold in little packages for a dollar or two, here's your chance. Splendid, reasonably priced crafts have a sizable niche here too.

## KING'S SQUARE AND THE LOYALIST BURIAL GROUND

Across Charlotte Street from the City Market are two maple-shaded, vest-pocket green spaces situated on separate kitty-corner blocks. At King's Square, the walkways are laid out like the stripes on the British Union Jack, radiating from the 1908 bandstand, the site of summertime concerts.

Across Sydney Street is the Loyalist Burial Ground, a surprisingly cheerful place with benches and flower gardens, scattered with old-style headstones dating back to 1784.

As busy as the square and burial ground are—alive with schoolchildren on field trips, bantering seniors, and moms with strollers—**Queen's Square,** three blocks south, is virtually deserted.

### TRINITY ANGLICAN CHURCH

A victim of the city's historic fires, this handsome Loyalist church (115 Charlotte St., 506/693-8558; Mon.–Fri. 9 A.M.–3 P.M.; free) was built in 1791, rebuilt in 1856, and rebuilt again in 1880 after the Great Fire. The sanctuary's famed treasure is the House of Hanover Royal Coat of Arms from the reign of George I, which had been rescued by fleeing Loyalists from the Boston Council Chamber in 1783 and rescued again from the 1877 runaway fire.

## West of Downtown

### FORT HOWE NATIONAL HISTORIC SITE LOOKOUT

The blockhouse of 1777 did double duty as harbor defense and city jail. The structure itself is a replica, but the rocky promontory site on Magazine Street nonetheless offers an excellent panoramic view of the city and harbor. To get there from downtown, cross the highway along Main Street.

### REVERSING FALLS

If ever there were a contest for Most Overhyped Tourist Attraction, this site would win grand prize. Tour buses and out-of-province license plates pack the parking lot, disgorging gaggles of camera-toting visitors to see…what? At low tide, the Bay of Fundy lies 4.4 meters below the Saint John River, and the river flows out to sea across a small falls (more like a rapids) here. During the slack tide, the sea and the river levels are equal and the rapids disappear. Then, as the slack tide grows to high tide, the waters of the rising sea enter Saint John Harbour, muscling the river inland for 100 kilometers and creating some turbulent currents (no falls). It's an unspectacular sight, and even the minimal physical-science interest can't be appreciated unless you're willing to hang around for 12 hours and watch the tide go through a full cycle. Nevertheless, throngs of visitors line up here for the requisite photo opportunity.

What all the hype does accomplish, however, is to draw all those tourists in to the friendly and helpful **Reversing Falls Visitor Information Centre** (Fallsview Dr., 506/658-2937; mid-May–mid-Oct. daily 8 A.M.–8 P.M.), which is probably as good a place as any to get information about the area. If you're interested in a capsule version of the sea and river encounter, check out the audiovisual ($2.50). To get there from downtown, cross Highway 1 via Main Street and turn left on Clesley Drive. The complex is on the far side of the bridge spanning the river.

For a reverse angle on Reversing Falls, go to **Fallsview Park,** which overlooks the spectacle from the east side of the river, off Douglas Avenue.

### CARLETON MARTELLO TOWER NATIONAL HISTORIC SITE

The massive circular stone tower (Fundy Dr. at Whipple St., Saint John West, 506/636-4011; June–early Oct. daily 10 A.M.–5:30 P.M.; adult $4, senior $3.50, child $2) served as a harbor defense outpost from 1812 and was declared a national historic site in 1924. The superstructure above it was a military intelligence center during World War II. Within, stone staircases connect the restored quarters and powder magazine. The observation decks provide splendid views of the harbor.

### PARTRIDGE ISLAND

This island near the mouth of Saint John Harbour, a national and provincial historic site and now a coast guard light station, was formerly a quarantine station for almost a million arriving immigrants during the 19th and 20th centuries, many of whom arrived sick with cholera, typhus, and smallpox. Some 2,000 newcomers who never made it any farther are buried here in six graveyards. A Celtic cross was erected for the Irish refugees, and a memorial stone commemorates Jewish immigrants. From the early 1800s up to 1947, the island was used as a military fortification. Most of the old wooden buildings have now been destroyed, and the island is off-limits to the public. If you're catching the ferry to Digby (Nova

Scotia), stand on the starboard (right-hand) side as the vessel pulls away from the terminal and you'll get a great view of the island.

## RECREATION

A visit to Saint John is about soaking up history and enjoying the services affiliated with a city, but there are a few things to keep you busy beyond sightseeing. The two parks detailed below have good walking trails, **Rockwood Park Golf Course** (506/634-0090; greens fees $37) is a challenging tree-lined layout, or you can try out a water sport.

## Parks

### ROCKWOOD PARK

This huge woodland park (506/658-2883; daily dawn–dusk), speckled with 13 lakes and laced with foot and horse trails, is across Highway 1 from downtown, with access from Exits 123, 125, and 128. In spring, yellow lady's slipper and colorful wild orchid varieties bloom on the forest floor, and the gardens and arboretum are in full glory. Activities in summer include fishing, boating, swimming, bird-watching, hiking, horseback riding, golfing at the 18-hole course, picnicking at lakeside tables, and camping. In winter, the ice skaters come out and the trails are taken over by cross-country skiers.

**Cherry Brook Zoo** (901 Foster Thurston Rd., 506/634-1440; daily 10 A.M.–dusk; adult $8, senior $7, child $6), at the park's northern end off Sandy Point Road, is stocked with lions, leopards, zebras, and other exotic animals. Part of the zoo is Vanished Kingdom Park, where you find replicas of extinct animals.

### ◖ IRVING NATURE PARK

Irving Nature Park occupies an unlikely setting. The remote reserve encompasses an entire peninsula dangling into Saint John Harbour, the province's busiest port. At the harbor's northeastern corner rises the skyline of New Brunswick's largest city. Across the harbor's center, oceangoing vessels enter and leave the port. Yet at the harbor's western corner, this speck of natural terrain remains blissfully

Irving Nature Park

© ANDREW HEMPSTEAD

remote and as undeveloped as it was when the city's founding Loyalists arrived centuries ago.

To get there, take Highway 1 out of the city to western Saint John and watch for the Catherwood Street turnoff (Exit 119). The narrow road angles south off the highway, takes a jog to the right (west), descends through a residential area, then lopes across an undeveloped marshland to the 225-hectare reserve. A sandy beach backed by the Saints Rest Marsh heralds the park's entrance. Many visitors park at the bottom of the hill and continue on foot. It is also possible to continue by road into the park, to a parking lot 500 meters from the beach, or to follow a one-way road that encircles the entire headland. Trails probe the park's interior and also wander off to parallel the water.

The reserve's mixed ecosystem offers interesting trekking terrain and draws songbirds, waterfowl, and migratory seabirds. More than 240 bird species are seen regularly; 365 species have been sighted over the past 20 years. Rare red crossbills and peregrine falcons are occasionally spotted in the marsh. Eastern North

America's largest cormorant colony lies offshore on Manawagonish Island. Semipalmated plovers like the reserve's quiet beaches and tidal flats. You can count on sandpiper varieties on the beach in July, greater shearwaters and Wilson's stormy petrels gliding across the water during summer, and a spectacular show of loons, grebes, and scoters during the autumn migration along the Atlantic flyway. Birds are the most noticeable but by no means the only wildlife to be found here. Deer, porcupines, red squirrels, and snowshoe hares inhabit the reserve. And starfish and sea urchins laze in the tidal pools.

## Water Sports

The **Dive Shack** (9 Lower Cove Loop, 506/634-8265; Mon.–Fri. 10 A.M.–6 P.M., Sat. 10 A.M.–3 P.M.) is the city's prime source for dive trips to the Bay of Fundy. The shop also rents equipment, runs courses, and offers weekend charters. Lower Cove Loop is an extension of Water Street south through downtown.

The top-notch facilities at the **Canada Games Aquatic Centre** (50 Union St., 506/658-4715) include a 50-meter pool with five diving boards, two shallower pools, two water slides, whirlpools, saunas, a fitness room, and a cafeteria. A day-use pass to the pool and fitness center costs $12; for the pool alone it's $7.50.

You'll find supervised swimming at Fisher Lake in **Rockwood Park,** at **Dominion Park** in Saint John West, and at **Little River Reservoir** off Loch Lomond Road in the city's eastern area. **Mispec Beach** at Saint John Harbour's eastern edge is unsupervised, and the water is cold, but it's a nice spot on a warm day and provides close-up views of ships from around the world entering and leaving the harbor. To get there, take Union Street and make a sharp right turn to Bayside Drive, and then turn onto Red Head Road.

# ENTERTAINMENT AND EVENTS
## Performing Arts

The city's pride and joy is the immaculately restored 1913 **Imperial Theatre** (24 King Square S., 506/674-4100). In its heyday, the theater hosted performances by the likes of Ethel Barrymore, John Philip Sousa, and Harry Houdini. After closing in the 1950s, it was reopened and used by the Full Gospel Assembly Pentecostal Church for 25 years. In 1994, decade-long renovations to restore the theater to its former glory were completed. Today it's once again the star venue of Saint John's performing-arts scene, hosting concerts by Symphony New Brunswick, stage productions of Theatre New Brunswick, and a variety of touring performers.

## Pubs and Nightclubs

Saint John may seem all historic and charming during the day, but remember it's primarily an international port, so be careful after dark, especially at the south end of downtown. That said, bars and restaurants along Market Square have a beautiful outlook with lots of outdoor tables that stay full with locals and visitors well

Built in 1913, the Imperial Theatre is now fully restored.

© ANDREW HEMPSTEAD

into the night on summer weekends, when musicians take to an outdoor stage. **Grannan's** (St. Patrick St., 506/634-1555; daily from 11 A.M.) forms a hub for the many nearby bars of many moods, and its indoor lounge has an inviting pub ambience. Adjacent **Cougar's Lounge** (506/693-6666) and **Saint John Ale House** (506/657-2337) also have wide portions of Loyalist Plaza packed with outdoor furniture. Toward the water, **Brigantine Lounge** (Hilton Saint John, Market Sq., 506/632-8564) is less pretentious than you might expect. It's open daily from 11:30 A.M. and offers basic food.

The Historic Trinity Royal area, bounded by Prince William, Princess, King, and Germain Streets, is another nightlife center, with nightclubs, pubs, lounges, and sports bars. One of the more welcoming places is **O'Leary's** (46 Princess St., 506/634-7135), a convivial Irish pub with the obligatory Guinness on tap and the sound of Celtic musicians filling the room Thursday–Saturday.

### Festivals and Events

In addition to free evening entertainment in Loyalist Plaza, summer brings the **Salty Jam** (www.saltyjam.com) music festival to Market Square, Pugsley Wharf, and other venues the second weekend of July.

The five-day **Atlantic National Exhibition** finishes the summer with a super-size county fair geared to families. It runs from late August to early September at the Exhibition Grounds (McAllister Dr., 506/633-2020).

On the fourth Sunday in October, Harbour Station, Saint John's main entertainment center, fills with the smells of the best in local cooking for the **Fundy Food Festival** (www.fundyfoodfestival.com). Admission is $5, and for nominal extra charges you can sample creations from local restaurants and food suppliers.

### SHOPPING

The city's main shopping district—along Charlotte, Union, Princess, Germain, and Prince William Streets—is filled with interesting outlets selling everything from Inuit art to Irish tartan. The local penchant for high-quality weaving and handmade apparel is particularly evident at **Handworks Gallery** (12 King St., 506/652-9787). In the vicinity is one of Atlantic Canada's preeminent antique dealers, **Tim Isaac Antiques** (97 Prince William St., 506/652-3222). Saint John is Canada's most Irish city, and Celtic wares are abundant. **House of Tara** (72 Prince William St., 506/634-8272) is stuffed with Irish imports, including plentiful jewelry and clothing (the tweeds are particularly attractive) and Belleek pottery. Walking up King Street from Market Square, the Inuit art and Canadian diamonds on display at **Arctic Echoes** (16 King St., 866/657-3246) are particularly eye-pleasing.

## ACCOMMODATIONS AND CAMPING

Ideally, you'll want to be within walking distance of historic old Saint John and the harbor. The area's bed-and-breakfasts often provide sumptuous accommodations for lower cost than many hotels. Lodgings beyond walking distance include the Fort Howe–area hotels, with great harbor vistas at reasonable prices, and the many budget choices on Manawagonish Avenue in Saint John West.

### $50-100

Of the bed-and-breakfast lodgings clustered near King's Square, none are better value than **Earle of Leinster** (96 Leinster St., 506/652-3275, www.earleofleinster.com; $82 s, $92 d), with congenial hosts and a very central location. This gracious brick Victorian townhouse has seven rooms with private baths. One of the rooms is a family suite. Amenities include laundry facilities, a game room with a pool table, a courtyard, and business services. Rates include a full breakfast.

Canada Select gives its ultimate five-star rating only sparingly, but ◖ **Homeport Historic Bed & Breakfast** (80 Douglas Ave., 506/672-7255 or 888/678-7678, www.homeport.nb.ca; $95–175 s or d) deserves every one of its five.

Set high on the hill overlooking the harbor and city, this lodging combines two mansions dating from the mid-1800s. From the impressive collection of antiques to the super-comfortable beds to the decanter of port left in the lobby for guests returning from dinner, it is obvious hosts Ralph and Karen Holyoke know how to make their guests feel like they're paying a lot more than they really are. Standard rooms are $95 s or d, but the Luxury Rooms at $140 are well worth the extra money. Rates include a full breakfast.

Around five kilometers from downtown, Manawagonish Avenue is lined with inexpensive motels—a reminder of the time that this was the main route west out of the city. To get there from the west, take Exit 100 from Highway 1 and follow Ocean Westaway toward the city; from downtown, take Exit 119 and follow Catherwood Street north. Choices in the $70–80 s or d range include **Balmoral Court Motel** (1284 Manawagonish Ave., 506/672-3019) and **Hillcrest Motel** (1315 Manawagonish Ave., 506/672-5310).

## $100-150

**Country Inn and Suites** (1011 Fairville Blvd., 506/635-0400, www.countryinns.com; from $105 s or d) is your typical midrange roadside motel, with clean, comfortable, and practical guest rooms. Standard rooms are $105 s or d, but the much-larger suites, with separate bedrooms and king beds, are good value at $134. A complimentary light breakfast is laid out for guests. Take Exit 117 from Highway 1.

## $150-200

Occupying a prime waterfront locale and linked to Market Square by an elevated walkway is **Hilton Saint John** (1 Market Sq., 506/693-8484 or 800/561-8282, www.hilton.com; $180 s or d), a 12-story high-rise dating to the mid-1980s. Most of its 200 rooms have water views and windows that open. They come with all the usual facilities—daily newspaper, coffeemaker, hair dryer, and more—while a waterfront restaurant, a lounge, and a

fitness room, and an indoor pool are downstairs. Check online for packages that include a buffet breakfast.

Rack rates at the **Delta Brunswick** (39 King St., 506/648-1981 or 877/814-7706, www.deltahotels.com) may be almost $200 per night, but reserve online and you'll pay a lot less. Part of the Brunswick Square Mall and one block back from the harbor, this modern hotel has 254 elegant rooms, as well as an indoor pool, a fitness room, and a restaurant and lounge.

### Campground

A five-minute drive from downtown, **Rockwood Park Campground** (Lake Drive S., 506/652-4050; May–Sept.; $20–29) has over 200 sites, most with electricity and water. Amenities include big communal bathrooms, kitchen shelters, fireplaces, and a campers' canteen. Available recreation includes golfing at the nearby course, swimming, boating at the lake, and hiking on trails around the lake. The park is just a five-minute drive from the city center. The easiest way to get there is to take Highway 1 Exit 121 or 125 and follow the signs north. No reservations are taken, but it rarely fills.

## FOOD

Market Square is the most obvious and convenient choice for visitors looking for a meal, but head uphill into the heart of downtown and you'll come across restaurants that thrive on good food and prices alone.

### Market

You won't know which way to turn once you've walked through the doors of the **Saint John City Market** (47 Charlotte St., 506/658-2820; Mon.–Thurs. 7:30 A.M.–6 P.M., Fri. to 7 P.M., Sat. to 5 P.M.), a city institution. Choose from a couple of old-fashioned cafés; a seafood market with live lobsters (they'll box them for you) and mussels for just $2 per pound; a delicatessen with sliced meats and gourmet cheeses; and Wild Carrot Café, with healthy juices and muffins.

**NEW BRUNSWICK**

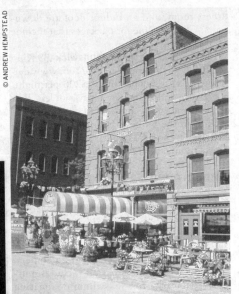

For the best variety of dining options, head to the waterfront and Market Square.

## Cheap Eats

Up the hill a little way from City Market, **Reggie's** (26 Germain St., 506/657-6270; daily 6 A.M.–6 P.M.) is a great old-fashioned diner in a historic building. It serves commendable homemade chowders, lobster rolls, corned beef hash, a huge menu of cooked breakfasts, and burgers, all at good prices.

If hunger strikes while you're out shopping, you'll find food courts with virtually infinite meal choices at Brunswick Square's **Courtyard** and at **Market Square.**

## Seafood

**Grannan's** (1 Market Sq., 506/634-1555; Mon.–Wed. 11 A.M.–11 P.M., Thurs.–Sat. 11 A.M.–midnight, Sun. noon–10 P.M.) is one of the Market Square restaurants with as many tables outside as in. The specialty is seafood, and everything is good. The chowder is expensive ($13.50) but delicious, while mains ranging $18–38 include blackened Creole salmon, seafood casserole, and snow crab.

**Billy's** (49 Charlotte St., 506/672-3474; daily for lunch and dinner) is tucked away at the back of the Saint John City Market. It's part fish market, part restaurant, so you know everything will be fresh. Everything is good—Atlantic Canada delicacies include Malpeque oysters served raw in their shells, fish cakes, seafood chowder, halibut broiled in a sweet pepper coulis, sautéed Digby scallops, cedar planked salmon for two, and a rich lobster and scallop penne pasta. Starters are around $10 and mains range $18–32.

## Italian

For well-priced solid Italian cooking, plan on dining at **D'Amico** (33 Canterbury St., Mon.–Thurs. 11:30 A.M.–11 P.M., Fri.–Sat. 11:30 A.M.–midnight, Sun. 4–10 P.M.). Most mains are under $20, including build-your-own pastas and wood-fired pizza.

## Thai

Saint John proves it's up to snuff with restaurant trends at **Lemongrass** (42 Princess St., 506/657-8424; daily lunch and dinner), a warmly decorated dining room one block up from the harborfront. You can't miss with *tod mun pla* (fish cakes infused with red curry and coriander) and either *phad yum* (seafood curry with lime leaves) or *hor neing pla* (steamed haddock with lemongrass and other herbs wrapped in a banana leaf) as a main. Expect to pay around $60 for two sans drinks.

## Mexican and Central American

Just a block off King Street, the city hustle and bustle drops off dramatically. Small, bright, and casual **Taco Pica** (96 Germain St., 506/633-8492; Mon.–Sat. 10 A.M.–10 P.M., mains $12–19) is a real find on a quiet side street in the Trinity Royal historic area, away from the tourist traffic. The Guatemalan proprietor offers a mouthwatering menu of recipes from his homeland, as well as dishes from Mexico and Spain. Try the *pepian* (a spicy Guatemalan beef stew) or Spanish paella, washed down with a Mexican beer.

**Mexicali Rosa's** (88 Prince William St., 506/652-5252; Mon.–Sat. 11:30 A.M.–11 P.M., Sun. noon–10 P.M.) is a popular hangout with locals looking for a Mexican meal in casual surroundings. For those on a budget, the chili con carne in a sourdough bread bowl ($8.50) is tempting, or splash out on creative offerings like Drunken Shrimp Fajitas ($17).

## Hotel Dining

The dining rooms in the major hotels are also safe bets, though pricier. **Shucker's** (Delta Brunswick, 39 King St., 506/648-1981; daily from 6:30 A.M.) offers tempting selections such as grilled Fundy Bay salmon fillet splashed with lemon butter or served with capers and cream. An alternative "Heart Smart" menu features low-fat poultry, seafood, and fruit-salad dishes. Tuesday through Thursday lunch is a buffet.

The maritime-themed **Turn of the Tide** (Saint John Hilton, Market Sq., 506/632-8564; daily 6 A.M.–10 P.M.) is right on the waterfront, with awesome views and a seafood and beef menu to match. Try the pan-fried Atlantic salmon served with stewed tomatoes and fiddleheads or one of the tenderloin steak variations.

# INFORMATION AND SERVICES
## Tourist Information

**Tourism Saint John** (506/658-2855 or 866/463-8639, www.tourismsaintjohn.com) does a great job of promoting the city, and its helpful website should be your first point of contact in planning your trip. It operates the city's main **Visitor Information Centre** (daily 9 A.M.–6 P.M., summer daily until 8 P.M.) at the eastern entrance to Market Square; it faces the corner of St. Patrick and King Streets. On the city's western approach (St. Andrews) is another information center, this one overlooking Irving Nature Park just beyond Exit 114 (mid-May–mid-Oct. daily 9 A.M.–5 P.M.).

## Books and Bookstores

**Saint John Library** (1 Market Sq., 506/643-7220; Mon.–Fri. 9 A.M.–5 P.M., plus weekends outside summer) is in the downtown Market Square complex. It holds a good selection of New Brunswick titles and offers free Internet access for visitors.

To purchase books about the province's natural, human, and cultural history, head for the **New Brunswick Museum** right by the library in Market Square (506/643-2300). **Coles** has three mall locations within the city, including downtown at Brunswick Square (39 King St., 506/658-9114). Used and antiquarian books are sold at **Book Broker** (196 Union St., 506/657-6310).

## Post Office

The main **post office** is at 125 Rothesay Avenue. **Lawton's Drugs** (Brunswick Sq., 506/634-1422) serves as one of the city's numerous retail postal outlets and has longer hours. **Shoppers Drug Stores** also have postal service outlets.

## Internet Services

Downtown hotels and most bed-and-breakfasts have wireless or modem Internet access, or head to **Saint John Library** (1 Market Sq., 506/643-7220; Mon.–Fri. 9 A.M.–5 P.M., plus weekends outside summer), where getting online is free.

## Money

You can pay with U.S. dollars at many local businesses, but for the best exchange rate head to one of the banks at the top end of King Street.

## Emergency Services

**Saint John Regional Hospital** (400 University Ave., 506/648-6000) is on the university campus near Rockwood Park. For the police or other emergencies, call 911. Convenient pharmacies include **Lawton's Drugs** (Brunswick Sq., 39 King St., 506/634-1422) and **Guardian Drugs** (114 River Valley Dr., 506/738-8406).

**NEW BRUNSWICK**

## GETTING THERE

### Air

**Saint John Airport** is 16 kilometers east of downtown. The airport is served by **Air Canada** (888/247-2262) from Halifax, Toronto, and Montréal. Car-rental companies represented are Avis, Budget, Hertz, and National, while other airport services include a restaurant and gift shop. The Passenger Facility Fee ($15) is incorporated into ticket prices of all departing passengers.

Taxis wait outside the airport for flight arrivals; the 25-minute cab ride to Market Square costs about $30.

### Bus

**Saint John Bus Terminal** (199 Chesley Dr., 506/648-3500) is the arrival and departure point for **Acadian** buses to and from Bangor (Maine), Fredericton, and Moncton. If you've arrived in Saint John by bus and catch the ferry to Digby (Nova Scotia), there will be an Acadian bus waiting to transport you to Halifax.

### Ferry

**Bay Ferries** (902/245-2116 or 888/249-7245, www.nfl-bay.com) sails the *Princess of Acadia* between Saint John and Digby (Nova Scotia) year-round up to three times daily in summer. It's a good option if you've driven through New Brunswick and want to explore Nova Scotia's Fundy Coast. The 3.5-hour crossing costs adult $40, senior and child $30, vehicle $100. To get to the terminal from Highway 1, take Exit 120 and follow the signs south along Market Street. The terminal has no café, so if you're looking for a snack while waiting in line, stop at the Tim Hortons along Market Street.

## GETTING AROUND

Saint John is a walking town in the historic area, but beyond there you'll need wheels. Highway 1 serves as the city's high-speed expressway and routes east–west traffic through Saint John from St. Stephen and Moncton. Highway 100 is the city's local traffic route, and it serves as a feeder route for Highway 7 to and from Fredericton. Driving is slow going most everywhere in Saint John, but it's worst during the 7–9 A.M. and 4:30–6 P.M. rush hours.

Parking garages and lots in the historic area are plentiful and inexpensive. Outdoor lots cost $1 an hour, indoor lots are slightly higher. Coming off Highway 1 at Exit 122, take the first right and you'll pass outdoor pay parking on your right, or continue to the bottom of the hill and turn left for underground parking.

### Bus

**Saint John Transit** (506/658-4700; $2.25 per sector) buses run throughout the city (Mon.–Fri. 6 A.M.–midnight, with limited service on weekends). The company also offers two-hour guided bus tours of Saint John twice daily (at 10 A.M. and 1 P.M.) from late June to early October. The cost is adult $18, child $7.

### Taxi

Cabs wait out front of the Delta and Hilton hotels, or call **Coastal Taxi** (506/635-1144), **Diamond Taxi** (506/648-8888), or **Royal Taxi** (506/652-5050). Fares are based on 14 city zones; expect to pay around $6 from Market Square to Fort Howe and $30 to the airport.

## SAINT JOHN TO ST. ANDREWS

In addition to the intrinsic beauty of the coast—with thick forests growing right down to the rocky shoreline—several detours spice up the 90-kilometer drive west to St. Andrews.

### Point Lepreau and Vicinity

The first spot of note west of Saint John is **Point Lepreau Nuclear Generating Station,** at the end of Highway 790. It opened in 1980 as Canada's first nuclear-power station. It currently supplies New Brunswick with 30 percent of its power needs.

A few kilometers beyond Highway 790, **New River Beach Provincial Park** (506/755-4042; May–Oct.) lies alongside the highway and has picnic tables, a long curving sandy beach, hiking trails through bogs and spruce woodlands, and boat-launching facilities.

A good-value accommodation along this stretch of highway is the **Clipper Shipp Beach Motel** (506/755-2211; Mar.–Nov.; $75 s or d). The rooms are basic—you're paying for a stunning waterfront location.

### St. George

The most impressive sight at St. George, 32 kilometers before reaching St. Andrews, is the thundering granite gorge of **Magaguadavic Falls.** Visitors can park and walk down a staircase beside the falls to watch salmon swimming upstream past a viewing window. The specialty at **Oven Head Salmon Smokers** (101 Ovenhead Rd., 506/755-2507;

Mon.–Sat. 8 A.M.–5 P.M.) is Atlantic salmon, cold-smoked to perfection over hickory and oak chips. The smokehouse wholesales to culinary notables such as the Fairmont Algonquin.

St. George is also the place to turn off Highway 1 for the short drive to the Deer Island ferry terminus at Letete. Highways 772 and 776 lead to Black Bay, picturesque **Blacks Harbour** (terminus for the Grand Manan Island ferry), and a welter of other islets. If you find yourself in Blacks Harbour in early September, don't miss the North American Sardine Packing Championship. Only in the Maritimes!

# St. Andrews and Vicinity

St. Andrews by the Sea, as it is marketed by the local tourism authority, is an immensely attractive seaside town of 1,800 people 90 kilometers west of Saint John. New Brunswick's first—and now definitive—resort town, St. Andrews sits at the end of a peninsula dangling into tranquil Passamaquoddy Bay, sheltered from the tumultuous Fundy by Deer Island and Letang Peninsula. The resort crowd revels in St. Andrews's version of old-time velvet-glove Canadiana, especially visible at the Fairmont Algonquin.

### History

The town has a special, almost sacred historic status among New Brunswickers. It was founded by Loyalists who sailed into the Fundy and followed the coastal curve to the peninsula's tip in 1783. The courageous journey was a technical wonder. The settlers, originally from England's former colonies farther south, had moved to what they believed was Canada at Castine, Maine. But a subsequent international boundary decision forced them to relocate once again. The pro-Crown settlers reloaded convoys with all their possessions, disassembled houses and reloaded the structures on barges, and set sail for a safe homeland. St. Andrews

was their creation. Most every street is named for George III or one of his kin. A few Loyalist houses remain and sit cheek-to-jowl with similar New England–style houses fronting narrow residential streets.

## SIGHTS

For a town that encourages relaxation, there's a lot to see and do. Many historic attractions are within walking distance of downtown accommodations, while others are just a short drive away. You could easily spend two days in town and still not have time to golf the hallowed fairways of Fairmont Algonquin Golf Course or go whale-watching. One of the most interesting things to do in St. Andrews is to watch the effect of the tide. I'm not suggesting you sit at the end of the Town Wharf for six hours, but take a peek at low or high tide, and then return six hours later—the effect is amazing.

### Historic Downtown

St. Andrews is a historic gem. Nearly half the buildings in the town core date back over 100 years, and most have been maintained or restored to mint condition. Water Street is the main avenue, following the shoreline through the five-block commercial district.

**NEW BRUNSWICK**

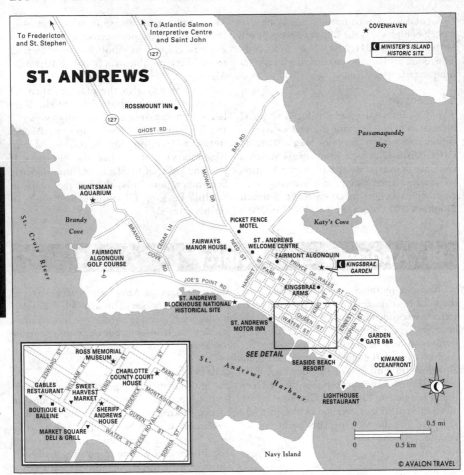

In the town's center, **Sheriff Andrews House** (63 King St., 506/529-5080; late June–early Sept. Mon.–Sat. 9:30 A.M.–4:30 P.M., Sun. 1–4:30 P.M.; donation) offers an attractive visual insight into the early Loyalist era. Costumed guides will show you around the county sheriff's Georgian-style 1820 house, which is simply but elegantly furnished in local period style.

The whitewashed **Charlotte County Court House** (Frederick St., 506/529-3843; July–Aug. Mon.–Sat. 9:30 A.M.–noon and 1–4:30 P.M.; free) dates to 1840 and is thought to be the country's oldest courthouse in continuous use.

**Ross Memorial Museum** (188 Montague St., 506/529-5124; early June–early Oct. Mon.–Sat. 10 A.M.–4:30 P.M.; donation), in an early-19th-century neoclassical brick home, preserves the furniture, porcelains, rugs, mirrors, paintings, and other items of Henry and Sarah Ross, discerning collectors of antiques and objets d'art.

## ◖ Kingsbrae Garden

Opened as recently as 1999, Kingsbrae Garden

Water Street, St. Andrews

(220 King St., 506/529-3335; mid-May–mid-Oct. daily 9 A.M.–6 P.M.; adult $10, senior and child $8.50) incorporates gardens that were once part of the Kingsbrae Arms estate, as well as additional land to create 11 hectares of tranquility on the hill above downtown. It is home to over 2,000 species—a place to feast your eyes on rhododendrons, roses, an orchard, a working windmill, an Acadian coastal forest, and a children's garden featuring miniature houses. The complex also includes a shop selling floral-themed gifts and a café overlooking the garden.

## St. Andrews Blockhouse National Historic Site

A pleasant walk along Water Street from downtown will lead you to St. Andrews Blockhouse (454 Whipple St., 506/529-4270; June–Aug. daily 10 A.M.–6 P.M.; adult $1, child $0.50). The fortification, the last survivor of 12 similar structures, was intended to protect the town from attack in the War of 1812, but nary a shot was fired in battle at this site. The interior depicts the War of 1812 era with re-created soldiers' quarters.

Even if you're not hot on history, the site is worth exploring for the wide grassy expanse out front, which edges the St. Croix River. Time your visit for the ebb (receding) tide, and you'll watch the revealing of a rocky peninsula and pools that had been fully submerged during high tide.

St. Andrews Blockhouse National Historic Site

## ST. CROIX ISLAND

In 1604, a French exploration party of 79 led by Samuel de Champlain sailed into the Bay of Fundy and named the Saint John River. After rejecting the site of the present city of Saint John as a proper spot for a settlement, the group spent the bitterly cold winter of 1604-1605 on Douchet's Island in the St. Croix River. The settlement marked the beginning of a French presence in North America. After a bitter winter in which hunger and scurvy claimed 35 lives, the remaining settlers packed up and headed for Nova Scotia's more agreeable side of the Fundy. There they established Port-Royal, the early hub of "Acadia," the name they gave this part of eastern Canada.

The St. Croix River, which drains into the Bay of Fundy at St. Andrews, forms the international border, and the site of the settlement is now protected as **St. Croix Island International Historic Site.** Beside Highway 127 nine kilometers north of St. Andrews, where views extend over the island, interpretive boards tell the story of the settlement. On the U.S. side, there's a viewing platform 13 kilometers south of Calais.

### ◖ Minister's Island Historic Site

This 200-hectare island (506/529-5081; adult $12, senior and student $10) in Passamaquoddy Bay was where Canadian Pacific Railway magnate William Van Horne built his summer retreat, **Covenhoven.** Completed in 1903, the 50-room home was built of locally quarried sandstone, and it, a windmill, a tidal swimming pool, and a barn remain. The island is only accessible at low tide, so the two daily tours depart at different times each day (check with the St. Andrews Welcome Centre for times). You will be asked to meet at the end of Bar Road, two kilometers northeast of town, from where you follow a lead vehicle across a strip of sand that is only exposed at low tide. The entry fee includes a guided tour.

## Huntsman Aquarium

Beyond the golf course, Huntsman Aquarium (Brandy Cove Rd., 506/529-1202; mid-May–Aug. daily 10 A.M.–6 P.M., Sept. Thurs.–Sun. 10 A.M.–5 P.M.; adult $7.50, senior $6.50, child $5) is part of the Huntsman Marine Science Centre, a nonprofit marine-biology study facility drawing researchers from far and wide. The aquarium is stocked with hundreds of local fish, crustaceans, mollusks, and marine plant species. A touch tank gives children gentle access to intertidal critters, while seals cavort in the outdoor pool. The center also offers environmental classes with guest lecturers and field/lab work (around $1,000 per week).

## Atlantic Salmon Interpretive Centre

On the road back to Saint John, the Atlantic Salmon Interpretive Centre (Chamcook Lake Rd., 506/529-1384; mid-May–mid-Oct. daily 9 A.M.–5 P.M.; adult $6, child $3) is part of a much larger research facility. Displays describe the life cycle of Atlantic salmon and breeding techniques. From the sun-filled room, paths lead upstream to Chamcook Lake and downstream to Passamaquoddy Bay.

## SHOPPING

Craft and gift shops abound. Whether you're looking for sweaters, souvenir T-shirts, locally produced pottery, or what have you, one of the de rigueur activities in St. Andrews is strolling along Water Street and drifting in and out of the shops. One of the nicest is **Boutique la Baleine** (173 Water St., 506/529-3926).

## RECREATION
### On the Water

Whale-watching is a popular activity here, and several companies offer cruises in search of finback, minke, and humpback whales. In addition to whales, you'll see harbor seals and lots of seabirds. All tours depart from the wharf at the foot of King Street.

**Quoddy Link Marine** (506/529-2600) has a stable covered boat that takes visitors on three-hour naturalist-narrated cruises. Light snacks

©ANDREW HEMPSTEAD

Whale-watching is a popular activity in St. Andrews.

and beverages, and use of binoculars and foul-weather gear, are included in the price of adult $50, senior $46, child $29. For the more adventurous, **Fundy Tide Runners** (506/529-4481) runs out to the whale-watching area in large inflatable Zodiacs for a similar price.

**Seascape Kayak Tours** (506/529-4866) offers sea-kayak classes and guided expeditions around Passamaquoddy Bay. Tour packages include a sunset paddle ($55 per person) and a full-day tour with lunch ($125).

## Golf
St. Andrews may not have the history of its Scottish namesake, but golfers have been drawn to the scenic fairways of the **Fairmont Algonquin Golf Course** (Brandy Cove Rd., 506/529-8165) for over 100 years. The course was thoroughly modernized in 2000, with a complete redesign that highlights the sparkling Bay of Fundy at every turn. Summer greens fees are $99, with discounts early and late in the season. Rates include access to the driving range and a power cart.

## ACCOMMODATIONS AND CAMPING
St. Andrews has a wealth of options, ranging from the eccentric (Salty Towers) to the extravagant (take your pick). Always make reservations for July and August.

### $50-100
A couple of inexpensive but clean and comfortable motels are along the road into town, including the **Picket Fence Motel** (102 Reed Ave., 506/529-8985, www.picketfencenb.com; $75–95 s or d).

### $100-150
For inexpensive no-frills waterfront accommodations, it's difficult to recommend anywhere but **⑅ Seaside Beach Resort** (339 Water St., 506/529-3846 or 800/506-8677, www.seaside.nb.ca; $120–150). Within walking distance of downtown, this complex comprises a collection of buildings dating back to the mid-1800s. There are 24 units, some of which are self-contained cabins, others larger structures complete with slanted floors and handmade windows. My favorite is Harbourview Two, which is right on the water and has two bedrooms and a small deck with a barbecue. All units have kitchens and older televisions.

**Garden Gate Bed and Breakfast** (364 Montague St., 506/529-4453, www.bbgardengate.com; $85–120 s or d) is a lovely late-19th-century home surrounded by mature gardens. Each of the four rooms has an en suite or private bathroom, and rates include a cooked breakfast.

Views from the sweeping lawns of **Rossmount Inn** (4599 Hwy. 127, 506/529-3351 or 877/529-3351, www.rossmountinn.com; $112–138 s or d) extend unimpeded across Passamaquoddy Bay. The three-story mansion holds a dining room, a lounge, an outdoor pool, and 18 guest rooms decorated in soothing cream colors and furnished with Victorian antiques. Outdoors, guests congregate on the patio or use the walking trails to explore the expansive 35-hectare grounds. The lodge is six kilometers northeast of town.

NEW BRUNSWICK

© ANDREW HEMPSTEAD

The large deck at Seaside Beach Resort is the perfect place to relax with a morning coffee.

## $150–200

Right on the edge of the bay and 200 meters from the heart of the village, **St. Andrews Motor Inn** (111 Water St., 506/529-4571, www.standrewsmotorinn.com; $160–200 s or d) is a modern three-story motel. The rates are high for a reason—most rooms have balconies with magnificent water views.

## Over $200

To experience St. Andrews' wealthy past without spending a fortune, make reservations at ☾ **Fairways Manor House** (109 Reed Ave., 506/529-4750, www.fairwaysmanorhouse .com; $175 s or d), which you pass just before entering town. Once owned by Edward Chandler Walker of Hiram Walker Distillery fame, the chateau-style mansion features luxurious guest rooms, a heated outdoor pool, a hot tub, and views across the golf course to the ocean. Rates include breakfast.

The Tudor-style **Fairmont Algonquin** (184 Adolphus St., 506/529-8823 or 800/257-7544, www.fairmont.com; from $300 s or d) is a classy Canadian resort, with manicured grounds dominating the hill above St. Andrews. Everything about it bespeaks gentility and class—verdant lawns dotted with flowerbeds, gardens, young couples in tennis whites leisurely sipping cool drinks on the veranda—and the tinkling of crystal is the loudest noise you'll hear in the formal dining room. Within, the public and guest rooms are arrayed with overstuffed furniture, oriental carpets, and gleaming dark furniture. The resort's image is very proper, and so are the members of the staff, who are snappily attired in Scottish ceremonial-style garb, replete with kilts. Amenities include multiple dining rooms, a lounge, an outdoor pool, tennis courts, a health spa, and squash/racquetball courts.

A member of the prestigious Relais & Chateaux group, the **Kingsbrae Arms** (219 King St., 506/529-1897, www.kingsbrae .com) features eight of the most luxurious guest rooms you'll find anywhere in Atlantic Canada. From the marble bathrooms to the refined room service, this is the place for a serious splurge. American plan rates (includes breakfast and dinner) start at $585 s or d.

## Campground

Through town to the east, and a 10-minute walk to downtown, **⟨ Kiwanis Oceanfront Camping** (Indian Point Rd., 506/529-3439, www.kiwanisoceanfrontcamping.com; $24–35) lives up to its name, with a front row of campsites that enjoy unimpeded water views. Amenities include showers, a playground, a grocery store, a kitchen shelter, Internet access, and a laundry.

## FOOD

While St. Andrews has cafés and restaurants to suit all tastes and budgets, seafood dominates local menus.

### Cafés

Locals head to places like **Sweet Harvest Market** (233 Water St., 506/529-6249; daily from 8 A.M.) for European-style breads, oversized cinnamon buns, and the daily muffin special.

Continuing east along the waterfront, **Market Square Deli & Grill** (211 Water St., 506/529-8241) has a coffee counter serving gourmet sandwiches made to order and hot drinks (daily 8 A.M.–7 P.M.) and a more substantial restaurant facing the town square (daily 11 A.M.–10 P.M.).

### Restaurants

If you're after casual seafood dining with water views, look no farther than **⟨ Gables Restaurant** (143 Water St., 506/529-3440; July–Aug. daily 8 A.M.–11 P.M., Sept.–May daily 11 A.M.–9 P.M.), which occupies a choice spot right on the bay. The waterfront wooden deck out back is a great place for lunch, and couldn't be more romantic in the evening—a great spot for sipping an after-dinner cognac and watching the lights shimmer across the water. The menu stays the same for lunch and dinner, with blackboard specials your best bet. Last time I was through, the seafood pie ($13) was delicious. The entrance is down an alleyway (if you pass a massive lobster woodcarving, you've found the right spot).

Also right on the water is the **Lighthouse Restaurant** (1 Patrick St., 506/529-3082; Wed.–Mon. 5–9 P.M.), on a small headland jutting into the ocean through town to the south (you can see the adjacent lighthouse from downtown). It's a big room, with basic furnishings and a casual vibe. Favorites include grilled teriyaki salmon ($19) and baked haddock wrapped in thin slices of smoked salmon ($24), or you can order boiled lobster from $25.

You don't need to be a guest at the Fairmont Algonquin (506/529-8823) to take advantage of its various eating options, including the **Passamaquoddy Room,** open in summer only for breakfast, lunch, and dinner. The resort's **Library Lounge** has a casual yet elegant atmosphere and opens to the terrace.

## INFORMATION

As you enter town from the west, the **St. Andrews Welcome Centre** (46 Reed Ave., 506/529-3556; daily 9 A.M.–6 P.M.) is tucked away in the trees on the left-hand side of the road beyond the Picket Fence Motel.

**NEW BRUNSWICK**

# Fundy Isles

The Fundy Isles are a world away from mainland living, an archipelago of islands spread across the New Brunswick side of the Bay of Fundy. Four islands—Deer, Campobello, Grand Manan, and White Head—are populated and linked to the mainland by ferry. They make an interesting diversion from coastal cruising and are little known outside Atlantic Canada.

## DEER ISLAND

The sea swirls mightily around Grand Manan but diminishes in intensity as the currents spin off around the coast of Maine to Deer Island, which lies closer to the United States than the Canadian mainland. Along with Campobello Island, sovereignty of the two islands was disputed for decades after the American Revolution; a treaty gave the islands to New Brunswick in the 1840s.

### Sights and Recreation

Wilder and with a lower profile than Campobello, Deer Island is nevertheless reached first from the New Brunswick mainland. It's devoted to fishing and is encircled with herring weirs (stabilized seine nets); other nets create the "world's largest lobster pounds." The **Old Sow,** the largest tidal whirlpool in the Western Hemisphere, can be viewed three hours before high tide from **Deer Island Point Park** at the island's south end.

### Accommodations

A great place to stay is **( Sunset Beach Cottage & Suites** (21 Cedar Grove Rd., 506/747-2972 or 888/576-9990, www.cottageandsuites.com; June–Sept.), which has an outdoor pool and a gazebo built right on the ocean. Accommodations are provided in five self-contained suites ($80 s or d) and one cottage ($700 per week), all with water views.

### Getting There

Ferries to Deer Island depart year-round from Letete, 15 kilometers from Highway 1 (turn off at Exit 56 four kilometers west of St. George). Ferries depart up to 20 times daily from 7 A.M. The government-run service is free and no reservations are taken. Between late June and early September, Deer Island is linked by ferry to Eastport (Maine) by **East Coast Ferries** (506/747-2159, www.eastcoastferries.nb.ca). Departures are hourly in each direction, and the cost is $16 per vehicle and driver plus $3 for each extra passenger.

## CAMPOBELLO ISLAND

Linked by a bridge to Lubec, Maine, Campobello is inextricably linked to the United States, but in summer a ferry links the island to Deer Island, making it a natural extension of your travels through the Fundy Isles.

Campobello, cloaked in granite, slate, and sandstone, was a favorite retreat of U.S. president Franklin Delano Roosevelt. The shingled, green and bell-pepper-red family vacation home is now the main attraction at the **Roosevelt Campobello International Park** (Hwy. 774, Welshpool, 506/752-2922; late May–mid-Oct. daily 10 A.M.–6 P.M.; free). The 34-room interior is furnished with authentic family trappings, made somehow all the more poignant as FDR was stricken with polio while on vacation here.

### Parks

East-facing 425-hectare **Herring Cove Provincial Park** (506/752-7010; May–mid-Oct.) has a long stretch of beach, six hiking trails, and a nine-hole golf course (506/752-7041; greens fees $24). Around half of the campground's sites come with electricity, and all have picnic tables and fire pits.

### Getting There

Aside from driving to the island from Maine, between late June and early September you can reach Campobello by ferry from Deer Island. **East Coast Ferries** (506/747-2159, www.eastcoastferries.nb.ca) schedules hourly crossings 9 A.M.–6 P.M. The fare for vehicle and driver is $16, plus $3 per passenger.

## ◖ GRAND MANAN ISLAND

As the Fundy Isles' largest and most southerly island, Grand Manan (pop. 2,700) gets the brunt of the mighty Fundy high tide. Pity the centuries of ships that have been caught in the currents during malevolent storms; near the island, shipwrecks litter the seafloor and pay homage to the tide's merciless power. Four lighthouses atop the island's lofty headland ceaselessly illuminate the sea lanes and warn ships off the island's shoals.

Apart from the surging tide, Grand Manan is blissfully peaceful. White, pink, and purple lupines and dusty pink wild roses nod with the summer breezes. Windswept spruce, fir, and birch shade the woodland pockets. Amethyst and agate are mixed with pebbles on the beaches at **Whale Cove, Red Point,** and **White Head Island** offshore. Dulse, a nutritious purple seaweed rich in iodine and iron, washes in at **Dark Harbour** on the western coast, and islanders dry and package the briny snack for worldwide consumption.

Offshore, every species of marine life known to the Bay of Fundy congregates in the bay's nutrient-rich mouth. Whales in pursuit of herring schools swim in on incoming currents—the right, finback, humpback, and minke whales cavort in the tempestuous seas. They're at their most numerous when the plankton blooms, mid-July through September.

### Bird-Watching

Birds of almost 350 species flutter everywhere in season, and each species has a place on this rock in the sea. Seabirds and waterfowl nest at the **Castalia Marsh** on the island's eastern side. Ducks and geese by the thousands inhabit the **Anchorage Beach** area, where a wet-heath bird sanctuary is speckled with ponds. Expect to see bald eagles and other raptors on the southern cliffs from mid-August through November. The eider, storm petrel, and Atlantic puffin prefer offshore islets.

Bird populations are thickest early April through June and late summer to autumn. A great way to see the birds is by hiking one of the 18 trails totaling 70 kilometers that crisscross the headland. Many wind through bird sanctuaries. Another incredible place for bird-watching is **Machias Seal Island,** the outermost bird-sanctuary island. Boat tours, restricted to a limited number of passengers, depart Grand Manan to see the archipelago's highest concentration of exotic bird species, including razorbill auks, arctic terns, and 900 pairs of nesting Atlantic puffins.

### Tours

While you can take whale- and bird-watching trips from St. Andrews, Grand Manan is where serious nature lovers base themselves. Space is limited and is always in demand on the following tours, so make reservations.

One of the finest, most well-established sightseeing outfits in town is **Sea Watch Tours** (North Head, 506/662-8552), which runs tour boats ($65 for a six-hour trip) to Machias Seal Island late June–early August. Whale-watching tours are scheduled July–September and also cost around $65.

### Accommodations and Camping

Though lodgings have blossomed across the island during recent years, it's smart to book ahead. **Compass Rose** (Route 776, North Head, 506/662-8570, www.compassroseinn .com; May–Oct.; $80–125 s, $90–135 d) sits atop a headland on the edge of North Head. Its six comfortable guest rooms are spread through two buildings, one of which was the island's original post office. Breakfast is served in a sunny dining room, and dinner is available with advance reservations.

**Shorecrest Lodge** (Route 776, North Head, 506/662-3216, www.shorecrestlodge .com; mid-May–mid-Nov.; $109–195 s or d) is a favorite with the bird-watching crowd (especially the late August through September migratory pelagic-bird season). The 10 rooms in this historic inn each have private bathrooms and frilly fabrics and wallpaper, while other amenities include a TV room, a veranda with water views, a library filled with field guides, and a restaurant open for dinner with advance reservations. A continental breakfast is included in the rates.

You'll need a vehicle to get to **Anchorage Provincial Park** (Seal Cove, 506/662-7022; May–Oct.), at the south end of the island. The park holds 100 unserviced ($24) or serviced ($28) campsites with toilets, hot showers, and kitchen shelters. Reservations are not accepted, so it's wise to call ahead to check on availability.

## Food

The accommodations detailed above provide dinner with reservations. For a quick pizza or burger, try **Fundy House Takeout** (23 Fleet St., Grand Manan, 506/662-8341; summer daily 9 A.M.–11 P.M.). **North Head Bakery** (North Head, 506/662-8862; Tues.–Sat.

6 A.M.–6 P.M.) has a great selection of cookies and cakes, plus bread baked daily from organic ingredients.

## Getting There

**Coastal Transport Ltd.** (506/642-0520, www.coastaltransport.ca) operates a ferry line between Blacks Harbour, 11 kilometers south of Exit 60 from Highway 1, to North Head. The 27-kilometer crossing takes about 90 minutes. The car/passenger ferries sail daily year-round, with up to six departures scheduled daily late June to early September. The round-trip fare (adult $10.70, child $5.30, vehicle from $32, bicycle $3.60) is collected when leaving the island. Reservations are not taken for travel to the island, so plan on arriving at least one hour prior to departure. Reservations *are* taken for the return journey, so call ahead to be sure of a spot, especially in July and August.

# Upper Fundy Coast

The impact of tidal action is extraordinarily dramatic on the Upper Fundy's coastline. The sea floods into the bay and piles up on itself, ravaging the shore at Mispec—where it has clawed into the land's edge to reveal gold veins—and pocking the coastline with spectacular caves at St. Martins. St. Martins also marks the starting point for the region's most challenging trek—to Fundy National Park. The backpacking trip involves just 40 kilometers, but expect to spend 3–5 days. In places the high tide washes out all beach access and forces hikers back inland.

Beyond the national park, the tide's strength increases as the bay forks into the narrow Chignecto Bay and Cumberland Basin. No place is safe during an incoming tide, especially the stretch of coast from Saint John to Hopewell Cape. At Alma, the village at the park's eastern edge, the sea rises waist-high in a half hour and continues rising to a height of 14 meters.

The Fundy orchestrates its final swan song at Hopewell Cape. Beyond the cape, its tidal impact is exhausted; some of the sea moves inland as a tidal bore and flows up the Petitcodiac River to Moncton, and the remainder washes Dorchester Peninsula's coastal marsh edges.

## SAINT JOHN TO FUNDY NATIONAL PARK

From Saint John, it's 55 kilometers northeast along Highway 1 to Exit 211, from where the boundary of Fundy National park is 22 kilometers southeast. This inland route misses St. Martins, a delightful old shipbuilding port reached from Saint John by following Highway 111 east from the airport.

### St. Martins

St. Martins, founded in 1783 as Quaco, became one of the busiest shipbuilding centers in the Maritimes in the 1800s, turning out more than 500 ships over the course of the 19th century.

## FUNDY BIRDING

In the Upper Fundy, where the tides are at their most dramatic, the setting belongs to a few remote villages and one of North America's most spectacular shows of migratory birds. The American bittern, Virginia rail, short-eared owl, marsh wren, and hundreds of other species soar across the wide stage. The bird-watching season varies according to species but is generally late March to late May and August through September.

One of the best bird-watching spots is **Grand Manan Island**. On the mainland, bird sanctuaries are scattered from upper Chignecto Bay's western coast across Shepody Bay to the Dorchester Peninsula and the Chignecto Isthmus. They are easily missed – signs are often obscure, and num-

bered roads may be the only landmarks. Many are managed by **Ducks Unlimited Canada** (506/458-8848), a nonprofit environmental group that manages around 20,000 hectares of wetlands in New Brunswick alone. Another good source of information is the **Canadian Wildlife Service,** which has its Atlantic head office at **Sackville Waterfowl Park** (17 Waterfowl Ln., Sackville, 506/364-5044, www .cws-scf.ec.gc.ca; Mon.-Fri. 8 A.M.-4 P.M.). At this location, there is a display room with details of species you're likely to spot in the adjacent wetland as well as down the road at the **Tintamarre Sanctuary,** a national wildlife area. A similar reserve is **Shepody National Wildlife Area** between Alma and Hopewell Cape.

---

Today the handsome little village is a fishing port, as evidenced by the stacks of lobster traps on the quay. At the harbor, two covered wooden bridges stand within a stone's throw of one another. The local tourist information office is housed in the lighthouse close by.

Some of the great attractions in the vicinity are the seaside caves scooped out of the red sandstone cliffs by the Fundy tides. The caves can be explored at low tide.

The village has two excellent accommodations, and being just a 40-minute drive from downtown Saint John, it's worth considering staying an extra night and using St. Martins as a base for a day trip to the city. The historic **Quaco Inn** (16 Beach St., 506/833-4772 or 888/833-4772, www.quacoinn.com; $99–200 s or d) has comfortable beach house quarters with 12 guest rooms, a dining room, a hot tub housed outdoors in a gazebo, and bicycles for rent. Overlooking the Bay of Fundy, the Victorian Gothic **St. Martins Country Inn** (303 Main St., 506/833-4534 or 800/565-5257, www.stmartinscountryinn.com; $110–180 s or d), former home of one of the seaport's most prosperous shipbuilding families, has aptly

been dubbed "the Castle" by locals. The beautifully restored mansion has 17 antique-furnished rooms, each with private bath and some with canopied beds. Breakfast is extra, or pay from $195 d for a package that includes accommodations, breakfast, and dinner.

## FUNDY NATIONAL PARK

This magnificent park is a bit out of the way but well worth the effort to get to. The 206-square-kilometer park encompasses a cross-section of Fundy environments and landforms: highlands; deeply cut valleys; swampy lowlands; dense forests of red and sugar maple, yellow birch, beech, red spruce, and balsam fir; and a shoreline of dizzying cliffs and sand and shingle beaches. For all its wilderness, though, Fundy National Park has a surprising number of civilized comforts, including rustic housekeeping chalets, a motel, a restaurant, and a golf course.

From Saint John, Highway 1 feeds into the TransCanada Highway, and the backcountry Highway 114 branches off east of Sussex, peels over the Caledonia Highlands, and plummets through woodlands to sea level. Thick woods rise on one side and conceal the park's deep valleys sown with rivers and waterfalls. Glimpses of the sea, cradled by beaches, appear on the road's other side; most of the 13-kilometer shoreline is wrapped with formidably steep sandstone cliffs.

## Park Entry

The park is open year-round, though full services operate (and entry fees are charged) only mid-May to mid-October. A one-day pass, valid until 4 P.M. the following day, is adult $8, senior $7, child $4.

## Hiking

Two dozen hiking trails wander the coastline or reach up into the highlands. The highlands hikes are easy-to-moderate treks, while the toughest trails lie along the coast, impeded by cliffs, ridges, fern glades, and thick forests.

Shorter, easier trails include the **Caribou Plain,** a 3.4-kilometer loop on flat terrain through forest and bog, and **Dickson Falls,** a 1.5-kilometer loop that offers views above and below the waterfall via a system of boardwalks and stairs. The moderately difficult **Goose River Trail** is 7.9 kilometers each way, along an old cart track to a wilderness campground at the mouth of Goose River in the park's southwestern corner. The 10-kilometer (each way) **Coastal Trail** is graded as difficult, but the rewards include lush fern glades and forest and great ridge-top views over the bay and coastal sea stacks. You can get more detailed information at park headquarters or the Wolfe Lake information center, both of which sell the useful *Fundy National Park Trail Guide.*

## Other Recreation

Beyond the grassed meadow below the Park Information Centre is the **Saltwater Pool** (summer 11 A.M.–7 P.M.; adult $3.50, senior $3, child $1.60), which is filled with heated saltwater piped in from the Bay of Fundy. If you prefer to be on the water rather than in it, head to **Bennett Lake,** where canoe, kayak, and rowboat rentals are $10 per hour.

**Fishing** is good for the plentiful trout found in the lakes and rivers; a national park fishing license, available at either visitor center, is required ($10 per day; $35 for an annual pass valid in all national parks).

**Fundy National Park Golf Course** (506/887-2970; mid-May–mid-Oct.) is a fun, old-fashioned nine-hole layout that tumbles down the hillside near the administration building and slices through the coastal forest like a green velvet glove whose fingers reach into the woodlands. The greens fee is $19 for nine holes, or you can play all day for $35. Adjacent to the golf course are **tennis courts** and **lawn bowling;** rental equipment is available at the pro shop.

## Accommodations

Lodging within the park and in the adjacent fishing village of **Alma** is well-priced. The best deal is at **Fundy Park Chalets** (506/887-2808, www.fundyparkchalets .com; late May–mid-Oct.; $99 s or d), which is beside the golf course's Seawinds Dining Room and within walking distance of the swimming pool. The 29 cabins are older, with basic cooking facilities and bathrooms. Early and late in the season, rates are reduced to $60 per night.

If you want to stay within the park but are looking for something a little more modern than the Fundy Park Chalets, consider **⦗** **Fundy Highlands Inn and Chalets** (8714 Hwy. 114, 506/887-2930 or 888/883-8639, www.fundyhighlandchalets.com; $89–105 s or d). This lodging two kilometers from the main facility area enjoys a lofty location high above the bay in the Caledonia Highlands. Choose between comfortable rooms in the main lodge or chalets with water views. All units have cooking facilities.

**Parkland Village Inn** (8601 Main St., 506/887-2313 or 866/668-4337, www.park-landvillageinn.com; $75–135 s or d) is a 50-year-old three-story motel with a waterfront location along Alma's main street. The rooms are simple but modern, and most have water views. The adjacent one-bedroom cottage is a steal at $125.

## Campgrounds

The park has four campgrounds. Reservations can be made through the **Parks Canada Campground Reservation Service** (905/426-4648 or 877/737-3783, www.pccamping.ca) for $11 per booking, but they are only really necessary for weekends in July and August.

**Headquarters Campground** (late June–early Sept.; $26–36) is within walking distance of the Park Information Centre, the swimming pool, the golf course, and Seawinds Dining Room. Facilities include showers, playgrounds, and full hookups. Back up Highway 114 a little way is **Chignecto North Campground** (mid-May–mid-Oct.; $26–36), with similar facilities.

At the end of Point Wolfe Road, six kilometers southwest of the Park Information Centre, **Point Wolfe Campground** (late June–early Sept.; $26) has a delightful beachside location and is linked to coastal hiking trails. It has showers but no hookups.

In the park's northwest corner, **Wolfe Lake Campground** (mid-May–mid-Oct.; $16) has basic facilities such as pit toilets and fire pits.

## Food

The only restaurant within the park is **Seawinds Dining Room** (506/887-2098; late May–mid-Oct. daily 11 A.M.–9:30 P.M.), across from the Park Information Centre beside the golf course. In all regards, it is a classically old-fashioned resort dining room, suited to families, well-priced, and with funky decorations that include three wrought-iron chandeliers, model ships, and the shell of a 13.5-pound lobster. Seafood dominates, with a lunchtime lobster roll and fries costing $10 and the dinner menu topping out at $19 for poached salmon covered with hollandaise sauce.

For locally harvested seafood to take back and cook at your campsite, head for **Butland's** (Main St., Alma, 506/887-2190), which sells live and cooked lobsters, scallops, salmon, and haddock. Also in Alma is **Tides** (Parkland Village Inn, 8601 Main St., 506/887-2313; daily for breakfast, lunch, and dinner), a casual dining room overlooking the Bay of Fundy.

## Information

The main **Park Information Centre** (506/887-6000, www.pc.gc.ca; spring and fall daily 8 A.M.–4:30 P.M., mid-June–early Sept. daily 8 A.M.–10 P.M., winter Mon.–Fri. 8:15 A.M.–4:30 P.M.) is on the park's eastern edge, just across the river from the village of Alma. In addition to handing out general park information, the center is home to various natural history displays and holds a large bookstore.

Entering from the northwest, you'll find a small visitor center beside picturesque Wolfe Lake (Hwy. 114; late June–mid-Aug. daily 10 A.M.–6 P.M.).

## ALMA TO HOPEWELL CAPE

It's 40 kilometers from Alma to Hopewell Cape, but for bird-watchers there is one important detour.

### Shepody National Wildlife Area

Shepody National Wildlife Area—New Brunswick's stellar bird-watching sanctuary—is made up of three different habitat areas. **Germantown/Beaver Brook Marshes,** 14.7 kilometers northeast of Alma, is the reserve's only inland area and spreads out on 686 hectares on Highway 114's east side. As you approach the area, look for Midway Road, the reserve's southern boundary. Turn right on Midway, cross the covered bridge, and park beyond at the second path. The nine-kilometer trail follows the marsh's edge alongside woodlands and fields rich with ducks and herons.

The 185-hectare **New Horton Marsh** attracts ducks and herons to a coastal setting. At Alma, take coastal Highway 915 for a 30-kilometer drive to the mudflats. The reserve's northern tip is situated where the road divides; one branch leads to inland Riverside-Albert, the other to Mary's Point Road farther out on

© ANDREW HEMPSTEAD

**At low tide, the boats in Alma end up on the drained ocean floor.**

the coast. A four-kilometer trek through the marsh starts on a dike off the latter road. **Note:** *Be wary of the tides:* the mudflats reach almost to the sea and quickly flood.

A few kilometers beyond New Horton Marsh, Mary's Point Road leads to **Mary's Point,** Canada's only shorebird reserve. Shorebirds by the hundreds of thousands set down on the 109-hectare coastal reserve, their numbers peaking mid-July through mid-August. Among the onslaught are about 9,000 blue herons and an uncountable number of cormorants, all of which swarm over the intertidal zone.

## HOPEWELL CAPE

The great Fundy tides have created a curiously compelling scene at Hopewell Cape, 40 kilometers northeast of Alma and 35 kilometers south of Moncton.

### ◖ Hopewell Rocks

Hopewell Cape is the place-name, and Hopewell Rocks (Hwy. 114, 506/734-3534; mid-May–mid-Oct. daily 9 A.M.–6 P.M.,

July–Aug. until 8 P.M.; adult $8, senior $7, child $6) is the name of the natural attraction. You pay the entry fee at the tollgate and then are directed to the main visitor center, where interesting displays describe the geology of the cape and its relationship to the Fundy tides.

Trails lead to a number of cliff-top lookouts, but the vast majority of visitors make a beeline for the **Flowerpot Rocks.** The walking trail takes around 20 minutes, or you can pay $1.25 each way to ride the oversized golf cart shuttle. Either way, next up is a steep descent down a stairway to the ocean floor. At the staircase's first landing, you overlook an otherworldly collection of giant natural arches and mushroom-shaped pillars jutting up from the sea floor. Known as "flowerpots," these sea-sculpted red shale and conglomerate sea stacks have been separated from the mainland cliffs by the abrasive tide. Many of the flowerpots are "planted" with stunted black spruce and balsam fir, looking somewhat like clipped haircuts stuck atop the stacks. At low tide, sightseers—dwarfed by the enormous pillars— roam the beach and retrieve seashells left by the tide. Be careful of falling rocks; the pillars and

© ANDREW HEMPSTEAD

The "flowerpots" at Hopewell Rocks are New Brunswick's most distinctive geological feature.

cliffs are continually eroding, and there's always a chance that rocks will loosen and tumble.

It's only possible to "walk on the ocean floor" (as it's promoted) around the flowerpots from three hours before low tide to two hours after. Catch the scene again at high tide and you'll understand why. The tide rises 16 meters here, fully flooding the area. All you'll see are the pillars' tree-covered crowns. Information centers in Fundy National Park and Moncton will be able to tell you when the tide is low at Hopewell Rocks, or check the website www .thehopewellrocks.ca. Be forewarned: When low tide falls during the middle of the day in July and August, the "ocean floor" gets *extremely* crowded.

## Accommodations and Food

Near the access road is **Hopewell Rocks Motel** (Hwy. 114, 506/734-2975 or 888/759-7070, www.hopewellrocksmotel.com; $105 s or d, family rooms $135), which has 33 rooms with water views, an outdoor swimming pool, and a restaurant with lots of seafood and dishes such as roast beef dinners under $15.

# SAINT JOHN RIVER VALLEY

The Saint John River originates in remote northern Maine near the Québec border and enters New Brunswick's northwestern corner alongside Highway 205, a backcountry road used more by loggers than sightseers. The young river tumbles along, over riverbed boulders and through glistening pools frequented by moose and white-tailed deer. It flows through Edmundston and then curves southeast through the French-flavored towns and villages of Madawaska until it's squeezed into a spuming torrent at the stony gorge at Grand Falls. The rest of the river's journey grows increasingly placid. It's tamed by hydro dams at Beechwood and Mactaquac, and it flows under the world's longest covered bridge at Hartland before draining into the Bay of Fundy at Saint John. That city was covered in the *Fundy Coast* chapter—here we concentrate on the river's interior course, which splits the inland provincial capital of Fredericton in two. This small genteel city of just 47,000 is a sightseer's delight, with a historically appealing downtown core, riverfront walking paths, and tree-lined streets feeding back to quiet residential areas of historic homes with open porches, bay windows, and gardens of pearl-colored peonies and scarlet poppies.

## PLANNING YOUR TIME

The vast majority of travelers who traverse the length of the Saint John River arrive overland through Québec and make this western

© ANDREW HEMPSTEAD

# HIGHLIGHTS

◖ **Historic Garrison District:** Filling two blocks of downtown Fredericton, this wide-open attraction lets visitors step back in time while surprising them with quirky attractions such as a 17-kilogram frog (page 219).

◖ **Beaverbrook Art Gallery:** Atlantic Canada's finest art gallery holds an impressive collection of Canadian work, as well as paintings by notables like Salvador Dalí (page 221).

◖ **Christ Church Cathedral:** In a land of grandiose churches, this is one of the most impressive. Come for summer music recitals, or simply wander through the gardens and crane your neck to search out the spire (page 221).

◖ **Kings Landing Historical Settlement:** Loyalist history comes alive at this outdoor museum that will easily fill a full day (page 228).

◖ **Hartland Covered Bridge:** The most memorable way to reach the quiet village of Hartland is by crossing the Saint John River via the world's longest covered bridge (page 228).

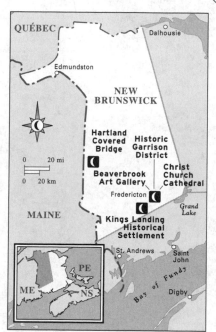

LOOK FOR ◖ TO FIND RECOMMENDED SIGHTS, ACTIVITIES, DINING, AND LODGING.

NEW BRUNSWICK

part of New Brunswick the first taste of the Maritimes. If you've flown into Halifax and caught the ferry across the Bay of Fundy, it will take a little over an hour to reach Fredericton, which should be your focus for a day of sightseeing. This will give you enough time to explore the **Historic Garrison District,** walk through **Beaverbrook Art Gallery,** and marvel at **Christ Church Cathedral. Kings Landing Historical Settlement** is only a short drive from the capital, but it would make for a long day to lump it in with the other city attractions in a single day. Besides, you'll want to continue upriver to **Hartland** for the opportunity to drive across the world's longest covered bridge.

NEW BRUNSWICK

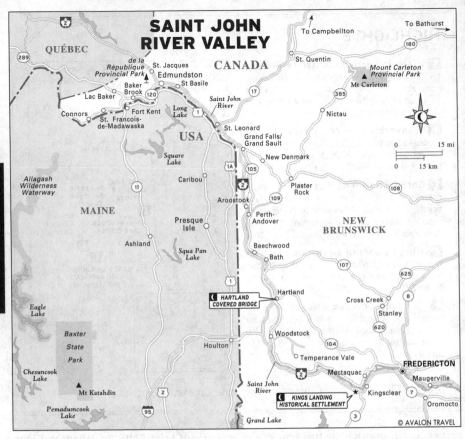

# Fredericton and Vicinity

Fredericton (pop. 50,000), in the southwestern heart of the province, is New Brunswick's legislative, cultural, and educational center, and one of the country's oldest settlements. The city is the exception to the usual rule of thumb that a province's busiest and largest city is the logical choice for the capital. Fredericton is hardly a metropolis. Rather, it's of modest size, elegant, picture book pretty, and very Anglo in tone and shape. "There is something subtle and elusive about it," Michael Collie wrote of Fredericton, "like a person who has had long sessions of psychoanalysis and has become more sophisticated and charming in the course of them."

Visitors flying in to New Brunswick will find Fredericton makes a good introduction to the province and a good sightseeing base. Roads lead from here to every part of the province. St. Andrews and Saint John on the Fundy are each just over an hour's drive south, and Moncton is 180 kilometers east. And it's always nice to return to Fredericton, the province's quintessential hometown.

© ANDREW HEMPSTEAD

Fredericton skyline

## HISTORY

Fredericton is one of North America's oldest cities, though early attempts at settlement were short-lived. The French tried settlements in the late 1600s. Joseph Robineau de Villebon, Acadia's governor, built a fur-trading fort on the northern bank of the Saint John River at the mouth of the Nashwaak River. Heavy winter ice wrecked the fortification, and the inhabitants fled to Port-Royal across the Bay of Fundy. In 1713, the Treaty of Utrecht awarded mainland Nova Scotia to the British, and Acadians fled back across the Fundy and founded Saint-Anne's Point (now site of Fredericton's historic area). The British demolished the village after the Acadian deportation. Malecite people camped along what is now Woodstock Road but moved upriver to the Kingsclear area before the Loyalists arrived in the late 18th century.

### The Capital's Fortuitous Beginning

The situation that created Fredericton as provincial capital was an interesting one. After the American Revolution, Loyalists by the thousands poured into New Brunswick at Saint John. England directed the mass exodus from New York, but military forces at Saint John were unprepared for the onslaught.

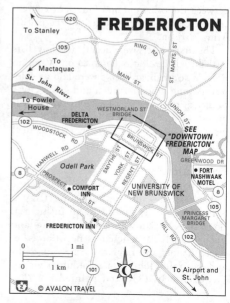

Arriving Loyalists and families, finding limited food and no housing, rioted. Stung by the backlash, the British directed subsequent emigrants 103 kilometers upriver to Saint-Anne's Point. The Loyalists arrived in the wilderness, founded a new settlement as a "haven for the king's friends," and named it Frederick's Town in honor of King George III's second son. Two years later, in 1785, provincial governor Thomas Carleton designated the little river town the colonial capital, and the people of Saint John were permanently miffed.

England had great plans for Fredericton. Surveyor Charles Morris drew up the first street grid between University Avenue and Wilsey Road. By 1786 the population center had shifted, and central Fredericton as you see it today was redrawn by another surveyor and extended from riverfront to George Street, bounded by University Avenue and Smythe Street.

Priorities were established. Space was set aside for the Church of England sanctuary and King's College, now the University of New Brunswick. Public commons were marked off between the riverfront and Queen Street, except for two blocks earmarked for the British Army garrison.

The first winters were brutal, and Loyalists buried their dead at Salamanca on Waterloo Row. Wooden boardwalks were laid as sidewalks along muddy streets, and sewage was funneled into the river. The colonial government began at Government House in 1787, and New Brunswick's first assembly met the next year at a coffeehouse.

## Expansion

The infamous Benedict Arnold lived awhile in Fredericton—and was burned in effigy at Saint John. Jonathan Odell, an influential Loyalist politician whose former estate land is now Odell Park, acted as negotiator between Arnold and England. American artist and naturalist John James Audubon visited Fredericton in 1830 and painted the *Pine Finch,* one of his best-known works, during his stay at Government House.

By 1800, wharves lined the riverfront from Waterloo Row to Smythe Street, and sloops, schooners, and brigantines sped between the capital and Saint John. Shipping lumber was a profitable early business, and Fredericton added foundry products, processed leather, carriages, and wagons to its economy in the 1800s.

Fredericton and Christ Church Cathedral had a tightly woven beginning. The town was barely three generations old when Queen Victoria got wind of the cathedral's construction. But with fewer than 10,000 inhabitants, the settlement was hardly the proper setting for the foundation of the first Anglican cathedral to be built on British soil since the Reformation. Royalty, of course, can do anything it wants, and Queen Victoria remedied the hitch. She elevated little Fredericton to the official "city" status required for an Anglican cathedral's setting. The city was incorporated in 1848, and in 1873 the city limits were extended to nearby towns, doubling the population. The city hall opened three years later.

## Fires and Floods

Fredericton had its share of scourges. At various times, flames consumed even the sturdiest stone buildings, from Government House to the Military Compound's Guard House. Great conflagrations leveled 300 downtown buildings in 1849, destroyed 46 houses and stores in 1854, and took the first Christ Church Cathedral's steeple in 1911. Even the Westmoreland Street Bridge was vulnerable, and the first bridge, built in 1885, burned in 1905.

River floods were equally devastating: Queen Street was frequently under water during spring's ice melt. Floods in 1887 and 1923 swamped the capital. The upriver Mactaquac Dam was built to divert the river's impact, but floods again threatened the capital during 1973–1974.

## The Town Evolves

England's plan for Fredericton as a miniature London was never fulfilled. Shipping and manufacturing diminished in the early 1900s, and Fredericton settled in as a prosperous genteel government town, university center, and haunt of the Anglo establishment. The **New Brunswick College of Craft and Design** started up in the 1940s and relocated to the renovated Military Compound in the 1980s. The **University of New Brunswick,** with 7,500 engineering, arts, education, business, and science students, overlooks the city from a steep hilltop and shares the campus with **St. Thomas University,** a Roman Catholic institution with 1,200 liberal-arts students.

William Maxwell Aitken, better known as Lord Beaverbrook, paved the way for Fredericton's cultural accomplishments. The **Beaverbrook Art Gallery** was a gift to the city in 1959, and **Lord Beaverbrook Playhouse** across the street followed in 1964. It became the home of Theatre New Brunswick, Atlantic Canada's only provincial repertory touring company.

## SIGHTS
### ◖ Historic Garrison District

This military compound (Queen St., 506/460-2129), a national historic site, dominates downtown, encompassing two long city blocks between the modern city to the south and the Saint John River to the north. Built in 1784 as headquarters for the British army, it is enclosed by a curlicue wrought-iron black fence that contains a variety of attractions.

At the corner of Queen and Carleton Streets, the stone **Officers' Quarters** was built in 1827. One street-level room is open to the public (July–Aug. daily 10 A.M.–6 P.M.; free), while around the back, low-ceilinged rooms once used to store ammunition now provide a home for vendors selling arts and crafts. Across the courtyard is the **Guard House,** a simple stone building (July–Aug. daily 10 A.M.–6 P.M.; free) that looks much like it would have in the

**NEW BRUNSWICK**

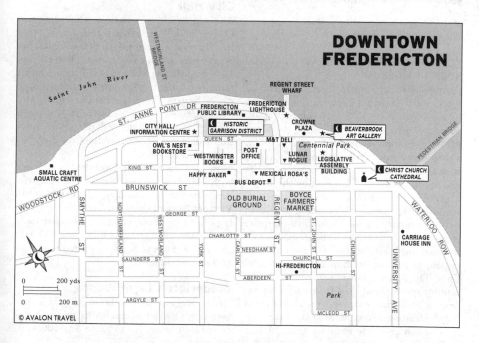

This wrought-iron arch forms the entranceway to the Historic Garrison District.

mid-1800s, complete—in summer—with costumed guards out front.

### YORK-SUNBURY HISTORICAL SOCIETY MUSEUM

Facing the Parade Square at the east end of the Historic Garrison District, this museum (Queen St., 506/455-6041; summer daily 10 A.M.–5 P.M.; adult $3, child $1) is housed within the former Officers' Quarters (1825), a three-story stone building unusually styled with a ground-level colonnade of white pillars and an iron handrail, designed by the Royal Engineers. The museum is devoted to provincial history from early Malecite and Mi'Kmaq to contemporary events. The unlikely surprise is the Coleman Frog, a 17-kilogram, 1.6-meter-long amphibian stuffed for posterity and squatting inside a glass showcase on the second floor. The believe-it-or-not frog was found a century ago by local Fred Coleman, who developed a friendship with the frog and fattened it up by feeding it rum pudding and June bugs in honey sauce—or so the story goes.

### SCHOOL DAYS MUSEUM

Step back into the classroom at the School Days Museum (corner Queen and York Streets, 506/459-3738; June–Aug. Mon.–Fri. 10 A.M.–4 P.M., Sat. 1–4 P.M.; free), across York Street from City Hall. In addition to a reconstructed classroom, you'll find an interesting display of one-room schools, textbooks and training manuals, and furniture from as early as the mid-1800s.

### NEW BRUNSWICK SPORTS HALL OF FAME

The John Thurston Clark Memorial Building is an impressive 1881 Second Empire French Revival edifice that once served as customs house and post office. The building now provides a home for the New Brunswick Sports Hall of Fame (503 Queen St., 506/453-3747; June–early Sept. Mon.–Fri. 8:30 A.M.–4 P.M.), with exhibits highlighting the province's best sporting men and women.

## City Hall

The red-brick city hall, at the corner of Queen and York Streets and across from the Historic Garrison District, is central to everywhere within downtown. The elegant 1876 building has been city offices, a jail, a farmers market, and an opera house. Its high tower houses the city's copper clock, and the decorative fountain in front—crowned by the figurine that Frederictonians have dubbed "Freddie, the little nude dude"—was added in 1885.

Inside, the **Council Chamber** is adorned with a series of 27 locally produced tapestries depicting the city's history. The **Fredericton Visitors Bureau** (506/460-2129), in the building's front vestibule, conducts chamber tours (mid-May–early Oct. daily 8:15 A.M.–7:30 P.M.; the rest of the year by appointment weekdays 8:15 A.M.–4:30 P.M.).

## Fredericton Lighthouse

Cross Regent Street from the Historic Garrison District to reach this privately operated lighthouse (615 Queen St., 506/460-

2939; May–June Mon.–Fri. 10 A.M.–4 P.M. and Sat.–Sun. noon–4 P.M., July to early Sept. daily 10 A.M.–9 P.M.; adult $2, child $1). The interior consists of 13 separate landings exhibiting shipping and river-sailing artifacts. The top level commands a magnificent riverfront view. At ground level, you'll find a gift shop, outdoor café serving light lunches, and bike rentals.

## Beaverbrook Art Gallery

On the east side of downtown is Beaverbrook Art Gallery (703 Queen St., 506/458-8545; Mon.–Sat. 9 A.M.–5:30 P.M., Sun. noon–5:30 P.M.; adult $8, senior $6, child $3), which was donated to the city by New Brunswick art maven Lord Beaverbrook, also known as William Maxwell Aitken. The gallery boasts an impressive 2,000-piece collection—the most extensive British fine-arts collection in Atlantic Canada, if not the nation. Among the British painters represented are Thomas Gainsborough, Sir Joshua Reynolds, John Constable, and Walter Richard Sickert. You'll find Graham Sutherland's sketches of Winston Churchill—drawn in preparation for Churchill's official portrait—and works by Atlantic Canada's Miller Brittain, Alex Colville, and Jack Humphrey. Also central to the collection are the oils of Cornelius Krieghoff, depicting social and domestic scenes of early life in Acadia. Lord Beaverbrook could not resist the European masters—Salvador Dalí's large-scale *Santiago El Grande* and Botticelli's *Resurrection* are prominently displayed.

## Legislative Assembly Building

The splendidly regal legislative building (Queen St., 506/453-2527) lies kitty-corner from the gallery. The sandstone French Revival building spreads across a manicured lawn, its massive wings pierced with high arched windows, and the upper floor and tower rotunda washed in glistening white. The building was completed in 1882 at a cost of $120,000, including construction and furnishings. The front portico entrance opens into an interior decorated in high Victorian style—the apex of expensive taste at the time. Glinting Waterford prisms are set in brass chandeliers, and the spacious rooms are wallpapered in an oriental design. The interior's pièce de résistance is the **Assembly Chamber,** centered around an ornate throne set on a dais and sheltered with a canopy.

John James Audubon's *Birds of America* is kept in the **Legislative Library.** One of four volumes is on display in a climate-controlled exhibit, and pages are periodically turned to show the meticulous paintings. Each of the building's nooks and corners has a story, which tour guides are eager to relate. Tours are offered through summer, daily 8:30 A.M.–6:30 P.M. Legislative sessions (February–May, October) are open to the public.

## Christ Church Cathedral

Gothic-styled cathedrals were designed to soar grandiosely toward heaven, and this storied stone cathedral is no exception. With a lofty copper-clad central spire and elegant linear stone tracery, the cathedral rises from a grassy city block at Church and Brunswick Streets (506/450-8500). Begun in 1845 and consecrated in 1853, this was the first entirely new cathedral founded on British soil since the Norman Conquest way back in 1066. It was rebuilt after a fire in 1911 and is still the place where the city's nabobs go to pay their respects to the benevolent powers that be. It's open year-round, with recitals taking place in summer Friday 12:10–12:50 P.M.

### Historic Cemeteries

The **Old Burial Ground** is bounded by Regent, Brunswick, George, and Sunbury Streets. The site—spliced with walkways beneath tall trees—is one of two historic burial grounds in town. This spread of greenery was the final resting place for Loyalist notables.

The **Loyalist Cemetery** (formerly the Salamanca graveyard), on an unmarked gravel road off Waterloo Row at riverfront, is simpler and marks the final resting place of the founding Loyalists who died in that first winter of 1783–1784.

# BY ANY OTHER NAME

Fredericton is known by many names. New Brunswickers have dubbed the city "North America's Last Surviving Hometown." You could debate the claim, perhaps, but it nonetheless does sum up local priorities.

The naming trend goes back to the 1800s, when locals ruefully joked that the city had a fire every Saturday night and dubbed it the "City of Fires." In 1911 one such fire destroyed the Christ Church Cathedral. The sanctuary was quickly rebuilt, its grandiose silhouette on the skyline leading to the moniker "Cathedral City."

Another Fredericton nickname, "City of Stately Elms," is a testament to Fredericton's leafy ambience. The quiet streets are lined mainly with elms, a choice that goes back to founding Loyalist times. They've survived centuries, even beating Dutch elm disease, which the city quelled in the 1960s and 1970s.

Fredericton's reputation as "Canada's Poets' Corner" is a tribute to native sons Bliss Carmen, Sir Charles G. D. Roberts, and Francis Joseph Sherman. And finally, the nickname "Canada's Pewtersmith Capital" singles out the city's preeminent craft, developed here first by pewtersmith Ivan Crowell in the 18th century.

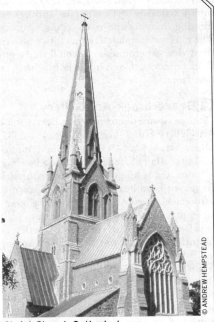

© ANDREW HEMPSTEAD

**Christ Church Cathedral**

## Odell Park

Of the 355 hectares of lush parkland throughout the city, Odell Park (Smythe St., 506/460-2038) is the choice spread, holding 16 kilometers of trails, formal lawns, duck ponds, a deer pen, barbecue pits, and picnic tables. The park is Fredericton's largest, covering 175 hectares (388 acres). It is best known for an arboretum holding every tree species in the province; a 2.8-kilometer walking trail divided in three loops wanders through the shady expanse.

## RECREATION

The riverfront **Small Craft Aquatic Centre** (Woodstock Rd., 506/460-2260; July–Aug. daily 6:30–9 A.M. and noon–8:30 P.M., shorter hours in spring and fall) rents recreational rowing shells, canoes, and kayaks; gives lessons; and leads kayak tours.

## ENTERTAINMENT AND EVENTS
### Performing Arts

Fredericton specializes in entertaining summertime visitors. Outdoor festivities center around the Garrison Historic District, where **Theatre-in-the-Park** takes to the boards July to early September. Their humorous and historical productions take place Monday–Friday at 12:15 P.M. and on weekends at 2 P.M. In summer, musicians—pipe bands and folk, country, and bluegrass groups—perform outdoors in Officers' Square every Tuesday and Thursday at 7:30 P.M., in front of the Guard House on Wednesday at 12:30 P.M., and in the Main Street Amphitheatre Wednesday at 7 P.M. Classic movies are screened outdoors every Sunday at 9 P.M. Storytellers weave local history into interesting yarns every Wednesday at 3 P.M. in Barracks Square. Best of all, this entire program is presented free of charge.

**Theatre New Brunswick,** the province's only professional English-speaking theater company, operates full-tilt during the autumn-to-spring theater season at **The Fredericton Playhouse** (686 Queen St., 506/458-8344).

## Pubs and Nightlife

Locals love their low-key pubs, and you will find many around the downtown core. The **Lunar Rogue** (625 King St., 506/450-2065) heads the list with English pub ambience, Canadian and British draft beer, and live music—usually with a Celtic flavor—several nights a week. A cluster of pubs surrounds Pipers Lane, an alley that connects the 300 blocks of King and Queen Streets. **Dolan's** (349 King St., 506/454-7474) offers an excellent menu of pub grub and slightly fancier fare, as well as Beamish on tap and live entertainment Thursday–Saturday. **Upperdeck Sports Bar** (1475 Pipers Ln., 506/457-1475) has a deck out in the sun and looks out on the comings and goings in Pipers Lane, three bars, pool tables, and bands on weekends.

Touring rock groups head for **Sweetwaters** (339 King St., 506/444-0121), where the cover charge is $8–25. Featuring five bars and two dance floors, the venue presents pulsating high-energy rock Thursday–Saturday. This place, along with **Rockin' Rodeo** (546 King St., 506/444-0122), is as hip as it gets in Fredericton.

## Festivals and Events

**Festival Francophone,** for three days late in May, celebrates Acadian language and culture with concerts, dancing, and children's activities. The festivities take place at Centre Communautaire Sainte-Anne (715 Priestman St., 506/453-2731).

The **Highland Games and Scottish Festival** (506/452-9244, www.highlandgames.ca), a local three-day Celtic tribute featuring pipe bands, highland dancing, Gaelic singing, heavy sports, clan booths, and more, takes over the city the last weekend of July.

**New Brunswick Day,** the first Monday in August, brings parades, street-food vendors, and fireworks to the Historic Garrison District.

Fredericton had its first fall fair in 1825, and the tradition continues at the **Fredericton Exhibition** (506/458-8819, www.frex.ca), with six days of country-fair trappings, including harness racing and stage shows, at the Fredericton Exhibition Grounds during early September.

The summer season finishes in a clamor of music, as the outdoor **Harvest Jazz and Blues Festival** (506/454-2583, www.harvestjazzandblues.com) takes over the downtown streets for five days in mid-September. It's billed as the biggest jazz and blues fest east of Montréal, and it features musicians from all over North America.

## SHOPPING

Shopping areas are concentrated downtown, mainly along Regent, Queen, York, King, and the adjacent side streets, plus on Woodstock Road and at the malls.

### Arts and Crafts

Several shops are known for craft specialties. **Aitkens Pewter** (408 Queen St., 506/453-9474) stocks handcrafted pewter hollowware, jewelry, and decorative ware. **Cultures Boutique** (383 Mazzuca's Ln., 506/462-3088) is a nonprofit operation featuring crafts produced by Third World artisans. It is off York Street between King and Queen Streets. For porcelain and stoneware, check out **Garden Creek Pottery** (1538 Woodstock Rd., 506/455-7631).

**Gallery Connexion** (686 Queen St., 506/454-1433) is a nonprofit artists' outlet with an eminent reputation for the province's arts. In a converted residence, **Gallery 78** (796 Queen St., 506/454-5192; closed Mon.) is the oldest commercial art gallery in New

**NEW BRUNSWICK**

Brunswick and stocks a collection of art from all over Canada.

## ACCOMMODATIONS AND CAMPING

In keeping with its status as a provincial capital, Fredericton has a choice of downtown chain hotels, each offering a wide range of modern services aimed at business travelers. Other options are historic inns dotted around the outskirts of downtown and regular motels along major arteries. The main concentration of the latter is three kilometers south of downtown at the junction of Regent and Prospect Streets (Exits 6A and 6B of Hwy. 8).

### Under $50

**HI-Fredericton** (621 Churchill Row, 506/450-4417, www.hihostels.ca), an affiliate of Hostelling International, is a restored heritage home five blocks south of the Historic Garrison District. Amenities include a kitchen, laundry, and living area. Guest rooms have a maximum of three beds, with most having just one or two. Members pay $20–25, nonmembers $23–30. Check-in is 7 A.M.–noon and 6–10 P.M.

### $50-100

Across the river from downtown, the **Fort Nashwaak Motel** (15 Riverside Dr., 506/472-4411 or 800/684-8999, www.fortnashwaakmotel.com; $75 s, $85 d) and, four kilometers downstream, the **Norfolk Motel** (Hwy. 2, 506/472-3278 or 800/686-8555, www.norfolkmotelonline.com; $70 s, $75 d) are basic cheapies.

### $100-150

The three-story Queen Anne Revival **Carriage House Inn** (230 University Ave., 506/452-9924 or 800/267-6068, www.carriagehouse-inn.net; $95 s, $105 d) is a restored three-story 1875 home southeast of downtown but still within walking distance. The 10 guest rooms are furnished with antiques; guests have use of a solarium and laundry. Breakfasts are a real treat.

None of motels around the junction of Regent and Prospect Streets offer anything extraordinary. Instead you get the reliability of chains such as the **Comfort Inn** (797 Prospect St., 506/453-0800 or 800/228-5150, www.choicehotels.ca; $105 s, $115 d). In the vicinity and one of the largest motels in the city is the four-story **Fredericton Inn** (1315 Regent St., 506/455-1430 or 800/561-8777, www.frederictoninn.nb.ca; $140 s or d), between the Regent and Fredericton shopping malls. It has 200 guest rooms, a dining room, lounge, pool, and whirlpool.

Around 20 kilometers west of downtown along Highway 102 (at Exit 274), **Riverside Resort** (35 Mactaquac Rd., 506/363-5111 or 800/561-5111, www.holidayfredericton.com; from $135 s or d) has a very un-city-like location within striking distance of Kings Landing. It's a sprawling property with a restaurant and lounge, and a health center with a heated indoor pool, a hot tub, and an exercise deck. Six two-bedroom chalets ($260 s or d) are also on the manicured grounds.

( **On the Pond** (Rte. 615, Mactaquac, 506/363-3420 or 800/984-2555, www.onthepond.com; from $145 s or d) is a luxurious country inn where the emphasis is on being pampered in a back-to-nature environment. Guests enjoy a wide variety of spa services, being close to Mactaquac Provincial Park and its golf course, and a fitness center. The eight guest rooms have an earthy Old World charm, with little niceties such as plush robes and inviting living areas. Bed-and-breakfast rates are $145 s or d, but check the website for spa and golf packages.

### $150-200

Along the river within striking distance of downtown attractions is the ( **Delta Fredericton** (225 Woodstock Rd., 506/457-7000 or 888/890-3222, www.deltahotels.com; from $199 s or d), which has an agreeable resort-style atmosphere centering on a large outdoor pool complex, complete with resort furniture and a poolside bar. It also has an indoor pool, a fitness room, two restaurants, and a lounge. Check the Delta website for discounted rooms, and maybe consider a splurge on a suite that will cost the same as a regular room in a big-city hotel.

### Over $200

One of Fredericton's better lodgings is the **Crowne Plaza Fredericton Lord Beaverbrook** (659 Queen St., 506/455-3371 or 800/561-7666, www.cpfredericton.com; $210–440 s or d), aimed squarely at those in town on government business. Don't let the dowdy exterior of this bulky hotel put you off—a massive revamp modernized the 165 guest rooms. Amenities include an indoor pool and fitness complex, two dining rooms, and a lounge.

### Campgrounds

The closest camping to Fredericton is at **Hartt Island RV Resort,** seven kilometers west of town on the TransCanada Highway (506/462-9400, www.harttisland.com; May–Oct.; $24–34), which is a great spot to enjoy river sports like canoeing and kayaking.

On the same side of the city, but on the north side of the river, **Mactaquac Provincial Park Campground** (Hwy. 105, 506/363-4747; mid-May–mid-Oct.; $21.50–24) is a huge facility 24 kilometers from downtown. In addition to 305 campsites, there's a golf course, hiking, biking, and fishing.

## FOOD

Fredericton has a reputation for so-so dining. Don't believe it. True, you won't find tony dining rooms by the dozens, and aside from at a few fine restaurants, the cooking is less than fancy. Nonetheless, you can sample virtually all the capital's fare without a qualm, and your dining dollar will go a long way too.

### Cafés and Cheap Eats

If you're planning a picnic, **M & T Deli** (602 Queen St., 506/458-9068; Mon.–Fri. 7:30 A.M.–4 P.M.) does an admirable job of sourcing big city delicacies such as New York–style bagels and Montréal smoked meats. Daily specials are well priced (it was shepherd's pie and salad for $6 when I stopped by).

**(** **Happy Baker** (520 King St., 506/454-7200; Mon.–Fri. 7:30 A.M.–5:30 P.M., Sat. 8 A.M.–4 P.M.) is worth searching out in the bowels of the Carleton Plaza high-rise. In addition to the usual array of coffee concoctions, you can order bakery treats and full meals like maple curry chicken penne for around $10.

Year-round **Boyce Farmers' Market** (665 George St., between Regent St. and Saint John St., 506/451-1815; Sat. 6 A.M.–1 P.M.) lures *everybody* with stalls heaped with baked goods, homemade German sausage, other local delicacies, and crafts.

### Pubs and Restaurants

The **Lunar Rogue** (625 King St., 506/450-2065; daily from 9 A.M.), one of Fredericton's most popular pubs, offers dining indoors or alfresco. The breakfasts are cheap and filling, and the Rogue serves lunches and worthy light dinners (Cornish pasties, stir-fry chicken, sirloin strip, and pub-grub specials such as barbecued chicken wings; $10–18.50) as well.

Across the street and a block down, **Mexicali Rosa's** (546 King St., 506/451-0686) is part of an eastern Canadian chain of colorful Mexican restaurants. Expect all the usual Americanized food at reasonable prices. It's a long way from Mexico, but the recipes nonetheless come off quite well. Margaritas and cold *cerveza* are available. Anyone hankering for pizza can step right next door to **BrewBakers** (546 King St., 506/459-0067; daily 11 A.M. until late), where the pizzas are baked in a wood-fired oven and accompanied by pastas and salads in a contemporary setting.

The dining rooms at the major hotels are good bets for fancier fare. At the Crowne Plaza (659 Queen St., 506/451-1804), the **Terrace Room** offers lunch and dinner buffets at moderate prices, while the **(** **Governor's Room** (dinner only, mains $26–36) serves a more upscale menu of French fare and nouvelle cuisine. At the Delta Fredericton, **Bruno's** (225 Woodstock Rd., 506/457-7000; 6:30 A.M.–11 P.M.) lures crowds for fare such as chicken saltimbocca—a sautéed stuffed chicken breast basted with white wine and served on linguine—and seafood, beef, and pasta. Look for moderately priced dinners and Sunday brunch, as well as an inexpensive weekday pasta lunch buffet and a Friday evening seafood buffet. Also at the Delta is **The Dip,** a poolside bar and grill open for inexpensive lunch and dinner daily in summer, weather permitting.

If you're staying along the motel strip south of downtown, the best place to eat without returning to the city is the **Lobster Hut** (City Motel, 1216 Regent St., 506/450-9900; Tues.–Sat. 11:30 A.M.–9:30 P.M.). The cooks boil, broil, stuff, fry, or serve cold the best lobsters in town, starting at $24—and the largest available lobsters can be requested with an advance phone call. Other entrées run $10–25.

## INFORMATION AND SERVICES
### Tourist Information
The main **Visitor Information Centre** is right downtown inside the lobby of city hall (397 Queen St.; late June–early Sept. daily 8 A.M.–8 P.M., early Sept.–mid-June Mon.–Fri. 8:15 A.M.–4:30 P.M.). For advance information, contact **Fredericton Tourism** (506/460-2041 or 888/888-4768, www.tourismfredericton.ca).

### Books and Bookstores
Stocking around 80,000 titles and newspapers from around the world, the downtown **Fredericton Public Library** (12 Carleton St., 506/460-2800; Mon.–Tues. and Thurs. 10 A.M.–5 P.M., Wed. and Fri. 10 A.M.–9 P.M.) has public Internet access.

Look no further than **Westminster Books** (445 King St., 506/454-1442) for local literature such as field guides and coffee-table books. Around the corner, **Owl's Nest Bookstore** (390 Queen St., 506/458-5509) has a fantastic selection of nonfiction used and out-of-print books.

### Services
In an emergency, call 911 or the **RCMP** (1445 Regent St., 506/452-3400). For medical emergencies, contact the **Dr. Everett Chalmers Hospital** (Priestman St., 506/452-5400) or

© ANDREW HEMPSTEAD

Start your exploration at city hall, where you'll find the main Visitor Information Centre.

**Fredericton Medical Clinic** (1015 Regent St., 506/458-0200).

Hours at the **post office** (570 Queen St., 506/444-8602) are Monday–Friday 8 A.M.–5 P.M.; the retail outlets at Kings Place and Fredericton Mall shopping centers have longer hours and are open Saturday.

Take your washing to **Spin & Grin** (516 Smythe St., 506/459-5552).

## GETTING THERE
**Fredericton Airport** is 14 kilometers southeast from downtown off Highway 102. Avis, Hertz, Budget, and National have counters near the baggage carousels. Other airport facilities include a restaurant, gift shop, and business center. A cab to downtown costs $18.

The airport is served by **Air Canada** (506/458-8561 or 888/247-2262), which has direct flights from Montréal, Toronto, and Halifax.

**Acadian** (101 Regent St., 506/458-6007) has daily bus service from Fredericton to Saint John, Moncton, and Edmundston. The small terminal is open daily 8 A.M.–8:30 P.M.; storage lockers are available for $1 per day.

## GETTING AROUND

**Fredericton Transit** (506/460-2200) has a web of bus routes connecting downtown with outlying areas daily except Sunday. Fare is $2 per sector.

Look for cabs cruising downtown streets and waiting at major hotels, or call **Trius Taxi** (506/454-4444).

**Car-rental** firms are plentiful. Chains in town include **Avis** (506/446-6006), **Budget** (506/452-1107), **Hertz** (506/446-9079), and **National** (506/453-1700).

Metered parking is plentiful in parking lots behind sites and curbside on Queen, King, upper York, Carleton, Regent, and Saint John Streets. The city provides free three-day parking passes for out-of-province visitors; the passes are available at city hall and the Legislative Assembly building, both on Queen Street.

## GAGETOWN AND VICINITY

The Saint John River downstream of Fredericton is dotted with islands, around which a skein of twisting channels is braided. It's beautiful countryside, and a delightful drive, with Gagetown, 40 kilometers from the capital, a good turnaround point.

The riverfront town of **Oromocto,** halfway to Gagetown, is built around Canadian Forces Base Gagetown, a military training installation located near the town center off Broad Road. The **CFB Gagetown Military Museum** (506/422-1304; July–Aug. Mon.–Fri. 8 A.M.–4 P.M. and Sat.–Sun. 10 A.M.–4 P.M., the rest of the year Mon.–Fri. noon–4 P.M.; free) has exhibits on the past and present of the Canadian armed forces since the late 18th century—weapons, uniforms, and other memorabilia.

From Oromocto, follow Highway 102 east along the river, cross divided Highway 2 (the TransCanada Highway), and you'll soon find yourself in the pretty riverfront town of Gagetown. Quite a bit goes on in this little town of 600 over the course of the season. Look for the four-day Queens County Fair in mid-September.

The **Queens County Museum** (69 Front St., 506/488-2966; June–mid-Sept. daily 10 A.M.–5 P.M.; $2) is in a handsome white wooden house that was the birthplace of Sir Leonard Tilley, one of the "Fathers of Confederation." The first floor is dutifully furnished with Loyalist antiques, and upstairs there are vintage county exhibits.

**NEW BRUNSWICK**

# Up the Saint John River

From Fredericton, Highway 2 (TransCanada Highway) wends north along the Saint John River, crossing it numerous times before reaching Edmundston after 270 kilometers. As part of the transcontinental highway, it's easy smooth driving, but leave the main route and you'll find beautiful rural scenery and a region dotted with small towns. The region's highlights are within day-tripping distance of Fredericton, so you could travel as far as Hartland to see the world's longest covered bridge and then spend the afternoon at Kings Landing.

## MACTAQUAC AND VICINITY

Stemming the flow of the Saint John River is **Mactaquac Dam,** part of a massive hydroelectric scheme 20 kilometers west of Fredericton. Completed in 1968, the dam rerouted the river and raised the water level 60 meters, flooding the valley and creating Mactaquac Lake Basin. Historic buildings from the flooded area found a new home at the Kings Landing Historical Settlement, a provincial heritage park that opened in 1974.

**Mactaquac Generating Station** (Hwy. 102, 506/462-3800; mid-May–early Sept.

daily 9 A.M.–4 P.M.), on the river's southern bank and just off the TransCanada Highway, offers free guided tours. Below the dam, the **Mactaquac Visitor Interpretation Centre** (Hwy. 102, 506/363-3021; mid-May–Aug. daily 9 A.M.–4 P.M.; free) releases 300,000 salmon fry annually.

## Mactaquac Provincial Park

Not all New Brunswickers were pleased with this massive river alteration, but the creation of 525-hectare Mactaquac Provincial Park, which opened the following year, was a sweetener. It's beside Highway 105 on the north side of the river 24 kilometers upriver from Fredericton.

The setting's pièce de résistance is the challenging 18-hole **Mactaquac Provincial Park Golf Course** (506/363-4926; greens fees $55), which is regarded as one of Canada's top 10 public courses. The park also offers hiking trails, supervised beaches, bike rentals, picnic areas, and bass fishing.

The wooded campground has over 300 sites ($21.50 unserviced, $24 with electrical hookups) with kitchen shelters, hot showers, a launderette, and a campers' store fronting the Mactaquac Lake Basin. The park and campground are open mid-May to mid-October and a day pass is $7 per vehicle.

## ◖ KINGS LANDING HISTORICAL SETTLEMENT

A marvelous counterpoint to Caraquet's Village Historique Acadien, this grand-scale living museum (506/363-4999; early June–mid-Oct. daily 10 A.M.–5 P.M.; adult $15.50, senior $13.50, child $10.50) is in a beautiful setting alongside the Saint John River, 35 kilometers west of Fredericton (take Exit 253 from Highway 2). The river valley was settled by Loyalists who arrived in New Brunswick in 1783, and it is this era through to the early 1900s that the village represents. Bring comfortable walking shoes, as the site spreads across 120 hectares with 70 houses and buildings—among them a sawmill, farmhouses, a school, a forge, and a printing office. Informative costumed "residents" depict rural New Brunswick life as it was lived in the 1800s. One of many interesting links to the past is an orchard where hybrid apples developed by Francis Peabody Sharp in the mid-1800s are grown. Demonstrations include horseshoeing, metal forging, cloth spinning and weaving, and farming. Special events include live theater, an Agricultural Fair in late August, the Provincial Town Criers' Competition in early September, and a Harvest Festival in early October to close out the season.

No one ever leaves the **Kings Head Inn** (506/363-4950) complaining about being hungry. At the riverside end of the village, this restaurant serves up hearty fare like salmon chowder ($7), crunchy almond fish cakes ($12), and divine desserts that include maple-brandy squash pie ($5).

## TO GRAND FALLS

West from Kings Landing, the TransCanada Highway follows the Saint John River along one of its loveliest stretches. Tourism New Brunswick refers to this stretch of highway as the **River Valley Scenic Drive.** The Saint John is wide and blue, bounded by green fields and forests of maple and hemlock.

### Woodstock

Just over 100 kilometers from Fredericton, Woodstock is an agricultural service center for this rich potato-producing region. The gracious 1884 red-brick courthouse is a dominant feature of the main street, but the **Log Cabin Restaurant** (539 Main St., 506/328-8553; daily 6 A.M.–9 P.M.) is where you'll find the law-abiding locals. A cooked breakfast is $5, or double everything in the Giant Breakfast for $8.

### ◖ Hartland Covered Bridge

North from Woodstock, give the TransCanada Highway a miss and stick to Highway 103, which hugs the west bank of the Saint John River for 30 kilometers, from where it makes a sharp right turn and crosses the world's longest covered bridge before emerging in the village of Hartland. The bridge is only wide enough for one-way traffic, so make sure no one else is driving toward you before entering the bridge. Built in 1901, covered in 1921, and now protected as a national historic site, it stretches 391 meters over the Saint John River. On the east side is an information center (summer daily 9 A.M.–6 P.M.) with displays on the bridge's history and on other covered bridges in New Brunswick. From this point, a walking trail leads upstream and then along the Becaguimac Stream.

### Grand Falls (Grand-Sault)

The otherwise placid Saint John River becomes a frothing white torrent when it plunges 23 meters over the stony cataract that gave Grand Falls, or Grand-Sault, its name. Below the falls, which have been harnessed to produce hydroelectric power, the tremendous force of the river has worn a two-kilometer-long, horseshoe-shaped gorge through 70-meter-high rock walls. Here, the river is at its narrowest, and the gorge's bottleneck impedes the water's force. The river pushes through the narrows in tumultuous rapids, like pent-up champagne bursting from the bottle.

The **Malabeam Reception Centre** (Madawaska Rd., 506/475-7769; early June–early Sept. daily 10 A.M.–6 P.M.; free) makes a convenient starting point for exploring the area. From the center's rear windows, you'll see the thundering cataracts tumbling through the gorge. A two-kilometer-long path leads along the gorge to **La Rochelle,** from where a rock staircase leads down to the cataract edge, where the agitated river swirls in the rocky wells. The river is most spectacular during spring runoff.

Several well-priced lodgings in Grand Falls make the town all the more appealing for overnight stays. The best choice is **Auberge Pres du Lac** (TransCanada Hwy., 506/473-1300 or 888/473-1300, www.presdulac.com; $80–140 s, $95–140 d), on the north side of town. It has 100 rooms and cottages opposite a manmade pond, an indoor pool, a small fitness room, and a sauna.

## EDMUNDSTON AND VICINITY

Originally settled by Acadian refugees on the site of a Malecite village, Edmundston (pop. 17,000) was first called Petit Sault for the rapids here at the confluence of the Saint John and Madawaska Rivers.

### Sights and Recreation

For an insight into the area's checkered history and "mythical Madawaska," stop in at the **Madawaska Museum** (195 Blvd. Hébert, 506/737-5282; July–Aug. daily 9 A.M.–8 P.M.; Sept.–June Wed.–Thurs. 7–10 P.M. and Sun. 1–5 P.M.; adult $4, child $2). But to truly experience the local Acadian-flavored culture, come for the five-day **Foire Brayonne** (www.foirebrayonne.com), on the weekend closest to August 1. Over 100,000 people show up for the celebration of Brayon foods, music, dance, sports, and other entertainment.

### Accommodations

The ritziest hotel in town is the large **Chateau Edmundston** (100 Rice St., 506/739-7321 or 800/576-4656, chateauedmundston .com; from $110 s or d), which has an indoor pool, a hot tub, a sauna, laundry facilities, a restaurant, and a lounge. With similar facilities is **Quality Inn Edmundston** (919 Canada Rd., 506/735-5525 or 800/563-2489, www.choice-hotels.ca; $95–115 s or d). Both are accessed from Exit 18 of the TransCanada Highway.

### Saint-Jacques

North of Edmundston, about halfway to the Québec border, is Saint-Jacques, home of **de la République Provincial Park,** where the highlight is the **New Brunswick Botanical Garden** (Exit 8 of the TransCanada Hwy., 506/737-5383; June–Sept. 9 A.M.–6 P.M., July–Aug. 9 A.M.–8 P.M.; adult $14, senior $12, child $7). If you've admired the flower-filled setting at the Montréal Botanical Garden, you will see a resemblance here. The formal garden complex on 17 hectares was designed by the same skilled Michel Marceau. It brims with 60,000 plants of 1,500 species. Roses, perennials, and rhododendrons bloom among the prolific posies all the quiet woodlands you could ever want, as well as the rustic **Camping RJ Belanger** (510 Church Rd., 506/992-2136; mid-May–mid-Sept.). The lakeshore complex lies several kilometers north of the river and has eight cabins ($65–85 s or d), campsites ($22.50–27.50), a dining room and canteen, and swimming, canoeing, and kayaking.

## MOUNT CARLETON PROVINCIAL PARK

This remote 17,000-hectare park is a popular spot for hiking and wilderness camping. It is off Highway 385, 105 kilometers northeast of Perth-Andover (on the TransCanada Highway halfway between Hartland and Grand Falls). If you're looping around the province between Campbellton and the Saint John River Valley via Highway 17, you can reach the park by following Highway 180 east from Saint Quentin to Highway 385.

The park surrounds the Maritimes' highest point of land, **Mount Carleton** (820 meters). If you're keen on reaching the summit, wear sturdy shoes and bring a jacket to combat the winds. The easiest, marked ascent goes up a 4.4-kilometer trail through a spruce, fir, and yellow birch forest. The mountain's peak rises above the tree line and the view is marvelous, overlooking the adjacent mountains and lakes from a summit strewn with mountain cranberries and wild blueberries. Other trails in the 62-kilometer network include a 300-meter path to Williams Falls.

The park's main campground (506/235-6040; mid-May–early Sept.) has 88 campsites ($19), flush toilets, showers, kitchen shelters, a dump station for RVs, a playground, a boat-launching ramp, and unsupervised swimming on Nictau Lake.

The Saint John River is a quiet waterway surrounded by pristine forest.

in nine gardens, all orchestrated with classical music in a romantic vein. Other park facilities include an outdoor swimming pool, tennis courts, and a campground ($21.50–24).

Targeted at visitors entering New Brunswick from Québec, the **Provincial Visitor Information Centre** (506/735-2747; mid-May–early Oct. daily 10 A.M.–6 P.M., July–Aug. daily 8 A.M.–9 P.M.) is alongside the TransCanada Highway nine kilometers south of the border.

## Lac-Baker

Lac-Baker is in New Brunswick's remote northwestern corner, near where the Saint John River flows into the province from the northern reaches of Maine. Here you'll find

# ACADIAN COAST

Along the eastern edge of New Brunswick is the Acadian Coast—a French-flavored realm of seaports, barrier beaches, sand dunes, salt marshes, sandy pine-clad shores, and rocky coastline. Northumberland Strait is the shallow, narrow sea strip between New Brunswick's southeastern coast and Prince Edward Island. Here the coastline attracts summertime sunbathers, swimmers, and windsurfers to welcoming beaches and waters warmed by the Gulf Stream. Farther north, the warm sea mixes with the cooler Gulf of St. Lawrence. Here the Labrador Current swirls in the open gulf, and the swift currents arrive ashore with low rolls of surf. Offshore, barrier islands hold sheltered seaports. Farthest north, the Baie des Chaleurs ("Bay of Warmth") is the shallow sea pocket between northern New Brunswick and Québec's Gaspé Peninsula.

The essence of French-speaking Acadia is entwined in its dining and festivals. To understand the region's cultural roots, visit the Village Historique Acadien at Caraquet, where early Acadian life has been re-created with authentic buildings and costumed animators. In the south, Moncton, northern New Brunswick's trendy urban commercial and educational center, is Caraquet's bustling modern counterpoint—a very successful Acadia of the new millennium. Acadian pride runs high, and everywhere in the region the Acadian flag—the red, white, and blue French tricolor with a single gold star—is displayed prominently. But other ethnic groups are represented here as well, including the Irish.

NEW BRUNSWICK

# HIGHLIGHTS

**( Bore Park:** OK, you don't *have* to visit Bore Park, but it's a good place to watch the tidal bore, and as it's home to the region's main information center, you can load up with brochures (page 235).

**( Magnetic Hill:** Magnetic Hill itself is mildly intriguing, but the surrounding commercial attractions – think zoo, water park, minigolf – make this a spot you'll want to take the family (page 237).

**( Sackville Waterfowl Park:** Birdwatchers will be enthralled with the many and varied bird species that call this reserve home (page 242).

**( Parlee Beach:** Buff – and not so buff – bods flock to Parlee Beach for its long expanse of sand, warm swimming water, and holiday vibe (page 244).

**( Le Pays de la Sagouine:** The literary world learned about Acadian life from the novels of Antonine Maillet, and this energetic historic park in her hometown brings the writing to life (page 245).

**( Lamèque International Baroque Music Festival:** Even if, like me, you're not an aficionado of early music, the remote setting and the haunting sounds of this musical extravaganza will stay with you (page 252).

**( Village Historique Acadien:** Experience Acadian life up close and personal at this outdoor museum (page 252).

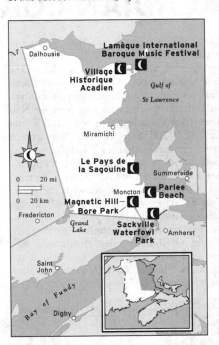

LOOK FOR **(** TO FIND RECOMMENDED SIGHTS, ACTIVITIES, DINING, AND LODGING.

Stretched-out distances notwithstanding, getting around is easy and very manageable. Highway 11 lopes along most of the three coasts from seaport to seaport, with the sea almost always within view. End to end, it's an easygoing 10-hour drive one way between Campbellton and Shediac, if you take your time. But by all means, take the side roads branching off the main route and amble even closer to the seas to explore the seaports and scenery. For example, Highway 11 diverges from the coast and cuts an uninteresting beeline between Miramichi and Bouctouche. Coastal Highway 117 is far

more scenic, running through Kouchibouguac National Park and curling out to remote Point Escuminac—a lofty shale plateau at Miramichi Bay's southeastern tip, frequented, in season, by thousands of migratory seabirds.

## PLANNING YOUR TIME

Moncton, at the south end of the Acadian Coast, is central to the entire Maritimes region, so you'll probably pass through at least once on your Atlantic Canada vacation. The bustling downtown core is well worth exploring, with **Bore Park** a good starting point. If

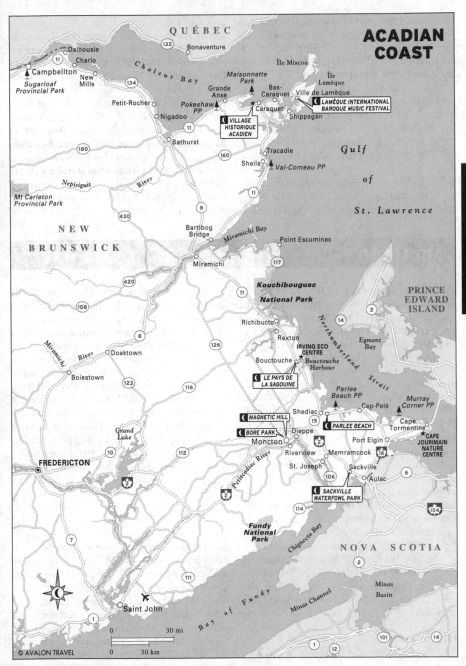

NEW BRUNSWICK

you're traveling with children, they'll definitely want you to stop at the city's **Magnetic Hill** commercial attractions. Getting back to nature, another nearby highlight for bird-watchers is **Sackville Waterfowl Park.**

If you look at a map of New Brunswick, you'll see that the Acadian Coast extends the entire length of the province (it's 320 kilometers from Moncton to Campbellton), so to avoid returning along the coastal highway, plan on combining time along the Acadian Coast with the drive down the Saint John River Valley to Fredericton—in effect two of three legs of a loop around the entire province. This circuit will take four days

at an absolute minimum, and preferably six. If the weather is warm, factor in some beach time, and there's no better place for this than **Parlee Beach,** just a short drive from Moncton. As you drive north, it is impossible not to be intrigued by the pockets of Acadian culture. The best place to learn more about this culture's tragic history and revitalized present are **Le Pays de la Sagouine** and **Village Historique Acadien.** The final highlight of the Acadian Coast is the **Lamèque International Baroque Music Festival,** and if you're anywhere near the region in late July, I encourage you to attend this unique event.

# Moncton

With a population of 65,000 (130,000 in Greater Moncton), this bustling city is the geographic center of the Maritimes. It does an admirable job of promoting its many and varied attractions, and it exudes a vitality and energy unlike anywhere else in the province. Visitors can take in two very different natural attractions—one related to the colossal Fundy tides, the other to a quirk of nature—while children will be attracted to Atlantic Canada's largest theme park. The bustling downtown core is packed with well-priced accommodations, good restaurants, and a lively nightlife.

Moncton lies 155 kilometers northeast along the Fundy Coast from Saint John and 175 kilometers east from the capital, Fredericton. It's also centrally located to other provinces, with the Nova Scotia border 37 kilometers southeast and the Confederation Bridge to Prince Edward Island 92 kilometers to the east.

The city is officially bilingual. About 30 percent of the population speaks French as a first language. So while most everyone also speaks English, knowledge of French will help the visitor.

## History

The site of modern-day Moncton was along a

Mi'Kmaq portage between the Bay of Fundy and Northumberland Strait, but the first permanent settlers were Acadians, who arrived in the 1740s. The British captured nearby Fort Beauséjour in 1755 and deported the Acadians in 1758. It was settled by Germans soon after, but it wasn't until the 1840s, when shipbuilding became a major business, that the town began its real growth. Moncton began its first real boom when the Intercolonial Railway chugged into New Brunswick and designated the town as the railroad's Atlantic hub. By 1885, the city was an industrial center with a tannery, soap factory, cotton mill, brass works, sugar refinery, foundries, lumberyards, and riverside wharves.

Moncton has maintained its economic edge through the decades, and the wealth has spilled over into the suburbs of Dieppe and Riverview. Riverview keeps a low profile. Dieppe is another story. After World War II, returning soldiers renamed the town, formerly Leger Corner, to honor their fallen comrades who died on the beaches at Dieppe, France. The suburb now rivals Moncton in economic importance and is the site of the airport, Atlantic Canada's largest amusement center, and one of the region's largest shopping malls.

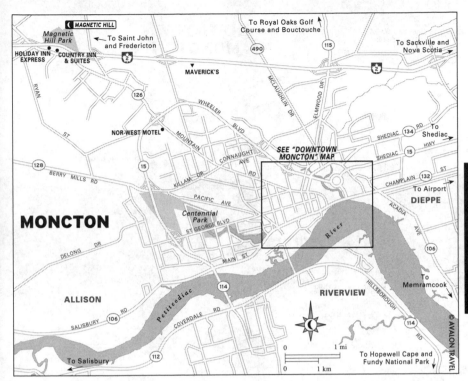

**NEW BRUNSWICK**

## DOWNTOWN SIGHTS

Downtown Moncton is centered on the north side of "The Bend," a sharp turn in the Petitcodiac River. The busy and bustling **Main Street,** a block in from the river, has brick sidewalks, old-time lampposts, and park benches beneath fledgling trees. The following sights are located at the riverfront and outward. There's no parking on Main Street. Instead, use one of the adjacent side streets and plug a loonie ($1 coin) for an hour into a metered parking slot, or park in one of the nearby lots.

### ◖ Bore Park

The huge Bay of Fundy tides reach Moncton twice daily, when a tidal bore, a lead wave up to 60 centimeters high, pulses up the Petitcodiac River. Within an hour or so, the muddy bed of the Petitcodiac—locally dubbed the "Chocolate River"—will be drowned under some 7.5 meters of water. The tourist information center on Main Street can provide a tidal schedule. While the Moncton tourism folks put watching the tidal bore on their list of mustsee attractions, many locals call it the Total Bore. In any case, the sight is most impressive at those times of the month when the tides are highest—around the full and new moons.

The best place to witness the tidal phenomenon is off Main Street at Bore Park, which is dotted with shade trees and park benches. This is also the site of the main tourist information center (where you can find out what time the tidal bore will arrive) and the start of a riverside boardwalk.

### Moncton Museum

Artifacts from the city's history—from the age of the Mi'Kmaq to World War II—and touring national exhibits are displayed at the

NEW BRUNSWICK

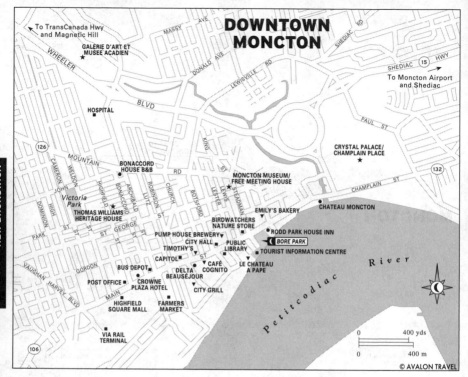

former city hall (20 Mountain Rd., 506/856-4383; Mon.–Sat. 9 A.M.–4:30 P.M. and Sun. 1–5 P.M.; donation). When the building was modernized, the city architect concocted an interesting arrangement that combined the building's original native-sandstone facade with an updated interior.

Adjacent to the Moncton Museum, the tidy small **Free Meeting House** (Moncton's oldest building) dates to 1821 and served as a sanctuary for religious groups as diverse as Anglicans, Adventists, Jews, and Christian Scientists. If you're interested in seeing the interior, ask at the museum.

## Thomas Williams Heritage House

A century ago, the Intercolonial Railroad brought the movers and shakers to town. Among them was Thomas Williams, the railroad's former treasurer. His 12-room Second Empire–style

mansion (103 Park St., 506/857-0590; May and Sept. Mon., Wed., and Fri. 10 A.M.–3 P.M., June Tues.–Sat. 9 A.M.–5 P.M. and Sun. 1–5 P.M., July–Aug. Mon.–Sat. 9 A.M.–5 P.M. and Sun. 1–5 P.M.; donation) was built in 1883 and is now open to the public. Elegantly furnished with period pieces, it's a showpiece of the good old days. The Verandah Tea Room serves tea, coffee, and muffins in summer.

## Galerie d'Art et Musée Acadien

The Acadian region is as creatively avant-garde as it is historic. At the Université de Moncton, in the Clément Cormier Building, this gallery and museum (off Wheeler Blvd., 506/858-4088; June–Sept. Mon.–Fri. 10 A.M.–5 P.M., Sat.–Sun. 1–5 P.M.; $2) touch upon numerous aspects of Acadian culture in the combined exhibits. The university itself spreads across a large campus north of downtown. It is Atlantic

© ANDREW HEMPSTEAD

The aptly named Church Street in Moncton is dotted with numerous churches.

Canada's sole French-speaking university and grants degrees in business, fine arts, science, education, nursing, and law.

## ◖ MAGNETIC HILL

If you've got children, Magnetic Hill will be the focus of your time in Moncton. To get there from downtown follow Mountain Road northwest; from the TransCanada Highway take Exit 488. The namesake Magnetic Hill (506/853-3540; mid-May–early Sept. daily 8 A.M.–8 P.M.; $3 per vehicle) is just a hill, but if you believe your eyes, you'll agree it's one of the world's oddest. Is Magnetic Hill magnetic? It must be. The unassuming dirt road, which seems to defy the rule of logic, is said to be Canada's third-most-popular natural tourist attraction, behind Niagara Falls and the Canadian Rockies.

The hill's slope plays tricks on anything with wheels. Set your car at the hill's "bottom," shift into neutral, and release the brake. The car appears to coast backward *up* the hill. Cars aren't the only things that defy gravity

here. A stream alongside the road seems to flow uphill too.

The illusion baffled Monctonians for decades. Before the 1900s, the local farmers fought the incline when they tried to haul wagons "down" the hill. Several decades later, reporters from Saint John discovered Magnetic Hill. Their newspaper coverage of the "natural phenomenon" brought a slew of spectators, and the stream of nonbelievers hasn't stopped since.

If you think a strange and otherworldly force powers Magnetic Hill, think again. For the record, the whole countryside hereabouts is tilted. Magnetic Hill forms the southern flank of 150-meter-high Lutes Mountain northwest of Moncton. The hill is an optical illusion, and believe it or not, the hill's top crest is lower than where the hill's "bottom" starts. Try to walk the hill with your eyes closed. Your other senses will tell you that you are traveling down rather than up.

## Commercial Attractions

So many tourists arrived to observe the illogical hill that an adjacent gift shop was opened in the 1970s, and the area quickly grew into a concentration of family-oriented attractions.

**Magnetic Hill Zoo** (506/877-7718; mid-June–early Sept. daily 9 A.M.–8 P.M.; adult $11.50, senior $10, child $8) bills itself as the largest zoo in Atlantic Canada. It houses some 100 animal species, including zebras, reindeer, tigers, camels, wolves, and gibbons. A petting zoo entertains the wee ones and the crowds gather daily at 2:30 P.M. for Meet the Ranger.

**Magic Mountain Water Park** (506/857-9283; mid-June–mid-Aug. daily 10 A.M.–7 P.M., mid-Aug.–early Sept. daily 10 A.M.–6 P.M.; $23 for those over 48 inches tall and $17 for those under) has an outdoor wave pool, numerous chutes, tube rides, and mini-golf. (No, the water here does not run uphill.)

**The Boardwalk** (506/852-9406; summer daily 9 A.M.–dusk) offers go-kart rides, mini-golf, batting cages, a driving range, and a playground. **Wharf Village** (506/858-8841) is a

NEW BRUNSWICK

shopping area featuring arts and crafts and a family-style restaurant overlooking an artificial pond.

## RECREATION
### Centennial Park
At the western side of town, this 180-hectare spread of greenery (St. George Blvd., 506/853-3516; daily 9 A.M.–11 P.M.) makes a pleasant place to picnic and relax amid woodlands with hiking trails and a lake with a sandy beach. Summer activities include lawn bowling, swimming, tennis, and canoeing or paddling on the lake. In winter, lighted trails invite cross-country skiers, skaters, and hockey players to take to the frozen lake.

### Fun Parks
The area has sprouted other amusements besides those at Magnetic Hill. A short, narrow river tributary separates Moncton from adjacent Dieppe, where **Crystal Palace** (Paul St., Dieppe, 506/859-4386; Mon.–Fri. noon–8 P.M., Sat.–Sun. 10 A.M.–8 P.M.) rises from the far side of the Highway 15 rotary. This complex is an architectural wonder, a geodesic dome of angled glass walls with the Crystal Palace Amusement Park (adult $20, child $16 for unlimited rides) and a science center within. **Champlain Place,** Atlantic Canada's largest one-level shopping mall is next door.

## ENTERTAINMENT AND EVENTS
### Theater
In the mid-1990s the **Capitol** (811 Main St., 506/856-4379) was transformed from a dowdy downtown movie theater to a gracious symbol of the past. Today, this lovely old grande dame, ornately decorated with frescoes and murals, glitters with concerts, ballets, shows, and film festivals. Check www.capitol.nb.ca for a schedule.

### Bars and Nightclubs
Most of the drinking and dancing action happens along Main Street, where the college crowds gather at bars and nightclubs where tables spill onto the streets. The **Pump House Brewery** (5 Orange Ln., 506/855-2337) is a little quieter than most and has a sun-drenched patio out front. For a quiet drink, **Le Galion,** in Château Moncton (100 Main St., 506/870-4444) is a good choice. With seating inside and out, you get to enjoy the river scenery up close and can sip a beer while waiting for the tidal bore in a bright, contemporary setting. On the top floor of the Crowne Plaza Hotel, **Top Side** (1005 Main St., 506/854-6340) is a typical hotel lounge, with the bonus of city and river views.

**Oxygen** (125 Westmorland St., 506/854-0265) is generally regarded as one of the province's hottest destinations for dance parties, with DJs spinning disks on weekends. **Ziggy's** (938 Mountain Rd., 506/858-8844) is a little more upscale and tends to attract a (slightly) older crowd.

### Festivals and Events
One of the city's most loved gatherings is the mid-August **Atlantic Seafood Festival** (506/855-8525, www.atlanticseafoodfestival.com), hosted by venues as varied as the main street and hotel dining rooms. As the name suggests, the emphasis is on local seafood. You can watch oyster-shucking demonstrations, cheer on your favorites in various cooking competitions, and take part in the street party.

The mid-September **Festival International du Cinéma Francophone en Acadie** (506/855-6050, www.ficfa.com) is a major French-language film festival.

Moncton hosts the **World Wine & Food Festival** (506/532-5333, www.wineexpo.ca) over the first week of November. It brings together wine representatives from around the world with celebrity chefs, but the ambience is anything but pompous as the general public gathers to soak up the worldly atmosphere.

## SHOPPING
Major shopping malls in the area include Dieppe's **Champlain Place** (corner of Paul St. and Champlain St.) and **Moncton Mall** (1380

Mountain Rd., 506/858-1380), but to sample the local flair for arts and crafts, you'll need to look elsewhere. Artisans market wares at the downtown **Farmers' Market** (Robinson St., Sat. 7 A.M.–1 P.M.). **Gifts Galore** (569 Main St., 506/857-9179) carries a little bit of everything—glass, pottery, pewter, T-shirts, and more. It helps to speak French at some shops, such as **Galerie Sans Nom** (Aberdeen Cultural Centre, 140 Botsford St., 506/854-5381), a co-operative where the emphasis is on contemporary arts and crafts.

Between downtown and Bore Park, **Birdwatchers Nature Store** (527 Main St., 506/388-2473) stocks binoculars and field guides.

## ACCOMMODATIONS AND CAMPING

Lodgings are conveniently concentrated in two main areas—downtown and at the city's northwestern corner near Magnetic Hill. Overall, prices are reasonable, especially for the larger downtown properties.

### $50-100

**Bonaccord House Bed and Breakfast** (250 Bonaccord St., 506/388-1535; $48 s, $65 d) is a charming meld of Victoriana with four guest rooms, a balcony, and a veranda, located in a tree-shaded residential area. Breakfast is included and you can walk to downtown in 10 minutes.

### $100-150

The five-story **Rodd Park House Inn** (434 Main St., 506/382-1664 or 800/565-7633, www.roddhotelsandresorts.com; $115 s or d, extra for river views) overlooks Bore Park with 97 elegant rooms, a river-facing café, a lounge, and an outdoor pool. The rooms aren't particularly large, but the location still makes this place good value.

On the eastern edge of downtown, **◖ Château Moncton** (100 Main St., 506/870-4444 or 800/576-4040, www.chateau-moncton.nb.ca; $120–150 s or d) is a distinctive red-roofed chateau-style lodging overlooking the tidal bore. Guests enjoy 97

modern and spacious rooms with high-speed Internet access, an exercise room, voice messaging, free local calls, and daily newspapers. The hotel also has a riverside deck and a pleasant lounge.

The motels clustered around Magnetic Mountain (take Exit 488 from the TransCanada Highway) are mostly within this price range. With the most facilities is **Holiday Inn Express** (2515 Mountain Rd., 506/384-1050 or 800/465-4329, www.ichotelsgroup.com; $115 s or d), with an indoor pool, restaurant, lounge, hot tub, sauna, and business center.

The folks at **Nor-West Motel** (1325 Mountain Rd., 506/384-1222 or 800/561-7904, www.norwestmotel.com; $105 s or d) have done a great job of upgrading an older motel out near Magnetic Hill, with colorful flower arrangements out front adding to the appeal. A light breakfast is included in the rates.

**Country Inn and Suites** (2475 Mountain Rd., 506/852-7000 or 888/201-1746, www.countryinns.com; from $135 s or d) has 77 spacious, nicely appointed guest rooms with free in-room movies, work desks, and small fridges. A daily newspaper and light breakfast are included in the rates.

### $150-200

**◖ Crowne Plaza Hotel** (1005 Main St., 506/854-6340 or 877/227-6963, www.ichotelsgroup.com; $179 s or d) comes complete with contemporary decor, the best beds in town, high-speed Internet access, CD clock radios, and many other niceties. The top floor is a restaurant and lounge. Other amenities include an indoor pool and fitness room. Check online for specials well under $150.

**Delta Beauséjour** (750 Main St., 506/877-7195 or 877/890-3222, www.deltahotels.com; from $189 s or d) is equal to the Crowne Plaza in style, service, and facilities, but everything is a little less new. On the plus side, the 310 guest rooms are spacious. Other facilities include three eateries, a piano bar, and an indoor pool. Disregard the rack rate and reserve online to pay around $150 for bed and breakfast.

**Ramada Palace Hotel** (499 Paul St., Dieppe, 506/858-8584 or 800/561-7108, www.crystalpalacehotel.com) is part of the Crystal Palace amusement park, which makes it the perfect place for families looking for a break from New Brunswick's natural and historic wonders. Most of the 115 guest rooms ($179 s or d) are fairly standard, but the themed fantasy suites—one employs a rock-and-roll theme complete with a replica of a 1959 pink Cadillac for a bed—are the highlight for those willing to pay extra ($249 s or d). Other amenities include an indoor pool, a restaurant, and a lounge.

## Campground

Shediac, 20 kilometers northeast of Moncton, is covered in the *Strait Coast* section, but the beachside campground within **Parlee Beach Provincial Park** (506/533-3363; $27) makes a great alternative to city camping—although it does get busy. The turnoff is on the east side of Shediac. Amenities include hot showers, a playground, and over 165 sites.

# FOOD

You might stumble on a few Acadian dishes, but most local restaurants keep it simple and straightforward, appealing to the college crowd with cheap food and energetic service.

## Cafés

Main Street is the place to head for a coffee at a street-side table, and no one pours better drinks than **Timothy's World Coffee** (735 Main St., 506/854-7210; Mon.–Fri. 7 A.M.–10 P.M., Sat. 9 A.M.–10 P.M.).

Across the road from Timothy's, **Café Cognito** (700 Main St., 506/854-4888; Mon.–Fri. 7:30 A.M.–5:30 P.M., Sat. 10 A.M.–4 P.M.) also has excellent coffee, along with chai lattes and sandwiches made to order.

Once you have your sandwich to go from Café Cognito, plan on a picnic in Bore Park, but also pick up a sweet treat from **Emily's Bakery** (34 King St., 506/857-0966; Mon. 9 A.M.–4 P.M., Tues.–Fri. 9 A.M.–5:30 P.M., Sat. 9 A.M.–4:30 P.M.).

## Restaurants

Most of the pubs along Main Street serve food, but the offerings at the **Pump House Brewery** (5 Orange Ln., 506/855-2337; daily from 11:30 A.M.) are a notch above the rest. Highlights are the wood-fired pizzas, such as roast vegetable ($9) and smoked turkey ($9). Fish-and-chips is $10, steaks average $15, and all the usual Mexican pub food is in the $6.50–12 range.

Take a break from seafood at stylish **Maverick's** (Future Inns, 40 Lady Ada Blvd., 506/855-3346; daily 7:30 A.M.–9 P.M.), out on the main highway through town. An extra thick cut of prime rib is $21–26, a tender rib eye is $28, and strip loin is $23–31—and they all come exactly how you ordered them. The menu also offers top-notch seafood, including boiled lobster. A well-rounded wine list adds to the appeal. **City Grill** (130 Westmoreland, 506/857-8325; daily from 4 P.M.) also caters to a beef-eating clientele, but it's less intimate.

Le Château à Pape is one of Moncton's finest restaurants.

Beside Bore Park, an old home has been given a nationalistic red-and-white makeover and now operates as **Le Château à Pape** (2 Steadman St., 506/855-7273; daily from 4 P.M.). The European cooking is old-fashioned and polished. The menu is replete with seafood and steak, with most mains under $25.

The two major downtown hotels have dining rooms. **T-bones** (Crowne Plaza Hotel, 1005 Main St., 506/854-6340; daily 6:30 A.M.–2 P.M. and 5–10 P.M.) has a predictable wide-ranging menu that don't offend anyone, with choices that include everything from stir-fried vegetables ($18) to T-bone steaks ($32). **Windjammer** (Delta Beauséjour, 750 Main St., 506/877-7137; Mon.–Sat. from 5:30 P.M.) has a slightly more adventurous European-influenced menu—minus the views. Mains are in the $27–42 range.

## Magnetic Hill Dining

Overlooking the pond at Wharf Village is **Wharf Village Restaurant** (506/859-1812; May–Oct. daily 10 A.M.–8 P.M.), which does a fine job feeding theme-park visitors with family fare at good value for the dollar (daily specials cost around $7). Seating is outside on a covered deck or inside with basic decor. On the right side of the restaurant is a self-service counter with soup and sandwiches to go.

# INFORMATION AND SERVICES
## Tourist Information

The city's main **Tourist Information Centre** (506/853-3590 or 800/363-4558, www .gomoncton.com; mid-May–early Sept. daily 8:30 A.M.–5:30 P.M.) is on the east side of downtown in Bore Park.

## Books and Bookstores

**Moncton Public Library** is at Blue Cross Centre (644 Main St., 506/869-6000; summer Mon. and Fri. 9 A.M.–5 P.M. and Tues.–Thurs. 9 A.M.–8:30 P.M., the rest of the year Mon.–Sat. 9 A.M.–5 P.M., Tues.–Thurs. 9 A.M.–8:30 P.M.). If you're looking for French-language reading material, **Librairie Acadienne** has it at the Université de Moncton's Taillon Building (Archibald St., 506/858-4140).

The city's largest bookstore is **Chapters** (499 Paul St., Dieppe, 506/855-8075), east of downtown in the Champlain Place complex. Also here is the smaller **Coles** bookstore (506/854-7397).

## Services

**Moncton Hospital** is on the road between downtown and Magnetic Hill (135 MacBeath Ave., 506/857-5111). **Hôpital Dr. Georges L. Dumont** is the French hospital (330 University Ave., 506/862-4000). For the **RCMP**, call 911 or 506/857-2400.

For postal services go to the main **post office** (281 St. George St. at Highfield St.). The VIA Rail terminal behind Highfield Square on Main Street has **storage lockers,** as does the Acadian bus terminal (961 Main St.). **St. George Laundromat** (66 St. George Blvd.) is open daily 8:30 A.M.–9 P.M.

# GETTING THERE
## Air

**Greater Moncton Airport** is 10 kilometers from downtown Moncton on Champlain Street/Highway 132 (a continuation of Main Street in Moncton) in adjacent Dieppe. The airport has a food court, lounge, modem hookups, and car rental desks (Avis, Budget, Hertz, and National). A metered taxi ride with **Air Cab** (506/857-2000) to Main Street in Moncton costs about $15 one-way.

The airport is served by **Air Canada** (888/247-2262) from Halifax, Montréal, and Toronto and by **WestJet** (800/538-5696) from Toronto, Hamilton, and Calgary.

## Train and Bus

Moncton is served by **VIA Rail** (506/857-9830 or 800/561-3952) on its route between Montréal and Halifax. The terminal is behind Highfield Square on Main Street.

By virtue of its central location, Moncton is a hub for **Acadian** buses (961 Main St., 506/859-5060). Services run to Saint John,

Fredericton, Charlottetown, Halifax, and along the Acadian Coast to Campbellton.

## GETTING AROUND

**Codiac Transit** (506/857-2008) operates local bus service (Mon.–Sat. 6:20 A.M.–7 P.M., Thurs.–Fri. 6:20 A.M.–10:15 P.M.).

**Air Cab** (506/857-2000) charges $2.15 to start and about $1 per kilometer.

Major car rental companies with downtown and airport desks are **Avis** (506/855-7212), **Budget** (506/857-3993), **Hertz** (506/858-8525), and **National** (506/382-6114).

# Southeast from Moncton

Geologically, the area southeast of Moncton is related to the Bay of Fundy, but as it is separated from the rest of the Fundy Coast, I've included coverage here. Unless you choose to stop at the attractions detailed below you'll cross over to Nova Scotia in a little over 30 minutes and be in Halifax in three hours.

## MEMRAMCOOK

Take Highway 106 southeast from Moncton for 20 kilometers to reach the village of Memramcook and **Monument-Lefebvre National Historic Site** (488 Centrale St., 506/758-9808; June–mid-Oct. daily 9 A.M.–5 P.M.; adult $4, senior $3.50, child $2), which is dedicated to the memory of Father Camille Lefebvre, founder of Canada's first French-language university. Within the historic Monument-Lefebvre building on the Memramcook Institute campus, **Acadian Odyssey** explains Acadian survival with a series of exhibits and displays.

## SACKVILLE

The 17th-century settlers who founded Sackville, 45 kilometers southeast of Moncton, emigrated from around the estuaries of western France, so they were experienced in wresting tidelands from the sea. By creating an extensive system of dikes called *aboideaux,* they reclaimed thousands of acres of Chignecto Isthmus marsh and brought the extremely fertile alluvial lands into agricultural production. Their raised dikes can be seen around Sackville and into Nova Scotia.

Mount Allison Academy (later University) was founded here in 1843; a "Female Branch" was opened 11 years later. In 1875, the university gained the distinction of being the first in the British Empire to grant a college degree to a woman.

The beautiful campus is still at the heart of this town, surrounded by stately houses and tree-shaded streets. A number of artists have chosen Sackville as their home, and one of the best places to see their work is at Mount Allison University's **Owens Art Gallery** (61 York St., 506/364-2574; Mon.–Fri. 10 A.M.–5 P.M., Sat.–Sun. 1–5 P.M.). The Owens ranks as one of the major galleries in the province and emphasizes avant-garde work by local, regional, and national artists.

### ◖ Sackville Waterfowl Park

If you're short on time and can stop at only one of the area's several wildlife sanctuaries, make it the Sackville Waterfowl Park, a 22-hectare reserve where over 170 bird species have been recorded. The main entrance, just a few blocks north of downtown, is easy to miss. Here you'll find interesting park displays. From this point, the sanctuary (open daily dawn to dusk) spreads out with trails routed through bushes and bleached wooden walkways crossing wetlands. Ducks, herons, teals, and bitterns are common, while the possibility exists for spotting loons, Canada geese, sandpipers, and peregrine falcons.

Boardwalks provide easy access to Sackville Waterfowl Park.

## Accommodations and Food

For a place to stay, consider **⟨ Marshlands Inn** (55 Bridge St., 506/536-0170, www .marshlands.nb.ca; $95–115 s or d), among the province's best-value lodgings. The inn, built in the 1850s, got its name from an early owner, who named the mansion in honor of the adjacent Tantramar Marshes. The resplendent white wooden heritage inn sits back from the road under shady trees and offers 20 guest rooms furnished with antiques and a dining room of local renown. Open daily for guests and nonguests, the dining room is smart and elegant, with many steak and seafood choices ($18–24), as well as a dish of seafood crepes ($23).

## SACKVILLE TO AULAC

Another prime birding site is not far from Sackville. From Dorchester, 14 kilometers west of Sackville on Highway 106, turn off on Highway 935. The backcountry gravel road loops south around the **Dorchester**

Peninsula—the digit of land separating Shepody Bay from the Cumberland Basin.

Some 50,000 semipalmated sandpipers nest from mid-July to mid-September between Johnson Mills and Upper Rockport, as the road loops back toward Sackville. Roosting sites lie along pebble beaches and mudflats, and the birds are most lively at feeding time at low tide. Smaller flocks of dunlins, white-rumped sandpipers, and sanderlings inhabit the area late September to October.

Across the Chignecto Isthmus is an incredibly fertile habitat so rich in waterfowl and birds that the early Acadian settlers described the area as a *tintamarre* ("ceaseless din"), which is now known as **Tantramar Marshes.** A few roads haphazardly thread through the marshes, and there's no official approach to bird-watching here. Head off the TransCanada Highway anywhere and wander; you can't go wrong on any of the backcountry roads from the Sackville area to the province's border crossing.

## AULAC AND VICINITY

The last town before crossing into Nova Scotia is Aulac, on the Bay of Fundy side of the TransCanada Highway at the turnoff to the Confederation Bridge.

### Fort Beauséjour

Eight kilometers east of Sackville, a signpost marks the turnoff from the TransCanada Highway to the Fort Beauséjour National Historic Site (111 Fort Beauséjour Rd., 506/364-5080; June–mid-Oct. daily 9 A.M.–5 P.M.; adult $4, senior $3.50, child $2), overlooking the Cumberland Basin just west of the Nova Scotia border. Continue on the road to the fort ruins, which mark France's last-ditch military struggle against the British, who threatened Acadia centuries ago. France lost the fort in 1755 after a two-week siege. The Brits renamed it Fort Cumberland and used it in 1776 to repel an attack by American revolutionaries. The fort stood ready for action in the War of 1812, though no enemy appeared. Fort Cumberland was abandoned in the 1830s,

NEW BRUNSWICK

and nature soon reclaimed the site. Some of the ruins have since been restored. Facilities include a picnic area and a museum–visitor center with exhibits on what life was like in the old days.

### Tintamarre Sanctuary

Tintamarre National Wildlife Area fans out beyond the fort ruins. Continue on Highway 16 for about 10 kilometers to Jolicure, a village at the reserve's edge. No trails penetrate the 1,990-hectare mix of marshes, uplands, old fields, forests, and lakes. A few dikes provide steady ground through some of the terrain, but you are asked to stay on the roads encircling the area to do your bird-watching. Amid the cattails, sedges, and bulrushes, sightings include migratory mallards, grebes, red-winged blackbirds, yellow warblers, swamp swallows, common snipes, black ducks, Virginia rails, and bitterns; short-eared owls take wing at dusk. Bring binoculars—and insect repellent. The area is thick with mosquitoes.

# Strait Coast

The Strait Coast runs from Cape Tormentine, New Brunswick's easternmost extremity, to Miramichi, 143 kilometers northeast of Moncton. It fronts Northumberland Strait, the narrow body of water separating New Brunswick from Prince Edward Island, and so it's no surprise the main towns and attractions revolve around the water.

## CAPE TORMENTINE TO SHEDIAC

Most travelers drive, literally, over the top of Cape Tormentine on their way to Prince Edward Island via the **Confederation Bridge.**

### Cape Jourimain Nature Centre

Nestled below the southern end of the Confederation Bridge, this interpretive center (5039 Hwy. 16, 506/538-2220; mid-May–mid-Oct. daily 9 A.M.–5 P.M.; adult $6, senior $5, child $4) sits at the gateway to a 675-hectare national wildlife area, home to a reported 170 species of birds. The center has varying ecology exhibits, is the starting point for an 11-kilometer trail system, and has a restaurant.

The nearest camping is at **Murray Beach Provincial Park** (Hwy. 955, 506/538-2628; May–Sept.; $24–28), 13 kilometers west toward Shediac. In addition to a good swimming beach, amenities include over 100 campsites on a wooded bluff, showers, a laundry, and a playground.

### Continuing West

A few fine quiet beaches dot the **Cap-Pelé** area, farther west on Highway 15. At Gagnon Beach, **Camping Gagnon Beach** (506/577-2519 or 800/658-2828; late May–mid-Sept.; $24–28) has 208 sites with full hookups plus a separate wooded tenting area.

## SHEDIAC

The self-proclaimed "Lobster Capital of the World," 20 kilometers northeast of Moncton, Shediac backs up its claim with the **world's largest lobster**—an 11-meter-long, cast-iron sculpture by Winston Bronnum, sitting beside the road into town. For the real stuff, head for the town's restaurants, which have a reputation for some of the province's best lobster dinners.

### ◖ Parlee Beach

The little town can be crowded on weekends—this is *the* beach getaway for Moncton residents. **Parlee Beach Provincial Park** (506/533-3363) protects one of many beaches strung out to the east. This placid three-kilometer-long beach is popular for the warmth of the water, which reaches 24°C in summer. Access is from the eastern edge of Shediac, along an access road that ends at a massive parking lot behind low sand dunes. Behind the beach are changing rooms, a café, and a restaurant, while down on the beach swimming is supervised. Access is $9 per vehicle per day (collected in summer only).

## Accommodations and Camping

The beautiful white **Auberge Belcourt Inn** (303 Main St., 506/532-6098; $95–115 s or d) boasts special provincial status as a heritage inn. The inn sits back from the road beneath stately trees, with seven Victorian-era rooms and a dining room. It's near the western edge of town, just a quick stroll from the beach.

In the heart of Shediac, **( Tait House** (293 Main St., 506/532-4233 or 888/532-4667, www.maisontaithouse.com; from $150 s or d) is a beautifully restored 1911 mansion with guest rooms that feature many historic features complemented by contemporary features such as polished hardwood floors and plush mattresses topped with white linens. The in-house restaurant offers a menu of local ingredients prepared with cooking styles from throughout Europe.

**Parlee Beach Provincial Park** (Hwy. 133, 506/533-3363; $31) is within walking distance of the beach. It has hot showers, a playground, and more than 165 sites. Reservations are not accepted, so plan to arrive around lunchtime to secure a spot.

## Food

Near the end of the road out to Point-de-Chêne Marina (turn off the highway on the east side of town), you find **( Captain Dan's** (506/533-2855; daily 11 A.M.–10 P.M.), a super-casual, perennially crowded bar and grill with a beachin' atmosphere and great food. Hang loose, watch the boats, and feel your blood pressure drop.

## BOUCTOUCHE

North of Shediac, Highway 11 zips through a wooded corridor, sacrificing scenery for efficiency. For a taste of the slower pace of rural coastal Acadia, strike out on any of the local

Le Musée de Kent is a good place to learn about Acadian history.

© ANDREW HEMPSTEAD

highways (such as 530, 475, or 505) to the east, which hug the coast and lead to quiet beaches at Saint-Thomas, Saint-Edouard-de-Kent, and Cap-Lumière. Along the way, the two routes come together at Bouctouche, 30 kilometers north of Shediac. You can learn about two centuries of Acadian culture at **Le Musée de Kent** (150 Chemin du Couvent, 506/743-5005; July–early Sept. Mon.–Sat. 9 A.M.–5:30 P.M., Sun. noon–6 P.M.; adult $3, senior $2, child $1), in a restored 1880 convent two kilometers east of downtown, but the two main local attractions are Le Pays de la Sagouine and Irving Eco-Centre.

## ( Le Pays de la Sagouine

Author Antonine Maillet is renowned in the literary world for her colorful descriptions of Acadian life, and so there is no better place for re-creating the ambience of her work than this lively outdoor theme park in her hometown of Bouctouche. Le Pays de la Sagouine (57 Acadie St., 506/743-1400; June–Aug. daily 10 A.M.–8 P.M., Sept. daily 10 A.M.–6 P.M.;

adult $15, senior $14, child $9) is on a peninsula and islet with a hamlet of houses and other buildings, a reception center, and a crafts shop. The highly recommended guided tour (included in admission) leaves daily at 11 A.M. and 3 P.M. Evening dinner theater (in French) is the site's big draw; you'll have a choice of seafood, Canadian, or—the best bet—traditional Acadian fare. And your meal will be accompanied by Acadian music, which might be in any number of styles. The show only is adult $40, child $22, or pay $69 and $45 respectively for park admission, dinner, and show.

### Irving Eco-Centre

Continue through town beyond Le Musée de Kent and turn north up the coast to reach Irving Eco-Centre (Hwy. 475, 506/743-2600), which preserves the ecosystem surrounding a 12-kilometer-long sand dune along Bouctouche Bay. The ecosystem was a public relations gesture created by New Brunswick megacorporation J. D. Irving Ltd. (petroleum, logging, you name it). A two-kilometer-long wheelchair-accessible boardwalk leads from an interpretive center through the dunes. Other trails traverse forest and marshland. Naturalists work on-site May–November, doing ecology research and leading school field trips and such. Bird-watchers will spot great blue herons, piping plovers, and long-winged terns, among other species.

## KOUCHIBOUGUAC NATIONAL PARK

The Northumberland Strait coast ends at Kouchibouguac National Park (506/876-2443), a 238-square-kilometer gem of a park that takes its name from the Mi'Kmaq word for "river of the long tides"—a reference to the waterway that meanders through the midsection of the low-lying park. Some pronounce it "KOOSH-ee-buh-gwack," others say "kee-gee-boo-QUACK," Parks Canada says it's "Kou-she-boo-gwack," and you'll hear many other variations.

Slender barrier islands and white beaches and dunes, laced with marram grass and false heather, face the gulf along a 25-kilometer front. A gray seal colony occupies one of the

Kouchibouguac National Park

offshore islands. In the park's interior, board-walks ribbon the mudflats, freshwater marshes, and bogs, and nature trails probe the wood-lands and fields.

## Park Entry

Entry fees are charged mid-May to mid-October. A one-day pass costs adult $8, senior $7, child $4 to a maximum of $20 per vehicle.

## Recreation

The land and coast are environmentally sensitive; park officials prefer that you stay on the trails and boardwalks or use a bike to get around on the 30 kilometers of biking and hiking trails. Naturalist-led programs and outings are organized throughout summer. Check at the Visitor Reception Centre and campgrounds for a schedule.

Trails that explore the park's varied ecosystems include the short **Kelly's Beach Boardwalk,** the **Pines** and **Salt Marsh** trails, and the 1.8-kilometer **Bog** trail. You can take longer hikes on the **Clair-Fontaine** (3.4 kilometers), **Osprey** (5.1 kilometers), and **Kouchibouguac** (14 kilometers—allow five hours) trails.

The Black, St. Louis, Kouchibouguac, and other rivers that weave through the park are wonderful to explore by canoe, kayak, rowboat, or paddleboat. Those watercraft, as well as fishing equipment and bicycles, are available at **Ryan's Rental Centre** (506/876-3733; mid-June–early Sept. daily 8 A.M.–9 P.M.). Fishing in the national park also requires a license: $10 per day or $35 for an annual license. **Swimming** is supervised at Kelly's Beach in summer; swimming at Callander's and other beaches is unsupervised.

## Camping

Within the park are two campgrounds. Finding a site shouldn't be a problem except in July and August. At these times reservations through the **Parks Canada Campground Reservation Service** (905/426-4648 or 877/737-3783, www.pccamping.ca) are wise. The cost is $11 per booking plus the campsite fee.

**South Kouchibouguac Campground** (mid-May–mid-Oct.; $28–33) offers 265 unserviced sites and 46 sites with power hookups. Civilized comforts include showers, flush toilets, kitchen shelters, firewood ($7 per bundle), launderettes, and a campers' store near the beach.

**Côte-à-Fabien Campground** (mid-June–early Sept.; $14) has 32 primitive campsites but few facilities and no hookups.

## Information

Make your first stop the **Visitor Reception Centre** (1 km inside the main entrance off Hwy. 134, 506/876-2443, www.pc.gc.ca; last two weeks of May daily 9 A.M.–5 P.M., June–early Sept. daily 8 A.M.–8 P.M., early Sept.–mid-Oct. daily 9 A.M.–5 P.M.). For a memorable introduction, be sure to see the 20-minute slide presentation, *Kouchibouguac,* which takes the viewer on a seasonal trip through the park's sublime beauty and changing moods. Campsite registration is handled at the center, and information on activities, outdoor presentations, and evening programs is posted here too.

NEW BRUNSWICK

# Miramichi River

The gorgeous Miramichi ("meer-ma-SHEE") River and its myriad tributaries drain much of the interior of eastern New Brunswick. The river enjoys a wide reputation as one of the best (if not *the* best) Atlantic salmon waters in the world. In the early 17th century, Nicolas Denys, visiting the Miramichi estuary, wrote of the salmon, saying: "So large a quantity of them enters into this river that at night one is unable to sleep, so great is the noise they make in falling upon the water after having thrown or darted themselves into the air."

Leaving the conurbation of Miramichi near the river's mouth, Highway 8 follows the river valley southwest for most of its length. Most of the valley is lightly populated.

## MIRAMICHI

Don't get too confused if that old road map of New Brunswick you're using doesn't seem to jibe with the signs you're seeing out the car window. No, the cities of Chatham and Newcastle didn't disappear; in 1995 they amalgamated into a single municipal entity called Miramichi. The former Chatham is now Miramichi East, and the former Newcastle is Miramichi West.

Old French maps of this area show the Miramichi River as the Rivière des Barques, the "River of Ships." From as early as the last quarter of the 18th century, the locally abundant timber and the deepwater estuary have made this an excellent location for the shipbuilding industry. The Cunard brothers began their lucrative shipbuilding empire at Chatham in 1826 and built some of the finest vessels of their day. The industry thrived for half a century and then faltered and faded, leaving no physical evidence—outside of museums—that it ever existed.

### Sights

At Miramichi East (Chatham), before Highway 11 crosses to the north side of the

Miramichi skyline

# SALMON FISHING ON THE MIRAMICHI

Fly-fishing is the only method allowed for taking Atlantic salmon. Fish in the 13- to 18-kilogram range are not unusual; occasionally, anglers land specimens weighing up to 22 kilograms. The salmon season runs from mid-May to mid-October. Nonresidents are required to hire guides, who are plentiful hereabouts.

Riverside fishing resorts, which let you drop a line in rustic elegance, are a popular way to enjoy the piscatorial experience. They're not cheap, however. One of the best and most historic is **Upper Oxbow Outdoor Adven-** **tures** (near Trout Brook, 506/622-8834 or 888/227-6100, www.upperoxbow.com), which has been in operation since 1823 and through five generations of the same family. The company has day trips ($330-500 s or d) inclusive of guides and equipment, but most anglers stay overnight on packages that typically cost around $600 per person for two days.

A more luxurious option is **Pond's Resort** (Porter Cove Rd., Sillikers, 506/369-2612 or 877/971-7663, www.pondsresort.com), charging around $550 per person per day for lodging, meals, and guided fishing.

NEW BRUNSWICK

river, **St. Michael's Basilica** (10 Howard St., 506/778-5150; daily 8 A.M.–4 P.M.; free) is a distinctive sandstone church overlooking the river.

Across the river, **Rankin House Museum** (2224 King George Hwy., 506/773-3448; June–early Sept. Mon.–Fri. 9 A.M.–5 P.M.; free) has a surprisingly large collection of memorabilia collected from throughout northeastern New Brunswick. Ask here for a brochure detailing buildings of historical interest within walking distance of the museum.

Farther southwest along Highway 8 is **Newcastle,** a pleasant river town with lots of old buildings that center on a small square where you find a memorial to Lord Beaverbrook. One of the most powerful newspaper men in British history, he was raised at what is now known as **Beaverbrook House** (518 King George Hwy., 506/624-5474; June–Aug. Mon.–Fri. 9 A.M.–5 P.M., Sat. 10 A.M.–5 P.M.), which is now a small museum dedicated to his life and links to New Brunswick. If you're traveling with children, head down to **Ritchie Wharf,** an old shipbuilding center that has been converted to a playground.

## Festivals and Events

In the mid-19th century, Middle Island, a river island just east of town, was the destination of thousands of Irish emigrants, many of them fleeing the catastrophic potato famine of the 1840s. Their descendants are still in the region, and since 1984 the area has celebrated its Irish heritage with **Canada's Irish Festival** (506/778-8810, www.canadasirishfest.com). The three-day event in mid-July includes concerts, dances, a parade, lectures and music workshops, booths selling Irish mementos and books, and the consumption of a good deal of beer.

The first week of August is the **Miramichi Folksong Festival** (www.miramichifolksongfestival.com), which opens with an outdoor gospel concert and continues with a shindig of traditional and contemporary singing, dancing, and fiddling.

## Accommodations and Camping

Step back in time at the **( Governor's Mansion Inn** (62 St. Patrick's Dr., Nelson, 506/622-3036 or 877/647-2642, www .governorsmansion.ca; $59–109 s or d), which is made up of two historic homes in a quiet out-of-town setting across the road from the Miramichi River. Some rooms share bathrooms while the largest have private four-piece bathrooms, separate sitting areas, and river views.

At the upper end of the price range is the **Rodd Miramichi River** (1809 Water St., Miramichi East, 506/773-3111 or 800/565-7633, www.roddhotelsandresorts.com; $125–165 s or d), a modern riverside complex where rooms are painted in warm heritage colors. Amenities include a restaurant and indoor pool.

**Enclosure Campground** (10 km south of town along Hwy. 8, 506/622-8638; $20–25) has 100 campsites, hiking trails, a beach, a heated pool and spa, kitchen shelters, a canteen, and a playground.

## Food

**Rodd Miramichi River** (1809 Water St., Miramichi East, 506/773-3111), on the south side of the river, has a restaurant with dependable breakfast, lunch, and dinner, but to eat with the locals, head to the nearby **Old Town Diner** (1724 Water St., 506/773-7817; daily 7 A.M.–7 P.M.), where a cooked breakfast with all the coffee you can drink is just $6.

## Information

**Miramichi Visitor Centre** (King St., 506/778-8444 or 800/459-3131; May–Aug. daily 10 A.M.–8 P.M., Sept. daily 10 A.M.–5 P.M.) is beside Highway 11 as it enters town from the south.

# MIRAMICHI TO FREDERICTON

From Miramichi, it's 180 kilometers south along the Miramichi River to Fredericton, the capital of New Brunswick. It's a handy highway if you're planning to drive a loop around the province, but aside from the rural scenery, the biggest draw to the actual drive is salmon fishing.

## Doaktown

Crossing through the deep interior of the province, Highway 8 runs alongside the famed salmon-rich Miramichi River to Doaktown, 86 kilometers southwest of Miramichi. Squire Robert Doak from Scotland founded the town and gave it a boom start with grist- and paper mills in the early 1800s. The squire's white wooden house with some original furnishings and nearby barn have been set aside as **Doak Historic Site** (Hwy. 8, 506/365-4363; late June–early Sept. Mon.–Sat. 9:30 A.M.–4:30 P.M., Sun. 1–4:30 P.M.; donation).

Also in town, the **Atlantic Salmon Museum** (263 Main St., 506/365-7787; June–Aug. daily 9 A.M.–5 P.M., Sept. Mon.–Sat. 10 A.M.–4 P.M.; adult $5, senior $4, child $3) will be especially interesting to anglers. Exhibits depict the life cycle and habitat of this king of game fish, as well as the history of the art of catching it (including a collection of rods, reels, and gaudily attractive flies). Live salmon specimens at various stages of development swim in the aquariums.

## Boiestown

Another well-conceived museum is the **Central New Brunswick Woodmen's Museum** (Hwy. 8, 506/369-7214; mid-May–early Oct. daily 9:30 A.M.–5:30 P.M.; adult $6, senior $5, child $3), which spreads over 15 acres along Highway 8 near Boiestown. The museum's exhibits explain forestry's past and present. Among the buildings are replicas of a sawmill, a blacksmith shop, a wheelwright shop, a trapper's cabin, a bunkhouse, and a cookhouse. A Forestry Hall of Fame remembers the Paul Bunyans of New Brunswick's timber industry, and a miniature train makes a 15-minute loop through the grounds.

# Baie des Chaleurs

North of Miramichi Bay, the Acadian peninsula juts northeast into the Gulf of St. Lawrence. One side of the peninsula faces the Gulf of St. Lawrence, while the other side fronts the Baie des Chaleurs. In contrast to the wild Gulf of St. Lawrence, the shallower Baie des Chaleurs is warm and calm. Busy seaports dot the eastern coast of the bay—the region's commercial fishing fleets lie anchored at Bas-Caraquet, Caraquet, and Grande-Anse. Interspersed between the picturesque harbors are equally beautiful peninsulas, coves, and beaches. Swimming is especially pleasant along the sheltered beaches, where the shallow sea heats up to bathtub warmth in summer. Across the bay, Québec's Gaspé Peninsula is usually visible, sometimes with startling clarity when conditions are right. From Bathurst west, the fishing villages give way to industrial towns.

## ACADIAN PENINSULA
### Bartibog Bridge
It's a 20-minute drive on Highway 11 from Miramichi to this bayside town, where **MacDonald Farm Historic Site** (600 Hwy. 11, 506/778-6085; late June–early Sept. daily 9:30 A.M.–4:30 P.M.; adult $2.50, senior and child $1.50) re-creates a Scottish settler's life in 1784. Guides take visitors through the two-story stone farmhouse, fields, orchards, and outbuildings.

### Val-Comeau Provincial Park
Farther north up Highway 11, Val-Comeau Provincial Park comprises lush sphagnum bogs, formed when the last ice sheet melted and pooled without a place to drain on the flat terrain. Seabirds inhabit the nutrient-rich marshes; the park is known for bird-watching, and there is an observation tower for good views. Val-Comeau also offers a campground (506/393-7150; June–mid-Sept.; $23–28), with 55 sites, swimming areas, and a playground.

### Shippagan
New Brunswick's largest commercial fishing fleet is based in this sheltered bay at the tip of the Acadian Peninsula, 100 kilometers northeast of Miramichi. The **Aquarium and Marine Centre** (100 Aquarium St., 506/336-3013; mid-May–Sept. daily 10 A.M.–6 P.M.; adult $8, senior $6, child $5) opens up the world of gulf fishing with exhibits and viewing and touch tanks holding 125 native fish species.

## ACADIAN DEPORTATION

In the mid-1700s, decades of war between England and France were winding down in England's favor. The British demanded unqualified oaths of allegiance from the Acadians, who refused and claimed neutrality. Instead, they fled Nova Scotia for Acadia's more peaceful north. The British followed, burning villages and crops as they went. The Acadian deportation began in 1755, when about 1,100 Acadians were deported to England's other colonies in South Carolina, Georgia, and Pennsylvania. Guerrilla warfare raged as the Acadians fought for their lives and then fled to the hinterlands.

Refugee camps sprang up, the most well-known of which were Beaubears Island, now a national historic site on the Miramichi River, and the nearby swatch of land today home to Enclosure Park (at Derby Junction, five kilometers west of Miramichi), one of the province's most important archaeological sites. Many Acadians died of scurvy and starvation.

The Peace of Paris in 1763 ushered in an uneasy truce. France surrendered its mainland possessions, but during the ensuing decades about 3,800 Acadians returned to the region. The deportation officially finished in 1816.

**Camping Shippagan** (4 km west of town, 506/336-3960; June–Sept.) enjoys a great location, right on the water with a nice beach. Its 153 basic campsites cost $20 for tenters and $24–30 with hookups (glorious sunsets included). Amenities include firewood, showers and washrooms, a licensed restaurant, kitchen shelters, a picnic area, Laundromat, and organized activities.

## ÎLE LAMÈQUE

Offshore of Shippagan, Île Lamèque noses into the gulf at the brow of the Acadian Peninsula. Connected to the mainland by a bridge, the island changes with the seasons: Spring brings a splendid show of wildflowers; summer brings wild blueberries ripening on the barrens; autumn transforms the landscape to a burnished red. The spruce trees here are bent and dwarfed by the relentless sea winds, but oysters, moon snails, blue mussels, and jackknife clams thrive along the beautiful white sandy beaches.

### ◖ Lamèque International Baroque Music Festival

Île Lamèque is best known for this late July festival (506/344-5846 or 800/320-2276, www.festivalbaroque.com), as unlikely as that may seem out here among the peat bogs and fishing villages. It is the only festival in North America dedicated to the celebration of music from the baroque period (1600–1760) and has been attracting the world's best early music musicians since the early 1970s. The setting is superb—almost divine—within the acoustically perfect 1913 Church Sainte-Cecile.

### Accommodations and Camping

The fanciest digs on the island are at **Auberge des Compagnons** (11 rue Principale, Lamèque, 506/344-7766 or 866/344-7762; $115–190), a modern 16-room lodge with sweeping water views. The restaurant serves a buffet-style breakfast and fixed-price dinner, both of which are extra.

Campers should continue across the bridge to Île Miscou, a blissfully remote island barely touched by the modern world. **Plage Miscou** (22 Allée Alphonse, 506/344-1015; mid-May–Sept.) is a simple campground with limited facilities but a pleasant bay outlook. Tent sites are $17, hookups $28, and cottages from $690 per week.

## CARAQUET

From the south, Highway 11 lopes into town and turns into a boulevard lined with shops, lodgings, and sights. Established in 1758, picturesque Caraquet (pop. 4,200), 32 kilometers northwest of Shippagan, is northern New Brunswick's oldest French settlement and is known as Acadia's cultural heart.

### Sights and Recreation
#### ◖ VILLAGE HISTORIQUE ACADIEN

Ten kilometers west of Caraquet, Village Historique Acadien (14311 Rte. 11, Rivière du Nord, 506/726-2600; June–early Oct. daily 10 A.M.–5 P.M., daily 10 A.M.–6 P.M. in summer; adult $15, senior $13, child $8) provides a sensory journey through early Acadia. To recreate the period from 1780 to 1890, more than 40 rustic houses and other authentic buildings were transported to this 1,133-hectare site and restored. The buildings—including a church, a smithy, farmhouses, a school, a printing shop, a carpenter's shop, a gristmill, and others—are spread across woods and fields along the North River. You walk the dusty lanes or hop aboard a horse-drawn wagon to get from one building to the next, where informative costumed "residents" describe their daily lives, their jobs, and surroundings in French and English. Out in the park, two "post houses" serve sandwiches, snacks, and drinks. The site also holds **La Table des Ancêtres,** which serves typical Acadian dishes at reasonable prices.

#### THE ACADIAN MUSEUM AND CARREFOUR DE LA MER

The Acadian Museum (15 St-Pierre Blvd., 506/726-2682; June–mid-Sept. Mon.–Sat. 10 A.M.–6 P.M., Sun. 1–6 P.M.; adult $3, child $1) is a less ambitious look at local history than Village Historique Acadien but still makes a worthwhile stop. The adjacent Carrefour de la Mer (51 St-Pierre Blvd., 506/726-2688), whose name translates to "Crossroads of the Sea," holds the local information center, minigolf, a playground, and a restaurant.

### FISHING

Caraquet's fishing fleet is based at **Bas-Caraquet,** a 10-minute drive east on Highway 145 toward Île Lamèque.

### Festivals and Events

The town is also the place to be for early August's two-week **Festival Acadien** (www .festivalacadien.ca), one of the province's best-attended events. It includes the blessing of the huge fishing fleet by the local Roman Catholic clergy; jazz, pop, and classical music concerts; live theater; food and drink; and the Tintamarre, a massive street celebration on Acadia Day (August 15).

### Accommodations and Food

The distinctive three-story, crisply colored red and green 〖 **Hotel Paulin** (134 St-Pierre Blvd., 506/727-9981 or 866/727-9981, www .hotelpaulin.com; $195–315 s or d) is a family-run boutique hotel that has been entertaining guests since 1901. The 12 guest rooms have hardwood floors, comfortable beds, and a low-key but stylish decor. The top floor Waterfront Suites are huge. The downstairs restaurant oozes charm and opens nightly for creative table d'hôte dining.

## GRANDE-ANSE

Highway 11 continues to the coast, where it takes a turn west to Grande-Anse. For a swim in the warm bay, take Highway 320, the narrow road that diverges to the right, to **Maisonnette Park,** an exquisite spread of beach overlooking Caraquet across Baie Caraquet. The warmwater beach is a favorite, especially when the tide retreats to reveal sand dune fingers washed by shallow, sun-heated waters. Seabirds are everywhere: You'll see them in large numbers on nearby aptly named Bird Island, where the long bluffs at **Pokeshaw Community Park** overlook rookeries of squawking cormorants.

In town, **Musée des Papes** (140 Acadie St., 506/732-3003; mid-June–Sept. daily 10 A.M.–6 P.M.; adult $5, senior and child $2.50) commemorates the visit of Pope John Paul II to New Brunswick in 1985. Exhibits include vestments, chalices, and other ecclesiastical paraphernalia, plus a detailed scale replica of St. Peter's Basilica.

## BATHURST AND VICINITY

The town of Bathurst (pop. 12,000) sits by its own fine natural harbor at the vertex of Nepisiguit Bay, a broad gulf on the Baie des Chaleurs. It's 75 kilometers west of Caraquet, or 60 kilometers north of Miramichi as you shoot up Highway 8.

**Daly Point Wildlife Reserve** spreads across 40 hectares of salt marshes, woodlands, and fields northeast of town; an observation tower provides views of nesting ospreys, various seabirds, and songbirds. To get there, take Bridge Street (the Acadian Coastal Drive) east from Bathurst, then turn left on Carron Drive. Bring insect repellent.

### Bathurst to Campbellton

Highway 11 stays inland for the scenically dull 85-kilometer stretch between Bathurst and Charlo. Far preferable is coastal Highway 134, which runs through the fishing villages of Nigadoo, Petit-Rocher, Pointe-Verte, and Jacquet River. The coast between Bathurst and Dalhousie is famed for sightings of a phantom ship. Numerous witnesses over the years have described a ship under full sail engulfed in flames on the bay; sometimes the vision includes a crew frantically scurrying across the deck. Some say the vision dates from the Battle of Restigouche (1760)—the last naval engagement between France and England in this part of eastern Canada—when France's fleet was destroyed by the British.

〖 **La Fine Grobe Sur-Mer** (289 Main St., Nigadoo, 506/783-3138; daily 5–10 P.M.) enjoys a delightful setting on the beach, separated from the main road by a small but lovely wood. Georges Frachon has been cooking up delightful meals here since 1973. You can order French-inspired dishes like chateaubri-and, herb-crusted rack of lamb, and seafood pancakes, mostly under $25.

Farther northwest, in New Mills, the **Auberge Blue Heron** (Hwy. 134, 506/237-5560; May–Oct.; $70–120 s or d) has seven guest rooms furnished with antiques. Set back from the road in an oversized former farmhouse opposite Heron Island, it's a setting worthy of provincial heritage inn status.

**Eel River Bar,** south of Dalhousie, is one of the world's longest sandbars. With freshwater on one side and saltwater on the other, it's a popular spot for beach-walking and swimming.

# CAMPBELLTON

At the head of the Baie des Chaleurs, the New Brunswick and Gaspé coastlines meet near Campbellton (pop. 8,500), the area's largest town. A bridge here spans the broad mouth of the Restigouche River to connect with Québec's Highway 132. Highway 17 plunges deep into the unpopulated interior of New Brunswick, across the Restigouche Uplands. Along this route, it's 92 kilometers to Saint-Quentin, where you can veer east to Mt. Carleton Provincial Park or continue another 80 kilometers to join the Saint John River valley at Saint-Léonard.

## Sights and Recreation

**Galerie Restigouche** (39 Andrew St., 506/753-5750; adult $2) is a public art gallery displaying works by local, national, and inter-national artists, as well as natural history and science exhibits.

**Sugarloaf Provincial Park** (Exit 415 of Hwy. 11, 506/789-2366) overlooks the whole region and has a year-round chairlift with views to the 305-meter gumdrop-shaped peak of Sugarloaf Mountain. The park also has hiking trails, a luge ride ($3), tennis courts, and supervised swimming. In winter, the park is popular for snowmobiling, skating, and cross-country skiing. The park campground is open May–October and has 76 wooded sites for $21–28.

## Accommodations and Food

Campbellton's most individual accommodation is also the least expensive. **HI-Campbellton** (1 Ritchie St., 506/759-7044, www.hihostels.ca; mid-June–Aug.) is in an old lighthouse along the Restigouche River. It has 20 beds in dormitories, a small kitchen, and a common area. Members of Hostelling International pay $20 per night and nonmembers pay $24.

The centrally located **Super 8** (26 Duke St., 506/753-7606 or 877/582-7666, www.super8campbellton.com; $115–145 s or d) has an indoor swimming pool and restaurant.

Tide Head, a small town at the river's mouth seven kilometers west of Campbellton, is known for fiddleheads—fern fronds served as a springtime culinary delicacy. Here, **Sanfar Cottages** (Restigouche Dr., 506/753-4287; mid-May–Sept.; $55–65 s or d) has simple but tidy cabins, a picnic area with a gas barbecue, and a restaurant open for lunch weekdays and dinner daily.

# PRINCE EDWARD ISLAND

# CHARLOTTETOWN AND QUEENS COUNTY

As Atlantic Canada's smallest capital, Charlottetown (pop. 32,000)—the island's governmental, economical, cultural, and shopping center—makes no pretense of being a big city. Rather, this attractive town is walkable, comfortable, and friendly. Its major attractions include a beautiful harborside location, handsome public and residential architecture, sophisticated art and cultural happenings, and plentiful lodgings and appealing restaurants.

The city also makes a good sightseeing base for exploring surrounding Queens County, which is the definitive Prince Edward Island as you imagined the province would be. The region is temptingly photogenic, a meld of small seaports with brightly colored craft at anchor and farmland settings with limpid ponds and weathered barns. Along the

Gulf of St. Lawrence is Cavendish, the island's most popular tourist destination. Cavendish was the childhood home of Lucy Maud Montgomery, who created perfection on earth within the pages of her books, which centered on the spunky heroine Anne of Green Gables.

## PLANNING YOUR TIME

For many visitors, Queens County *is* Prince Edward Island. A typical itinerary may be that they catch the ferry to Wood Islands, spend one day in the capital, Charlottetown, and another in Cavendish before driving off the island via the Confederation Bridge. This is enough time in the capital to visit major attractions such as **Founders' Hall** and **Province House** while having enough time

© ANDREW HEMPSTEAD

# HIGHLIGHTS

**◖ Founders' Hall:** Canadians especially will enjoy learning about how the Dominion of Canada was created at this harborfront interpretive center (page 261).

**◖ Province House:** This historic sandstone building in the heart of Charlottetown hosted the Fathers of Confederation in 1864 and continues today as the provincial seat of government (page 262).

**◖ Victoria Park:** Take a break from history with a walk through this waterfront park (page 263).

**◖ International Shellfish Festival:** You can feast on seafood year-round in Charlottetown, but this late-September festival is the place to try all your favorites at once (page 265).

**◖ Confederation Players:** Performers dressed in period costume lead small groups of interested visitors through the streets of historic downtown Charlottetown (page 272).

**◖ Prince Edward Island National Park:** Stretching along the Gulf of St. Lawrence, this park is one of the island's few undeveloped tracts of land. Warm water, beaches and dunes, and red cliffs are the main draws (page 276).

**◖ North Rustico Harbour:** It's just a dot on the map, but this small fishing village is particularly photogenic. A lighthouse, kayak tours, and an excellent restaurant add to the appeal (page 278).

**◖ Green Gables House:** Northern Queens County is lovingly known as "Anne's Land," for Anne of Green Gables, one of the world's best-known literary characters (page 280).

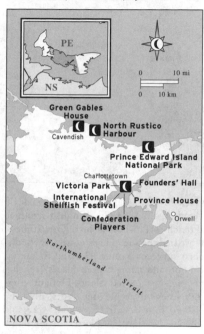

LOOK FOR ◖ TO FIND RECOMMENDED SIGHTS, ACTIVITIES, DINING, AND LODGING.

to join a **Confederation Players** tour and end the day with an evening walk through **Victoria Park.** If your travels coincide with the late September **International Shellfish Festival,** you may want to stay longer.

Cavendish, the most popular destination on all of Prince Edward Island, is just an hour's drive from the capital. This makes a day trip possible and means you can settle yourself into Charlottetown for two or more nights, taking advantage of the theater and many restaurants.

Cavendish does have many accommodations, but good dining rooms are severely lacking. Regardless of where you stay, your trip to Cavendish should include a drive through **Prince Edward Island National Park,** the short detour to **North Rustico Harbour,** and a visit to **Green Gables House.**

## HISTORY

In 1755, England deported the Acadians from Acadia (Prince Edward Island, Nova Scotia,

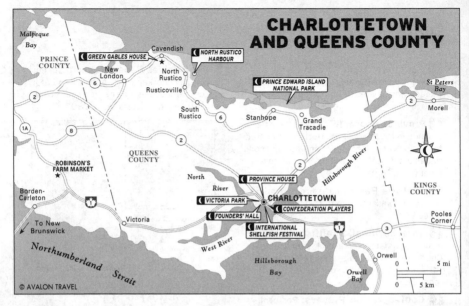

and New Brunswick) and swept the area again for Acadians in 1758. The English renamed the French fort at Port-la-Joye Fort Amherst and fortified the site. The English Crown dispatched surveyor Samuel Holland to survey, parcel out, and name various places and sites on the newly acquired island. Holland drew county lines on perplexing slants, dividing the island into 67 parcels, which were sold to absentee landlords at a lottery in England. Deciding Fort Amherst was difficult to defend, Holland moved the settlement across to the inner peninsula tip within Hillsborough Bay. He named it Charlotte, for the consort of King George III. The town's grid was laid out in 1764 and was named the island's capital the next year. During the American Revolution, American privateers sacked the capital, then added insult to injury when they stole the island's government seal and kidnapped the colonial governor.

Charlottetown has always been the island's main market town; the land now occupied by Province House and Confederation Centre was once the colony's thriving marketplace.

As in most early island towns, the majority of buildings were constructed of wood rather than stone, and many were subsequently leveled by fire. The stone buildings, however, survived. One of these is the small brick building at 104 Water Street—one of the capital's oldest buildings.

## Growth

Charlottetown's development paralleled the island's development. A road network was laid out by 1850. And by 1860, some 176 sawmills were transforming forests into lumber, greasing the island's economy and providing the raw materials for a thriving shipbuilding industry. As the center of government and commerce, the town was enriched with splendid stone churches and public buildings. The building of St. Peter's Anglican Church at Rochford Square transformed a bog into one of the capital's finest areas in 1869. Beaconsfield, a tribute of Second Empire and Victorian gingerbread style at Kent and West Streets, was designed by architect William Critchlow Harris for wealthy shipbuilder

# GETTING TO PRINCE EDWARD ISLAND

Most visitors to Prince Edward Island arrive by road, traveling either across the Confederation Bridge or on the ferry. You can also fly to Charlottetown.

## CONFEDERATION BRIDGE

The impressive Confederation Bridge (902/437-7300 or 888/437-6565, www .confederationbridge.com) is Prince Edward Island's most important transportation link to the rest of Canada. From Cape Jourimain (New Brunswick), 80 kilometers east of Moncton, the bridge stretches across Northumberland Strait to Borden-Carlton, which is in Prince County, 60 kilometers west of Charlottetown. Driving across the impressive 12.9-kilometer span takes around 10 minutes (views are blocked by concrete barriers erected as a windbreak).

The round-trip bridge toll is $41.50 per vehicle including passengers. Payment (credit card, debit card, or cash) is collected at Borden-Carlton upon leaving the island.

## BY FERRY

Prince Edward Island is also linked to the rest of Atlantic Canada by ferry. The mainland departure point is Caribou (Nova Scotia), near Pictou, a two-hour drive from Halifax. The ferry docks at Wood Islands, a scenic 62-kilometer drive southeast from Charlottetown. The 75-minute crossing is operated by **Northumberland Ferries** (902/566-3838 or 800/565-0201, www .peiferry.com) May to mid-December, with up to nine crossings in each direction daily during peak summer season. The round-trip fare is $61 per vehicle, regardless of the number of passengers. As with the bridge crossing, payment is made upon leaving the island. Therefore, take the ferry to PEI and return on the Confederation Bridge to save a few bucks.

## BY AIR

**Air Canada** (888/247-2262, www.aircanada .com) has direct flights to Charlottetown from Halifax, Montréal, Ottawa, and Toronto. **WestJet** (403/250-5839 or 888/937-8538, www .westjet.com) flies in from Toronto.

PRINCE EDWARD ISLAND

and merchant James Peake in 1877. The Kirk of St. James was architect James Stirling's tribute to early Gothic Revival. The brick Charlottetown City Hall, at Queen and Kent Streets, was a local adaptation of Romanesque Revival. While the downtown precinct remains a hotbed of historical buildings, there is one exception. The confederation centennial prompted the federal government to mark the event by establishing the Confederation Centre of the Arts in Charlottetown in 1964, and the new complex became PEI's proud showplace for theater, art exhibits, and other presentations.

# Sights and Recreation

Downtown Charlottetown is compact; plan on parking and exploring on foot. The waterfront area is the best place to leave your vehicle. Not only is it central, but you can make the harborside **Visitor Information Centre** (173 Water St., 902/368-4444; July–Aug. daily 8 A.M.–9 P.M., spring and fall daily 9 A.M.–6 P.M., winter Mon.–Fri. 9 A.M.–6 P.M.) your first stop.

## GETTING ORIENTED

The city, small as it is, may be baffling for a new visitor because of the way historic and newer streets converge. The town began with a handful of harborfront blocks. The centuries have contributed a confusing jumble of other roads that feed into the historic area from all sorts of angles.

From either direction, the **TransCanada Highway** (Route 1) will take you right into the heart of town. From the west, it crosses the North River, turns south at the University of Prince Edward Island campus and becomes University Avenue. From the east, take the Water Street exit to reach the information center.

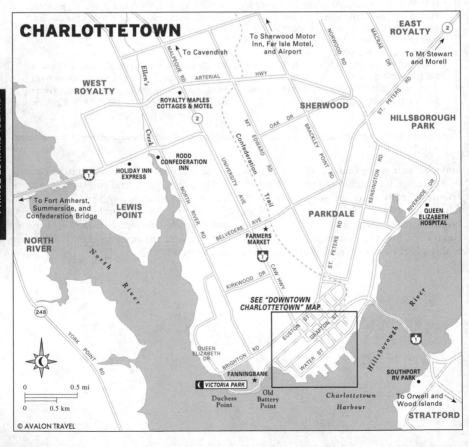

© AVALON TRAVEL

Extending from the harbor to Euston Street, the commercial area is pleasantly compact, attractive, and easily covered on foot. **Old Charlottetown** (or Old Charlotte Town, depending on who's describing the area) has been restored with rejuvenated buildings and brick walkways, lighted at night with gas lamps.

The most-sought-after residential areas, with large stately houses, rim Victoria Park and North River Road. Working-class neighborhoods fan out farther north beyond Grafton Street and are marked with small pastel-painted houses set close to the streets.

# DOWNTOWN
## ◖ Founders' Hall

Years of restoration saw a historic railway building transformed into Founders' Hall (6 Prince St., 902/368-1864; adult $7, senior $6, child $4), Charlottetown's number-one attraction. Located on the harbor beside the information center, this state-of-the-art facility combines the latest technology, dynamic audiovisuals, holo-visuals, and interactive displays to create a very different museum experience. You'll enter the Time Tunnel and travel back to 1864, when the Fathers of Confederation first met to discuss the union of Canada. You'll proceed through history, from the formation of each province and territory to modern times. Founders' Hall hours vary (Feb.–mid-May daily 10 A.M.–3 P.M., mid-May–mid-June daily 10 A.M.–5 P.M., mid-June–end of June daily 9 A.M.–6 P.M., July–mid-Aug. daily 8:30 A.M.–8 P.M., mid-Aug.–early Oct. daily 8:30 A.M.–6 P.M., early Oct.–Nov. daily 9 A.M.–3 P.M.).

## Downtown Waterfront

A rejuvenation project has seen much improvement in the downtown waterfront precinct, much of it spurred on by the establishment of Founders' Hall. The adjacent **Confederation Landing Park** is rimmed by a seaside boardwalk and filled with pleasant gardens and well-trimmed grass. The park is integrated with **Peake's Wharf,** where the Fathers of Confederation arrived on the island. This is

Founders' Hall

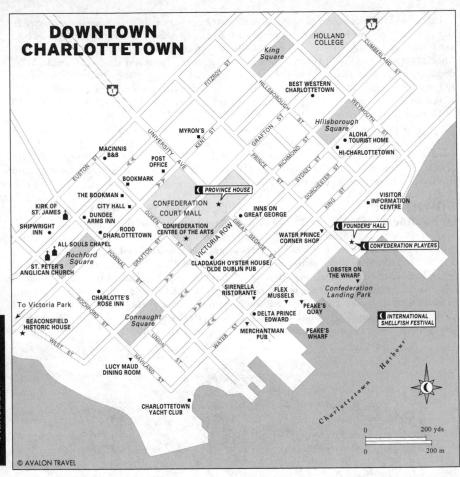

## DOWNTOWN CHARLOTTETOWN

PRINCE EDWARD ISLAND

© AVALON TRAVEL

now a tourist hub of sorts with restaurants and shops, and tour boats wait to take interested visitors on sightseeing trips.

## Province House

The nation of Canada began at Province House (corner Grafton St. and Great George St., 902/566-7626; June–Sept. daily 9 A.M.–5 P.M., Oct.–May Mon.–Fri. 9 A.M.–5 P.M.; free), four blocks up Great George Street from the harbor. Now protected as a national historic site, the buff sandstone neoclassical edifice at the high point of downtown was erected in 1847

to house the island's colonial legislature. It quickly became the center of public life on the island. It was the site of lavish balls and state functions, including the historic 1864 conference on federal union. The provincial legislature still convenes here; meetings are in session between mid-February and early May for 5 to 17 weeks, depending on how much provincial government haggling is underway.

In the late 1970s, Parks Canada undertook restoration of the age-begrimed building, a five-year task completed in 1983. Layers of paint came off the front columns. The double-hung windows throughout were refitted with glass panes from an old greenhouse in New Brunswick. About 10 percent of the original furnishings remained in the building before restoration and were retained. Most of the rest were replaced by period antiques obtained in the other provinces and the northeastern United States. A flowered rug was woven for Confederation Chamber, where the Fathers of Confederation convened. Every nook and corner was refurbished and polished until the interior gleamed. Today, Province House is one of Atlantic Canada's most significant public buildings.

## Confederation Centre of the Arts

Confederation Centre of the Arts (145 Richmond St., 902/628-1864) is the other half of the imposing complex shared by Province House. The promenades, edged with places to sit, are great places for people watching, and kids like to skateboard on the walkways.

The center opened in 1964 to mark the centennial of the Charlottetown Conference, as the confederation meeting became known in Canadian history. It's a great hulk of a place, compatible with its historic neighbor in its design and coloring. The center houses an art gallery, the provincial library, four theaters, and a café. The emphasis at the **Confederation Centre Art Gallery** (mid-June–Sept. daily 9 A.M.–5 P.M., Oct.–mid-June Wed.–Sat. 11 A.M.–5 P.M. and Sun. 1–5 P.M.; free) is the work of Canadian artists—expect to see some of island artist Robert Harris's paintings and Lucy Maud Montgomery's original manuscripts. A gift shop stocks wares by the cream of PEI's artisans.

## All Souls' Chapel

A few blocks west of Queen Street, this remarkable chapel next to **St. Peter's Anglican Church** (Rochford St., 902/628-1376; daily 8 A.M.–6 P.M.; free) was a joint Harris family creation. The architect William Harris styled it in island sandstone with a dark walnut interior. His brother Robert painted the murals

and deftly mixed family members and friends among the religious figures.

## Beaconsfield Historic House

This bright yellow 25-room mansion (2 Kent St., 902/368-6603; tours July–Aug. daily 10 A.M.–5 P.M.; adult $4.50, child $3.50) was built in 1877 from a William Critchlow Harris design. The building has survived more than a century of varied use as a family home, a shelter for "friendless women," a YWCA, and a nurses' residence. It was rescued in 1973 by the PEI Museum and Heritage Foundation, which turned it into foundation headquarters and a heritage museum. A good bookstore is on the first level, and genealogical archives are kept across the hall and also upstairs. Outside, you can sit on the wide front porch overlooking the harbor across the long lawn—it's a great place to have tea and scones.

## ◖ Victoria Park

Victoria Park, adjacent to Beaconsfield House, reigns as one of Charlottetown's prettiest settings, with 16 wooded and grassy hectares overlooking the bay at Battery Point. The greenery spreads out across the peninsula tip; to get there follow Kent Street as it turns into Park Roadway. The park's rolling terrain is the result of moraines, heaps of gravelly deposits left behind by ice-age glaciers.

Joggers like the park's winding paths, and birders find abundant yellow warblers, purple finches, and downy woodpeckers nesting in the maples, firs, oaks, pines, and birches. The white palatial mansion overlooking the water is Fanningbank (Government House), the lieutenant governor's private residence—nice to look at, but it's closed to the public.

## BEYOND DOWNTOWN
### Farmers' Market

The Farmers' Market (100 Belvedere Ave., 902/626-3373; July–Aug. Sat. 9 A.M.–2 P.M. and Wed. 10 A.M.–5 P.M.) is across from the university campus. The indoor market holds about 40 vendors selling everything from flowers and crafts to baked goods, produce, and fish.

### Fort Amherst-Port-la-Joye National Historic Site

Just four kilometers across the harbor from downtown, but a 35-minute drive via Routes 1 and 19, Fort Amherst–Port-la-Joye National Historic Site protects the site of the island's first European settlement. It all began in 1720, when three French ships sailed into Port-la-Joye (today's Charlottetown Harbour) carrying some 300 settlers. Most of them moved to the north shore and established fishing villages, but the rest remained here at the military outpost.

Within just four years, adverse conditions had driven out most of the French. The British burned Port-la-Joye in 1745 and took control of the island. The French later returned to rebuild their capital but were compelled to surrender Port-la-Joye to a superior British force in 1758. The British renamed the post Fort Amherst. After the British established the new capital at Charlottetown, Fort Amherst fell quickly into disrepair, and now no buildings remain. The grounds, which have picnic tables, are open June–August.

## OUTDOOR ACTIVITIES

Those looking for easy walking gravitate to the waterfront at the southwestern end of downtown. This is the starting point for a paved trail that extends to Old Battery Point and Victoria Park. While this area is also popular for biking, cyclists looking for longer rides will be impressed at how easy it is to reach the rural landscape beyond city limits. From downtown, the ride out to Brackley Beach (45 kilometers) is a good destination for a full-day ride.

**MacQueen's Bike Shop** (430 Queen St., 902/368-2453) provides complete bike and accessory rental and repairs and can also arrange cycle-touring packages. **Smooth Cycle** (330 University Ave., 902/566-5530) also offers rentals and repairs as well as drop-offs for the Confederation Trail. Both companies charge from $25 per day for a road bike.

# Entertainment and Events

Charlottetown once rolled up the sidewalks at night, but in recent years a rousing nightlife and pub scene has emerged, centered on drinking and dancing. Last call for drinks is at 1:30 A.M.; the doors lock at 2 A.M. For complete listings of all that's happening around the city, pick up the free weekly *Buzz* or the weekend editions of *The Guardian* newspaper.

## PUBS AND BARS

**Peake's Quay** (1 Great George St., 902/368-1330; daily from 11 A.M.) has a prime waterfront location, making it popular with both locals and visitors. While the service is often blasé, it's a good family-friendly environment with inexpensive food and lots of outdoor seating. Look for live music most weekends after 9 P.M. **Olde Dublin Pub** (131 Sydney St., 902/892-6992) has a popular deck and offers Celtic and Irish music Thursday–Saturday for a $5 cover charge.

**Mavor's** (145 Richmond St., 902/628-6107; Mon.–Sat. 11 A.M.–10 P.M.), in the Confederation Centre of the Arts, is a colorful space with over 40 wines by the glass, topnotch martinis, and a thoughtful menu of light meals under $15.

The **Selkirk Lounge** (Delta Prince Edward, 18 Queen St., 902/894-1208; daily noon–11 P.M.) is a sophisticated space within one of the city's top hotels. Piano players perform Tuesday–Saturday evenings; martinis and specialty coffees are highlights on a long menu of drinks.

The **42nd St. Lounge** (125 Sydney St., 902/566-4620) is another good choice for a quiet drink and conversation; ask one of the affable bartenders for a cognac, kick back in one of the overstuffed chairs, and listen to soft jazz on the sound system. Highly recommended.

## NIGHTCLUBS

A mainstay of the club scene is **Velvet Underground** (166 Prince St., 902/628-6898). Music plays Tuesday–Saturday, with the Saturday dance party attracting the biggest crowd. As closet-like as Myron's is cavernous, **Baba's Lounge** (upstairs at 81 University Ave., 902/892-7377) is a "hipoisie" hangout extraordinaire. "Intimate" is an understatement here; bodies writhe to the rhythm on a dance floor about the size of a postage stamp. Expect live music ranging from slightly alternative to modern rock.

## PERFORMING ARTS

The **Confederation Centre of the Arts** (145 Richmond St., 902/566-1267) is the performing-arts capital of the province and the site of the **Charlottetown Festival,** which runs from mid-June to late September. The festival is best known for the *Anne of Green Gables* musical; tickets cost $50–70. Also on the bill are repertory productions in the center's main theater and cabaret-style productions at the **MacKenzie Theatre,** the festival's second stage at University Avenue and Grafton Street.

## FESTIVALS AND EVENTS
### June

The June to mid-October **Charlottetown Festival** (902/628-1864, www.confederationcentre.com) presents musical theater and cabaret at the Confederation Centre and the nearby MacKenzie Theatre. Two musicals are presented, including one centering on *Anne of Green Gables.*

### July

The **Canada Day** long weekend (first weekend in July) is celebrated on the waterfront with a food fair, nationalistic displays, buskers, island music, and the **Festival of Lights** fireworks display.

Organized by the Charlottetown Yacht Club, **Race Week** (902/892-9065, www.cyc.pe.ca) runs Wednesday–Saturday in the middle of July. The program revolves around yacht races for various classes of boats, with other scheduled activities including shore games and nightly entertainment. Even if you're not involved in the event, watching the yachts racing across the harbor is a sight to behold.

### August

The mid-August **Old Home Week** (902/629-6623, www.oldhomeweekpei.com), Atlantic Canada's largest agricultural exposition, centers on Charlottetown Driving Park, northeast of downtown along Kensington Road. The city unofficially shuts down for the week-ending **Gold Cup Parade** through the streets of Charlottetown—said to be Atlantic Canada's biggest and best-attended parade. Daily grounds admission is a reasonable adult $7, child $4.

### September
#### ◖ INTERNATIONAL SHELLFISH FESTIVAL

Summer ends with the International Shellfish Festival (www.peishellfish.com), over the third weekend of September. Festivities along the waterfront include an oyster-shucking contest, a Chowder Challenge, "touch tanks," cooking classes, the World is Your Oyster children's program, sock-hanging, and chefs from the local culinary institute sharing their cooking skills with the public.

**PRINCE EDWARD ISLAND**

PRINCE EDWARD ISLAND

# Shopping

Centrally located and the largest city by far, Charlottetown is the island's shopping hub. Downtown is a pleasant blend of old and new shopping experiences, although the main concentration of shopping malls is north of downtown along University Avenue. Stores catering to islanders are normally open Monday–Saturday from about 9 A.M. to 5 P.M. while touristy ones open later in July and August and also operate on Sunday.

## ARTS AND CRAFTS

Local artists capture the island in masterful watercolors, acrylics, oils, and sculpture. Local crafts include finely made quilts, knits and woolens, stained glass, jewelry, pewter, pottery, and handsome furniture. The Anne doll is the most popular souvenir, and it's produced in innumerable variations for as little as $20 to as much as $800.

An exquisite handmade quilt costs $400–800—seldom a bargain. But well-crafted quilts are sturdily constructed and will last a lifetime with good care. Sweaters ($75–300) are especially high quality. One of the best sources is **Northern Watters Knitwear,** which operates a downtown factory outlet (150 Richmond St., 902/566-5850).

The **P.E.I. Crafts Council** is a driving force behind local arts and crafts. It counts about 100 provincial craftspeople among its esteemed ranks. **Island Crafts Shop** (156 Richmond St., 902/892-5152) functions as the council members' outlet. A thorough browse among quilts, glassware, sculpture, clothing, knitted apparel, and jewelry ad infinitum will provide you an insight into what's available in the city and province. Craftspeople demonstrate their trades at the shop from time to time. The wares here tend to be one-of-a-kind. If you don't see exactly what you want, you could go directly to the maker; the membership list is available at the shop.

# Accommodations and Camping

You'll find every kind of lodging, from plain budget places to sumptuous expensive rooms, in Charlottetown's 100-plus lodgings. Also, unlike elsewhere in the province, most are open year-round.

Unless noted otherwise, prices given below are for a double room; sales tax is not included in these prices.

## DOWNTOWN
### Under $50

Charlottetown's lone hostel is **HI-Charlottetown** (60 Hillsborough St., 902/367-5749, www.hihostels.ca; dorm beds $27–30, $65–70 d), a converted residential home just two blocks east of Province House. Facilities include a living room with a fireplace, a recreation room, and wireless Internet.

### $50-100

Operated by the same owners as HI-Charlottetown and in the same vicinity, **Aloha Tourist Home** (234 Sydney St., 902/892-9944 or 866/892-9944, www.alohaamigo.com; $56–68 s or d) is an inexpensive downtown accommodation for those looking for private rooms. The renovated home has four guest rooms with single or double beds, two shared bathrooms, a shared kitchen, a lounge area, and free wireless Internet throughout.

One of the least expensive of Charlottetown's historic accommodations with en suite rooms is **MacInnis Bed and Breakfast** (80 Euston St., 902/892-6725), a homey, centrally located choice with a veranda that overlooks pleasant gardens. It offers two regular guest rooms ($85 s or d) and a top-floor one-bedroom suite ($135 s or d).

## $100-150

The elegant 1860s 【 **Shipwright Inn** (51 Fitzroy St., 902/368-1905 or 888/306-9966, www.shipwrightinn.com; $149–249 s or d) was originally the home of shipbuilder James Douse. The inn has eight rooms and suites, all with private baths and furnished in richly colored nautical themes (my favorite is the Chart Room, with an 1830s four-poster walnut bed, heavy drapes, and historic sea charts on the walls). Rates include a full breakfast.

What makes **Elmwood Heritage Inn** (121 North River Rd., 902/368-3310 or 877/933-3310, www.elmwoodinn.pe.ca; $149–259 including breakfast) stand out is the setting. Still within easy walking distance of downtown, it is in a parklike setting, surrounded by mature gardens and with a row of stately elm trees leading up from the wrought-iron entry gates to the front door. Built for the grandson of Samuel Cunard in 1889, the mansion boasts 28 very Victorian guest rooms, many with jetted tubs and fireplaces.

**Best Western Charlottetown** (238 Grafton St., 902/892-2461 or 800/528-1234, www.bestwesternatlantic.com; $145–185 s or d) is a three-block jaunt from Province House. It has 143 midsized rooms fronting both sides of the street, connected beneath the road by a tunnel. Facilities include a pub-style restaurant, indoor pool, sauna, hot tub, and launderette.

## $150-200

A restored Queen Anne Revival mansion awash with antiques, **Dundee Arms Inn** (200 Pownal St., 902/892-2496 or 877/638-6333, www.dundeearms.com; $145–220 s, $155–230 d) has been taking in guests since the early 1970s. Conveniently located between downtown and Victoria Park, its other pluses include a good restaurant and comfortable beds. Note that half the 18 rooms are in a modern addition out back of the original home, but these are still stylishly decorated and come with wireless Internet, bathrobes, and more.

**Charlotte's Rose Inn** (11 Grafton St., www.charlottesrose.ca, 902/892-3699 or 888/237-3699) is a three-story 1884 home on a quiet residential street. Original hardwood floors, high ceilings, and Victorian-era furnishings add to the charm. The four en suite guest rooms rent for $155–205 s or d, including a cooked breakfast.

## Over $200

A few steps from Province House, 【 **Inns on Great George** (58 Great George St., 902/892-0606 or 800/361-1118, www.innsongreatgeorge.com; $209–349 s or d) comprises 53 guest rooms spread through 13 beautifully restored buildings dating to as early as 1811. The lobby is in a building that was originally known as the Pavilion Hotel, at the corner of Great George and Sydney Streets. It was here that the Fathers of Confederation stayed during the 1864 Charlottetown Conference. This building also has a large lounge area and a fine-dining restaurant. Rooms in this and buildings running up Great George Street and beyond have been beautifully restored, with the addition of modern amenities like air-conditioning and high-speed Internet access.

**Rodd Charlottetown** (75 Kent St., 902/894-7371 or 800/565-7633, www.roddhotelsandresorts.com; $230 s or d) is a grand red-brick 1931 Georgian gem with magnificent woodwork and furnishings made by island craftspeople. It offers 115 rooms and suites and a restaurant, whirlpool, indoor pool, and rooftop patio. As always with these top-end properties, check the website for the best deals.

Like the nearby Confederation Centre, the **Delta Prince Edward** (18 Queen St., 902/566-2222 or 888/890-3222, www.deltahotels.com; $240 s or d) stands out for its boxy look amid the gracious buildings of downtown. Inside are 211 well-decorated rooms. The more expensive Delta Rooms have king beds and water views. It offers all the amenities of a full-service hotel, including underground valet parking ($19 per day), a day spa, a fitness room, an indoor pool, a lounge, and a restaurant. Disregard the rack rates and check online—you should find packages that include accommodations and either theater tickets or greens fees for around $200 d.

**PRINCE EDWARD ISLAND**

Rodd Charlottetown, a grand 1931 Georgian hotel

## NORTH OF DOWNTOWN

Staying downtown has its perks, but if you're looking for a well-priced motel room or are traveling with a family, staying on the north side is a good alternative.

### $50-100

**Sherwood Motor Inn** (281 Brackley Point Rd., 902/892-1622 or 800/567-1622) is a reliable cheapie opposite the airport turnoff eight kilometers north of downtown. It comprises a strip of dated motel rooms ($65–75 s or d) and a newer two-story building filled with air-conditioned rooms ($85–105 s or d).

A little closer toward the city, **Fair Isle Motel** (Rte. 2, 902/368-8259 or 800/309-8259; Apr.–Nov.; $40–56 s, $50–66 d), an old roadside motel where rooms overlook landscaped gardens. If you've picked up fresh seafood at Lobster on the Wharf, take advantage of this motel's barbecues for a great outdoor dinner.

I doubt too many Canadian capitals boast a cottage complex surrounded by expansive lawns within city limits, but Charlottetown does, in the form of ◖ **Royalty Maples Cottages & Motel** (Rte. 2, 902/368-1030, www.royaltymaples.com; May–Nov.), which is one kilometer north of the junction of Routes 1 and 2. The 10 one- and two-bedroom cottages ($95–125 s or d) each have a full kitchen, living area, and air-conditioning. Six motel rooms go for $75 s or d per night.

### $100-150

At the busy intersection of Routes 1 and 2, four kilometers north of downtown along University Avenue, is **Rodd Confederation Inn** (TransCanada Hwy., 902/892-2481 or 800/565-7633, www.roddhotelsandresorts .com; $125–160 s or d). This spread-out property features 31 regular guest rooms and 31 suites (the latter are better value). Other facilities include a heated outdoor pool, playground, pub, and restaurant.

### $150-200

The **Holiday Inn Express** (200 TransCanada Hwy., 902/892-1201 or 800/465-4329, www .ichotelsgroup.com; $155–210 s or d) maintains the same standards and facilities expected of this worldwide chain. The modern rooms have air-conditioning and high-speed Internet access, and rates include a continental breakfast. Families can take advantage of children's suites, complete with Nintendo systems and bunk beds separate from the main bedroom. Other amenities include an indoor pool and a sundeck.

## CAMPGROUNDS
### East

The only campground within city limits is **Southport RV Park** (20 Stratford Rd., Stratford, 902/569-2287; mid-May–mid-Oct.; $22–34 per night). This facility sprawls along the east bank of the Hillsborough River, a short five-minute drive east from downtown. It has tent and full-hookup spaces, a Laundromat, a kitchen shelter, and views back across the water to downtown.

## West

( **Holiday Haven Campground** (Rte. 248, 2 km east of Cornwall, 902/566-2421, www.holidayhaven.pe.ca; June–early Oct.) spreads across 25 beautiful hectares along the West River. Amenities include an outdoor swimming pool, a playground, hayrides, showers, a launderette, and a kitchen shelter. All sites are $28 per night.

Follow the TransCanada Highway west from downtown toward the Confederation Bridge and you'll pass the entrance to **Strathgartney Provincial Park** (Rte. 1, Churchill, 902/675-7476; mid-June–early Sept.) after 20 kilometers. The park's 55 hectares encompass inland woodlands spliced by (and providing delightful views of) the Strathgartney River (with fishing). Facilities include unserviced campsites ($22) and two-way hookup sites ($25), hiking trails, hot showers, a launderette, kitchen shelters, and a nearby campers store.

# Food

Island fare is *good,* and while it centers on homegrown produce and seafood from the surrounding ocean, everything comes together in the capital, with an excellent array of dining opportunities for all budgets. The center of the eating action is **Victoria Row,** a block of vintage buildings along Richmond Street between Queen and Great George Streets. The street is pedestrian-only through summer. The restaurants set up outdoor tables while musicians play to the assembled crowd of diners.

Even if you're not in town for the **International Shellfish Festival** (third weekend of September), you'll find local delicacies such as lobster and Malpeque oysters on menus throughout the city. Local produce and dairy products are delicious. Chefs make the most of island-grown succulent berries, locally produced maple syrup, and thick, sweet honey.

## CAFÉS

On pedestrian-only Victoria Row, **Cafe Diem** (128 Richmond St., 902/892-0494; Apr.–Oct. daily 8 A.M.–10 P.M.) is centrally located for a break from sightseeing. On the menu are dozens of coffee concoctions, light lunches such as sandwiches and bagels, and a tempting array of sweet treats. This is also the city's most central Internet café.

**Just Juicin'** (62 Queen St., 902/894-3104; Mon.–Sat. 8 A.M.–5 P.M., Sun. noon–5 P.M.) started out mixing up fresh juices but now also offers the healthy (smoked salmon bagels) to the heavy (rich chocolate cake).

At the Confederation Centre of the Arts, ( **Mavor's** (145 Richmond St., 902/628-6107; daily 8 A.M.–8 P.M.) is a striking room where you can get your fill of Starbucks coffee, complete with the fancy names. The kitchen opens daily except Sunday at 11 A.M., serving up fresh and wholesome food, with ethnic influences showing through in dishes such as blue mussels steamed in Thai curry broth. Also good: the thin-crust smoked salmon pizza ($12) and sweet potato wedges with a side of sour cream ($6.50).

**Beanz Espresso Bar** (38 University Ave., 902/892-8797; Mon.–Fri. 6:30 A.M.–6 P.M., Sat. 8 A.M.–6 P.M., Sun. 9 A.M.–4 P.M.) gets rave reviews for its coffee, but the soups, salads, sandwiches, and old-fashioned pastries draw me back every time I'm in Charlottetown.

## SEAFOOD

( **Flex Mussels** (2 Lower Water St., 902/569-0200; daily noon–midnight) is a unique and tasty stop. Mussels are the specialty. They are steamed open to order in one of 50 flavors, including Parisienne (Pernod, tarragon, and basil), Wild Turkey (roasted corn, green onions, kumquats, and bourbon), Maine (baby clams, cream, and parsley), and Cajun (spicy Creole sauce, red wine, shrimp, and okra). The cost is $12–16 per pound, with delicious fries a worthwhile $4.50 extra. Want to watch a mussel grow? Then check out the company's mussel-cam at www.flexmussels.com.

**❰ Water Prince Corner Shop** (141 Water St., 902/368-3212; May–Oct. daily 9 A.M.–8 P.M., July–Aug. until 10 P.M.) looks like a regular convenience store from the outside, but inside the ocean-blue clapboard building is a casual dining space where the emphasis is on fresh seafood at reasonable prices. It's all good—lobster burgers, lobster dinners, seafood chowder, steamed clams, and more.

**Fishbones** (136 Richmond St., 902/628-6569; daily from 11 A.M. for lunch and dinner) is a fresh, casual restaurant along pedestrian-only Victoria Row. Start at the oyster bar before moving on to a set menu of contemporary creations such as the grilled salmon brushed with maple butter. Other highlights include a rich seafood stew and baked halibut topped with salsa. Mains are in the $18–27 range.

The **❰ Claddagh Oyster House** (131 Sydney St., 902/892-9661; Mon.–Fri. for lunch, daily for dinner) is authentically Irish, starting with owner Liam Dolan from County Galway. Seafood is the specialty ($17–30), with the Lobster spaghetti ($29) a rich-tasting splurge.

For its harborfront location alone, **Lobster on the Wharf** (2 Prince St., 902/368-2888; May–Oct. 11:30 A.M.–10 P.M.) is a longtime favorite with visitors and locals alike from its waterfront foundations, but the venerable restaurant has been rebuilt, complete with an extra level and a large deck. As the name suggests, lobster is the specialty (the lobster risotto is delicious), but the fish-and-chips in tempura batter ($18) is also excellent.

## PUB DINING

Taking full advantage of its harborfront locale is the upstairs **Peake's Quay** (1 Great George St., 902/368-1330; daily from 11 A.M.), with informal indoor and outdoor dining and an enviable seafood selection ($11–22); try the scallops sauced with honey butter. Peake's Quay is also arguably the hottest nightspot

in town, drawing locals, landlubber tourists, and yachties (who tie up at the adjacent marina) alike to see and be seen while listening or dancing to top touring bands, so plan on dining early.

**The Merchantman Pub** (23 Queen St., 902/892-9150; Mon.–Sat. from 11:30 A.M.) has a nice atmosphere, a wide-ranging menu that includes some Thai and Cajun dishes, and a good beer selection. But the place seems a little overpriced, probably due to its location across the street from the upscale Delta Prince Edward.

## CANADIAN

The **❰ Lucy Maud Dining Room** (4 Sydney St., 902/894-6868; Tues.–Fri. 11:30 A.M.–1:30 P.M., Tues.–Sat. 6–8 P.M.) is part of the Culinary Institute of Canada, a respected school that attracts students from across the country. Turn a blind eye to the rather institutional room, concentrate on the water views, and sit back to enjoy enthusiastic service and well-priced meals that blend contemporary and Continental. Expect to pay $35 for a four-course meal.

If you want to dine in one of the city's best restaurants but don't want to pay for an expensive dinner, eat breakfast at **The Selkirk** (Delta Prince Edward, 18 Queen St., 902/894-1208; Mon.–Sat. 7 A.M.–2:30 P.M. and 6–9 P.M., Sun. 11 A.M.–2 P.M.). The buffet is $17, or try dishes as traditional as fish cakes with baked beans ($14) or as creative as lobster eggs Benedict ($18). Things go upscale in the evening. That's when you can order pork tenderloin ravioli or smoked duck and asparagus salad to start, followed by pan-fried arctic char topped with fruit salsa or salmon marinated in whiskey and maple syrup and then grilled on a cedar plank. Starters are mostly under $15 and mains range $25–33.

The **Griffon Room** (Dundee Arms Inn, 200 Pownal St., 902/892-2496; daily for breakfast, lunch, and dinner) is away from the tourist crush within a restored three-story manor that combines an old-fashioned setting with elegantly conceived fine cuisine emphasizing red meats and seafood. If you feel like a break from seafood, you won't regret it with the roast pork tenderloin topped with peach relish. Mains are $21–32.

## ITALIAN

**Sirenella Ristorante** (83 Water St., 902/628-2271; Mon.–Fri. 11:30 A.M.–2 P.M., Mon.–Sat. 5 A.M.–10 P.M.) serves up traditional Northern Italian food in a simple but classy setting. The scallop, shrimp, and hot sauce linguine is delicious. The wine list is dominated by Italian reds and whites. Mains range $13–27. A children's menu and patio add to the appeal.

## ICE CREAM

Ice-cream fanciers whoop it up at 【 **Cow's,** a local ice-cream company that is renowned as much for its creamy treats wrapped in handmade waffle cones as for its colorful merchandise. Downtown outlets include opposite the Confederation Centre (corner of Queen St. and Grafton St., 902/892-6969) and at Peakes Wharf (902/566-4886). On your way off the island, you can also indulge at Gateway Village or aboard the ferry.

# Information and Services

## TOURIST INFORMATION

Charlottetown's main **Visitor Information Centre** is right beside the harbor (173 Water St., 902/368-4444; July–Aug. daily 8 A.M.–9 P.M., spring and fall daily 9 A.M.–6 P.M., winter Mon.–Fri. 9 A.M.–6 P.M.) answers questions and stocks a good supply of literature about the province and Charlottetown. Inside city hall, at the corner of Kent and Queen Streets, is a smaller seasonal information booth. The official island tourism website (www.peiplay.com) is a good source for advance planning.

## LIBRARY

Access to the centrally located **Confederation Centre Public Library** (902/368-4642; Mon. and Fri.–Sat. 10 A.M.–5 P.M., Tues.–Thurs. 10 A.M.–9 P.M., Sun. 1–5 P.M.) is from Richmond Street. It has a solid collection of island literature, newspapers from across North America, and free public Internet access.

## BOOKSTORES

**Bookmark** (172 Queen St., 902/566-4888; Mon.–Fri. 8:30 A.M.–9 P.M., Sat. 9 A.M.–5:30 P.M., Sun. noon–5 P.M.) is an excellent locally owned bookstore in the heart of downtown. You can pick up coffee-table books, *Anne of Green Gables,* and field guides.

For island literature and especially architecture and history coverage, check out the bookshop at **Beaconsfield Historic House** (2 Kent St., 902/368-6600; July–Aug. daily 10 A.M.–5 P.M., Sept.–June Wed.–Thurs. noon–5 P.M.).

**The Bookman** (177 Queen St., 902/892-8872) carries new, used, and rare books.

## HEALTH AND SAFETY

**Queen Elizabeth Hospital** is on Riverside Drive (902/894-2200). For **police** call 902/566-7112.

## POST AND INTERNET

The main **post office** is at 135 Kent Street (902/628-4400).

Most accommodations in the capital offer wireless or high-speed Internet access, or head to the **Confederation Centre Public Library** (902/368-4642; Mon. and Fri.–Sat. 10 A.M.–5 P.M., Tues.–Thurs. 10 A.M.–9 P.M., Sun. 1–5 P.M.). Across from the library, **Cafe Diem** (128 Richmond St., 902/892-0494; daily 8 A.M.–10 P.M.) has a row of computers along an upstairs indoor balcony; Internet access costs $6 per half hour.

## OTHER SERVICES

Coin laundries are plentiful; they're generally open daily 8 A.M.–11 P.M. Among them, **Better Than Home Laundromat** (73 St. Peters Rd., 902/628-1994) and **Mid Town Laundromat** (238 University Ave., 902/628-2329) offer drop-off service.

For all your digital camera needs, head to **PEI Photo Lab** (55 Queen St., 902/892-5107).

# Getting There and Around

## GETTING THERE

**Charlottetown Airport** is eight kilometers north of downtown along Brackley Point Road. **Air Canada** (888/247-2262) has direct flights from Toronto, Montréal, Ottawa, and Halifax while **WestJet** (888/937-8538) flies in from Toronto.

Though open daily 24 hours, it's a small airport sans banks or a duty-free shop. For sightseeing and other information, use the free phone line to the tourist office. Taxis wait outside during flight arrivals and charge about $12 for one person or $15 for two for the 15-minute drive to town. Avis, Budget, Hertz, and National rent vehicles at the airport, but their counters are not staffed between flights.

## GETTING AROUND

Use **Charlottetown Transit** (902/566-9962) to get anywhere in Greater Charlottetown for $2; buses run weekdays only.

Charlottetown taxis are plentiful; you'll pay $4–6 to get almost anywhere downtown. Taxis cruise the streets or wait at major downtown hotels. Taxi companies include **City Cab** (902/892-6567), **Co-op** (902/892-1111), and **Yellow Cab** (902/566-6666).

Local rental-car agencies include **Avis** (902/892-3706), **Budget** (902/566-5525), **Hertz** (902/966-5566), and **National** (902/628-6990).

## TOURS

### ◖ Confederation Players

The Confederation Players are keen local historians who dress in period costume to conduct walking tours of downtown Charlottetown from Founders' Hall (6 Prince St., 902/368-1864) mid-June through August. The regular one-hour tour departs daily at 11 A.M., 1 P.M., and 3:30 P.M.; the one-hour tour for French speakers departs at 1 P.M. The Ghostly Realm Tour departs Tuesday–Saturday at 7:30 P.M. All tours cost a reasonable $10 per person.

### Bus and Boat Tours

**Abegweit Tours** (902/894-9966) operates the red double-decker bus that lopes through Charlottetown on sightseeing tours ($10 for a one-hour tour). The bus stops at Confederation Centre on Queen and Grafton Streets, and it runs mid-June through September daily 10:30 A.M.–6:15 P.M.

**Peake's Wharf Boat Tours** (902/629-1864) operates a covered 42-foot boat from Peake's Wharf, at the foot of Great George Street. Options include a 70-minute sightseeing cruise (1 P.M.; $22), a 2.5-hour seal-watching cruise (2:30 P.M.; $30), and 70-minute evening and sunset cruises (6:30 P.M. and 8 P.M.; both $25). The tours run June to early September.

# The South Shore

From Charlottetown, Route 1 (TransCanada Highway) whisks travelers 56 kilometers southwest to Borden–Carleton, from where the Confederation Bridge provides a link to the rest of Canada. If you're arriving on the island via the bridge, consider veering off Route 1 at DeSable and following scenic Route 19 along the South Shore to Rocky Point and Fort Amherst–Port-la-Joye National Historic Site for views of the city skyline across sparkling Charlottetown Harbour.

## VICTORIA

Victoria (pop. 200), 40 kilometers west of Charlottetown, marks Queens County's southwestern corner. The town owed its start to shipbuilding, and by 1870 Victoria ranked as one of the island's busiest ports. As the demand for wooden ships faded, the seaport turned to cattle shipping—herds of cattle were driven down the coastal slopes to water's edge, where they were hoisted with slings onto waiting ships.

Today Victoria shows just a shadow of its former luster. The seaport slipped off the commercial circuit decades ago, and the settlement shrank to a handful of waterfront blocks. Happily, island craftspeople discovered the serene setting. It's still a quiet place where the fishing fleet puts out to sea early in the morning as the mist rises off the strait. But now the peaceful seaport also holds a modest arts colony, with outlets along the main street.

### Victoria Playhouse

If an evening at the theater sounds good, make plans to attend the **Victoria Playhouse** (Howard St., 902/658-2025, www.victoriaplayhouse.com), a repertory theater that showcases historically themed comedy and drama (adult $24, senior $22, child $18), as well as concerts of jazz and folk music.

### Accommodations

Next to the Victoria Playhouse, **Victoria Village Inn** (Howard St., 902/658-2483 or 866/658-2483, www.victoriavillageinn.com; $90–145 s or d) is an 1870s inn that was originally built for a sea captain. Awash with lustrous antiques, it offers four comfortable guest units—one with three bedrooms. The inn also has a restaurant open daily in summer for dinner.

Kitty-corner to the theater, the **Orient Hotel** (Main St., 902/658-2503 or 800/565-6743; mid-May–mid-Oct.; $80–150 s or d) has been taking in guests since 1900. It features a few smallish guest rooms (from $80) and larger suites ($130–150). Rates include a delicious breakfast, and tea and coffee throughout the day.

### Food

Enterprising locals remodeled the old general store and post office and opened ◖ **Landmark Café** (12 Main St., 902/658-2286; June–Sept. daily 11:30 A.M.–9 P.M.). You can't go wrong with any of the fresh seasonal cooking, but the soups and meat pies are especially good.

Walk out on Victoria Wharf to reach **Ruthie's Lobster House** (902/658-2200; June–Sept. daily 11:30 A.M.–2:30 P.M. and 5–9 P.M.), a haven for seafood and steaks. The adjacent **Ruthie's Pub** has live music most weekends.

Two kilometers east of the main wharf is **Morning Star Fisheries** (902/658-3045; summer daily 10 A.M.–7 P.M.), where you can purchase a cooked lobster and then enjoy it at the picnic area in nearby **Victoria Provincial Park.**

## BORDEN-CARLETON

The twin villages of Borden–Carleton, 56 kilometers west of Charlottetown, are the closest point to mainland Canada, and so have always been an important transportation hub. Back in the late 1700s, iceboats carrying mail and passengers crossed Northumberland Strait when the island was icebound from December to early spring. The voyages were filled with hair-raising tales of survival, and the iceboats—rigged with fragile sails and runners—were often trapped in the strait's ice. It wasn't until 1916 that the first vehicle ferry made the crossing, but in 1997, the Confederation Bridge opened and the ferry service was discontinued.

Since the opening of the bridge, Borden–Carleton, 56 kilometers west of Charlottetown, has seen much development as thousands of travelers peeling off the bridge come looking for food and information, and those leaving stop to stock up with last-minute souvenirs.

## Gateway Village

As you descend the final span of Confederation Bridge, 12-hectare Gateway Village soon comes into view. It is designed especially for bridge travelers, but well worth visiting even if you're on your way back to the mainland. With the theme of an island streetscape of the early 1900s, the shops are filled with island souvenirs, some tacky (T-shirts, Christmas decorations, etc.), some tasty (fresh lobster), and some trendy (wine from Rossignol Estate Winery). The epicenter for new arrivals is the cavernous **Gateway Village Visitor Information Centre** (902/437-8570; daily 9 A.M.–6 P.M., spring and fall until 8 P.M., summer until 10 P.M.), where friendly staff will help sort out the best way to spend your time while on the island. Displays within the center focus on various island experiences. Outside, amid the café tables and wandering visitors, free musical performances and craft demonstrations add to the appeal.

## Confederation Bridge

If you arrived in Borden–Carlton via the Confederation Bridge, you enjoyed a free ride. If you're leaving the island, it's time to pay. The toll is $41.50 per vehicle including passengers. Payment is collected at toll booths on the island side of the bridge. Have cash, credit card, or debit card ready.

## Accommodations

Around 13 kilometers west of town, south of Central Bedeque on Route 171, **Mid Isle Motel** (Rte. 171, 902/887-2525 or 877/877-2525, www.midisle.ca) offers 10 basic rooms for $60; a small adjacent café is open for breakfast.

◖ **Lord's Seaside Cottages** (Bells Point Rd. off Rte. 10, 902/437-2426 or 888/228-6765, www.lordsseasidecottages.com; June–Sept.; $100–130 s or d) is well worth the extra money. Sitting on Bells Point, a few kilometers west of Borden–Carleton, the eight simple cottages each have 1–3 bedrooms, a TV, and a deck with a barbecue. In June and September, you can rent any of the cottages for $550 per week—an excellent deal for families or two couples traveling together.

# Charlottetown to Cavendish

The most direct route between Charlottetown and Cavendish is to take Route 2 west from the capital for 25 kilometers, then head north from Hunter River on Route 13. This drive takes less than one hour to reach the coast. A more leisurely alternative, and the one followed below, begins by taking Route 2 northeast from Charlottetown to Grand Tracadie and then following Route 6 east along the coast to Cavendish. If you've been traveling through Kings County (on Eastern Prince Edward Island), Tracadie Cross, the turnoff for the coastal route, is just seven kilometers west of Mount Stewart.

## GRAND TRACADIE

Grand Tracadie is easily reached in around 40 minutes from Charlottetown. It is the eastern gateway to Prince Edward Island National Park but is best known for a historic inn that lies within the park, two kilometers from the town center.

## Accommodations and Food

Elegant green-roofed ◖ **Dalvay by the Sea**

(16 Cottage Cres., 902/672-2048 or 888/366-2955, www.dalvaybythesea.com; mid-June–early Oct.) appeals to guests who like an old-money ambience. The rustic mansion was built in 1895 by millionaire American oil industrialist Alexander MacDonald, who used the lodging as a summer retreat. Today the hotel, its antiques, and its spacious grounds are painstakingly maintained by the national park staff. Its 26 rooms rent for $180–200 s, $280–380 d, including breakfast and dinner. Four cottages on the grounds ($470–510 d including meals) are most popular with honeymooners.

The hotel's dining room is locally renowned, and nonguests are welcome with advance reservations. Entrées ($20–36) feature formal Canadian cuisine prepared with a French flair. The emphasis is on the freshest produce, best seafood, and finest beef cuts. Mains include a rack of lamb crusted with hazelnut and grainy mustard; the sticky date pudding topped with toffee sauce is an easy choice for dessert. In July and August, a grand afternoon tea is served daily 2–4 p.m. for $20 per person (children pay $6 for cookies and lemonade). Other hotel facilities include a well-stocked gift shop, a nearby beach, a tennis court, bike rentals, a lake with canoes, and nature trails.

## STANHOPE

From Grand Tracadie, there are two options for travelers heading west toward Cavendish: one along the coast within Prince Edward Island National Park, and the other through Stanhope.

### Accommodations

**Stanhope Bay and Beach Resort** (3445 Bayshore Rd., 902/672-2701 or 866/672-2701, www.stanhopebeachresort.com; June–mid-Oct.; from $164 s or d) overlooks Covehead Bay and the national park from north of town. Dating to 1855, the resort has 86 units spread through numerous buildings. The resort recently underwent major renovations, with all rooms stylishly redecorated in decor that gives a contemporary feel to the Victorian style. Amenities include tennis, croquet, an outdoor heated pool, bike and canoe rentals, and an adjacent golf course. Rates include a buffet-style breakfast and a discount on dinner.

## BRACKLEY BEACH

With its proximity to the national park, excellent beaches, golf, deep-sea fishing, and other attractions, Brackley Beach is a popular base.

Just south of town is **Dunes Studio Gallery and Cafe** (Rte. 15, 902/672-2586; June–Oct. daily 10 a.m.–6 p.m.), an architecturally distinctive building with the ocean-facing wall composed almost entirely of windows. Inside, a wide spiral walkway passes the work of around 70 artists, including island craftspeople who create stoneware, framed photography, gold jewelry, pottery, watercolors, woodcarvings, oils, and sculptures. It's worth browsing just for porcelains crafted by owner Peter Jansons. Make sure you make your way up to the rooftop garden. For some of the island's most creative modern cooking, plan on enjoying lunch or dinner at the sunken rear of the gallery, in the café (June–Oct. daily 11:30 a.m.–10 p.m.) overlooking the gardens. You'll need reservations for dinner on weekends.

### Accommodations and Camping

Distinctive red and white ◖ **Shaw's Hotel** (99 Apple Tree Rd., 902/672-2022, www.shawshotel.ca) overlooks the bay from a 30-hectare peninsula at the edge of Prince Edward Island National Park. This was the Shaw family's homestead in the 1860s, and it's still in the family, now protected as a National Historic Site. The property has 16 antique-furnished guest rooms in the main house, 25 adjacent historic cottages, and 15 newer upscale waterfront chalets. Rates start at $145 s or d for a room only, or you can pay from $115 per person to include breakfast and dinner. The ambience is informal and friendly—a nice place for meeting islanders and other visitors. The dining room at Shaw's Hotel is consistently good; start with a chowder appetizer and stick to the chef's daily choices, prepared from whatever seafood is in season ($22–28).

Camping is available nearby at the

12-hectare **Vacationland Travel Park** (east of Rte. 15 overlooking Brackley Bay, 902/672-2317 or 800/529-0066, www.vacationlandrv.pe.ca; mid-May–mid-Sept.; $29–43). Facilities include a dump station, store, canteen, Laundromat, heated pool, hot showers, mini-golf, and other recreational activities.

# ◖ PRINCE EDWARD ISLAND NATIONAL PARK

Prince Edward Island National Park's sandy beaches, dunes, sandstone cliffs, marshes, and forestlands represent Prince Edward Island as it once was, unspoiled by the crush of 20th-century development.

The park protects a slender 40-kilometer-long coastal slice of natural perfection, extending almost the full length of Queens County, as well as a six-square-kilometer spit of land farther east near Greenwich on the North Shore on eastern Prince Edward Island. The park also extends inland at Cavendish to include Green Gables House and Green Gables Golf Course. The main body of the park is book-ended by two large bays. At the eastern end, Tracadie Bay spreads out like an oversize pond with shimmering waters. Forty kilometers to the west, New London Bay forms almost a mirror image of the eastern end. In between, long barrier islands define Rustico and Covehead Bays, and sand dunes webbed with marram grass, rushes, fragrant bayberry, and wild roses front the coastline.

Sunrise and sunset here are cast in glowing colors. All along the gulf at sunrise, the beaches have a sense of primeval peacefulness, their sands textured like herringbone by the overnight sea breezes.

Getting around is easy. Route 6 lies on the park's inland side, connecting numerous park entrances, and the Gulf Shore Parkway runs along the coast nearly the park's entire length. You can drive through the park year-round. Cyclists will appreciate the smooth wide shoulders and light traffic along the Gulf Shore Parkway, which runs most of the length of the park.

## Park Entry

Between early June and mid-September, the entrance fee for a one-day pass is adult $8, senior $7, child $4, to a maximum of $16 per vehicle. (The park entry fee does not apply for Green Gables House but is collected from those staying at park campgrounds).

## Environmental Factors

The national park was established in 1937 to protect the fragile dunes along the Gulf of St. Lawrence and cultural features such as Green Gables House. Parks Canada walks a fine line, balancing environmental concerns with the responsibilities of hosting half a million park visitors a year. Boardwalks route visitors through dunes to the beaches and preserve the fragile landscape.

Bird-watchers will be amply rewarded with sightings of some of the more than 100 species known to frequent the park. Brackley Marsh, Orby Head, and the Rustico Island Causeway are good places to start. The park preserves nesting habitat for some 25 pairs of endangered piping plovers—small, shy shorebirds that arrive in early April to breed in flat sandy areas near the high-tide line. Some beaches may be closed in spring and summer when the plovers are nesting; it's vital to the birds' survival that visitors stay clear of these areas.

## Recreation

The unbroken stretches of sandy beaches—some white, others tinted pink by iron oxide—are among the best in Atlantic Canada. On warm summer days, droves of sunbathers laze on the shore and swim in the usually gentle surf. The busier beaches have a lifeguard on duty, but always be aware of undertows.

**Stanhope Beach,** opposite the campground, is wide and flat, and remains relatively busy throughout summer. Next up to the east, **Brackley Beach** is backed by higher sand dunes. The adjacent visitor center has changing rooms and a snack bar. **Cavendish Beach** is the busiest of all; those toward Orby Head are backed by steep red-sandstone cliffs.

Established **hiking trails** range from the

0.5-kilometer wheelchair-accessible Reeds and Rushes Trail, beginning at the Dalvay Administration Building near Grand Tracadie, to the eight-kilometer Homestead Trail beginning near the entrance to Cavendish Campground. The latter wends inland alongside freshwater ponds and through woods and marshes and is open to both hikers and bikers. Be wary of potentially hazardous cliff edges, and of the poison ivy and ticks that lurk in the ground cover.

If you'd like to learn more about the park's ecology, join one of the **nature walks** led by Parks Canada rangers. The treks lead through white spruce stunted by winter storms and winds, to freshwater ponds, and into the habitats of such native animal species as red fox, northern phalarope, Swainson's thrush, and junco.

## Campgrounds

The park's three campgrounds are distinctly different from one another. A percentage of sites can be reserved through the **Parks Canada Campground Reservation Service** (905/426-4648 or 877/737-3783, www.pccamping.ca) for $11 per reservation. During July and August and especially for weekends, reservations are recommended. The remaining sites are sold on a first-come, first-served basis.

**Stanhope Campground** (north of Stanhope; mid-June–early Oct.) is across the road from the ocean and has 95 unserviced sites ($25.50), 16 sites with two-way hookups ($32), and 14 sites with full hookups ($36). Amenities include showers, a playground, a grocery store, laundry facilities, and wooded tent sites.

Closest to Cavendish and center of the park's summer interpretive program is **Cavendish Campground** (late May–early Oct.). This, the most popular of the three campgrounds, has 230 unserviced sites ($25.50) and 78 hookup sites ($34–36). Campground facilities include a grocery store, kitchen shelters, launderettes, flush toilets, and hot showers.

## Information

The main **Cavendish Visitor Centre** is combined with the provincially operated Visitor Information Centre, 50 meters north of the Route 6 and Route 13 intersection in Cavendish (902/963-2391; mid-May–mid-Oct. daily 9 A.M.–5 P.M., July–Aug. daily 8 A.M.–10 P.M.). As well as general park information, displays depict the park's natural history, and a small shop sells park-related literature and souvenirs. Another source of information is the website www.pc.gc.ca.

## RUSTICO BAY

A decade after the French began Port-la-Joye near Charlottetown, French settlers cut through the inland forest and settled Rustico Bay's coastline. England's Acadian deportation in 1755 emptied the villages, but not for long. The Acadians returned, and the five revived Rusticos—Rusticoville, Rustico, Anglo Rustico, North Rustico, and North Rustico Harbour—still thrive and encircle Rustico Bay's western shore.

## Sights

For a glimpse at Acadian culture, check out the imposing two-story **Farmers' Bank of Rustico Museum** (Church Rd., Rustico, 902/963-3168; mid-June–Sept. Mon.–Sat. 9:30 A.M.–5:30 P.M., Sun. 1–5:30 P.M.; adult $4). Built in 1864 as Canada's first chartered people's bank (the precursor of today's credit unions), the building served as the early Acadian banking connection, then as a library. Exhibits at this national historic site include heritage displays plus artifacts from the life of the Reverend Georges-Antoine Belcourt, the founder.

## Accommodations and Camping

Accommodations at **Rustico Resort** (corner Rte. 6 and Rte. 242, Rustico, 902/963-2357, www.rusticoresort.com; May–Oct.) are usually filled with golfers, who stay in the cottages for $175 s or d, including breakfast and unlimited golf on the adjacent course. Other amenities include grass tennis courts, a heated pool, and a dining room with a lounge.

The 1870 **Barachois Inn** (2193 Church Rd., Rustico, 902/963-2194, www.barachoisinn.com;

May–Oct.; $160–200 s or d) overlooks Rustico Bay from just off Route 243. The main house holds four historically themed guest rooms while the adjacent McDonald House contains four larger, more modern rooms. Rates include a full breakfast.

**Cymbria Tent and Trailer Park** (Rte. 242, Cambria, 902/963-2458, www.cymbria.ca; mid-May–mid-Oct.) occupies a quiet 12-hectare location close to the beach four kilometers east of Rustico. Campsites are $26 unserviced, $30–35 with hookups. Facilities include a store, game room, playground, dump station, and hot showers.

### Food

**Fisherman's Wharf Lobster Suppers** (Rte. 6, North Rustico, 902/963-2669; June–mid-Oct. daily 11 A.M.–9 P.M.) is a cavernous 400-seat restaurant that attracts the tour bus crowd from Cavendish. Choose from three different sizes of lobster ($30–38), pay your money, and join the fray. The cost includes one full lobster and unlimited trips to the buffet counter, including chowder, mussels, hot entrées, salad, dessert, and hot drinks.

If your accommodation has cooking facilities, head to **Doiron Fisheries** (North Rustico dock, 902/963-2442; May–early Oct. daily 8 A.M.–8 P.M.) for lobsters, mussels, clams, fish, and delicious Malpeque Bay oysters.

## ◖ NORTH RUSTICO HARBOUR

This tiny village on the north side of Rustico Bay is one of my favorite spots on Prince Edward Island. It slopes down to the water, where you find a restored wharf with an interesting interpretive center, fishing charters, and sea-kayak rentals. Add to the scene an old wooden lighthouse and one of the region's best restaurants, and you have a destination as far removed from nearby commercial Cavendish as you could imagine.

### Sights and Recreation

While you should make sure to wander along the wharf and beyond the lighthouse to North

the lighthouse at North Rustico Harbour

Rustico Beach (which is within Prince Edward Island National Park), there is also **Rustico Harbour Fishery Museum** (318 Harbourview Dr., 902/963-3799; mid-May–Sept. daily 9:30 A.M.–5:30 P.M.; adult $4, child $2). This small well-designed facility, sitting on the main wharf, centers around a lobster-fishing boat. Displays tell the story of the Mi'Kmaq who lived across the bay on Robinsons Island for 1,500 years and also chronicle fishing since the arrival of Europeans.

Half a dozen charter fishing operators tie up at North Rustico Harbour. The average cost is a remarkably low $30 per person for a three-hour outing or $150 for a full day's charter, for cod, mackerel, flounder, and tuna. Most charters operate July to mid-September. The crew will outfit you in raingear if needed, provide tackle and bait, and clean and fillet your catch. **Aiden's Deep-sea Fishing** (902/963-3522) has been in business for decades and has three excursions scheduled daily.

North Rustico Harbour is the push-off point for kayak tours operated by **Outside**

© ANDREW HEMPSTEAD

PRINCE EDWARD ISLAND

**Expeditions** (902/963-3366; mid-May–mid-Oct.). A 90-minute paddle around the bay is $39 per person; a three-hour trip, with the chance of seeing abundant bird life, is $50; and a six-hour trip across to Robinsons Island is $100 including lunch.

## Food

A shack on the main dock has been converted to the 🌙 **Blue Mussel Café** (Harbourview Dr., 902/963-2152; mid-June–mid-Sept. daily 11:30 A.M.–8 P.M.), a tiny little restaurant where most of the tables are outside on a private corner of the wharf. The menu reads like a list of what fisherfolk haul in from local waters—salmon, haddock, mussels, lobster—and unlike at most other island restaurants, there's not a deep fryer in sight.

# Cavendish

Thanks to Lucy Maud Montgomery and a certain fictional character named Anne, Cavendish, 40 kilometers northeast of Charlottetown, is Prince Edward Island's most popular tourist destination. Unfortunately, those who come here expecting to find a bucolic little oasis of tranquility will be sorely disappointed. The once rural Cavendish area has become a maze of theme parks, fast-food outlets, and souvenir shops in parts, and the village has repositioned itself as an official resort municipality to try to grapple with fame. To dedicated readers of Montgomery's sentimental books, the village's lure is emotional. For others—those who don't know Anne of Green Gables from Anne Frank—it might best be avoided. Still, if you end up here and are looking for something to do, you'll have a multitude of choices—including heading into adjacent Prince Edward Island National Park, golfing at Green Gables Golf Course, or browsing through crafts shops.

Green Gables House is the most popular of many "Anne attractions" in and around Cavendish.

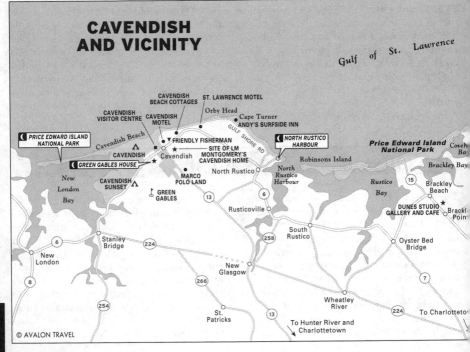

© AVALON TRAVEL

## UTOPIAN AVONLEA

Montgomery portrayed rural Cavendish as an idyllic "never land" called Avonlea, imbued with innocence and harmony. Beyond the crass commercialism, as you drive the rambling red-clay lanes and walk the quiet woods, meadows, and gulf shore, you'll have to agree the lady did not overstate her case. The most pastoral and historic places are preserved as part of **Prince Edward Island National Park.** Cavendish itself is home to two important Anne attractions, while others dot the surrounding countryside.

## ◖ Green Gables House

Located on the west side of the Route 6 and Route 13 intersection, Green Gables House (902/963-7874; May–Oct. daily 9 A.M.–5 P.M., July–Aug. until 6 P.M.; adult $8, senior $7, child $4) reigns as the idyllic hub of a Montgomery sightseeing circuit. The restored 19th-century farmhouse, once home of Montgomery's elderly cousins and the setting for her most famous book, *Anne of Green Gables,* is furnished simply and stolidly, just as it was described in the novel. A fire in 1997 badly damaged portions of the house, but repairs commenced immediately, and within a couple of weeks the landmark was back in perfect condition. Among other memorabilia in the pretty vintage setting are artifacts such as the author's archaic typewriter, on which she composed so many well-loved passages. Period-style gardens, farm buildings, and an interpretive center and gift shop complete the complex. Also on the grounds, the Balsam Hollow and Haunted Woods trails feature some of Montgomery's favorite woodland haunts, including Lover's Lane.

## Site of Lucy Maud Montgomery's Cavendish Home

Montgomery spent much of her childhood living with her grandparents in a small home one kilometer east of Green Gables House. "I wrote it in the evenings after my regular day's work was done," she recalled, "wrote most of it at the window of the little gable room that had been mine for many years." While the main building is long gone, the stone cellar remains. Surrounded by a white picket fence and by apple trees, it has been converted to a small museum and bookstore (Rte. 6, 902/963-2231; mid-May–mid-Oct. daily 9 A.M.–5 P.M., July–Aug. daily 9 A.M.–6 P.M.; adult $3, child $1) operated by Montgomery's descendants.

Montgomery is buried behind the adjacent United Church.

# RECREATION
## Golf

Little known outside Canada, Stanley Thompson was one of the world's great golf course architects of the mid-20th century. His best-known courses were those within the country's national park system. **Green Gables Golf Course** (Rte. 6, 902/963-4653) may not be as revered as Thompson-designed Highland Links (Cape Breton Highlands National Park) or Banff Springs (Banff National Park), but this old-fashioned layout within Prince Edward Island National Park is a gem of composition defined by water views and deep bunkers. Regular greens fees are $100 including a cart, or pay $55 after 3 P.M.

## Fun Parks

The only theme park with any relationship to Anne of Green Gables is **Avonlea** (Rte. 6, 902/963-3050; mid-June–Sept. daily 10 A.M.–5 P.M.; adult $20, senior $18, child $16). Staff in period costumes bring the life and times of Anne to life in musical shows that take place throughout the sprawling grounds. Visitors are invited to try their hand at milking a cow, learn how to barn dance, and tour an old-fashioned chocolate factory.

You'll see the rides of **Sandspit** amusement park (Rte. 6, 902/963-2626; last week of June daily 10 A.M.–6 P.M., July–early Sept. daily 10 A.M.–11 P.M.), east of the junction of Routes 6 and 13, long before arriving at the front gate. The huge park, a magnet for kids on vacation, features a roller coaster (The Cyclone—billed as the largest in the Maritimes), a carousel, and other rides, rides, rides. It's free to get in, but each ride costs a small amount. All-day ride packages cost $12–22, depending on your height.

And what tourist town would be complete without a **Ripley's Believe It or Not! Museum** (Cranberry Village, Rte. 6, 902/963-2242; June and Sept. daily 9:30 A.M.–5:30 P.M., July–Aug. daily 9 A.M.–10 P.M.; adult $9, senior $7, child $5.50) or a wax museum—in this case the

**PRINCE EDWARD ISLAND**

## LUCY MAUD MONTGOMERY

Lucy Maud Montgomery, known and beloved around the world as the creator of *Anne of Green Gables*, was born at New London, Prince Edward Island, in 1874, a decade after the Charlottetown Conference. When Lucy was only two, her mother died and her father moved to western Canada. Maud, as she preferred to be called, was left in the care of her maternal grandparents, who brought her to Cavendish.

Cavendish, in northern Queens County, was idyllic in those days, and Montgomery wrote fondly about the ornate Victorian sweetness of the setting of her early years. As a young woman, she studied first at the island's Prince of Wales College, later at Dalhousie University in Halifax. She then returned to the island as a teacher at Bideford, Lower Bedeque, Belmont, and Lot 15. In 1898 her grandfather's death brought her back to Cavendish to help her grandmother.

The idea for *Anne of Green Gables* dated to the second Cavendish stay, and the book was published in 1908. In 1911, Montgomery married the Rev. Ewen MacDonald at her Campbell relatives' Silver Bush homestead overlooking the Lake of Shining Waters. (The Campbell descendants still live in the pretty farmhouse and have turned their home into a museum.) The couple moved to Ontario, where Montgomery spent the rest of her life, returning to PEI only for short visits. Although she left, Maud never forgot Prince Edward Island. Those brief revisitations with her beloved island must have been painful; after one trip, she wistfully recalled in her journal:

*This evening I spent in Lover's Lane. How beautiful it was – green and alluring and beckoning! I had been tired and discouraged and sick at heart before I went to it – and it rested me and cheered me and stole away the heartsickness, giving peace and newness of life.*

Montgomery died in 1942 and was buried in Cavendish Cemetery. As an author, she left 20 juvenile books and myriad other writings. Her works have been published worldwide, translated into 16 languages. In Japan, Montgomery's writings are required reading in the school system – which accounts for the island's many Japanese visitors.

Montgomery wrote for children, and she viewed Cavendish and Prince Edward Island with all the clarity and innocence that a child possesses. Her books are as timeless today as they were decades ago. Some critics have described Montgomery's writings as mawkish. Contemporary scholars, however, have taken a new look at the author's works and have begun to discern a far more complex style. The academic community may debate her literary prowess, but no matter – the honest essence of Montgomery's writings has inspired decades of zealous pilgrims to pay their respects to her native Cavendish. To islanders, she is Lucy Maud, their literary genius, on a first-name basis.

adjacent **Wax World of the Stars** (Cranberry Village, Rte. 6, 902/963-2350), which has a similar admission price and hours.

## FESTIVALS AND EVENTS

**Lucy Maud Montgomery Festival** is a summer-long gathering (www.lmmontgomery-festival.com) that attracts Anne fans from around the world. Children especially will be enchanted by a schedule of events that includes re-creations of various events in Montgomery's life, a coloring competition in the local schoolhouse, Victorian-era lawn games, writing workshops, and an ice-cream picnic. Parents are catered to with book readings and carriage rides, and, of course, they are also invited to the ice-cream picnic.

## ACCOMMODATIONS AND CAMPING

While accommodations in Cavendish are plentiful, they book up well in advance for July and August. No place in Atlantic Canada sees a more dramatic drop in room rates for the shoulder seasons (mid-May–June and Sept.–mid-Oct.), while the rest of the year most accommodations close completely.

## Under $50

C **Andy's Surfside Inn** (Gulf Shore Rd., 902/963-2405; June–Nov.; $45–75 s or d) is a big old whitewashed home right on the ocean a few kilometers east of Cavendish along the coastal road. The rooms and facilities are older, but the setting can't be beat. Only one room has its own bathroom; other amenities include a deck, bikes, and a barbecue.

## $50-100

The **St. Lawrence Motel** (351 Gulf Shore Rd., 902/963-2053 or 800/387-2053, www.stlawrencemotel.com; mid-May–Sept.; $69–159 s or d) is within Prince Edward Island National Park between Cavendish and North Rustico. Set on eight hectares, this 16-room property overlooks the gulf a short walk from the water.

All but one of the units has a kitchen, and the largest have three bedrooms. The beach is a short walk down the road and on-site amenities include a recreation room, barbecues, and lawn games such as horseshoes and croquet. Rates include free park entry.

**Silverwood Motel** (Rte. 6, 902/963-2439 or 800/565-4753, www.silverwoodmotel.com; mid-May–mid-Oct.) has regular motel rooms for $94 s or d, one-bedroom units with kitchens for $114 s or d, and two-bedroom kitchen-equipped units for $144 s or d. There's also a pool and adjacent restaurant.

**Cavendish Motel** (corner Rte. 6 and Rte. 13, 902/963-2244 or 800/565-2243, www .cavendishmotel.pe.ca; May–Oct.; from 115 s or d) offers a mix of regularly revamped rooms with surprises such as big 27-inch TVs. Amenities include barbecues, a heated pool, a dining room, and a playground.

## Over $100

From C **Kindred Spirits Country Inn and Cottages** (Memory Ln., off Rte. 6, 902/963-2434

© ANDREW HEMPSTEAD

Kindred Spirits Country Inn and Cottages

or 800/461-1755, www.kindredspirits.ca; mid-May–mid-Oct.), guests can stroll along Lover's Lane to Green Gables House, just the way Lucy Maud Montgomery described in *Anne of Green Gables*. This grandly Victorian estate is also handy to the golf course, but also very private and far removed from busy Route 6. Bed-and-breakfast rooms in the main inn ($135–180 s or d) are decorated with stylish antiques. Some have balconies and fireplaces. Surrounding the inn are 14 kitchen-equipped cottages, each surrounded by green space. Rates range from $205 for a one-bedroom unit to $375 for a three-bedroom cottage with a whirlpool bath.

Overlooking the Gulf of St. Lawrence from within Prince Edward Island National Park is **Cavendish Beach Cottages** (Gulf Shore Rd., 902/963-2025, www.cavendishbeachcottages .com; early May–mid-Oct.; $155–209 s or d), a complex of 13 simply furnished yet modern cottages, each with a deck offering ocean views. The cottages, set back 200 meters from the beach, are just a few steps from the park's jogging and hiking trails. Off-season rates (late May and early October) start at $90.

## Campgrounds

What **( Cavendish Campground** (late May–early Oct.; $24–38) lacks in facilities it makes up for in location, close to the ocean within Prince Edward Island National Park and just a few kilometers from downtown Cavendish. Amenities include showers, kitchen shelters, and fire pits (firewood $8 per bundle). Even with over 300 campsites, it fills most summer days, so plan on arriving before noon or booking a site in advance. These can be made through the **Parks Canada Campground Reservation Service** (905/426-4648 or 877/737-3783, www.pccamping.ca) for $11 per reservation.

**Marco Polo Land** (Rte. 13, 902/963-2352 or 800/665-2352, www.marcopololand.com; late May–mid-Oct.; $28–42) is the island's definitive commercial campground, replete with resort trappings. Facilities at the 40-hectare park include over 400 campsites ($24–31), tennis courts, mini-golf, a full-sized outdoor pool, a wading pool, a restaurant, a campers' store, a Laundromat, and hot showers.

The 465-site **Cavendish Sunset Campground** (Rte. 6, 902/963-2440 or 800/715-2440, www.cavendishsunsetcampground.com; mid-June–early Sept.; $30–38) is big, bold, and very family-friendly. It has all the amenities of Marco Polo Land except the restaurant.

## FOOD
### Lobster Supper

Lobster suppers are casual good-value gatherings held across the island. They can be very commercial or simply an annual gathering of locals in a church basement. A great compromise is the **( New Glasgow Lobster Supper** (Rte. 258, 902/964-2870; June–mid-Oct. 4–8:30 P.M.), eight kilometers southeast of Cavendish along Route 13. In operation since 1958, this one fills the local community hall with up to 500 diners at a time. It even has its own lobster holding pond, allowing the tradition to continue beyond lobster-fishing season. Choose the size of lobster (between one and two pounds) and then have it boiled up while you feast on a buffet of mussels, clam chowder, salad, breads, and nonalcoholic drinks for a set price ($30–42 per person).

### Other Dining Options

One cannot live on lobster alone, so if you're in town more than one night, you'll need to find somewhere else to eat once you've participated in a lobster supper. The best restaurant in the region is the **( Blue Mussel Café** (Harbourview Dr., 902/963-2152; mid-June–mid-Sept. daily 11:30 A.M.–8 P.M.), six kilometers east at North Rustico Harbour, or if you have cooking facilities at your accommodation (even just a barbecue), pick up fresh seafood at **Doiron Fisheries** (North Rustico dock, 902/963-2442; May–early Oct. daily 8 A.M.–8 P.M.).

In Cavendish itself, most restaurants are

family-style and very touristy—great if you have children, but that's about it. The most popular of these is the **Friendly Fisherman** (corner Rte. 6 and Rte. 13, 902/963-2234; mid-June–mid-Oct. daily 8 A.M.–8 P.M.). It advertises very cheap breakfasts, but the crowds come mainly for dinner buffets. Adult pay from $15 and children pay $2 per year of their age.

For do-it-yourself meals, take your choice of markets along major highways; shops at **Cavendish Beach Shopping Plaza** answer most needs. The main excuse to stop at **Cavendish Boardwalk,** another mall, is for an ice cream at **Cow's** (902/963-2692).

## INFORMATION AND SERVICES

Cavendish has no downtown. Instead, services such as restaurants and gas stations are scattered along a five-kilometer stretch of Route 6 southeast from the junction with Route 13. For chores such as grocery shopping, banking, and posting mail, plan on doing that back in Charlottetown.

The provincial **Visitor Information Centre** (corner Rte. 6 and Rte. 13, 902/963-7830; June and Sept. daily 9 A.M.–5 P.M., July–Aug. daily 9 A.M.–8 P.M.) represents local operators and accommodations. Tourism Prince Edward Island shares the building with Parks Canada (902/963-2391), which hands out park information.

## VICINITY OF CAVENDISH

Hamlets encircle Cavendish. The rural scenery is lovely, and exploring the beaches and back roads should help you sharpen your appetite for a night at one of PEI's famed lobster-supper community halls, which are scattered hereabouts.

### Stanley Bridge

For seaworthy sightseeing, check out **Stanley Bridge Marine Aquarium** (Rte. 6, 902/886-3355; mid-June–Sept. daily 9:30 A.M.–8 P.M.; adult $7.50, child $4.50), five kilometers

southwest of Cavendish. The privately operated aquarium has native fish species in viewing tanks and exhibits on natural history and oyster cultivation; seals are kept outside in penned pools. Part of the complex is an oyster bar with a deck built over the water.

In the vicinity, shoppers like the **Stanley Bridge Studios** (Rte. 6, 902/886-2800), where shelves and floor space overflow with woolen sweaters, quilts, apparel, stoneware, porcelain, jewelry, and Anne dolls. **Old Stanley Schoolhouse** (corner Rte. 6 and Rte. 224, 902/886-2033) handles island-made quilts, weaving, pottery, pewter, folk art, and sweaters.

### New London

The **Lucy Maud Montgomery Birthplace** (corner Rte. 6 and Rte. 20, 902/886-2099; mid-May–Oct. daily 9 A.M.–5 P.M.; adult $3, child $1) lies 10 minutes from Cavendish at what was once Clifton. The author was born in the unassuming house in 1874. The exhibits include her wedding dress, scrapbooks, and other personal items.

Old-fashioned tea rooms dot the countryside around Cavendish, and none are more welcoming than **( Blue Winds Tea House** (10746 New London Rd., 902/886-2860; Fri.–Wed. 11:30 A.M.–6 P.M., Thurs. 2–5 P.M.), on the south side of the village. Here, the soups are made from scratch, breads and pastries are baked daily, and recipes for treats such as New Moon Pudding are taken from historic cookbooks. On Thursday, afternoon tea is served for $11 per person.

### Park Corner

**Anne of Green Gables Museum** (Rte. 20, 902/436-7329; May–Oct. daily 11 A.M.–4 P.M., summer 9 A.M.–4 P.M.; adult $3, child $1), eight kilometers northwest of New London, is another Montgomery landmark and the ancestral home of the author's Campbell relatives. The estate spreads out in a farmhouse setting in the pastoral rolling countryside, with the Lake of Shining

Waters, described in *Anne of Green Lakes,* in front of the main buildings. Montgomery described the house as "the big beautiful home that was the wonder castle of my dreams," and here she was married in 1911. The museum's exhibits include Montgomery's personal correspondence and first editions of her works.

The adjacent **Shining Waters Tea Room** (902/886-2003) serves island-style light fare, and the crafts shop sells Montgomery souvenirs as well as wind chimes, quilts, and other crafts.

# PRINCE COUNTY

Prince County encompasses the western third of Prince Edward Island. Like Kings County in the east, it is well off the main tourist path. Along the southern portion of Prince County, the land is level, and the pastoral farmlands flow in gentle serene sweeps to the strait coastline. Thick woodlands span the county's midsection, and you'll see fields of potatoes that blossom in July and green carpets of wheat nodding in the summer breezes. The northern tip is a remote and barren plain with a windswept coast, where farmers known as "mossers" use stout draft horses to reap Irish moss (a seaweed) from the surf.

Summerside, the province's second-largest town, boasts an ample supply of lodgings, restaurants, and nightlife. Just west of there is the province's largest Acadian area, the Région Évangéline. Count on high-quality crafts and wares at town boutiques and outlying shops throughout the region; the region's craftspeople are renowned for quilts, knitted apparel, Acadian shirts, and blankets.

Route 2, PEI's main expressway, enters Prince County at the town of Kensington, glides past the seaport of Summerside on a narrow isthmus, and leads inland for 100 kilometers to finish at the village of Tignish, near the island's northwestern tip. The highways up and down the east and west coasts come together to be known as Lady Slipper Scenic Drive, one of the provincial scenic sightseeing routes (it's signposted with a red symbol of the orchidlike flower). The county's most idyllic scenery—and some of the island's most spectacular sea views—lie along this route, at the sea's edges

© ANDREW HEMPSTEAD

# HIGHLIGHTS

◖ **College of Piping:** Students from around the world gather at this school to learn the art of bagpiping and highland dancing, and visitors are more than welcome to watch (page 290).

◖ **Tyne Valley:** A gem of composition, this small village straddling the Tyne River comprises neat homes, arts and crafts shops, and an inviting lodge (page 292).

◖ **Green Park Shipbuilding Museum and Yeo House:** An attraction that is as scenic as it is historic, this waterfront estate was once the center of a thriving shipbuilding industry (page 293).

◖ **Our Lady of Mont-Carmel Acadian Church:** This magnificent church rises high above the trim Acadian homes of Mont-Carmel (page 295).

◖ **Prince Edward Island Potato Museum:** Learn about the province's main agricultural crop at this museum; it is more interesting than the name might suggest (page 297).

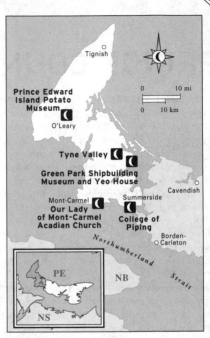

LOOK FOR ◖ TO FIND RECOMMENDED SIGHTS, ACTIVITIES, DINING, AND LODGING.

of Northumberland Strait and the Gulf of St. Lawrence. Around 50 meandering side roads lead off the coastal route to connect with Route 2 and others. You may become temporarily lost on the roads, but not for long—the blue sea invariably looms around the next bend.

## PLANNING YOUR TIME

It's possible to reach the northern tip of Prince County on a day trip from Charlottetown, but a more sensible option if you have just one day would be to concentrate on the southern half of the county. A suggested route would be to stop in Summerside to visit the **College of Piping,** drive through Région Évangéline past the spectacular **Our Lady of Mont-Carmel Acadian Church,** and jog north to picturesque **Tyne Valley** and the nearby **Green Park Shipbuilding Museum**

**and Yeo House.** The main reason to explore further is for the coastal scenery, especially along the Northumberland Strait. Other attractions include the **Prince Edward Island Potato Museum,** golfing at Mill River, and the feeling of accomplishment of driving to the end of the road at North Cape.

Tourist services are more limited in Prince County than elsewhere in the province. You should be able to find somewhere to stay with a few days' notice, but for top picks such as **West Point Lighthouse** (West Point) and **Doctor's Inn** (Tyne Valley), plan on being disappointed if you arrive without reservations. You won't need reservations at my favorite two Prince County eateries—**Flex Mussels** (Summerside) and the **Seaweed Pie Café** (Miminegash)—but you will need a sense of adventure for the latter.

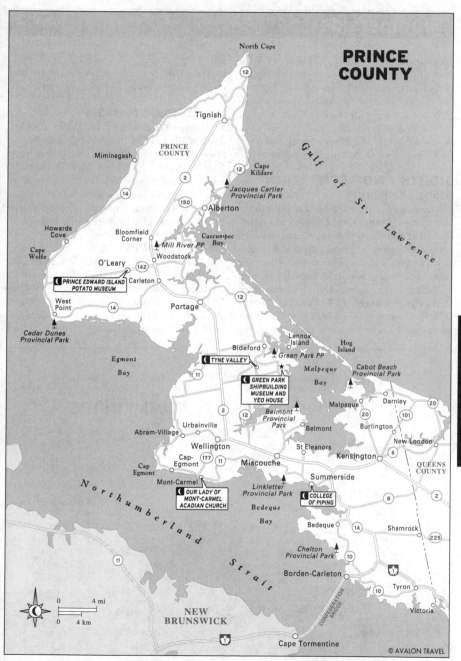

PRINCE EDWARD ISLAND

PRINCE COUNTY

North Cape

12

Tignish

PRINCE COUNTY

Miminegash

2

12  Cape Kildare

*Jacques Cartier Provincial Park*

150

Alberton

*Gulf of St. Lawrence*

14

Howards Cove

Bloomfield Corner

*Cascumpec Bay*

*Mill River PP*

Cape Wolfe

Woodstock

O'Leary

142

Carleton

**PRINCE EDWARD ISLAND POTATO MUSEUM**

West Point

14

Portage

12

*Cedar Dunes Provincial Park*

*Egmont Bay*

11

Bideford

**TYNE VALLEY**

Lennox Island

*Green Park PP*

Hog Island

*Malpeque Bay*

*Cabot Beach Provincial Park*

**GREEN PARK SHIPBUILDING MUSEUM AND YEO HOUSE**

2

12

*Belmont Provincial Park*

Belmont

Malpeque

20

Darnley

101

20

Burlington

New London

Urbainville

Abram-Village

Wellington

Cap-Egmont

177

11

Miscouche

St Eleanors

Kensington

6

QUEENS COUNTY

Cap Egmont

Mont-Carmel

**OUR LADY OF MONT-CARMEL ACADIAN CHURCH**

*Linkletter Provincial Park*

Summerside

**COLLEGE OF PIPING**

8

2

*Northumberland*

*Bedeque Bay*

Bedeque

1A

Shamrock

225

*Chelton Provincial Park*

10

11

*Strait*

Borden-Carleton

10

Tyron

Victoria

NEW BRUNSWICK

0    4 mi

0    4 km

CONFEDERATION BRIDGE

Cape Tormentine

© AVALON TRAVEL

# Summerside

Summerside (pop. 17,000), 72 kilometers west of Charlottetown and 30 kilometers northwest of the Confederation Bridge, is Prince Edward Island's second-largest town and its main shipping port. It's got all the bustle yet none of the seaminess usually associated with seaports. Stately old homes anchor wide lawns, and quiet streets are edged with verdant canopies.

## SIGHTS AND RECREATION
### Along the Harbor

The tourist's Summerside lies along Harbour Drive, where **Spinnakers' Landing** was developed after a military base was phased out. The complex comprises numerous shops and restaurants, an outdoor stage built over the water, a nautical-themed playground, and a lighthouse.

Taking its name from the Mi'Kmaq word for hot spot, **Eptek Art & Cultural Centre** (130 Harbour Dr., 902/888-8373; July–Aug. Mon.–Sat. 9 A.M.–5 P.M., Sun. noon–5 P.M., the rest of the year Tues.–Sat. only; admission varies) has a spacious main gallery hosting touring national fine arts and historical exhibits.

## Wyatt House Museum

The home of Wanda Lefurgey Wyatt until her death at 102 in 1998, this grandly restored 1867 home (85 Spring St., 902/432-1327; June–Sept. Mon.–Sat. 10 A.M.–5 P.M.; adult $5.50, child $4.50) allows you to step back into the lives of a well-to-do family with long ties to the Summerside community. Adding to the charm are guided tours led by costumed guides.

## ☪ College of Piping

The College of Piping (619 Water St. E., 902/436-5377, www.collegeofpiping.com), affiliated with Scotland's College of Piping in Glasgow, attracts students from around the world to its teaching programs of highland dancing, step dancing, fiddling, and

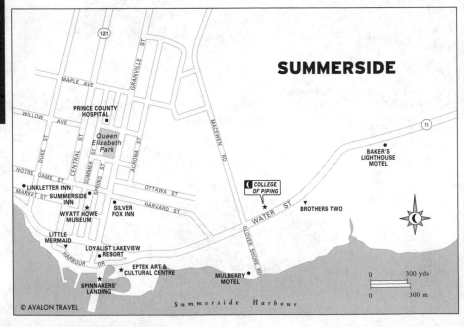

bagpiping. Students perform for the public at a series of summer concerts that take place daily at 11:30 A.M., 1:30 P.M., and 3:30 P.M. ($5 per person). Another program open to the public is the Highland Storm ceilidh (July–Aug. Tues.–Thurs. 7 P.M.; adult $24, senior $20, child $15). The college also offers short-term summer classes (about $25 per hour) in highland dancing, piping, and drumming. Check the website for a schedule.

## ACCOMMODATIONS AND CAMPING
### $50-100

Summerside's least expensive motel is **Baker's Lighthouse Motel** (802 Water St., 902/436-2992; $65 s, $75 d), two kilometers east of downtown. The rooms are plain but clean and comfortable. There's also a laundry and barbecues.

On the same side of town, but within walking distance of the waterfront, is the **Mulberry Motel** (6 Water St. E., 902/436-2520 or 800/274-3825). Each of the 13 guest rooms is spacious and has basic cooking facilities. On the downside, the televisions are very small, but for $75 s, $80 d, that's of little consequence.

**Summerside Inn** (98 Summer St., 902/436-1417 or 877/477-1417, www.summersideinn .net; $85–100 s or d) is a stately mansion three blocks from the harbor that has been converted to a bed-and-breakfast. The tasteful restoration has included stained-glass windows, hardwood floors, and period antiques. Four of the six guest rooms have en suite bathrooms with the remaining two sharing a single bathroom. Rates include a cooked breakfast.

### $100-150

The 1890 Queen Anne Revival **☾ Silver Fox Inn** (61 Granville St., 902/436-1664 or 800/565-4033, www.silverfoxinn.net; $110–140 s or d) reigns locally as one of the seaport's "fox houses," built with a silver fox fortune and designed by architect William Critchlow Harris. The comfortable lodging has six guest rooms furnished with antiques and also with air-conditioning, TVs, and phones. With its wing-backed chairs and shelves of reading material, the living area is a relaxing place to spend the evening.

The 108-room **Linkletter Inn** (311 Market St., 902/436-2157 or 800/565-7829; $120–170) is centrally located and offers large rooms (some with kitchenettes), a restaurant, a lounge, and amenities for the physically challenged.

Across the road from Spinnakers' Landing, **Loyalist Lakeview Resort** (195 Harbour Dr., 902/436-3333 or 800/361-2668, www.lakeviewhotels.com; $135–170 s or d) features 103 spacious motel rooms decorated with a distinct country inn–style decor. It offers a good range of amenities—tennis, an indoor pool, a fitness room, bike rentals, a pub, and a restaurant—making it a good choice for those looking for city-type accommodations.

### Campground

Summerside's closest campground is in **Linkletter Provincial Park,** eight kilometers west of town (Rte. 11, 902/888-8366; mid-June–mid-Sept.). This 30-hectare park on Bedeque Bay has 84 serviced and unserviced sites ($22–28), hot showers, a Laundromat, a dump station, a kitchen shelter, and a nearby store.

## FOOD

Away from the water, **Brothers Two** (618 Water St. E., 902/436-9654; daily 11 A.M.–9:30 P.M.) has been Summerside's social hub for decades. It's no-frills family-style seafood dining at its best. Mains range $15–24 and come as simple as meatloaf and as fancy as scallops poached in white wine. If it's a warm evening, talk your way to a table on the rooftop patio.

## INFORMATION

In the heart of harborfront Spinnakers' Landing, the **Visitor Information Centre** (Harbour Dr., 902/888-8364, www.city .summerside.pe.ca; late June–early Sept. daily 9:30 A.M.–9:30 P.M.) is well signposted as you come into town.

The **Rotary Regional Library** (192 Water St., 902/436-7323; Mon.–Fri. 10 A.M.–5 P.M.) has public Internet access.

# Malpeque Bay

Sheltered from the open gulf by the long, narrow sandbar of Hog Island, the shallow waters of broad Malpeque Bay are tranquil and unpolluted. The bay's long fretted coastline is deserted, nearly bereft of development apart from three small provincial parks. Conditions are perfect for the large oyster fishery that thrives here. Ten million Malpeque oysters—Canada's largest source of the shellfish—are harvested each year. The purity of the bay water in part accounts for the excellent flavor of the oysters, which has made them famed worldwide as a gustatory treat. You'll find them served in a variety of ways at restaurants in the region.

## KENSINGTON

Kensington lies at the intersection of five roads, including the trans-island Route 2. Summerside is 15 kilometers to the southwest, Charlottetown is 48 kilometers to the east, and Cavendish is 38 kilometers to the northeast.

### Sights

Make your first stop **Kensington Railyards,** where you'll find the **Welcome Centre** (902/836-3031 or 877/836-3031, www .kata.pe.ca; May–Oct. daily 9 A.M.–9 P.M.) and a **farmers market** (July–Sept. Sat. 10 A.M.–2 P.M.), a good place to come for fresh produce, baked goods, snacks, and crafts.

On the main road through town, **Kensington Water Gardens** (Rte. 2, 902/836-3336; mid-June and Sept. daily 10 A.M.–5 P.M., July–Aug. daily 9 A.M.–7 P.M.; adult $6, child $3) is a popular spot with children. It features Tudor-style castles large and small, and kid-friendly water attractions.

## CABOT BEACH PROVINCIAL PARK

From Kensington, Route 2 loops around the head of Malpeque Bay to the Tyne Valley, but Cabot Beach Provincial Park is worth a short detour (10 minutes).

This 140-hectare park (902/836-8945; late June–early Sept.), 30 kilometers north of Summerside on Route 105, is the most worthwhile attraction along the east side of Malpeque Bay. It occupies a gorgeous setting on a peninsula tip just inside the bay, including a coastline of sandy beaches broken by rocky headlands. At the park's day-use area is **Fanning School** (mid-June–mid-Sept. daily 10 A.M.–dusk; free), a schoolhouse built in 1794 and unique (for the time) for having two stories. Finally closed in 1969, it's now open to the public. Facilities at the park campground include over 150 sites (unserviced sites $22, hookups $25–28), a supervised ocean beach, a launderette, hot showers, kitchen shelters, and a nearby campers' store.

## ◖ TYNE VALLEY

Quiet and bucolic, the crossroads hamlet of Tyne Valley (pop. 200), at the intersection of backcountry Routes 12, 178, and 167, lies on the west side of Malpeque Bay, a 50-minute drive from Summerside and uncountable kilometers from the rest of the modern world.

In the 1800s, Tyne Valley began as a Green Park suburb. Two generations of the Yeo family dominated the island's economy with their shipbuilding yards on Malpeque Bay, and the empire begun by James Yeo—the feisty, entrepreneurial English merchant who arrived in the 1830s—spawned the next generation's landed gentry.

The empire's riches are gone, but the lovely landscape remains, like a slice of Lucy Maud Montgomery's utopian Avonlea, transplanted from Cavendish to this corner of Prince County. To get there, follow Route 12 around Malpeque Bay, or from Route 2, turn east on Route 132 or 133. The paved and red-clay roads ripple across the farmlands like velvet ribbons on plump quilts.

The quiet village stirs to life on the first weekend of August with the **Tyne Valley Oyster Festival,** a three-day tribute to

Malpeque oysters. Daytime oyster-farming exhibits and evening oyster and lobster dinners are accompanied by talent shows, oyster-shucking demonstrations, fiddling and step-dancing contests, a parade, and a dance.

## Accommodations and Food

◖ **Doctor's Inn** (Rte. 167, 902/831-3057; $55 s, $70 d) belonged to the village doctor during the late 1800s, and the inn's luster still sparkles, polished by innkeepers Jean and Paul Offer, who lovingly tend to almost one hectare of vegetable and fruit gardens. The inn has a formal front entrance, but everyone arrives at the side kitchen door and enters the busy kitchen fray, as the Offers process, can, and preserve the backyard's produce. Beyond the door to the dining room, the inn's interior gleams with antiques. A four-course dinner is served with advance reservations ($45 per person with wine) in the elegant, spacious dining room. Upstairs are three welcoming guest rooms.

## VICINITY OF TYNE VALLEY
### Green Park Provincial Park

Take Route 12 northeast from Tyne Valley and continue north through the hamlet of Port Hill to reach this beautiful park, protecting a peninsula that juts into Malpeque Bay. From the end of the road (at the Shipbuilding Museum), a three-kilometer hiking trail brings you as deep into the bay as you can go without getting your feet wet. (Wear sneakers anyway, and bring insect repellent; mosquitoes flourish in the marsh pools.) The trail starts among white birches, short and stunted due to the bay's winter winds and salt. Beyond there, the path wends through hardwood groves, brightened with a ground cover of pink wild roses, bayberries, and goldenrod. Eventually the trail gives way to marshes at the peninsula's tip. The small inland ponds at the bay's edge are all that remains of a local effort to start oyster aquaculture decades ago. Marsh hay and wild grasses bend with the sea winds. Minnows streak in tidal pools, and razor clams exude streams of continuous

bubbles from their invisible burrows beneath the soggy sand.

A 58-site **campground** (902/831-2370; late June–early Sept.; $22–28) fronts the bay beneath tree canopies on a sheltered coastal notch. It offers a launderette, kitchen shelters, hot showers, Frisbee golf, a river beach, and nature programs.

## ◖ Green Park Shipbuilding Museum and Yeo House

This heritage attraction (902/831-7947; early June–early Sept. daily 9 A.M.–5 P.M.; adult $5, child $2.50) lies on the edge of the provincial park. The Yeo House sits back on a sweep of verdant lawn. It's a gorgeous estate, fronted by a fence that rims the curving road. Inside, rooms are furnished with period antiques. Up four flights of stairs, the cupola—from which James Yeo would survey his shipyard—overlooks the grounds and sparkling Malpeque Bay. Behind the house, the museum has exhibits explaining the history and methods of wooden shipbuilding, Prince Edward Island's main industry in the 19th century. From these buildings, it's a short walk through a meadow to the water, where outdoor displays include a partially finished vessel cradled on a frame, plus historic shipbuilding equipment.

## Bideford

The modest **PEI Shellfish Museum** (Rte. 166, 902/853-2181; late June–early Sept. Sun.–Fri. 10 A.M.–4 P.M.; adult $3, child $1.50) lies at the end of a red-clay road four kilometers north of Tyne Valley. Everything you could ever want to know about oysters and mussels is explained. A small aquarium contains mollusks, lobsters, snails, and inshore fish; outside, experimental farming methods are underway in the bay.

## Lennox Island

A causeway off Route 163 brings you to this small island, home to 250 people of Mi'Kmaq ancestry intent on cultivating oysters, spearing eels, trapping, and hunting while pursuing recognition of the 18th-century treaties with England that entitled them to their land. The province's Mi'Kmaq are said to have been the first native Canadians converted to Christianity. Their history is kept alive at the **Mi'Kmaq Cultural Centre** (902/831-2702; summer Mon.–Sat.

10 A.M.–7 P.M., Sun. noon–6 P.M.). The 1895 **St. Anne's Roman Catholic Church,** a sacred tribute to their patron saint, grips the island's coastline and faces the sea. A crafts shop just north of the church markets Mi'Kmaq baskets, silver jewelry, pottery, and other wares.

# Région Évangéline

The bilingual inhabitants of the Région Évangéline, the province's largest Acadian area, date their ancestry to France's earliest settlement efforts. The region offers French-flavored culture at more than a dozen villages spread west of Summerside between Route 2 and the strait seacoast. Miscouche, the commercial center, is a 10-minute drive west of Summerside on Route 2, and 30 minutes from the seaport along the coastal Route 11 is Mont-Carmel, the region's seaside social and tourist hub.

## MISCOUCHE

As you approach from the east, the high double spires of **St. John the Baptist Church** announce from miles away that you've left Protestant, Anglo Prince Edward Island behind and are arriving in Catholic territory.

The village of 700 inhabitants at the intersection of Routes 2 and 12 began with French farmers from Port-la-Joye in the 1720s, augmented with Acadians who fled England's Acadian deportation in 1755. The settlement commands a major historical niche among Atlantic Canada's Acadian communities and was the site of the 1884 Acadian Convention, which adopted the French tricolor flag with the single gold star symbolizing Mary.

### Musée Acadien

On the east side of town, Musée Acadien (Rte. 2, 902/436-2881; July–Aug. 9 A.M.–7 P.M.; adult $3.50) is geared as a genealogical resource center and also has exhibits of early photographs, papers, and artifacts, and a book corner (mainly in French) with volumes about Acadian history and culture since 1720. Don't miss the documentary on events leading up to the 1755 Acadian deportation; it's screened on demand.

## MONT-CARMEL

Two kilometers south of Miscouche and 24 kilometers west of Summerside, the backcountry Route 12 meets the coastal Route 11 (Lady Slipper Drive), which lopes south and west across Acadian farmlands to this hamlet, best

St. John the Baptist Church rises high above the town of Miscouche.

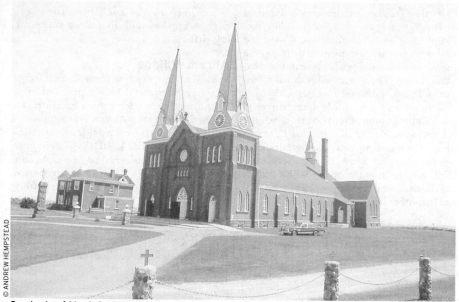

© ANDREW HEMPSTEAD

Our Lady of Mont-Carmel Acadian Church is an architectural highlight of Région Évangéline.

known for Le Village, a complex of lodgings with a restaurant. Mont-Carmel, 16 kilometers from Miscouche, makes a handy sightseeing base for touring the Région Évangéline.

## ◖ Our Lady of Mont-Carmel Acadian Church

This magnificent church, between Route 11 and the red cliffs fronting Northumberland Strait, reflects the cathedral style of France's Poitou region, which is renowned for its Romanesque churches featuring elaborate exteriors. The cathedral is open Sunday during Mass. For permission to enter at other times, ask at the **Musée Religieux** (902/854-2260; July–Aug. daily 1–5 P.M.), across the road.

# CONTINUING ALONG ROUTE 11
## Cap-Egmont

A few kilometers west of Mont-Carmel is the village of Cap-Egmont, best known for the very un-Acadian **Bottle Houses** (Rte. 11, 902/854-2987; early June–late Sept. daily 9 A.M.–6 P.M., July–Aug. 9 A.M.–8 P.M.; adult $4, senior

© ANDREW HEMPSTEAD

Cape Egmont Lighthouse is perched on red cliffs high above Northumberland Strait.

$3, child $1). They are the work of Edouard Arsenault, who in the 1970s mortared together 25,000 glass bottles of all colors, shapes, and sizes to form three astonishing buildings—a chapel with altar and pews, a tavern, and a six-gabled house. The structures qualified for inclusion in *Ripley's Believe It or Not.*

Turn off on the west side of the village to reach **Cape Egmont Lighthouse.** Although it's not open to the public, this light sits in a commanding position overlooking Northumberland Strait. Built in 1884, it is the same design as the one at Wood Islands (where the ferry from Nova Scotia docks), and like other lighthouses around the island it has been moved back from the ocean edge as erosion took its toll on surrounding cliffs.

## Abram-Village

From Cap-Egmont, the scenic coastal Route 11 wends north for 10 kilometers and turns inland to this hamlet known for crafts. **La Co-op d'Artisanat d'Abram Village** (Abram's Village Handcraft Co-op), at the intersection of Routes 11 and 124 (902/854-2096; mid-June–mid-Sept. Mon.–Sat. 9 A.M.–6 P.M., Sun. 1–5 P.M.) is the area's definitive crafts source, with weavings, rugs, Acadian shirts, pottery, and dolls.

# Western Prince County

Beyond Summerside and the Région Évangéline, Route 2 cuts into the interior out of sight of the seas. Nonetheless, most backcountry roads off the main route eventually finish at the water. To the west, the Northumberland Strait is the pussycat of summer seas, and the warm surf laps peacefully along the southern and western coastlines. The Gulf of St. Lawrence, however, is more temperamental, with a welter of rolling waves breaking onto the north shore.

For sightseeing information, stop at the provincial **Visitor Information Centre** in Portage (Rte. 2, 902/831-7930; July–Aug. daily 9 A.M.–7 P.M., June and Sept. daily 9 A.M.–4:30 P.M.), which is 43 kilometers north of Summerside.

## MILL RIVER PROVINCIAL PARK

As you exit Route 2 at Woodstock, you enter a wooded realm on a ribbon of a road into Mill River Provincial Park. The park meshes lush landscapes with contemporary-style resort trappings and full recreation facilities, including the championship-quality Mill River Golf Course.

### Recreation

Campers, resort guests, and day visitors all have access to the park's sports facilities. The eight tennis courts (lighted for night games) beside the hotel are free (but hotel guests get first dibs). At the campground, there's a marina with rentals (canoes and rowboats for $7 per hour and $28 per day).

The 18-hole, par-72 **Mill River Golf Course** (902/859-8873 or 800/377-8339) is generally regarded as one of Canada's top 50 courses and has hosted many national events through the years. The course spans 6,747 yards and is open May through October. During July and August, you'd be wise to make reservations 48 hours in advance. Greens fees range $50–60.

On warmer days, **Mill River Fun Park** (902/859-3915; July–early Sept. daily 11 A.M.–7 P.M.; $9 per person), is a good place for families looking for watery fun on waterslides and in outdoor pools.

### Accommodations and Food

The three-story **Rodd Mill River** (Rte. 2, 902/859-3555 or 800/565-7633, www.roddhotelsandresorts.com; Jan.–Oct.; $130–275 s or d) is a sleek wood-sided hotel with 90 spacious and modern rooms and suites. Guests are attracted to the resort-style activities—golf, tennis, canoeing, swimming, and more—detailed in *Recreation*. The resort's **Hernewood Dining Room** boasts regionally renowned dining that draws an appreciative clientele from Summerside; expect a reasonably priced menu (from $16.50) featuring seafood specialties with a dish-of-the-day emphasis on salmon, halibut, or lobster (usually around $20).

The park's riverfront **campground** (902/859-8790; mid-June–late Sept.) has 72 sites: 18 unserviced ($22), 18 with two-way hookups ($25), and 36 with full hookups ($28). Amenities include kitchen shelters, hot showers, a launderette, and summer interpretive programs.

## O'LEARY

On Prince Edward Island, O'Leary is synonymous with potatoes. Legend has it that the hamlet took its name from an Irish farmer who settled here in the 1830s. By 1872, rail service connected the hamlet with the rest of the island, and with that link in place, O'Leary was on its way to becoming Canada's largest potato producer.

O'Leary straddles backcountry Route 142, a five-minute drive from Route 2 and 50 minutes from Summerside. You might expect mountains of potatoes; rather, O'Leary (pop. 900) is a tidy place, nestled in the midst of surprisingly attractive fields of low-growing potato plants. If you're in the area during the autumn harvest, you'll see the fields lighted by tractor headlights as the farmers work late at night to harvest the valuable crop before the frost.

### ( Prince Edward Island Potato Museum

Don't be put off by the name; this museum (Parkview Dr. off Rte. 142, 902/859-2039; mid-May–mid-Oct. Mon.–Sat. 9 A.M.–5 P.M., Sun. 1–5 P.M.; adult $6, child $3) is an interesting stop that depicts the history of Prince Edward Island's most famous crop. The museum explains the story of the potato's humble beginnings in South America, the way the crop is grown and harvested, and how science has played a hand in the potatoes we eat today. A barn, a schoolhouse, and a chapel are out back.

## WEST POINT AND VICINITY

Route 14 exits Route 2 at Carleton, eight kilometers west of Portage, doglegs west across the verdant farmlands, and heads to West Point at the island's western tip. From there, the scenic coastal route hugs the strait shore and brings some of the island's most magnificent sea views—a total distance of 80 kilometers to Tignish. Potato fields peter out at the strait coastline, which is definitely off the beaten tourist route. The coast's long stretches of beach are interspersed with craggy red cliffs.

**Cedar Dunes Provincial Park** fronts Northumberland Strait 30 kilometers from Route 2. It's only a small park, but it has

Cliffs fringe the west coast of Prince Edward Island, and in spots stairs lead down to narrow beaches where locals gather to swim and sunbathe.

a beach backed by sand dunes and a small campground (902/859-8785; late June–early Sept.) with 20 tent sites ($22) and another 39 two-way hookup sites ($25), a supervised beach, an activities program, a nature trail, kitchen shelters, a nearby campers' store, and hot showers.

## West Point Lighthouse

Within Cedar Dunes Provincial Park is one-of-a-kind **(** West Point Lighthouse** (Cedar Dunes Park Rd., 902/859-3605, www.westpointlighthouse.com; June–Sept.; $100–145 s or d), the only place in Canada where you can stay overnight in a lighthouse. There's just one guest room in the actual lighthouse ($145 s or d), but eight others are spread through adjacent buildings. The complex also has a small museum, a gift shop, and a dining room serving basic and well-priced seafood.

## West Point to Miminegash

Beyond West Point, Route 14 cleaves to the coastline and heads north, first to **Cape Wolfe** (where British General James Wolfe is said to have stepped ashore on the way to battle the French in 1759) and then to **Howards Cove,** fronted with precipitous cliffs of burnished red. The distance from West Point to Miminegash is 36 kilometers.

## MIMINEGASH

Nestled beside a body of water protected from the winds of Northumberland Strait by low dunes, Miminegash is renowned as the home of people who earn a living from collecting seaweed. Storm winds whip the sea on this side of the island into a frenzy, churning sea-floor plants into a webbed fabric that floats to the surface and washes to shore. This seaweed, known as **Irish moss,** is used commercially as a stabilizer in ice cream and other foods. It is harvested from the sea by boat, and also from along the shore—after a storm you may see workers raking the surf's edge, reaping the Irish moss and hauling it away with the help of draft horses. You

can learn about Irish moss farming at the **Irish Moss Interpretive Centre** (Rte. 152, 902/882-4313; early June–late Sept. daily 10 A.M.–7 P.M.; adult $3, child $1.50).

Part of the Irish Moss Interpretive Centre, the **(** Seaweed Pie Café** (Rte. 152, 902/882-4313; early June–late Sept. daily 10 A.M.–7 P.M.) serves light meals such as chowder and its namesake ($3.50 per slice).

## ROUTE 12 NORTH TO TIGNISH

None of the three highways that lead north through Prince County to Tignish are particularly busy, but Route 12, along the Gulf of St. Lawrence, is the least traveled. It branches off Route 2 just beyond the village of Portage, 42 kilometers from Summerside.

## Alberton

The seaport of Alberton (pop. 1,200) is the northern area's largest town. Named for Albert, Prince of Wales, the town began in 1820 with 40 families who worked at the shipyards in nearby Northport. Deep-sea fishing aficionados will readily find charter boats here. The **Alberton Museum** (457 Church St., 902/853-4048; June–Sept. Mon.–Sat. 10 A.M.–5:30 P.M., Sun. 1–5 P.M.; donation) is in a historic stone building that was originally a courthouse and jail. Exhibits delve into the town's history with antiques, clothing, and farm tools. The fox farming display is particularly interesting.

On the south side of Alberton, **Travellers Inn** (Rte. 12, 902/853-2215 or 800/268-7829; $85 s or d) has better-than-average motel trappings with 14 regular motel rooms and 13 kitchen-equipped units ($85–155), an indoor heated pool, a hot tub, and a pleasant atmosphere. The motel's restaurant serves basic beef and seafood dishes.

## Jacques Cartier Provincial Park

It's only a short hop from Alberton back to Route 2, then 16 kilometers north to Tignish, but a worthwhile detour is to continue north on Route 12 to this coastal provincial park

(902/853-8632; late June–early Sept.), occupying the site where explorer Cartier is believed to have stepped ashore in 1534. The campground rims the gulf. It offers a supervised ocean beach, 23 unserviced campsites ($22), 30 sites with two-way hookups ($25), hot showers, a launderette, varied programs, and Frisbee golf.

## TIGNISH AND VICINITY

Stories of legendary riches and the fur that created a haute-couture sensation almost a century ago embellish the lore of the remote northern peninsula. The world's first successful silver fox breeding began in the Tignish area in 1887. Charles Dalton—later knighted by the queen—was the innovator, and he joined with Robert Oulton from New Brunswick to breed the foxes. The pelts sold for thousands of dollars in fashion salons worldwide. From 1890 to 1912, the Dalton and Oulton partnership kept a keen eye on the venture and the number of silver fox breeding pairs. As luck would have it, generosity was their downfall: Their empire fell apart when one of the partners gave a pair of the breeding foxes to a relative. The cat—the fox, that is—was out of the bag. That single pair begat innumerable descendants that were sold worldwide, and breeding became an international business.

The area earned itself another major entry in national history when local fishermen organized Canada's first fishermen's union; the cooperative still processes and markets the bulk of the island's tuna. During summer, expect to see the "mossers"—Irish-moss harvesters clad in high rubber boots—in town.

Tignish (pop. 800) is simply laid out with Church Street/Route 2 as the main street. The town is 20 minutes from Alberton, a half hour from O'Leary, and 80 minutes from Summerside.

### Sights

Make your first stop the **Tignish Cultural Centre** (Maple St., 902/882-1999; late

## RAIL TO TRAIL

A joy for hiking and biking, the **Confederation Trail** spans Prince Edward Island, extending from Tignish in the west to Elmira in the east, a distance of 279 kilometers. Spur trails, including those leading to Charlottetown's downtown waterfront and the Confederation Bridge, add an additional 80 kilometers.

The trail was developed on a decommissioned rail line. The advantages of creating the trail on a rail line were twofold – there are no hilly sections, and the route passes through dozens of towns and villages. Add a base of finely crushed gravel, extensive signage, picnic tables, benches, and lookouts and you get one of the finest opportunities for outdoor recreation in all of Atlantic Canada.

The Confederation Trail is well promoted by both the provincial tourism authority and **Island Trails** (www .islandtrails.ca), a nonprofit organization that manages the system. Accommodations in villages along the route provide a handy base for traversing sections of the trail or as an overnight stop for those traveling longer distances. Some, such as **Trailside Inn** (Mount Stewart, 902/676-3130 or 888/704-6595, www .trailside.ca), have been specifically developed for trail travelers by offering beds and bike rentals.

May–early Sept. daily 8 A.M.–4 P.M.), which tells the natural and human history of the area, holds the usual array of tourism brochures, and offers public Internet access. Nearby, the **St. Simon and St. Jude Church** (902/882-2049; daily 8 A.M.–7 P.M.) is the town's stellar attraction, notable for its frescoes of the apostles and its mighty pipe organ. The organ, built by Louis Mitchell of Montréal, features 1,118 pipes from six inches to 16 feet in length. It was installed in 1882, and until the 1950s the organ was pumped by hand.

PRINCE EDWARD ISLAND

## Accommodations

Right in town, an old red-brick convent has been converted to the **Tignish Heritage Inn** (Maple St., 902/882-2491; $80–110 s or d). The rooms are basic but adequate, and the inn has amenities such as a lounge area, laundry, and a kitchen, as well as a continental breakfast; it is a good place to spend the night before returning south.

## North Cape

Some 16 kilometers north of Tignish, Route 12 ends at North Cape, the northern tip of Prince County. The dominant artificial feature, the **Atlantic Wind Test Site,** juts up from the windy plain with a federal project complex that tests and evaluates wind turbines. The adjacent **North Cape Interpretive Centre** (Rte. 12, 902/882-2746; July–Aug. daily 10 A.M.–8 P.M.; adult $3, senior and child $1.50) describes the science behind the wind turbines and also has a small aquarium.

Four kilometers before the cape, **Island's End Motel** (42 Doyle Rd., Sea Cow Pond, 902/882-3554, www.islandsendmotel.com; $65–95) overlooks the Gulf of St. Lawrence and is within walking distance of a beach. The most unique unit is a converted fishing boat, which has been dry-docked and renovated into a spacious and comfortable place to rest your head.

# EASTERN PRINCE EDWARD ISLAND

The eastern third of Prince Edward Island, much of it within Kings County, is cut off geographically from the rest of the province by the Hillsborough River. One of this region's main attractions is the lack of crowds. It has none of the hype of Cavendish, and its activities and sights are more limited. If you're looking for sightseeing and recreation combined with natural attractions—coastal windswept peninsula beaches, seal colonies, sand dunes, and, inland, an improbable herd of provincial bison—you'll find that and more.

A two-lane highway circumnavigates the entire region, with farmlands laid out on the intensely red earth on one side, and the sea and sapphire-blue sky on the other. The eastern shore, from Cardigan through to Murray Harbour, is tattered with little offshore islands and dozens of deeply indented bays and river estuaries. The region's southern climate is warm, humid, and almost tropical; islanders refer to this region as the "banana belt," and even such crops as wine grapes and tobacco thrive here. The long northern coast is nearly straight and uninterrupted, except at large St. Peter's Bay, where a tract of coast is protected as part of Prince Edward Island National Park. The northeast area is relatively remote, lightly populated and developed, and, inland, thickly wooded. As any islander will tell you, the county's northern portion is "far out"; i.e. far out of sight and out of mind from mainstream Prince Edward Island. The pastoral inland countryside is beautiful. It is cultivated in farms of corn, berries, grains, potatoes, and tobacco, and is rimmed on the north by forests and tracts of provincial woodlot plantations.

# HIGHLIGHTS

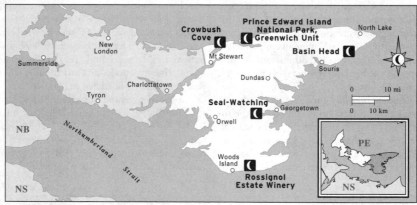

◖ **Rossignol Estate Winery:** Unlike the typical wine country scenery, the vineyard at Rossignol is perched atop red cliffs high above Northumberland Strait – and the wine isn't bad either (page 306).

◖ **Seal-Watching:** Seal colonies inhabit islands along the southeast coast, but none are more accessible than near Montague (page 308).

◖ **Basin Head:** The unlikely combination of a fascinating fisheries museum and silica-filled

sand that "sings" as you walk across it makes for a stop that all ages will enjoy (page 311).

◖ **Prince Edward Island National Park, Greenwich Unit:** The Greenwich Unit of the island's only national park protects a moving sand dune system that is slowly burying a coastal forest (page 313).

◖ **Crowbush Cove:** Prince Edward Island is dotted with golf courses, but the best is the oceanfront Links at Crowbush Cove (page 314).

LOOK FOR ◖ TO FIND RECOMMENDED SIGHTS, ACTIVITIES, DINING, AND LODGING.

## PLANNING YOUR TIME

Distances throughout the eastern portion of the island are much shorter than they may first appear when poring over the provincial road map. It is possible to drive around the entire region (under 400 kilometers) in one day from Charlottetown or to reach Souris, in the far eastern corner, in one hour from the capital. Visitors arriving on the island by ferry land at Wood Islands, from where most make a beeline for the capital, less than an hour's drive to the west, but this is a good starting point for exploring the region by heading in the opposite direction to Murray Harbour and beginning the convoluted coastal route

north and then west along the North Shore. Aside from exploring the provincial parks and admiring the coast-meets-farmland scenery, the three highlights of the drive are taking a **seal-watching trip** from Montague, visiting the museum at **Basin Head,** and admiring the wilderness of **Prince Edward Island National Park.**

Even though Prince Edward Island is tiny, the eastern portion of the province is well off the main tourist route. This means you will find well-priced accommodations. For this reason, it's a good place to take a break from touring. An ideal scenario would be to book a cabin for a couple of days and plan on

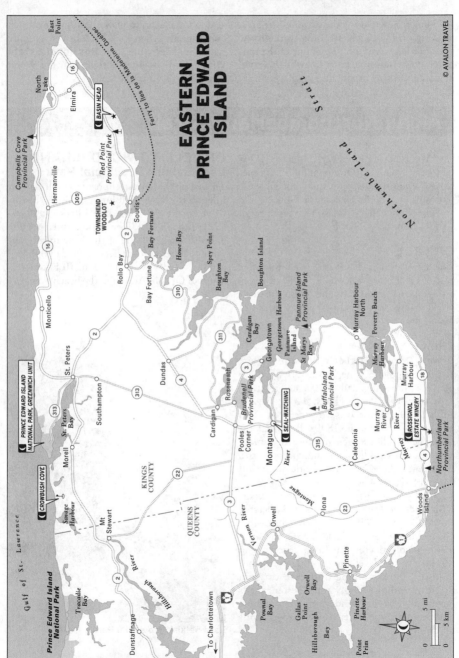

EASTERN PRINCE EDWARD ISLAND

© AVALON TRAVEL

PRINCE EDWARD ISLAND

spending time exploring the surrounding area, relaxing on the beach, strolling through the surrounding towns, golfing at one of the top-notch golf courses such as **Crowbush Cove,** or doing nothing at all. Larger villages have seafood markets, so plan on doing your own cooking, and then kick back in the evening with a glass of wine from **Rossignol Estate Winery,** which you pass right near the Wood Islands ferry terminal.

# Along Northumberland Strait

The TransCanada Highway (Highway 1) extends east from Charlottetown for 62 kilometers to Wood Islands. This small village is the termination point for ferries from Nova Scotia, and also the starting point for touring through Kings County.

## ORWELL

The small village of Orwell, 27 kilometers east of Charlottetown, has a couple of interesting historic attractions and is also the turn-off for those cutting across Kings County to Montague.

### Sights

**Orwell Corner Historic Village** (Hwy. 1, 902/651-8515; June Mon.–Fri. 9 A.M.–4:30 P.M., July–Aug. daily 9:30 A.M.–5:30 P.M., Sept.–mid-Oct. Sun.–Thurs. 9 A.M.–5 P.M.; adult $7.50, child $3) is a restored Scottish village representing the 1890s. Buildings include the farmhouse, general store, dressmaker's shop, blacksmith's shop, church, and barns. In summer, there's a *ceilidh* (Celtic music and dancing) Wednesday at 8 P.M.

Off Highway 1 beyond the historical village is **Sir Andrew MacPhail Homestead** (Fletcher Rd., 902/651-2789; June–Oct. Sun.–Fri. 10 A.M.–6 P.M., Sat. 10 A.M.–8 P.M.), the summer home of a doctor of national renown who was involved in developing the island's potato industry. Three walking trails lead through the surrounding woods, and a restaurant is open daily (except Monday and Tuesday) for lunch and afternoon tea as well as weekends for dinner.

## ORWELL TO WOOD ISLANDS
### Lord Selkirk Provincial Park

Tucked on the eastern shore of Orwell Bay, an inlet off the larger Hillsborough Bay, is beach-front Lord Selkirk Provincial Park (902/659-7221; June–Sept.). The park, named for the Scottish leader of one of the early immigrant groups, is right off the TransCanada Highway, a stone's throw west of Eldon, 10 kilometers south of Orwell. Although the beach here isn't

**Lord Selkirk Provincial Park**

© ANDREW HEMPSTEAD

good for swimming, it's great for walking, beachcombing, and clam digging. The park's campground has unserviced sites ($22) and hookups ($25), a swimming pool, nine-hole golf course, mini-golf, laundry, kitchen shelters, fireplaces, and a nearby campers' store.

A naturalist program runs throughout summer, and the first weekend of August the park is the site of the annual **Highland Games,** which include piping, dancing competitions, Scottish athletic competitions, and lobster suppers. The park is open late June through early September.

## Point Prim

**Point Prim Lighthouse** (902/659-2412; July–Aug.; free) is at the end of Route 209, which peels off the TransCanada Highway and runs 10 kilometers down the long slender peninsula jutting into Hillsborough Bay. It's Prince Edward Island's oldest lighthouse and Canada's only circular brick lighthouse tower. The view overlooking the strait from the octagonal lantern house at the top is gorgeous.

The **Chowder House** (Point Prim, 902/659-2023; mid-June–mid-Sept. daily 9 A.M.–8 P.M.) serves fresh local clams and mussels, chowder, sandwiches, and homemade breads and pastries.

# WOOD ISLANDS

Not an archipelago of islands at all but a little village 62 kilometers east of the capital, this is where the ferry service from Nova Scotia unloads its cargo of vehicles and people.

Along the main highway through town is the **Plough the Waves Centre** (902/962-3761; mid-May–mid-Oct. daily 9 A.M.–6 P.M.), which holds the local information center and public Internet terminals.

## Wood Islands Lighthouse

Ferry travelers will spot this traditional red-and-white lighthouse long before arriving at Wood Islands (stand on the starboard side for the best views). Dating to 1876, it is part of a small provincial park right beside the

© ANDREW HEMPSTEAD

**Wood Islands Lighthouse is near the ferry dock.**

ferry dock. You can climb to the top of the lighthouse (902/962-3110; June–early Sept. daily 9:30 A.M.–6 P.M.; free) and admire displays that tell the story of the ferry service and rum-running.

## Accommodations

**Meadow Lodge Motel** (Hwy. 1, 2 km west of the ferry, 902/962-2022 or 800/461-2022; mid-May–Sept.) is a convenient accommodation if you're leaving the island early or arriving late. Standard motel rooms are $73–83 s or d, and a two-bedroom kitchen-equipped unit is $90.

## Getting There

Between May and mid-December (the rest of the year, ice in Northumberland Strait restricts shipping) ferries depart Wood Islands 5–9 times daily for Caribou, Nova Scotia. The crossing takes 75 minutes, but expect to wait at least that long again during peak travel periods (July and August weekends). The round-trip

PRINCE EDWARD ISLAND

fare is $61 per vehicle, including passengers. For a schedule, contact **Northumberland Ferries** (902/566-3838 or 877/635-7245, www.peiferry.com).

## WOOD ISLANDS TO MURRAY HARBOUR

From Wood Islands, Route 4 continues into Kings County, making a sharp left inland to Murray River. Route 18 sticks to the coast, wrapping around Murray Head before leading into the town of Murray Harbour and then into Murray River.

### Northumberland Provincial Park

Just three kilometers from Wood Islands, Northumberland Provincial Park (Rte. 4, 902/962-7418; late June–early Sept.) fronts the ocean, near enough to the terminal to see the ferries coming and going to Caribou. The park offers rental bikes, hayrides, a nature trail, a stream for fishing, an ocean beach with clam digging, and miniature golf. Facilities at the well-equipped campground include 60 sites (tent sites $22, hookups $25–28), a launderette, kitchen shelters, a nearby campers' store, and hot showers.

### ◖ Rossignol Estate Winery

Beyond the park, the highway crosses into Kings County and quickly reaches Prince Edward Island's only commercial winery (Rte. 4, 902/962-4193; May–Oct. Mon.–Sat. 10 A.M.–5 P.M., Sun. 1–5 P.M.). Try not to let the glorious ocean views distract you from the task at hand—tasting a wide range of reds and whites (including chardonnay and pinot cabernet), along with fruit wines and deliciously sweet blackberry mead. The winery produces 45,000 bottles annually and does everything right, including using oak barrels for aging. No tours are offered, but you are free to wander down the red dirt path leading to the ocean cliffs. The cellar door has tastings and sales.

# Murray Harbour to Souris

From Wood Islands, you'll pass through tiny hamlets like Little Sands and White Sands, marked more by road signs than clusters of houses, as Route 18 approaches Murray Harbour. Enormous numbers of seals live in this well-sheltered harbor, and they love to loll about on offshore islands.

The Murray family settled the area and has namesakes everywhere: The Murray River flows into Murray Harbour, whose entrance is marked by Murray Head; seal colonies cluster on the harbor's Murray Islands; and the three seaport villages are Murray Harbour, Murray River, and Murray Harbour North.

## MURRAY HARBOUR

On the south side of the bay is the small village of Murray Harbour. Beyond town to the east is **Beach Point Lighthouse,** from where seals are often visible.

Set on a five-hectare property, ◖ **Fox River**

**Cottages** (239 Machon Point Rd., 902/962-2881, www.foxriver.ca; May–Oct.; $775–925 per week July–Aug., $125–150 s or d nightly the rest of the season) offers four two-bedroom housekeeping cottages with screened porches overlooking the Fox River. Amenities include a canoe, rowboat, and laundry. Also in the area, **Harbour Motel** (Mill Rd., 902/962-3660, www.harbourmotelpei.com; $75 s or d) has seven kitchen-equipped units within walking distance of town.

Easily the best place to eat in town, **Brehauts Restaurant** (Rte. 18, 902/962-3141; Apr.–Oct. daily 8 A.M.–10 P.M.) has a big deck overlooking the river. The menu is strong on seafood, simply prepared and well priced.

## MURRAY RIVER

The oval-shaped harbor is centered on the town of Murray River, hub of the island's southeast corner.

## Sights

Children will love **King's Castle Provincial Park** (Rte. 348; mid-June–mid-Oct. daily 9 A.M.–9 P.M.) on the banks of the Murray River east of town. A grassy meadow is filled with concrete storybook characters, trails lead through the woods, and there's a riverside beach (complete with hot showers). A covered picnic shelter is the perfect spot for lunch.

If you like woodland walking, stretch your legs at **Murray River Pines,** a provincial woodlot near town. The site off Route 4 is remote. Look for an abandoned mill, the former provincial Northumberland Mill and Museum, now closed; the woodlot is inland behind the site. A 30-minute hike on the red-clay road leads to dense groves of red and white pines, abutted by stands of balsam, red maple, and red spruce. The largest pines date to the 1870s, when England's Royal Navy cut down most of the forest for masts. Somehow these trees survived, and they have become havens for birds of all kinds, including blue herons, kingfishers, swallows, blue jays, and chickadees.

## Recreation

From the downtown wharf along Route 4, **Marine Adventures** (902/962-2494 or 800/496-2494; June–Sept.) operates a tour boat to the seal colonies of the Murray Islands. Along the way, you'll pass mussel farms and often spot seals and bald eagles. The trip costs adult $20, senior $15, child $12.

The **Old General Store** (Main St., 902/962-2459; July–Aug. Mon.–Sat. 9:30 A.M.–5:30 P.M., Sun. noon–5 P.M.; shorter hours in spring and fall) ranks as one of the island's best crafts sources and stocks folk art, linens, and domestic wares. It's open mid-June to mid-September.

## Accommodations and Camping

On a small lake east of town, **Forest and Stream Cottages** (Rte. 18, 902/962-3537 or 800/227-9943, www.forestandstreamcottages.com; May–Oct.; $85–125 s or d) comprises six simple but tidy cottages, each with a kitchen, a bedroom, and a covered porch. Rowboats are supplied, and there's a playground.

Continue through town to the northeast to reach **( Seal Cove Campground** (87 Mink River Rd., 902/962-2745, www.sealcovecampground.ca; June–Sept.), which overlooks offshore seal colonies. When you're done watching seals, there's a nine-hole golf course ($18 for a full-day greens fees), an outdoor pool, kayak rentals, and a playground to keep everyone busy. Tent sites are $28, hookups $35.

## MURRAY RIVER TO MONTAGUE

Route 4 is the most direct road between Murray River and Montague, but Route 17 is more scenic.

Through the village of Murray Harbour North, **Poverty Beach,** at the end of a spur off Route 17, is a long narrow sandbar that separates the sea from the harbor. It's quiet, remote, and wrapped in a sense of primeval peacefulness. The peninsula is worth a trek, but think twice about swimming in the surf; powerful sea currents can be dangerous, and no lifeguards are around to rescue floundering bathers.

### Panmure Island

Panmure Island, a remote and windswept wilderness, lies 15 kilometers north of Poverty Beach. It is linked to the mainland by a narrow strip of land, traversed by Route 347, which rambles out along the flag-shaped peninsula that wags between St. Marys Bay, Georgetown Harbour, and the sea. A supervised beach fronts the strait, and a wisp of a road angles into the interior and emerges at the waterfront with views of Georgetown across the harbor. Back on the mainland is **Panmure Island Provincial Park** (902/838-0668; late June–early Sept.). A campground here has 22 unserviced sites and 16 two-way hookup sites ($22–25), supervised ocean swimming off a beautiful white-sand beach, a launderette, a campers' canteen, fireplaces, and hot showers.

## Buffaloland Provincial Park

Halfway between Murray River and Montague along Route 4, the 40-hectare Buffaloland Provincial Park (year-round; free) may seem deserted at first glance. If you look closely, though, you'll spot bison and white-tailed deer roaming the woodlands. The namesake herd began with 14 bison imported from Alberta in 1970 as part of a federal experiment to help preserve the almost-extinct species. There's still no population explosion, but the herd numbers 24 buffalo now. No guarantees, but mid-afternoon the bison herd often emerges to feed near the Route 4 fence.

# MONTAGUE

Montague, 46 kilometers east of Charlottetown and 28 kilometers north of Wood Islands, is the largest town in Kings County, yet the population is under 2,000. The town is defined by the Main Street bridge over the Montague River. In fact, the town began as Montague Bridge in 1825, when the bridge was made of logs and the area had just four farms. Shipbuilding brought riches to the town, and many a schooner and other sailing craft was launched here on the broad river.

The town is uncomplicated, pretty, clean, and friendly. Everything important lies along Main Street, which slices through town and proceeds up, over, and down the bridge.

## Sights and Recreation
### GARDEN OF THE GULF MUSEUM

The Garden of the Gulf Museum (564 Main St., 902/838-2467; June–Sept. Mon.–Sat. 10 A.M.–5 P.M.; adult $3) is housed in an old post office overlooking Montague River at the bridge. The building is an impressive hulk of red brick with a steeply pitched roof, showing its French architectural influence. The collection includes exhibits on local history, including the colorful story of Trois Rivières, which was established nearby in 1732 by French entrepreneur Jean Pierre de Roma.

### ◖ SEAL-WATCHING

**Cruise Manada** (902/838-3444) leave from the town's marina on Route 4 or from the Brudenell

River resort wharf on Route 3. Both two-hour cruises sail 1–3 times daily. An onboard narrator provides information on local history and wildlife such as harbor seals, great blue herons, gulls, and ospreys. Tickets are adult $24, senior $22.50, children 5–13 $12.50.

## Accommodations and Food

Overlooking the water, **Lanes Cottages** (33 Brook St., 902/838-2433 or 800/268-7532, www.lanescottages.com; $79–105 s or d) is a pleasant cluster of units with basic cooking facilities. Amenities include a playground and a Laundromat.

The deliberately rustic riverside **Lobster Shanty** (102 Main St., 902/838-2463 or 800/418-9430) has older motel rooms ($89 s or d) and chalets (from $169). The motel's riverview restaurant reigns as one of the region's best dining rooms, although it's a bit touristy.

## Information

The junction of Routes 3 and 4, five kilometers north of Montague, is known as **Pooles Corner**. Here you find a provincial **Visitor Information Centre** (902/838-0670; June daily 9 A.M.–5 P.M., July–Aug. daily 9 A.M.–7 P.M.; Sept. 9 A.M.–4:30 P.M.).

# BRUDENELL RIVER PROVINCIAL PARK

This 30-hectare park-cum-resort occupies a gorgeous pastoral setting on the peninsula that juts out into Cardigan Bay between the Brudenell and Cardigan Rivers. You enter the park from Route 3 three kilometers east of Pooles Corner, and the road winds through manicured grounds to the resort's main house and nearby chalets.

## Recreation

Golfers enjoy walking the fairways of two golf courses (902/652-8965 or 800/377-8336; May–Oct.), Brudenell River and the newer Dundarave course, which plays to a challenging 7,300 yards from the back tees. The courses both rank among Atlantic Canada's superior golf greens and have been the site of various national and CPGA tournaments. Greens fees are $70 and $80 respectively.

Other park activities include canoeing ($35 a day), windsurfing ($45 for a partial day), horse-back riding (902/652-2396; $28 for a one-hour beach ride), indoor and outdoor pools, tennis, and boat tours. All park activities are open to campers, resort guests, and day visitors alike.

## Accommodations and Food

The epicenter of the resort complex is **Rodd Brudenell River** (902/652-2332 or 800/565-7633, www.roddhotelsandresorts.com; May–Dec.; $140–260 s or d). Dating from the early 1990s, the resort holds three types of rooms: regular motel rooms in the main lodge; Countryside Cabins, which are simple free-standing units grouped together in strange configurations; and two-bedroom cottages with kitchens and fireplaces. Check the website for deals and packages. The resort's licensed **Stillwaters** is casually upscale and specializes in seafood entrées ($20–29); try the poached salmon awash in lemon sauce and, for dessert, shortbread squares topped with lemon meringue or the homemade parfait.

The modern units at ◖ **Brudenell Fairway Chalets** (Rte. 3, 902/652-2900 or 866/652-2900, www.fairwaychalets.com) are more like mini houses rather than chalets. Each has two or three bedrooms ($224 and $275 s or d, respectively), a well-designed kitchen, a lounge with TV, washing and drying facilities, and a deck with a barbecue. On the edge of the park, it's close to the golf course and also has its own pool and playground.

## Campground

The park isn't all resort. Continue beyond the main entrance to reach **Brudenell River Provincial Park Campground** (902/583-2020; late June–late Sept.). Tent sites are spread through a wooded area ($22) while hookup sites ($25–30) have plenty of room to maneuver big rigs. Amenities include hot showers, kitchen shelters, a launderette, interpretive programs, a riverfront beach, and a walking trail that links the campground to the resort.

# VICINITY OF BRUDENELL RIVER PARK
## Georgetown

At the end of Route 3, beyond the park, Georgetown was once a major shipbuilding center. The naming of Georgetown was surveyor Samuel Holland's tribute to George III of England. The port boasted one of the island's most perfectly created deepwater harbors. Its early economy was built with British money, however, and when England's economy had a short-lived collapse, Georgetown lost its economic edge and never regained it. Georgetown slid into the shadows, replaced by Montague first as a shipbuilding and shipping center and then as the area's principal market town. It is now best known for the **King's Playhouse** (65 Grafton St., 902/652-2053; mid-July–mid-Sept.), a repertory company that stages dramas and comedies in a downtown theater year-round.

## Cardigan

At this hamlet five kilometers north of the provincial park, the **lobster suppers** are well worth partaking in. You'll find them at the Olde Store (902/583-2020; late June–late Sept.; adult $26, child $16).

At the former railway station, **Cardigan Craft Centre** (902/583-2930; June–mid-Oct. Mon.–Sat. 10 A.M.–5:30 P.M.) is a reliable source of high-quality crafts, including handmade textiles, stained glass, and warm sweaters. Also in the station is a tearoom (Mon.–Sat. 10 A.M.–4 P.M.).serving inexpensive lunches.

# BAY FORTUNE

Around 60 kilometers north of Cardigan along the Kings Byway, Fortune River flows into Bay Fortune, whose name originated long before the fortunes of Broadway fueled the local retreats of producer David Belasco and playwright Elmer Harris. Upriver six kilometers is the hamlet of Dingwells Mills, where *Johnny Belinda,* one of Harris's most successful Broadway plays and later a movie, was set.

## Accommodations and Food

The **◖ Inn at Bay Fortune** (Rte. 310, 902/687-3745 or 888/687-3745, www.innatbayfortune.com; late May–mid-Oct.; $150–325 s or d) has earned an international reputation thanks to the care lavished on the property by innkeeper David Wilmer. The estate was once the summer home of Elmer Harris, who designed the 19th-century version of a motel to house the entourage of thespians who traveled with the renowned playwright. The 18 guest rooms, 14 with fireplaces, are impeccably furnished and fill with natural light. The most sought-after is the two-level Tower Suite, which has sweeping water views from the upstairs lounge. Rates include a cooked breakfast.

A strong sense of conviviality pervades the inn's dining room, which is regarded as one of Canada's finest restaurants. Meals are served on the front enclosed porch during summer or inside with tables arranged before the fireplace when the weather is cooler. The creative menu features entrées emphasizing local produce from both the land and the sea (try scallops topped with strawberry and balsamic salsa), accompanied by a sophisticated wine list. Although you don't need to be a guest to dine here, many are, staying as part of a package (check the website).

# Souris and Vicinity

Any islander will tell you that the fishing town of Souris is "far out," the end of the line on the beaten tourist track. The town (pop. 1,200), notched on the strait seacoast 80 kilometers east of Charlottetown and 44 kilometers north of Montague, garners unqualified raves for its setting. Consider Souris as a base for touring throughout the northeast. The location translates as good value for the dollar in lodgings and dining. The restaurants are plainly furnished and specialize in seafood platters, ranked by islanders among the province's best and freshest.

## History

Unaware of the benevolent climate in the region's southern area, early French settlers from Port-la-Joye made their way up the Hillsborough River by 1724. Conditions were wretched. Plagues of field mice ravaged the fields and Souris village through the 1750s. Though the infestations eventually petered out, a reputation for rodents followed the seaport through the centuries and gave the village its name; *souris* is French for mouse. By 1800 the town emerged as a shipbuilding center and retained the role until the Great Age of Sail ended in the late 19th century. Simultaneously, canning as a method of preserving food developed as a seaport specialty, and for decades islanders stuffed lobster ad infinitum into cans for international export.

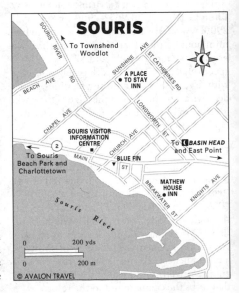

## SIGHTS AND RECREATION

The town overlooks Northumberland Strait from sloping headlands, bounded in part by grasslands that sweep down to the water and in other parts by steeply pitched red cliffs. On the southern boundary, the Souris River rushes toward the sea with a gush of red-colored water and pours into the blue strait, like a palette of blended watercolor pigments.

### Townshend Woodlot

Townshend Woodlot is a 106-hectare spread that closely resembles the island's original Acadian forest. In 1970 the International Biological Program designated the setting as one of the island's finest examples of old-growth hardwood groves. To get there, take Route 305 three kilometers north to the hamlet of Souris Line Road. The woodlot plantation lies off the road, fairly well hidden and obscurely marked—you may want to ask for directions in Souris. Acquired by the province in 1978, the woodlot lacks a clear hiking route, but it's easily walkable on a level grade of sandy loam. The groves meld beech trees—a species that once dominated half the island's forests—with yellow birch, red maple, and sugar maple, whose dark brown trunks stretch up as high as 32 meters. Eastern chipmunks nest in underground tunnels. Dwarf ginseng—rare on the island—and nodding trillium thrive.

### ◖ Basin Head

Formed by the winds, most sand dunes grow and creep along, albeit at a snail's pace. Basin Head's dunes are known as "walking" dunes for their windblown mobility. The high silica content of the sand here causes it to squeak audibly when crunched underfoot. Islanders poetically describe the phenomenon as "singing sands." The beaches at both Basin Head and adjacent Red Point Provincial Park are composed of singing sands. At Basin Head, the dunes are high and environmentally fragile; visitors should stay off the dunes and tread instead along the beach near the water's edge.

Behind the Basin Head dunes, **Basin Head Fisheries Museum** (Rte. 16, 902/357-7233; mid-June–late Sept. daily 9 A.M.–5 P.M.; adult $4, child $3.50) sits high on the headland overlooking an inlet. Here you'll find boats, nets, and a museum with expertly conceived exhibits detailing the historic inshore fishing industry and local coastal ecology. Behind the museum, a boardwalk leads across the dunes to the ocean.

Northeast of town, Basin Head is a popular destination for local cruise operators. Daytime sailings feature coastal bird-watching, and sunset cruises are timed to take in the colorful twilight. Cruises (usually around $30 per person) depart the Souris town wharf regularly, with all-day **lobster-fishing** expeditions offered in summer ($100 per person, with all gear supplied). Call the Souris Visitor Information Centre (902/687-7030) for a list of operators.

## FESTIVALS AND EVENTS

The highlight of the event calendar is the **Souris Regatta** in mid-July, which features a sailing regatta, tub races, a midway, wood-carving demonstrations, and an arm-wrestling competition. That same weekend, musicians from across the island gather southeast of town at Rollo Bay for the **Prince Edward Island Bluegrass & Old Time Music Festival** (www.bluegrasspei.com).

## ACCOMMODATIONS AND CAMPING

### Under $50

As lodging prices are reasonable throughout the island, finding a place to stay for backpackers is less important than elsewhere in the region. That said, ◖ **A Place to Stay Inn** (9 Longworth St., 902/687-4626) is excellent in all regards. The downstairs of this large home within walking distance of town has been converted into a lodge, with separate male and female dorms, a kitchen, a living room with TV, bike rentals, a deck with a barbecue, and a laundry. Dorm beds are $20 per person.

## $50-100

Guests at **A Place to Stay Inn** (9 Longworth St., 902/687-4626) may share the building with backpackers, but the two sections are completely separate. The upstairs guest rooms share bathrooms and breakfast is included in the rate of $65–70 s or d.

Fronting the ocean and within walking distance of a beach and Platter House Restaurant, **Lighthouse and Beach Motel** (Rte. 2, 902/687-2339 or 800/689-2339, www.lighthouseandbeachmotel.com; mid-June–mid-Sept.; $70–100 s or d) offers regular motel rooms with a light breakfast included in the rates. An old lighthouse on the property is rented by the week ($700) and has a jetted tub, separate bedrooms, and a kitchen. This lodging is two kilometers west of town.

A further six kilometers west is **Rollo Bay Inn** (Rte. 2, 902/687-3550 or 877/687-3550; $89–99 s or d). This lodging combines a re-created Georgian setting with 15 rooms, housekeeping units, and suites on spacious grounds with a licensed restaurant serving basic island cuisine.

## $100-150

The lovely **Matthew House Inn** (15 Breakwater St., 902/687-3461, www.matthewhouseinn .com; late June–early Sept.; $110–175 s or d) sits on landscaped gardens within sight of the water. Built in 1885 by a local entrepreneur, its historic character has been preserved through meticulous restoration. My favorite of the guest rooms is Number 8, which has a soothing pastel-blue color scheme that blends perfectly with the polished hardwood floors and antique bed. Rates include a full breakfast.

### Campground

**Red Point Provincial Park** (13 km east of Souris off Rte. 16, 902/357-2463; late June–early Sept.) has a campground with 32 tent sites ($22) and 58 powered sites ($28). Amenities include kitchen shelters, fireplaces, and hot showers.

## FOOD

The **( Blue Fin** (10 Federal Ave., 902/687-3271; daily 8 A.M.–8 P.M.) is partly protected from the tourist crowd by its tucked-away location off the main street. But for well-priced simple seafood dishes, it's well worth searching out. The seafood chowder ($7) and the fish-and-chips ($10) are both excellent.

## INFORMATION

**Souris Visitor Information Centre** (95 Main St., 902/687-7030; June–Oct. daily 9 A.M.–5 P.M.) is in a historic building in the middle of town.

# North Shore

If you like photogenic landscapes, windy seacoasts washed with tossing surf, and weathered seaports, consider northeastern Kings County for a revealing glimpse of this seafaring island as it once was. Beyond Souris, the strait seacoast stretches 25 kilometers to windswept East Point, the island's easternmost point. On the equally remote gulf coast in this region, you'll find few tourists, a dozen tiny seaports, and a handful of lonesome lighthouses that stand as sentinels along the 75-kilometer-long coastline, strewn with centuries of shipwrecks.

## FAR EAST
### East Point

At the northeastern tip of Prince Edward Island, 25 kilometers northeast of Souris, Northumberland Strait and the Gulf of St. Lawrence meet in a lathered flush of cresting seas, sometimes colored blue and often tinged with red from oxide-colored silt. Here stands the 20-meter-high octagonal tower of **East Point Lighthouse** (off Rte. 16, 902/357-2106; mid-June–Aug. daily 10 A.M.–6 P.M.; guided tours adult $3, senior $2, child $1), which is still in use. The first lighthouse at this spot was built in 1867, but erosion has forced subsequent structures to be moved farther back from the cliff edge.

## Elmira
**Elmira Railway Museum** (Rte. 16A, 902/357-7234; mid-June–early Sept. daily 9 A.M.–5 P.M.; $2) is the end of the line. Literally. This is where a rail line that once spanned Prince Edward Island came to an end. The original station now serves as the unspoken testament to the island railroad's halcyon years, with the province's only exhibits and documentation on rail service. It also holds a small gift shop and café, and has bike rentals. The bikes are for use on the **Confederation Trail,** the old rail bed, which has been converted to a walking and bike path that extends 279 kilometers to the other end of the island.

## North Lake and Vicinity
North Lake harbor is one of four departure points for deep-sea fishing; anglers try for trophy catches of bluefin tuna. Expect to pay $20–30 per person for a three- to four-hour trip or about $400 for an eight-hour charter with four aboard. Trips depart daily during the July to mid-September season from North Lake, Naufrage, Launching, and Red Head harbors. **North Lake Tuna Charters** (902/357-2055), at North Lake harbor, is among the best.

**Bluefin Motel** (Rte. 16, 902/357-2053; July–Sept.; $70 s or d) caters to anglers with 10 basic rooms and a beach with clam digging.

**Campbells Cove Provincial Park** (Rte. 16, 5 km west of Elmira, 902/357-3080; late June–early Sept.) fronts the gulf with a beach, hot showers, kitchen shelters, and 48 serviced and unserviced sites ($22–28).

## GULF SHORE
### St. Peters
If you're in the area in late July or early August, check out the port's five-day **Blueberry Festival,** an islander favorite with concerts, entertainment, blueberry dishes, lobster and beef barbecue, and a pancake brunch.

**St. Peters Park** (Rte. 2, 902/961-2786;

---

# ÎLES DE LA MADELEINE

Souris is the departure point for ferries to Québec's Îles de la Madeleine (Magdalen Islands), in the Gulf of St. Lawrence, 105 kilometers from the northern tip of Prince Edward Island and 215 kilometers from the closest point of Québec. This remote archipelago comprises 12 islands, six of which are linked by rolling sand dunes, and totals 200 square kilometers. The islands are renowned as a remote wilderness destination, featuring great beaches and abundant bird life. Villages dot the islands, and each has basic tourist services.

**CTMA Ferry** (418/986-3278 or 888/986-3278, www.ctma.ca) operates the MV *Madeleine* car/passenger ferry between Souris and the islands April through January. The 134-kilometer crossing takes five hours, with a schedule that includes 6-8 sailings weekly in each direction. Most runs leave Souris at 2 P.M. and leave Cap-aux-Meules for the return at 8 A.M. One-way passenger fares are adult $44, senior $36, child $22, vehicle from $82.

For information on the Magdalens, contact the local **tourism office** (128 Chemin Débarcadère, Cap-aux-Meules, 418/986-2245). This office also maintains an excellent website, www.ilesdelamadeleine.com, with detailed island information and links to accommodations.

---

**PRINCE EDWARD ISLAND**

mid-June–Sept.; $22–28 per night) has a campground with a choice of 11 unserviced sites and more than 70 full-hookup sites. Amenities include a launderette, kitchen shelters, free firewood, two swimming pools, mini-golf, and hot showers.

## ◖ Prince Edward Island National Park, Greenwich Unit
This national park has three units. (For the other two, see *Charlottetown to Cavendish* and *Cavendish* in the *Charlottetown and Queens*

*County* chapter.) Known as the Greenwich Unit, this six-square-kilometer tract of land encompasses a fragile dune system and wetlands, with a 4.5-kilometer trail leading over the dunes. Wind is slowly pushing the dunes back into the forest, burying trees that over time become bleached skeletons—an intriguing and unique sight. At the end of the road is **Greenwich Interpretation Centre** (902/963-2391; July–mid-Aug. daily 9 A.M.–8 P.M., June and mid-Aug.–Oct. daily 9 A.M.–5 P.M.). Admission to the park is adult $8, senior $7, child $4. To get there, take Route 313 west from St. Peters along the north side of St. Peters Bay.

## MORELL AND VICINITY

Berries are the focus at Morell, 40 minutes from Charlottetown. The St. Peters Bay seaport makes much of the harvest at mid-July's six-day **Strawberry Festival,** with a parade, concerts, dances, barbecues, strawberry desserts, and other community events.

### ◖ Crowbush Cove

Along the coast just west of Morell is **Links at Crowbush Cove** (902/368-5761; May–Oct.), a highly acclaimed, 18-hole, par-73 golf course. A true links course in the Scottish tradition, Crowbush challenges players with 9 water holes and 8 holes surrounded by dunes. Greens fees are $80–100. Overlooking the golf course is ◖ **Rodd Crowbush Golf & Beach Resort** (902/961-5600, www.roddhotelsandresorts .com; mid-May–mid-Oct.), comprising contemporary rooms in the main lodge and 32 two-bedroom cottages spread along the course.

Amenities include spa services, a fitness center, an indoor pool, tennis courts, and a restaurant overlooking the ocean. Most guests stay as part of golf packages, from $220 per person per night.

## MOUNT STEWART

Located on the Hillsborough River, 35 kilometers northeast of Charlottetown, Mount Stewart grew as a shipbuilding center in the second half of the 19th century. Today, instead of shipyards, the draw is the **Confederation Trail,** a rail bed that has been converted to a hiking and biking trail that spans the entire island. Mount Stewart is a good place to base yourself for a day or overnight trip along a short section of the trail.

The main attraction in town is the **Hillsborough River Eco-Centre** (104 Main St., 902/676-2050; July–Aug. daily 10 A.M.–6 P.M.; free), which has displays on the river and its ecosystem, public Internet access, and a gift shop. Make sure to climb the tower out back for sweeping views up and down Prince Edward Island's major river.

The ◖ **Trailside Inn** (109 Main St., 902/676-3130 or 888/704-6595, www.trailside .ca; mid-June–late Sept.; $75 s or d) is named for the Confederation Trail, which passes through town. In a restored general store, the four rooms each have private bathrooms, hardwood floors, and televisions. For those looking at traveling the trail, this is a handy place to rent bikes ($25 the first day plus $10 per additional day). The in-house café (Fri.–Sun. from 4 P.M.) serves hearty country-style cooking and often hosts local musicians.

# NEWFOUNDLAND AND LABRADOR

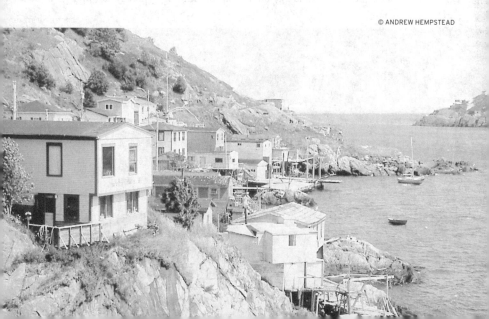

# ST. JOHN'S AND THE AVALON PENINSULA

St. John's, the provincial capital, is a colorful and comfortable city. Situated on the steep inland side of St. John's Harbour, the city's rooftops form a tapestry: Some are gracefully drawn with swooping mansard curves, some are pancake-flat or starkly pitched, while others are pyramidal with clay pots placed atop the central chimneys. Against this otherwise picture-perfect tapestry, the tangle of electrical wires strung up and down the hillside is a visual offense.

Contrasts of color are everywhere. House windows are framed in deep turquoise, red, bright yellow, or pale pink and are covered with starched white lace curtains. Window boxes are stuffed to overflowing with red geraniums and purple and pink petunias. Along the streets, cement walls brace the hillside, and any blank surface serves as an excuse for a pastel-painted mural. The storefronts on Water Street, as individual as their owners, stand out in Wedgwood blue, lime green, purple, and rose. At streetside, public telephone booths are painted the bright red of old-time fire hydrants.

As the Newfoundlanders say, St. John's offers the best for visitors—another way of saying that Newfoundland is short on cities and long on coastal outports. But without question, St. John's thrives with places for dining, nightlife, sightseeing, and lodging—more than anywhere else across the island and Labrador. Simply put, the Newfoundlanders have carved a contemporary, livable, and intriguing niche in one of North America's most ancient ports. Come to St. John's for some of Atlantic Canada's most abundant high-quality shopping; unusual

© ANDREW HEMPSTEAD

# HIGHLIGHTS

**( The Rooms:** A museum, an art gallery, and spectacular harbor views are wrapped up together in this magnificent complex showcasing the very best of everything Newfoundland and Labrador (page 321).

**( Signal Hill:** The sweeping ocean and city views alone make the drive to the top of Signal Hill worthwhile (page 325).

**( Johnson Geo Centre:** Descend underground in a glass-sided elevator at this Signal Hill attraction; the ancient geological world of the province comes to life (page 325).

**( Quidi Vidi:** With its charming fishing shacks and rugged shoreline, you could be in a Newfoundland "outport" (remote fishing village), but you're not – downtown is just over the hill (page 326).

**( Witless Bay Ecological Reserve:** Jump aboard a tour boat and head out to this reserve where you're almost guaranteed whale, puffin, and seal sightings (page 341).

**( Colony of Avalon:** Integrated with the seaside village of Ferryland, this ongoing archaeological dig is slowly uncovering one of North America's oldest European settlements (page 342).

**( Shamrock Festival:** The joyous sounds of Newfoundland music permeate all aspects of life on "The Rock," but at the late July Shamrock Festival, you can get up close and personal not just with music but also with the people and their love of life (page 343).

**( Cape St. Mary's Ecological Reserve:** Even if you have no real interest in birds, the sights and sounds of thousands of birds on this offshore rock stack are a spectacle to remember (page 344).

LOOK FOR **(** TO FIND RECOMMENDED SIGHTS, ACTIVITIES, DINING, AND LODGING.

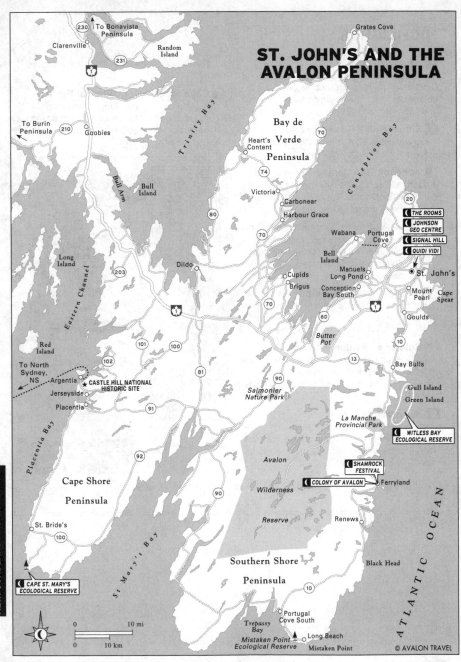

# ST. JOHN'S AND THE AVALON PENINSULA

NEWFOUNDLAND AND LABRADOR

dining in lush surroundings; interesting maritime history displayed in fine museums; rousing nightlife and music; and an emerging eclectic fine-arts scene.

And when you're done with the city, there's the rest of the Avalon Peninsula to discover. Within day-tripping distance of downtown you can go whale-watching at Witless Bay Ecological Reserve, watch archaeologists at work at Ferryland, walk in to North America's most accessible bird sanctuary at Cape St. Mary's, and drive through delightfully named villages like Heart's Desire.

## PLANNING YOUR TIME

Whether you arrive by air, by ferry, or overland from the west, St. John's is a definite destination in itself. It has all the amenities of a major city, including top-notch accommodations, a good range of restaurants, and lively nightlife. Sightseeing will easily fill two days, with at least half a day spent at **The Rooms,** a museum and art gallery complex as good as any in the country. Don't miss the drive up to **Signal Hill National Historic Site,** and stop at **Johnson Geo Centre** along the way. The **Fluvarium** is a good rainy-day diversion. While the village of **Quidi Vidi** gives a taste of the rest of the province without leaving city limits, the rest of the Avalon Peninsula is well worth exploring. The options are relatively straightforward—either use St. John's as a base for day trips or plan on an overnight excursion. Two highlights—a whale-watching trip to **Witless Bay Ecological Reserve** and a visit to the historic **Colony of Avalon**—can easily be combined into day trip, but if you're visiting in late July, don't miss the **Shamrock Festival,** an outdoor concert beside the Colony of Avalon. **Cape St. Mary's Ecological Reserve** is also within a couple of hours' drive of St. John's, although if you're arriving by ferry from Nova Scotia, it's only a short detour from the main route into town. If you're arriving by air, five days is the minimum amount of time to allow for exploring the city and Avalon Peninsula. If

## THE NEWFOUNDLAND DOG AND LABRADOR RETRIEVER

The large long-haired Newfoundland dog is believed to have originated with the early Portuguese, who brought mountain sheepdogs across the Atlantic with them. Considered one of North America's finest show dogs, the Newfoundland is better-known locally as a working dog. Its swimming prowess in rescuing shipwrecked fishers and sailors from stormy seas has inspired local legends.

Contrary to the name, the Labrador retriever originated on the island of Newfoundland as a descendant of the Newfoundland dog. The retriever was known as the "lesser Newfoundland," "St. John's dog," or "St. John's water dog" until its debut in London at the English Kennel Club in 1903.

you're arriving by ferry with your own vehicle, plan on spending three days on the Avalon Peninsula and seven days traveling through the central and western portion of the province to the ferry terminal at Port-aux-Basques. Add two days' ferry travel from North Sydney (Nova Scotia) and you can create a 12-day itinerary with no backtracking.

## HISTORY

St. John's officially dates to 1497, when Newfoundlanders say the explorer John Cabot sailed into the harbor and claimed the area for England. Portugal's Gaspar Côrte-Real arrived about 1500 and named the harbor (or a tributary river) the Rio de San Johem, which appeared on a 1519 Portuguese map. Although undocumented, European fishermen probably knew about the port in Cabot's time—perhaps before. By the early 1540s, St. John's Harbour was a major port on Old World maps, and the French explorer Jacques Cartier anchored there for ship repairs.

## The British Presence

The British—who arrived, conquered, and re-mained for centuries—have had the greatest impact here. By 1528 the port had its first resi-dence, and the main lanes were the Lower Path (Water Street) and Upper Path (Duckworth Street). Fishing thrived, but settlement was slow. Early on, the defenseless port was ready game for incursions by other European impe-rialists, and in 1665 the Dutch plundered the town. Nevertheless, by 1675 St. John's had a population of 185, as well as 155 cattle and 48 boats anchored at 23 piers. The English pro-tected the harbor with Forts William, George, Castle, and Battery. They blocked the har-bor's Narrows with chains and nets, and used lofty Signal Hill as a lookout to monitor both friendly and hostile ships.

By 1696 the French emerged as England's persistent adversary. Based at Plaisance (Placentia), the French launched destructive attacks on St. John's in 1696, 1705, and 1709. Simultaneously, England developed Halifax, Nova Scotia, as a naval hub, and by 1762 dis-patched a fleet that vanquished the French at the Battle of Signal Hill, North America's final land battle of the Seven Years' War.

## The Early Port

St. John's was a seamy port through most of its early years. In a town bereft of permanent settlement and social constraints, 80 taverns and innumerable brothels flourished on Water Street, with a few stores on Duckworth Street and Buckleys Lane (George Street). The port's inhabitants were a motley mix of Spaniards, Portuguese, French, and British; as the latter gained dominance, Anglo immigration was encouraged.

Almost 4,000 settlers from England and Ireland arrived in the early 1800s, followed by another 10,000 in 1815. The new immigrants had fled the poverty of the British Isles, but they found the St. John's cupboard equally bare. They rioted en masse, and uncontrol-lable fires worsened conditions.

St. John's history has been punctuated with great fires. Those early conflagrations were fueled by various sources. Fish caught on the Grand Banks were often brought to port and laid out to dry on street-side fish flakes (wooden racks). During the great fires from 1816 to 1819, sparks ignited the flakes' dry timbers and tree boughs, sending fires racing across the hillside. In 1846 the scene repeated itself when sparks ignited barrels of seal and codfish oil.

## Troubles and Triumphs

St. John's, like Halifax, was a British gar-rison town. With no foreseeable enemy, England withdrew the troops in 1870. The Royal Newfoundland Constabulary, mod-eled after England's occupying police force in Ireland, made its headquarters at Fort Townshend in 1871.

In 1892, another huge fire destroyed the city from Water Street to the East End, leveling 1,572 houses and 150 stores and leaving 1,900 families homeless. St. John's rebuilt *again*. The stores, commercial buildings, and merchant mansions were re-created in Gothic Revival and Second Empire styles. The Anglican Cathedral of St. John the Baptist, on the site of the first 1720 church, was rebuilt within the Gothic stone walls.

The fire coincided with rail transportation's emergence, and St. John's was designated as the island's rail headquarters in 1892. The main Water Street rail station was styled with a flourish of Victorian gingerbread. In 1907, the fledgling Newfoundland Museum found a permanent home in the twin-towered brick building on Duckworth Street.

## Inheritances and Additions

St. John's was beautiful at the turn of the 20th century. From the British military oc-cupation, the city inherited grandiose build-ings. The Georgian-style Commissariat House on King's Bridge Road was built in 1821; the stately pillared Colonial Building on Military Road now houses the provin-cial archives. St. Thomas's Anglican Church, built first in 1699 as Fort William's garri-son church, was torched by the French, then rebuilt in 1836. Prosperous citizens donated choice land for Bannerman and Bowring Parks. Trolley cars tooled along the downtown streets and served as public transit until 1948. Atop Signal Hill, the city added Cabot Tower in 1897 as a tribute to both the 400th anniversary of Cabot's discovery and Queen Victoria's Diamond Jubilee.

### World War II and After

St. John's thrived during World War II. Fort Pepperell served as the operations headquarters for military bases across the island and Labrador. As defenses against the German submarines that stalked the harbor entrance and local waters, Signal Hill and Cape Spear were fortified with antiaircraft batteries, and nets were stretched across the Narrows' 174-meter-wide entrance. After the war, the U.S. Northeast Command, followed by NATO's 64th Air Division, occupied Fort Pepperell until the base was deactivated in 1960.

Newfoundland joined the Confederation in 1949. An infusion of federal funding and 4,000 civil service posts buoyed the city's economy. In the 1960s, the city lost its commercial and residential cores as people and business fled to the suburbs, with their new malls, industrial parks, and housing. In 1966 downtown merchants and private parties galvanized interest in an almost abandoned downtown with the Downtown Development Corporation, and in 1985 the federal government initiated the Main Street Program, Canada's first urban-rejuvenation project.

### The Contemporary City

St. John's today is a handsomely historic and stylishly new city with a metropolitan-area population of around 200,000. The town grew up from the harbor, which is still the city's most colorful part—a promenade aside a long string of ships at anchor. Water and Duckworth Streets offer a colorful array of storefronts, while the lively night scene continues until early morning at the bars, pubs, and clubs on pedestrian-friendly George Street. The city hall, built at a cost of $3.5 million, opened in 1970 on New Gower Street, but even more dramatic is The Rooms, the provincial museum and art gallery complex that dominates the hilly skyline.

# Sights

Most of St. John's best sightseeing revolves around the city's long and colorful history. In addition to traditional sights such as The Rooms (the provincial museum) and national historic sites, go beyond the ordinary and plan on sipping a pint of beer at the Crow's Nest and joining a guided walking tour of downtown—both excellent ways to soak up the seafaring ambience of this historic city.

## DOWNTOWN

Although adding to the charm in many ways, the layout of downtown defies modern logic. The streets follow footpaths laid out by European fishermen and sailors centuries ago, when towns were not planned but simply evolved for everyone's convenience. Water Street (one of North America's oldest streets) and the other main streets rise parallel to the waterfront and are intersected by roads meandering across the hillside. Historic stone staircases climb grades too steep for paved roads.

### ◖ The Rooms

One of Canada's finest cultural facilities, The Rooms (9 Bonaventure Ave., 709/757-8000; June–mid-Oct. Mon.–Sat. 10 A.M.–5 P.M. and Sun noon–5 P.M., mid-Oct.–May Tues.–Sat. 10 A.M.–5 P.M. and Wed.–Thurs. until 9 P.M.; adult $7.50, senior $5, child $4) combines the provincial museum, art gallery, and archives under one roof. Styled on the simple oceanfront "fishing rooms" where Newfoundlanders would process their catch, this complex is anything

NEWFOUNDLAND AND LABRADOR

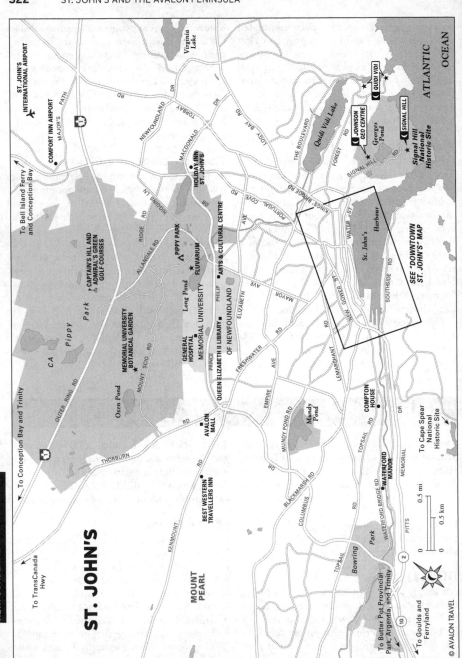

© AVALON TRAVEL

The Rooms is St. John's premier cultural attraction.

but basic. Sitting on the site of a 1750s fort, from a distance it is nothing short of spectacular to see the ultramodern "rooms" rising above the rest of the city like a mirage. The interior is no less impressive, with huge windows allowing uninterrupted views across the city and harbor. Displays in the museum component encompass the entire natural and human history of Newfoundland and Labrador, from glaciation to modern-day cultural diversity. The art gallery spreads across two floors. More than 7,000 works of art are displayed, with touring exhibits adding to the artistic mix. If you're a history buff with time to spare, include a visit to the archives, which contain more than 500,000 historic photos, plus government and shipping records, maps and atlases, family histories, and personal diaries.

### Basilica Cathedral Museum

The early Roman Catholics aimed to make an impact on the skyline of St. John's and did so in the mid-1800s with the Basilica Cathedral of St. John the Baptist (200 Military Rd., 709/754-2170; Mon.–Sat. 10 A.M.–5 P.M.; free), one block toward downtown from The Rooms. The Romanesque cathedral, built of stone and shaped like a Latin cross with twin 43-meter-high towers, is now a national historic site. In addition to the museum, guided tours point out the ornate ceilings embellished with gold leaf, numerous statues, and other features.

### Anglican Cathedral of St. John the Baptist

This Anglican cathedral (16 Church Hill, 709/726-5677; mid-June–Sept. daily 10:30 A.M.–4:30 P.M.; free) is a national historic site revered by locals (and said to be haunted by a resident ghost). English architect Sir George Gilbert Scott designed the impressive Gothic Revival edifice in Newfoundland bluestone. The cornerstone was laid in 1847, and the Great Fire of 1892 almost gutted the structure. Reconstruction within the walls started the next year. Of special interest are the carved furnishings and sculpted arches and a gold communion service presented by King William IV.

### James J. O'Mara Pharmacy Museum

Inside the splendidly restored and gleaming Apothecary Hall, the James J. O'Mara Pharmacy Museum (488 Water St., 709/753-5877; mid-June–Aug. daily 10 A.M.–5 P.M.; free) recalls a pharmacy of 1895.

### Newman Wine Vaults

In the late 1700s, wine that had been stored in St. John's was transported back to London, where it was deemed to have a much improved flavor. As a result, a number of wine vaults were constructed in the city, and cases of wine were brought across the Atlantic to mature. The last remaining of these is Newman Wine Vaults (436 Water St., 709/739-7870; June–Aug. Tues.–Sat. 10 A.M.–4:30 P.M.; free), on the west side of downtown. Ensconced in a more modern shell, the two vaults, held together by mortar from crushed seashells, are the oldest buildings in St. John's.

NEWFOUNDLAND AND LABRADOR

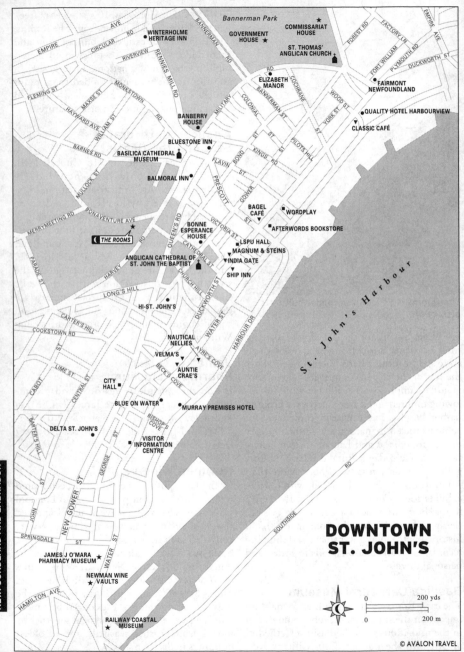

**DOWNTOWN ST. JOHN'S**

0    200 yds
0    200 m

© AVALON TRAVEL

## Railway Coastal Museum

The Newfoundland Railway was a vital link for islanders between 1898 and the last scheduled passenger service in 1969. It extended the length of the island (roughly following the modern-day TransCanada Highway), terminating in the east at what is now the Railway Coastal Museum (495 Water St. W., 709/753-5877; summer daily 10 A.M.–5 P.M., the rest of the year Tues.–Sat. 10 A.M.–5 P.M.; adult $6, senior $5, child $4). Symbolizing the grandeur of its onetime importance, the city's main railway station forms the backbone of the museum, with historic photographs and memorabilia from days gone by. It is west of the New Gower Street overpass.

## Government House

One of few structures that escaped damage in the Great Fire of 1892, Government House (Military Rd.; grounds daily dawn–dusk) is the residence of the province's lieutenant governor. The impressive 1831 building was constructed of red sandstone quarried from Signal Hill and features a moat, ceiling frescoes, and floral gardens. This, the Commissariat House, and St. Thomas's Anglican Church are on the northern edge of downtown, a steep five-block walk from the waterfront.

## Commissariat House

Now protected as a provincial historic site, the three-story Commissariat House (King's Bridge Rd., 709/729-6370; mid-May–early Oct. daily 10:30 A.M.–5:30 P.M.; adult $3) began in 1818 as a residence and office for Fort William's assistant commissary general. Over the years, it was used as the St. Thomas's Church rectory, a nursing home, and a hospital. The interior, furnished with antiques, has been restored to the style of the 1830s.

## St. Thomas's Anglican Church

The St. Thomas's Anglican Church (corner King's Bridge Rd. and Military Rd., 709/576-6632; free) is known as the Old Garrison Church. Dating to the 1830s, the city's oldest church houses a cast-iron Hanoverian coat of arms over the door, attesting to the royal lineage. Sanctuary tours are available July–August (Mon.–Sat. 9:30 A.M.–5:30 P.M.).

## ◖ SIGNAL HILL

This distinct geological feature rises high above the Narrows, at the mouth of St. John's Harbour. On a clear day, it's plainly visible from throughout town, but more importantly it offers stunning views back across the city, down the coast, and out into the Atlantic Ocean. Although Signal Hill is only a little over two kilometers from the city center, it's a steep walk, so plan on driving.

### ◖ Johnson Geo Centre

What better place for a geology museum than underground? Access to the Johnson Geo Centre (175 Signal Hill Rd., 709/724-7625; Mon.–Sat. 9:30 A.M.–5 P.M., Sun. noon–5 P.M.; adult $10.25, senior $8, child $6), almost at the top of Signal Hill, is a glass-sided elevator that descends below the rocky landscape to a cavernous room where one entire wall exposes the 550-million-year-old bedrock. Displays describe the entire geological history of the province, from the oldest rocks on earth to modern oil-and-gas exploration. Highlights include a *Titanic* room, where you can watch footage from exploration of the famous wreck.

### Signal Hill National Historic Site

In the 1700s, this hill, once known as the Lookout, served as part of a British signaling system; news of friendly or hostile ships was flagged from Cape Spear to Signal Hill, where the message was conveyed to Fort William in town. In 1762 the Battle of Signal Hill marked the Seven Years' War's final North American land battle, with England victorious and France the loser.

The hilltop is pocked with historical remnants. England's Imperial Powder Magazine stored gunpowder during the Napoleonic Wars, and the Queen's Battery—an authentic outport tucked beneath the cliff—guarded the harbor Narrows from 1833. Public hangings were held at Gibbet Hill, the slope overlooking

© ANDREW HEMPSTEAD

Cabot Tower sits on the high point of Signal Hill.

Deadman's Pond. The pond served as the port's reserve water supply in the event of a siege. The most distinctive feature is **Cabot Tower** (709/772-5367; Apr.–mid-Jan. daily 9 A.M.–5 P.M., June–Aug. daily 9 A.M.–8 P.M.; adult $4, senior $3.50, child $2), where Guglielmo Marconi received the first transatlantic wireless message.

For hiking, the **North Head Trail** peels off the hill and follows along the cliffs to Fort Chain Rock. The Cuckold's Cove Trail wends across Signal Hill's leeward side to Quidi Vidi Village.

## QUIDI VIDI

The Atlantic's watery inroads permeate the St. John's area. Aside from the city's famed harbor, another sizable pocket of the sea—**Quidi Vidi Lake**—lies nearby. Its azure-blue waters meet a boulder-bound coastline, all within the bustling city limits. Quidi Vidi Lake ("kiddie viddie" is the local pronunciation) is best known as the site of the Royal St. John's Regatta, held on the first Wednesday in August. The lake's choppy water also lures windsurfers. Locals enjoy strolls along the grassy banks. To get there, follow Water Street west under Pitts Memorial Drive and turn left onto Route 11 (Blackhead Road).

Beyond the lake is picturesque **Quidi Vidi Village.** Wander the narrow winding streets of this fishing village, and you'll never believe a provincial capital lies just over the hill.

### Quidi Vidi Battery

Quidi Vidi Battery (Cuckhold's Cove Rd., 709/729-2977; mid-May–Sept. daily 10 A.M.–5:30 P.M.; adult $3) sits high on a hill above Quidi Vidi, overlooking the lake and village. The site owes its origin to the French, who built the battery in their effort to capture St. John's in 1762. France lost, and the British took the battery and rebuilt it in 1780. The site has been restored to the War of 1812 glory years, when England fortified the battery in anticipation of a U.S. attack that never materialized. The battery is now staffed by guides dressed in period uniforms of the Royal Artillery.

## SOUTH OF DOWNTOWN
### Bowring Park

Arguably the city's prettiest park, Bowring has hosted significant guests for many tree-planting ceremonies, including a visit from Queen Elizabeth for the Cabot celebrations in 1997. Crocus and hyacinth beds make a colorful impact during spring, swans glide across the tranquil ponds in summer, and the setting is transformed into a canvas of dappled oranges and reds during autumn. Statues are everywhere, the most famous being of Peter Pan. It's a replica of the original in England's Kensington Gardens, and it serves as a memorial to Sir Edgar Bowring's godchild, who died in an offshore shipwreck.

To get there, stay south on Water Street until the road splits into Waterford Bridge and Topsail Roads; continue on Waterford Bridge Road for three kilometers to the park's entrance.

NEWFOUNDLAND AND LABRADOR

© ANDREW HEMPSTEAD

Quidi Vidi

## Cape Spear National Historic Site

Cape Spear's eminently photogenic lighthouse (off Rte. 11, 709/772-5367; mid-May–mid-Oct. daily 10 A.M.–6 P.M.; adult $4, senior $3.50, child $2) crowns a windy 75-meter-high promontory above the Atlantic Ocean. Built in 1839, the lighthouse ranks as the province's oldest extant beacon and was used until 1955, when the original lighting apparatus was moved to a more efficient building nearby. The keeper's living quarters have been restored, while the adjacent visitors center displays antiques and maritime artifacts.

Outside the lighthouse, the precipitous slopes hold the rusting remains of World War II gun batteries. Hiking trails fan out from the peak. The 10-kilometer trail to Maddox Cove starts here and winds south along the coast, through gullies, bakeapple bogs, and berry patches. If you're lucky, you'll see a family of shy foxes in the high grasses.

The cape, North America's most easterly point, lies six kilometers southeast of St. John's Harbour as the crow flies and 15 kilometers

around Route 11's coastal curve. To get there, follow Water Street to the exit for Pitts Memorial Parkway and turn left to Route 11 (Blackhead Road).

## PIPPY PARK

Civilization ends and wilderness begins at this preserve, which covers 1,343 hectares of woodlands, grasslands, and rolling hills on the steep hilltop plateau overlooking St. John's. In addition to the Fluvarium and the botanical garden, the park is laced with hiking trails and is home to two golf courses. Developed along the rim of the hill, the park fronts Confederation Parkway/Prince Philip Drive and encompasses Memorial University's campus and the government Confederation Building complex. Barrens, marshes, woodlands, ponds, and streams make for a splendid landscape. Moose, muskrat, mink, snowshoe hare, meadow voles, and common shrews roam the hilly terrain, which is studded with balsam fir, spruce, and juniper. The green-winged teal, black and pintail duck, sora rail,

NEWFOUNDLAND AND LABRADOR

American bittern, gyrfalcon, and pie-billed grebe are among the birds lured to Long Pond, the oval lake near the park's edge. Long Pond marks the start of the seven-kilometer Rennies River Trail across the city's hillside to Quidi Vidi Lake.

## Fluvarium

This eco-attraction (Nagle's Pl., 709/754-3474; June–Sept. Mon.–Fri. 9 A.M.–5 P.M., Sat.–Sun. noon–5 P.M.; adult $5.50, senior $4.50, child $3.50) overlooks Long Pond from just north of Prince Philip Drive. It's contained in a handsome eight-sided wooden building wrapped with an open porch; you enter on the second floor, a spacious room with ecological exhibits depicting Atlantic salmon and other fish species, marsh birds, and carnivorous plants. The center's pièce de résistance is down a winding stairway. Nine windows pierce the walls and provide spectators a below-water-level look at the brook and brown trout, arctic char, and salmon in Nagle's Hill Brook. It's an innovative variation on the traditional aquarium.

## Memorial University Botanical Garden

The 38-hectare Memorial University Botanical Garden (306 Mt. Scio Rd., 709/737-8590; May–Sept. daily 10 A.M.–5 P.M., Oct.–Apr. Mon.–Fri. 10 A.M.–4 P.M.; adult $5, senior $3, child $1.15) is the province's only botanical garden. Garden environments include heather beds, a cottage garden, a rock garden, and a wildflower garden. Hiking trails wind through a boreal forest and a fen, both resplendent with native flowers, shrubs, and trees. The gardens feature a medley of soft colors. Blue forget-me-not, white turtlehead and rhododendron, and pink Joe-pye-weed bloom among spirea, northern wild raisin, dogwood, and high-bush cranberry. White birch, chokecherry, trembling aspen, ash, willow, and maple surround the botanical medley. To get to the gardens, follow Allandale Road north past Prince Philip Drive and turn west on Mount Scio Road.

# WEST OF DOWNTOWN
## Bell Island

One of many islands in Conception Bay, west of St. John's, nine-kilometer-long Bell has a long history of mining. **No. 2 Mine** (709/488-2880; June–Sept. 11 A.M.–7 P.M.; adult $10, senior $8, child $3), which stopped operating in 1949, remains as one of the world's most productive submarine (underground) iron ore mines. The striking black-and-white photography of Yousuf Karsh is a highlight of the aboveground museum, while underground the main shaft has been restored and is open for inspection. Guided tours include the use of a hard hat, but you should bring your own sweater.

Newfoundlanders boast an incredible flair for artistic expression, an ability displayed by the **Bell Island murals.** Large-scale scenes painted on the sides of buildings depict the community's life and people during the ore-mining decades. Look for the half dozen murals in different locations across the tiny island's northeastern corner, mainly in and near **Wabana,** the largest settlement. One assumes the murals were painted from historical photographs, yet there's a sense of real life to each painting—from a car's black luster to the animated figures and even the clear gleam of a miner's eyes.

To get to Bell Island, follow Route 40 west to Portugal Cove, 15 kilometers from downtown. The ferry (709/895-6931) operates year-round. In summer, sailings are every 20–40 minutes 7 A.M.–11:30 P.M. The fare is $7 per vehicle and driver, plus $3.50 per additional passenger.

# Recreation

Don't let bad weather prevent you from enjoying the outdoors—the locals certainly don't. Sure, it may be foggy or raining, but in many ways this adds to the St. John's experience when you're out hiking or striding the local fairways.

## HIKING AND BIKING

The hilly streets of downtown St. John's aren't conducive to walking and biking, but if you're looking for wilderness, you don't need to travel too far from the city. A five-minute drive from downtown is **Pippy Park.** Follow Allendale Road north over the TransCanada Highway and look for the parking area beyond the golf course entrance. From this point, hiking trails loop past numerous lakes and through native forest.

Alongside the TransCanada Highway 36 kilometers south of downtown is **Butter Pot Provincial Park,** a 2,800-hectare wilderness of forests, bogs, and barrens—a taste of the interior a 30-minute drive from the city. The name Butter Pot is a local term for a rounded hill, many of which occur within the park boundary, including along Butter Pot Hill Trail, a 3.3-kilometer walk to a 300-meter-high summit. Along the way you'll see signs of ancient glacial action, including displaced boulders known as erratics, while at the summit, hikers

are rewarded with views extending north to Bell Island. This trail starts beside Site 58 of the park campground. With minimal elevation gain, the Peter's Pond Trail parallels a small lake from the day-use area; you can turn around after one kilometer or continue to Butter Pot Hill. A day pass is $5 per vehicle.

## SCUBA DIVING

Situated on Atlantic Canada's oldest ship routes, the St. John's area is incredibly rich in shipwrecks. What's more, the waters here are as clear as the Caribbean—20- to 30-meter visibility is common—and reasonably warm from summer to autumn, although a wetsuit is advisable. One of the most accessible wreck diving sites is **Lance Cove,** on Bell Island, where four iron-ore carriers were torpedoed by German U-boats during World War II. Also in Conception Bay are much older whaling boats and a number of wrecks close enough to be accessible for shore diving. Based at Conception Bay South, **Ocean Quest** (17 Stanley's Rd., 709/834-7234, www.ocean-questcharters.com) takes divers to the bay and other dive sites for a full-day boat charter rate of $190 per person inclusive of rental gear. This company also operates a dive school, a dive shop, and a resort.

# Entertainment and Events

## NIGHTLIFE

It's said St. John's has more pubs, taverns, and bars per capita than anyplace else in Atlantic Canada. Spend any time wandering through downtown after dark, and you'll probably agree. The city's international port status is partly the reason. Even better, these watering holes serve double duty as venues for music of various styles, including traditional Newfoundland, folk, Irish, country, rock, and jazz. The weekly entertainment newspaper

*Town Cryer* (www.thetowncryer.net) has entertainment listings.

A local band of note is **Great Big Sea,** which combines modern rock and traditional Newfoundland folk to create a sound and atmosphere that draws sellout crowds throughout Canada.

### Pubs

The energetic pub scene centers on a one-block stretch of George Street off Water

Street. The weekend starts late Friday evening, picks up again on Saturday afternoon, and lasts until 2 A.M. (and at some places keeps up through Sunday).

Among George Street's abundance of pubs and eating establishments, **Trapper John's** (2 George St., 709/579-9630) ranks as a city entertainment mainstay, hosting notable provincial folk groups and bands. The patrons will gladly initiate visitors to Newfoundland with a "screech-in" ceremony for free. **Green Sleeves Pub** (14 George St., 709/579-1070) doubles as a weekend hub for traditional, rock, and Irish concerts and jam sessions. **Fat Cat Blues Bar** (5 George St., 709/739-5554; Tues.–Sun. from 8 P.M.) presents concerts, open mic, blues rock, and women's jam sessions.

Escape the frat-house atmosphere of George Street by pulling up a barstool at one of the cozy pubs dotted through surrounding downtown streets. Although it doesn't look like much from the outside, **Erin's Pub** (186 Water St., 709/722-1916) is a friendly place renowned for Celtic and local artists performing nightly except Sunday. Across the road, **Nautical Nellies** (201 Water St., 709/738-1120) lives up to its name with decorations such as a scale model of the *Titanic* and cabinets filled with knotted rope. It's one of the most popular spots off George Street, so expect a crowd, especially on weekends.

The **Ship Inn** (265 Duckworth St., 709/753-3870) is a dimly lit room that has been a venue for local and provincial recording acts for years and continues to draw Newfoundland's hottest up-and-coming jazz, blues, and folk musicians. These same artists, as well as literary types, are the main customers—you just never know who might be on stage or in the audience.

In the vicinity of the Ship Inn, the **Crow's Nest** (709/753-6927; Tues.–Thurs. 4:30–7:30 P.M., Fri. noon–10 P.M., Sat. 2–8 P.M.) opened in 1942 as a retreat for naval officers, but this once-exclusive club is now open to interested visitors (dress code is "smart casual"). The old-fashioned room is a treasure trove of naval memorabilia, which includes a periscope from a German U-boat that was

## "SCREECHED IN"

Newfoundlanders dote on the codfish, and visitors are invited to pledge piscatorial loyalty to King Cod in hilarious induction ceremonies conducted on tours and in touristy restaurants. The tradition dates to the early 1900s, when a visiting U.S. naval officer followed the lead of his St. John's host by downing a glass of rum in one gulp. His reaction to swallowing the unlabeled rum was a mortified screech. And so the tradition was born, as U.S. servicemen docked in St. John's came ashore to sample the "screech."

To be "screeched in" in proper style, a visitor dons fishing garb, downs several quick shots of Screech rum, kisses a cod, joins in singing a local ditty, poses for a photograph, and receives an official certificate. It's strictly tourist nonsense, but visitors love it. Mostly due to its authentic atmosphere, **Trapper John's** (2 George St., 709/579-9630) is one of the best places to be "screeched in."

captured off St. John's during World War II. The club is on the fourth floor of an old brick warehouse between Water and Duckworth Streets; the entrance is opposite the war memorial.

## PERFORMING ARTS

The **Resource Centre for the Arts** (LSPU Hall, 3 Victoria St., 709/753-4531, www.rca.nf.ca) stages productions by the resident RCA Theatre Company and also hosts professional touring groups throughout the year. Ticket prices vary depending on the event but are always reasonable.

The **Arts and Culture Centre** (corner Allandale Rd. and Prince Philip Dr., 709/729-3900) presents a wide range of theater, music, and dance on its Main Stage, with artists and troupes from across Canada. The center is also home to the **Newfoundland Symphony Orchestra** (709/722-4441), which has a September–April season.

## FESTIVALS AND EVENTS
### Summer

The city shines as a music-festival venue. The biggest and best is early July's nine-day **Festival 500** (709/738-6013, www.festival500.com), held in odd-numbered years. Highlights include the noontime medley of harbor ship horns; citywide theater, workshops, and dance; and Newfoundland, folk, electronic, jazz, New Age, and African concerts.

St. John's shares a **Shakespeare by the Sea Festival** (709/743-7287) with Los Angeles and Sydney, Australia. The Newfoundland version takes place for three weeks in July, Friday–Sunday at 6 P.M. Expect outdoor productions of the Bard's best by the acclaimed Loyal Shakespearean Company. The venue changes annually but may be as dramatic as Cape Spear National Historic Site.

The **Signal Hill Tattoo** is a tribute to the landmark Battle of Signal Hill that ended the war between the English and French in North America. The military event is staged dramatically with military drills by foot soldiers, artillery detachments, fife and drum bands, and more. It all takes place up at Signal Hill National Historic Site early July–mid-August on Wednesday, Thursday, Saturday, and Sunday at 11 A.M. and 3 P.M.

Beginning the last Thursday in July, Prince Edward Plaza on George Street is the outdoor setting for the weeklong **George Street Festival** (www.georgestreetfestival.com), which offers performances by top entertainers.

The **Royal St. John's Regatta** (709/576-8921, www.stjohnsregatta.org) is a city tradition that dates back to 1818, making it North America's oldest organized sporting event. What began as a rowing contest has morphed into a world-class event drawing rowers from around the world. Held at Quidi Vidi Lake on the first Wednesday in August, the event draws up to 50,000 spectators and is so popular the city long ago declared the day a civic holiday.

### Winter

Most of the winter action centers on **Mile One Stadium** (50 New Gower St., 709/576-7657), where the St. John's Fog Devils hockey franchise competes a couple of levels below the National Hockey League.

# Shopping

An abundance of arts and crafts stores can be found in downtown St. John's. Aside from these, east along Duckworth Street beyond downtown is a string of interesting shops specializing in Newfoundland music, pet paraphernalia, and the like. My favorite is **Living Planet** (116 Duckworth St., 709/739-6810), which stocks souvenirs with a politically incorrect Newfoundland slant.

## ARTS AND CRAFTS

Crafts shops downtown offer every conceivable craft available, and new developments continually increase the variety. One of the best places to start is **Devon House** (59 Duckworth St., 709/753-2749), in a historic building below the Fairmont Newfoundland. An outlet for the Craft Council of Newfoundland and Labrador, it displays an excellent sampling of traditional and contemporary wares.

For designer pieces, check out retail sales outlets in the artists' studios, such as **Woof Design** (181 Water St., 709/722-7555), which specializes in mohair, woolen, and angora apparel, plus whalebone carvings and other crafts. Other shops operate as cottage-industry outlets. **Nonia Handicrafts** (286 Water St., 709/753-8062) is among the best crafts shops, carrying hand-woven apparel, weavings, parkas, jewelry, hooked mats, domestic wares, and handmade toys. The **Cod Jigger** (245 Duckworth St., 709/726-7422), a similar cooperative, is another good source for parkas, hooked mats, bone and talc carvings, quilts, knits, mittens and hats, crocheted items, and jewelry.

Other shops sell a variety of wares: Grenfell parkas from St. Anthony, books about Newfoundland, local Purity-brand candies, tinned biscuits or seafood, bottles of savory spice, pottery and porcelain, handmade copper and tin kettles, model ships, soapstone and stone carvings, fur pelts and rugs, apparel, folk art, and hand-woven silk, wool, cotton, and linen. Expect to find most of these goods at **Melendy's Kuffer Korner** (336 Water St., 709/753-8021) and the **Downhome Shoppe & Gallery** (303 Water St., 709/722-2970).

Top-notch private galleries are plentiful. **Christina Parker Gallery** (7 Plank Rd., 709/753-0580) showcases Newfoundland's avant-garde spectrum; for more traditional art, plan on visiting the **Emma Butler Gallery** (111 George St., 709/739-7111).

## OUTDOOR GEAR

**The Outfitters** (220 Water St., 709/579-4453) sells an excellent range of outdoor wear, including winter jackets. It also has canoes, kayaks, and skis, and is a clearinghouse for information about outdoor recreation around the island.

# Accommodations and Camping

While St. John's may not have a huge selection of budget accommodations, it does provide an excellent choice of historic bed-and-breakfasts that offer excellent value. A few major chains are represented downtown (and are also well-priced), while you find all the familiar chains along major arteries. As elsewhere in Atlantic Canada, demand for rooms is highest in summer, and you should make reservations far in advance. While the larger downtown properties supply parking, at smaller properties you may be expected to use metered street parking.

## DOWNTOWN
### Under $50

Ensconced in one of the city's famously photogenic pastel-colored townhouses is **HI-St. John's** (8 Gower St., 709/754-4789, wwwhihostels.ca), an affiliate of Hostelling International. Within walking distance of downtown, dorm rooms are spacious and come with a maximum of four beds. Other facilities include a well-equipped kitchen, a small backyard with a barbeque, and Wi-Fi access. Rates are $23.50 for members and $27.50 nonmembers. The double room is $60 or $64 respectively.

### $50-100

**Compton House** (26 Waterford Bridge Rd., 709/739-5789, www.comptonhouse.travel; $79–189 s, $89–199 d) once served as the mansion of C. A. Pippy, the merchant who donated St. John's local hilltop to the city for a park. The house has been grandly restored. Each of the 11 guest rooms has a private bath, and two have a whirlpool and fireplace or a full kitchen. Located south of downtown, it is a little longer walk to the harbor than from those bed-and-breakfasts in the vicinity of Military Road, but there are no hills to negotiate.

Opposite Bannerman Park, **Elizabeth Manor** (21 Military Rd., 709/753-7733 or 888/263-3768, www.elizabethmanor.nl.ca; $80–200 s or d) was built in 1894, following the Great Fire of 1892. Completely revamped in 2004, it now offers four spacious en suite guest rooms, a sundeck, and a library with art and books about the province. Rates include a full breakfast.

A restored Queen Anne–style townhouse, the **Balmoral Inn** (38 Queen's Rd., 709/754-5721 or 877/428-1055, www.balmoralhouse.com; $99–149 s or d) offers four large guest rooms, each with a fireplace, private bath, antique furnishings, TV, Internet access, and an expansive view of the harbor. Rates include a full breakfast and the use of off-street parking.

## $100-150

( **Bonne Esperance House** (20 Gower St., 709/726-3835 or 888/726-3835, www.bonneesperancehouse.ca; $135–250 s or d) combines three adjoining townhouses to create an inviting lodging in a very central location. Although the building dates to the late 1800s, the rooms are brightly decorated, and there's a tranquil garden out back. Each room has an en suite bathroom, TV, and phone.

**Waterford Manor** (185 Waterford Bridge Rd., 709/754-4139, www.waterfordmanor .nf.ca; $100–260 s or d), a beautiful Queen Anne–style mansion near Bowring Park, is furnished with antiques of the late 19th century. The seven guest rooms vary greatly in size, but all have TVs and en suite bathrooms. The Riverview Room ($140 s or d) is an excellent value.

Backing onto Bannerman Park and with a beautiful rear garden, ( **Banberry House** (116 Military Rd., 709/579-8006 or 877/579-8226, www.banberryhouse.com; $139–169 s or d) oozes style throughout. My favorite of six guest rooms is the Labrador Room, which is filled with stylish mahogany furniture (including a work desk) and has a super-comfortable bed, a four-piece bath, and garden views. Rates include a full Newfoundland breakfast.

The **Bluestone Inn** (34 Queen's Rd., 709/754-7544 or 877/754-9876, www.thebluestoneinn.com; $149–179 s or d) is a restored townhouse with a delightful street-side patio out front. The four guest rooms are comfortable and well furnished, and each has a fireplace. Rates include a full breakfast; there's also a private bar.

If you're traveling with children but want to stay downtown, **Quality Hotel-Harbourview** (2 Hill O'Chips, 709/754-7788 or 800/228-5151, www.choicehotels.ca; $140 s or d) is a good choice. It has 162 midsized rooms, a popular restaurant overlooking the harbor, free outdoor parking, and free local calls. Rooms with harbor views are $160, but check online for deals.

## $150-200

In a graciously restored 1905 Queen Anne mansion across from Bannerman Park, **Winterholme Heritage Inn** (79 Rennies Mill Rd., 709/739-7979 or 800/599-7829, www .winterholme.com; $159–229 s or d) offers 12 guest rooms, each with bold color schemes, jetted tubs, and TV/DVD combos.

Instead of a hotel with a restaurant, **Blue on Water** (319 Water St., 709/754-2583 or 877/431-2583, www.blueonwater.com; from $169 s or d) is a restaurant with seven upstairs rooms. The location is as central as it gets, and no expense has been spared in creating a luxurious sanctuary within seven guest rooms. The decor is slick and contemporary—think 400-thread-count sheets, high-speed Internet connections, and flat-screen TVs. On the downside, the nearest parking is a public lot behind the property, there is no elevator, and check-in is within the restaurant. But once you're in your room, you'll think you're paying a lot more than you really are.

Across the road from the heart of the downtown waterfront, a row of 1846 wooden warehouses has been transformed into ( **Murray Premises Hotel** (5 Becks Cove, 709/738-7773, www.murraypremiseshotel.com; $189–259 s or d). The 28 rooms fill the top two floors. Each is super-spacious and features luxurious touches such as maple furniture, heated towel racks and jetted tubs in the oversized bathrooms, and TV/DVD combos. In-room coffee, complimentary newspapers, and a choice of downstairs eateries add to the appeal.

Closer to the airport than to the waterfront, **Holiday Inn St. John's** (180 Portugal Cove Rd., 709/722-0506 or 800/933-0506, www .ichotelsgroup.com; $155 s or d) is handy to Pippy Park, Memorial University, and the Confederation Building complex. The 256 guest rooms were last revamped in 2004; other amenities include indoor and outdoor pools,

NEWFOUNDLAND AND LABRADOR

a restaurant, a lounge, a laundry, a business center, a hairdresser, and a shopping arcade. Outside of summer, check online for rooms around $100.

### Over $200

**Fairmont Newfoundland** (corner King's Bridge Rd. and Military Rd., 709/726-4980 or 800/257-7544, www.fairmont.com; from $234 s or d) has an auspicious location, on the former site of Fort William. The first Hotel Newfoundland, one of Canadian Pacific's deluxe properties, opened in 1925. After many years' service, it was demolished to make room for this handsome hotel. Opened in 1982, the hillside property has over 300 guest rooms, two restaurants, a lounge, a fitness center (with an indoor pool, table tennis, squash courts, a sauna, and a whirlpool), a shopping arcade with a hairdresser, and free parking.

**Delta St. John's** (120 New Gower St., 709/739-6404 or 800/268-1133, www.deltahotels.com; $240 s or d) is an avant-garde high-rise that offers 276 rooms and suites; restaurants and a pub; fitness facilities that include an indoor heated pool, exercise equipment, a whirlpool, a sauna, and squash courts; a shopping arcade; and free covered parking. Check the website for deals.

## AIRPORT
### $100-150

**Comfort Inn Airport** (106 Airport Rd., 709/753-3500, www.choicehotels.ca; $129–149 s or d) is conveniently located across from St. John's International Airport and features 100 rooms and suites, a restaurant and lounge, a business center, a fitness center, airport transfers, and free continental breakfast.

## CONCEPTION BAY
### $100-150

**◖ Ocean Quest Adventure Resort** (17 Stanley's Rd., Conception Bay South,

709/834-7234 or 866/623-2664, www.oceanquestcharters.com; $110 s, $130–165 d) is a purpose-built accommodation that revolves around divers and their needs, but everyone is welcome. The rooms feature clean contemporary layouts, and one has a jetted tub. The downstairs common area has a library of books, a TV where you can watch dive videos, a kitchen, and a deck with a propane barbecue. Attached to the accommodation is a dive shop and dive school with an indoor heated pool. Rates include breakfast, but many guests stay as part of a package that includes diving.

## CAMPGROUNDS

**Pippy Park Trailer Park** (Nagle's Pl., 709/737-3669, www.pippypark.com; May–Sept.; $24–34), 2.5 kilometers northwest of downtown, fills on a first-come, first-served basis. It offers more than 150 sites, most of which are private and well spaced. Amenities include a general store, a playground, and washrooms. The Fluvarium (great for children) is across the road, while trails lead from the campground to all corners of Pippy Park.

**Butter Pot Provincial Park,** along the TransCanada Highway 36 kilometers south of downtown, has a 126-site campground. The cost is $18 per night, with showers and laundry facilities provided. Each private site has a fire pit and a picnic table (firewood costs $5 per bundle). Activities include hiking and water sports such as lake swimming and canoeing (rentals available). Three playgrounds will keep the young ones occupied.

Farther out, but in a beautiful lakeside location, **◖ La Manche Provincial Park** (Rte. 10; late May–late Sept.; $14) has campsites spread around two forested loops. Although there are no showers or hookups, the facility fills every summer weekend. In addition to kayaking and fishing, campers take advantage of trails leading along La Manche River and down to an abandoned fishing village.

# Food

No one would describe the St. John's dining scene as sophisticated, but it is better—by far—than anywhere else in the province. As you might imagine, seafood features prominently on most menus. Cod is a staple, while in better restaurants you find Atlantic salmon, mussels, scallops, halibut, and lobster.

## CAFÉS AND CHEAP EATS
### Coffee and Cafés
The **☾ Bagel Café** (246 Duckworth St., 709/739-4470; daily from 8 A.M.) feels more like a restaurant than a coffeehouse. All breakfasts are under $10, including heart-smart options like poached eggs and cereal with low-fat yogurt. The rest of the day, potato bakes make a tasty treat for well under $10, or order something more substantial, like lasagna for $11.

If you're looking for good coffee in a modern city-style setting, stop by **Hava Java** (216 Water St., 709/753-5282; Mon.–Fri. 7:30 A.M.–11 P.M., Sat.–Sun. 9 A.M.–11 P.M.), which is in the heart of busy Water Street.

Walk a few blocks east and step back in time a few decades at the **Classic Café East** (73 Duckworth St., 709/579-4444), open daily 24 hours. It gets crowded with all types, who come seeking delicious lobster dinners, seafood chowder, cod tongues, and other traditional Newfoundland fare at moderate prices in a cozy atmosphere. The cheesecakes are also good.

### Delis
You'll find plenty of places to pick up do-it-yourself picnic ingredients. For a tantalizing overview of Newfoundland cuisine, head to **☾ Bidgoods** (Rte. 10, Goulds, 709/368-3125; Mon.–Sat. 9 A.M.–6 P.M.), on the south side of the city. This 50-year-old store stocks every taste sensation known to the province, including seal flipper pie, caribou, salted fish, salmon, and cod tongues and cheeks. Not much is prepackaged here, but the produce (especially west coast strawberries), berry preserves, shellfish,

smoked or pickled fish, and sweet tea biscuits make delicious picnic additions.

Back downtown, **☾ Auntie Crae's** (272 Water St., 709/754-0661; summer Tues.–Sat. 8 A.M.–7 P.M., the rest of year daily 8 A.M.–5:30 P.M.) is a deli with a difference. It stocks all the goodies you would expect to find in a Newfoundland deli as well as bakery and lunch items, in-house roasted coffee, and dry goods. Many customers pick up their order and move on to the adjacent Common Room, which is not really a restaurant but somewhere to sit down and eat lunch. Noontime entertainment draws big crowds every Tuesday.

The lower end of Freshwater Road has a concentration of bakeries and delicatessens. **Stockwood's Bakery and Delicatessen** (316 Freshwater Rd., 709/726-2083) stocks fresh sandwiches, cold plates, salads, cakes, and baking supplies and is open 24 hours a day. For a selection of fancier cakes and pastries, stop by **Manna European Bakery & Deli** (342 Freshwater Rd., 709/739-6992). Both are open Monday–Saturday from 9 A.M.

Head to the **Seafood Shop** (7 Rowan St., Churchill Sq., 709/753-1153) for fresh and packaged seafood such as cod, shrimp, halibut, mussels, and scallops.

## Pub Grub
**☾ Nautical Nellies** (201 Water St., 709/738-1120; Sun.–Thurs. 5–9 P.M.) has some of the best pub grub in town, but it doesn't serve food during the busy weekend evenings. The rest of the week, enjoy a pile of steamed mussels, crab spring rolls with jalapeño dipping sauce, pan-fried cod with a side of scrunchions (tiny pieces of fried pork fat), or British dishes like steak and kidney pie. All mains are under $15. On Thursday, a basket of mussels is just $2.

The **Ship Inn** (265 Duckworth St., 709/753-3870) is a cozy neighborhood pub best known for its live music, but you can order simple lunches (daily noon–3 P.M.) from the blackboard menu.

## RESTAURANTS
### Seafood

While seafood dominates local menus, few better restaurants specialize in it. For inexpensive fish-and-chips—with a side of gravy—head to **Ches's Snacks** (9 Freshwater Rd., 709/722-4083). Here, tender deep-fried fillets and crisp french fries (from $6.50) are served in an atmosphere of Formica and bright lights.

**Velma's** (264 Water St., 709/576-2264; daily 8 A.M.–9:30 P.M.) is an informal favorite with locals. Don't expect anything too creative. Instead, you can order just about everything deep-fried or pan-fried, including cod tongues and scallops.

Ensconced in the Murray Premises complex, the **Hungry Fisherman** (Harbour Dr., 709/726-5791; daily 8 A.M.–9:30 P.M.) goes beyond the deep fryer to offer dishes such as halibut sautéed with rum-soaked raisins. Mains range $19–31.

### Contemporary

**C** **Blue on Water** (319 Water St., 709/754-2583; daily for breakfast, lunch, and dinner) is a smallish modern space with a bright atmosphere that contrasts greatly with the historic stone buildings that surround it. At breakfast, modern cooking is combined with traditional foods in dishes such as kippered mackerel baked with cream and shallots. Lunches in the $8–15 range include gourmet sandwiches and a delicious seafood bouillabaisse. In the evening, things get serious with starters like lobster salad with warm garlic mayonnaise and mains like salmon stuffed with roasted red peppers and spinach ($26). The wine list covers all bases.

The chic industrial-style signage out front is a giveaway—**Magnum & Steins** (284 Duckworth St., 709/576-6500; Mon.–Fri. noon–2 P.M., daily 6–10 P.M.) is clearly unlike any other restaurant in the city. If you're looking for a traditional Newfoundland experience, eat elsewhere. If you're looking for creative city-style cooking and top-notch presentation, this place is a welcome break from deep-fried seafood. Starters such as brie, leek, and apple wrapped in a phyllo crust average $10 while mains range $23–34 (the beef and lamb dishes are all excellent).

### East Indian

Fine East Indian cuisine can be found at **India Gate** (286 Duckworth St., 709/753-6006; daily for lunch and dinner). The extensive menu includes tandoori dishes; prawns, lamb, beef, and chicken cooked in the masala, korma, and vindaloo styles; and a wide array of vegetarian entrées. Prices are inexpensive to moderate, portions are generous, and the atmosphere is quiet and relaxed.

### Hotel Dining

The **Cabot Club** (Cavendish Sq., 709/726-4944; daily 6–10 P.M.), the Fairmont Newfoundland's signature dining room, combines a superb view of the harbor's Narrows with an elegant menu (mains $24–35) featuring classic steak dishes such as chateaubriand, as well as local delicacies like caribou and scallops baked with a partridgeberry and molasses glaze. **BonaVista,** the hotel's more casual dining room, lures locals with buffet breakfasts and lunches, a Thursday Newfoundland buffet, and Friday-night prime rib.

The Delta St. John's **Mickey Quinn's** (120 New Gower Rd., 709/739-6404; daily 6:30 A.M.–2 P.M. and 5–9 P.M.) serves up casual cuisine with harbor views.

# Information and Services

## INFORMATION
### Tourist Information

The provincial tourism office (709/729-2830 or 800/563-6353, www.newfoundlandlab-rador.com) and **Destination St. John's** (709/739-8899 or 877/739-8899, www.desti-nationstjohns.com) are both good sources of information when planning your trip.

There's an information booth at the airport (open whenever flights are arriving) and another just beyond the ferry dock at Argentia (open for all ferry arrivals). The local **Economic Development and Tourism** department operates a downtown visitor center (348 Water St., 709/576-8106, www.stjohns.ca; year-round Mon.–Fri. 9 A.M.–4:30 P.M. with extended hours in summer daily 9 A.M.–5 P.M.).

### Libraries

The city's largest library is Memorial University of Newfoundland's **Queen Elizabeth II Library** (Westerland Rd., 709/737-7425; Mon.–Thurs. 8:30 A.M.–11:30 P.M., Fri. 8:30 A.M.–5:45 P.M., Sat. 10 A.M.–5:45 P.M., Sun. 1:30–9:30 P.M.). To get there, turn into the campus at Westerland Road off Prince Philip Drive and head for the massive building with windows tiered like steps.

### Bookstores

Books about St. John's and the province are plentiful. **Wordplay** (221 Duckworth St., 709/726-9193; Mon.–Sat. 10 A.M.–6 P.M., Sun. noon–5 P.M.) is one of the best and oldest independents, with both new and used books along with public Internet access. For secondhand and rare editions, check out **Afterwords Bookstore** (245 Duckworth St., 709/753-4690). The Canadian bookstore giant **Chapters** stocks over 100,000 titles at its St. John's megastore (70 Kenmount Rd., 709/726-0375), where you'll also find an in-house café, discounted books, and public-accessible computers to help search out specific titles and subjects. Affiliated with Chapters is **Coles** (Avalon Mall, 48 Kenmount Rd., 709/753-3394), a much smaller store with bestsellers and local-interest titles.

St. John's has no specialty travel bookstores, but **Travel Bug** (155 Water St., 709/738-8284) stocks a good range of travel guides, and **The Outfitters** (220 Water St., 709/579-4453) sells provincial field guides for all interests.

## SERVICES
### Health and Safety

Local hospitals under the jurisdiction of the Health Care Corporation of St. John's include the **General Hospital** (300 Prince Philip Dr., 709/737-6300), **Janeway Child Health Centre** (Janeway Pl., 709/778-4222), and **St. Clare's Mercy Hospital** (154 LeMarchant Rd., 709/777-5000).

The **Royal Newfoundland Constabulary** (911 or 709/729-8333) deals with police matters within city limits while the **Royal Canadian Mounted Police** (709/772-5400) protect the rest of the province.

### Post and Internet

The city has three main **post offices.** For buying stamps and mailing letters, the best bet is the office at 354 Water Street (709/758-1003; Mon.–Fri. 8 A.M.–5 P.M.).

All of the bigger hotels and most bed-and-breakfasts have in-room or wireless Internet access or business centers. Other options for checking email include the libraries or **Wordplay** (221 Duckworth St., 709/726-9193; Mon.–Sat. 10 A.M.–6 P.M., Sun. noon–5 P.M.).

NEWFOUNDLAND AND LABRADOR

# Getting There and Around

Even though St. John's sits on the far eastern edge of the North American continent, it is a transportation hub for air travel through the province and for shipping routes across the Atlantic Ocean.

## GETTING THERE
### Air

**St. John's International Airport** (www.stjohnsairport.com) is off Portugal Cove Road, a simple 15-minute drive northwest from downtown. The airport is a large modern facility, with ATMs, a currency exchange center, an information booth (open daily until the arrival of the last flight), a restaurant and lounge, a duty-free shop, a newsstand, and car-rental desks for all the major companies (Avis, Budget, Discount, Hertz, National, and Thrifty). Taxis charge a flat rate to any of the major downtown hotels: $20 for the first person, $5 per each additional person.

St. John's is served by direct **Air Canada** (709/726-7880 or 888/247-2262) flights from Halifax, Montréal, and Toronto, with connections made through these three cities from its worldwide network. **WestJet** (888/937-8538) uses Halifax as its eastern hub, from where regular connections can be made to St. John's. Local airlines include **Provincial Airlines** (709/576-3943 or 800/563-2800, www.provair.com), with flights between Halifax and St. John's plus onward flights throughout the province; **Air Labrador** (709/758-0002 or 800/563-3042, www.airlabrador.com), linking St. John's to Labrador; and **Air Saint-Pierre** (902/873-3566, www.airsaintpierre.com), with daily shuttle services to the St-Pierre and Miquelon Islands.

### Bus

Although there is no scheduled service between the ferry terminal at Argentia and St. John's, **DRL Coachlines** (709/738-8088) operates long-haul bus service just about everywhere else on the island, including along the TransCanada Highway to the distant ferry terminal at Port-aux-Basques (14 hours; $123 each way).

### Ferry

One of two ferry services to Newfoundland from North Sydney (Nova Scotia) docks at **Argentia,** a 130-kilometer drive south of the capital. Ferries are operated by **Marine Atlantic** (709/227-2431 or 800/341-7981, www.marine-atlantic.ca) two times weekly mid-June to mid-October. The trip over from the mainland takes 14 hours and costs adult $110, senior $90, child $50, and from $210 for vehicles. Dorm beds and cabins are also available.

## GETTING AROUND

Locals complain that downtown parking space is scarce. Not so, the city says, countering that there are 1,500 parking slots at the Municipal Parking Garage on Water Street, other downtown garages, and on the streets. Some 800 street spaces are metered for loonies (the $1 coin) and quarters; when the time is up, the cops are quick to ticket expired meters.

### Bus

**MetroBus** (709/570-2020) operates an extensive bus network that leads from downtown to all outer suburbs. Transfers are valid for 90 minutes of travel in one direction. The cost is adult $2.25, child $1.75 per sector.

### Taxi

Cabs wait at the airport ($28 to downtown for one person, then $6 for each additional) and also out front of major hotels like the Delta St. John's and Fairmont Newfoundland. Travel within downtown runs $5–8. Major companies include **Gullivers** (709/722-0003), **Citywide** (709/722-0003), **Jiffy** (709/722-2222), and **Co-op** (709/726-6666).

## Car Rental

All major rental-car companies are represented in St. John's, but check local restrictions, such as bans on traveling in certain parts of the island. One advantage to renting in St. John's rather than elsewhere in Newfoundland is that rentals originating in the capital usually (but not always) come with unlimited kilometers.

**Islander RV** (709/738-7368 or 888/848-2267, www.islanderrv.com) charges $184 per day for a two-person camper and from $234 for an RV that sleeps six. Per day, 150 free kilometers are included, and there's a seven-day minimum rental during summer.

## TOURS
### Sightseeing Tours

**British Island Tours** (709/738-8687; June–Sept.) operates distinctive red double-decker buses along a loop through the city, with 14 stops that include Signal Hill and Quidi Vidi. Tours depart June–September daily at 9:15 A.M. and 1:15 P.M. from the Delta St. John's and 9:30 A.M. and 1:30 P.M. from the Fairmont Newfoundland. The cost is adult $25.50, senior $23, child $15.

**McCarthy's Party** (709/579-4444) has been on the sightseeing-tour scene for decades. From June to August the company offers daily 2.5-hour guided tours to Signal Hill, the cathedrals, and other major sites.

**City & Outport Adventures** (709/754-8687, www.newfoundlandtours.com) combines city and coastal sightseeing year-round in three- or four-day packages. It also offers daily 2.5-hour tours (around $30) with pickup service from anywhere in St. John's.

### Walking Tours

One of many informal walking tours of downtown St. John's is **Boyle's Walking Tours** (709/364-6845; mid-June–mid-Sept.), led by the very prim and proper Sir Cavendish Boyle. One tour departs daily at 10 A.M. from Cavendish Square, while the Rum, Romance, and Rebellion Tour departs Thursday at 7:30 P.M. from the gazebo opposite LSPU Hall (Victoria St.). Both tours cost $10, cash only.

The **Haunted Hike** (709/685-3444; June–mid-Sept.; $5) departs Sunday–Thursday at 9:30 P.M. from the west entrance to the Anglican church at the corner of Duckworth Street and Church Hill. With the Reverend Thomas Wyckham Jarvis leading the way, you'll explore the darkened back streets learning of murders, mysteries, and ghosts. It's an experience you won't forget in a hurry.

# Avalon Peninsula

If sightseeing time is short and you must bypass the rest of Newfoundland, consider the Avalon Peninsula as a manageable stand-in. Although it is known by a single name, it is actually four peninsulas, two jutting southward and two northward. The city of St. John's sprawls across one, and that city and surrounding areas have been covered above, while highlights of the remaining three follow.

## BACCALIEU TRAIL

This route hugs the northern Avalon coastline, winding around Conception Bay to the town of Carbonear and then looping south along the east side of Trinity Bay back to the TransCanada Highway. The loop makes an ideal day trip from St. John's (around 200 kilometers), but accommodations en route may tempt you to stay longer.

## Brigus

Picturesque Brigus lies across Conception Bay from Conception Bay South, or around 50 minutes' drive via the TransCanada Highway and Route 63. The town's most famous native son, Captain Robert Bartlett, was an Arctic explorer who accompanied Robert Peary on his 1908 North Pole expedition. Bartlett's house is

# NEWFOUNDLAND'S COD INDUSTRY: A CHRONOLOGY

Newfoundland's rich cod-fishing heritage began with waters so thick with fish they could, it was said, be harvested by the bucketful. This wealth of resources engendered long-running battles between nations for fishing rights, and the battles continue to this day. The seemingly endless supply of cod resulted inevitably in overharvesting on a massive scale. Now, despite moratoriums placed on the fisheries through the 1990s, fish numbers remain low. Recent aquaculture endeavors are proving moderately successful, as are various diversification programs, and there is hope that the industry will rebound.

- **1550s:** Basque and Portuguese fleets begin fishing the Strait of Belle Isle and the Grand Banks.

- **1600s:** French and English fleets begin fishing the Grand Banks and the waters of the Avalon Peninsula.

- **1890s:** Ninety percent of Newfoundland's workforce is involved in the fishing industry.

- **1908:** The powerful Fishermen's Protective Union is established by William Coaker. (The union's power will diminish by 1932.)

- **1949:** Newfoundland joins the Canadian Confederation. As a result, it cedes exclusive fishing rights to its waters.

- **1960s:** Overharvesting by foreign trawler fleets results in depletion of cod stocks.

- **1971:** The Newfoundland Fishermen, Food and Allied Workers' Union is established and becomes the first provincial fishers union to wield effective power.

- **1986:** Aquaculture industries begin experimental cod farming and find limited success.

- **1990:** Severe decline in northern cod stocks reaches lowest levels on record.

- **1992:** A two-year moratorium on commercial cod fishing is enacted.

- **1994:** Yearly cod catch has declined by 90 percent in five years. The moratorium of 1992 is extended. Province-wide, scores of fisheries and processing plants are closed.

- **1997:** Cod farms continue to supply juvenile cod to fishery waters, an enterprise that will continue to be necessary even if wild cod stocks return to healthy numbers.

- **1999:** Cod fisheries reopen, and the fishing sector experiences its best year ever, employing 15,000 Newfoundlanders and adding over $500 million to the economy.

- **2001:** As cod numbers return to normal in some areas, factors outside Newfoundland's control affect the industry, such as poor market conditions, which forced the July closure of the shrimp fishery.

- **2005:** The Fisheries Diversification Program reaps benefits for the entire province, as the emphasis moves from cod fishing to cold-water shrimp, crabs, and shellfish.

now **Hawthorne Cottage National Historic Site** (corner South St. and Irishtown Rd., 709/528-4004; July–Aug. daily 9 A.M.–7 P.M.; adult $5, senior $4.50, child $3). Built in 1830, the cottage is a rare intact example of the *cottage orné* (decorative) style.

Numerous small town cafés dot the Baccalieu Trail, but none is more welcoming than **Country Corner** (14 Water St., 709/528-1099; daily from 10 A.M.), where a bowl of steaming cod chowder, a generous slice of pie, and a cup of tea is just $7.

## Cupids

Plantation owner John Guy established Cuper's Cove in 1610, making what is now called Cupids the oldest British settlement in Canada. At the **Cupids Cove Archaeological Site,** an ongoing dig continues to unearth the remains of Guy's plantation. Visitors are welcome to view the dig on 20-minute guided tours. These leave on demand (June–early Oct. daily 9 A.M.–4:30 P.M.) and cost adult $3, child $1. Artifacts can be seen at the **Cupids Museum** (Seaforest Dr., 709/528-3500; mid-June–mid-Oct. daily 10 A.M.–5 P.M.; adult $2, child $1).

## Harbour Grace

Once the second-largest town in Newfoundland, Harbour Grace suffered a series of setbacks when seven fires besieged the town over the span of a century. Many of its oldest buildings survived and now make up the **Harbour Grace Heritage District.** Named Havre de Grace by the French in the early 16th century, the town boasts both pirates and pilots in its heritage. **Conception Bay Museum** (Water St., 709/596-1309; June–Sept. daily 10 A.M.–5 P.M.; donation) occupies the former site of the lair of Peter Easton, a notorious pirate of the early 1600s. Three centuries later, in 1932, Harbour Grace gained notoriety when Amelia Earhart took off from the local airfield to become the first woman to fly solo across the Atlantic. The grassed runway of Harbour Grace airfield is now a national historic site.

## Grates Cove

The peninsula's northernmost village, Grates Cove retains the look and feel of Ireland perhaps more than any other Irish-settled community, thanks to the hundreds of rock walls erected as livestock and farm enclosures by early settlers.

Off the eastern end of the peninsula's tip, the **Baccalieu Island Ecological Reserve** shelters 11 species of seabirds, including Leach's storm petrels, black-legged kittiwakes, gannets, fulmars, and puffins.

## Heart's Content

The first successful transatlantic telegraph cables came ashore in 1866 at Heart's Content, 23 kilometers northwest of Carbonear. The original cables, which extended from Valentia Island on the west coast of Ireland, are still visible at the shoreline. The restored **Heart's Content Cable Station** (Rte. 80, 709/583-2160; mid-May–early Oct. daily 10 A.M.–5:30 P.M.; adult $3, child $1) displays some of the original equipment.

## Dildo

Best known for its risqué name (thought to have been bestowed by Captain Cook in reference to a phallic-shaped offshore island), Dildo lies at the head of Trinity Bay, 12 kilometers north of the TransCanada Highway. The history of the 19th-century codfish hatchery on Dildo Island—the first commercial hatchery in Canada—is depicted at the **Dildo and Area Interpretation Centre** (Rte. 80, 709/582-2687; June–Sept. daily 10 A.M.–6 P.M.; adult $2, child $1), along with a display of Dorset Inuit harpoon tips estimated to be 1,700 years old. Out front is a replica of an 8.5-meter-long squid pulled from local waters.

High above Trinity Bay, **◖ Inn by the Bay** (78 Front Rd., 709/582-3170 or 888/339-7829, www.innbythebaydildo.com; May–late Dec.; $99–199 s or d) stacks up as equal to the best bed-and-breakfasts in St. John's in all regards—with sweeping water views as a free extra. No stone has been left unturned in transforming this 1888 home into an eight-room inn, right down to super-comfortable beds topped with feather-filled duvets and striking antiques that fill the Veranda Sunroom. Rates include a full breakfast and afternoon tea; dinner is available for an extra $25 per person.

# ST. JOHN'S TO FERRYLAND

From downtown St. John's, it's a little over 70 kilometers to Ferryland, the ideal turnaround point for a day trip from the capital—except that there are a couple of stops en route worth as much time as you can afford.

## ◖ Witless Bay Ecological Reserve

Newfoundland's seabird spectacle spreads across three offshore islands near Witless Bay, 30 kilometers south of St. John's. Overwhelming displays of more than a million pairs of Atlantic puffins, Leach's storm petrels, murres, black-legged kittiwakes, herring gulls, Atlantic razorbills, black guillemots, and black-backed and herring gulls are the attraction here. The season spans May–August and peaks from mid-June to mid-July. Whale numbers in local waters have increased dramatically in the last two decades, and this is mirrored in the number of operators running whale-watching trips. Between May and September, you are most likely to see humpbacks, but killer, fin, and minke whales are also present throughout the reserve. Seeing icebergs is also a possibility.

The closest tour operator to St. John's is **O'Brien's** (709/753-4850 or 877/639-4253), which is based at Bay Bulls, 31 kilometers south. It is a well-organized operation, complete with a choice of vessels and an onshore gift shop and restaurant. The cost is $60 per person for trips aboard the covered vessel and $70 per person in rigid-hulled Zodiacs, including pickups at any St. John's lodging. The former is a more leisurely trip, with live Newfoundland music, while the latter gets to the whales quicker. The village of Bauline East, 15 kilometers south of Bay Bulls, is a lot closer to the birds and whales, meaning less time spent reaching the reserve. Here, **Colbert's** (709/334-3773) departs regularly from the local wharf on one- to two-hour trips for around $40 per person. You can make reservations, but during quieter times, boats leave on demand.

## La Manche Provincial Park

This park was established in the 1960s to protect a scenic valley 53 kilometers south of St. John's along Route 10. The valley comes to an abrupt end at a cove surrounded by high cliffs, and here lies the most interesting aspect of the park. In 1840 a small village developed at the head of the cove, complete with a school, general store, and wooden flakes for drying fish. In 1966 a wild winter storm destroyed most of the settlement. The government resettled the residents, and today concrete foundations and a reconstructed suspension bridge are all that remains. To get there, drive down the fire

road beyond the park campground; from the gate it's 1.5 kilometers to the cove (allow one hour for the round-trip). The campground (late May–late Sept.; $14) has 69 campsites spread around two loops. There are no showers or hookups.

## FERRYLAND

This east coast port, 72 kilometers south of St. John's, is one of Canada's oldest fishing villages, and the site of the colony founded by Sir George Calvert in 1621. To him, the region was akin to King Arthur's heavenly paradise, a haven for the beleaguered Roman Catholics from England. Or so he thought. Once settled at Ferryland, Calvert's colony endured diminishing supplies and harsh winters. His wife and son and a number of other colonists headed south to Maryland, and Calvert followed, leaving the plantation and the name of Avalon. Today, Ferryland is one of the most attractive communities on the Avalon Peninsula, but an archaeological dig in the heart of the community draws most visitors.

### ◖ Colony of Avalon

An ongoing archaeological dig and a sparkling interpretive center combine to make the drive from St. John's worthwhile. The **Colony of Avalon Interpretation Centre** (709/432-3200; mid-May–early Oct. daily 9 A.M.–5 P.M., July–Aug. daily 9 A.M.–7 P.M.; adult $5, child $2.50) is a big two-story building where display panels tell the story of Ferryland's long history, with the help of hundreds of artifacts used by the original settlers. Upstairs is a laboratory where you can watch archaeologists at work documenting the finds. The herb garden out front replicates one from the era of the original Colony of Avalon.

From the interpretive center, it's a short walk through the modern-day village to the dig site, where you can watch archaeologists at work weekdays mid-June to mid-October. Admission to the interpretive center includes a 90-minute guided walk around the site, where you can see the remnants of a cobblestone street and the site of Calvert's mansion.

## ℂ Shamrock Festival

The two-day Shamrock Festival (709/432-2052, www.ssfac.com) crowds the town on the last full weekend in July. Thousands of music fans gather within a roped-off area in the heart of the village (along with a few hundred on a distant hillside) to listen to some of Newfoundland's top musicians. The atmosphere is both welcoming and unforgettable—you'll find yourself surrounded by the lilt of Irish accents, the smells of an outdoor fair mixed with fresh ocean air, and the sounds of foot-stomping Celtic music. A plastic cup of Quidi Vidi beer rounds out the experience.

### Food

Ferryland doesn't have a great deal of visitor services, but as most visitors are day trippers from the capital, this isn't a problem.

Originally a fish plant, **Colony Café** (Rte. 10, 709/432-3030; May–Sept. 11 A.M.–8 P.M.) sits in the heart of the village, just steps from the dig site. It offers dependable cooking at reasonable prices. Traditional meals such as cod tongues with scrunchions are mostly under $10 at lunch and $10–16 in the evening.

Earn you lunch by walking up to the headland through town to reach ℂ **Lighthouse Picnics** (709/363-7456; mid-June–early Sept. daily 11:30 A.M.–6 P.M.), which operates out of the 1870 red-and-white lighthouse. Order food as simple as daily-baked muffins, or a full picnic lunch of gourmet cheeses, fish cakes, and strawberry shortcake. Picnic baskets—along with blankets—are supplied.

## CONTINUING ALONG THE IRISH LOOP

From Ferryland, Route 10 continues south for 58 kilometers then heads west and north as Route 90 to St. Catherines. From this point, you can head south to Cape St. Mary's or north past Salmonier Nature Park back to the TransCanada Highway. While almost 50 percent of Newfoundlanders are of Irish descent, the strong accents and Celtic traditions are more prevalent here than elsewhere in the province.

## Mistaken Point Ecological Reserve

At the southern end of the Avalon Peninsula, Mistaken Point Ecological Reserve lies alongside a remote coastline. To explore the area, turn off Route 10 at Portugal Cove South and follow the unmarked gravel road 16 kilometers to Long Beach, where the reserve's gently rolling headland stretches to the sea. Bring a warm jacket to fend off the strong winds, and be ready for thick fog banks from June to mid-July. Hikers enjoy the trails that meander across the reserve, and photographers relish the offshore boulders and turbulent surf. The rocks at the ecological reserve, acclaimed as one of Canada's most important fossil sites, contain impressions of 20 different species of multicelled marine creatures that lived 620 million years ago.

## Salmonier Nature Park

The facility, on Route 90 halfway between the TransCanada Highway and St. Catherines (709/229-7189; June–Aug. daily 10 A.M.–6 P.M., Sept. daily 10 A.M.–4 P.M.; free) is well worth searching out. A two-kilometer boardwalk and wood-chip trail runs through a sample forest and across bogs, which back up to the Avalon Wilderness Reserve. Moose, caribou, lynx, bald eagles, snowy owls, otters, beavers, mink, and other indigenous species are exhibited in natural-habitat enclosures.

## CAPE SHORE

The Cape Shore juts into Placentia Bay west of the main body of the Avalon Peninsula. It's 215 kilometers from the TransCanada Highway, south through Salmonier to St. Bride's, and back to the TransCanada Highway 33 kilometers west of the starting point. The highlight of the region is the bird colony at Cape St. Mary's, but if you're arriving by ferry from North Sydney (Nova Scotia), you'll dock at Argentia, along the western side of the Cape Shore.

### Argentia

Argentia, 8 kilometers north of Placentia and 130 kilometers south of St. John's via Route

© ANDREW HEMPSTEAD

If your Newfoundland travels take you far from the main roads, you may come across a deserted "outport." Many of these remote coastal villages have been abandoned over the last few decades, with residents leaving behind everything.

100 and the TransCanada Highway, is the arrival point for ferries from Sydney, Nova Scotia. Formerly a U.S. naval base, the bay is now dominated by the ferry terminal, but trails lead to lookouts, abandoned bunkers, and good vantage points for watching local bird life.

**Marine Atlantic** (709/227-2431 or 800/341-7981, www.marine-atlantic.ca) arrives at Argentia two times weekly during a mid-June to mid-October sailing season. One-way fares for the 14-hour sailing from North Sydney (Nova Scotia) are adult $110, senior $90, child $50, and from $210 for vehicles. Beyond the ferry terminal is a provincial **Visitor Information Centre** (709/227-5272) that opens in conjunction with ferry arrivals. From Argentia, drive south through Placentia to reach Cape St. Mary's or head northwest along Route 100 to the TransCanada Highway,

which leads into downtown St. John's (allow 90 minutes from Argentia).

## Placentia

France chose the magnificent coastal forest area overlooking Placentia Bay for its early island capital, Plaisance, and colonists and soldiers settled here in 1662. The early military fortification crowned a high hill overlooking the port at what is now Jerseyside. The French launched assaults on St. John's from Le Gaillardin, the first small fort of 1692, and then from Fort Royal, the massive stone fortress built the following year. England gained possession of the settlement in 1713 and renamed it Placentia. The hill on which the fortress stands became known as Castle Hill. Exhibits at the visitor center of **Castle Hill National Historic Site** (709/227-2401; mid-May–mid-Oct. daily 9 A.M.–6 P.M.; adult $4, senior $3.50, child $2) document French and English history at Placentia. Guided tours are offered in summer. Picnic tables are available, and trails run along the peak's fortifications and the bay's stone beach.

## St. Bride's

The closest accommodation to Cape St. Mary's is **Bird Island Resort** (Rte. 100, 709/337-2450 or 888/337-2450, www.birdislandresort .com; $75–120 s or d), in St. Bride's, 20 kilometers north. Overlooking Placentia Bay, the resort comprises five motel rooms, 15 kitchen-equipped cottages, lawn games, a convenience store, and a launderette.

## ◖ Cape St. Mary's Ecological Reserve

This seabird reserve lies at the Cape Shore's southern tip, 16 kilometers down an unpaved road off Route 100. If you're traveling down from St. John's, allow at least three hours; from the ferry terminal at Argentia, head south for 75 kilometers (allow at least an hour). At the end of the road is an interpretive center (709/277-1666; mid-May–early Oct. daily 9 A.M.–5 P.M.; adult $7 includes a guided hike). From this point, a one-kilometer trail leads across the steeply banked headland to North America's most accessible bird sanctuary. You'll hear the birds long before they come into view. And then all of a sudden, Bird Rock emerges in front of you—a 60-meter-high sea stack jammed with some 60,000 seabirds. The rocky pyramid seems to come alive with fluttering, soaring birds, whose noisy calls drift out to sea on the breezes. Expect to see northern gannets in one of North America's largest colonies (11,000 nesting pairs), common and thick-billed murres, and black-legged kittiwakes, along with some razorbills, black guillemots, great black-backed gulls, and herring gulls. **Warning:** The trail is often slippery and comes very close to precipitous cliffs, so be *very* careful. Also, be prepared for bad weather by dressing warmly and in layers.

# CENTRAL AND WESTERN NEWFOUNDLAND

Visualize the island of Newfoundland as not one island but two, similarly shaped but different in size—a mammoth main island and a smaller one. This chapter covers the former—everything west of the Avalon Peninsula. The "two islands" are linked by an isthmus that begins an hour's drive west from St. John's. Beyond the turnoff to the delightfully named village of Come by Chance, the TransCanada Highway enters the meaty part of the island. Think of this highway as a long Main Street. The horseshoe-shaped route edges the interior and connects the Avalon Peninsula with Channel-Port-aux-Basques—a 905-kilometer journey. Well-marked side roads split off the main highway and whisk drivers onto the peninsulas. Aside from the Burin Peninsula's efficient Route 210 and the Northern Peninsula's relatively uncomplicated Route 430, the other side roads to the peninsulas and coastlines meander interminably.

The appeal of raw wilderness aside, this vast part of Newfoundland caters to numerous interests. Majestic icebergs wander into fjords and coves on the northern coastlines. All along the seacoasts, photogenic lighthouses perch atop precipitous cliffs overlooking the surf. Sightseers line up for boat tours led by knowledgeable skippers or academically trained guides, whose vessels nose among whales, seals, and icebergs. If you're interested in a quick trip to France, Fortune on the Burin Peninsula lies a two-hour boat ride from St-Pierre, the capital of France's archipelago province of St-Pierre and Miquelon. The ancient world heaved and formed richly diverse landscapes at Gros Morne

# HIGHLIGHTS

**◖ Trinity:** Step back in time at this quintessential Newfoundland village with brightly painted, saltbox-style houses lining its narrow lanes (page 352).

**◖ Iceberg-Viewing:** You can see icebergs from various points along the northern Newfoundland coast, but one of the most reliable spots is Twillingate (page 357).

**◖ Marble Mountain:** If, for some strange reason, you find yourself in Newfoundland during the winter, make your way to this small resort with a big-time reputation for steep slopes and deep snow (page 362).

**◖ Tablelands:** This geological phenomenon is too complicated to describe in a single sentence – but you'll be lost for words scrambling through this moonlike terrain anyway (page 369).

**◖ Boat Tours in Gros Morne National Park:** Take to Western Brook Pond in Gros Morne National Park for neck-straining views of an ancient glacially carved fjord (page 370).

**◖ Port au Choix National Historic Site:** Watch history uncovered at Port au Choix, which has been inhabited by humans for over 4,500 years (page 374).

**◖ Thrombolites of Flowers Cove:** Never heard of thrombolites? Most people haven't. But don't blink – even though they occur in only two places on earth, they're not signposted as you drive north along the Viking Trail (page 376).

**◖ L'Anse aux Meadows:** Follow in the

footsteps of the Vikings by exploring the tip of the Northern Peninsula (page 378).

**◖ Burnt Cape Ecological Reserve:** Scenic in a wild and rugged Newfoundland kind of way, this remote limestone outcrop is home to more rare and endangered species of plants than anywhere else in Atlantic Canada (page 380).

LOOK FOR ◖ TO FIND RECOMMENDED SIGHTS, ACTIVITIES, DINING, AND LODGING.

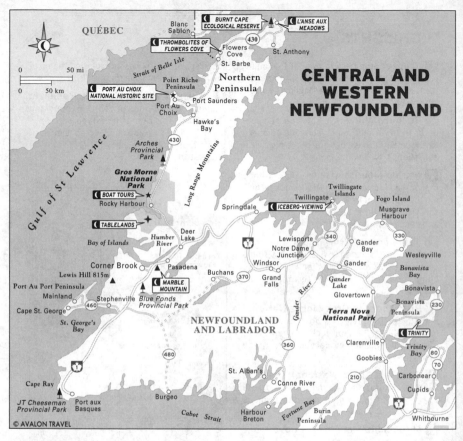

National Park. A millennium ago, the Vikings arrived and established a coastal camp (North America's first European settlement), now re-created at L'Anse aux Meadows National Historic Site.

## PLANNING YOUR TIME

While the previous chapter covered a small corner of the province, distances in this chapter will prove to be important when planning how and where to spend your time. For example, from St. John's, it's 640 kilometers to Deer Lake, 905 kilometers to the ferry terminal at Port-aux-Basques, and almost 1,100 kilometers to St. Anthony at the tip of the Northern Peninsula.

The time you spend in the central and western regions of Newfoundland obviously ties in with your travels to St. John's and the Avalon Peninsula. Traveling to the Bonavista Peninsula and villages like **Trinity** can be a two-day trip from the capital, but travel any farther west and you're committed to driving clear across the island. If you're catching the ferry from Port-aux-Basques, allow at least five days to get there from the capital. This would allow a night at Trinity, a detour from the TransCanada Highway to go **iceberg-viewing** at Twillingate, and a couple of days exploring **Gros Morne National Park,** where highlights include hiking through the **Tablelands** and taking a **boat tour on Western Brook Pond.**

What this five-day suggestion doesn't take into consideration is the **Northern Peninsula,** which is one of my favorite places in all of Canada. It's 470 amazing kilometers from Deer Lake to the tip of the peninsula. With time spent exploring the region's beautiful coastline, as well as stops at **Port au Choix National Historic Site,** the **thrombolites of Flowers Cove, L'Anse aux Meadows,** and **Burnt Cape Ecological Reserve,** add at least four days to your cross-province schedule from St. John's to Port-aux-Basques. If you're returning a rental vehicle to St. John's, give the stretch of highway south from Deer Lake a miss, but still add two days to the total trip. By flying in and out of Deer Lake, you can concentrate your time in Gros Morne National Park and the Northern Peninsula—an ideal scenario for outdoors lovers.

If you happen to be visiting Atlantic Canada in winter—maybe for a conference in Halifax—and are a keen skier or snowboarder, you may want to consider adding **Marble Mountain** to your itinerary. Book flights to Deer Lake, and plan on schussing down the slopes of Atlantic Canada's biggest and steepest ski resort.

# Burin Peninsula and Vicinity

The 200-kilometer-long Burin Peninsula angles like a kicking boot off Newfoundland's southeastern coastline. The peninsula's interior is a primeval, barren moonscape—if the moon held water, that is—for every hollow and depression in these barrens is filled with bogs, marshes, and ponds. But the coastline rims the edge of the Grand Banks, historically one of the most fertile fishing regions in North America. Along the shore are scattered fishing villages and several burgeoning towns. Marystown, one of the fastest-growing towns in the province, is supported by one of the largest fish-processing plants in eastern Canada, and its shipyard supplies vessels to the booming North Atlantic oil industry. St. Lawrence is the exception to the region; as Canada's only producer of fluorspar, it has relied on mining as much as on marine-related industries. For the most part, however, fishing has been the mainstay of the peninsula's communities since the 1500s.

## BOAT HARBOUR

A cottage industry here produces hand-hooked scenic mats made of reused fabric scraps. The mats and other homemade wares are sold at reasonable prices at the **Placentia West Craft Shop** (Rte. 210, 709/443-2312; summer daily 8:30 A.M.–6 P.M.), about one kilometer south of the Boat Harbour intersection.

## BURIN

Near the "heel" of the boot-shaped peninsula, Burin, settled in the early 1700s, lies in the lee of offshore islands. The islands generally protect the town from the open Atlantic, though they weren't enough to stop a destructive tidal wave in 1929. The islands also were a refuge for pirates, who could escape their pursuers among the dangerous channels. During his mapping expeditions of the Newfoundland coast in the 1760s, Captain James Cook used Burin as a seasonal headquarters. A high hill above the town, where watch was kept for smugglers and illegal fishing, still bears his name—Cook's Lookout.

In early July, the **Festival of Folk Song and Dance** (709/891-1546) kicks off three days of Irish-inspired song and dance, children's games, seafood meals, and crafts shows and sales. The festival ranks among Newfoundland's most popular heritage events.

A friendly accommodation is the **Wheelhouse Inn** (204 Main St., 709/891-2000 or 877/891-3810, www.wheelhouseinn.com; $79–89 s or d). The three guest rooms are spacious and modern, each with a private bathroom that holds a shower/tub combo, a phone with modem connection, and a TV. Other amenities include a lounge with a fireplace and a recreation room anchored with a pool table. Rates include a cooked breakfast.

NEWFOUNDLAND AND LABRADOR

## GRAND BANK

Grand Bank, on the "toe" of the Burin boot, is the best known of the peninsula's towns. Settled in the 1650s by the French and taken over by the British in the early 1700s, Grand Bank (pop. 2,600) has always been associated with the rich fishing grounds of the same name, the Grand Banks to the south and west of Newfoundland.

The **Heritage Walk** visits the province's largest number of Queen Anne–style homes outside of St. John's. The historic district's architectural treasures include the 1905 **Masonic Lodge,** the 1917 **Thorndyke House** (with its Masonic symbolism integrated into the interior design), and the **George C. Harris House** (16 Water St., 709/832-1574). The latter is a 1908 Queen Anne building housing the town's museum. Complementing the Heritage Walk is the Nature Trail, leading to a lookout and salmon spawning beds, and the Marine Trail, which closely follows the shoreline of Fortune Bay to the **Mariners' Memorial.**

The **Provincial Seamen's Museum** (54 Marine Dr., 709/832-0917; May–mid-Oct. daily 9:30 A.M.–4:30 P.M.; free) is difficult to miss. Styled as an angular white sailing ship, the museum has exhibits on the Grand Banks fisheries and maritime history, with photographs, ship models, and other artifacts.

## ST-PIERRE AND MIQUELON

Centuries of fierce British and French battles ended in the mid-1700s with Britain's dominance firmly stamped across eastern Canada—*except* on St-Pierre and Miquelon, a trio of islands 25 kilometers south of the Newfoundland mainland. Today, this geopolitical oddity is not part of Atlantic Canada but rather a *département* of France and the last toehold of France's once-vast holdings in North America.

St-Pierre and Miquelon is French in all regards. Unlike traveling to French regions of Canada, there is a lot more than a foreign language to deal with. Canadians require photo identification such as a driver's license or passport. Entry for all other nationalities mirrors entry requirements for France; i.e. a passport is required for U.S. citizens.

Legal tender is the euro (€), but most businesses accept U.S. and Canadian dollars at fair bank rates. To make an approximate conversion yourself, multiply euros by 1.4 to get the price in Canadian or U.S. dollars. For example, a hotel room quoted at €100 will cost around US$140 or C$140.

Electrical current throughout St-Pierre and Miquelon is 220 volts, although the bigger hotels have converters.

The islands even have their own time zone— 30 minutes ahead of Newfoundland time.

### Sights

St-Pierre and Miquelon consists of three islands, with a combined land area of about 242 square kilometers. Tiny St-Pierre is the name of the smallest island, as well as a bustling town (pop. 6,300). The topography of this triangular island includes hills, bogs, and ponds in the north, and lowlands in the south. The larger islands are Miquelon, which is home to a village of the same name (pop. 600), and uninhabited Petite Miquelon (also called Langlade). These two islands are joined by a sand-dune isthmus.

The capital, St-Pierre, is the most popular destination. It dates to the early 1600s, when French fishermen, mainly from Brittany, worked offshore. The port's mood and appearance are pervasively French, with bistros, cafés, bars, brasseries, wrought-iron balconies, and an abundance of Gallic pride. St-Pierre borders a sheltered harbor filled with colorful fishing boats and backed by narrow lanes that radiate uphill from the harbor. The cemetery, two blocks inland from rue du 11 Novembre, has an interesting arrangement of aboveground graves, similar to those in New Orleans. The **St-Pierre Museum** (15 rue Docteur Dunan), open by chance, documents the islands' history.

One of the islands' greatest attractions, of course, is the low duty rates on French wines and other goods. Visitors may bring back $200 worth of duty-free purchases after a 48-hour visit. You'll find shops with French wines, perfumes, and jewelry.

## Accommodations

Because the number of guest rooms is limited, make all lodging arrangements before arriving. The least expensive way to do this is as part of a package booked through **St. Pierre Tours** (709/832-0429). Starting from $180 per person per night (from $60 for extra nights), packages include bus shuttle from St. John's, the Fortune-to-St-Pierre ferry, and lodgings.

Among the dozen small hotels, pensions, and bed-and-breakfasts, the largest lodging is the 42-room **l'Hôtel Robert** (14 rue du 11 Novembre, 508/41-24-19), within walking distance of the ferry wharf. Having hosted the American gangster Al Capone in the 1920s, this red-brick lodging oozes historic charm. Rates of €90 s or d include breakfast.

**Hôtel Île de France** (6 rue Maître Georges Lefèvre, 508/41-03-50, www.hoteliledefrance .net; €95 s, €105 d) has stylish rooms with modern furnishings and Wi-Fi access. The hotel has a restaurant and a lounge with live entertainment on weekends.

## Food

Make your way through the streets of St-Pierre and it's difficult not to be tempted by the sweet smells coming from the many patisseries and cafés. One of the best choices for a casual meal is **Le Feu de Braise** (14 rue Albert Briand, 508/41-91-60), a bright bistro open daily for lunch and dinner.

A step up in price, but also a little more formal and with well-presented dishes, is **Le Cabestan** (1 bis rue Marcel Bonin, 508/41-21-00; daily from 6 P.M.), where *Zarzuela de poissons,* a delicious fish-filled bouillabaisse, costs €22. Choosing dessert is a cinch—the crème brûlée with pistachios is to die for.

## Information

Once on the island, the best source of information is the **St-Pierre & Miquelon Tourist Office** (rue Antoine Soucy, 508/41-02-00, www.st-pierre-et-miquelon.info). The website has links to island accommodations.

## Getting There

**Air Saint Pierre** (902/873-3566, www .airsaintpierre.com) flies year-round between St-Pierre and St. John's for $280 round-trip. The airline also flies into St-Pierre from Halifax, Sydney (Nova Scotia), and Montréal.

The *Atlantic Jet* (709/832-2006 or 800/563-2006, www.spmexpress.net) is a high-speed passenger ferry that operates between Fortune, on the Burin Peninsula, to St-Pierre once daily in July and August and on Friday and Sunday April–June and in September. The round-trip fare is adult C$99, child C$47. The *Atlantic Jet* also departs St-Pierre Tuesday, Friday, and Sunday at 8 A.M. for Miquelon. The return trip departs Miquelon at 7 P.M.; €22 roundtrip.

# Bonavista Peninsula

The Bonavista Peninsula rises off the eastern coastline as a broad, bent finger covered with verdant woods, farmlands, and rolling hills. Paved Route 230 runs along the peninsula's length, from the TransCanada to the town of Bonavista at the tip; Route 235 returns to Highway 1 along the peninsula's west side.

## CLARENVILLE

Founded in 1890, Clarenville, along the TransCanada Highway 190 kilometers from St. John's, serves as the gateway to the Bonavista Peninsula. The town is relatively new compared to the rest of Newfoundland and offers few reasons to stop other than to rest your head for the night.

Along the TransCanada Highway are two larger motels. From St. John's, the first of these is the **Clarenville Inn** (134 TransCanada Hwy., 709/466-7911 or 877/466-7911, www.clarenvilleinn.ca; $85 s, $95 d), which fronts the highway with 64 rooms, a steakhouse, a lounge and patio bar, and an outdoor heated pool. In town itself, the **Rest Land Motel** (Memorial Dr., 709/466-7636; from $75 s or d) has a mix of midsized motel rooms and kitchen-equipped units. On the site is a restaurant and pub, and across the road is a shopping mall.

## **◖ TRINITY**

Just three years after John Cabot bumped into Newfoundland, Portugal commissioned mariners Gaspar and Miguel Côrte-Real to search for a passage to China. That mission failed, but Gaspar accidentally sailed into Trinity Bay on Trinity Sunday in 1501. In 1558, merchants from England's West Country founded a settlement on the same site, making Trinity even older than St. Augustine, Florida.

The attractive village (pop. 500) has changed little since the late 1800s, much to the delight of moviemakers who spent the spring of 2001 in town filming *The Shipping News*. White picket fences, small gardens, and historic homes are everywhere. The best photo

© ANDREW HEMPSTEAD

**a church in historic Trinity, one of the most charming communities in all of Atlantic Canada**

vantage point of Trinity is from the Route 239 coastal spur, the narrow road also known as Courthouse Road. The road peels across the headlands, turns a quick corner, and suddenly overlooks the seaport. Ease into the turn so you can savor the view. (To get your photograph, park your car in the village and walk back up the road.) Once down in the village proper, park your car and explore on foot.

### Sights

The **Trinity Interpretation Centre** (Rte. 239, 709/729-0592), in a handsomely restored building, has historical exhibits about the village. **Lester-Garland Premises** (West St., 709/464-2042; June–Oct. daily 10 A.M.–5:30 P.M.) is a restored 1820s general store. Emma Hiscock and her two daughters lived in the restored mustard-and-green **Hiscock House** (late June–early Sept. daily

10 A.M.–5:30 P.M.), a block inland from the government wharf. They operated a forge, retail store, and telegraph office in the saltbox-style house in the 1800s. These three attractions are operated by the province; combined admission is adult $4, child $2.

The following other historic buildings scattered through the village are looked after by the Trinity Historical Society (709/464-3599). They are open similar hours, but admission is with a different pass (adult $2.50, child $1). **Lester Garland House** has been restored to its 1820s appearance and now houses a museum. The **Green Family Forge** (Church Rd.), in a restored 1895 building, is a blacksmith museum displaying more than 1,500 tools, products, and other artifacts of the blacksmith trade. Also on Church Road is an 1880 saltbox-style house that now serves as the **Trinity Historical Society Museum,** displaying more than 2,000 fishing, mercantile, medical, and fire-fighting artifacts. All of these historic properties/museums are open mid-June to mid-September and charge $3 adult, $5 family.

### Entertainment and Events

The summer solstice kicks off Rising Tide Theatre's **Summer in the Bight** (709/464-3232), presenting original musical and dramatic productions written and performed by some of Newfoundland's best writers and actors. The theater is a re-created fishing shed on Green's Point, at the eastern side of the village. Performances are scheduled 2–3 times a week and cost $16 ($31 for the dinner theater).

### Accommodations and Food

Right on the water, the ( Artisan Inn (High St., 709/464-3377 or 877/464-7700, www .artisaninntrinity.com; May–Oct.; $115–135 s or d) is set up as a retreat for artists—if views from the oceanfront studio don't inspire you, nothing will—but everyone is welcome. It offers two en suite rooms and a kitchen-equipped suite. The adjacent Campbell House holds an additional three guest rooms. Rates include breakfast, and dinner is available with advance

notice. Check the website for art and photography workshops.

The **Village Inn** (Taverner's Path, 709/464-3269) is open in summer for dinner. You could start with pan-fried capelin (arctic salmon), then try fish and brewis (salted cod topped with crispy fried chunks of pork) as a main. Order Figgy Duff (steamed pudding) for dessert and you have a traditional three-course meal for under $35.

## PORT UNION

The only town in Canada to have been established by a labor union, Port Union lies 32 kilometers past Trinity. The oldest part of town is across the bay from the fish-processing plant. Turn right as you enter the village and you'll soon find yourself in Port Union South, passing through a narrow street of boarded-up company warehouses. Beyond these is **Port Union Historical Museum** (Main St., 709/469-2159; mid-June–Aug. daily 11 A.M.–5 P.M.; free), housed in a waterfront railway station. Once you've read up on the town's history, backtrack and take a left turn through a narrow rock cleft to Bungalow Hill.

## BONAVISTA

Fifty kilometers from Trinity up Route 230, Bonavista (pop. 5,000) is a surprisingly large town that sprawls across the far reaches of the Bonavista Peninsula. The town began in the 1600s as a French fishing port, but many believe **Cape Bonavista,** six kilometers north of town, was the first landfall of Giovanni Caboto (better known as John Cabot), who visited the region in 1497.

### Sights

Along the harbor, **Ryan Premises** (corner Ryan's Hill and Old Catalina Rd., 709/468-1600; mid-May–mid-Oct. daily 10 A.M.–6 P.M.; adult $4, senior $3.50, child $2) was where merchant James Ryan established his salt-fish enterprise in the mid-1800s. The site's collection of white clapboard buildings includes a fish store and a re-created retail shop. Across the road is the original manager's residence. All buildings are filled with exhibits and artifacts of the era. In the salt shed, local crafters demonstrate such skills as furniture making; their goods can be purchased in the retail shop.

Signposted through town, the 1871 **Mockbeggar Plantation** (Mockbeggar Rd., 709/468-7300; June–Oct. daily 10 A.M.–5:30 P.M.; adult $3, child $1.50) is a whitewashed waterfront building surrounded by a white picket fence. It has been a residence, carpenter's shop, and fish store.

Beyond Mockbeggar Plantation, the photogenic 1843 **Cape Bonavista Lighthouse** (Rte. 230, 709/468-7444; early June–early Oct. daily 10:30 A.M.–5:30 P.M.; free) crowns a steep and rocky headland. The keeper's quarters inside the red-and-white-striped tower have been restored to the 1870 period. A climb up steep steps leads to the original catoptric light with Argand oil burners and reflectors.

### Accommodations
Bonavista makes a pleasant day trip from Trinity, but if you want to stay longer, there are numerous options. The most luxurious by far, and one of the finest accommodations in all of Newfoundland, is ◖ **Elizabeth J. Cottages** (Harris St., 709/468-5035 or 866/468-5035, www.elizabethjcottages.com; $274 s or d). The cottages enjoy an absolute oceanfront setting on the edge of town; their design was inspired by the old saltbox homes still common throughout the region, but beyond the layout, no expense has been spared in creating a luxurious environment in which to soak up the sweeping ocean views. The two-bedroom units are awash in natural light, common with niceties such as 450-thread-count sheets, plush bathrobes, and baskets of breakfast provisions. Other features include private decks with slick outdoor furniture and barbecues, modem hookups, TV/DVD combos, and laundry facilities.

If your tastes are a little simpler, **Oceanside Cabins** (Cape Shore Rd., 709/468-7771; $75 s, $85 d) will suffice.

# Clarenville to Deer Lake

It's 450 kilometers from Clarenville to Deer Lake. The TransCanada Highway linking these two towns cuts across the interior in a rambling inland path, sometimes angling north to touch a deeply carved bay or reaching into the interior to amble amid the plateau's seemingly endless stretches of tree-blanketed hills. The best chance to get up close and personal with this region is Terra Nova National Park, but there are also many worthwhile detours, such as to Twillingate, famous for its iceberg-watching tours.

## TERRA NOVA NATIONAL PARK
The TransCanada Highway enters Terra Nova National Park 35 kilometers north of Clarenville, and for the next 50 kilometers it travels within the park boundary. But to really see the park, divert from the highway to remote bodies of fish-filled freshwater, through forests inhabited by moose and bears, and to the rugged coastline where kayakers glide through protected water and bald eagles soar overhead.

### Park Entry
You don't need a pass to drive through the national park, but if you plan on stopping for any reason, you must pay adult $6, senior $5, child $3, which is valid until 4 P.M. the following day.

### Marine Interpretation Centre
Make your first stop the Marine Interpretation Centre (709/533-2942; mid-May–June daily 10 A.M.–4 P.M., July–Aug. daily 9 A.M.–7 P.M., Sept.–early Oct. daily 10 A.M.–4 P.M.; free with park admission). Overlooking Newman Sound at the Saltons Day Use Area, it is one kilometer

off the TransCanada Highway, 35 kilometers north of where it first enters the park. The center features small aquariums, touch tanks, live feed from an underwater camera, exhibits on the various marine habitats within the park, interactive computer displays, and films, plus a restaurant and gift shop. The center's gift shop sells topographical maps of the park and stocks books about the province's flora, fauna, and attractions.

## Hiking

More than a dozen trails thread through the park, providing some 60 kilometers of hiking. Most are uncomplicated loop routes that meander easily for an hour's walk beneath tree canopies. From the Marine Interpretation Centre, the one-kilometer **Heritage Trail** leads along Salton's Brook and a three-kilometer (one-way) trail leads to picturesque and quiet **Blue Hill Pond.** Another three-kilometer trail follows the edge of **Sandy Pond,** starting from 13 kilometers south of the Marine Interpretation Centre. The longest trek, the 55-kilometer **Outport Trail,** requires backcountry camping skills. Most hikers spend one or two nights on the trail, which is notable for the opportunities to see icebergs and whales.

## Water Sports

At the Marine Interpretation Centre, you find a wharf, from where tour boats and kayakers depart for trips along Newman Sound. Handy amenities at the wharf include washrooms with hot showers and coin laundry facilities. You won't need to use the hot showers after a trip with **Ocean Watch Boat Tours** (709/533-6024). The three-hour morning trip (9 A.M. departure) noses among the fjord fingers looking for icebergs and whales, while the two afternoon trips (departing at 1 and 4 P.M.) are geared to sightseeing. The shorter sunset tour (7 P.M.) explores an abandoned outport. The season runs mid-May through October, and the tours cost from $40 per person.

Take a break from the saltwater by planning to spend time at **Sandy Pond,** a shallow body of water 13 kilometers south of the Marine Interpretation Centre and 12 kilometers north of the southern park boundary. This day-use area has canoe and kayak rentals (709/677-2221; $5 for 30 minutes), allows swimming, and is encircled by a three-kilometer walking trail (allow one hour).

## Accommodations and Food

While there are no accommodations within park boundaries, the following two options lie on the edge of the park.

The village of Charlottetown occupies a pocket of oceanfront land 15 kilometers north of the park, outside the official park boundary. Here you find the trim **Clode Sound Motel** (709/664-3146, www.clodesound.com; May–Oct.; $85–140 s or d). It has 19 rooms with up to three bedrooms in each, a swimming pool, a playground, a tennis court, and barbecue pits. Also on the premises is a highly regarded restaurant/bakery that serves wonderful desserts created with apples from the motel's 90-year-old orchard.

Just beyond the south end of the park is **Terra Nova Golf Resort** (TransCanada Hwy., 709/533-2525, www.terranovagolf.com; May–Oct.; $125 s or d), a full-service resort built alongside Twin Rivers Golf Course, where golfers get to walk some of Canada's finest fairways for the bargain price of $48 midweek and $56 on weekends. Other amenities include tennis courts, an outdoor heated pool, hiking trails, a restaurant, and a pub. The 83 guest rooms feature solid furnishings and a contemporary feel. Children are catered to with a schedule of activities that includes treasure hunts, craft sessions, and picnic lunches.

Overlooking Newman Sound from the back of the Marine Interpretation Centre is **Starfish Eatery** (709/533-9555; June–Sept. daily 10 A.M.–7 P.M.), with tasty chowders and small but inexpensive plates of fish-and-chips.

## Camping

Wooded **Newman Sound Campground** has 387 full- and semi-serviced campsites (tents $26, hookups $30), kitchen shelters, heated washrooms with hot showers, a Nature House (June–Sept. daily 10 A.M.–5 P.M.), a launderette, a café, an interpretive program, and a grocery store. Reservations are taken for 40 percent of the sites through Parks Canada (905/426-4648 or 877/737-3783, www.pccamping.ca). The cost is $11 per reservation, plus the camping fee. The campground turn-off is 30 kilometers north of the southern park boundary. A 4.5-kilometer trail along Newman Sound links the campground with the Marine Interpretation Centre.

At the park's northern edge, head east on Route 310 to reach **Malady Head Campground** ($21.50 per site). The facility has a kitchen/activity area and playground.

## GANDER

The town of Gander is halfway between Newfoundland's two largest cities (350 kilometers from St. John's and 357 kilometers from Corner Brook). It was founded in 1951, when the military decided to convert Gander Airport to civilian operations, and so today, it's fitting that the main attractions revolve around air travel.

### Gateway to North America

When aircraft cross the Atlantic Ocean from Europe, they enter North American airspace somewhere off the coast of Newfoundland. In the early days of aviation, this meant that the planes needed somewhere to refuel, and so Gander grew as a stopping point for all types of aviation. Although commercial transatlantic flights no longer need to refuel at Gander, the airport retains its importance, such as after the terrorist attacks of September 11, 2001, when 39 commercial planes carrying over 6,500 crew and passengers were diverted to Gander. Even if you're not departing on one of the scheduled Air Canada or Provincial Airlines flights, it's worth dropping by **Gander International Airport,** on the eastern side of downtown, to view the historic displays and admire the massive mural inside the main terminal.

Gleaming full-size models of World War II Hudson, Voodoo, and Canso water bombers, a Beech 18 aircraft, and a reconstructed

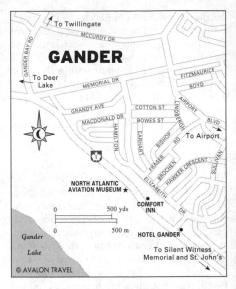

De Havilland Tiger Moth greet visitors to the **North Atlantic Aviation Museum** (TransCanada Hwy., 709/256-2923; mid-May–early Sept. daily 9 A.M.–9 P.M.; adult $5, senior and child $4). Inside, exhibits on Gander's strategic role in World War II and the development of transatlantic aviation include early equipment, uniforms, photographs, and a reconstructed DC-3 cockpit.

The **Silent Witness Memorial,** four kilometers east of town and one kilometer south along an unpaved road, marks the site of an aviation disaster. On a cold December day in 1985, the airport was a scheduled refueling stop for a DC-8 flight from the Middle East. The flight carried the U.S. 101st Airborne Division, better known as the Screaming Eagles, who were returning home from a United Nations peacekeeping mission in the Sinai. The plane, with 248 soldiers and an eight-member crew, crashed shortly after takeoff between the highway and Gander Lake. A group of statues, of an American soldier and two children, backed by Canadian, U.S., and Newfoundland flags, overlooks the lake. The memorial spreads across the rocky hillside, and flower bouquets lie here and there.

## Accommodations and Food

Gander is a convenient stop for travelers crossing Newfoundland's interior, and it provides a wide choice of accommodations. The two-story **Comfort Inn** (112 TransCanada Hwy., 709/256-3535, www.comfortinn.com; $90 s, $95 d including a continental breakfast buffet) has 66 large rooms. The spacious **Hotel Gander** (TransCanada Hwy., 709/256-3931 or 800/563-2988, www.hotelgander.com) offers 152 rooms and suites ($94–150 s or d), a restaurant, a lounge with entertainment, an indoor pool, and an exercise room.

Beside the Comfort Inn is **Jungle Jim's** (112 TransCanada Hwy., 709/651-3444; daily 11 A.M.–11 P.M.). If you can get the waitstaff's attention through the vines and bamboo decorations, order fish-and-chips for $12 or ribs for $17.

## NORTH TO TWILLINGATE

From Gander, Route 330 heads north to Gander Bay, where Route 331 curves farther northwest and lopes onto the northern archipelago as Route 340, better known as the Road to the Isles.

### Boyd's Cove

Boyd's Cove, 70 kilometers north of Gander at the intersection of Routes 331 and 340, is a small village with a large attraction: **Boyd's Cove Beothuk Interpretation Centre** (709/656-3114; mid-May–early Oct. daily 10 A.M.–5:30 P.M.; $3). Designed to mimic the shapes of 300-year-old Beothuk dwellings, the center lies at the end of a two-kilometer gravel road. The detour is worth it, though, for the artifacts, dioramas, films, and exquisitely expressive paintings depicting the history of the Beothuk people. Take the 20-minute walk down to the site of the 17th-century Beothuk encampment, excavated in the early 1980s. Eleven house pits, clearly defined by earthen walls, were discovered here, along with countless artifacts such as beads, stone tools, and iron.

### TWILLINGATE

Beyond Boyd's Cove, causeways link an archipelago of islands lying close to the mainland. Along the way, narrow Route 430 passes farmland (where you might catch a glimpse of the rare Newfoundland pony); gentle, island-filled bays; and tiny outports to finish at South and North Twillingate islands. The archipelago's most northwesterly point, the islands are washed by the Atlantic and shouldered by Notre Dame Bay. The road crosses the southern island and eases into the tiny port at Twillingate Harbour.

Cross the causeway to Twillingate (pop. 3,500) on the northwestern island. Main Street runs alongside the scenic harbor before it zips north and climbs to Long Point.

### Sights and Recreation
#### TWILLINGATE MUSEUM AND CRAFT SHOP

If you're interested in local lore, stop at Twillingate Museum and Craft Shop (709/884-2825; mid-May–early Oct. daily 9 A.M.–9 P.M.; adult $2.50, child $1.50). The gleaming, white-painted wooden building sits back from the road behind the 1839 St. Peter's Anglican Church and is bordered by a white picket fence—altogether as proper as a former Anglican manse should be. The museum's extensive exhibits include historic fishing gear and tools, antique dolls, and several rare Dorset Inuit artifacts. One room is devoted to the career of Dr. John Olds, Twillingate's famous expatriate surgeon who came from the United States to pioneer medicine in remote Newfoundland. The intriguing medical artifacts include a collection of early 20th-century pharmaceuticals and glass eyes.

#### ◖ ICEBERG-VIEWING

Icebergs, which wander offshore and sometimes ditch at land's end in Notre Dame Bay, are one of Twillingate's main claims to fame. If you're interested in getting up close, take one of the three daily cruises offered by **Twillingate Island Boat Tours,** based at the Iceberg Shop (50 Main St., 709/884-2242 or 800/611-2374, www.iceburgtours.ca). Tours operate May through September with departures daily at 9:30 A.M., 1 P.M., and 4 P.M. They are operated by Cecil Stockley, who steers the MV *Iceberg Alley* to

## ICEBERGS ON PARADE

The spectacular icebergs that float past Newfoundland and Labrador every summer originate from southwestern Greenland's ice cap, where great chunks of ice calve off the coast and cascade into the bone-chilling Davis Strait. The young bergs eventually drift out to the Labrador Sea, where powerful currents route them south along the watery route known as Iceberg Alley. The parade usually starts in March, peaks in June and July, and in rare cases continues into November.

Although no one actually counts icebergs, an educated guess has 10,000-30,000 of them migrating down from the north annually. Of those, about 1,400-2,000 make it all the way to the Gulf Stream's warm waters, where they finally melt away after a two- to four-year 3,200-kilometer journey.

No two bergs are exactly the same. Some appear distinctly white. Others may be turquoise, green, or blue. Sizes vary too: A "growler" is the smallest, about the size of a dory, and weighs about 1,000 tons. A "bergy bit" weighs more, about 10,000 tons. A typical "small" iceberg looms 5-15 meters above water level and weighs about 100,000 tons. A "large" ice mass will be 51-75 meters high and weigh 100-300 million tons. Generally, you'll see the largest bergs – looking like magnificent castles embellished with towers and turrets – farther north; the ice mountains diminish in size as they float south and eventually melt. No matter what the size, what you see is just a fraction of the whole – some 90 percent of the iceberg's mass is hidden beneath the water.

Occasionally, a wandering berg may be trapped at land's edge or wedged within coves and slender bays. Should you be tempted to go in for a closer look, approach with caution. As it melts and its equilibrium readjusts, an iceberg may roll over. And melting bergs also often fracture, throwing ice chips and knife-sharp splinters in all directions.

---

wherever icebergs have grounded themselves in the vicinity of Twillingate. The tours cost adult $40, child $25 and last two hours.

You may also see an offshore iceberg from Back Harbour, the semicircular bay a short walk behind the museum. Otherwise, head for Long Point, the high rocky promontory that juts into the Atlantic Ocean beside Notre Dame Bay. Take Main Street north and follow the narrow road to **Long Point Lighthouse,** the local iceberg vantage point. Bring rubber-soled shoes for scrambling across the boulders, and don't forget your camera—the beacon backed by the sea and sky makes a beautiful picture, particularly at sunset.

### Accommodations

Visitors to Twillingate often find themselves captivated by the town's charm, and because of this, numerous accommodations can be found. **( Harbour Lights Inn** (189 Main St., 709/884-2763, www.harbourlightsinn .com; Apr.–mid-Oct.; $85–140 s or d) is a restored early-19th-century home overlooking the harbor. The nine-room inn features non-smoking rooms with private baths and wireless Internet access; two suites have whirlpool baths. Rates include a cooked breakfast.

If you prefer more privacy, consider **Cabins by the Sea** (11 Hugh Ln., 709/884-2158, www.cabinsbythesea.com; $80 s or d), comprising seven small self-contained cabins overlooking the ocean.

## GRAND FALLS-WINDSOR

Grand Falls–Windsor lies almost exactly halfway along the Newfoundland leg of the TransCanada Highway: St. John's is 428 kilometers to the east, and Port-aux-Basques is 476 kilometers to the west. For the sake of government, the two towns have been merged to form one municipality, but keep in mind that Windsor lies north of the TransCanada Highway and Grand Falls south.

### Sights

Grand Falls offers the most sightseeing. Turn south off the highway at Cromer Avenue to the **Mary March Provincial Museum** (22 St. Catherine St., 709/292-4522; May–mid-Sept. daily 9 A.M.–4:30 P.M.; $2.50), where exhibits about the area's Beothuk people, natural history, geology, and regional industry fill the modern center.

The town is aptly named for its **Grand Falls,** a thunderous white-water gush from the Exploits River as it speeds alongside the town. To see the falls, take Scott Avenue off the TransCanada Highway or drive through town, turn west at the pulp and paper mill, and head north on a narrow gravel lane. You can get a close look at the salmon that inhabit the river at the **Salmonid Interpretation Centre** (709/489-7350; mid-June–mid-Sept. daily 8 A.M. to dusk; adult $4, child $2.50), on the south side of the river. The main floor's exhibits explain the salmon's life cycle and habitat, while on the observation level you can watch the migratory salmon through the viewing windows.

## Accommodations and Food

On the residential outskirts of Windsor, **Carriage House Inn** (181 Grenfell Heights, 709/489-7185 or 800/563-7133, www.carriagehouseinn.ca; $89–119 s or d) comprises 10 spick-and-span guest rooms, with full breakfast included in the rates. Outside you'll find a covered veranda, a pool, a sundeck, and stables.

**Mount Peyton Hotel** (214 Lincoln Rd., 709/489-2251 or 800/563-4894, www.mountpeyton.com; $90–144 s or d) has an array of accommodations on both sides of the TransCanada Highway, including 102 hotel rooms, 32 motel rooms, and 16 housekeeping units. The motel's dining room is locally known for seafood, locally grown vegetables, and for dessert, berries in all forms.

**Hotel Robin Hood** (78 Lincoln Rd., 709/489-5324, www.hotelrobinhood.com; $90–110 s or d) is Grand Falls–Windsor's newest hotel. Small and charming, it's set off from the road and run by a couple from Nottingham, England. The 14 rooms, all air-conditioned and with private baths,

are comfortable and spacious. Friar Tuck's Restaurant serves up British-style meals, including, of course, fish-and-chips.

## Information

The **Visitor Information Centre** (709/489-6332, www.grandfallswindsor.com; May–mid-Oct. daily 9 A.M.–9 P.M.) is along the TransCanada Highway on the west side of town.

## THE BEOTHUKS

Across the island's central area, the arrival of Europeans foretold grave consequences for the Beothuks, who had migrated from Labrador in A.D. 200 and spread across the Baie Verte Peninsula to Burnside, Twillingate, and the shores of the Exploits River and Red Indian Lake.

In 1769 a law prohibiting murder of the indigenous people was enacted, but the edict came too late. The Beothuks were almost extinct, and in 1819 a small group was ambushed by settlers near Red Indian Lake. In the ensuing struggle, a 23-year-old woman named Demasduit was captured, and her husband and newborn infant were killed. The government attempted to return her to her people when she contracted tuberculosis, but she was too ill, and she died in Botwood. In 1823 her kinswoman, Shanawdithit, was also taken by force. Shanawdithit told a moving tale of the history and demise of her people, punctuating it with drawings, maps, and a sampling of Beothuk vocabulary before she died in 1829, the last of her race.

You'll hear mention of the Beothuks throughout central Newfoundland, but two attractions concentrate on these almost mythical people – **Boyd's Cove Beothuk Interpretation Centre,** 70 kilometers north of Gander on the road to Twillingate, and Grand Falls' **Mary March Regional Museum,** which is named for Demasduit's European given name.

# Deer Lake to Port-aux-Basques

It's 270 kilometers from the western hub of Deer Lake south to the ferry terminal at Port-aux-Basques. Along the way is Newfoundland's second-largest city, Corner Brook; Atlantic Canada's premier ski resort; and many interesting provincial parks and scenic detours.

## DEER LAKE

Deer Lake, 640 kilometers west of St. John's and 270 kilometers from Port-aux-Basques, is a busy transportation hub at the point where Route 430 spurs north along the Northern Peninsula. The town lies at the north end of its namesake lake, a long body of water that flows into the Humber River. Along the lakeshore is a sandy beach and shallow stretch of water that offers pleasant swimming in July and August. The only commercial attraction is the **Newfoundland Insectarium** (2 Bonne Bay Rd., 709/635-4545; mid-May–mid-Oct. daily 9 A.M.–5 P.M., July–Aug. daily 9 A.M.–6 P.M.; adult $10, senior $8.50, child $6.50). Inside this converted dairy displays include active beehives and a collection of butterflies. To get there, take Exit 16 from the TransCanada Highway and follow Route 430 for a short distance to Bonne Bay Road.

### Sir Richard Squires Provincial Park

Take Route 430 for eight kilometers to reach the turnoff to this remote park, which is then a further 47 kilometers from civilization. The park protects a short stretch of the upper reaches of the Humber River; salmon are the main draw. Even if you're not an angler, watching them leap up three-meter-high Big Falls makes the drive worthwhile. Camping is $18 per night.

### Accommodations and Camping

**Deer Lake Motel** (15 TransCanada Hwy., 709/635-2108 or 800/563-2144, www.deerlakemotel.com; $85–130 s or d) is your typical low-slung roadside motel, with basic rooms and its own restaurant and lounge.

Take the Nicholsville Road exit to reach **Deer Lake RV Park** (197 Nicholsville Rd., 709/635-5885; late June–early Sept.; $15), close to the lake and with showers and a playground.

### Information

Along the highway through town (beside the Irving gas station, with its big moose out front) is **Deer Lake Information Centre** (TransCanada Hwy., 709/635-2202; June–Sept. daily 8 A.M.–8 P.M.).

### Getting There

**Deer Lake Airport** is western Newfoundland's air hub. Located on the north side of town, just off the TransCanada Highway, it has Avis, Budget, Thrifty, and National car-rental desks (make reservations well in advance). The airport is served by **Air Canada** (888/247-2262) from Halifax and Montréal and **Provincial Airlines** (709/576-3943 or 800/563-2800, www.provair.com) from throughout Newfoundland and Labrador.

## CORNER BROOK AND VICINITY

Corner Brook, 50 kilometers south of Deer Lake and 690 kilometers from the capital, lies at the head of the Humber Arm, 50 kilometers inland from the Gulf of St. Lawrence. The city is picturesquely cupped in a 20-square-kilometer bowl sloping down to the water, but most of the best natural attractions lie outside city limits, including the area around Marble Mountain and along Route 450 to Lark Harbour. The city ranks as Newfoundland's second largest, combining Corner Brook (pop. 24,000) with outlying settlements on the Humber Arm (another 20,000). It began as a company town, developing around a harborfront pulp and paper mill still in operation, and has grown to become western Newfoundland's commercial, educational, service, and governmental center.

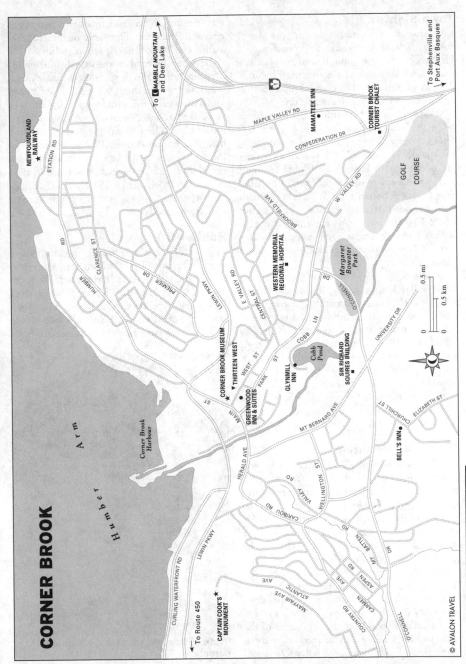

CORNER BROOK

NEWFOUNDLAND AND LABRADOR

© AVALON TRAVEL

## Town Sights

First things first—making your way down to the harborfront from the TransCanada Highway is simple enough, but to visit the main downtown sights, orient yourself by stopping at the information center and deciding exactly what you want to see and do.

**Captain Cook's Monument** is a lofty lookout with views that provide a feeling for the layout of the city. On the road to the monument, the traveler is rewarded with glorious views as far as the Bay of Islands. Follow O'Connell Drive across town, turn right (north) on Bliss Street, make another right on Country Road, turn left onto Atlantic Avenue with another left to Mayfair Street, and right to Crow Hill Road. The monument itself commemorates Cook's Bay of Islands explorations with a plaque and sample chart.

In the wide bowl containing downtown, West Valley Road roughly divides the city in half. Near the bottom end of this thoroughfare and overlooking Remembrance Square is the staid old **Corner Brook Museum** (2 West St., 709/634-2518; summer daily 9 A.M.–5 P.M., the rest of the year weekdays only; adult $5, child $3), housed in a historic building that has served as a post office, courthouse, and customs house through the years. Displays center around the various local industries and their impact on the city's growth.

## ◖ Marble Mountain

Driving south from Deer Lake, you pass Marble Mountain (709/637-7601, www.ski-marble.com) 12 kilometers before reaching Corner Brook. The mountain rises from the east side of the highway, while on the other side of the road is the small community of Steady Brook, which fronts the Humber River. The resort is Atlantic Canada's largest and best-known alpine resort, and although the lifts don't operate in summer, the area is worth a stop during the warmer months. The highlight is **Steady Brook Falls,** accessible via a steepish trail that begins from the far corner of the main parking lot. The falls are reached in about 15 minutes. From there, a 3.5-kilometer (one-

way) unmarked trail continues and brings you nearer to the peak. The views of the Humber Valley and Bay of Islands are splendid.

Between December and April, four chairlifts, including a high-speed detachable quad, whisk skiers from throughout Atlantic Canada and as far away as Toronto up 520 meters of vertical to access 27 runs, a terrain park, and a half-pipe. The base area is dominated by a magnificent four-story 6,400-square-meter day lodge, home to a ski and snowboard school, rental shop, café, restaurant, and bar. Lift tickets cost adult $49, senior $37, child $25. Check the website for packages that include accommodations and flights.

## Route 450

This winding highway follows the south shore of Humber Arm for 50 kilometers, ending at the fishing village of **Lark Harbour.** From the TransCanada Highway, Route 450 begins at Exit 4 and bypasses the city; from downtown take the Lewin Parkway west to reach Route 450. Rather than official attractions, this drive

Route 450 ends at the fishing village Lark Harbour.

© ANDREW HEMPSTEAD

Glynmill Inn

is worthwhile for its water-and-mountains scenery and picturesque fishing villages.

Almost at the end of the road is **Blow Me Down Provincial Park.** The park isn't extraordinarily windy, as the name might imply. Legend holds that a sea captain saw the mountain centuries ago and exclaimed, "Well, blow me down." The name stuck. From the park, sweeping views across the Bay of Islands make the drive worthwhile. You'll see the bay's fjord arms and the barren orange-brown Blow Me Down Mountains, as well as bald eagles and ospreys gliding on the updrafts, and perhaps caribou and moose roaming the preserve's terrain. The remote park has 28 campsites ($11), pit toilets, a lookout tower, and hiking trails.

## Accommodations and Camping
### CORNER BROOK

With the exception of the historic Glynmill Inn, Corner Brook motels serve casual highway travelers and those in town on business. A scenic alternative is to stay out at Marble Mountain.

**Bell's Inn** (2 Fords Rd., 709/634-1150 or 888/634-1150, www.bellsinn.ca; $80–100 s or d) offers eight nonsmoking rooms, each with private bath and TV, in an attractive clapboard house with a large garden. Breakfast is included and guests also have use of a kitchen.

The gracious **Glynmill Inn** (Cobb Ln., 709/634-5181 or 800/563-4400, www.glynmillinn.ca; from $105 s or d) lies near the historic Townsite residential area. It's a charming inn banked with gardens of red geraniums. Rambling ivy, with leaves as large as maple leaves, covers the half-timber Tudor-style exterior. The wide front steps lead to an open porch, and the English-style foyer is comfortably furnished with wing chairs and sofas. All the rooms are comfortably furnished, but the older ones feature old-time spaciousness and antique marble in the bathroom.

**Mamateek Inn** (64 Maple Valley Rd., 709/639-8901 or 800/563-8600, www.mamateekinn.ca; from $105 s or d) is handy to the TransCanada Highway and has adequate guest rooms, some with views down to Humber Arm. Rooms at the adjacent **Comfort**

NEWFOUNDLAND AND LABRADOR

**Inn** (41 Maple Valley Rd., 709/639-1980 or 800/228-5150, www.choicehotels.ca; $110 s or d) are of a similar standard. Both these places have restaurants, the former with distant water views.

**Greenwood Inn & Suites** (48 West St., 709/634-5381 or 800/399-5381, www.greenwoodcornerbrook.com; from $150 s or d) is right downtown and across the road from Thirteen West, the city's best restaurant. This full-service hostelry also has its own English-style pub with sidewalk tables, a restaurant, outdoor and indoor heated pools, spa facilities, a fitness room, high-speed Internet access, and underground parking.

## MARBLE MOUNTAIN

Across the highway from Marble Mountain, 12 kilometers northeast of Corner Brook, is ◖ **Marble Inn** (21 Dogwood Dr., Steady Brook, 709/634-2237 or 877/497-5673, www.explorenewfoundland.com), a modern riverside complex that combines regular motel rooms (from $119 s or d) with self-contained cabins ($139) and luxurious suites ($329 s or d). Amenities include an indoor pool, fitness room, spa services, and a restaurant. The lodge has its own dock, along with canoe and kayak rentals and guided salmon-fishing trips.

Also at Steady Brook is **Marble Villa** (709/637-7601 or 800/636-2725, www.skimarble.com), which is right at the base of the alpine resort. Naturally, winter is high season, when most guests stay as part of a package. The rest of the year, the self-contained units rent from $129 s or d.

**George's Mountain Village** (709/639-8168, www.georgesskiworld.com) has a limited number of campsites under the shadow of Marble Mountain. It's part of a complex that includes a restaurant, gas station, and sports shop. Powered sites are $20 and cabins $115 s or d.

## Food

Beyond the fast-food places along all main arteries are some surprising dining options. The very best of these is ◖ **Thirteen West** (13 West St., 709/634-1300; daily 11:30 A.M.–2:30 P.M.

and 5:30–9:30 P.M.), housed in a restored residence in the heart of the old business core. The array of entrées reaches far beyond the typical Newfoundland dinner menu. You could start with warm pear salad ($11), then move on to pan-seared hazelnut-crusted pork tenderloin ($25), with delicious apple strudel ($7) to finish.

The Glynmill Inn (Cobb Ln., 709/634-5181) has two restaurants. The more formal of the two is the downstairs **Wine Cellar** (daily for dinner), a cozy setting with a fine wine list. The dining room serves up some of the city's best unadorned beef. Entrées ($22–31) include grilled juicy filet mignon served in 12-ounce cuts. Upstairs, the more casual **Carriage Room** specializes in Newfoundland fare with cooked breakfasts and then fried, poached, or broiled salmon, cod, halibut, and lobster the rest of the day.

## Information and Services

Take Exit 6 from the TransCanada Highway and follow the signs to **Corner Brook Tourist Chalet** (11 Confederation Dr., 709/639-9792; daily Mon.–Fri. 8:30 A.M.–4:30 P.M., longer hours in summer), the city's main information center.

The **post office** is on Main Street near Park Street. **Corner Brook Library,** in the Sir Richard Squires Building (Mt. Bernard Ave., 709/634-0013; Tues.–Thurs. 10 A.M.–8:45 P.M., Fri. 10 A.M.–5:45 P.M.), has public Internet access.

**Western Memorial Regional Hospital** (709/637-5000) is at 1 Brookfield Avenue. For the **RCMP,** call 709/637-4433.

## Getting There and Around

Deer Lake, an hour's drive north of Corner Brook, has the region's main airport. **DRL Coachlines** (709/634-7422) operates bus service along the TransCanada Highway, with daily stops in Corner Brook (at the Confederation Dr. Irving gas station). Departures from St. John's at 8 A.M. arrive in Deer Lake at 5:15 P.M.

The city has half a dozen cab companies whose cabs wait at lodgings, cruise business streets, and take calls. **City Cabs** (709/634-6565) is among the largest outfits.

# CORNER BROOK TO PORT-AUX-BASQUES

It's 220 kilometers between Corner Brook and Port-aux-Basques, a two-hour drive without stops. If you're catching the ferry back to Nova Scotia, remember you need to be at the terminal at least one hour before the departure time.

## Stephenville

With a population of more than 8,000, Stephenville, 50 kilometers south of Corner Brook and then 40 kilometers west along Route 460, is the business hub for the Bay St. George–Port au Port region. In the center of town is **Beavercraft** (108 Main St., 709/643-4844), renowned for Winterhouse sweaters ($120–175), designed locally and produced by cottage-industry knitters. The shop is also a source for thrummed mittens ($20–30) and caps. This revived traditional craft combines a knitted woolen facing backed with raw fleece. The shop shelves are stuffed with top-quality wares, including Woof Design sweaters, Random Island Weaving cotton placemats, King's Point Pottery platters and bowls, and handmade birch brooms.

Stephenville offers a selection of hotels and restaurants to travelers heading out onto the Port au Port Peninsula. The best of these is **Dreamcatcher Lodge** (14 Main St., 709/643-6655 or 888/373-2668, www.dreamcatcherlodge.net), comprising three buildings filled with a mix of motel rooms ($79 s, $85 d) and kitchen-equipped units ($99). The in-house restaurant is open Monday–Saturday 11 A.M.–9 P.M.

## Barachois Pond Provincial Park

One of the province's most popular parks, 3,500-hectare Barachois Pond is home to a 3.2-kilometer hiking trail through birch, spruce, and fir trees to Erin Mountain's barren summit. Be on the lookout for the rare Newfoundland pine marten along the way. The view at 340 meters overlooks the Port au Port Peninsula. There's also a summertime interpretive program with guided walks and evening campfires, a lake for swimming and fishing, mini-golf, and 150 unserviced campsites ($18). Park entry is $5 per vehicle per day.

## Port-aux-Basques

Just over 900 kilometers from its starting point in St. John's, the TransCanada Highway reaches its western terminus at Port-aux-Basques, a town of about 5,000 with a deepwater port used by French, Basque, and Portuguese fishing fleets as early as the 1500s. Arriving in town from the north, the main highway continues two kilometers to the ferry terminal, and a side road branches west, past hotels and fast-food restaurants to the township proper. Here you'll find a cluster of commercial buildings along the harbor, including the **Gulf Museum** (118 Main St., 709/695-7560; July–Aug. daily 10 A.M.–8 P.M.; $3). The highlights of this small museum are an astrolabe (a navigation aid dating to the early 1600s) and remnants from the SS *Caribou*, a ferry torpedoed by a German submarine as it crossed the Cabot Strait during World War II. Beyond the museum, turn left at the church and climb through a residential area to a lookout that affords 360-degree views of the town, the open ocean, and the ferry terminal.

### ACCOMMODATIONS AND CAMPING

Just over two kilometers from the ferry terminal is **Shark Cove Suites** (16 Currie Ave., 709/695-3831; $80 s or d), a small complex of simple units. Each has a kitchen and a lounge with a TV/VCR combo. Originally a Holiday Inn, **Hotel Port aux Basques** (Grand Bay Rd., 709/695-2171 or 877/695-2171, www.hotelpab.com; $85 s, $95 d) sits on the corner where the highway branches to the ferry terminal. If you're camping, your best choice is six kilometers north of town at **J. T. Cheeseman Provincial Park,** where over 100 sites ($18) are spread along a picturesque stream. Facilities are limited, but the park is fronted by a long beach and is a nesting ground for the endangered piping plover.

NEWFOUNDLAND AND LABRADOR

## INFORMATION

Housed in a distinctive pyramid-shaped building just north of the turnoff to town is a provincial **Visitor Information Centre** (709/695-2262), open in summer daily 9 A.M.–8 P.M. and for all ferry arrivals.

## Continuing to the Mainland by Ferry

Port-aux-Basques is the northern terminus of year-round **Marine Atlantic** (709/227-2431 or 800/341-7981, www.marine-atlantic .ca) ferry service from North Sydney (Nova Scotia). It's the shorter and least expensive of the two crossings to Newfoundland from North Sydney. One-way fares and rates for the five- to seven-hour sailing are adult $31, senior $28, child $15.50, vehicle under 20 feet $96.50. Extras include reclining chairs ($10, only on some sailings), bunk beds ($16), and cabins ($75–109).

# Gros Morne National Park

UNESCO World Heritage Sites are scattered across the world. Egypt boasts the pyramids. France is known for Chartres Cathedral. Australia has the Great Barrier Reef. And Newfoundland boasts 1,085-square-kilometer Gros Morne National Park, a spectacular geological slice of the ancient world.

Gros Morne is on Newfoundland's west coast, 72 kilometers northwest from the town of Deer Lake. While the geological history will amaze you, there's also a wealth of hiking and boating tours, and cross-country skiing in winter. Even though the park is remote, it is surrounded by small towns that cater to visitors with lodging and restaurants to suit all budgets. There's even a dinner theater.

## The Land

The park fronts the Gulf of St. Lawrence on a coastal plain rimmed with 70 kilometers of coast edging sandy and cobblestone beaches, sea stacks, caves, forests, peat bogs, and breathtaking saltwater and freshwater fjords. The flattened Long Range Mountains, part of the ancient Appalachian Mountains, rise as an alpine plateau cloaked with black and white spruce, balsam fir, white birch, and stunted tuckamore thickets. Bare patches of peridotite, toxic to most plants, speckle the peaks, and at the highest elevations the vegetation gives way to lichen, moss, and dwarf willow and birch on the arctic tundra.

Innumerable moose, arctic hares, foxes, weasels, lynx, and a few bears roam the park. Two large herds of woodland caribou inhabit the mountains and migrate to the coastal plain during winter. Bald eagles, ospreys, common and arctic terns, great black-backed gulls, and songbirds nest along the coast, while rock ptarmigans inhabit the mountain peaks. You might see willow ptarmigans on the lower slopes or, especially during the June to early July capelin run, a few pilot, minke, or humpback whales offshore.

## Park Entry

Gros Morne National Park is open year-round, although all but one campground and the two information centers operate only in the warmer months. A **National Parks Day Pass** is adult $10, senior $8.50, child $5 to a maximum of $20 per vehicle. It is valid until 4 P.M. the day following its purchase. A **Viking Trail Pass** (adult $45, senior $36, child $24) is valid for park entry and admission to the many Northern Peninsula historic sites for seven days from the date of purchase. Passes can be purchased at the information center at Rocky Harbour or the Discovery Centre at Woody Point.

## ROUTE 430

This is the main route up the Northern Peninsula. From Wiltondale it's 86 kilometers to park's northern extremity; from Rocky Harbour it's 51 kilometers. The highway

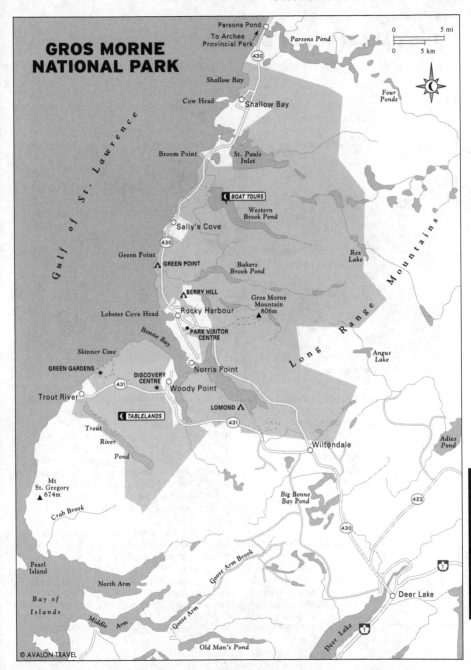

# GROS MORNE NATIONAL PARK

Parsons Pond
To Arches
Provincial Park
*Parsons Pond*
430

*Shallow Bay*

Cow Head
Shallow Bay

*Four
Ponds*

0        5 mi
0        5 km

Broom Point
St. Pauls
Inlet

BOAT TOURS

*Western
Brook Pond*

*Gulf of St. Lawrence*

Sally's Cove
430

Green Point
GREEN POINT

*Bakers
Brook Pond*

*Rex
Lake*

BERRY HILL
Rocky Harbour

Gros Morne
Mountain
806m

Lobster Cove Head
PARK VISITOR
CENTRE

*Bonne Bay*

*Skinner Cove*

GREEN GARDENS
DISCOVERY
CENTRE
431

*Angus
Lake*

Norris Point

Trout River
Woody Point

LOMOND

TABLELANDS
431

*Trout
River
Pond*

Wiltondale

*Adies
Pond*

Mt
St. Gregory
674m

*Crab Brook*

*Big Bonne
Bay Pond*

422

Pearl
Island

*North Arm*

*Goose Arm Brook*

430

Bay of
Islands

*Goose Arm*

*Middle Arm*

*Old Man's Pond*

Deer Lake

*Deer Lake*

© AVALON TRAVEL

*Long Range Mountains*

NEWFOUNDLAND AND LABRADOR

# THE GALÁPAGOS OF GEOLOGY

© ANDREW HEMPSTEAD

the moonlike Tablelands

"What the Galápagos are to biology, Gros Morne is to geology," declared Britain's Prince Edward when he visited and dedicated Gros Morne National Park as an UNESCO World Heritage Site in 1987.

Long before Newfoundland was an island, it was a landlocked part of a great supercontinent formed during Precambrian times. When the supercontinent broke apart, the land plates drifted, and a rift formed that filled with water – the Iapetus Ocean. After another 50 million years, give or take, the land plates reversed direction and moved toward each other. As the landmasses were pushed together, Newfoundland, not yet an island, perched high and dry near the center of another supercontinent. At that point, Newfoundland's only distinctive characteristic was a mountain rib – the budding Appalachian Mountains that now rim North America's eastern edge.

Strewn among the mountains now protected by Gros Morne National Park was a colossal geological heritage: remnants from the world's first supercontinent and parts of the Iapetus Ocean's seafloor. East of the mountains, the island's central plateau portion was made up of a great rectangular swatch of the crumpled ancient seabed, 200-250 kilometers in width and length.

Between then and now, the eons added a few more topographical touches. The retreating ice sheet uncovered the Labrador Trough, scooped out the Strait of Belle Isle, cut fjords into the coastlines, and pocked the interiors to create myriad lakes, such as spectacular Western Brook Pond.

traverses terrain typical of the island's rocky seacoast and verdant hills and mountains, a distinct contrast to the southern area. Unusual groups of faulted and folded rock layers lie along this coastline.

## Lobster Cove Head

The point of land north of Rocky Harbour is Lobster Cove Head. Its layers formed as the North American plate slid beneath the eastern Eurasian/African plate 450–500 million years ago. Exhibits inside **Lobster Cove Head Lighthouse** (late May–mid-Oct. daily 10 A.M.–5:30 P.M.) depict local lore, geological facts, and ancient natural history, but the views from outside are what makes a visit worthwhile, especially as the sun sets over Bonne Bay and the Gulf of St. Lawrence beyond.

## Rocky Harbour to Cow Head

More dramatically formed coastal rock lies farther north. **Green Point,** 17 kilometers beyond Lobster Cove, presents a tilted, textured surface of ribbon limestone and shale embedded with fossils from the Cambrian and Ordovician Periods.

Continuing north is the parking lot for the short trail to Western Brook Pond. One kilometer farther is where Western Brook drains into the Gulf of St. Lawrence. You'll find a sandy beach and an oceanfront picnic area. The headland immediately to the north is **Broom Point;** along the access road is a platform and telescope, which you can train on the mountains that rise from Western Brook Pond.

## Cow Head

Cow Head, 10 kilometers north of Broom Point, features an angled formation similar to that of Green Point, with limestone breccia (jumbled limestone chunks and fossils) spread across a small peninsula. The areas are richly textured. At Cow Head, the breccia looks like light-colored rock pillows scattered across a dark rock surface, while Green Point's surface is a rich green and textured like crushed velvet. The rock layers at both places originated during deepwater avalanches as the Iapetus Ocean formed 460–550 million years ago. In

the village itself, beside **St. Mary's Church,** is a small botanical garden.

## ROUTE 431

From Wiltondale, 31 kilometers north of Deer Lake, Route 431 leads west, entering the park after 13 kilometers.

## Discovery Centre

If you've entered the park on Route 431, make your first stop the Discovery Centre, on the hill above Woody Point (709/458-2417; mid-May–June daily 9 A.M.–5 P.M., July–Aug. daily 9 A.M.–6 P.M., Sept.–early Oct. daily 9 A.M.–5 P.M.; included in park entry fee). This modern facility showcases everything the national park is renowned for. The main display area holds an impressive 3-D map of the park, geological samples and descriptions, a human history display, and a theater. A gift shop sells park literature, and a café specializes in regional cuisine. Outside, a short trail leads through a garden planted with species native to the park.

## ◖ Tablelands

The Tablelands, the park's most prized geological tract, lies along Route 431, halfway between Woody Point and Trout River. It's an odd sight, more resembling Hudson Bay's bleached, brown barrens than verdant Newfoundland. The 12-by-7-kilometer chunk once lay beneath the ancient Iapetus Ocean. Violent internal upheavals eventually thrust the unearthly landscape to the surface. The parched yellow and tan cliffs and boulders that resulted are formed of peridotite, an igneous rock found in the earth's mantle. You can get a good idea of the landscape from the parking lot, but I encourage you to take a stroll along the easy Tablelands Trail. It's four kilometers each way, but you only need walk a short way to get a feeling for the starkness of the moonlike terrain.

## Trout River

After leaving the Tablelands behind, Route 431 descends to the small fishing village of

Trout River, on a protected bay 18 kilometers from Woody Point. A boardwalk rims the stony beach, leading past weatherworn wooden buildings to the mouth of the Trout River, where wharves are filled with lobster pots and fishing gear. Fronting the boardwalk are historic buildings open to the public, including the bright yellow 1898 Jacob A. Crocker House. Across the river, turn right over the bridge and look for a small sign on the left. This marks the start of a short trail (10 minutes round-trip) leading to the Old Man, a rock stack that is visible from town.

## RECREATION

More than 100 kilometers of marked and unmarked hiking trails lead novice to expert trekkers into the park's nooks and crannies. Several privately operated boat tours probe the fjords. A provincial fishing license (available at any sports store) opens up angling for brook trout and arctic char on the fast-flowing streams and rivers.

If you'd like to know more about Gros Morne's natural history and geology, plan on attending a scheduled interpretive program and evening campfire talk; see the information center for a schedule.

### Hiking

Even if you're not a keen hiker, you can enjoy short interpretive walks at **Broom Point** (32 kilometers north of Rocky Harbour) and the **Tablelands,** as well as the two-kilometer circuit of **Lobster Cove Head.** If you're planning on taking a boat tour on Western Brook Pond, you'll need to lace up your hiking boots for the three-kilometer walk to the dock. But it is the following two longer hikes that get most of the attention.

Between the Tablelands and Trout River are two trailheads for the **Green Gardens.** This feature originated as lava from erupting volcanoes in the Iapetus Ocean. The hike has two trailheads. The longer option (16 kilometers round-trip; allow six hours) begins from Route 431 on the west side of the Tablelands. Four kilometers farther west is another trailhead for the Green Gardens. This is a nine-kilometer loop (four hours). Regardless of which trail you take, the trails emerge on a high headland cloaked in rich green grasses overlooking the gulf. Below the headland, sea stacks and sea caves (accessible only at low tide) rise from the beach floor beside cliffs pocked with pillow lava, the solidified remnants of molten rock from 100 kilometers beneath the ancient seafloor.

Feeling fit? If so, the hike to the 806-meter bald summit of **Gros Morne Mountain** (eight kilometers one way; allow eight hours for the round-trip) may be what you're looking for. Beginning from Route 430 just east of the main information center, the first hour's walking is across flat terrain. Tightly packed boulders mark the beginning of the actual ascent, which takes 2–2.5 hours. Unexpectedly, the trail empties at a corner of the flattened peak. The air is clear and exhilarating, but surprisingly chilly. Far below, climbers scramble fitfully up the rocky ascent. To the west rise the Long Range Mountains. Looking south, you'll see a sapphire fjord, laid like an angled ribbon across the green woodlands. The summit is bare shale, limestone, and quartzite rock sprinkled with wild grass tufts. Check weather forecasts before heading out, and be prepared by carrying raingear, a first-aid kit, and extra food, clothing, and drinking water.

### ◖ Boat Tours

Like Scandinavia, Gros Morne National Park is famous for fjords, fringed sea arms carved by the last ice sheet and shouldered by forests and cliffs. Unlike their Scandinavian counterparts, the most spectacular are actually landlocked fjord lakes and are known as "ponds." These ponds—**Trout River, Ten Mile, Bakers Brook,** and **Western Brook**—were carved by the ice sheets. But in each case, when the enormous ice sheet melted out, the coastline—which had been compressed by the sheer weight of the glacier—rebounded like a sponge, rising above sea level and cutting the fjord off from the sea.

**Bontours** (709/458-2016 or 888/458-2016) offers a cruise on spectacular Western Brook

Pond. Tickets can be booked by phone or in person at the Ocean View Motel in Rocky Harbour. To get to Western Brook Pond, you must drive 30 kilometers north from Rocky Harbour to a marked parking lot. From this point, it's a three-kilometer hike to the boat dock. During July and August, three tours depart daily (10 A.M., 1 P.M., and 4 P.M.), while in June and September there's just one tour daily (1 P.M.). Plan on leaving Rocky Harbour at least 90 minutes before the scheduled departure time. This tour lasts two hours and costs adult $45, child $20.

In the park's southern reaches, **Tableland Boat Tour** (709/451-2101) cruises 15-kilometer-long Trout River Pond, passing between the Tablelands and the Gregory Plateau's towering cliffs. Cruises leave three times daily in July and August. **Seal Island Boat Tour** (709/243-2278) provides tours of St. Paul's Inlet and the coastline beyond on a similar schedule. These tours depart from the main wharf in St. Pauls, 34 kilometers north of Rocky Harbour. Both companies charge adult $35, child $15.

## Other Tours

**Gros Morne Adventures** (709/458-2722 or 800/685-4624, www.grosmorneadventures .com) leads geology and natural-history tours through the park June through September. The six-day backpacking adventure costs $1,295 per person, and the six-day hiking trip (with lodge accommodations) costs $1,695. In both cases, transfers from Deer Lake Airport and all meals are included. Kayaking is another specialty; a day with instructions and lunch costs around $125 per person, an overnight trip is $345, and kayak rentals from the company's Norris Point base cost $50–60 per day.

## ENTERTAINMENT AND EVENTS

To immerse yourself in the culture of Newfoundland, plan on spending an evening at the **Gros Morne Theatre Festival** (709/639-7238, www.theatrenewfoundland.com), which runs June through mid-September at Cow Head, 48 kilometers north of Rocky Harbour.

The festival comprises two plays and more than 40 professional actors, with performances that tell the story of people and events that have helped shape the province. Tickets cost adult $20–25, child $10–12.50. A free shuttle bus runs to the theater from Rocky Harbour, with pickups made at Berry Hill Campground.

In Rocky Harbour, the **Anchor Pub** (Ocean View Motel, Main St., 709/458-2730) has traditional Newfoundland music Wednesday and Friday nights. The cover charge is minimal, and it gets surprisingly crowded.

## ACCOMMODATIONS

Rocky Harbour, 72 kilometers from Deer Lake, has the best choice of accommodations and is centrally located for exploring the park.

### Rocky Harbour

Those not camping will find a variety of accommodations in Rocky Harbour, the park's major service area. For bed-and-breakfast accommodations, **Evergreen B&B** (4 Evergreen Ln., 709/458-2692 or 800/905-3494; $55 s, $65 d) has four guest rooms and a large patio with barbecue facilities. It's open year-round, and rates include a full breakfast.

**Parsons' Harbour View Cabins** (Harbour Dr., 709/458-2544 or 877/458-2544; May–Oct.; $60–70) comprises three motel rooms, three simple cabins, and a restaurant.

The **Ocean View Motel** (Main St., 709/458-2730 or 800/563-9887, www.oceanviewmotel .com; from $85 s, $95 d) enjoys a prime location across from the water in the heart of Rocky Harbour. Rooms in the older wing are high-quality and spacious, while those in the newer wing offer ocean views. The motel also has a downstairs bar, an upstairs restaurant, a booking desk for Western Brook Pond boat tours, and a super-funky old-fashioned elevator.

A short walk from the harbor, the units at **Mountain Range Cottages** (32 Parsons Ln., 709/458-2199, www.mountainrangecot-tages.com; mid-May–mid-Oct.; $100–130 s or d) are excellent value. Each of 10 simple but modern cottages has a full kitchen, a dining table, two separate bedrooms, a bathroom, and a balcony equipped with outdoor furniture and a barbecue.

Continue around the southern side of Rocky Harbour to reach **Gros Morne Cabins** (Main St., 709/458-2020 or 888/603-2020, www.grosmornecabins.com; $100–150 s or d), a modern complex of 22 polished log cabins strung out along the bay. Unfortunately, they don't take advantage of the wonderful location (small windows and no balconies), but each has a kitchen and separate bedrooms. Other amenities include a playground and laundry, while across the road is a general store and bakery.

### Cow Head
In Cow Head, 48 kilometers north of Rocky Harbour, **Shallow Bay Motel and Cabins** (193 Main St., 709/243-2471 or 800/563-1946, www.shallowbaymotel.com; $80–120 s or d) lies close to long stretches of sandy beach, hiking trails, and Arches Provincial Park. The rooms are basic but comfortable, and the cabins have full kitchens. Amenities include a large restaurant and a small outdoor pool.

### Along Route 431
A luxurious lodging that seems a little out of place within this remote national park, **Sugar Hill Inn** (115 Sexton Rd., Norris Point, 709/458-2147 or 888/299-2147, www.sugarhillinn.nf.ca; $145–225 s or d) is nevertheless a treat. The 11 guest rooms and cottage are accentuated with polished hardwood floors and earthy yet contemporary color schemes. The King Suite has a vaulted ceiling, jetted tub, and sitting area with a leather couch. Breakfast is included in the rates, while dinner—a grand three-course affair—is extra. Sugar Hill is on the left as you descend to Norris Point.

One block back from the water in the heart of the village of Woody Point is **Aunt Jane's B&B** (1 Water St., 709/453-2485; mid-May–mid-Oct.; $50–70 s or d), a charming 1880s home that contains five guest rooms, four with shared bathrooms. Aunt Jane's is one of numerous other guest houses in town marketed as **Victorian Manor Heritage Properties** (same contact). One of these is **Uncle Steve's,** a trim three-bedroom home with a kitchen and a TV lounge. It costs $150 per night, with a three-night minimum.

### Trout River
At the end of Route 431 and a 10-minute walk along the river from the ocean, **Tableland Resort** (709/451-2101, www.tablelandresortandtours.com; May–Oct.; $90 s or d) has seven two-bedroom cottages, a restaurant, and a laundry.

## CAMPGROUNDS
Almost 300 campsites at five campgrounds lie within Gros Morne National Park. No electrical hookups are available, but each campground has flush toilets, fire pits (firewood costs $7 per bundle), at least one kitchen shelter, and a playground. All campgrounds except Green Point have hot showers.

A percentage of sites at all but Green Point can be reserved through Parks Canada (905/426-4648 or 877/737-3783, www.pccamping.ca) for $11 per reservation—reassuring if you're visiting the park in the height of summer. The remaining sites fill on a first-come, first-served basis.

### Route 430
Across Route 430 from Rocky Harbour, **Berry Hill Campground** (June–Oct.; $26) has 146 sites, showers, kitchen shelters, and a playground. It fills quickly each summer afternoon, mainly due to its central location.

◖ **Green Point Campground** ($16), 12 kilometers north of Rocky Harbour, is the only park campground open year-round, and is the only one without showers. But the oceanfront setting more than makes up for a lack of facilities.

At the park's northern extremity, **Shallow Bay Campground** (mid-May–early Oct.; $26) offers full facilities and 50 sites within walking distance of the services of a small town.

## Route 431

**Lomond Campground** (mid-May–early Oct.; $26) edges Bonne Bay's east arm. It is popular with anglers but also is the start of three short walking trails, including one along the Lomond River.

Turn left at the end of Route 431 to reach **Trout River Pond Campground** (mid-June–mid-Sept.; $26), which is close by the Trout River boat tour dock. It's only a small facility (40 sites), but it has a beautiful setting.

## Commercial Campground

**Juniper RV Campground** (West Link Rd., 709/458-2917; mid-May–Sept.; $18–24) is a full-service campground in Rocky Harbour. It offers 15- and 30-amp pull-through sites, tent camping, laundry facilities, hot showers, a kitchen shelter, and free firewood. The campground also has a 15-bed hostel, where beds are $14 per person per night.

## FOOD
### Rocky Harbour

If you rise before 7:30 A.M., head to **Ⓒ Fisherman's Landing** (Main St., 709/458-2060; daily 6 A.M.–11 P.M.), across from the wharf, for a $5 cooked breakfast special that includes juice and coffee. The rest of the day, it's traditional Newfoundland cooking at reasonable prices—grilled pork chops with baked potatoes and boiled vegetables ($13), poached halibut ($18), pan-fried cod tongues ($19), and more. House wine is sold by the glass, but some bottles are under $20. A few tables have water views.

### Cow Bay

Part of the Shallow Bay Motel complex, the **Bay View Family Restaurant** (193 Main St., 709/243-2471; daily 7 A.M.–9 P.M.) does indeed have bay views, but only from a few of the tables. Dining choices are as simple as a Newfie Mug (tea and molasses bread), but you can also order more recognizable meals, such as blackened salmon with Cajun spices ($14) and T-bone steaks ($18).

### Woody Point

The **Lighthouse Restaurant** (Water St., 709/453-2213; daily 11 A.M.–8 P.M.) has simple seafood meals such as a poached cod dinner for $14 and deep-fried scallops for $12. It's across from the waterfront.

### Trout River

Along the waterfront in this end-of-the-road fishing village, the **Seaside Restaurant** (709/451-3461; mid-May–mid-Oct. daily noon–10 P.M.) enjoys sweeping water views. The restaurant has a reputation for consistently good food. The seafood chowder is overflowing with goodies, and fish-and-chips were cooked to perfection. Expect to pay around $30 for three courses.

## INFORMATION AND SERVICES

The **Park Visitor Centre** (Rte. 430, 709/458-2417; mid-May–late June daily 9 A.M.–5 P.M., late June–early Sept. daily 9 A.M.–9 P.M., early Sept.–mid-Oct. daily 9 A.M.–5 P.M.) stocks literature, sells field guides, presents slide shows, and has changing exhibits on the park's geology, landscapes, and history. It's along Route 430 just before the turnoff to Rocky Harbour.

The **Discovery Centre** (details in the *Route 431* section) is another source of park information. For pretrip planning, go to the Parks Canada website (www.pc.gc.ca) or check out the business links at www.grosmorne.com.

Rocky Harbour has a launderette, an ATM, and a general store.

## GETTING THERE AND AROUND

The nearest airport is in Deer Lake, 72 kilometers from Rocky Harbour. It is served by **Air Canada** (888/247-2262) from Halifax and Montréal. Rental car companies with airport desks include Avis, Budget, Thrifty, and National. Each allows 200 free kilometers per day, meaning you'll be unlikely to rack up extra charges on a trip to the park.

# Northern Peninsula

North of Gros Morne National Park, the Northern Peninsula sweeps northeast across mountainous flat-topped barrens and ends in tundra strewn with glacial boulders. Route 430 (also known as the **Viking Trail**) runs alongside the gulf on the coastal plain and extends the peninsula's full length, finishing at St. Anthony, 450 kilometers north of Deer Lake.

As you drive this stretch of highway, you'll notice, depending on the time of year, either small black patches of dirt or tiny flourishing vegetable gardens lining the road. These roadside gardens belong to the people of the nearby villages; because of the region's nutrient-poor soil, people plant their gardens wherever they find a patch of fertile ground.

## NORTH FROM GROS MORNE
### Arches Provincial Park

Right beside the highway, just north of Gros Morne National Park, this intriguing geological feature is well worth the drive, even if you're not planning on traveling up the Northern Peninsula. Two arches have been eroded into a grassed rock stack that sits along the rocky beach. At low tide you can climb underneath, but most visitors are happy to stand back and snap a picture.

### Daniel's Harbour

Around 15 kilometers north of Arches Provincial Park is the village of Daniel's Harbour. It has an interesting little harbor, and historic buildings such as Nurse Myra Bennett Heritage House, once home to a woman known throughout Newfoundland and Labrador as the "Florence Nightingale of the North" for her medical exploits.

On the south side of town is **Bennett Lodge** (Rte. 430, 709/898-2211, www.bennettlodge.com; $65–70 s or d), nothing more than a modular motel with a restaurant and dimly lighted lounge. But it's one of the least expensive motels on the Northern Peninsula

and has ocean views through the small guest room windows.

## PORT AU CHOIX

Around 150 kilometers north of Rocky Harbour, a road spurs west off Route 430 for 10 kilometers to Port au Choix, a small fishing village with a human history that dates back over 4,500 years. The historic site related to these early residents is the town's main attraction, but the local economy revolves around the ocean and cold-water shrimp (those tasty little shrimp you see in salads and the like).

### ( Port au Choix National Historic Site

The Maritime Archaic people and the later Dorset and Groswater Inuit migrated from Labrador, roamed the Northern Peninsula, and then settled on the remote cape beyond the modern day town of Port au Choix. Today, the entire peninsula is protected, with trails leading to the various dig sites. Start your exploration at the Visitor Reception Centre (709/861-3522; mid-June–early Oct. daily 9 A.M.–6 P.M.; adult $8, senior $6.60, child $4), which is signposted through town. Here, the three cultures are represented by artifacts, exhibits, and a reconstruction of a Dorset Inuit dwelling. Dig sites are scattered over the peninsula, with a 3.5-kilometer trail leading from the center to the most interesting site, Phillip's Garden. First discovered in the 1960s, archaeological digs here revealed Dorset dwellings and an incredible wealth of Maritime Archaic cultural artifacts buried with almost 100 bodies at three nearby burial grounds. The digs continue to this day, and through summer you can watch archaeologists doing their painstaking work (if you're lucky, you may even see them uncover an ancient artifact). Free guided hikes depart daily at 1 P.M. If you drive through town beyond the shrimp-processing plant, you pass an Archaic cemetery and a parking lot from where Phillip's Garden is a little closer (2.5 kilometers one-way).

## Museum of Whales and Things

Along the main road into town, this small museum (709/861-3280; Mon.–Sat. 9 A.M.–5 P.M.; donation) is the work of local man Ben Ploughman, who has, as the name suggests, collected a 15-meter-long sperm whale skeleton, as well as other "things." In an adjacent studio, Ploughman makes and sells driftwood creations.

## Accommodations

As the town of Port au Choix continues to unfold its rich archaeological heritage, it also continues to expand its visitor services. One of these is **Jeannie's Sunrise Bed and Breakfast** (84 Fisher St., 709/861-2254 or 877/639-2789, www.jeanniessunrisebb.com; $50–80 s or d), owned by lifelong Port au Choix resident Jeannie Billard. Each of the six rooms is bright and spacious and has its own TV. The less expensive rooms share a bathroom. Rates include a full breakfast, and dinner is available on request.

**Sea Echo Motel** (Fisher St., 709/861-3777, www.seaechomotel.ca; $82–108 s or d) has 30 fairly standard motel rooms with wireless Internet, three cottages, and a restaurant.

## Food

As you cruise through town, it's difficult to miss the ( **Anchor Café** (Main St., 709/861-3665; summer daily 9 A.M.–11 P.M., spring and fall daily 10 A.M.–10 P.M.), with its white ship's bow jutting out into the parking lot. With the cold-water shrimp plant across the road, this is the place to try this local delicacy ($5 for a shrimp burger). You can also eat like locals have done for generations (corned fish with sides of brewis, pork scrunchions, and a slice of molasses bread for $15) or try a Moratorium Dinner (a reference to the cod-fishing ban), such as roast turkey ($13). Also good is the cod and shrimp chowder ($6.50).

Along the same road, the **Sea Echo Motel** (Fisher St., 709/861-3777; daily 7 A.M.–9 P.M.) has a nautically themed restaurant with similar fare.

Back toward the highway a few hundred meters, **Dot's Pantry** (56 Fisher St., 709/861-3735; Mon.–Fri. 7 A.M.–8 P.M., Sat. 8 A.M.–6 P.M.) is easily missed. Inside the nondescript building, you find a surprising selection of cakes and pastries, as well as pizza slices and sandwiches made to order.

## PLUM POINT

At Plum Point, 60 kilometers north of Port au Choix, Route 430 continues north and Route 432 spurs east toward Roddickton. The latter is the longer route to St. Anthony, but an abundance of moose makes it an interesting alternative.

### Bird Cove

Although visited by Captain Cook in 1764 and settled permanently by Europeans in 1900, Plum Point's first residents made a home for themselves as early as 4,500 years ago. These Maritime Archaic people were prehistoric hunters and gatherers who spent summers on the edge of Bird Cove. The two adjacent village sites, discovered as recently as the 1990s, were rare because they presented archaeologists with an undisturbed look at life many thousands of years ago. Shell middens, spear points used to hunt sea mammals, and tools used for woodworking have all been excavated. A boardwalk with interpretive panels leads around the site. To get there, drive to the end of the road, loop left past the grocery store, and take the unpaved road on the right-hand side of the light brown house. The boardwalk is on the left, a little under one kilometer from the grocery store.

### Dog Peninsula

Beyond the general store, stay right as the road loops around and you soon find yourself at a bridge linking the Dog Peninsula to the mainland. The peninsula is laced with walking trails that follow the shoreline and pass through the remains of an 1880s settlement. You can complete the first loop (turn right at the far end of the bridge) in around 30 minutes, even with time spent skimming a few of the super-flat stones into Bird Cove.

## Accommodations and Food

Out on the highway, the **Plum Point Motel** (709/247-2533 or 888/663-2533; $84–102 s or d) has 40 motel rooms and 18 basic cabins. With a few water-view tables, the in-house restaurant (daily 7 A.M.–9 P.M.) serves the usual array of cooked breakfasts, included salted cod, tea, and toast for $10. Most mains are under $16.

## ST. BARBE

St. Barbe, 30 kilometers north of Plum Point and 300 kilometers north of Deer Lake, is where ferries depart for Labrador. There's little to see or do in town, but accommodations are provided at the **Dockside Motel** (709/877-2444 or 877/677-2444, www.docksidemotel .nf.ca; $78–90 s or d), which isn't at the dock at all. Instead, it's on the road leading down to the waterfront. Rooms are basic but adequate and the simple in-house restaurant is open daily for breakfast, lunch, and dinner.

## Catching the Ferry to Labrador

If you are planning on exploring the Labrador Straits region, make ferry reservations long before arriving in St. Barbe. The ticket office is at Dockside Motel, and even with reservations, you'll need to check in before heading down to the dock. The **MV Apollo** ferry (709/877-2222 or 866/535-2567, www.tw.gov.nl.ca/ferryservices) sails from St. Barbe once or twice daily between early May and early January. The crossing takes around two hours. The one-way fare is a reasonable vehicle and driver $23, extra adults $7.50, senior and child $6. Across the road from the Dockside Motel is a fenced compound with hookups for RVs and a drop-off area for those catching the ferry and not wanting to travel with full rigs.

## ST. BARBE TO ST. ANTHONY

It's 110 kilometers between St. Barbe and St. Anthony. For the first 50 kilometers, Route 430 hugs the Strait of Belle Isle, passing a string of fishing villages clinging tenuously to the rocky coastline. Tourist services are minimal, but there are a couple of worthwhile stops, and you should take the time to wander through one or more of these outports to get a feeling for the sights, sounds, and smells that go with living along this remote stretch of coastline.

## Deep Cove Wintering Interpretation Site

Just beyond the turnoff to the modern-day village of Anchor Cove is an observation platform and trail that leads to the site of an 1860s village where residents of Anchor Cove would spend the winter. Only the weathered remains of a few wooden homes are left, but it is interesting as one of the rare cases of European seasonal migration. It takes around 10 minutes to reach the site from Route 430.

## ⟨ Thrombolites of Flowers Cove

The picturesque village of Flowers Cove, its low profile of trim homes broken only by the occasional church spire, lies 13 kilometers north of St. Barbe. Turn onto Burns Road from Route 430 to reach the red-roofed Marjorie Bridge. Beyond the bridge, a boardwalk leads along the cove to an outcrop of thrombolites. Resembling flowerlike-shaped boulders, they are actually the remnants of algae and bacteria that have been dated at 650 million years old, making them among the earliest forms of life on earth. While the actual thrombolites are of course interesting, it is the complete lack of surrounding hype for what is one of the world's rarest fossils (the only other place they occur is on the remote west coast of Australia) that makes visiting the site even more unforgettable.

## ST. ANTHONY

Although you will want to continue north to L'Anse aux Meadows, St. Anthony (pop. 3,000), 450 kilometers north of Deer Lake, is the last real town and a service center for the entire Northern Peninsula. Most attractions revolve around Dr. Wilfred Grenfell, a medical missionary from England who established

The thrombolites of Flowers Cove are the world's oldest living organisms.

hospitals along both sides of Labrador Straits in the late 1800s. His impact on St. Anthony was especially powerful. It was here, in 1900, that Grenfell built his first year-round hospital and established a medical mission headquarters. St. Anthony still serves as the center of operations for the International Grenfell Association, which continues to build hospitals and orphanages and funds other community endeavors across the country.

The main natural attraction is **Fishing Point Park,** through town. From this lofty point, you have the chance to spy whales or icebergs.

## Grenfell Historic Properties

Start your discovery of everything Grenfell at the **Grenfell Interpretation Centre** (West St., 709/454-4010; mid-May–mid-Oct. daily 9 A.M.–8 P.M.; adult $5, senior $4, child $3). This large facility details Grenfell's many and varied accomplishments, from the establishment of his first hospital at Battle Harbour to the work of the association that carries his name today. Grenfell also helped foster financial independence for remote outports through profitable organizations such as **Grenfell Handicrafts,** which still produces hand-embroidered cassocks, fox-trimmed parkas, hooked rugs, and jackets that are sold at a gift shop across from the admissions desk of the Grenfell Interpretation Centre.

Exit the museum through the tea room and you come across the tiny **Dock House Museum** (July–Aug. daily 10 A.M.–4 P.M.; free). Displays here describe how Grenfell's ships were pulled from the water for repairs after long voyages to remote communities.

A tribute to the life and works of Dr. Grenfell lives in the **Jordi Bonet Murals,** impressive ceramic panels adorning the walls of the rotunda at the entrance to Curtis Memorial Hospital, which is across the road from the Grenfell Interpretation Centre.

Exhibits at the stately green and white **Grenfell House Museum** (mid-May–early June daily 9 A.M.–6 P.M., early June–Sept. daily 9 A.M.–8 P.M.; donation), his home for many years, describe Grenfell's home and family life. The home is on the far side of the hospital, a five-minute walk from the Interpretation Centre. A trail starting from behind the home leads to Tea House Hill, where viewing platforms provide sweeping harbor views.

### Tours

As the gateway to Iceberg Alley, St. Anthony is the place to take to the water in a tour boat. **Northland Discovery** (709/454-3092 or 877/632-3747; mid-May–Sept.) departs three times daily from behind the Grenfell Interpretation Centre. When there's a lack of icebergs (mid-June through August is the best viewing period), the captain concentrates on searching out humpback, minke, and fin whales, as well as seabirds. The covered vessel is stable and has washrooms. The 2.5-hour tours cost adult $50, child $20, which includes hot drinks.

### Accommodations

**Fishing Point B&B** (Fishing Point Rd., 709/454-3117 or 866/454-2009; $60 s or d) is through town and within walking distance of Lightkeeper's, the best place to eat in town. Built in the 1940s, the converted fisherman's home is set right on the harbor and has four guest rooms with shared bathrooms.

**Haven Inn** (14 Goose Cove Rd., 709/454-9100 or 877/428-3646, www.haveninn.ca; $92–133) has 30 rooms in various configurations on a slight rise off Route 430. Rooms are fairly standard, but each has a coffeemaker and hair dryer. The in-house restaurant dishes up inexpensive breakfasts. The nearby **Vinland Motel** (West St., 709/454-8843 or 800/563-7578; $86 s, $95 d) has rooms of a similar standard, a restaurant, a lounge, a small exercise room, and a laundry.

## Food

On the lower level of the Grenfell Interpretation Centre is **Lady Anne's Tea Room,** open daily from 10 A.M. for light meals, but the time to visit is Thursday–Saturday at 6 P.M. for a "Newfie Mug-Up" ($10) that includes traditional treats, cold drinks with iceberg ice, and musical entertainment.

Drive through town to reach **( Lightkeeper's** (Fishing Point Rd., 709/454-4900; summer daily 11:30 A.M.–9 P.M.), which, true to its name, follows a red and white color theme that extends all the way down to the salt and pepper shakers. Housed in a converted light-keeper's residence overlooking the ocean (you may even spot icebergs June through August), this tiered dining room is casual and well priced. Starters such as crab claws with garlic butter are under $12, and mains like seafood linguine range $16–30.

**Haven Inn** (14 Goose Cove Rd., 709/454-9100; daily 7 A.M.–9 P.M.) has a small bright dining room that catches the morning sun. Cooked breakfasts are $8, and mains such as cod dinners cost around $15.

## ( L'ANSE AUX MEADOWS

At the very end of Route 436 lies L'Anse aux Meadows, 48 kilometers from St. Anthony

L'Anse aux Meadows National Historic Site protects the place where Vikings first landed on the North American continent.

and as far as you can drive up the Northern Peninsula. It was here that the Vikings came ashore over 1,000 years ago—the first Europeans to step foot in North America. Two Viking attractions make the drive worthwhile, but there's also a fine restaurant and lots of wild and rugged scenery.

## L'Anse aux Meadows National Historic Site

Long before archaeologists arrived, Newfoundlanders were aware of the odd-shaped sod-covered ridges across the coastal plain at L'Anse aux Meadows. George Decker, a local fisherman, led Norwegian scholar-explorer Helge Ingstad and his wife, archaeologist Anne Stine Ingstad, to the area in the 1960s. The subsequent digs uncovered eight complexes of rudimentary houses, workshops with fireplaces, and a trove of artifacts, which verified the Norse presence. National recognition and site protection followed, leading to the creation of a national historic site in 1977 and to UNESCO designating it a World Heritage Site the following year.

A Visitor Reception Centre (Rte. 436, 709/623-2608; June–early Oct. daily 9 A.M.–6 P.M.; adult $12, senior $10, child $6) has been developed above the site. Here, you can admire excavated artifacts, view site models, and take in an audiovisual presentation. A gravel path and boardwalk lead across the grassy plain to the site of the settlement, where panels describe the original uses of buildings now marked by depressions in the grass-covered field. Just beyond is a settlement of re-created buildings overlooking Epaves Bay. Costumed interpreters reenact the roles and work of the Norse captain, his wife, and four crewmembers.

## Norstead

Just beyond the turnoff to L'Anse aux Meadows National Historic Site is Norstead (Rte. 436, 709/623-2828; mid-June–mid-Sept. daily 9 A.M.–6 P.M.; adult $8, senior $6.50, child $4), the re-creation of a Viking port of trade.

Aside from the Viking theme, it has little resemblance to how the Vikings of L'Anse aux Meadows lived, but is still well worth visiting. Right on the water, you can see a full-size replica of a Viking ship, listen to stories in the dimly lit Chieftains Hall, watch a blacksmith at work, and sample bread as it comes from the oven in the dining hall. The costumed interpreters bring this place to life, and you can easily spend an hour or more listening and watching them at work and play.

## Accommodations and Camping

L'Anse aux Meadows the village comprises just a smattering of homes on the headland. For overnight accommodations, there are a few choices back toward St. Anthony, all more enjoyable than staying in one of St. Anthony's nondescript motels.

The closest accommodations are in Hay Cove, a cluster of houses two kilometers before the end of the road. Stay in one of five guest rooms at **Marilyn's Hospitality Home** (709/623-2811 or 877/865-3958; Apr.–Nov.) and enjoy breakfast for just $40–65 s or d. Also in Hay Cove, **Viking Village Bed and Breakfast** (709/623-2238 or 877/858-2238; $62 s, $78 d) has five en suite guest rooms, ocean views, a TV lounge, and laundry facilities.

The units at **Southwest Pond Cabins** (Rte. 436, Griquet, 709/623-2140 or 800/515-2261, www.southwestpondcabins.com; May–Oct.; $70 s or d) overlook a small lake nine kilometers from L'Anse aux Meadows. Each of eight spacious wooden cabins has a kitchen, separate bedrooms, satellite TV, and a bathroom. Other amenities include a playground, barbecues, and a grocery store.

At the top of the list for originality is ◖ **Quirpon Lighthouse Inn** (Quirpon Island, 709/634-2285 or 877/254-6586, www.linkumtours.com; May–Oct.), a converted light-keeper's residence and modern addition that house a total of 11 guest rooms. Access is by boat from Quirpon (turn off Route 436 six kilometers beyond Griquet), with the trip over taking around

NEWFOUNDLAND AND LABRADOR

45 minutes. Instead of cable TV, you get to watch icebergs float by and whales frolicking in the surrounding waters. Rates are $250 s, $350 d, inclusive of traditional Newfoundland meals and boat transfers.

One of the few commercial campgrounds this far north is **Viking RV Park** (Rte. 436, Quirpon, 709/623-2425; May–Oct.), where tent campers pay $15 and RVs wanting hookups are charged $22 per night.

### Food

Amazingly, at the end of the road is one of the finest dining rooms in all of Newfoundland, the 🄲 **Norseman Restaurant** (709/754-3105; late May–late Sept. daily noon–9 P.M.). Admittedly, the ocean views add to the appeal, but the food is fresh and creative, the service professional, and the setting casual yet refined. Starters include a smooth shellfish-less seafood chowder ($9), smoked char ($14), and lots of salads. Ordering lobster takes a little more effort than usual—you'll be invited to wander across the road with your waitress to pick one from an ocean pound. Other entrées ranging $12–33 include cod baked in a mustard and garlic crust and grilled Labrador caribou brushed with a red-wine glaze. Still hungry? It's hard to go past a slice of freshly baked pie filled with local berries.

The 🄲 **Dark Tickle Company** (Rte. 436, Griquet, 709/623-2354; June–Sept. daily 9 A.M.–6 P.M., Oct.–May Mon.–Fri. 9 A.M.–5 P.M.) uses locally harvested berries to create a delicious array of jams, preserves, sauces, and even chocolates and wines. You can watch the various processes in creating the finished product, but you'll also want to sample and purchase them from the attached store.

## RALEIGH

Between St. Anthony and L'Anse aux Meadows, Route 437 branches off Route 436 to the delightfully named Ha Ha Bay and the small town of Raleigh.

© ANDREW HEMPSTEAD

**Burnt Cape Ecological Reserve is remote, but well worth the drive for intriguing flora and stunning ocean views.**

### 🄲 Burnt Cape Ecological Reserve

Encompassing a barren landscape of limestone, this park is an unheralded highlight of the Northern Peninsula. The plant life is especially notable, as many species would normally only be found in Arctic regions, while others such as Long's Braya and Burnt Cape cinquefoil are found nowhere else in the world. A geological oddity are *polygons,* circular patterns of small stones formed by heavy frosts. On the western edge of the cape are sea caves, some big enough to hold pools of water when the tide recedes. Looking straight ahead from the parking lot, you'll see aquamarine pools of water at the base of the cliffs, known locally as the Cannon Holes. The sun reflecting on the limestone bedrock warms the trapped seawater, and you'll often see locals taking a dip on hot days.

To get there, turn left in downtown Raleigh, round the head of Ha Ha Bay, and follow the rough unpaved road up and through the barrens. The end of the road is a semi-official parking lot high above the ocean four kilometers from the interpretive board at the entrance to the reserve. As there are no marked trails and many of the highlights are hidden from view, a much better option is to visit the site with a guide. Tours depart from Pisolet Bay Provincial Park (just before Raleigh) June–September daily at 9:30 A.M. and 2 P.M. The cost is just $5 per person. For reservations, drop by the office at Pisolet Bay Provincial Park or call 709/454-7795.

## Accommodations and Camping

The only accommodation in town is a good one—**Burnt Cape Cabins** (709/452-3521, www.burntcape.com; $120 s or d), which are in town and beside a café (daily 8 A.M.–9 P.M.) serving inexpensive seafood. Each of the two modern cabins has a TV, Internet access, and comfortable beds.

Just before Route 437 descends to Raleigh, it passes **Pisolet Bay Provincial Park** (709/454-7570; June–mid-Sept.), which offers 30 sites, a kitchen shelter, washrooms with showers, and a lake with a beach and swimming. Camping is $18, or a day pass is $5.

NEWFOUNDLAND AND LABRADOR

# LABRADOR

Spanning 294,330 square kilometers, two and a half times the size of Newfoundland island and three times the size of the three Maritime provinces, Labrador dominates Atlantic Canada. This, the mainland portion of Newfoundland and Labrador, resembles an irregular wedge pointing toward the North Pole, bordered on the east by 8,000 kilometers of coastline on the Labrador Sea, and on the west and south by the remote outskirts of Québec. Thorfinn Karlsefni, one of several Norse explorers who sailed the coastline around A.D. 1000, is said to have dubbed the region Helluland for the large flat rocks, and Markland for the woodlands. Jacques Cartier described the coastline as a "land of stone and rocks" during a 1534 voyage.

Labrador can be divided into three geographical destinations. Along the Strait of Belle Isle, the narrow passage between Labrador and Newfoundland, is a string of communities fronting the Strait of Belle Isle. Known as the Labrador Straits and linked to Newfoundland by ferry, this region was a Basque whaling center in the 1500s. Modern sightseers have rediscovered the strait and its archaeological treasures at Red Bay and L'Anse Amour. Spruce forests, interspersed with bogs and birch and tamarack stands, dominate the wilderness of central Labrador. The watery complex of Lobstick Lake, Smallwood Reservoir, Michikamau Lake, and the Churchill River and its tributaries are the main geographical features. The Churchill flows out of the western saucer-shaped plateau and rushes eastward, widening into Lake Melville at the commercial hub of Happy Valley–Goose Bay, which

# HIGHLIGHTS

◖ **L'Anse Amour:** North America's oldest known burial site and an imposing stone lighthouse combine to make the short detour to the "cove of love" a highlight (page 387).

◖ **Red Bay National Historic Site:** Four Spanish galleons lie in Red Bay; onshore displays tell their story and that of what was at one time the world's largest whaling port (page 388).

◖ **Battle Harbour:** Known locally as "outports," dozens of remote communities throughout Newfoundland and Labrador have been abandoned over the last few decades. Battle Harbour is one of the few that encourages tourism (page 388).

◖ **North West River:** A short drive from Happy Valley–Goose Bay, this small community is home to a museum filled with local history, while down along the river you can watch the Innu hauling in the day's catch (page 392).

◖ **Nain and the Far North:** Labrador's northernmost town is no scenic gem, but reaching this remote outport aboard the MV *Ranger* is an adventure in itself (page 395).

LOOK FOR ◖ TO FIND RECOMMENDED SIGHTS, ACTIVITIES, DINING, AND LODGING.

grew from an important military base. In western Labrador, iron-ore mining developed in the late 1950s. The twin cities of Labrador City and Wabush started as mining towns, and together they now serve as the region's economic and transportation center. With a population of 11,300, Labrador City/Wabush is Labrador's largest municipality. Between Labrador City and Happy Valley–Goose Bay a massive hydroelectric plant, developed in the late 1960s, spawned another company town—Churchill Falls. Linked to the outside world by ferry, the North Coast is dotted with tiny Inuit settlements.

Many visitors to Labrador are anglers, who rank the sportfishing among the world's best. The fishing is said to be Atlantic Canada's finest: It's not uncommon to land an *ouananiche* (landlocked salmon) weighing four kilograms. Brook trout here range 3–4 kilograms, lake trout to 18 kilograms, northern pike 9–14 kilograms, and arctic char 5–7 kilograms.

## PLANNING YOUR TIME

Mostly due to its remote location, Labrador is the least visited region of Atlantic Canada. It can be divided into three regions—Labrador Straits, across the Strait of Belle Isle from Newfoundland's Northern Peninsula; Central Labrador, along the TransLabrador Highway, and the North Coast. While the northern regions attract serious adventurers, the main attractions lie along the Labrador Straits, easily accessible by ferry from the

NEWFOUNDLAND AND LABRADOR

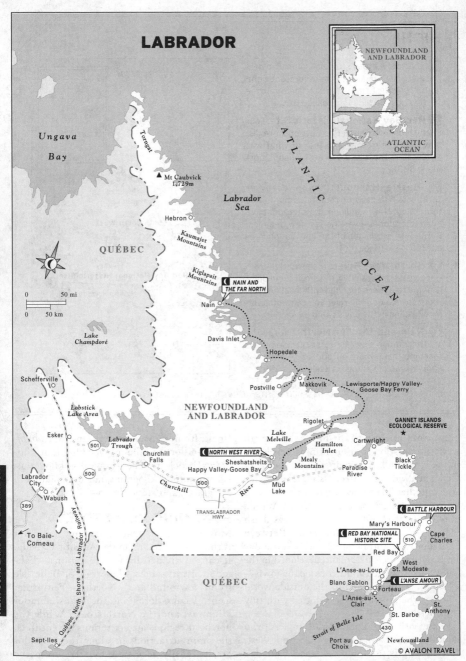

# LABRADOR

NEWFOUNDLAND AND LABRADOR

ATLANTIC OCEAN

*Ungava Bay*

Torngat

▲ Mt Caubvick 1,729m

*Labrador Sea*

Hebron

*Kaumajet Mountains*

QUÉBEC

*Kiglapait Mountains*

☾ **NAIN AND THE FAR NORTH**

Nain

0   50 mi
0   50 km

*Lake Champdoré*

Davis Inlet

Hopedale

Scheffervile

Postville   Makkovik

Lewisporte/Happy Valley-Goose Bay Ferry

*Lobstick Lake Area*

NEWFOUNDLAND AND LABRADOR

Esker

*Labrador Trough*

501

Rigolet

GANNET ISLANDS ECOLOGICAL RESERVE ★

*Lake Melville*

☾ **NORTH WEST RIVER**

Churchill Falls

Sheshatsheits
Happy Valley-Goose Bay

500

*Hamilton Inlet*

Cartwright

Black Tickle

Labrador City

Wabush

500

*Churchill*   *River*

*Mealy Mountains*

Paradise River

389

To Baie-Comeau

TRANSLABRADOR HWY

Mud Lake

☾ **BATTLE HARBOUR**

Mary's Harbour

Cape Charles

☾ **RED BAY NATIONAL HISTORIC SITE**

510

Red Bay

West St. Modeste

L'Anse-au-Loup

Blanc Sablon

Forteau

☾ **L'ANSE AMOUR**

QUÉBEC

L'Anse-au-Clair

St. Anthony

St. Barbe

430

Sept-Iles

Québec North Shore and Labrador Railway

*Strait of Belle Isle*

Port au Choix

Newfoundland

© AVALON TRAVEL

Northern Peninsula. Along a 120-kilometer stretch of highway is a string of picturesque fishing villages. Some are more historic than others. At **L'Anse Amour** you can view North America's oldest known burial site; **Red Bay National Historic Site** tells the story of a Basque whaling port. One of the most moving experiences in all of Atlantic Canada is a visit to **Battle Harbour,** an island fishing community that was abandoned in the late 1960s. Today, you can relive the glory days of this remote port, and even stay overnight. Unlike many other destinations, getting to and traveling around Labrador is part of the adventure, and nothing is more out there than catching the ferry to **Nain,** Labrador's most remote community.

Getting around Labrador requires some advance planning. The communities of Labrador Straits are linked by Route 510 from Blanc Sablon, where ferries land from Newfoundland. The 510 extends north through Cartwright for 250 kilometers to Goose Bay. The 520-kilometer unpaved TransLabrador Highway crosses Central Labrador from Labrador City to Happy Valley–Goose Bay. Intraprovincial ferry routings are to be tweaked when a highway link is completed between Cartwright and Goose Bay in 2009. Deciding *when* to travel to Labrador is easy. July and August are the only two months that you will find all attractions open. June and September are shoulder months, when weather is a little cooler, and attractions begin opening and closing. Also beware that transportation is conducted on a weather-permitting basis. Early-season ice packs and late-season storms can delay the ferries. The region's smaller aircraft need daylight and good visibility for flights. An absence of both may ground flights for days.

# Labrador Straits

The communities of Labrador Straits lie across the Strait of Belle Isle from Newfoundland. They are linked by a 160-kilometer stretch of paved road that extends between Blanc Sablon (Québec) and Mary's Harbour. From Mary's Harbour an unpaved road loops inland and continues north to Cartwright, from where ferries ply the open ocean and then Lake Melville to Goose Bay. In 2009, a highway, currently under construction from a point 87 kilometers south of Cartwright to Goose Bay, is to replace the ferry.

## Getting There by Ferry

The **MV *Apollo*** ferry (866/535-2567, www .tw.gov.nl.ca/ferryservices) links the Labrador Straits to Newfoundland. Ferries depart St. Barbe, 300 kilometers north of Deer Lake, once or twice daily between early May and early January. The crossing takes around two hours. The arrival point is Blanc Sablon, in Québec but just a five-minute drive from L'Anse-au-Clair, within Labrador. If the weather is pleasant, find a spot outside and keep an eye out for whales. Inside, you find a café and gift shop. The one-way fare is vehicle and driver $23, extra adult $7.50, senior and child $6. Reservations are not required but definitely recommended for travel in July and August. Even with a reservation, upon arrival at St. Barbe you should check in at the ferry office. It is within the Dockside Motel (on the right before the terminal) and opens two hours before scheduled departures. At Blanc Sablon, the ferry office is at the terminal, along with a craft shop, food concession, and information booth.

## L'ANSE-AU-CLAIR

Founded in the early 18th century by French sealers, L'Anse-au-Clair is the closest strait community to the Québec border. Fishing is still the livelihood for the population of about 300, although crafts also contribute to its economy. For these, head to **Moore's Handicrafts** (8 Country Rd., 709/931-1022;

summer daily 8:30 A.M.–10 P.M.), signposted across from the information center. Pieces to look for include hand-knit woolens, winter coats, cassocks, and moccasins.

## Sights and Recreation

The **Gateway to Labrador Visitor Centre** (709/931-2013; mid-June–Sept. daily 9:30 A.M.–5:30 P.M.), the region's interpretive center seen as you enter town from Québec, is in a handsomely restored, early-20th-century Anglican church. Inside, exhibits, photographs, fossils, and artifacts represent the area's fishing heritage.

The information center can also point out two interesting walks. The shorter of the two is to the "Jersey Rooms," site of an early 1700s sealing station operated by men from Jersey. Only stone foundations and a stone walkway remain, but the two-kilometer trail also offers sweeping ocean views. The trailhead is signposted beyond the wharf. At the far end of the beach, a trail leads across the barrens to Square Cove, where the boilers are all that remains of a 1954 shipwreck. In August, wild strawberries are a bonus along this three-kilometer (each way) walk.

## Accommodations and Food

Turn at the information center to reach the **Beachside Hospitality Home** (9 Lodge Rd., 709/931-2338), which isn't right on the water, but the beach is just one block away. Three guest rooms share two bathrooms, the living room has satellite TV, and a continental breakfast is included in the rates of $40 s, $50 d.

The largest accommodation along the Labrador Straits is the **Northern Light Inn** (58 Main St., 709/931-2332 or 800/563-3188, www.northernlightinn.com; from $90 s or d), which has 54 comfortable rooms. The inn's restaurant (daily 7 A.M.–10 P.M.) is well-priced throughout the day, with dinner mains topping out at $24 for steamed crab legs with mashed potato and vegetables. Other dinner offerings are as simple as spaghetti and meatballs and as fishy as pan-fried halibut.

The Gateway to Labrador Visitor Centre is in this church on the hill leading down to L'Anse-au-Clair.

## FORTEAU

Established as a cod-fishing settlement by islanders from Jersey and Guernsey in the late 1700s, Forteau remains a fishing community, not only in the cod industry but also as a base for anglers fishing the salmon- and trout-filled Forteau and Pinware Rivers.

The **Bakeapple Folk Festival,** held over three days in mid-August, is always popular. The gathering includes traditional music, dance, storytelling, crafts, and Labrador foods.

## Accommodations and Food

Forteau's accommodations include the **Grenfell Louie A Hall Bed and Breakfast** (3 Willow Ave., 709/931-2916, www.grenfellbandb.ca; May–Oct.; $50–65 d), in a nursing station built by the International Grenfell Association. The five guest rooms are comfortable but share bathrooms. Other amenities include an antique-filled dining room and a lounge room

# THE GRENFELL LEGEND

Labrador's harsh living conditions and lack of medical care attracted Dr. Wilfred Grenfell, the British physician-missionary. Dr. Grenfell worked with the Royal National Mission to Deep Sea Fishermen on the North Sea. A visit in 1892 convinced him that serving the people of remote Labrador and northern Newfoundland was his calling. He established Labrador's first coastal hospital at Battle Harbour the next year, followed by a large mission at St. Anthony. From the mission, he sailed along the coast in mission boats, treating 15,000 patients in 1900 alone. By 1907 he had opened treatment centers at Indian Harbour, Forteau, North West River, and seven other remote settlements. For his efforts, he was knighted.

Dr. Grenfell initiated a policy of free medical treatment, clothing, or food in exchange for labor or goods. Funded by private contributions and the Newfoundland government, he opened cooperative stores, nursing homes, orphanages, mobile libraries, and lumber mills. He also initiated the Grenfell Handicrafts programs and home gardening projects. In 1912, he formed the International Grenfell Association to consolidate the English, Canadian, and American branches that funded his work. The physician was subsequently knighted a second time, in 1927, and also awarded recognition by the Royal Scottish Geographical Society and other notable organizations.

where you can watch films on the Grenfell legacy or read up on local history.

Along the highway in the center of town, **Seaview Restaurant and Cabins** (33 Main St., 709/931-2840; $90 s, $95 d) has motel rooms, not cabins, but they are comfortable, and each has a TV and telephone. The restaurant (daily 9 A.M.–10 P.M.) has a few local specialties, such as caribou burgers and halibut chowder.

# L'ANSE AMOUR

Just off Route 510, this tiny community comprises just four houses, all owned by members of the Davis family, residents since the 1850s. The bay was originally named Anse aux Morts ("Cove of the Dead") for the many shipwrecks that occurred in the treacherous waters offshore. A mistranslation by later English settlers resulted quite charmingly in the name L'Anse Amour ("Cove of Love").

## Maritime Archaic Burial Mound National Historic Site

Turn off Route 510 to L'Anse Amour and watch for a small interpretive board on the right. Here, in 1973, archaeologists uncovered a Maritime Archaic burial site of a 12-year-old boy dated to 6900 B.C., which makes it North America's oldest known funeral monument. The dead boy was wrapped in skins and birch bark, and placed faced down a pit. Items such as a walrus tusk were excavated from the pit, and other evidence points to a ceremonial feast. The artifacts found here are on display at The Rooms in St. John's.

## Point Amour Lighthouse

At the end of the road is Point Amour Lighthouse (709/927-5825; summer daily 10 A.M.–5:30 P.M.). The strait's rich sea has attracted intrepid fishing fleets through the centuries: The early Basques sailed galleons into Red Bay, followed by English and French fleets, and eventually Newfoundlanders arrived in schooners to these shores. By 1857, shipwrecks littered the treacherous shoals, and the colonial government erected this 33-meter-high beacon, Atlantic Canada's tallest. Now restored, the stone lighthouse and light keeper's residence (now the interpretive center) feature displays and exhibits on the history of those who have plied the strait's waters. The 122-step climb to the top (the final section is a ladder) affords excellent views of the strait and the surrounding land.

## Accommodations

One of the village's four homes operates as

NEWFOUNDLAND AND LABRADOR

( **Lighthouse Cove B&B** (709/927-5690; $40 s, $45 d), with three rooms open year-round for travelers. The hosts, Rita and Cecil Davis, are very hospitable, spending the evening with guests relating stories of the area and their family's long association with the cove. When you make a reservation, be sure to reserve a spot at the dinner table (extra) for a full meal of traditional Labrador cooking using game such as moose and caribou. Breakfast, included in the rate, comes with homemade preserves.

## RED BAY

Little evidence is left today, but 400 years ago Red Bay was the world's largest whaling port. Not discovered until the 1970s, four Spanish galleons at the bottom of the bay have taught archaeologists many secrets about the whaling industry and early boat construction; an excellent two-part historic site brings the port to life. The village itself, 40 kilometers north of L'Anse Amour, has limited services.

It is estimated that between 1540 and 1610 around 2,500 Basque men (from an area of Spain near the French border) would make the crossing from Europe each year, traveling in up to 30 galleons that returned to Europe filled with whale oil. The Basques came to harvest right whales, which migrated through the Strait of Belle Isle. Most of the men lived aboard the galleons, but evidence shows some built simple shelters on the mainland and Saddle Island, where red roof tiles still litter the beaches.

### ( Red Bay National Historic Site

Four Spanish galleons lie in Red Bay, including the well-preserved *San Juan*. Archaeologists have done extensive research on all four, and they now lie in the cold shallow water covered with tarpaulins. While you can't view the actual boats, two excellent facilities combine to make up Red Bay National Historic Site (709/920-2051; June 15–Oct. 15 daily 9 A.M.–6 P.M.; adult $7.50, senior $5.25, child $3.60). Coming off the highway, the first of the two historic site buildings is a modern structure centering on a *chalupa*, a wooden whaling

boat recovered from the bottom of Red Bay. You can watch a documentary on the galleon *San Juan* and have staff point out where each of the galleons is located. Keep your receipt and head toward the waterfront, where the main collection of artifacts is held. Displays describe how the four galleons, each from a different era, have helped archaeologists track ship design through the 16th and 17th centuries. Highlights include a scale model of the *San Juan,* pottery, and remains of a compass and sandglass.

### Accommodations and Food

The single lodging choice at Red Bay is ( **Basin View B&B** (Rte. 510, 709/920-2002), a modern home overlooking the bay from a rocky shoreline just before reaching the town itself. The three downstairs rooms share a single bathroom. The upstairs guest room has a private bathroom but less privacy as it is on the main level of the house. Rates are $45–70 s or d, which includes a light breakfast.

Down by the harbor but without water views, **Whaler's Restaurant** (709/920-2156; daily 8 A.M.–9 P.M.) is one of the region's better dining rooms. The seafood chowder ($4.50) is good, as is the beef soup ($3). For a main, the fish-and-chips ($12) is delicious while the pork chop dinner ($10) is simple and hearty.

## MARY'S HARBOUR

Beyond Red Bay, Route 510 is unpaved for 80 kilometers to Mary's Harbour. This small fishing village, where the local economy revolves around a crab-processing plant, was isolated until 2000, when the road was completed.

The main reason to travel this far north is to visit Battle Harbour, and as the ferry leaves from Mary's Harbour, the local **Riverlodge Hotel** (709/921-6948; $85–95) makes a sensible overnight stop. The 15 rooms are simple but comfortable, and the in-house restaurant has pleasant views across the St. Mary's River.

## ( BATTLE HARBOUR

On a small island an hour's boat ride from Mary's Harbour lies Battle Harbour, a remote

© ANDREW HEMPSTEAD

Battle Harbour is a remote coastal village that was abandoned in the 1960s, but is now open to visitors.

yet intriguing outport village that is well worth the effort to reach.

Established as a fishing village in 1759, it was one of the earliest European settlements on the Labrador coast. By 1775, Battle Harbour's cod-fishing industry had made the settlement the economic center of the region, a status that faded and then rebounded a century later with the arrival of seasonal fishers from Newfoundland. By 1848 Battle Harbour was the capital of Labrador, an important trade and supply center where up to 100 vessels would be tied up in port at any one time. Thanks to the work of missionary Wilfred Grenfell, the residents had year-round medical services and, by 1904, state-of-the-art communications thanks to the Marconi Wireless Telegraph Company, which erected a station here in 1904.

In the late 1960s, with the inshore fishery in decline, Battle Harbour residents were resettled on the mainland at Mary's Harbour, leaving the community an abandoned outport. A few local families continued to spend summers on the island, but it wasn't until 1990 that the

Battle Harbour Historic Trust took over the site and began an ambitious restoration program that continues to this day. Now protected as a national historic site, Battle Harbour allows a glimpse into the past. Around 20 structures have been restored, including an Anglican church, the original mercantile salt fish premises, the loft from where Edward Peary told the world of his successful expedition to reach the North Pole, a general store, and a massive fish flake. A boardwalk links many of the restored buildings, tapering out near the back of the village where a dozen or so homes stand in varying states of disrepair and a trail leads through a rock cleft to a cemetery.

## Accommodations and Food

In addition to restoring many of the most important buildings, the **Battle Harbour Historic Trust** (709/921-6216, www.battle-harbour.com) does a wonderful job of providing visitor services, including accommodations, meals, and transportation.

On a rise overlooking the town and Great

Caribou Island, a merchant's home has been converted to the ◖ **Battle Harbour Inn.** Three of the five guest rooms have double beds ($145 d) and two have single beds ($125 s). Other buildings with beds include the Cookhouse ($35 for a bunk bed); the Grenfell Cottage, which has harbor views and a kitchen ($115 s, $125 d); the RCMP Cottage, which also has a kitchen ($115 s, $125 d); the three-bedroom Isaac Smith Cottage, which is lighted by oil lamps and heated by wood fire ($325); and the very private two-bedroom Spearing Cottage ($180).

Meals are provided in a dining room above the general store. Breakfast ($10), lunch ($15), and dinner ($25) are all hearty meals with plenty of cross-table conversation between diners. Day-trippers are more than welcome at lunch. At the general store itself, you can buy snacks and provisions.

## Getting There and Around

The trip between Mary's Harbour and Battle Harbour takes around one hour aboard a small enclosed ferry. The ferry departs Mary's Harbour daily at 11 A.M. and 7 P.M., with the latter sailing designed for overnight guests. Return trips depart Battle Harbour at 9 A.M. and 4 P.M. The round-trip fare is adult $60, child $30, plus a $7 island interpretation fee that includes a two-hour guided tour of the site.

# CARTWRIGHT

Most travelers incorporate Cartwright, 237 kilometers north of Mary's Harbour along an unpaved road, into their itineraries as part of a loop that includes driving the TransLabrador Highway through to Québec along a new stretch of highway set to open in 2009.

## Sights

The town was named for 18th-century merchant adventurer and coastal resident Captain George Cartwright; **Flagstaff Hill Monument,** overlooking the town and Sandwich Bay, still has the cannons Cartwright installed to guard the harbor 200 years ago.

**Gannet Islands Ecological Reserve,** off the coast, is a breeding colony for common murres, puffins, black-legged kittiwakes, and the province's largest razorbill population. North of Cartwright lies the spot where Norse sailors first laid eyes on the coast: Wunderstrands, a remarkable 56-kilometer stretch of sandy golden beach. The local tour operator, **Experience Labrador** (709/653-2244 or 877/938-7444), has an overnight sea-kayaking trip to Wunderstrands for $350 per person. The company has many other scheduled sea-kayaking trips and charges $250 per day for boat tours.

## Accommodations and Food

The **Cartwright Hotel** (3 Airport Rd., 709/938-7414, www.cartwrighthotel.ca) holds 10 basic motel rooms ($100 s, $110–140 d), each with cable TV and a coffeemaker. The hotel also has a restaurant offering everything from fried chicken to Atlantic salmon. Also at the hotel is the Eagle's Nest Lounge, which hosts a dance on Saturday night.

# Central Labrador

## HAPPY VALLEY-GOOSE BAY

Happy Valley–Goose Bay (pop. 7,500) spreads across a sandy peninsula bordered by the Churchill River, Goose Bay, and Terrington Basin at the head of Lake Melville. Although remote, it is linked to the outside world by an unpaved highway and scheduled ferry and air services.

During World War II, Canadian forces selected the Goose Bay site and, with assistance from the British Air Ministry and the U.S. Air Force, built a massive airbase and two airstrips there. Before the war ended, 24,000 aircraft set down for refueling during the transatlantic crossing. Currently operated by the Canadian Armed Forces, 5 Wing Goose Bay Airport serves as a training center for Canadian, British, Dutch, Italian, and German air forces, the latter four countries with no airspace of their own suitable for low-level flight training. Goose Bay is also an important refueling stop for transatlantic flights, with a runway long enough to accommodate space shuttle landings in an emergency. The town last hit the headlines on September 11, 2001, when the airport filled with commercial flights that were diverted from their intended destinations.

Happy Valley–Goose Bay originally evolved as two distinct areas: Goose Bay, rimming an important air base, and adjacent Happy Valley, which became the base's residential and commercial sector. In 1961 the two areas joined as Happy Valley–Goose Bay and elected the first town council, which was Labrador's first municipal government. The distinction between the two areas remains firm, so be prepared to consult a map as you wander around. Goose Bay connects to Happy Valley by the L-shaped Hamilton River Road, the main drag.

### Town Sights

In the Northern Lights Building, the **Northern Lights Military Museum** (170 Hamilton River Rd., 709/896-5939; Tues.–Sat. 9 A.M.–5:30 P.M.) offers exhibits pertaining to military history from World War I to the Vietnam War. Displays include uniforms, medals, documents, weapons, and photographs. Across the

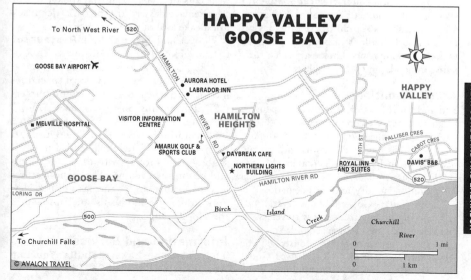

© AVALON TRAVEL

**NEWFOUNDLAND AND LABRADOR**

hall, the **Trapper's Brook Animal Display** exhibits stuffed native animals and birds—from beavers and bears to bald eagles. Also in the building is the **Labrador Institute** (709/896-6210), an arm of Memorial University of Newfoundland. Of interest to the public is an archive of historic maps and photographs, along with a crafts display.

## ◖ North West River

This community of 500, northeast of Goose Bay 38 kilometers on Route 520, was the center of the area until the 1940s. The settlement began as a French trading post in 1743, and the inhabitants are descendants of French, English, and Scottish settlers.

Within town are two worthwhile sights. The **Labrador Interpretation Centre** (Portage Rd., 709/497-8566; Tues.–Sun. 1–4 P.M.; free) is filled with interesting exhibits that catalog the natural and human history of "the Big Land." Beyond the center, Portage Road leads to piers and pleasant views. If you'd like to meet some of the locals, arrive in late afternoon, when the Innu fishers collect the day's catch from nets strung across the waterway. Within an original Hudson's Bay Company building, the **Labrador Heritage Museum** (Portage Rd.; summer Wed.–Sun. 8:30 A.M.–4:30 P.M.; adult $2, child $1) provides an insight into Labrador's early years with photographs, manuscripts, books, artifacts, furs, native minerals, and other displays.

## Accommodations

Bed-and-breakfasts offer the least-expensive lodgings. **Davis' Bed and Breakfast** (14 Cabot Cres., Happy Valley, 709/896-5077; $40–50 s, $50–60 d) has four guest rooms with private baths. Rates include a continental breakfast (a full breakfast costs extra). Facilities include a dining room, laundry, and outside patio.

Happy Valley–Goose Bay has several motels catering mostly to business travelers. In general, rooms are of an acceptable standard and expensive, but not outrageously so. The **Royal Inn and Suites** (3 Royal Ave., Goose Bay, 709/896-2456 or 888/440-2456, www

.royalinnandsuites.ca) is my pick of the bunch. It has 29 bright modern rooms starting at $83 s, $93 d. Business Class Suites ($125 s, $135 d) have separate bedrooms, TV/DVD combos, kitchens, and high-speed Internet.

The town's two other motels are side by side on Hamilton River Road opposite Loring Drive, the airport's access road. The **Labrador Inn** (380 Hamilton River Rd., 709/896-3351 or 800/563-2763, www.labradorinn.nf.ca; $95–125) has 74 basic to deluxe rooms, a restaurant, a lounge, and airport shuttles.

## Food

Fast-food places line Hamilton River Road, including the ubiquitous and ever-popular **Tim Hortons** (220 Hamilton River Rd., 709/896-5666) coffee-and-doughnut place. Farther down the hill, the **Daybreak Café** (178 Hamilton River Rd., 709/896-0936) serves up hearty breakfasts and healthy lunches daily from 7 A.M.

Hungry locals who love beef head for **Tricia Dee's Steak and Rib** (96 Hamilton River Rd., 709/896-3545; daily for lunch and dinner), where diners enjoy prime beef from western Canada and barbecued ribs. All manner of steak cuts are prepared any way you'd like. For a homemade dessert, try the dark, rich black forest cake ($6) or fruit or cream pies.

The casual ◖ **Caribou Restaurant** (Aurora Hotel, 382 Hamilton River Rd., 709/896-3398) features a menu of typical Canadian dishes and a few local specialties like lunchtime moose and caribou burgers ($8); dinner mains range a reasonable $15–27. Next door in the Labrador Inn, **Banniken's** (380 Hamilton River Rd., 709/896-3351; daily for breakfast, lunch, and dinner) is slightly more formal, with linen tablecloths laid out in the evening. The menu features lots of Labrador cuisine and pasta dishes, New York sirloin, T-bone steaks, and ribs—all in the $18–31 range.

## Information and Services

The **Labrador-Lake Melville Tourism Association** (709/896-3489, www.

# LAYING CLAIM TO LABRADOR

For centuries the French Canadians have asserted, "Labrador is part of Québec." And the British and the Newfoundlanders have traditionally countered, "Never!"

Labrador is a choice piece of property, and Québec has been a longtime avid suitor of North America's northeastern edge. Québec's interest in Labrador dates to 1744, when the French cut a deal with the British: Québec got jurisdiction over Labrador, but the island of Newfoundland got fishing rights in Labrador's coastal waters. The Treaty of Paris of 1763 went one step further, however, and awarded all of Labrador (not defined by a precise border) to Newfoundland. Newfoundland's claim gained more substance in 1825, when the British North America Act set Labrador's southern border with Québec at the 52nd parallel.

In the 1860s, when the Dominion of Canada was formed, the dispute over Labrador, formerly between France and England, now involved the new Confederation of Canada. Québec never disputed England's sovereignty over Labrador, but instead continued to question the location of the border. In 1898 the Québec border was unofficially as far east as what is now the town of Happy Valley–Goose Bay.

## FOR SALE: LABRADOR

Newfoundland put Labrador up for sale in 1909 for $9 million, but there were no takers. In the ensuing years, Labrador's precise border became a tedious issue for England, and so in 1927 a judicial committee in London set Labrador's border at the "height of the land,"

the watershed line separating the Atlantic Ocean from Ungava Bay, the current provincial border of today. In the decision, Labrador acquired the wedge-shaped "Labrador Trough," a delta area rich in iron ore deposits and rivers perfect for harnessing hydroelectric power.

## QUÉBEC'S CLOUT EMERGES

The only road access to Labrador is through Québec, so it is no surprise that that province became a major player in Labrador's economy. Québec bought into Labrador's hydroelectric fortune in the early 1970s. Québec's provincial Hydro-Québec now earns $200 million annually from within Labrador, while Newfoundland, another company shareholder, earns $12 million. Ironically, Newfoundland and Labrador receives none of the energy.

To this day, the province's western border remains to be fully surveyed, and Québec does not consider the issue settled. A fragile status quo exists between the two provinces, but the renaming of Newfoundland to Newfoundland and Labrador in 2001 brought official recognition to Labrador as part of Newfoundland.

## NUNATSIAVUT

In 2004, Labrador's Inuit people were successful in a land-claim process that took 30 years before coming to fruition. Led by the **Labrador Inuit Association** (709/922-2942, www.nunatsiavut.com), the indigenous people now have special rights to 142,000 square kilometers of land that extends north from Lake Melville to Torngat Mountains National Park. The latter was established as part of the claim.

tourismlabrador.com) operates a helpful information center along the main drag (365 Hamilton River Rd.; June–Sept. Mon.–Fri. 8 A.M.–8 P.M., Sat.–Sun. 8 A.M.–5 P.M.).

**Melville Hospital** (also called Grenfell Hospital), is at Building 550, G Street (near 5th Avenue). For the **RCMP** (149 Hamilton River Rd.), call 709/896-3383. **Post offices** are located on Hamilton River Road and at the airport.

## Getting There and Around

**Air Canada** (888/247-2262) flies into Goose Bay from Halifax and Toronto. **Air Labrador** (709/758-0002 or 800/563-3042, www.air-labrador.com) has direct flights between the capital, St. John's, and Goose Bay, as well as via Deer Lake. This airline also flies from Montréal to Wabash and then on to Goose Bay as well as between Blanc Sablon and Goose Bay. **Provincial Airlines** (709/576-3943 or

800/563-2800, www.provair.com) has flights to Goose Bay from as far away as Montreal and St. John's.

**Budget** (709/896-2973) and **National** (709/896-5575) have rental cars in town and out at the airport, but neither company allows its vehicles on the TransLabrador Highway. **Deluxe Cabs** (709/896-2424) charges around $6 per trip anywhere within Goose Bay, and $15 between the airport and Happy Valley.

## CHURCHILL FALLS

Churchill Falls, 288 kilometers west of Goose Bay, is a relatively modern town constructed to serve the needs of workers at one of North America's largest hydroelectric schemes. The waters of the Churchill River drop more than 300 meters over a 32-kilometer section—ideal for generating hydroelectric power. In an incredible feat of engineering, the water is diverted underground to the massive generators, which produce 5,220 megawatts of electricity. Organized tours of the facility (around two hours) can be arranged at the town office (709/925-3335).

The 21-room **Churchill Falls Inn** (709/925-3211 or 800/229-3269; $85 s, $95 d) is a modern lodging attached to the main town office complex. Rates include use of an indoor pool.

## LABRADOR CITY AND WABUSH

Continuing west from Churchill Falls, the twin towns of Labrador City and Wabush, five kilometers apart, lie 530 kilometers from Goose Bay and just 23 kilometers from the Québec–Labrador border. Labradorians knew of the area's iron-ore potential in the late 1800s, and massive ore deposits were discovered in 1958. The Iron Ore Company of Canada and Wabush Mines, served by the two towns, together rank as the Canadian steel industry's largest supplier. The two extract 20 million metric tons of iron ore a year.

Lodging in the two towns is limited to just over 100 rooms in three motels. **Two Seasons Inn** (Avalon Dr., Labrador City, 709/944-2661 or 800/670-7667, www.twoseasonsinn.com; $97 s, $105 d) has 37 standard rooms, airport shuttle service, a restaurant, and all the amenities of a big-city hotel. The **Wabush Hotel** (9 Grenfell Dr., Wabush, 709/282-3221, www.wabush-hotel.com; $98 s, $108 d) is an imposing property dating to the 1960s. The 68 rooms have been revamped a few times since, and services include a Chinese/Canadian buffet lunch and dinner in its restaurant and a convenience store.

At **Duley Lake Family Park** (10 km west of Labrador City, 709/282-3660; late May–Sept.), choose between campsites on either the lake or river for $12 per night. The campground has a sandy beach, boating, fishing, and picnicking. **Grande Hermine Park** (45 km east of Labrador City, 709/282-5369; June–Aug.) offers 45 powered sites and 30 unserviced sites from $12 per night. Facilities include a boat launch, a convenience store, and paddleboat rentals.

# North Coast

Labrador's northern coast evokes images of another world. It's the Labrador you might imagine: raw and majestic with the craggy Torngat, Kaumajet, and Kiglapait mountain ranges rising to the north.

The 1763 Treaty of Paris ceded the Labrador coastline to Britain's Newfoundland colony, but the imprint of European architecture only reached the northern seacoast when the Moravians, an evangelical Protestant sect from Bohemia, established mission stations with prefabricated wooden buildings starting in the early 19th century. It is in these remote north coast villages—Rigolet, Postville, Makkovik, and Nain—that the original inhabitants, the Inuit, have settled. Few aspects of these towns have changed over the last century, and the lifestyle of northern peoples here remains traditional.

## Getting There

Access to Labrador's north coast is by air or sea. The communities are linked to the outside world by **Air Labrador** (709/753-5593 or 800/563-3042, www.airlabrador .com) from Goose Bay, or by a cargo and passenger ferry that takes two days to reach its northern turnaround point, Nain. Riding the ferry, the **MV Northern Ranger,** is a real adventure. The one-way fare for an adult between Goose Bay and Nain is $143. A single berth in a cabin costs $80, while a private cabin costs from $450. For more information, call 800/563-6353. The website www .tw.gov.nl.ca/ferryservices lists a schedule and prices, with distances included to make calculations easy.

## MAKKOVIK

After stopping at Rigolet, the MV *Northern Ranger* starts its long haul through open ocean, reaching Makkovik (pop. 400) 18 hours after leaving Goose Bay. The ferry makes a 90-minute stop on the way north and a three-hour stop on the return

journey. Makkovik was first settled in the early 1800s by a Norwegian fur trader; the Moravians constructed a mission here in 1896. Today this two-story building holds the **White Elephant Museum** (July–Aug. daily 1–5 p.m., or call 709/923-2262 for an appointment). Local shops such as the **Makkovik Craft Centre** (709/923-2246) sell Inuit crafts, including fur caps, boots and mittens, parkas, moose-hide moccasins, and bone and antler jewelry.

Right on the water, the **Adlavik Inn** (7 Willow Creek Ln., 709/923-2389, www .labradorabletours.com; $95 s, $130 d) has the only five guest rooms in town, so call ahead if your itinerary includes an overnight stay in Makkovik. Rooms have TVs and phones, and meals are served in an adjacent dining room.

## HOPEDALE

Around 110 nautical miles north of Makkovik and 122 miles short of Nain, the MV *Northern Ranger* makes a two-hour stop at Hopedale, just enough time to go ashore and visit the 1782 **Hopedale Mission National Historic Site** (709/933-3777; $6), containing the oldest wooden frame building east of Québec. Here, a restored Hudson's Bay Company storeroom has been converted into a museum; other site highlights include huts, a residence, and a graveyard. It generally opens whenever the ferry is in town.

Accommodations are provided at **Amaguk Inn** (709/933-3750, www.labradoradventures .com), which charges $105 s, $115 d for one of its 12 rooms. Meals are available at the inn for both guests and nonguests.

## ◖ NAIN AND THE FAR NORTH

With stunning coastal scenery, stops at remote villages, and the chance to see whales and icebergs, the long trip north aboard the MV *Northern Ranger* ferry is a real adventure, but after two days on board, the captain's announcement of imminent arrival in Nain is welcome. In the early 1900s, an epidemic of Spanish flu—introduced from a supply ship—destroyed a third of the indigenous population on the northern coast. The Inuit who survived resettled at Nain, which now has a population of just over 1,000 and is the northernmost municipality on the Labrador coast. Life is rugged this far north—electricity is provided by diesel generator; fuel and wood are used for domestic heat; local transportation is by boat in the summer and snowmobile in the winter. The only roads are within the town itself. The settlement's history is depicted at the **Nain Piulimatsivik** (Inuit for "Nain Museum") through Inuit and Moravian artifacts, vessels, and other displays.

## Accommodations and Food

For an overnight stay, there's just one option, the **Atsanik Lodge** (Sand Banks Rd., 709/922-2910; $115 s, $135 d). Each of the 25 rooms has cable TV, a phone, and a private bathroom. The lodge also has a lounge, restaurant, and laundry. It's open year-round. Other services include three retail shops, a takeout food joint, and a snowmobile dealership.

## Getting There

If you've arrived on the ferry, you'll have just three hours ashore to explore the town before the return journey. The alternative is to take the ferry one way and an **Air Labrador** (709/753-5593 or 800/563-3042) flight the other. The one-way fare to Goose Bay is $300 plus around $120 in taxes.

## Voisey Bay

Prior to the cod-fishing moratorium, the fishing industry dominated Nain, but now mining at Voisey Bay, 35 kilometers south, appears to be the economic engine of the future. It is home to world's largest known deposit of nickel and copper, with the main processing facility completed in early 2006.

## Continuing North

Labrador's northernmost remaining Moravian mission is protected at **Hebron Mission National Historic Site,** on the shores of remote Kangershutsoak Bay, 140 nautical miles north of Nain. Building began on the mission complex, including a church, residence, and store, in 1829. The mission remained in operation until 1959. **Nature Trek Canada** (250/653-4265, www.naturetrek.ca) stops in on its guided tours along the northern Labrador coastline.

# BACKGROUND
# AND ESSENTIALS

# BACKGROUND

## The Land

Atlantic Canada as a whole forms one-twentieth of the country's total area. The provinces, and the distances separating them, are far larger than they may seem at first glance, compared against the vastness of the whole of Canada. Nova Scotia, for example, is the country's second-smallest province, yet it will take you a long day to drive from Yarmouth, at the southern tip, to Cape Breton Highlands National Park, at the other end of the province. And from Cape Breton, it's a six-hour ferry ride to the next landfall—the island of Newfoundland—which itself lies nearer to Liverpool, England, than to Toronto.

### In the Beginning

Six hundred million years ago, the collision of the North American and European continental plates pushed up the Appalachian Mountains. The range's ribs, starting far to the south in Alabama, extend through New England and the Maritime provinces to the Gaspé Peninsula, whose highlands spread across Cape Breton and as far as Newfoundland. Geologists believe that the range was originally taller and more rugged than the modern Rockies. Glaciation and eons of erosion, however, have ground down the once-mammoth summits such that the rather modest 820-meter Mount

© ANDREW HEMPSTEAD

© ANDREW HEMPSTEAD

Some of the world's oldest rock is exposed in Labrador and along Newfoundland's Northern Peninsula.

Carleton, in New Brunswick, is today the Maritimes' highest point. The highest peak in the Atlantic provinces, northern Labrador's desolate Mount Caubvick, rises 1,729 meters above the Labrador Sea. Otherwise, great swaths of the region's terrain are mostly low and undulating, dipping and swelling in innumerable variations.

One of the reasons for this was glacial ice, uncountable trillions of tons of it, formed over the last four ice ages. Glaciers up to an estimated three kilometers thick weighed down on the elastic bedrock as recently as 14,000 years ago, submerging the coasts and counteracting the inexorable thrust of tectonic uplift.

Some 350 million years ago, as the tectonic plates shifted, a great slab of the earth's crust slumped, forming the valley that would be flooded by a rising sea to form the Bay of Fundy only 6,000 years ago.

## A Watery Wonderland

More than any other region of Canada, the

Atlantic provinces are defined by water, which divides and yet also unifies them. The planet's mightiest tides surge through the Bay of Fundy between New Brunswick and Nova Scotia. The Cabot Strait separates Nova Scotia's Cape Breton and the island of Newfoundland's southern coastline. The unexpectedly warm Northumberland Strait, heated by the Gulf Stream, is a broad blue parenthesis dividing Prince Edward Island from Nova Scotia and New Brunswick. On the island's north side spreads the Gulf of St. Lawrence. The Baie des Chaleurs, its warmth owing to its shallow depth, lies between northeastern New Brunswick and Québec's Gaspé Peninsula.

Along Labrador's coast, currents from the chilly Labrador Sea move southward and fork into a channel known as the Strait of Belle Isle, which separates the island of Newfoundland from the mainland, while the rest of the current washes along Newfoundland's eastern coast.

If it were possible to walk the profoundly reticulated coastlines of the four provinces, following every cove, bay, point, and peninsula, the footsore traveler would eventually log some 40,000 kilometers before returning to the starting point.

The sea's pervasive presence is felt throughout the region, but the ties to the ocean are perhaps strongest in Nova Scotia and Newfoundland, whose outer coasts confront the open Atlantic. The waters off Newfoundland in particular—the Gulf of St. Lawrence and the Grand Banks along the continental shelf—are among the most productive fisheries in the world, for five centuries an unbelievably rich resource for tuna, mackerel, herring, lobster, and cod.

Prince Edward Island, of course, is surrounded by water, so fishing is a major industry. But agriculture is an equally important component of the economy, the benevolent result of the last ice age, which blessed the land with a deep fertile loam. New Brunswick faces the sea on two sides and joins the mainland with a massive sweep of land rich in forests and ores, hence an economy comprised of fishing, forestry, and mining.

# COLOSSAL FUNDY TIDES

The world's highest tides rise in the upper Bay of Fundy, with up to a 17-meter vertical gain at the head of the bay. The tides work on roughly a six-hour cycle, and each peak or low arrives 50 minutes later each day. Twice daily, six hours after high tide, the bay is empty, but then the Fundy surges onward and water funnels into the bay and up numerous rivers. The upper Fundy is split into two arms by Cape Chignecto, the wedge-shaped point that angles into the bay. On its west side, Chignecto Bay with its raw lonesome coastline penetrates inland and finishes at Cumberland Basin near Amherst. On the cape's other side, the bay compresses itself first into the Minas Channel. It is here in the upper reaches of the bay that the tides are highest. By the time rising water funnels into the head of the bay, it is in the form of a **tidal bore** (lead wave) that rides inland up the area's rivers. The arriving wave can be a dainty, ankle-high ripple or an upright wall of knee-high water, depending on the tide.

Due to the convoluted coastline, viewing the phenomena is possible at dozens of points around the Bay of Fundy, including Truro (Nova Scotia) and Moncton (New Brunswick), where riverside parks have been set aside for watching the bore. At Hopewell Rocks (New Brunswick), you can "walk on the ocean floor" at low tide. If you're feeling more adventurous, you can even take a rafting trip down the Shubenacadie River (Nova Scotia) as the bore moves upstream. Tide tables are posted in shops and storefronts throughout the region. Tides are highest around the full or new moon.

**Warning:** The Bay of Fundy at low tide can be perilously alluring, when the coastal sea floor looks tranquilly bare and mudflats glisten like glass. High tide's arrival is subtle and hardly noticeable. The distant tidal stirrings alert sea birds, and they cry out and wheel and turn across the sky. But then the sea moves in relentlessly, swelling and pushing forward into the bay at 6 knots per hour – and up to 13 knots in tidal rips. The incoming sea can wash across the empty bay faster than a person can swiftly walk. Only a foolhardy sightseer walks the mudflats; the high tide stops for nothing.

© ANDREW HEMPSTEAD

When the tide goes out, boats are left high and dry on the ocean floor.

# CLIMATE

Maritime weather varies from province to province, and from region to region within the provinces. As a rule, though, extremes are moderated by proximity to the sea. The months from June through September are generally the most pleasant and popular for visiting. The regions' landscapes and seascapes are recast by the changing seasons. In springtime, occasional banks of thick fog blanket the coast from Yarmouth to St. John's. In summer, a pervasive balminess ripens the blueberry fields from Cumberland County in Nova Scotia to Newfoundland's Codroy Valley. Autumn brings the last burst of Indian summer, coloring the forests until winter's sea winds swirl in and send the leaves tumbling away to finish another year.

## Nova Scotia

The province has a pleasant, modified continental climate, moderated by air and water currents from the Gulf Stream and the Arctic. Summers are warm and winters are mild. Cape Breton is subject to more extreme weather than the mainland. Precipitation province-wide averages 130 centimeters, falling mainly as rain during autumn and as snow in winter.

Spring high temperatures range –2.5 to 9°C, though the days begin to warm up toward the end of March. Summer weather has a reputation for changing from day to day; daytime highs range up to 30°C, while nights are cool, averaging 12°C. Inland areas are generally 5°C warmer during the day. The coasts often bask in morning fog. Caribbean hurricanes, having spent their force farther south, limp through the region, bringing to the northwestern Atlantic short spells of rain and wind.

In autumn, the evenings start to cool, but pleasant days continue through September at up to 18°C. The days are cool to frosty October through mid-November. Winter lasts from late November through early March, with temperatures averaging –10 to 4°C.

## New Brunswick

New Brunswick's continental climate contrasts hot summers with cold winters. Extremes are moderated by the surrounding seas, more so near the coast than in the interior. Summer means warm days and cool nights, with an average daytime high temperature of 23°C in June, 26°C in July, and 25°C in August. July is the sunniest month. September and October are pleasantly warm, with increasingly cool days toward November. Winter is cold.

Precipitation throughout the province averages 115 centimeters annually. The Bay of Fundy coast is steeped in dense fog about 70 days a year.

## Prince Edward Island

The island basks in a typical maritime climate with one major exception: Its growing season of 110–160 days is Atlantic Canada's longest. The island also gets more than its share of year-round breezes, pleasant and warm in summer but fiercer come fall. Spring is short, lasting from early to mid-May until mid-June. Summer temperatures peak in July and August, when temperatures range 18–23°C; an unusually warm day can reach 35°C, while the other extreme can be quite cool at just 5°C. Autumn brings with it Atlantic Canada's brightest and most dramatic fall foliage. Winter temperatures can dip below 0°C in December and January.

Annual precipitation amounts to 106 centimeters, with half of that falling from May to October.

## Newfoundland and Labrador

The climate is harsher and more extreme here than in the Maritimes. A sultry summer day can be interspersed with chilly breezes, brilliant sun, dark clouds, and showers from light to drenching. The island's eastern and southern seacoasts are often foggy due to the offshore melding of the warm Gulf Stream and cold Labrador current.

Overall, the island has cool, moist, maritime weather. Summer days average 16–21°C, dropping to 9–12°C at night, but hot spells are common, and the swimming season starts by late June. The island's low-lying interior and coastal areas are warmest and sunniest. Annual

# SUMMER TEMPERATURES
**(IN DEGREES CELSIUS)**

| | JULY | | AUGUST | |
| --- | --- | --- | --- | --- |
| | Low | High | Low | High |
| Charlottetown, PEI | 14 | 23 | 14 | 23 |
| Corner Brook, NL | 12 | 22 | 12 | 21 |
| Fredericton, NB | 10 | 23 | 12 | 25 |
| Halifax, NS | 14 | 23 | 14 | 23 |
| Happy Valley-Goose Bay, NL | 10 | 21 | 9 | 19 |
| Moncton, NB | 10 | 25 | 12 | 24 |
| Saint John, NB | 12 | 22 | 11 | 22 |
| St. John's, NL | 11 | 21 | 12 | 20 |
| Sydney, NS | 12 | 23 | 13 | 23 |
| Yarmouth, NS | 12 | 20 | 12 | 21 |

rainfall averages 105 centimeters. Frost begins by early October on the southern coast, earlier farther north. Snowfall averages 300 centimeters a year.

Winter high temperatures average −4°C to 0°C, warm enough to turn snow to rain, while nighttime lows can tumble to −15°C. Expect year-round blustery winds along Marine Drive and nearby Cape Spear.

Labrador's climate is continental and subject to great extremes. Summers are short, cool to sometimes hot, and brilliantly sunny with periodic showers. A July day averages 21°C, but temperatures have been known to rise to 38°C at Happy Valley–Goose Bay. Temperatures drop rapidly after mid-August. By November, daytime highs at Goose Bay fall to 0°C. Winter is very cold and dry. Daytime high temperatures average −20°C in the subarctic, −18°C to −21°C in the interior, and −51°C in the western area.

## ENVIRONMENTAL ISSUES

The northeastern Atlantic fisheries have been the economic engine driving exploration and development of these coasts for centuries. In days past, codfish were said to carpet the sea floor of the shallow Grand Banks, and those who caught them—first with lines from small dories, then with nets, and finally from great trawlers that scour the sea—have hauled in untold millions of tons of not only cod but also flounder, salmon, pollack, haddock, anchovies, and dozens of other species. Today the fish are in serious trouble and so too, inexorably, are the people and communities whose lives have revolved around them.

Today, the state of local fisheries—most notably the collapse of cod stocks—is the most important environmental issue facing the region. The beginning of the end was the arrival of "factory ships" in the 1960s, which could harvest up to 200 tons of cod per hour. By the late 1980s the cod stock had been mostly obliterated, and by the early 1990s a moratorium was put in place until the fisheries had recovered. Unfortunately, what was not fully understood at that time was that overfishing was only a part of the problem. Cod are a groundfish, and the factory ships had been bottom trawling—scooping up the cod in nets with an opening up to one kilometer wide that dragged along the sea floor and decimated the very ecosystem that was a breeding ground for the fish. It is widely thought that the cod stock will never fully recover, especially in the waters around the island of Newfoundland.

## Contacts

An excellent website for learning more about the state of the ocean is www.seachoice.org. For information on general environmental issues in Atlantic Canada, contact the following organizations: **Canadian Parks and Wilderness Society Nova Scotia** (www .cpawsns.org), **Greenpeace** (www.greenpeace .ca), **Ecology Action Centre** (www.ecology-action.ca), and **Nova Scotia Environmental Network** (www.vws.org), and **Newfoundland & Labrador Environment Network** (www .nlen.ca). There are also a number of local environmentally aware groups, such as the **Southeast Environmental Association** on Prince Edward Island (www.seapei.ca).

# Flora and Fauna

To a great extent, it was the land's natural resources—and the potential riches they represented—that attracted Europeans to Canada over the centuries. Since time immemorial, mammals, fish, and varied plant species had, of course, fed and clothed the indigenous peoples, who harvested only enough to sustain themselves. But the very abundance of the wildlife seemed to fuel the rapacity of the newcomers, driving them to a sort of madness of consumption—and hastening the exploration and settlement of the newfound continent.

Cod, flounder, mackerel, herring, and scores of other fish species in unbelievable numbers first lured brave seafarers across the Atlantic as early as the 15th century. The great whales, too, fell victim to widespread slaughter. Later, the fur-bearing mammals—mink, otters, ermines, beavers, and seals—became a currency of trade and the sine qua non of fashionable attire. Birds, too, by the millions in hundreds of species, represented money on the wing to the newcomers. Some, like the flightless great auk of the northeastern coast, were hunted to extinction.

But much remains, in sometimes astonishing abundance and variety, thanks to each species' own unique genius for survival, to blind luck, to the shifting vagaries of public tastes, and even to the occasional glimmer of human enlightenment.

## FLORA

The receding glaciers of the last ice age scoured the land and left lifeless mud and rubble in their wake. Overall, the climate then was considerably cooler than it is today, and the first life forms to recolonize in the shadow of the glaciers were hardy mosses, lichens, and other cold-tolerant plants. Junipers and other shrubs later took root, and afterward came coniferous trees—hardy fast-growing spruce and fir—that could thrive here despite the harsh climate and relatively brief growing season. In the boggy interiors sprouted moisture-loving willows and tamaracks. As the climate warmed and the soil grew richer, broadleaf deciduous trees arrived, filling in the outlines of the forests still seen and enjoyed today.

## Forests

Maritime Canada's forests abound with ash, balsam fir, birch, beech, cedar, hemlock, maple, oak, pine, and spruce. Thick woodlands now

© ANDREW HEMPSTEAD

"Tuckamore" is a local name for spruce trees stunted by the harsh northern climate.

blanket over 81 percent of Nova Scotia and 93 percent of New Brunswick, whose interior conifer forests in places resemble vast impenetrable fields of dark green wheat. Prince Edward Island, by contrast, is the country's least-forested province, with its land area about equally divided between farmlands and woodlands.

Newfoundland's forests are dominated by black spruce and balsam fir, with occasional stands of larch, pin cherry, pine, paper and white birch, aspen, red and mountain maple, and alder. In Newfoundland's alpine and coastal areas, you may encounter the formidable "tuckamore," a thicket composed of stunted, hopelessly entangled fir and spruce. Labrador's southern forests are cloaked with spruce, tamarack, juniper, and birch. White spruce 30 meters tall dominate the central area, while stunted black spruce, a mere meter tall, form a stubble along the timberline area. Farther north on the arctic tundra, dwarf birch and willow are common.

With so many provincial tree varieties, visitors may easily be confused. For a helpful general introduction, visit Odell Park Arboretum in Fredericton, New Brunswick, where a 2.8-kilometer trail winds through woods made up of every tree native to the area.

## Wildflowers and Other Plants

Trees, of course, are only part of the picture. Along the forest margins, raspberry and blackberry thickets proliferate, among other benefits providing welcome snacks for summertime hikers. Throughout the spring and summer months, the Maritimes host magnificent wildflower shows that change subtly week by week. Common wildflowers throughout New Brunswick and Nova Scotia—seen especially along roadsides in summertime—include lupine, Queen Anne's lace, yarrow, pearly everlasting, and daisies. The showy spikes of purple loosestrife, a pretty but aggressive and unwelcome pest, can be seen everywhere.

Bayberries and wild rose bloom on the Chignecto Isthmus during June. The bayberry bush grows clusters of dimpled fruits close along woody stems and releases a pleasant spicy aroma popular in potpourri and Christmas candles. The yellow beach heather colors the Northumberland Strait dunes and sandy plains, and the rhodora (miniature rhododendron) brightens coastal marshes. Another dune resident, the beach plum, grows snowy white to pinkish flowers in June, which produce fruit welcomed by birds, beasts, and man in late summer and early fall. Nutrient-rich bogs in northeastern New Brunswick nurture plant exotics, especially at Lamèque and Miscou Islands, where the wild cranberry and insectivorous pitcher plant and sundew grow among peat moss beds.

Prince Edward Island is like one large garden when late spring and summer's warm temperatures urge columbines, bachelor buttons, pansies, lilacs, wild roses, pink clover, and the delicate lady's slipper (the provincial flower) into blossom.

Across Newfoundland's marshes and bogs, you'll see white and yellow water lilies, rare orchid species, purple iris and goodwithy, and insectivorous plants (such as the pitcher plant, the provincial flower). Daisies, blue harebells, yellow goldenrod, pink wild roses, and deep pink fireweed thrive in the woodlands. Marsh marigolds, as brightly yellow as daffodils, are native to the western coast's Port au Port Peninsula. Low dense mats of crowberry are common throughout Newfoundland and Labrador. The late-autumn crop of blue-black fruits is a favorite food of curlews, plovers, and other migrants preparing for their long flights to the Caribbean and South America.

Yellow poppies, heather buttercups, miniature purple rhododendrons, violets, and deep blue gentian, mixed among the white cotton grass, brighten Labrador's arctic tundra; farther south, the daisy-like arnica and purple saxifrage grow in plateau-rock niches.

You may encounter poison ivy. Mushrooms are everywhere; be absolutely certain you know the species before sampling—the chanterelles are culinary prizes, but the amanitas are deadly poisonous.

## Along the Shore

Near the coasts, familiar plants—spruces, hardy cinnamon ferns, northern juniper—take on a stunted, gnarled look from contending with the unmitigated elements. It can take endurance and adaptation to survive here amid often harsh conditions. Trees and bushes lie cropped close to the ground or lean permanently swept back by the wind as if with a giant hairbrush.

Living on or near the beach requires specialization too. Maram grass, also called American beach grass, is abundant all along the Atlantic coast. Its extensive root systems help to stabilize the sand dunes on which it grows. Another important dune plant, the beach heather, grows in low mats that trap sand and keep the dunes in place. Small, abundant yellow flowers color large patches from May to July. Beach pea, seaside goldenrod, dusty miller, and sea rocket are a few of the other plants that can manage on the less-than-fertile soils just above the high-tide line. Lower down grow cord grass and glasswort, whose systems can tolerate regular soakings of saltwater.

Within the intertidal zone, there's a different world altogether amidst the surging seawater and tide pools. The great disparities between high and low tides help to make the rocky coasts of the Maritimes among the richest and most varied anywhere in the world. Low tide exposes thick mats of tough rubbery rockweed, or sea wrack, for a few hours each day. Farther out (or deeper down) is the lower intertidal zone of coral-pink to reddish-brown Irish moss and brilliant green sea lettuce, which carpet the rocks and harbor populations of starfish, crabs, and sea urchins.

The deepest stratum of plant life is what marine biologists call the laminarian zone, typified by the giant brown kelps such as the common horsetail kelp. These algae attach to rocks at depths up to 40 meters and grow rapidly toward the surface, their broad leathery fans and air bladders lilting with the rise and fall of the swells. Storms can prune the upper extremities or tear entire plants from their moorings to wash ashore with populations of tiny mollusks, crustaceans, and other creatures that made their homes among the fronds.

## LAND MAMMALS

Around 70 different land mammals call Atlantic Canada home. The ones you're most likely to come across are moose, deer, black bears, and beavers, which are widespread in all provinces except Prince Edward Island (where raccoons, coyotes, and foxes are the largest species).

### Moose

The giant of the deer family is the moose, an awkward-looking mammal that appears to have been designed by a cartoonist. It has the largest antlers of any animal in the world, stands up to 1.8 meters tall at the shoulder, and weighs up to 500 kilograms. Its body is dark brown, and it has a prominent nose, long spindly legs, small eyes, big ears, and an odd flap of skin called a bell dangling beneath its chin. Each spring the bull begins to grow palm-shaped antlers that by August will be fully grown. Moose are solitary animals that prefer marshy areas and weedy lakes, but they are known to wander to higher elevations searching out open spaces in summer. They forage in and around ponds on willows, aspen, birch, grasses, and all aquatic vegetation. Although they may appear docile, moose will attack humans if they feel threatened.

Moose are present in Nova Scotia and New Brunswick but are most common in Newfoundland, where they are naturally suited to the terrain. Ironically, they are not native to the island. The estimated 150,000 or so that thrive in the province today are descended from a handful of individuals introduced in 1878 and 1904 as a source of meat. On the mainland, they are most common in Cape Breton Highlands National Park (Nova Scotia).

### White-Tailed Deer

Populations of deer are not particularly large in Nova Scotia or New Brunswick and were nonexistent by the late 1800s, but they came back in the ensuing years. The color of the white-

## CAUTION: MOOSE ON THE LOOSE

© ANDREW HEMPSTEAD

Some locals won't drive on rural roads between dusk and dawn. The reason? Moose on the loose.

About 400 moose-and-car collisions occur annually in Newfoundland alone, where the moose population is 150,000 and growing. Rural New Brunswick and Cape Breton Island are other trouble spots. A moose collision is no mere fender-bender. These animals are big and heavy, and hitting one at speed will make a real mess of your car (it doesn't do the unfortunate moose much good either). Consequences can be fatal to both parties.

Seventy percent of collisions occur between May and October. Accidents occur mainly 11 P.M.-4 A.M. (but that's no guarantee collisions won't happen at any hour). If you must drive after dark in areas frequented by moose, use the high beams, scan the sides of the road, and proceed with caution.

Provincial governments post signs marked with the figure of a moose along the most dangerous stretches of highway.

tailed deer varies with the season but is generally light brown in summer, turning dirty gray in winter. The white-tailed deer's tail is dark on top, but when the animal runs, it holds its tail erect, revealing an all-white underside.

Whitetails frequent thickets along the rivers and lakes of interior forests.

## Black Bears

Black bears number around 3,000 in Nova Scotia, 8,000 in New Brunswick, and 8,000–10,000 in Newfoundland and Labrador (there are no bears on Prince Edward Island). Black bears are not always black in color (they can be brown), causing them to be called brown bears when in fact they are not. Their weight varies considerably, but males average 150 kilograms and females 100 kilograms. Their diet is omnivorous, consisting primarily of grasses and berries but supplemented by small mammals. They are not true hibernators, but in winter they can sleep for up to a month at a time before changing position. During this time, their heartbeat drops to 10 beats per minute, body temperature drops, and they lose up to 30 percent of their body weight. Females reach reproductive maturity after five years; cubs, usually two, are born in late winter, while the mother is still asleep.

## Polar Bears

Polar bears are often sighted along the Labrador coast during the spring breakup of pack ice, but their range is out of reach to most travelers. These largest members of the bear family weigh up to 600 kilograms and measure over three meters from head to toe.

## Caribou

Standing 1.5 meters at the shoulder, caribou have adapted perfectly to the harsh arctic climate. They weight up to 150 kilograms and are the only member of the deer family in which both sexes grow antlers. The only region of Atlantic Canada where caribou are present is Newfoundland and Labrador; 12 herds roam the island and are most plentiful in the Avalon Wilderness Reserve and across the Northern Peninsula. Four caribou herds inhabit Labrador, the most famous of which is the George River herd. Its 500,000 caribou migrate eastward from Québec in late spring to calve in the Torngat Mountains. This

Black bears are widespread in all Atlantic Canada provinces except Prince Edward Island.

calving ground is currently under consideration for a national park.

## Lynx

The elusive lynx is an endangered species across Atlantic Canada. It is present in low numbers in all provinces except Prince Edward Island. Easily identifiable by its pointy black ear tufts and an oversized tabby cat appearance, the animal has broad padded paws that distribute its weight, allowing it to float on the surface of snow. It weighs up to 10 kilograms but appears much larger because of its coat of long, thick fur. The lynx is a solitary creature that prefers the cover of forest, feeding mostly at night on small mammals.

## Beavers

One of the animal kingdom's most industrious mammals is the beaver. Growing to a length of 50 centimeters and tipping the scales at around 20 kilograms, it has a flat rudderlike tail and webbed back feet that enable it to swim at speeds up to 10 kilometers per hour. Once hunted for their fur, beavers can be found in flat forested areas throughout Atlantic Canada. They build their dam walls and lodges of twigs, branches, sticks of felled trees, and mud. They eat the bark and smaller twigs of deciduous plants and store branches underwater, near the lodge, as a winter food supply.

## SEA LIFE

The ocean water that surrounds the four provinces nurtures an astonishing abundance and variety of sea creatures, from tiny uncounted single-celled organisms up through the convoluted links of the food chain to the earth's largest beings—whales.

## Tidal Zones

Along the shores, the same conditions that provide for rich and diverse plant zones—rocky indented coasts, dramatic tidal variations—also create ideal habitats for varied animal communities in the tidal zone. Between the highest and lowest tides, the Maritime shore is divided into six zones, each determined by the amount of time it is exposed to air. The black zone, just above the highest high-water mark, gets its name from the dark band of primitive blue-green algae that grows here. The next zone is called the periwinkle zone, for the small marine snails that proliferate there. Able to survive prolonged exposure to air, the periwinkles can leave the water to graze on the algae. The barnacle zone, encrusted with the tenacious crustaceans, while also exposed several hours daily during low tides, receives the brutal pounding of breaking waves. Next is the rockweed zone—home to mussels, limpets, and hermit crabs (which commandeer the shells of dead periwinkles)—and the comparatively placid Irish moss zone, which shelters and feeds sea urchins, starfish, sea anemones, crabs, and myriad other animals familiar to anyone who has peered into the miniature world of a tide pool. Last is the laminarian zone, where lobsters, sponges, and fishes thrive in the forests of kelp growing in the deep churning water.

## Fish

Beyond the tidal life zones lie the waters of the continental shelf and then the open sea. Flowing south from the Arctic, cold oxygen-laden currents also carry loads of silica, ground out of the continental granite by the glaciers and poured into the sea by coastal rivers. Oxygen and silica together create an ideal environment for the growth of diatoms, the microscopic one-celled plants that form the bedrock of the ocean's food chain. In the sunlight of long summer days in these northern latitudes, the numbers of diatoms increase exponentially. They are the food source for shrimp and herring, which in turn support larger fish, such as mackerel, Atlantic salmon, and tuna.

## Whales

Not all the creatures that swim in the Atlantic Ocean are cold-blooded. About 20 whale species cruise offshore. The so-called baleen or toothless whales—minke, humpback, beluga, and right whales—are lured by the massive food stocks of plankton and tiny shrimp called krill, which the whales strain from the water through their sieve-like curtains of baleen. The toothed whales—a family that includes dolphins, orcas (killer whales), and fin and pilot whales—feed on the vast schools of smelt-like capelin, herring, and squid. In the last three decades, whaling has been halted by Canadian law and international moratoriums, and populations of these beleaguered mammals are undergoing very encouraging comebacks.

Today's lucrative whaling industry is based not on butchering but on simply bringing curious onlookers to observe the wonderful animals up close. Prime whale-watching areas are the Bay of Fundy—especially around Grand Manan Island and Brier Island—and off the shores of Cape Breton. Minke, pilot, finback, orca, and humpback whales are the most populous species. The whales that frequent local waters arrive from the Caribbean between June and mid-July and remain through October; the season peaks during August and September. On Newfoundland's western coast, fin, minke, humpback, and pilot whales are sighted off Gros Morne National Park.

## Seals

Gray and harbor seals inhabit Nova Scotian and Prince Edward Island waters at various times of the year. Whale-watching tours often include a stop at an offshore seal colony, although you may also spot one unexpectedly, such as while dining at a waterfront restaurant in Halifax. One spot you'll be guaranteed sightings is on a seal-watching trip from Eastern Kings County (Prince Edward Island), where the waters are calm and the seals abundant.

Harp seals, after fattening themselves on fish off the Labrador and Greenland coasts, migrate to northern Newfoundland and the Gulf of St. Lawrence in January and February. The females arrive first, living on the ice and continuing to feed in the gulf before giving birth to their pups. These snowy white, doe-eyed pups became the poster children of the conservation movement in the 1970s. The slaughter of the young pups—carried out by sealers who bashed in their heads with clubs—galvanized protests against it and finally embarrassed the

Canadian government into restricting the killing in the mid-1980s. Even with the Canadian government quietly allowing hunting to resume in 1996, seal numbers have rebounded dramatically in the last two decades, and the current population stands at around five million.

## BIRDS

If you're an avid birder, Atlantic Canada's bird life may leave you breathless. In addition to hundreds of year-round resident species, the Atlantic migratory route stretches across part of the region, bringing in millions of seasonal visitors for spectacular and sometimes raucous displays.

Among the richest areas is the Bay of Fundy. In July, waterfowl, such as the American black duck and green-winged teal, and shorebirds, including the greater yellowlegs, descend on the Mary's Point mudflats at Shepody National Wildlife Area. Across Shepody Bay, 100,000 sandpipers stop at the Dorchester Peninsula to grow fat on their favorite food—tiny mud shrimp—before continuing on to South America. With over 300 species, Grand Manan Island is a prime bird-watching site. The show is thickest during September, when migrants arrive in force. Ornithologist and artist John James Audubon visited the island in 1833 and painted the arctic tern, gannet, black guillemot, and razorbill—annual visitors that can still be seen here.

Even greater numbers of seabirds, the region's densest concentrations, gather on the coastlines of Newfoundland's Avalon Peninsula, most notably at Cape St. Mary Sea Bird Sanctuary. Species found there include common and arctic terns, kittiwakes, great and double-crested cormorants, Leach's storm petrels, razorbills, guillemots, murres, gannets, and 95 percent of North America's breeding Atlantic puffins.

Each species has found its niche, and each is remarkable in its own way. The black-and-white murre, for example, is an expert diver that uses its wings as flippers to swim through the water chasing fish. This behavior can sometimes get the birds caught up with the fish in nets. The murre's cousin, the comical-looking

Atlantic puffin, borrows the penguin's tuxedo markings but is nicknamed the "sea parrot" for its distinctive triangular red-and-yellow bill. Puffins make Swiss cheese of the land, as they nest in burrows they've either dug out themselves or inherited from predecessors. In Labrador, ruffled and spruce grouse, woodpeckers, ravens, jays, chickadees, nuthatches, and ptarmigans are a few of the inland birds you may spot.

In New Brunswick's interior, crossbills, varied woodpecker species, boreal chickadees, and gray jays nest in the spruce and fir forests. Ibises, herons, and snowy egrets wade among lagoons and marshes. Among Nova Scotia's 300 or so bird species, the best known is the bald eagle. About 250 pairs nest in the province, concentrated on Cape Breton—the second-largest population on North America's

east coast, after Florida. The season for eagle watching is July and August. Other birds of prey include red-tailed, broad-winged, and other hawks; owls; and the gyrfalcon in Newfoundland and Labrador. Peregrine falcons were reintroduced to Fundy National Park in 1982. They nest in seaside cliffs and attack their prey in "stoops," kamikaze dives in which the falcon can reach speeds of over 300 kilometers per hour.

The noisy blue jay, Prince Edward Island's official provincial bird, is at home throughout the province, but the island's showiest species is the enormous, stately great blue heron, which summers there from May to early August. The rare piping plover may be seen (but not disturbed) on the island's national park beaches, and arctic terns nest along the coast near Murray Harbour.

# History

## THE EARLIEST INHABITANTS

Atlantic Canada's earliest inhabitants arrived in Labrador about 9,000 years ago, camping near the large rivers and hunting seals and walrus during the summer. Archaeological research documents that these Maritime Archaic people hunted seals and whales along the Strait of Belle Isle and hunted caribou inland around 7500 B.C. They eventually crossed the strait to the island of Newfoundland's northern portion and established encampments such as Port au Choix, where their burial grounds and artifacts date to 2300 B.C. Around 1000 B.C., these people died out. A thousand years later, the Dorset people, ancestors of today's Inuit, arrived from the north. They survived until about A.D. 600. The Beothuk, called Red Indians for their use of ocher in burial rituals, came to Newfoundland.

### Mi'Kmaq

Culturally and linguistically related to Algonquian people, the largest language group in Canada, the Mi'Kmaq made a home throughout present-day Nova Scotia, New Brunswick, and as far west as Québec. They were coastal dwellers who fished with spears and hook and line while also collecting shellfish from the shoreline. Hunting was of lesser importance for food but held a great degree of status among other members of the group. Canoes with sails were built for summer travel, while in winter toboggans (a word that originates from the Mi'Kmaq word *topaghan*) and snowshoes were essential.

Like aboriginal peoples across North America, the Mi'Kmaq practiced a kind of spiritual animism, deeply tied to the land. The trees, animals, and landforms were respected and blessed. Before food could be consumed or a tree felled, for example, it was appreciated for its life-sustaining sacrifice. Mythology also played an important part in spiritual life, along with rituals, shamanism, and potlatch ceremonies.

# THE FIRST EUROPEANS

Brendan the Navigator, a fifth-century Irish monk, may have been the first European to explore the area; he sought Hy-Brazil, the "wonderful island of the saints," and later accounts of his voyage, recorded in the medieval best-seller *Navigatio Sancti Brendani,* describe a land with coastal topography similar to Newfoundland's.

Atlantic Canada's link to the Vikings is more certain. Driven out of Scandinavia, it's believed by overpopulation, Norse seafarers settled in Iceland and began to establish settlements in Greenland. Around A.D. 1000 they sailed in long stout ships, called *knorrs,* southwest from Greenland and down the Labrador coastline, and established a temporary settlement at L'Anse aux Meadows on Newfoundland's Northern Peninsula. There they built at least eight houses and two boatsheds of cut turf, and lived off the land. It is not known how long they lived here, but they stayed long enough to construct a forge for crafting implements from iron ore they dug and smelted here. It may have been hostilities with the native people that drove them out. The remnants of their settlement would remain unrecognized until the 1960s.

"Newfoundland" as a place-name originated with the Italian explorer Giovanni Caboto— better known today as John Cabot. Sailing westward from Bristol with a sanction to claim all lands hitherto "unknown to Christians," he sighted the "New Founde Lande" in 1497 and claimed it in the name of his employer, King Henry VII of England. His first landfall probably lay in the northern part of the island. He and his men explored the coast and also sighted Prince Edward Island and Nova Scotia before returning to England. In the summer of 1997, celebrations in St. John's and across Newfoundland celebrated the 500-year anniversary of the event.

## The Fabulous Fisheries

So abundant were the cod fisheries of the Grand Banks, the shallow undersea plateaus south and east of Newfoundland, that John Cabot claimed that a man had only to lower a basket into the sea and haul it up full. His report exaggerated the truth only slightly. Although the specifics have not been documented, European fishermen are believed to have preceded Cabot by decades. Legends in Newfoundland describe the Basques as whale hunters in the Strait of Belle Isle as early as the 1470s. France's fishing exploits are better known. In the early 1500s, French fleets roamed the seas from the Grand Banks—where they caught cod and dried them on Newfoundland's beaches—to inland rivers such as the salmon-rich Miramichi in what is now New Brunswick. England's fishing fleets were equally active, leading one diplomat to describe Newfoundland as "a great ship moored near the Grand Banks for the convenience of English fishermen."

England also dabbled in other commercial interests in Newfoundland. A group of merchants from England's West Country settled Trinity in the mid-1500s. Cupids, England's first chartered colony on the island, began in 1610. In contrast, St. John's evolved independently and belonged to no nation; the port served as a haven and trading center for all of Europe's fishing fleets, and Signal Hill, the lofty promontory beside the harbor, dates as a lookout and signal peak from the early 1500s.

## French Interests

Ultimately, France was more interested in trading posts and settlements than in fishing. The French Crown granted Sieur de Monts a monopoly to develop the fur trade, and in 1604 the nobleman-merchant, with explorer Samuel de Champlain, led an exploratory party to the mouth of the Bay of Fundy. The expedition established a camp on an island in the St. Croix River (the river that now separates New Brunswick from Maine). The group barely survived the bitter first winter and relocated across the Bay of Fundy, establishing Port-Royal as a fur-trading post in the Annapolis basin the following spring.

The grant was canceled, and while most of the expedition returned to France in 1607, a group of French settlers took their place at

Port-Royal in 1610. The French dubbed the area Acadia, or "Peaceful Land."

The French settlement and others like it ignited the fuse between England and France. John Cabot had claimed the region for England, but explorer Jacques Cartier also claimed many of the same coastlines for France several decades later. For France, the region was a choice piece of property, a potential New France in the New World. On the other hand, England's colonial aspirations centered farther south, where colonization had begun at Virginia and Massachusetts. England didn't *need* what is now Atlantic Canada, though the region offered much with its rich fisheries, but it was a place to confront the expansion of the French, England's most contentious enemy in Europe.

In terms of military strength, the British had the upper hand. An ocean separated France from its dream of settlement, while England's military forces and volunteer militias were located along the eastern seaboard. In 1613, a militia from Virginia plundered and burned the buildings at Port-Royal. The French relocated the site to a more protected site farther up the Annapolis River, built another fort named Port-Royal, and designated the setting as Acadia's colonial capital in 1635.

## France's Sphere Develops

The French Acadian settlements quickly spread beyond the Port-Royal area to the Fundy and Minas Basin coastlines. The merchant Nicholas Denys, whose name is entwined with France's early exploration, established a fortified settlement on Cape Breton at St. Peters, and also at Guysborough in 1653. So many Acadians settled at Grand-Pré that it became the largest settlement and hub of villages in the area. Other settlements were established across Acadia on Cape Breton, the Cobequid Bay and Cape Chignecto coastlines, and from the Restigouche Uplands to the Baie des Chaleurs in what's now northern New Brunswick.

France needed a military center and created it in the mid-1600s at Plaisance, one of the earliest and most important fishing ports on the Avalon Peninsula in Newfoundland. Here, they erected another tribute to the French Crown and named the new fortification Fort Royal.

British reprisals against the French increased. The British hammered Port-Royal again and again, and in 1654, a militia from New England destroyed some of the Acadian settlements. In Newfoundland, France's presence at Plaisance prompted the British to counter by building forts around St. John's in 1675.

## The Treaty of Utrecht

Hostilities between England and France in the New World mirrored political events in Europe. Fighting ebbed and flowed across Atlantic Canada as the powers jockeyed for control on the European continent. Queen Anne's War (1701–1713), the War of Austrian Succession (1745–1748), and the Seven Years' War (1756–1763) were all fought in Europe, but corresponding battles between the English and French took place in North America as well (where they were known collectively as the French and Indian Wars).

The Treaty of Utrecht in 1713 settled the Queen Anne's War in Europe. Under the terms of the treaty, England fell heir to all of French Acadia (though the borders were vague). In Newfoundland, Plaisance came into British hands and was renamed Castle Hill. The treaty awarded France the token settlements of the offshore Île Saint-Jean (Prince Edward Island) and Île Royale (Cape Breton). Acadia became an English colony. Nova Scotia (New Scotland) rose on the ashes of New France and the fallen Port-Royal; the British took the fort in 1710, renamed it Fort Anne, and renamed the settlement Annapolis Royal. The town was designated the colony's first capital until Halifax was established and became the capital in 1749.

The French military regrouped. They fled from the peninsula and began to build (and never finish) the Fortress of Louisbourg on Île Royale's Atlantic seacoast in 1719. Once again, the French envisioned the fortification as a New Paris and France's major naval base, port city, and trading center in North America.

Simultaneously, they sent 300 fishermen and farmers across the Northumberland Strait to create a new settlement at Port-la-Joye; the enclave, at what is now Charlottetown's southwestern outer edge, was intended to serve as the breadbasket for the Fortress of Louisbourg.

The British quickly responded. A fort at Grassy Island on Chedabucto Bay was their first effort, a site close enough to the Fortress of Louisbourg to watch the arrivals and departures of the French fleets. By 1745, Louisbourg represented a formidable threat to England, so the Brits seized the fortress and deported the inhabitants. But no sooner had they changed the flag than the French were moving back in again. The War of Austrian Succession in Europe ended with the Treaty of Aix-la-Chapelle in 1748, which, among other things, returned Louisbourg to France.

### Full-Fledged War

Peace was short-lived. Eight years later, in 1756, the Seven Years' War broke out in Europe, and once more both powers geared for confrontation in Atlantic Canada. Britain's Grassy Island fort was strategically located but too small a military base. In 1749 a British convoy sailed into Halifax Harbour, established England's military hub in the North Atlantic in the capacious harbor, and named Halifax the capital of Nova Scotia. Fort Edward near the Fundy seacoast went up in the midst of an Acadian area and guarded the overland route from Halifax. Fort Lawrence on the Chignecto Isthmus, between Nova Scotia and New Brunswick, was built to defend the route to the mainland. The fort defiantly faced two of France's most formidable forts: Fort Beauséjour and Fort Gaspéreau.

The stage was set for war, and the region's civilian inhabitants, the Acadian farmers, were trapped in the middle. Decades before, England had demanded but not enforced an oath of allegiance from the Acadians who lived under their jurisdiction. By the 1750s, however, the British decided to demand loyalty and also readied a plan to evict the Acadians from their land and replace noncompliant French inhabitants with Anglo settlers. In 1755, the British swept through the region and enforced the oath. In a show of force, more than 2,000 troops from Boston captured Fort Beauséjour and renamed it Fort Cumberland.

### The Acadian Deportation

England's actions unleashed chaos on the Acadians. Those who refused to sign the oath of allegiance were rounded up and deported, and their villages and farmlands were burned. By October, 1,100 Acadians had been deported, while others fought the British in guerrilla warfare or fled to the hinterlands of Cape Breton, New Brunswick, and Québec.

The Acadians being deported were herded onto ships bound for the English colonies on the eastern seaboard or anyplace that would accept them. Some ships docked in England, others in France, and others in France's colonies in the Caribbean. As the ports wearied of the human cargo, many of them refused the vessels entry, and the ships returned to the

© ANDREW HEMPSTEAD

Port-Royal National Historic Site in Nova Scotia is a re-creation of the first permanent European settlement north of Florida.

high seas to search for other ports willing to accept the Acadians. In one of the period's few favorable events, the Spanish government offered the refugees free land in Louisiana, and many settled there in 1784, where they became known as Cajuns.

Refugee camps, rife with disease and malnutrition, sprang up across the Maritimes. Beaubears Island, on New Brunswick's Miramichi River, began as a refugee center. About 3,500 Acadians fled from Nova Scotia to Île du Saint-Jean (Prince Edward Island); 700 lost their lives on two boats that sank on the journey. Many deported Acadians returned, only to be deported again, some as many as seven or eight times.

Exact deportation numbers are unknown. Historians speculate that 10,000 French inhabitants lived in Acadia in 1755; by the time the deportation had run its course in 1816, only 25 percent of them remained. The poet Henry Wadsworth Longfellow distilled the tragedy in *Evangeline,* a fictional story of two lovers divided by the events.

### England's Final Blow

In 1758, the British moved in for the kill. They seized the Fortress of Louisbourg and toppled Port-la-Joye, renaming it Fort Amherst. The French stronghold at Québec fell the next year. In the ultimate act of revenge, the British troops returned to Louisbourg in 1760 and demolished the fortress stone by stone so it would never rise again against England. New France was almost finished; bereft of a foothold in Atlantic Canada, the French launched a convoy from France and captured St. John's in 1762. The British quickly swooped in and regained the port at the Battle of Signal Hill, the final land battle of the Seven Years' War. Finally, the bitter French and Indian Wars were finished.

### Postwar Developments

Atlantic Canada, as you see it now, then began to take shape. After the British had swept the Acadians from their land, prosperous "planters," gentlemen-farmers from New England, were lured to the lush Annapolis Valley with free land grants. Merchants settled Yarmouth in the 1760s, and other Anglo settlers went to Prince Edward Island. The island, formerly part of Nova Scotia, became an English colony in 1769.

Some of the Acadians had evaded capture, and settlements such as the Pubnico communities south of Yarmouth date to the pre-deportation period. But most of the region's surviving Acadian areas began after the refugees returned and settled marginal lands no one else wanted, such as the rocky seacoast of La Côte Acadienne (the Acadian Coast) in western Nova Scotia.

England lucked out. Even the inglorious defeat in the American Revolution benefited the British. Loyalists (Americans loyal to England) by the thousands poured into Nova Scotia and New Brunswick. The influx was so great in Saint John and Fredericton that New Brunswick, originally part of Nova Scotia, became an English colony, and Saint John became the first incorporated city in Canada.

### An Uneasy Peace

Even as peace settled across Atlantic Canada, the specter of war loomed again in Europe. Ever wary of their contentious enemy, the British feared a French invasion by Napoleon's navies in Atlantic Canada. In Halifax, the British built up the harbor's defenses at the Halifax Citadel and other sites. At St. John's, the British fortified Signal Hill with the Queen's Battery.

As if Britain didn't have enough problems with the Napoleonic Wars, at the same time the War of 1812 ensued as England and the United States wrangled over shipping rights on the high seas. More British fortifications went up, this time across the Bay of Fundy in New Brunswick with harbor defenses such as the Carleton Martello Tower at Saint John, the blockhouse at St. Andrews, and other strongholds at more than a dozen strategic places.

## TOWARD CONFEDERATION

The Napoleonic Wars ended in June 1815 with Napoleon's defeat at Waterloo. Atlantic

Canada emerged unscathed. The war years had fostered shipping, and Halifax earned a questionable reputation as the home port of privateers who raided ships on the high seas and returned to port to auction the booty at the harbor. In Newfoundland, many ships had been lost on the treacherous shoals outside St. John's Harbour, prompting the British to build the lofty Cape Spear Lighthouse in 1836.

In 1864 a landmark event in Canada's history took place in Atlantic Canada. The "Fathers of the Confederation"—from New Brunswick, Nova Scotia, Prince Edward Island, Ontario, and Québec—met at Province House in Charlottetown. The small city owes its fame as the birthplace of Canada to the discussions of a potential joint dominion that followed. In 1867, England gave the union its blessing and signed the British North America Act (now known as the Constitution Act); the Dominion of Canada was born on July 1 as a confederation of Québec, Ontario, New Brunswick, and Nova Scotia united under a parliamentary government.

Under the leadership of its first prime minister, Sir John A. MacDonald, Canada expanded rapidly. The acquisition of Ruperts Land from the Hudson's Bay Company in 1869 increased its total land area sixfold. Manitoba and British Columbia joined the Confederation in 1870 and 1871 respectively. Prince Edward Island, having initially declined to become a Confederation member, joined the dominion in 1873. Alberta and Saskatchewan followed in 1905, and nearly a half century later, in 1949, Newfoundland became Canada's 10th province.

As a condition of participation in the Confederation, British Columbia and New Brunswick insisted that the government build a railroad across Canada to facilitate trade, transport, and communication. Work on the daunting project began in 1881, and in 1885, just four years later, the last spike was driven in the Canadian Pacific Railway. Linking Vancouver with Montréal, which in turn connected with regional lines in New Brunswick, Nova Scotia, and Prince Edward Island, the railroad united the country in a way no act of confederation could.

## WHERE CANADA BEGAN

In the fall of 1864, the colonial capital of Prince Edward Island hosted the Charlottetown Conference, which led to the establishment of the Dominion of Canada. The delegates who became Canada's founding Fathers of Confederation agreed that the city was the ideal neutral site for the conference. Islanders were neither for nor against the idea of a dominion. But just in case the fledgling idea of forming a union did come to something, the islanders appointed several delegates to represent them.

The other delegates arrived by sea in groups from New Brunswick, Nova Scotia, and Upper and Lower Canada, now Ontario and Québec. Their respective ships docked at the harbor, and one by one the delegates walked the short blocks up Great George Street to the Colonial Building, as Province House was known then. The meeting led to the signing of the British North America Act in London in 1867 and the beginnings of modern Canada on July 1 of that year. The initial four provinces were Nova Scotia, New Brunswick, Québec, and Ontario. Prince Edward Island originally passed on membership and didn't join the Confederation until 1873. Other latecomers included Manitoba (1870), British Columbia (1871), Alberta (1905), Saskatchewan (1905), and Newfoundland and Labrador (1949).

## World Wars and the Depression

Atlantic Canada became a hotbed of controversy during World War I, when the sensitive issue of Francophone rights was raised. The federal government had decided to initiate a military conscription, and French Canadians were afraid that the draft would decrease their already minority population. The measure was a failure, as both French- and English-speaking men of conscription age avoided the draft. By war's end, however, 63,000 Canadians had died in battle, and another 175,000 were wounded. During the war, the nation had supplied Britain with much of its food and also produced large quantities of munitions, ships, and planes—an experience that helped move Canada from a primarily agricultural economy to an industrial one. Afterward, Canada emerged stronger, more independent, and with a greater sense of self-confidence. The Atlantic provinces enjoyed a brief brush with prosperity as mining and manufacturing expanded.

But the Maritimes were not immune to the Great Depression of the 1930s, which hit Canada even harder than the United States. Many businesses collapsed under the financial crisis. When World War II erupted, Canada followed Britain's lead in joining the war against Hitler. Nearly one-tenth of the population of about 11.5 million served in the war effort. Atlantic Canada again took part in shipping much of the munitions and food supplies for the Allies, and the regional and national economies were again revived.

In 1959 the completion of the St. Lawrence Seaway, a project jointly undertaken by the United States and Canada, opened a new sea lane between the Great Lakes and the Atlantic. Three years later, the new TransCanada Highway spanned the country from sea to sea. Linking Vancouver Island with St. John's, Newfoundland, the highway joined all 10 provinces along a single route and made the country just a little smaller.

## A Constitution and Autonomy

Starting in 1867, the British North America Act required the British parliament's approval for any Canadian constitutional change. On November 5, 1981, Canada's federal government and the premiers of every province except Québec agreed on a Canadian Constitution and Charter of Rights and Freedoms. The Canada Act formally went into effect on April 17, 1982, removing the last vestiges of the British parliament's control. Canada remains, however, a member of the Commonwealth.

## Old Divisions in Modern Times

The formation of the Parti Québécois in 1968 signaled a popular new militancy among French-speaking separatists in Québec, who desired a political and cultural divorce from the rest of Canada. The Official Languages Act recognized French as the country's second official language after English, but this act only bandaged over deep wounds. Referenda on the question of Québec secession in the 1980s and 1990s have failed to resolve the issue; a provincial vote on the question in 1995 saw the drive for separation defeated by a margin of barely 1 percent. It's difficult to predict which way the pendulum will swing, should there be another vote, but the national government, in any case, has indicated that it will honor the will of the Québécois. In Atlantic Canada, attitudes toward separation are mixed; the general consensus, even in officially bilingual New Brunswick, seems to run in favor of continued Canadian unity, but that consensus is undermined by a growing impatience with Québec's demands for what many Canadians see as preferential treatment from the federal government.

# Government and Economy

## GOVERNMENT

Canada is a constitutional monarchy. The federation of 10 provinces and three territories operates under a parliamentary democracy in which power is shared between the federal government, based in Ottawa, and the provincial governments. Canada's three nonprovincial territories (Nunavut, Yukon, and the Northwest Territories) exercise delegated—rather than constitutionally guaranteed—authority. The power to make, enforce, and interpret laws rests in the legislative, executive, and judicial branches of government respectively.

## Federal Government

Under Canada's constitutional monarchy, the formal head of state is the queen of England, who appoints a governor general to represent her for a five-year term. The governor general stays out of party politics and performs largely ceremonial duties such as opening and closing parliamentary sessions, signing and approving state documents on the queen's behalf, and appointing a temporary replacement if the prime ministry is vacated without warning. The head of government is the prime minister, who is the leader of the majority party or party coalition in the House of Commons. In 2008 Stephen Harper of the Conservative Party was elected for a second term. Harper is Canada's 22nd prime minister.

The country's legislative branch, the Parliament, is comprised of two houses. The House of Commons, with 295 members, is apportioned by provincial population and elected by plurality from the country's districts. The Senate comprises 104 members appointed by the governor general (formerly for a life term, though retirement is now mandatory at age 75) on the advice of the prime minister. Legislation must be passed by both houses and signed by the governor general to become law.

Fredericton's Government House

© ANDREW HEMPSTEAD

National elections are held whenever the majority party is voted down in the House of Commons or every five years, whichever comes first. Historically, it has been unusual for a government to last its full term.

## Provincial and Local Governments

Whereas the federal government has authority over defense, criminal law, trade, banking, and other affairs of national interest, Canada's 10 provincial governments bear responsibility for civil services, health, education, natural resources, and local government. Each of the nation's provincial Legislative Assemblies (in Newfoundland and Labrador, the body is called the House of Assembly) consists of a one-house legislative body with members elected every four years. The nominal head of the provincial government is the lieutenant governor, appointed by the governor general of Canada. Executive power, however, rests with the cabinet, headed by a premier, the leader of the majority party.

## ECONOMY

Traditionally, the economy of Atlantic Canada revolved around resources-based industries such as fishing, forestry, and mining. Although communities established around fishing and farming areas continue to thrive, the economy today is a lot more diverse. In addition to all the stalwarts discussed below, other growing sectors include information technology, the medical field, and the film industry.

### Fishing

Canada was once the world's largest fish-exporting country, but poor resource management and overfishing have destroyed its once-bounteous supplies. Even so, fisheries and fish processing still remain the third-biggest contributor to Nova Scotia's gross domestic product (GDP), and cod, haddock, herring, and lobster are caught inshore and off the Atlantic's Scotian Shelf. The province is Canada's largest lobster exporter.

New Brunswick's fisheries produce groundfish, lobster, crab, scallops, and herring. The newest aquaculture developments are Atlantic salmon farms and blue mussel beds. Blacks Harbour–area canneries on the Bay of Fundy rank first in Canada's sardine production.

Newfoundland and Labrador's fisheries, a chronic boom-or-bust industry, contribute some $500 million yearly to the economy, with catches of mackerel, flounder, capelin, herring, squid, eel, fish roe, sole, salmon, perch, turbot, halibut, lobster, and farmed mussels and rainbow trout. Labrador also produces half of Canada's commercial char. Since the 1990s, when the cod industry came to a standstill, Newfoundland fisheries have diversified. Now scallops and shrimp make up a good percentage of the catch.

Prince Edward Island also has an important fishing industry, especially in lobster and shellfish such as farmed blue mussels.

### Natural Resources

Atlantic Canada's fisheries have declined as a consequence of modern fishing methods as well as foreign competition. As a result, the area has turned to its other resources: timber, coal, and other minerals. New Brunswick harbors Canada's largest silver, lead, and zinc reserves, and also mines potash, coal, and oil shale. Peat moss is collected in northeastern New Brunswick, especially from Lamèque and Miscou Islands—enough to make the province the world's second-largest exporter of this fuel.

Mining contributes $1 billion to New Brunswick's economy and is the second-largest segment of Nova Scotia's. Over 30 mines and quarries in Nova Scotia are worked for their coal, limestone, and tin.

Nova Scotia's extensive forests supply a substantial lumber and paper industry; among the largest operators are Bowater (half-owned by the *Washington Post*) on the South Shore and the Irving Forest Products pulp mills at Abercrombie Point, Point Tupper, Brooklyn, Hantsport, and East River.

Western Labrador's mines contribute about 80 percent of Canada's share of iron ore. Other Newfoundland metals and minerals include copper, lead, zinc, gold, silver, chromium, limestone, gypsum, aluminum silicate, and asbestos. Newfoundland also holds Canada's sole commercial deposit of pyrophyllite, used in the production of ceramics. Newfoundland is economically on the bottom rung of Canada's per-capita income, yet the province is sitting on a gold mine when it comes to natural resources. Offshore oil fields started producing in 2000, and the extraction rate is 600,000 barrels per day.

## Agriculture

Agriculture contributes $230 million to New Brunswick's GDP; Victoria and Carleton Counties' seed potatoes make up 20 percent of Canada's total potato crop and are exported to Mexico, Portugal, and the United States. The benevolent spring floods wash the Saint John River valley with rich silt, helping to sustain a healthy mixed farming economy. The farms at Maugerville yield two crops each season. Other agricultural products include livestock (exported to France, Britain, Denmark, and the United States), dairy products, and berries.

Although just 8 percent of Nova Scotia's land is arable, agriculture contributes heavily to the economy. The province produces fruit (including Annapolis Valley apples), dairy products, poultry, hogs, and Canada's largest share of blueberries.

Diminutive PEI ranks first in Canada's potato production. Half of the crop is grown in Prince County, and the remainder is produced by farms scattered across the province. Local farmers travel abroad to 32 nations to advise their foreign counterparts on varieties and farming methods. The province harvests 10 million oysters annually, and most are exported. The island's beauty may be attributed to its investments in agriculture, which contributes about 9.5 percent to the gross domestic product. The sector yields $120 million a year and employs 4,000 islanders on 2,200 farms, each of which averages 140 hectares. Grains, fruit, beef, pigs, sheep, and dairy products are other components of mixed farming production.

## Power

Water is ubiquitous in the Atlantic provinces (one-third of all the world's freshwater is found in Canada), and hydroelectricity is a cheap, clean export. Québec Hydro alone sells over $1 billion worth of electricity a year to New England. The Mactaquac Generating Station, on the Saint John River near Fredericton, New Brunswick, is the Maritimes' largest hydroelectric station.

## Tourism

Tourism ranks as the fastest-growing sector of the economy across Atlantic Canada. Tourism contributes $1.6 billion to Nova Scotia's annual economy alone. Most visitors enter the region through New Brunswick, Atlantic Canada's land gateway, and arrive by car, RV, or tour bus. Only 25 percent fly in; air arrivals are increasing, however, as long-distance air links improve beyond Atlantic Canada. Most visitors (40 percent) are from the neighboring provinces, while central and western Canada contribute 25 percent, and the United States adds almost 25 percent. Together, these tourists contribute some $2.8 billion to the regional economy and support 90,000 jobs.

# People and Culture

While the topography of this region—the dense forests, mountains, and rugged coast-line—has tended to separate people and isolate them in scattered settlements, centuries of sometimes turbulent history have bound the Atlantic Canadians together: the mutual grief of the early wars, the Acadian deportation, immigration upheavals, and the abiding hardships common to resource-based economies. In the same sense, these and other factors have given each population an indisputable identity that makes it difficult to generalize about the diverse peoples of this part of Canada. Senator Eugene Forsey's observations on the country as a whole are equally applicable to Atlantic Canada: "I think our identity will have to be something which is partly British, partly French, partly American, partly derived from a variety of other influences which are too numerous even to catalogue."

In spite of diversity, the region still shares a common identity as a place apart from the rest of Canada. A foreign nation borders it to the southwest, and Atlantic Canada is separated from the body of its nation by the insular bastion of Québec. Although the country began in the east and was nourished by its resources for centuries, Canada's general prosperity has not been fully shared here. Atlantic Canada experiences higher unemployment, higher underemployment, and lower income than any of the other provinces. Unlike the rest of the country, the provinces of Atlantic Canada share economies that rise and fall largely on the vicissitudes of the fisheries and other natural resources.

## DEMOGRAPHY

A few statistics say much about the region. The entire population of the country numbers some 33.5 million—smaller than California's population. Atlantic Canada's four provinces make up less than a tenth of that figure (7.2 percent of Canada's total population), with a combined total of about 2 million.

## NATIONAL HOLIDAYS

| | |
|---|---|
| **New Year's Day** | January 1 |
| **Good Friday** | late March to mid-April |
| **Easter Monday** | late March to mid-April |
| **Victoria Day** | Monday closest to May 24 |
| **Canada Day** | July 1 |
| **Labour Day** | first Monday in September |
| **Thanksgiving** | second Monday in October |
| **Remembrance Day** | November 11 |
| **Christmas Day** | December 25 |
| **Boxing Day** | December 26 |

## Nova Scotia

Nova Scotia's population is 920,000. It is the seventh most populous province and is home to 3.2 percent of Canada's total population. Distribution is closely divided between urban and rural, with a full third of Nova Scotians concentrated in and around Halifax.

Four of five Nova Scotians trace their lineage to the British Isles. Some 49 original Scottish families, from Archibald to Yuill, are still on the rolls of the Scottish Societies Association of Nova Scotia, which does genealogical surveys.

After the American Revolution, 25,000 United Empire Loyalists poured into Nova Scotia. Several thousand African Americans arrived during the War of 1812, followed by Irish immigrants from 1815 to 1850. Recent worldwide immigration has added more than 50 other ethnic groups (including Poles, Ukrainians, Germans, Swiss, Africans, and Lebanese) to the province's cultural milieu, making it the most cosmopolitan in the region. About 8,000 black people live in Nova Scotia today, many of them descendants of immigrants from the colonial United States.

## New Brunswick

The province, with a population of 740,000, is in a sense a miniature Canada, a provincial composite of Anglophones and Acadian Francophones who harmoniously coexist— the exception rather than the rule in a nation whose two dominant cultures are so often at odds. One suspects the harsh history that divided New Brunswick at its inception has run its course and has mellowed. As Canada's only officially bilingual province, it steps to an agreeable duple beat.

The duality repeats itself in numerous ways. New Brunswick has an Anglophone region and another equally distinctive Acadian Francophone counterpart. The distinctions were set in stone centuries ago when the British evicted the Acadians from their original settlements and resettled the Loyalists. The Anglophone cities, towns, and settlements lie along the Fundy seacoast and throughout most of the Saint John River valley. The French-speaking Acadian region lies beyond, on the province's outer rim in the northwestern woodlands along the Saint John River and on the coastlines of the Baie des Chaleurs, the open gulf, and the sheltered strait. Today, English is the first language of about 65 percent of New Brunswickers, while French is the mother tongue for about 33 percent.

## Prince Edward Island

Although it's anything but crowded, Prince Edward Island (PEI, population 135,000) is Canada's most densely populated, with nearly

## MAGICAL MUSIC

The thousands of Gaelic speakers who migrated to the New World during the 1700s and 1800s brought many traditions with them, none more distinctive than their Celtic music. Many cherished songs describing life on the land have been passed down through the generations, while new lively tunes create a spirited mix of music heard throughout the region and beyond.

The lively fiddle performances of Cape Breton-born **Natalie MacMaster** bring crowds the world over to their feet. Also from Cape Breton Island are **The Rankins,** who infuse a variety of styles into their music, and grunge-fiddler **Ashley MacIssac,** whose sound crosses from Celtic to garage rock and heavy metal. Across on "The Rock," **Great Big Sea** is renowned for its energetic rock-meets-Celtic live performances. In addition to the big names, bands like **Beolach** and the **Irish Descendents** are worth watching for,

while bands churning out lively foot-stomping beer-drinking tunes can be heard in pubs throughout Atlantic Canada.

### CEILIDHS

A *ceilidh* (pronounced "KAY-lee") was originally an informal gathering, usually on a Friday or Saturday night, that would bring together young people who would dance the night away to lively Celtic music in a local hall. In rural areas of Cape Breton Island, they remain an important part of the social scene. At Mabou, on the island's west coast, the local community hall fills with the sound of fiddle music every Tuesday through summer, while the following night, the foot-stomping fun happens down the road at the local museum. Passing through on Thursday? Then plan for a lively evening of entertainment at the Inverness Fire Hall Ceilidh.

© ANDREW HEMPSTEAD

Pockets of Acadian culture are strongest along the Fundy Coast of Nova Scotia, northwest of Moncton in New Brunswick, and in the southwestern corner of Prince Edward Island.

24 people per square kilometer. At the same time, Prince Edward Island is the most rural province, with fewer than two in five residents living in urban areas. PEI's people are also said to be Canada's most homogeneous. The province's ancestry is 80 percent Anglo—a third Irish and the remainder Scottish. Acadians represent 17 percent of the population (5 percent of them speak French). Southeast Asians, Germans, and a thriving population of about 500 Mi'Kmaq (most living on Lennox Island on the north shore and at Scotchfort) together constitute about 2 percent of the population. PEI still lures immigrants, mainly from other Atlantic Canada provinces and Ontario.

## Newfoundland and Labrador

In contrast to relatively crowded Prince Edward Island, this province, with a population of 510,000, has less than 1.5 people per square kilometer. Ninety-five percent of the population is concentrated on the island of Newfoundland (known as "The Rock").

In Labrador, Inuit, Innu, and Anglo-Labradorians inhabit the sparsely settled eastern coastline and remote central interior. The people of the island of Newfoundland are an overwhelmingly Anglo and Celtic cultural mix (96 percent), whose psyche is linked to the sea and the Grand Banks fisheries. A small number of Mi'Kmaq also live on the island.

An insular mentality still informs the provincial character, and over 50 years after joining the Confederation, residents of The Rock may refer to their countrymen as "Canadians"—outsiders from another nation. They even inhabit their own time zone, Newfoundland time, a quirky half hour ahead of Atlantic time.

Though a full-fledged province since 1949, Newfoundland was a colony of England's for centuries. This is why you'll still hear a clipped King's English accent in St. John's, a West Country dialect in some of the small remote fishing villages (called outports), and a softly brushed Irish brogue on the Avalon

Peninsula. Some 60 dialects and subdialects have been documented throughout the province, many of them incorporating colorful expressions and vocabulary that are unique to Newfoundland. In addition, the map of the province is decorated with one-of-a-kind place-names: Blow Me Down, Joe Batt's Arm, Happy Adventure, Jerry's Nose, and dozens of other toponymic oddities.

# NATIVE PEOPLES AND MÉTIS

The first European explorers to reach North America found a land that was anything but uninhabited. Tribes or nations of aboriginals had been here for millennia, from coast to coast and up into the continent's subarctic and Arctic regions.

Various names are used to describe aboriginal Canadians, and all can be correct in context. The government still uses the term *Indian,* regardless of its links to Christopher Columbus and the misconception that he had landed in India. *Native* is generally considered acceptable only when used in conjunction with *people, communities,* or *leaders. Indigenous* or *aboriginal* can have insulting connotations when used in certain contexts.

## Mi'Kmaq

When Europeans first arrived, perhaps 20,000 Mi'Kmaq lived in the coastal areas of the Gaspé Peninsula and the Maritimes east of the Saint John River. The name Mi'Kmaq (also Micmac) is thought to have derived from the word *nikmaq,* meaning "my kin-friends," which early French settlers used as a greeting for the tribe. The aboriginal Mi'Kmaq fished and hunted, and became involved with the fur trade in the 18th century.

The Mi'Kmaq historically had practiced little or no agriculture, and attempts by the British to convert them into farmers fared poorly. Later, they found employment building railways and roads and in lumbering and fisheries. Today the Mi'Kmaq number an estimated 15,000 in the Maritime provinces, Newfoundland, and parts of New England.

## Maliseet

Culturally and linguistically related to the Mi'Kmaq (both are members of the widespread Algonquian language group), the Maliseet (or Malicite) inhabited the Saint John River valley in New Brunswick and lands west to the St. Lawrence and what is now Maine. For the first century after contact, the Maliseet got on well with European fishers and traders, although Old World diseases greatly reduced their numbers.

As the fur trade dwindled, Maliseet women adopted agriculture, while the men continued to hunt and fish. Increasing white settlement along the Saint John, however, displaced the Maliseet from their traditional lands, eventually leaving them destitute. In the 19th century, the first Indian reserves were created for them, at Fredericton, Oromocto, Kingsclear, and other New Brunswick locations.

## Inuit

The Inuit (formerly known as Eskimos—a name many consider pejorative) inhabit the northern regions of Canada from Alaska to Greenland. Their ancestors arrived in the Arctic in the 11th century, and today they number roughly 25,000 in eight main tribal groups. They share a common language—Inuktitut—with six dialects. Until the late 1930s, when a court ruled that their welfare was the responsibility of the federal government, the Inuit were largely ignored by Canada, principally because they occupied inhospitable lands in the far north that nobody else wanted.

In the late 18th century, Moravian missionaries in Labrador established the first lasting contact with the Inuit, followed by commercial whalers and explorers. The Europeans initiated cultural and technological changes in the traditional societies (including almost universal conversion to Christianity) that continue to this day. In the northern reaches of Labrador, the Inuit today live in small remote settlements and still maintain some traditional practices: hunting seals, caribou, and whales, and other aspects of Inuit culture.

## Métis

The progeny of native people and Caucasians, the Métis (named for an old French word meaning "mixed") form a diverse and complex group throughout Canada. They date from the time of earliest European contact; in Atlantic Canada, unions between European fishermen and native women—sometimes casual, sometimes formal—produced Métis offspring by the early 1600s.

In the 17th century, the French government encouraged this mixing, seeing it as conducive to converting the native people to Christianity and to more speedily increasing the population of New France. Samuel de Champlain said, "Our young men will marry your daughters, and we shall be one people." That policy had changed by the 1700s, however, and France then *discouraged* mixed unions, in part because of the increased availability of white women in North America. This policy led to the development of distinct Métis settlements, mainly around the Great Lakes (these settlements would later grow into cities such as Chicago, Milwaukee, Sault Ste. Marie, and Detroit).

Recent census figures estimate Métis numbers at about 60,000. Some identify themselves with the aboriginals, some with whites, while others consider themselves members of a society and culture distinct from both.

## LANGUAGE

Although Canada is constitutionally bilingual, English is the language of choice for most of the country and for the majority of Atlantic Canadians. (In 2008, French was the mother tongue of about 18 percent of Canadians, while the figure in Québec was 88 percent.) The Official Languages Acts of 1969 and 1988 established French and English as equal official languages and designated rights for minority language speakers throughout the country.

In Atlantic Canada, English is the first language for the majority. But in officially bilingual New Brunswick, French is the home tongue for a substantial portion of the population—about 28 percent—and the province's two languages and cultures have managed to coexist in reasonable harmony. Francophones are smaller minorities in Prince Edward Island (about 5 percent), Nova Scotia (4 percent), and Newfoundland (less than 1 percent).

The French spoken here is not a patois; it's closely tied to the language that was brought to the continent by the original settlers from France. Visitors who have studied standard Parisian French may have a little trouble with the accent, syntax, and vocabulary here (the differences are not unlike those between American and British English). Still, travelers who make an effort at speaking French will find the Francophones here patient and appreciative.

Some Dutch is spoken on Prince Edward Island, and with the arrival of Asian immigrants starting around the 1960s, Chinese, Vietnamese, Punjabi, Hindi, Urdu, and other tongues can be overheard in urban areas. The Inuit of Labrador continue to speak Inuktitut, and the Mi'Kmaq of the other provinces maintain their native language—with varying success.

## Canada Eh!

Canadian English is subtly different from American English, not only in pronunciation but also in lexicon. For instance, Canadians may say "serviette," "depot," and "chesterfield" where Americans would say "napkin," "station," and "couch." Spelling is a bit skewed as well, as Canadians have kept many British spellings—e.g., colour, kilometre, centre, cheque. "Eh?" is a common lilt derived from British and Gaelic in which each sentence ends on a high note, as though a question had been asked. At the same time, Canadian English has been profoundly influenced by its neighbor to the south. Nevertheless, you'll find that language variations pose no serious threat to communication.

# RELIGION

Atlantic Canada's cultural diversity is also reflected in religion. Though Christian faiths have predominated since the first Europeans settled here, and despite Canada's less-than-sterling history of religious tolerance, the Maritime territories have offered sects and a variety of denominations—including oppressed minority groups such as Mennonites, Doukhobors, Eastern European and Russian Jews, and others—an opportunity to start anew. The domination of organized religions (primarily the Roman Catholic Church and various Protestant churches) over the lives of Canadians has waned substantially since the 1960s. Partly this is due to the overall drop nationally in church membership over the past several decades, but it could also be an effect of Canada's increasingly multicultural population. In the Atlantic provinces, church affiliation is still high, and the Catholic and Protestant churches, in particular, still play substantial roles in the lives and communities of people throughout the region.

# ESSENTIALS

## Getting There

Visitors to Atlantic Canada have the option of arriving by road, rail, ferry, or air. The main gateway city for flights from North America and Europe is Halifax (Nova Scotia), from where flights leave for other provincial capitals. Ferries land at Yarmouth (Nova Scotia) from Maine, while the main rail line enters the region in New Brunswick and terminates at Halifax.

Unless otherwise noted, telephone numbers given in this section are the local (North American) contacts.

### BY AIR

Most long-haul international and domestic flights into eastern Canada set down at Toronto, Ottawa, or Montréal, with connecting or ongoing flights to Atlantic Canada.

### Air Canada

Air Canada (888/247-2262, www.aircanada .ca or aircanada.com in the U.S.) is one of the world's largest airlines, serving five continents. The company has one of the world's easiest-to-understand fare systems, with simplified fare levels and multiple ways of searching for flights and fares online. It offers direct flights to Halifax from Montréal, Ottawa, Toronto, Calgary, Boston, Detroit, and New York City. All other flights from North America are routed through Toronto or Montréal, with

connections made to Halifax, Saint John, Fredericton, Bathurst, Charlottetown, and St. John's. From Europe, Air Canada flies from London to Halifax. From the South Pacific, Air Canada operates flights via Honolulu from Sydney and in alliance with Air New Zealand from Auckland and other South Pacific islands to Honolulu, where passengers change to an Air Canada plane for the flight to Vancouver and onward connections to the east coast. Asian cities served by direct Air Canada flights include Beijing, Hong Kong, Nagoya, Osaka, Seoul, Shanghai, Taipei, and Tokyo. All terminate in Vancouver. Air Canada's flights originating in the South American cities of Buenos Aires, Santiago, and Sao Paulo are routed through Toronto.

### WestJet

Canada's second-largest airline, WestJet (403/250-5839 or 888/937-8538, www.westjet .com), is a low-cost carrier that operates along the same lines as Southwest. Based in Calgary, its flights extend as far east as St. Johns, with flights routed through Toronto to Halifax.

### U.S. Airlines

Air Canada offers the most flights into Atlantic Canada from the United States, but Halifax is also served by **American Eagle** (800/433-7300, www.aa.com), from New York City; **Continental** (800/231-0856, www.continental .com), from Newark; and **Northwest** (800/225-2525, www.nwa.com), from Detroit.

### BY RAIL

**Amtrak** (800/872-8725, www.amtrak.com) has service from New York City to Toronto (via Buffalo), and from New York City to Montréal.

### VIA Rail

Once you're in Canada, rail travel is handled by VIA Rail (416/366-8411 or 888/842-7245, www.viarail.ca). VIA Rail has replicated the famous transcontinental route's deluxe trappings and service with its Easterly class aboard the **Ocean.** The *Ocean* departs Montréal, follows the St. Lawrence River's southern shore to northern New Brunswick, cuts across the province to Moncton, speeds into Nova Scotia via Amherst and Truro, and finishes at Halifax. The trip takes 21 hours. The train has a variety of economy classes (called Comfort), but it is the Easterly class that gets all the attention. These luxuriously restored vintage carriages include a domed car with three small salons (one of which is a replica of the transcontinental's mural lounge), a dining car with art deco trappings, and a more informal car designed for lighter dining. Rates range from $140 each way in Comfort class to $520 in Easterly class, the latter including sleeping-car accommodations and all meals.

### Passes

If you're planning on extensive rail travel within Canada, the least expensive way to travel is on a **Canrailpass,** which allows unlimited travel

---

## AIR TAXES

The Canadian government collects a variety of "departure taxes" on all flights originating from Canada. These taxes are generally not in the advertised fare, but they will be included in the ticket purchase price. First up is the **Air Travellers Security Charge,** $5-10 each way for flights within North America and $25 round-trip for international flights. At the time of writing, all Canadian airlines were adding $25-50 per sector for a fuel surcharge and $3 for an insurance surcharge. **NAV Canada** also dips its hand in your pocket, collecting $9-20 per flight for maintaining the country's navigational systems. Additionally, passengers departing Halifax International Airport must pay an **Airport Improvement Fee** of $10, while those departing Bathurst (New Brunswick) pay $40, the highest such fee in Canada. Additionally, if your flight transits through Toronto, you pay an additional $8 improvement fee for that airport.

## CUTTING FLIGHT COSTS

Ticket structuring for air travel is so complex that finding the best deal requires some time and patience (or a good travel agent). In the first place, to get an idea of what you will be paying, call the airlines or check their websites and compare fares. **Air Canada** (www .aircanada.com) has a streamlined fare structure that makes it easy to find the fare that serves your needs and budget. Also look in the travel sections of major newspapers – particularly in weekend editions – where budget fares and package deals are frequently advertised. While the Internet has changed the way many people shop for tickets, having a travel agent that you are comfortable in dealing with – who takes the time to call around, does some research to get you the best fare, and helps you take advantage of any available special offers or promotional deals – is an invaluable asset in starting your travels off on the right foot.

Within Canada, **Travel Cuts** (866/246-9762, www.travelcuts.com) and **Flight Centre** (888/967-5302, www.flightcentre.ca),

both with offices in all major cities, including Halifax, consistently offer the lowest airfares available, with the latter guaranteeing the lowest. Flight Centre offers a similar guarantee from its U.S. offices (866/967-5351, www .flightcentre.us), as well as those in the United Kingdom (tel. 0870/499-0040, www.flight-centre.co.uk), Australia (tel. 13/31-33, www .flightcentre.com.au), and New Zealand (tel. 0800/24-35-44, www.flightcentre.co.nz). In London, **Trailfinders** (215 Kensington High St., Kensington, tel. 0845/058-5858, www.trail-finders.com) always has good deals to Canada and other North American destinations. Reservations can be made directly through airline or travel agency websites, or use the services of an Internet-only company such as **Travelocity** (www.travelocity.com) or **Expedia** (www .expedia.com).

When you have found the best fare, open a **frequent flyer** membership with the airline – **Air Canada** (www.aeroplan.com) has a very popular reward program that makes rewards easily obtainable.

---

anywhere on the VIA Rail system for 12 days within any given 30-day period. During high season (June 1–October 15) the pass is adult $879, senior (older than 60) and child $791, with extra days (up to three are allowed) $75 and $68 respectively. The rest of the year, the pass costs adult $549, senior and child $494, with extra days $47 and $42 respectively. VIA Rail has cooperated with Amtrak (800/872-7245) to offer a North American Rail Pass, with all the same seasonal dates and discounts as the Canrailpass, and similarly priced passes.

On regular fares, discounts of 25–40 percent apply to travel in all classes October–June. Those older than 60 and younger than 25 receive a 10 percent discount that can be combined with other seasonal fares. Check for advance-purchase restrictions on all discount tickets.

The VIA Rail website (www.viarail.ca) provides route, schedule, and fare information, takes reservations, and offers links to towns

and sights en route. Or pick up a train schedule at any VIA Rail station.

## BY BUS

North America's main bus line, **Greyhound** (800/231-2222, www.greyhound.ca or www .greyhound.com), doesn't provide service to Atlantic Canada. Instead, you will need to get yourself to a gateway city such as Montréal, Toronto, or Bangor (Maine) and connect with **Acadian Lines** (902/454-9321 or 800/567-5151, www.acadianbus.com), which provides service from these three cities to locations throughout the three Maritimes provinces.

### Passes

Acadian Lines honors all Greyhound passes. Greyhound's **Discovery Pass** comes in many forms. The Canada Discovery Pass is sold in periods of seven days ($329), 15 days ($483), 30 days ($607), and 60 days ($750) and allows unlimited travel throughout the country, as well as on select rail routes and from U.S. gateway cities south of the 49th parallel. Passes can be bought 14 or more days in advance online, seven or more days in advance from any Canadian bus depot, or up to the day of departure from U.S. depots.

## BY FERRY

From the United States (and even from Toronto), the most direct driving route to Halifax includes a ferry trip between Maine and Yarmouth (Nova Scotia), thereby saving the drive around the Bay of Fundy.

North America's fastest vehicular ferry, *The Cat* (902/742-6800 or 888/249-7245, www .catferry.com) crosses between Portland (Maine) and Bar Harbor (Maine) and Yarmouth in 5.5 and three hours respectively. It runs three or four times weekly from each port June–mid-October. From Portland, peak-season one-way fares (July–August) are adult US$99, senior US$79, child US$55, vehicle under 6.6 feet US$164. From Bar Harbor, fares are adult US$69, senior US$58, child US$48, vehicle under 6.6 feet US$115.

## BY CAR

The intricacies of driving in Canada, including basic road rules and information on rentals, are covered under *Getting Around*.

### Principal Routes into Atlantic Canada

The majority of visitors drive to Atlantic Canada. From the United States, Highway 9 heads east from Bangor, Maine, and enters New Brunswick—Atlantic Canada's principal land gateway—at St. Stephen, near the Fundy coast. The TransCanada Highway from central Canada (another main entry route) is more roundabout, following the St. Lawrence River through Québec to enter northwestern New Brunswick at Saint-Jacques near Edmundston. Once in New Brunswick, you can take the Confederation Bridge to Prince Edward Island or continue driving east into Nova Scotia.

Labrador can be reached from Québec on Highway 389, from Baie-Comeau, on the St. Lawrence River's northern bank. The 581-kilometer drive takes nine hours; the two-lane road wends through the province's wilderness to enter western Labrador at Labrador City.

# Getting Around

Driving, whether it be your own vehicle or a rental car, is by far the best way to get around Atlantic Canada. This section talks about driving in Canada, as well as the public transportation options.

## BY AIR

**Halifax International Airport,** 35 kilometers from Halifax, serves as Atlantic Canada's principal regional air hub. Other airports are located at Saint John, Moncton, Bathurst, Yarmouth, Sydney, Charlottetown, and St. John's. **Air Canada** (888/247-2262, www .aircanada.ca) and its code-share subsidiary, Air Canada Jazz, saturate the region with frequent flights. **WestJet** (403/250-5839 or 888/937-

8538, www.westjet.com) also flies between all major Atlantic Canada cities.

**Provincial Airlines** (709/576-3943 or 800/563-2800, www.provair.com) serves all of Newfoundland and Labrador with direct flights from Halifax and St. John's. **Air Labrador** (709/758-0002 or 800/563-3042, www.airlabrador.com) links the remote towns of Labrador to the outside world, flying in from St. John's, Deer Lake, and Montréal.

Air travel is the public transportation mode of choice throughout the provinces. While the airlines haven't put bus or ferry travel (or trains, yet) out of business, the airports are usually crowded, and regional flights are often filled.

## BY BUS

Getting around Atlantic Canada is made possible by **Acadian Lines** (902/454-9321 or 800/567-5151, www.acadianbus.com), which links all major cities and towns, as well as many minor ones. Buses operate seven days a week year-round. No passes are offered, but fares are reasonable.

All major cities have public transportation systems that revolve around scheduled bus service. If you have a day on your hands and no other plans, consider an early-morning bus to an unexplored area and a late-afternoon or early-evening return to the city. Few outsiders do it, but mixing among the locals on a bus circuit is a terrific way to explore a city.

## BY FERRY

In addition to the ferries linking Maine and Nova Scotia, the following services can be

## CONFEDERATION BRIDGE

The 13-kilometer-wide strait between New Brunswick's Cape Jourimain and Prince Edward Island is spanned by the Confederation Bridge, Canada's longest bridge (and the world's longest continuous multispan bridge). Replacing a busy ferry route that had been in operation since 1832, the bridge was completed after four years of construction and a cost of $1 billion. Building a road link to the rest of Canada was the subject of debate for decades, with passionate opinions running on both sides of the issue. Open now since 1997, there's little question that the link has increased traffic to the island. Whether the growing volume of visitors will dramatically alter the island's way of life, as opponents warned, remains to be seen.

The bridge toll is $41.50 per vehicle including passengers. The fee is collected on leaving the island — in effect the amount is for the round-trip. Payment can be made in cash or by debit or credit card. Check out the bridge at www.confederationbridge.com.

© ANDREW HEMPSTEAD

incorporated into your Atlantic Canada travels.

## Across the Bay of Fundy

**Bay Ferries** (902/245-2116 or 888/249-7245, www.nfl-bay.com) handles the busy Bay of Fundy crossing between Saint John (New Brunswick) and Digby (Nova Scotia), a shortcut that saves drivers a few hours' driving time. The ferries operate once or twice daily year-round; one-way high-season fares are adult $40, senior $25, child $24, vehicle $80 plus a $20 fuel surcharge. Reservations are essential through summer.

## To Prince Edward Island

**Northumberland Ferries** (902/566-3838, www.peiferry.com) operates 5–9 sailings daily between Caribou (Nova Scotia) and Wood Islands in eastern Prince Edward Island. The crossing takes just over one hour. The fare is $61 per vehicle, regardless of the number of passengers. You pay when leaving the island, so take the ferry to PEI and return on the Confederation Bridge to save a few bucks.

## To and Around Newfoundland and Labrador

**Marine Atlantic** (902/794-5254 or 800/341-7981, www.marine-atlantic.ca) operates two routes between North Sydney (Nova Scotia) and Newfoundland. The shorter passage, to Port-aux-Basques, takes 5–6 hours and costs adult $31, senior $28, child $15.50, vehicle under 20 feet $96.50. Summer-only sailings between North Sydney and Argentia take around 14 hours and cost adult $110, senior $90, child $50, and from $210 for vehicles.

The **Department of Transportation and Works** (www.tw.gov.nl.ca) operates ferries on 16 routes within Newfoundland and Labrador. Some are short runs that link populated islands to the rest of the province, while others, such as the 4.5-day round-trip to remote Nain, are real adventures.

A ferry links the island of Newfoundland to Labrador.

© ANDREW HEMPSTEAD

## DRIVING IN CANADA

U.S. and International Driver's Licenses are valid in Canada. All highway signs give distances in kilometers and speeds in kilometers per hour (km/h). Unless otherwise posted, the maximum speed limit on the highways is 100 km/h (62 miles per hour).

Use of safety belts is mandatory, and motorcyclists must wear helmets. Infants and toddlers weighing up to 9 kilograms must be strapped into an appropriate children's car seat. Use of a child car seat for larger children weighing 9–18 kilograms is required. Before venturing north of the 49th parallel, U.S. residents should ask their vehicle insurance company for a Canadian Non-resident Inter-provincial Motor Vehicle Liability Insurance Card. You may also be asked to prove vehicle ownership, so carry your vehicle registration form.

If you're a member in good standing of an automobile association, take your membership card—the Canadian AA provides members of related associations full services, including free maps, itineraries, excellent tour books, road- and weather-condition information, accommodations reservations, travel agency services, and emergency road services. For more information contact the **Canadian Automobile Association** (613/247-0117, www.caa.ca).

**Note:** Drinking and driving (with a blood-alcohol level of 0.08 percent or higher) in Atlantic Canada can get you imprisoned for up to five years on a first offense and will cost you your license for at least 12 months.

## Car Rental

All major car-rental companies have outlets at Halifax International Airport, in downtown Halifax, and at airports and cities across Atlantic Canada. Try to book in advance, especially in summer. Expect to pay from $50 a day and $250 a week for a small economy car with unlimited kilometers.

Major rental companies with outlets in Atlantic Canada include: **Avis** (800/974-0808, www.avis.ca), **Budget** (800/268-8900, www.budget.com), **Discount** (800/263-2355, www.discountcar.com), **Dollar** (800/800-4000, www.dollar.com), **Enterprise** (800/325-8007, www.enterprise.com), **Hertz** (800/263-0600, www.hertz.ca), **National** (800/227-7368, www.nationalcar.com), **Rent-a-wreck** (800/327-0116, www.rentawreck.ca), and **Thrifty** (800/847-4389, www.thrifty.com).

## RV and Camper Rental

Consider renting a camper-van or other recreational vehicle for your trip. With one of these apartments-on-wheels, you won't need to worry about finding accommodations each night. Even the smallest units aren't cheap, but they can be a good deal for longer-term travel or for families or two couples traveling together. The smallest vans, capable of sleeping two people, start at $175 per day with 100 free kilometers (62 miles) per day. Standard extra charges include insurance, a preparation fee (usually around $60 per rental), a linen/cutlery charge (around $60 per person per trip), and taxes. Major agencies with rental outlets in Halifax include **Cruise Canada** (800/671-8042, www.cruisecanada.com) and **Canadream** (800/461-7368, www.canadream.com). Both of these companies also have rental outlets across the country.

While you can take these vehicles across to Newfoundland on the ferry, you can also rent from St. John's–based **Islander RV** (709/738-7368 or 888/848-2267, www.islanderrv.com), which charges $184–325 per day for campers and RVs.

# Visas and Officialdom

## ENTRY FOR U.S. CITIZENS

Citizens and permanent residents of the United States are required to carry a passport for both entry to Canada and for reentry to the United States. At press time, the U.S. government was developing alternatives to the traditional passport. For further information, see the website http://travel.state.gov/travel. For current entry requirements to Canada, check the Citizenship and Immigration Canada website (www.cic.gc.ca).

## OTHER FOREIGN VISITORS

All other foreign visitors must have a valid passport and may need a visa or visitors permit depending on their country of residence and the vagaries of international politics. At present, visas are not required for citizens of the United States, British Commonwealth, or Western Europe. The standard entry permit is for six months, and you may be asked to show onward tickets or proof of sufficient funds to last you through your intended stay. Extensions are available from the **Citizenship and Immigration Canada** office in Halifax. This department's website (www.cic.gc.ca) is the best source of the latest entry requirements.

## ENTRY BY PRIVATE AIRCRAFT OR BOAT

If you're going to be entering Canada by private plane or boat, contact the **Canada Border Services Agency** (204/983-3500 or 800/461-9799, www.cbsa.gc.ca) in advance for a list of official ports of entry and their hours of operation.

## CLEARING CUSTOMS

Visitors are allowed to bring in personal items that will be used during a visit, such as cameras, fishing tackle, and equipment for camping, golf, tennis, scuba diving, etc. You can also take the following into Canada duty-free: reasonable quantities of clothes and personal effects, 50 cigars and 200 cigarettes, 200 grams of tobacco, 1.14 liters of spirits or wine, food for personal use, and gas (normal tank capacity). Pets from the United States can generally be brought into Canada, with certain caveats. Dogs and cats must be more than three months old and have a rabies certificate showing date of vaccination. Birds can be brought in only if they have not been mixing with other birds, and parrots need an export permit because they're on the endangered species list.

Handguns, automatic and semiautomatic weapons, and sawn-off rifles and shotguns are not allowed into Canada. Visitors with firearms must declare them at the border; restricted weapons will be held by customs and can be picked up on exit from the country. Those not declared will be seized and charges may be laid. It is illegal to possess any firearm in a national park unless it is dismantled or carried in an enclosed case. Up to 5,000 rounds of ammunition may be imported but should be declared on entry.

On reentering the United States, if you've been in Canada more than 48 hours, you can bring back up to US$400 worth of household and personal items, excluding alcohol and tobacco, duty-free. If you've been in Canada fewer than 48 hours, you may bring in only up to US$200 worth of such items duty-free.

For further information on all customs regulations contact **Canada Border Services Agency** (204/983-3500 or 800/461-9799, www.cbsa-asfc.gc.ca).

# Recreation

In Atlantic Canada's great outdoors, just about every form of recreation is feasible and first-rate: bicycling and hiking, mountaineering, scuba diving, houseboating, river rafting and canoeing, ocean and river kayaking, sailing, windsurfing, rockhounding, bird-watching, hunting, fishing, hockey, tennis, golf—you name it. No matter what the temperature—35°C in summer or −15°C in winter—people can be found throughout the year enjoying some form of recreation.

Spectator sports popular in the Atlantic provinces include minor-league professional ice hockey, harness racing, and rugby.

## PARKS

The region's national and provincial parks come in a wide range of personalities and offer an equally eclectic array of activities and facilities, from wilderness backpacking at New Brunswick's Mt. Carleton Provincial Park to lounging in luxury at Cape Breton Highlands' Keltic Lodge resort.

### National Parks

Atlantic Canada has eight of Canada's 43 national parks. **Cape Breton Highlands National Park,** in Nova Scotia, is one of the most spectacular but is also very accessible; ocean panoramas, abundant wildlife, and an extensive network of hiking trails are the highlights. In the same province, **Kejimkujik National Park** is the only one not on the ocean, which means visitors trade kayaks for canoes to explore the extensive system of freshwater lakes. In New Brunswick, **Fundy National Park** is

## NATIONAL PARK PASSES

Permits are required for entry into all Canadian national parks. These are sold at park gates, at all park information centers, and at campground fee stations.

Day passes (under $10 per person) are the best deal for short visits, but if you're planning to visit a number of parks throughout Atlantic Canada, consider an annual **National Parks of Canada Pass**, good for entry into all of Canada's national parks for one year from the date of purchase. The cost is adult $67.70, senior $57.90, child $33.30 up to a maximum of $136.40 per vehicle. The **Discovery Package** pass (adult $84.40, senior $72.60, child $42.20 to a maximum of $165.80 per vehicle) is a good choice for history buffs. It allows unlimited entry into both national parks and national historic sites for a full year from purchase. For more information on park passes, check the **Parks Canada** website (www.pc.gc.ca).

renowned for the world's highest tides, while **Kouchibouguac National Park** fronts the calm waters of Northumberland Strait. The beaches of **Prince Edward Island National Park** are a popular destination for vacationing families. Newfoundland and Labrador has three parks—**Terra Nova,** renowned by kayakers; **Gros Morne,** where spectacular cliffs rise above inland "ponds"; and **Torngat Mountains,** protecting the remote northern tip of Labrador.

For information on these parks, including detailed trip planners, visit the **Parks Canada** website (www.pc.gc.ca).

### Provincial Parks

Protecting areas of natural, historical, and cultural importance, Atlantic Canada's many hundreds of provincial parks also provide a wide variety of recreational opportunities. All provide day-use facilities such as picnic areas and washrooms, while many also have playgrounds, canoe rentals, and concessions. A good number also have campgrounds and summer interpretive programs.

You'll find lots of information about provincial parks from local information centers and in general tourism literature. You can also contact the following:

- **Nova Scotia:** Department of Natural Resources, 902/662-3030, www.novascotia-parks.ca

- **New Brunswick:** Department of Tourism and Parks, 506/462-5924, www.tourism-newbrunswick.ca

- **Prince Edward Island:** Department of Tourism, 902/368-4444, www.tourismpei.com

- **Newfoundland and Labrador:** Department of Environment and Conservation, Parks and Natural Areas Division, 709/729-2664, www.env.gov.nl.ca/parks

## HIKING

Hiking is one of the most popular activities in Atlantic Canada. Not only are there hundreds of trails to explore, but it's free and anyone can do it. The hiking season in the Maritime provinces spans spring to autumn; hiking in Newfoundland and Labrador is relegated for the most part to the height of summer, except for the hardiest adventurers. Coastal areas are generally free of pesky insects, but insect repellent is wise inland from May through September. As national and provincial parks protect the most spectacular scenery, it'll be no surprise that this is where you find the best hiking. One standout is **Cape Breton Highlands National Park,** on Nova Scotia's Cape Breton Island. Here you can find anything from short interpretive trails along raised boardwalks to strenuous slogs that end at high ocean lookouts.

## FISHING

Sportfishing in Atlantic Canada is legendary, especially for Atlantic salmon in Newfoundland

# A PHOTOGRAPHER'S DREAM

Atlantic Canada has incredible light for photography. The sky turns from a Wedgwood color to sapphire blue – a beautiful background for seacoast photographs. Rise at dawn to take advantage of the first rays of sunlight hitting picturesque villages such as popular **Peggy's Cove** (home to the "world's most photographed lighthouse"), near Halifax, and **St. Andrews,** in New Brunswick, as well as remote gems such as **Battle Harbour** in Labrador. Nature photographers will revel in the fall colors of **Cape Breton Highlands National Park,** the red sand beaches of **Prince Edward Island National Park,** and Newfoundland's moody **Gros Morne National Park.**

While photography is simplest when the weather is favorable – and that's more often than not – don't pass up a morning basking in thick mist, as bright sun illuminates the sky behind the thick clouds. The fog breaks apart gradually, and when it does, the sun radiates like a spotlight, illuminating the sparkling dampness that clings briefly to the landscape.

and Labrador, New Brunswick, and Cape Breton Island. Fishing guides, tours, lodges (from rustic to luxurious), and packages are available throughout these regions. Expect to pay $250–500 a day for a guide. An all-inclusive week's package has the highest price and usually includes license fees, lodging, meals, a guide, and, for remote locations, fly-in transportation. Typical is Labrador's **Rifflin' Hitch Lodge,** a 50-minute flight southeast from Goose Bay (www.rifflinhitchlodge.nf.ca). Located on the Eagle River, one of the richest Atlantic salmon rivers in North America, the lodge supplies anglers with some of the world's best fishing and all the comforts of home. Guests enjoy luxuries such as gourmet meals

and a hot tub, comfortable private rooms, and fishing from the shore or boats at a ratio of one guide to every two guests.

## Salmon

Just one species of salmon is native to the tidal waters of Atlantic Canada—the Atlantic salmon. It is anadromous, spending its time in both freshwater and saltwater. The salmon spend up to three years in local rivers before undergoing massive internal changes that allow them to survive in saltwater. They then spend 2–3 years in the open water, traveling as far as Greenland. After reaching maturity, they begin the epic journey back to their birthplace, to the exact patch of gravel on the same river from where they emerged. It is the returning salmon that are most sought after by anglers, with New Brunswick's **Miramichi** watershed the most famed of all river systems. Atlantic salmon grow to 36 kilograms, although their landlocked relatives rarely exceed 10 kilograms.

## Other Saltwater Species

**Flounder** are caught in shallow waters, where they bury themselves in the sand. Growing to 40 centimeters long, these groundfish are easily caught, and just as easy to lose. Clams and worms are favored baits. **Mackerel,** living in shallow waters throughout summer, are easy to catch using spinning rods. Mackerel charters departing from North Rustico Harbour (Prince Edward Island) are extremely inexpensive.

## Freshwater Fish

**Speckled trout** (also known as brook trout) are widespread throughout the region and are fun to catch and tasty to eat. They tend to gravitate to cooler water, such as spring-fed streams, and can be caught on spinners or flies. A 3.4-kilogram specimen, one of the largest ever caught, is on display in Halifax's Museum of Natural History. Introduced in the late 1800s, **rainbow trout** are in lakes and rivers across Atlantic Canada. Many easily accessible lakes across Atlantic Canada are stocked with trout each spring. Most are rainbows because they are easy to raise and adapt to varying conditions. You can catch them on artificial flies, small spinners, or spoons. Sherbrooke Lake and Dollar Lake, both near Halifax, have healthy populations of **lake trout,** but the biggest of the species are in Newfoundland and Labrador. Introduced from Europe, **brown trout** are found in some streams and larger lakes, with the regional record a 13-kilogram fish caught in Newfoundland.

Long and lean, **striped bass** inhabit rivers and estuaries throughout the region. There is a definite art to catching the species—it is estimated it takes an average of 40–50 hours of fishing to catch one. The regional record is a 28.6-kilogram monster pulled from the lower reaches of the Saint John River (New Brunswick). **Smallmouth bass** are a popular sport fish introduced to the waterways of New Brunswick and southwestern Nova Scotia from farther west. They live in clear, calm water, usually with a gravelly bottom. Common throughout North America, **whitefish** are easily caught in most rivers and lakes, although they rarely exceed 15 centimeters in length. **Atlantic whitefish** (also called Acadian whitefish) are endemic to southwestern Nova Scotia. It is a protected species, so angling for them is prohibited; carry an identification chart if fishing these waters. **Yellow perch** (also known as lake perch) are identified by wide vertical stripes. Most often caught in shallow rivers and lakes in Nova Scotia and New Brunswick, they are fun to catch and tasty.

## Fishing Licenses and Regulations

Each province has its own licensing system and regulations with which you should familiarize yourself with before casting a line.

**Nova Scotia:** The recreational fishery is managed by the Department of Fisheries and Aquaculture (902/485-5056, www.gov.ns.ca/natr). A freshwater license for nonresidents costs 12.46 for one day, $31.74 for seven days, or $57.45 per year. Residents pay $24.13 for an annual license.

**New Brunswick:** A three-day nonresident license to fish for salmon is $40; to fish all other species for three days is $25. A seven-day license is $82 and $35 respectively, and an annual license is $140 and $55. It is illegal for nonresidents to fish for salmon in New Brunswick rivers without a guide, while other waters are set aside as "Crown Reserve"—for the fishing pleasure of residents only. For information, check the government website www.gnb.ca.

**Prince Edward Island:** The Department of Environment, Fishery, and Forestry (902/368-6080, www.gov.pe.ca) charges $7 per day or $20 for an annual license for a trout fishing season that runs from mid-June to mid-September.

**Newfoundland and Labrador:** Contact the Department of Environment and Conservation (709/772-4423, www.env.gov.nl.ca) for information on fishing in both fresh and tidal waters. An important point to note is that nonresidents are prohibited from fishing farther than 800 meters from a provincial highway without a guide or direct resident relative.

Fishing in **national parks** requires a separate license, which is available from park offices and some sports shops; $8 for a seven-day license, $25 for an annual license.

## CYCLING AND MOUNTAIN BIKING

Reasonably good roads and gorgeous scenery make Atlantic Canada excellent road biking territory, while mountain biking has caught on among the adventurous as a way to explore more remote areas of the region. Except on main arteries, particularly the TransCanada Highway, car traffic is generally light. Cyclists, nonetheless, should remain vigilant: Narrow lanes and shoulders are common, and in some areas, drivers may be unaccustomed to sharing the road with bicycles.

Touring opportunities, through a variety of terrain, are numerous in Nova Scotia; probably the ultimate trip is the five- to six-day trek around Cape Breton Island's Cabot Trail. In New Brunswick, following the Saint John River valley and the complex of lakes north of Saint John makes for pleasant touring. The narrow roads that slice through Prince Edward Island's gentle countryside are sublime avenues for biking, while the Confederation Trail, extending from one end of the island to the other, is specifically designed for biking; **Smooth Cycle** (330 University Ave., Charlottetown, 902/566-5530, www.smoothcycle.com) is a good source of trail information. It also rents bikes decked out with panniers and provides drop-offs to points along the trail.

Many shops rent decent- to good-quality road and mountain bikes, but if you plan to do some serious riding, you'll probably want to bring your own. An outstanding information resource is **Atlantic Canada Cycling** (902/423-2453, www.atlanticcanadacycling. com). The organization publishes extensive information on cycling routes (including descriptions and ratings of highways and byways throughout Atlantic Canada), tours, races, clubs, and equipment, while its website has links to local operators and a message board.

## Guided Tours

Nova Scotia–based **Freewheeling Adventures** (902/857-3600 or 800/672-0775, www.freewheeling.ca) leads agreeable arrangements of guided trips in small groups, each accompanied by a support van to carry the luggage and, if necessary, the weary biker. Owners Cathy and Philip Guest plan everything—snacks, picnics, and meals at restaurants en route, and overnights at country inns. Expect to pay around $200–300 per person per day for an all-inclusive tour. The trips pass through some of Atlantic Canada's prettiest countryside, including the Cabot Trail, the Annapolis Valley, Prince Edward Island, and Newfoundland's Northern Peninsula.

# WATER SPORTS

This ocean-bound region has no shortage of beaches, and most waterside provincial parks have a supervised **swimming** area. The warmest beaches are found along the Baie des Chaleurs ("Bay of Warmth") and the Northumberland Strait. The Bay of Fundy and Atlantic shores

© ANDREW HEMPSTEAD

The Pinware River, in Labrador, is one of Atlantic Canada's most pristine salmon streams.

tend to be much cooler, although conditions vary considerably throughout the region.

With so much water surrounding and flowing through the provinces, **boating** opportunities are nearly infinite. Sailing is popular in the Bay of Fundy, around Passamaquoddy Bay, and in spacious Halifax and Sydney harbors, as well as in protected inland areas such as Bras d'Or Lake and the extensive inland waterways of New Brunswick's Saint John River and Mactaquac Lake.

## Canoeing and Kayaking

Canoeing is a traditional form of transportation that remains extremely popular throughout Atlantic Canada. You can rent canoes at many of the more popular lakes, including those protected by Kejimkujik National Park. If you bring your own, you can slip into any body of water whenever you please, taking in the scenery and viewing wildlife from water level. Coastal kayaking is another adventure, especially among the rock towers at Hopewell

Rocks and along Cape Breton Island's turbulent Atlantic coast.

## Tidal Bore Rafting

Instead of white-water rafting, Atlantic Canada is known for wild and woolly trips on the tidal bore created by the world's highest tides in the Bay of Fundy. **Shubenacadie River Adventure Tours** (902/261-2222, www .shubie.com) offers trips for varying levels of adrenaline rush in motorized Zodiacs, riding the bore as it rushes upriver before blasting back across its face. Trips last three hours and cost $70 per person.

## Surfing

Nova Scotia is home to a small but dedicated population of surfers who hit the waves of the province's east coast year-round. **Lawrencetown Beach** (known as L-town to the locals), less than an hour's drive north of Halifax, is the best-known spot, with beach breaks along the long stretch of sand and a right-hander breaking off the rocky point. Other surf spots are scattered along the province's east coast. Water temperatures rarely rise above 16°C, meaning a 4/3-millimeter

or 3/2-millimeter wetsuit is necessary, even in midsummer. Boards and wetsuits can be rented from shops at Lawrencetown Beach as well as from the Rossignol Surf Shop (White Point Beach Lodge, 902/683-2140, www .surfnovascotia.com), south of Halifax. Locals will be more than happy to tell you the cleanest, most consistent waves roll through in winter, but with air temperatures that drop to −20°C and water temperatures hovering around 0°C, only the keenest surfers take to the water.

## WINTERTIME SPORTS

Winter is definitely low season for tourism in Atlantic Canada. Outdoor recreation is severely limited by the weather, although snow-related sports are popular with the locals. In addition to downhill skiing and boarding, skating on frozen ponds is popular, while locals cheer for minor-league ice hockey teams scattered throughout the region.

## Skiing and Snowboarding

The alpine resorts of Atlantic Canada may lack the vertical rise of their western counterparts, but snowfall is high and outsiders

© ANDREW HEMPSTEAD

Surfers gravitate to Lawrencetown Beach in Nova Scotia for some of Canada's finest waves.

will be greeted with open arms wherever they choose to ski. Day passes top out at $40, and each resort has day lodge facilities and rentals. Vertical rises range 180–300 meters, and the season generally runs from Christmas to late March.

Nova Scotia has three downhill resorts. Closest to Halifax is **Ski Martock,** south of the Annapolis Valley; **Wentworth** is near the New Brunswick border; and **Cape Smokey** has spectacular ocean views from its Cape Breton Island location.

In New Brunswick, **Crabbe Mountain,** west of Fredericton, and **Mont-Farlagne,** near Edmundston, have loyal followings.

Atlantic Canada's biggest and best-known resort is **Marble Mountain,** in western Newfoundland (709/637-7601, www.skimarble.com), which has impressive enough mountain statistics to attract skiers and boarders from throughout eastern and central Canada. The resort receives up to five meters of snow each season. Four lifts (including the region's only high-speed quad) offer a vertical rise of 520 meters, with the longest run being over four kilometers. Amenities include a massive day lodge, on-hill accommodations, a terrain park, and a respected ski school. On the mainland, just outside Labrador City, **Smokey Mountain** is a small hill developed in the 1960s by the local mining company.

## Cross-Country Skiing

The region's national parks and many of the provincial parks stay open year-round. In winter, hiking routes are transformed by snow into excellent cross-country ski trails, many of which are groomed by local ski clubs that charge a nominal fee for their use. **Ski Tuonela,** on Nova Scotia's Cape Breton Island (902/929-2144, www.skituonela.com), is one of North America's only lift-served telemark hills. In addition to a rope tow, the resort has 20 kilometers of groomed trails, a day lodge, and overnight accommodations. Organizations with handy websites loaded with information and links to ski clubs are **Canada Trails** (www .canadatrails.ca) and **Cross Country Canada** (www.cccski.com).

# SPECTATOR SPORTS

Windsor, Nova Scotia, claims its place in history as the birthplace of ice hockey (known simply as "hockey" in Canada). Although the region is home to no National Hockey League (NHL) teams, the exploits of the Toronto Maple Leafs, Montréal Canadiens, and other NHL franchises are passionately followed here. In the Atlantic provinces you can also see lively play from the Québec Major Junior Hockey League's Halifax Mooseheads, Moncton Wildcats, and St. John's Fog Devils; NHL farm teams in Fredericton and Saint John, and high-quality college and amateur teams in cities and towns throughout the region. The season runs October–March; check with local tourist-information offices for game schedules and ticket information.

# SHOPPING
## Arts and Crafts

Quilts, sweaters, hooked rugs, porcelains, and wooden carvings are deftly mixed among the watercolors, oils, and sculptures in many arts and crafts venues. The hand-woven tartans of Loomcrofters (the weavers who designed the New Brunswick provincial and Royal Canadian Air Force tartans) at Gagetown, New Brunswick, and the work of the Madawaska Weavers, in New Brunswick's Acadian northwest, are well known on the provincial fashion scene.

New Brunswick's craftspeople specialize in yarn portraits, glass-blowing, pottery, wood sculptures, and pewter goods. The tourism department publishes the *Crafts Directory,* available at any tourism office. Antique buyers should head to Nova Scotia, where many historic sites and homes have been converted into antiques shops. The Nova Scotia tourism department produces a buyer's guide, available at tourism offices. Newfoundland is known for a wide selection of labradorite jewelry as well as down jackets. The basketry work of the Mi'Kmaq of Lennox Island (Prince Edward

Island) has received much attention. PEI shops also carry beadwork, leather goods, silver jewelry, pottery, handcrafted furniture, and woodcarvings.

On Prince Edward Island, *Anne of Green Gables* is a common theme, but there is also a wide range of more traditional crafts. The best of these are knitted sweaters created by **Great Northern Knitters** (13 Queen St., Charlottetown, 902/566-5302), which also has a store in Halifax (1781 Lower Water St., 902/422-9209). The **P.E.I. Crafts Council** website (www.peicraftscouncil.com) has an address book of island craftspeople.

## Business Hours

Shopping hours are generally Monday–Saturday 9 A.M.–6 P.M. Late shopping in most areas is available until 9 P.M. on Thursday and Friday, and supermarkets open 24 hours have begun to appear in a few towns. Generally, banks are open Monday–Wednesday 10 A.M.–4 P.M. and Thursday–Friday 10 A.M.–5 P.M. A few banks may open on Saturday, but all are closed on Sunday. Nova Scotia is the only Canadian province that disallows Sunday shopping, although exceptions are made for essential services like gas stations and in "tourist areas" such as the Halifax waterfront.

# Accommodations

Atlantic Canada has all the chain hotels you know, as well as a range of accommodations that showcase the region—historic bed-and-breakfasts, grand resorts, riverside cottages, and luxurious fishing lodges. This section will give you a taste of the choices and some hints on reserving a room. Throughout the travel chapters of this book, I detail my favorites in all price ranges.

## Lodging Reservations

Many large local, national, and international hotel, resort, and motel groups have properties in Atlantic Canada; if you want to make advance reservations at any of their lodgings, simply phone the toll-free reservation center or book online using their websites.

## HOTELS, MOTELS, AND RESORTS

International, Canadian, and regional lodging chains are represented in Atlantic Canada. At the more expensive properties, expect all the requisite amenities and services—swimming pools, air-conditioning, in-room Internet access, room service, complimentary toiletries, restaurants, and bars. This type of accommodation can be found in central locations in all cities and major tourist areas. Rates at four- or

five-star hotels start at $150 s or d in high season. Prices for a basic motel room in a small town start at $45 s, $50 d, rising to $100 for a room in a chain hotel within walking distance of a major city's downtown core.

The big chains are represented in Atlantic Canada, as well as the following that you may not be familiar with.

## Best Western

OK, I assume you have heard of the world's largest motel chain, but the website www .bestwesternatlantic.com is helpful in providing direct links to 14 local properties.

## Choice Hotels Canada

Choice Hotels (800/424-6423, www.choice-hotels.ca) owns 275 properties across Canada. It operates seven brands, including Sleep, with smallish but clean, comfortable, and inexpensive rooms; Comfort, where guests enjoy a light breakfast and newspaper with a no-frills room; Quality, a notch up in class with a restaurant and lounge; and Econo Lodge, older properties that have been renovated to Choice's standard and often have a pool and restaurant.

## Delta Hotels and Resorts

This Canadian-owned company is a class

Fairmont Algonquin, St. Andrews, New Brunswick

operation; expect fine hotels with splendid facilities in notable settings. Locations include Saint John, Fredericton, and Moncton, New Brunswick; Halifax and Sydney, Nova Scotia; and St. John's, Newfoundland. Reservations can be made by calling 416/874-2000 or 877/814-7706, or online at www.deltahotels .com. Check the Delta website for package deals offered year-round.

### Fairmont Hotels and Resorts

Fairmont (506/863-6310 or 800/257-7544, www.fairmont.com) is North America's largest operator of luxury hotels and resorts. The company is represented in Atlantic Canada by the Fairmont Algonquin, a gorgeous, Tudor-style resort spread across manicured grounds and gardens at St. Andrews, New Brunswick. Besides the Algonquin, the group's only other Atlantic Canada property is in St. John's, Newfoundland.

### Maritime Inns and Resorts

With package deals and locations in Pictou, Antigonish, Port Hawkesbury, and the Cape Breton resort town of Baddeck, these properties (902/752-5644 or 888/662-7484, www.mari-timeinns.com) are popular with holidaying Maritimers. Generally, packages include meals and activities such as golfing for around $100 per person per day.

### Rodd Hotels and Resorts

This locally owned hotel company (902/892-7448 or 800/565-7633, www.roddhotel-sandresorts.com) is Prince Edward Island's lodgings standard bearer. The handsome Loyalist Country Inn at Summerside is the newest hotel; the Rodd Charlottetown in the capital is the oldest. Two full-facility resorts are situated within provincial-park settings at either end of the island: near Cardigan (Roseneath, Brudenell River Provincial Park) and O'Leary (Woodstock, Mill River Provincial Park). Other Rodd locations include two more properties in Charlottetown; one in Moncton, New Brunswick; and two in Yarmouth, Nova Scotia.

### Signature Resorts

Nova Scotia's provincial government owns three stunning resorts. They appeal to the

# GETTING A GOOD DEAL ON ACCOMMODATIONS

Rates quoted through this guidebook are for a standard double room in the high season (usually July and August, but sometimes as early as June and as late as September). Almost all accommodations are less expensive outside of these busy months, with some discounting their rates by up to 50 percent. You'll enjoy the biggest seasonal discounts at properties that rely on summer tourists, such as those in Lunenburg or along the Northumberland Strait. The same applies in Halifax on weekends – many of the big downtown hotels rely on business and convention travelers to fill the bulk of their rooms; when the end of the week rolls around, the hotels are left with rooms to fill at discounted rates Friday, Saturday, and Sunday nights.

While you have no influence on the seasonal and weekday/weekend pricing differences detailed above, *how* you reserve a room *can* make a difference in how much you pay. First and foremost, when it comes to searching out actual rates, the Internet is an invaluable tool. All hotel websites listed in *Moon Atlantic Canada* show rates, and many have online reservation forms. Use these websites to search out specials, many of which are available only on the Internet. Don't be afraid to negotiate during slower times. Even if the desk clerk has no control over rates, there's no harm in asking for a bigger room or one with a better view. Just look for a VACANCY sign hanging out front.

Most hotels offer auto association members an automatic 10 percent discount, and whereas senior discounts apply only to those older than 60 or 65 on public transportation and at attractions, most hotels offer discounts to those age 50 and older, with chains such as Best Western also allowing senior travelers a late checkout. "Corporate Rates" are a lot more flexible than in years past; some hotels require nothing more than the flash of a business card for a 10-20 percent discount.

When it comes to frequent-flyer programs, you really do need to be a frequent flyer to achieve free flights, but the various loyalty programs offered by hotels often provide benefits simply for signing up.

---

carriage trade—travelers who like the understated ambience of a resort lodge with a tony rustic setting and furnishings, gourmet dining, a remote location with manicured grounds, and the genteel sports of golf or fly-fishing. Provincial resorts in Nova Scotia are the Pines Resort at Digby; the Keltic Lodge at Ingonish Beach, Cape Breton; and Liscombe Lodge at Liscomb Mills. The website www.signatureresorts.com has links to all three.

## BED-AND-BREAKFASTS

Atlantic Canada is blessed with hundreds of bed-and-breakfasts. Concentrations are located across Prince Edward Island and in historic towns such as Annapolis Royal (Nova Scotia) and St. John's (Newfoundland and Labrador). Styles run the gamut from historic mansions to rustic farmhouses, and as a result, amenities can also vary greatly. Regardless, guests can expect hearty home cooking, a peaceful atmosphere, personal service, knowledgeable hosts, and conversation with like-minded travelers. They are usually private residences, with hosts that live on-site and up to eight guest rooms. As the name suggests, breakfast is included in quoted rates; ask before booking whether it is a cooked or continental breakfast. Rates fluctuate enormously—from $40 s, $50 d for a spare room in an otherwise regular family home to over $200 in a historic mansion.

### Finding and Reserving a Room

My favorite bed-and-breakfasts are recommended within the travel chapters of this book. You can also use provincial accommodations guides and local information centers to find out about individual properties. **Select Inns of Atlantic Canada** (www.selectinns.ca) is an organization of mid- to top-end bed-and-breakfasts, with online reservations and lots of information on specific properties. The

**Canadian Bed and Breakfast Guide** (www .canadianbandbguide.ca) is a regularly updated database, although listings aren't recommendations as such. Finally, **Bed and Breakfast Online** (www.bbcanada.com) doesn't take bookings, but links are provided and an ingenious search engine helps you find the accommodation that best fits your needs.

Before reserving a room, it is important to ask a number of questions of your hosts. The two obvious ones are whether or not you'll have your own bathroom and how payment can be made (many establishments don't accept debit cards or all credit cards).

## BACKPACKER ACCOMMODATIONS

As accommodation prices are reasonable throughout Atlantic Canada, there is less of a need to find a dorm bed than in other parts of North America. While privately operated backpacker lodges come and go with predictable regularity, Hostelling International operates five hostels in the region.

### Hostelling International

The curfews and chores are long gone in this worldwide nonprofit organization of 4,200 hostels in 60 countries. Hostelling International Canada has hostels in Nova Scotia at Halifax, South Milford (near Kejimkujik National Park), and Wentworth; in New Brunswick at Fredericton and Campbellton; in Charlottetown on Prince Edward Island; and in St. John's, Newfoundland. For a dorm bed, members of Hostelling International pay $15–25 per night, nonmembers pay $17–30. Generally, you need to provide your own sleeping bag or linen, but most hostels supply extra bedding (if needed) at no charge. Accommodations are in dormitories (2–10 beds), although single and double rooms are often available for an additional charge. Each also offers a communal kitchen, lounge area, and laundry facilities, while some have Internet access, bike rentals, and organized tours.

You don't *have* to be a member to stay in an affiliated hostel of Hostelling International, but membership pays for itself after only a few nights of discounted lodging. Aside from discounted rates, benefits of membership vary from country to country but often include discounted air, rail, and bus travel; discounts on car rental; and discounts on some attractions and commercial activities. For Canadians, the membership charge is $35 annually, or $175 for a Friend (lifetime) Membership. For more information contact HI–Canada (604/684-7111, www.hihostels.ca).

Joining the Hostelling International affiliate of your home country entitles you to reciprocal rights in Canada, as well as around the world; click through the links at www.hihostels.com to your country of choice.

## CAMPING

Camping out is a popular summer activity across Atlantic Canada, and you'll find campgrounds in all national parks, many provincial parks, on the outskirts of cities and towns, and in most resort areas. Facilities at park campgrounds vary considerably, but most commercial operations have showers and water, electricity, and sewer hookups.

**National parks** provide some of the nicest surroundings for camping. All sites have picnic tables, fire grates, toilets, and fresh drinking water, although only some provide showers. Prices range $18–38 depending on facilities and services. A percentage of sites can be reserved through the **Parks Canada Campground Reservation Service** (877/737-3783, www .pccamping.ca). Backcountry camping in a national park costs $8 per person per night.

Whenever possible, reservations for campsites—especially at the national parks and most popular provincial parks—should be made at least six weeks in advance. Most provincial parks, however, do not accept reservations, but instead assign sites on a first-come, first-served basis. At those parks, it's best to arrive before noon to ensure yourself a spot. Most provincial parks are open mid-May to mid-October. Most privately owned campsites accept reservations, which are more likely to be held if you send a small deposit.

# Tips for Travelers

## EMPLOYMENT AND STUDY

International visitors wishing to work or study in Canada must obtain authorization *before* entering the country. Authorization to work will only be granted if no qualified Canadians are available for the work in question. Applications for work and study are available from all Canadian embassies and must be submitted with a nonrefundable processing fee. The Canadian government has a reciprocal agreement with Australia for a limited number of **holiday work visas** to be issued each year. Australian citizens aged 30 and younger are eligible; contact your nearest Canadian embassy or consulate. For general information on immigrating to Canada check the **Citizenship and Immigration Canada** website (www.cic.gc.ca).

## WHAT TO TAKE

You'll find little use for a suit and tie in Atlantic Canada. Instead, pack for the outdoors. At the top of your must-bring list should be **hiking boots.** Even in summer, you should be geared up for a variety of weather conditions, especially at the change of seasons or if you'll be spending time along the coast. Do this by preparing to **dress in layers,** including at least one pair of fleece pants and a heavy long-sleeved top. For breezy coastal sightseeing, a sweater or windbreaker, hat, sunscreen, and comfortable shoes with rubber soles will come in handy. For dining out, **casual dress** is accepted at all but the most upscale restaurants.

Electrical appliances from the United States work in Canada, but those from other parts of the world will require a **current converter** (transformer) to bring the voltage down. Many travel-size shavers, hairdryers, and irons have built-in converters.

## VISITORS WITH DISABILITIES

A lack of mobility should not deter you from traveling to Atlantic Canada, but you should definitely do some research before leaving home.

If you haven't traveled extensively, start by doing some research at the website of the **Access-Able Travel Source** (www.access-able .com), where you will find databases of specialist travel agencies and lodgings in Canada that cater to travelers with disabilities. **Flying Wheels Travel** (507/451-5005 or 877/451-5006, www.flyingwheelstravel.com) caters solely to the needs of travelers with disabilities. The **Society for Accessible Travel and Hospitality** (212/447-7284, www.sath.org) supplies information on tour operators, vehicle rentals, specific destinations, and companion services. For frequent travelers, the membership fee (US$45 per year) is well worthwhile. *Emerging Horizons* (www.emerginghorizons .com) is a U.S. quarterly magazine dedicated to travelers with special needs.

**Access to Travel** (800/465-7735, www .accesstotravel.gc.ca) is an initiative of the Canadian government that includes information on travel within and between Canadian cities. The website also has a lot of general travel information for those with disabilities. The **Canadian National Institute for the Blind** (www.cnib.ca) offers a wide range of services from its Halifax (902/453-1480) and Fredericton (506/458-0060) offices. Finally, the **Canadian Paraplegic Association** (877/324-3611, www.canparaplegic.org) is another good source of information; provincial head offices include Halifax (902/423-1277), Moncton (506/858-0311), Charlottetown (902/368-3955), and St. John's (709/753-5901).

## TRAVELING WITH CHILDREN

Regardless of whether you're traveling with toddlers or teens, you will come upon decisions affecting everything from where you stay to your choice of activities. Luckily for you,

Atlantic Canada is very family-friendly, with indoor and outdoor attractions aimed specifically at the younger generation, such as Magnetic Hill just outside Moncton. Children familiar with *Anne of Green Gables* will love Cavendish, Prince Edward Island, the setting of the tale and now a major tourist destination packed with places highlighted in the book and also many commercial attractions.

Admission prices for children are included throughout the travel chapters of this book. As a general rule, these reduced prices are for those ages 6 to 16. For two adults and two-plus children, always ask about family tickets. Children under 6 nearly always get in free. Most hotels and motels will happily accommodate children, but always try to reserve your room in advance and let the reservations desk know the ages of your brood. Often, children stay free in major hotels, and in the case of some major chains—such as Holiday Inn—eat free also. Generally, bed-and-breakfasts aren't suitable for children, and in some cases don't accept kids at all. Ask ahead.

Let the children help you plan your trip; look at websites and read up on Atlantic Canada together. To make your vacation more enjoyable if you'll be spending a lot of time on the road, rent a minivan (all major rental agencies have a supply). Don't forget to bring along favorite toys and games from home—whatever you think will keep will keep your kids entertained when the joys of sightseeing wear off.

The various provincial tourism websites have sections devoted to children's activities within each province. Another handy source of online information is **Traveling Internationally with Your Kids** (www.travelwithyourkids.com).

# Health and Safety

Atlantic Canada is a healthy place. To visit, you don't need to get any vaccinations or booster shots. And when you arrive you can drink the water from the faucet and eat the food without worry.

If you need an ambulance, call 911 or the number listed on the inside front cover of local telephone directories. All cities and most larger towns have hospitals—look in each travel chapter of this book for locations and telephone numbers.

## INSURANCE AND PRESCRIPTIONS

Intraprovincial agreements cover the medical costs of Canadians traveling across the nation. As a rule, the usual health-insurance plans from other countries do not include medical-care costs incurred while traveling; ask your insurance company or agent if supplemental health coverage is available, and if it is not, arrange for coverage with an independent carrier before departure. Hospital charges vary from place to place but can be as much as $3,000 a day, and some facilities impose a surcharge for nonresidents. Some Canadian companies offer coverage specifically aimed at visitors.

If you're on medication, take adequate supplies with you, and get a prescription from your doctor to cover the time you will be away. You may not be able to get a prescription filled at Canadian pharmacies without visiting a Canadian doctor, so don't wait till you've almost run out. If you wear glasses or contact lenses, ask your optometrist for a spare prescription in case you break or lose your lenses, and stock up on your usual cleaning supplies.

## SEXUALLY TRANSMITTED DISEASES

AIDS and other venereal and needle-transmitted diseases are as much of a concern in Atlantic Canada as anywhere in the world today. Take exactly the same precautions you would at home—use condoms, and don't share needles.

## GIARDIA

Giardiasis, also known as beaver fever, is a real concern for those who drink water from backcountry water sources. It's caused by an intestinal parasite, *Giardia lamblia,* that lives in lakes, rivers, and streams. Once ingested, its effects, although not instantaneous, can be dramatic; severe diarrhea, cramps, and nausea are the most common. Preventive measures should always be taken and include boiling all water for at least 10 minutes, treating all water with iodine, or filtering all water using a filter with a small enough pore size to block the *Giardia* cysts.

## WINTER TRAVEL

Travel through Atlantic Canada during winter months should not be undertaken lightly. Before setting out in a vehicle, check antifreeze levels, and always carry a spare tire and blankets or sleeping bags.

**Frostbite** can occur in a matter of seconds if the temperature falls below freezing and if the wind is blowing. Layer your clothing for the best insulation against the cold, and don't forget gloves and, most important, a warm hat, which can offer the best protection against heat loss. Frostbite occurs in varying degrees. Most often it leaves a numbing, bruised sensation, and the skin turns white. Exposed areas of skin such as the nose and ears are most susceptible, particularly when cold temperatures are accompanied by high winds.

**Hypothermia** occurs when the body fails to produce heat as fast as it loses it. Cold weather combined with hunger, fatigue, and dampness create a recipe for disaster. Symptoms are not always apparent to the victim. The early signs are numbness, shivering, slurring of words, dizzy spells, and in extreme cases, violent behavior, unconsciousness, and even death. The best treatment is to get the patient out of the cold, replace wet clothing with dry, slowly give hot liquids and sugary foods, and place the victim in a sleeping bag. Prevention is a better strategy; dress for cold in layers, including a waterproof outer layer, and wear a warm wool cap or other headgear.

## CRIME

The provinces of Atlantic Canada enjoy one of the country's lowest crime rates. Violent crimes are infrequent; the most common crime is petty theft. If you must leave valuable items in your car unattended, keep them out of sight, preferably locked in the vehicle's trunk. Women have few difficulties traveling alone throughout the region.

Remember that cities such as Halifax, Saint John, and St. John's are international ports with seamy (albeit interesting) bars and taverns at or near the working area of the waterfront; keep your wits about you, especially late at night. Better yet, leave these night scenes to the sailors and others who frequent the areas.

Both possession and sale of illicit drugs are considered serious crimes and are punishable with jail time and/or severe fines. Furthermore, Canadians consider drinking while driving equally serious; the penalty on the first conviction is jail and/or a heavy fine. A conviction here or in your home country can be grounds for exclusion from Canada.

### Royal Canadian Mounted Police (RCMP)

Despite the romantic image of the staid redjacketed officer on horseback, Mounties (as they are most often called) nowadays favor the squad car as their mount of choice and a less colorful uniform. They are as ubiquitous a symbol of the country as the maple leaf, and are similar to the highway patrol or state police in the United States. They operate throughout all the country's provinces and territories (except Ontario and Québec), complementing the work of local police.

# Information and Services

## MONEY

Unless noted otherwise, **prices quoted in this book are in Canadian currency.** Canadian currency is based on dollars and cents, with 100 cents equal to one dollar. Canada's money is issued in notes ($5, $10, and $20 are the most common) and coins (1, 5, 10, and 25 cents, and $1 and $2). The 11-sided, gold-colored $1 coin is known as a "loonie" for the bird featured on it. The unique $2 coin ("toonie," for "two loonies") is silver with a gold-colored insert.

The safest way to carry money is in the form of travelers checks from a reputable and well-known U.S. company such as American Express, Visa, or Bank of America; those are also the easiest checks to cash. Cash only the amount you need when you need it. Banks offer the best exchange rates, but other foreign-currency exchange outlets are available. It's also a good idea to start off with a couple of travelers checks in Canadian dollars so you're never caught without *some* money if you don't make it to a bank on time.

Visa and MasterCard credit and debit cards are also readily accepted throughout the region. By using these cards you eliminate the necessity of thinking about the exchange rate—the transaction and rate of exchange on the day of the transaction will automatically be reflected in the bill from your credit-card company. On the downside, you'll always get a better exchange rate when dealing directly with a bank.

## Costs

The cost of living in Atlantic Canada is lower than elsewhere in the country. For you, the visitor, this will be most apparent when paying for accommodations and meals. By planning ahead, having a tent, or traveling in the shoulder seasons, it is possible to get by on around $100 per person per day or less. Gasoline is sold in liters (3.78 liters equals one U.S. gallon) and is generally $1.30–1.50 a liter for regular unleaded.

## CURRENCY EXCHANGE

For the best exchange rate, take your foreign currency to a bank. Current exchange rates (into CDN$) for major currencies are:

US$1 = $1.20

AUS$1 = $0.84

€1 = $1.62

HK$10 = $1.54

NZ$1 = $0.70

UK£1 = $1.78

¥100 = $1.36

On the Internet, check current exchange rates at www.xe.com/ucc.

**Tipping** charges are not usually added to your bill. You are expected to add a tip of 15 percent to the total amount for waiters and waitresses, barbers and hairdressers, taxi drivers, and other such service providers. Bellhops, doormen, and porters generally receive $1 per item of baggage.

## Harmonized Sales Tax (HST)

In the spring of 1997, the Harmonized Sales Tax, a tax levied on most goods and services, supplanted the "goods and services" and provincial sales taxes in Nova Scotia, New Brunswick, and Newfoundland and Labrador. Originally pegged at 15 percent, the GST portion has since been reduced by two percent, making the HST 13 percent. The provincial sales tax on Prince Edward Island is two percent higher at 10 percent, and is billed separately from the GST. All Canadian residents must pay the tax, as must visitors.

## MAPS

Driving maps such as those published by **MapArt** (www.mapart.com) and **Rand McNally** (www.randmcnally.com) are available at bookstores, gas stations, and even some grocery stores across Atlantic Canada. In Halifax, **Maps and Ducks** (Historic Properties, 1869 Upper Water St., 902/422-7106) and **Trail Shop** (6210 Quinpool Rd., 902/423-8736) are specialty map stores.

Nautical maps are handled by the **Canada Hydrographic Service,** a division of Fisheries and Oceans Canada, but it doesn't sell directly to the public. To request a map catalog and a list of dealers, call 613/995-4413 or check www.charts.gc.ca. This department also distributes *Sailing Directions,* a composite of general navigational information, port facility descriptions, and sailing conditions (in English or French) for the entire region.

## TOURISM OFFICES

The website of the **Canadian Tourism Commission** (www.canada.travel) is loaded with general information and provides travel information for individual provinces. The following provincial government offices provide more detailed information and will send out free information packages and maps:

- **Tourism Nova Scotia:** 902/425-5781 or 800/565-0000, www.novascotia.com

- **Tourism New Brunswick:** 800/561-0123, www.tourismnewbrunswick.ca

- **Prince Edward Island Tourism:** 902/368-4444 or 800/463-4734, www.tourismpei.com

- **Newfoundland and Labrador Tourism:** 709/729-0862 or 800/563-6353, www.newfoundlandlabrador.com

## COMMUNICATIONS AND MEDIA
### Postal Services

**Canada Post** (www.canadapost.ca) issues postage stamps that must be used on all mail posted in Canada. First-class letters and postcards sent within Canada are $0.54, to the United States $0.98, to other foreign destinations $1.65. Prices increase along with the weight of the mailing. You can buy stamps at post offices (closed weekends), some hotel lobbies, airports, many retail outlets, and some newsstands.

### Telephone Services

The country code for Canada is 1, the same as the United States. Provincial area codes are: Nova Scotia, 902; New Brunswick, 506; Prince Edward Island, 902, Newfoundland and Labrador, 709. These prefixes must be dialed for all long-distance calls, even in-province calls. Toll-free numbers have the 800, 888, 877, or 866 prefix, and may be good for the province, Atlantic Canada, Canada, North America, or, in the case of major hotel chains and car rental companies, worldwide.

To make an international call from Canada, dial the prefix 011 before the country code or dial 0 for operator assistance.

Public phones accept 5-, 10-, and 25-cent coins; local calls are $0.35–0.50, and most long-distance calls cost at least $2.50 for the first minute. The least expensive way to make long-distance calls from a public phone is with a **phone card.** These are available from convenience stores, newsstands, and gas stations.

### Internet Access

If your Internet provider doesn't allow you to access your email away from your home computer, open an email account with **Hotmail** (www.hotmail.com) or **Yahoo** (www.yahoo.com). Although there are restrictions on the size and number of emails you can store, these services are handy and best of all, free.

Free public Internet access is available throughout Atlantic Canada through the

**Community Access Program (CAP).** To find out addresses and hours of the over 1,000 locations across the region, call 866/569-8428 or go to http://cap.ic.gc.ca.

All major hotels and many bed-and-breakfasts have high-speed or Wi-Fi access from guest rooms. Those that don't—usually mid- and lower-priced properties—often have an Internet booth in the lobby. You'll also find Internet booths and Wi-Fi access in many cafés.

## Newspapers and Magazines

Atlantic Canada is too expansive and diverse to be well covered by one newspaper, but plenty of regional and big-city papers are available. The *Globe and Mail* and *National Post* are distributed throughout the Atlantic provinces, and Halifax's *Chronicle Herald* is found throughout Nova Scotia. Publications for the other provinces are listed under each specific province.

Canada's best-selling and most respected newsmagazine is *Maclean's*. *L'Actualité* is the French counterpart. *Newsweek, Time,* and other big American publications are available at drugstores, bookstores, and corner groceries.

# WEIGHTS AND MEASURES

Canada uses the metric system, with temperature measured in degrees Celsius, liquid measurements in liters, solid weights in kilograms and metric tons, land areas in hectares, and distances in kilometers, meters, and centimeters. This newfangled system hasn't completely taken hold everywhere, and many locals still think in terms of the imperial system; expect to hear a lobster described in pounds, local distances given in miles, and the temperature expressed in Fahrenheit degrees.

The electrical voltage is 120 volts. The standard electrical plug configuration is the same as that used in the United States: two flat blades, often with a round third pin for grounding.

## Time Zones

Even though Nova Scotia was home to Sir Sandford Fleming, the man who devised time zones, the province didn't receive any special favors. It is on **Atlantic standard time (AST),** the same as New Brunswick and Prince Edward Island. **Newfoundland standard time (NST),** 30 minutes ahead of Atlantic standard time, is used on the island of Newfoundland and the southeastern Labrador communities on the Strait of Belle Isle; the rest of Labrador is on AST.

Atlantic standard time is one hour ahead of eastern standard time and four hours ahead of Pacific standard time.

# RESOURCES

## Suggested Reading

### NATURAL HISTORY

Grescoe, Taras. *Bottomfeeder*. Toronto: Harper Collins, 2008. An insight into the fisheries industry made more readable by the author's firsthand accounts of visits to the world's most important fisheries, including Nova Scotia.

Griffin, Diane. *Atlantic Wild Flowers*. Toronto: Oxford University Press, 1984. A glorious combination of text by Griffin and photography by Wayne Barrett and Anne MacKay—a must for every naturalist who revels in wildflowers.

Hare, F. K., and M. K. Thomas. *Climate Canada*. Toronto: John Wiley & Sons, 1974. One of the most extensive works on Canada's climate ever written. Includes a chapter on how the climate is changing.

Lyell, Charles. *Geological Observations on the U.S., Canada, and Nova Scotia*. New York: Arno Press, 1978. During an early 1840s visit, Lyell thought enough of Nova Scotia's unusual landscape and geology to give it equal space among the nations in this insightful account.

MacAskill, Wallace R. *MacAskill Seascapes and Sailing Ships*. Halifax: Nimbus Publishing. Cape Breton's famed photographer captures the misty moods of fishermen, schooners, seaports, and seacoasts.

Saunders, Gary. *Discover Nova Scotia: The Ultimate Nature Guide*. Halifax: Nimbus Publishing, 2001. Perfect for a daypack, this handy guide includes maps, trail descriptions, and the natural wonders of Nova Scotia's parks.

Thurston, Harry. *Tidal Life: A Natural History of the Bay of Fundy*. Halifax: Nimbus Publishing, 1998. The lavishly illustrated contents describe natural habitats formed by the famed Fundy tides.

Towers, Julie, and Anne Camozzi. *Discover Nova Scotia: Wildlife Viewing Sites*. Halifax: Nimbus Publishing, 1999. Another of Nimbus's popular "Discover Nova Scotia" titles, this one gives detailed directions to over 100 sites.

### HUMAN HISTORY

Andrieux, J. P. *St. Pierre and Miquelon: A Fragment of France in North America*. Ottawa: O.T.C. Press, 1986. One of the most thorough books about France's overseas province, the small volume details sightseeing within a historical context and is illustrated with historical photographs.

Beamish, Peter. *Dances with Whales*. St. John's, Newfoundland: Robinson-Blackmore, 1993. Describes the methodology involved in studying the various species' habits, peculiarities, and migrations. Stay at Trinity's Village Inn and Dr. Beamish will be your host.

Bedford, David, and Danielle Irving. *Tragedy of Progress: Marxism, Modernity and the Aboriginal Question*. Toronto: Fernwood Books,

2000. Catalogs the struggle for justice by native Canadians. Although published in Ontario, the book's New Brunswick–based authors provide plenty of local content.

Boileau, John. *Half Hearted Enemies*. Halifax: Formac Publishing, 2005. Examines the intriguing story of how Nova Scotia and New England continued to trade through the War of 1812.

Brasseaux, Carl A. *The Founding of New Acadia*. New Orleans: Louisiana State University Press, 1997. A little academic, but this book will make interesting reading for anyone who wants to learn about the links between Cajuns and the Acadians of Atlantic Canada.

Campbell, Gary. *The Road to Canada*. Fredericton, New Brunswick: Goose Lane Editions, 2005. Tells the story of how river transportation—specifically the Saint John and St. Lawrence Rivers—opened up central Canada for settlement.

Campey, Lucille H. *After the Hector*. Edinburgh: Birlinn Publishing, 2005. An account of those who arrived in Pictou aboard the *Hector* and how their Scottish Highlands heritage helped them adapt and thrive in the New World.

Collie, Michael. *New Brunswick*. Toronto: Macmillan, 1974. Much has changed in the 30-plus years since this book was written, but much still rings true. Collie provides a poetic, highly personal, and often moving overview of the province, its history, and the psyche of its people.

Conrad, Margaret. *A History of Atlantic Canada*. Oxford, U.K.: Oxford University Press, 2005. A concise history of the four Atlantic provinces by a local history professor.

Daigle, Jean, ed. *Acadians of the Maritimes*. Moncton, New Brunswick: Chaire d'Études Acadiennes, Université de Moncton, 1995. The history of the Acadians in Atlantic Canada is a tangled tale of upheaval and survival, cultural clashes and passions. Daigle's collection of Acadian literature is among the best on the bookshelves.

Davidson, James. *Great Heart: The History of a Labrador Adventure*. Tokyo: Kodansha International, 1997. In 1903 an adventure across the Ungava-Labrador Peninsula came to a tragic end with the death of leader Leon Hubbard. This highly readable story was written from original expedition diaries and notes taken by Hubbard's wife, who spent years searching for the truth about his death.

De Mont, John. *Citizens Irving: K. C. Irving and His Legacy, The Story of Canada's Wealthiest Family*. Toronto: Doubleday Canada, 1991. The Irving family is *very* private, and this unofficial biography is stuffed with well-documented unfavorable and favorable facts, legends, and speculation.

Faragher, John Mack. *A Great and Noble Scheme: The Tragic Story of the Expulsion of the French Acadians from Their American Homeland*. New York: WW Norton, 2005. In this hefty 560-page book, Faragher describes the evolution of Acadia, the horrors of the deportation, and the resulting pockets of Acadian culture that thrive to this day.

Finnan, Mark. *Oak Island Secrets*. Halifax: Formac Publishing, 2002. One of many books devoted to the world's longest treasure hunt, which continues on a small island south of Halifax.

Hicks, Brian. *Ghost Ship: the Mysterious True Story of the* Mary Celeste *and Her Missing Crew*. New York: Random House, 2005. The latest of dozens of books devoted to unraveling the story of the world's most famous mystery ship, including its early history and launch from Nova Scotia.

Kert, Faye. *Trimming Yankee Sails* Fredericton, New Brunswick: Goose Land Editions, 2005. Stories of privateers from Saint John, including the 1863 capture of the passenger liner SS *Chesapeake*.

Ledger, Don. *Swissair Down*. Halifax: Nimbus Publishing, 2000. The story of the September 1998 crash of a Swissair jetliner off the village of Peggy's Cove from a pilot's point of view.

MacDonald, M. A. *Rebels and Loyalists: The Lives and Material Culture of New Brunswick's Early English-Speaking Settlers, 1758–1783*. Fredericton, New Brunswick: New Ireland Press, 1990. MacDonald's slice of history is narrow, and his view is interestingly pervasive.

Major, Kevin. *As Near to Heaven by Sea: A History of Newfoundland and Labrador*. Toronto: Penguin, 2002. Lively yet full of detail, this is an excellent introduction to Newfoundland and Labrador's long and colorful history.

Nunn, Bruce. *History with a Twist*. Halifax: Nimbus Publishing, 2002. Light yet interesting reading that covers a few dozen tales from Nova Scotia's past. And if you're looking for more, there's *More History with a Twist* by the same author.

Oickle, Vernon. *Busted: Nova Scotia's War on Drugs*. Halifax: Nimbus Publishing, 1997. Stories of local lawmen and their struggle to curb the trade of illicit drugs along Nova Scotia's remote coastline.

Parker, Mike. *Guides of the North Woods*. Halifax: Nimbus Publishing, 2005. If you enjoy history and hunting or fishing, you'll enjoy sitting around a campfire reading tales of outdoorsmen from the last century.

Paul, Daniel N. *We Were Not the Savages*. Toronto: Fernwood Books, 2000. A fascinating look at the unhappy relationship between the Mi'Kmaq and Europeans.

Rompkey, Ronald. *Grenfell of Labrador: A Biography*. Toronto: University of Toronto Press, 1991. Sir Wilfred Grenfell, the physician/missionary whose work left an indelible imprint on the province's remote areas, has had several biographers, but none as meticulous and incisive as Rompkey.

Thomas, Peter. *Lost Land of Moses: The Age of Discovery on New Brunswick's Salmon Rivers*. Fredericton, New Brunswick: Goose Lane Editions, 2001. Thomas combines his knowledge of New Brunswick history with his love of angling.

Tuck, James A., and Robert Grenier. *Red Bay, Labrador: World Whaling Capital, A.D. 1550–1660*. St. John's, Newfoundland: Atlantic Archaeology, 1989. Archaeological discoveries form the gist for relating the early Basque whaling industry. Splendid color photography and black-and-white graphics.

## CULTURE AND CRAFTS

Bolger, F. W. P. *Spirit of Place: Lucy Maud Montgomery and Prince Edward Island*. Toronto: Oxford University Press, 2000. Among the best of the photography books depicting Montgomery's island. Augmented with text, Bolger matches selected Montgomery quotes with glossy pictures by Wayne Barrett and Anne MacKay.

Carter, Pauline. *The Great Nova Scotia Cookbook*. Halifax: Nimbus Publishing, 2001. This in-depth look at local cuisine includes many traditional dishes incorporating modern trends in cooking.

Gallant, Melvin, and Marielle Cormier-Boudreau. *A Taste of Acadie*. Fredericton, New Brunswick: Goose Lane Editions, 1991. Traditional Acadian recipes.

Gillis, Stephen, and John Gillis. *No Faster than a Walk: The Covered Bridges of New Brunswick*. Fredericton, New Brunswick: Goose Lane Editions, 1997. Currently out of print, but found in many secondhand bookstores, this photo-filled guide highlights the province's significant covered bridges.

Harper, Marjory. *Myth, Migration and the Making of Memory: Scotia and Nova Scotia*. Halifax: John Donald Publishers, 2000. Explores Nova Scotia's Scottish heritage and the importance of the province's links to Scotland through the years.

Heibron, Alexandra, ed. *Lucy Maud Montgomery Album*. Markham, Ontario: Fitzhenry and Whiteside, 1999. Thoroughly researched, this huge compilation includes everything there is to know about Montgomery, her writing, and her home province. It was released in 1999 to commemorate the 125th anniversary of her birth.

MacDonald, Edward. *If you're Stronghearted: PEI in the Twentieth Century*. Charlottetown: PEI Museum Heritage Foundation, 2000. This hardcover book tells the story of the people of Prince Edward Island, their culture, and a changing economy through a turbulent 100 years that ended with the construction of a bridge to the outside world.

Montgomery, Lucy Maud. *The Alpine Path*. Markham, Ontario: Fitzhenry and Whiteside, 1999. Some of Montgomery's most vivid descriptions of the island are found in this recounting of the author's life.

Montgomery, Lucy Maud. *Anne of Green Gables*. Toronto: HarperCollins, 2005. The juvenile story that started Montgomery's popularity as an author is as interesting today as when it was written.

Mowat, Claire. *The Outport People*. Toronto: Key Porter Books, 2005. The wife of famed Canadian writer Farley Mowat describes the couple's time living in a remote Newfoundland village in the form of a fictional memoir.

Parsons, Catriona. *Gaidhlig Troimh Chomhradh (Gaelic Through Conversation)*. Englishtown, Nova Scotia: Gaelic College of Celtic Arts and Crafts. The Cape Breton Island college's mission is to keep the language alive, and it does so with this text and accompanying cassette tapes as well as a number of other books and varied literature.

Perlman, Ken. *The Fiddle Music of Prince Edward Island*. Pacific, Missouri: Mel Bay Productions, 1996. Over 400 traditional Celtic and Acadian tunes.

Proulx, E. Annie. *The Shipping News*. New York: Touchstone, 1994. Pulitzer Prize–winning story of a widowed journalist rebuilding his life on the Newfoundland coast. Reprinted in hardcover in 1999.

Rootland, Nancy. *Anne's World, Maud's World: The Sacred Sites of L. M. Mongomery*. Halifax, Nova Scotia: Nimbus Publishing, 1998. This thought-provoking book reflects on how Montgomery's island home was reflected in her writing, with references to many sites that remain today.

Story, G. M., W. J. Kirwin, and J. D. A. Widdowson, eds. *Dictionary of Newfoundland English*. Toronto: University of Toronto Press, 1990. The Newfoundlanders use their own version of the King's English—from "aaron's rod," a roseroot's local name, to "zosweet," a Beothuk word for the ptarmigan. This remarkably researched compilation translates words and adds historical, geographical, and cultural insights.

## RECREATION GUIDES AND GUIDEBOOKS

*Canoe Routes of Nova Scotia*. Halifax: Canoe Nova Scotia and Camping Association of Nova Scotia, 1983. A description of canoe routes for novice to expert paddlers.

Dunlop, Dale, and Alison Scott. *Exploring Nova Scotia*. Halifax: Formac Publishing, 2003. Golf, cycling, rockhounding, and more—it's all covered in the well-researched book.

Eiselt, Marianne, and H. A. Eiselt. *A Hiking Guide to New Brunswick*. Fredericton: Goose Lane Editions, 1999. Extensively detailed with abundant maps, the guide describes 90 hikes throughout the province.

Haynes, Michael. *Hiking Trails of Nova Scotia.* Fredericton, New Brunswick: Goose Lane Editions, 2002. The eighth edition of this comprehensive yet compact guide details around 50 trails throughout the province. Each description, up to five pages long, is accompanied by a map.

Hempstead, Andrew. *Moon Nova Scotia.* Berkeley, California: Avalon Travel, 2009. Expands on Nova Scotia coverage in this guidebook.

Lawley, David. *A Nature and Hiking Guide to Cape Breton's Cabot Trail.* Halifax: Nimbus Publishing, 1994. The first half of this 200-page book covers all major trails along the Cabot Breton Trail. The second half delves into the region's natural history, complete with descriptions of all flora and fauna.

Lebrecht, Sue. *Trans Canada Trail Guide to Prince Edward Island.* Ottawa: Canadian Geographic, 2004. On the island, the Trans Canada Trail follows an abandoned rail bed and is known as the Confederation Trail. This book details everything you'll need to know for a walking or biking trip along its length.

Maryniak, Barbara. *A Hiking Guide to the National Parks and Historic Sites of Newfoundland.* Fredericton, New Brunswick: Goose Land Editions, 1996. Details 50 trails in the two national parks and historic sites such as Signal Hill.

Maybank, Blake. *Birding Sites of Nova Scotia.* Halifax: Nimbus Publishing, 2005. This thorough field guide makes the province's bird life easy to identify through detailed descriptions and habitat maps.

O'Flaherty, Patrick. *Come Near at Your Peril: A Visitor's Guide to the Island of Newfoundland.* St. John's, Newfoundland: Breakwater Books, 1994. Often hilarious and always insightful, the author meanders across the island, explains the sights as no one but a Newfoundlander sees them, and reveals travel's potential tangles and torments.

Sienko, Walter. *Nova Scotia & the Maritimes by Bike.* Seattle: Mountaineers Books, 1995. Detailed description of 21 routes, with details of highlights along the way.

Tracy, Nicholas. *Cruising Guide to the Bay of Fundy and the Saint John River.* Toronto: Stoddart Publishing, 1999. A useful guide to Fundy and Saint John sailing.

## MAGAZINES, MAPS, AND ATLASES

*Canadian Geographic.* Ottawa: Royal Canadian Geographical Society (www.cangeo.ca). Bimonthly publication pertaining to Canada's natural and human histories and resources.

*Cummins' Atlas of Prince Edward Island, 1928.* Charlottetown: P.E.I. Historical Foundation, 1990. All the details are here, from maps and lists to history.

*Downhome.* St. John's, Newfoundland. Monthly magazine of everything Newfoundland and Labrador, from family stores to hints on growing gardens in northern climes (www. downhomelife.com).

*Explore.* Toronto. Bimonthly publication of adventure travel throughout Canada (www. explore-mag.com).

Hamilton, William B. *Place Names of Atlantic Canada.* Toronto: University of Toronto, 1996. Includes definitions for thousands of place-names throughout the region. Divided by province and then sorted alphabetically.

MapArt. Driving maps for all of Canada, street atlas for major cities, and folded maps of Atlantic Canada (www.mapart.com).

*Meacham's Illustrated Historical Atlas of the Province of Prince Edward Island, 1880.* Charlottetown: P.E.I. Historical Foundation, 1989. A helpful guide to tracing family roots.

*Nature Canada.* Ottawa. Quarterly magazine of the Canadian Nature Federation (www .cnf.ca).

*Nova Scotia Atlas.* Halifax: Formac Publishing, 2001.This comprehensive atlas breaks the province down into 90 topographical style maps, including geographical features and all public roads. The back-matter includes an index of 14,500 place-names and a short description of all provincial and national parks.

Rand McNally. Products include the *Atlantic Canada Road Atlas* and *Halifax & Nova Scotia Communities StreetFinder,* as well as folded maps of various Atlantic Canada regions (www.randmcnally.com).

*Saltscapes.* Dartmouth, Nova Scotia. Classy lifestyle magazine for Canada's east coast. Seven issues annually (www.saltscapes .com).

# Internet Resources

## TRAVEL PLANNING

### Canadian Tourism Commission
**www.canada.travel**
Official tourism website for all of Canada.

### Newfoundland and Labrador Tourism
**www.newfoundlandlabrador.com**
The first place to go when planning your trip to the region's largest province. This site includes a distance calculator, order forms for brochures, and detailed events calendars.

### Nova Scotia Department of Tourism, Culture, and Heritage
**www.novascotia.com**
Everything you need to begin planning your trip to Nova Scotia.

### Prince Edward Island Tourism
**www.peiplay.com**
Visitor guides are available online, along with information especially for children, online reservations, and package deals.

### Tourism New Brunswick
**www.tourismnewbrunswick.ca**
A searchable database of accommodations, information on provincial parks, and event listings make this a worthwhile site for planning your trip.

## PARKS

### Department of Environment and Conservation
**www.env.gov.nl.ca/parks**
Newfoundland and Labrador is dotted with provincial parks and wilderness preserves, and this website details them all.

### Department of Natural Resources
**www.novascotiaparks.ca**
This department manages Nova Scotia's provincial park system. The website details seasons and fees, and has a handy search tool to make finding parks easy.

### Parks Canada
**www.pc.gc.ca**
Official website of the agency that manages Canada's national parks and national historic sites. Information includes general information, operating hours, and fees.

### Parks Canada Campground Reservation Service
**www.pccamping.ca**
Use this website to make reservations for campsites in national parks.

# GOVERNMENT

### Atlantic Canada online
www.acol.ca

An alliance of the four provincial governments to disseminate databases of information to the public.

### Citizenship and Immigration Canada
www.cic.gc.ca

Check this government website for anything related to entry to Canada.

### Environment Canada
www.weatheroffice.gc.ca

Five-day forecasts from across Canada, including over 200 locations across Atlantic Canada. Includes weather archives such as seasonal trends, hurricane history, and sea ice movement.

### Government of Canada
www.gc.ca

The official website of the Canadian government.

# ACCOMMODATIONS

### Bed and Breakfast Online
www.bbcanada.com

Easy-to-use tools for finding and reserving bed-and-breakfasts that suit your budget and interests.

### Hostelling International–Canada
www.hihostels.ca

Canadian arm of the worldwide organization.

# TRANSPORTATION

### Acadian
www.acadianbus.com

Where Greyhound buses terminate, Acadian takes over, with inexpensive service throughout Nova Scotia, New Brunswick, and Prince Edward Island.

### Air Canada
www.aircanada.ca

Canada's national airline.

### Halifax International Airport
www.flyhalifax.com

The official airport website is www.hiaa.ca (with information on airport services), but the airport authority also maintains this site. It includes images of departure and arrival boards, tools to help reach Halifax using the most direct flights, and virtual flight maps that show the location of all incoming and outgoing flights.

### Marine Atlantic
www.marine-atlantic.ca

Use this website to make advance reservations for ferry travel between Nova Scotia and Newfoundland.

### VIA Rail
www.viarail.ca

Passenger rail service across Canada, including from Montréal through New Brunswick to Halifax.

### WestJet
www.westjet.com

Before booking with Air Canada, check out this airline for flights into Atlantic Canada from points west.

# CONSERVATION

### Atlantic Canada Conservation Data Centre
www.accdc.com

Some good information on what and where you're likely to see various species, but mostly composed of charts and databases.

### Canadian Parks and Wilderness Society
www.cpaws.org

A national nonprofit organization that is instrumental in highlighting conservation issues throughout Canada.

### Canadian Wildlife Service
**www.ns.ec.gc.ca/wildlife**

Government website that details every bird and animal species present in Atlantic Canada. Includes pictures and distribution information.

### Ducks Unlimited Canada
**www.ducks.ca**

Respected wetlands protection organization represented by chapters in each of the four Atlantic Canada provinces.

### Sierra Club of Canada-Atlantic Canada Chapter
**www.sierraclub.ca/atlantic**

Dedicated to preserving wilderness throughout the region. Currently active in fighting oil and gas development offshore from Cape Breton Island.

### Starving Ocean
**www.fisherycrisis.com**

Filled with Canadian content, this private website contains articles related to seals, humpback whales, and the decline in cod stocks.

## PUBLISHERS

### Acorn Press
**www.acornpresscanada.com**

The most prolific publisher of Prince Edward Island-related books, including both fiction and nonfiction.

### Creative Book Publishing
**www.creativebookpublishing.com**

This St. John's book publisher has expanded from its stable of local titles to include a catalog of over 200 books, many related to life in Newfoundland and Labrador.

### Goose Lane Editions
**www.gooselane.com**

While all the best books on Atlantic Canada are detailed under *Suggested Reading,* check the web-site of this prolific Fredericton-based publisher for contemporary titles about the region.

### Nimbus Publishing
**www.nimbus.ns.ca**

Respected publisher of numerous Nova Scotia books, including lots of natural and human history titles.

## OTHER INTERNET RESOURCES

### Acadian Genealogy Homepage
**www.acadia.org**

One of the best websites for everything Acadian. Includes detailed census reports dating to 1671 and links to books about this unique culture.

### Howard Dill Enterprises
**www.howarddill.com**

Dill, the world's preeminent super-sized pumpkin grower, sells his record-breaking seeds through this website. He also gives growing tips and uploads photos of his massive vegetables.

### Lucy Maud Montgomery Institute
**www.lmmontgomery.ca**

This institute promotes everything Anne (as in *Anne of Green Gables*). The website www .gov.pe.ca/lmm is a source of tourist-oriented information about the famous author.

### Off da Rock
**www.offdarock.com**

A lighthearted look at everything Newfoundland, including jokes, slang, and music.

### Titanic-The Unsinkable Ship and Halifax
**http://titanic.gov.ns.ca**

Maintained by the government of Nova Scotia, this website includes everything from full passenger lists to local links as obscure as a plaque in the Halifax YMCA that commemorates the sinking with the wrong date.

# Index

# List of Maps

# www.moon.com

DESTINATIONS | ACTIVITIES | BLOGS | MAPS | BOOKS

**MOON.COM** is all new, and ready to help plan your next trip! Filled with fresh trip ideas and strategies, author interviews, informative blogs, a detailed map library, and descriptions of all the Moon guidebooks, Moon.com is all you need to get out and explore the world—or even places in your own backyard. As always, when you travel with Moon, expect an experience that is uncommon and truly unique.

# MAP SYMBOLS

| | | | | | | | |
|---|---|---|---|---|---|---|---|
| ▭▭▭ | Expressway | ◖ | Highlight | ✗ | Airfield | ⚲ | Golf Course |
| ▭▭▭ | Primary Road | ○ | City/Town | ✈ | Airport | P | Parking Area |
| ▭▭▭ | Secondary Road | ◉ | State Capital | ▲ | Mountain | ▲ | Archaeological Site |
| ▭ ▭ ▭ | Unpaved Road | ⊛ | National Capital | ✦ | Unique Natural Feature | ⛪ | Church |
| - - - - | Trail | ★ | Point of Interest | | | ⛽ | Gas Station |
| ⋯⋯⋯ | Ferry | • | Accommodation | 🗻 | Waterfall | | Glacier |
| ▬▬▬ | Railroad | ▼ | Restaurant/Bar | ▲ | Park | | Mangrove |
| ▬▬ | Pedestrian Walkway | ■ | Other Location | T | Trailhead | | Reef |
| ▥▥▥ | Stairs | ⋀ | Campground | ⛷ | Skiing Area | | Swamp |

# CONVERSION TABLES

°C = (°F − 32) / 1.8
°F = (°C × 1.8) + 32
1 inch = 2.54 centimeters (cm)
1 foot = 0.304 meters (m)
1 yard = 0.914 meters
1 mile = 1.6093 kilometers (km)
1 km = 0.6214 miles
1 fathom = 1.8288 m
1 chain = 20.1168 m
1 furlong = 201.168 m
1 acre = 0.4047 hectares
1 sq km = 100 hectares
1 sq mile = 2.59 square km
1 ounce = 28.35 grams
1 pound = 0.4536 kilograms
1 short ton = 0.90718 metric ton
1 short ton = 2,000 pounds
1 long ton = 1.016 metric tons
1 long ton = 2,240 pounds
1 metric ton = 1,000 kilograms
1 quart = 0.94635 liters
1 US gallon = 3.7854 liters
1 Imperial gallon = 4.5459 liters
1 nautical mile = 1.852 km

°FAHRENHEIT  °CELSIUS

WATER BOILS (100 / 210-212)

WATER FREEZES (0 / 32)

INCH 0 1 2 3 4

CM 0 1 2 3 4 5 6 7 8 9 10

## MOON ATLANTIC CANADA

Avalon Travel
a member of the Perseus Books Group
1700 Fourth Street
Berkeley, CA 94710, USA
www.moon.com

Editor: Erin Raber
Series Manager: Kathryn Ettinger
Copy Editor: Christopher Church
Graphics and Production Coordinator: Lucie Ericksen
Cover Designer: Nicole Schultz
Map Editor: Albert Angulo
Cartography Director: Mike Morgenfeld
Cartographers: Kat Bennett, John Twena,
    Chris Markiewicz, Suzanne Service
Indexer: Greg Jewett

ISBN-13: 978-1-59880-153-8
ISSN: 1082-5150

Printing History
1st Edition – 1995
5th Edition – May 2009
5 4 3 2 1

JAN 2 5 2010

## KEEPING CURRENT

If you have a favorite gem you'd like to see included in the next edition, or see anything
that needs updating, clarification, or correction, please drop us a line. Send your
comments via email to feedback@moon.com, or use the address above.